American Political Thought

Fourth Edition

Kenneth M. Dolbeare

THE EVERGREEN STATE COLLEGE

CHATHAM HOUSE PUBLISHERS, INC.
Chatham, New Jersey

DEDICATED TO

Edward Artinian

American Political Thought
Fourth Edition

CHATHAM HOUSE PUBLISHERS, INC.
Box One, Chatham, New Jersey 07928

Publisher: Patricia Artinian
Managing editor: Katharine Miller
Production supervisor: Melissa A. Martin
Cover design: Quentin Fiore
Composition: Bang, Motley, Olufsen
Printing and binding: R.R. Donnelley & Sons Company

Library of Congress Cataloging in Publication Data

American political thought / [compiled by] Kenneth M. Dolbeare. — 4th ed.
    p. cm.
  Includes bibliographical references.
  ISBN 1-56643-059-3 (paper)
  1. Political science—United States—History—Sources.
I. Dolbeare, Kenneth M.
JA84.U5A73 1998
320'.0873—dc21

97-51407
CIP

Manufactured in the United States of America
10 9 8 7 6 5 4 3

Contents

PART III
RECONSTRUCTION AND INDUSTRIALIZATION: 1865–1900

Preface

OF ALL THE courses taught in the college political science curriculum, I believe a course in American political thought explains the most about the political world Americans live in today. Here we encounter ourselves—our past, the origins of our current values and beliefs, and the ways in which we think about the range of the possible for the future. Over almost four centuries, these values and beliefs—truly a unique set of ideas—have become so deeply rooted and powerful in our political culture and practice that they often go unrecognized. This collection is designed to bring to light the vital components of our ideas, the ways they have developed and changed, and how they will affect our future.

For this fourth edition, I have sought to do three things: First, I have tried to respond to new scholarship and to shifting political concerns in the country. Second, I have endeavored to stress the continuities in our political thought, particularly those of constitutional structure and its modification. And finally, I have attempted to balance the length and character of selections more carefully, eliminating what I now recognize as some of my own pedagogical idiosyncrasies. No authors or documents have been eliminated entirely, but some careful editing has trimmed about thirty pages of original materials, chiefly from Richard Henry Lee, Thomas Jefferson, Herbert Croly, John Dewey, and Ronald Reagan.

These changes have facilitated the addition of about forty-five new pages, including seven major new selections:

1. Benjamin Franklin, our first great statesman, with his experience with the Iroquois and his efforts toward a strong national union, first colonial and ultimately independent;
2. The Articles of Confederation, separate but linked to Franklin;
3. Ralph Waldo Emerson, the intellectual giant who contributed so much to our individualism and our notions of nature, spirit, and the higher self;
4. The Populist movement, with its radical democratic goals;
5. The Progressive movement, with its practical constitutional and structural reforms;
6. Franklin Roosevelt's Economic Bill of Rights, the unrealized aspirations of the late New Deal; and
7. The constitutional amendments of the post–World War II era—those ratified *and* those not ratified—and the California initiative Proposition 209, eliminating affirmative action as state policy, which together serve as a summary of the tensions between change and continuity that characterize that most recent period.

I have also tightened and updated my introductory essays and the bibliographies, while following the earlier outline and style. In my first or general framework essay, I have sought to go a bit further by tentatively offering some continuing themes in American political thought that might help us analytically, perhaps even enable us to escape from the outdated and confusing "liberal-conservative" dichotomy and indeed all straight-line spectrums.

The basic plan of the book, however, remains the same. There are now forty-five relatively extensive original selections, organized into the same five major sections. This is a product of my continuing conviction that, although the tradeoff means some important figures can be addressed only in essays or must be omitted entirely, it is essential to have enough of each thinker to understand better his or her premises, assumptions, goals, and methods. My criteria for selection included linkage with the enduring themes of American political thought (see the first essay), traditional scholarly treatment, and my own convictions generated in more than thirty years of teaching this course.

The five sections, each of which is a block of time introduced with a context-setting essay, have been arbitrarily (but in quite standard ways) defined to connect social and economic changes with the development of responsive political ideas, some new and some adaptations. My goal is to enable readers to see today's values and beliefs taking shape, cumulating, and then crystallizing and being projected into the future, as a not-inevitable process of human struggle and choices.

The first period ("From Colony to Constitution") is the longest in the book and might readily have been broken down into several parts. But the antecedents of American political thought, widely scattered as they are, do come together in the founding era. This coherent development is evident in the selections that address the American colonial experience and the Revolution, as well as their fusion in the still-shaping achievement of that brief period.

The nineteenth century has been broken into two parts, separated by the Civil War. In the first ("Development and Democracy"), we focus on the rise of democracy, the beginnings of movement from agrarian to capitalist society, and the several dimensions of abolitionism. The second period ("Reconstruction and Industrialization") is dominated by the radically different pressures of industrialization, immigration, and various forms of popular protest.

After the watershed election of 1896, two crucial new factors are added: the shift from laissez-faire to the positive state and the new American role in international affairs. The effects of these drastic changes continue essentially unabated through the crisis of the Great Depression and World War II, so it seems appropriate to end this part ("The Rise of the Positive State") only at 1945.

The fifth and final part ("The Postwar Period: Change versus Continuity") thus begins with the Cold War and continues to the present. This section has been modified least in the fourth edition because it was so extensively reconstructed, with an entirely new introductory essay, for the third edition. The basic theme remains the old adage: The more things change, the more they stay the same.

I have had much help in preparing this collection over the course of four editions. Many students, colleagues, reviewers, and friends have helped to shape this final product, and only a few can be named here. The early contributions of Larry Spence and Booth Fowler are still evident, as is the hard work of Cyndi Daniels, Sandy Blanchard, and Jeff Bradley. For this edition, my colleague Mike Cummings and my co-author in another work, Janette

Hubbell, made substantial contributions. The book owes its existence to an old and good friend, however, and so this edition is warmly dedicated to the late Ed Artinian, who rescued it at a timely moment, nurtured and established it over the years, and always gave it the benefit of his truly distinctive publishing acuity and commitment. ⌇

Introduction
American Political Thought — Two Approaches

THE GOALS OF studying American political thought, as suggested in the Preface, include understanding the origins and evolution of today's dominant values and beliefs, what these mean for the way Americans address problems of the present and future, and what any serious challengers may offer in the way of alternatives. We can do this more analytically and efficiently if we first clarify what we are looking for and why—a task that requires some reflection on the nature of political thinking generally. In this essay, I set forth two approaches, each of which (when filled out with careful definitions) I consider capable of providing the analytic depth and perspective that will reveal the essence of evolving American political thought. One is the classical approach, involving the traditional liberal-conservative spectrum and its groundings in certain basic values. The other is a deliberate effort to avoid the confusions and possible datedness of that spectrum by focusing instead on four concepts or themes that have characterized American political thinking and practice from the origins to the present: dignity, democracy, ideology, and power.

The Classical Approach

The classical approach assumes that certain basic assumptions give rise to more or less coherent systems of political values and beliefs, and identifies distinctive mixes of such values and beliefs with long-established labels. Assumptions about *the nature of human beings* and about *the purposes of social life* are fundamentally building blocks of political thinking. If people are assumed to be naturally good, intelligent, reasonable, and mutually concerned with each other's well-being and development, then a community of equals with a minimum of coercion will seem possible and desirable. *Anarchists* think it is. If people are assumed to be self-interested and acquisitive by nature, however, ways will have to be found to harness their rational but competitive striving so that the general good can also be provided for, and thus a balance achieved between private and public interests. *Liberals* think they have found such ways. And if people are assumed to be more self-indulgent and emotional than rational, there must be some means of causing them to be guided by the few people who possess wisdom and talent so that the needs of the society as a whole can be served instead. *Conservatives* advocate such means.

In each case, assumptions about human nature have merged with a related sense of the purposes of social order to form the core of well-known systems of political thought. Some of these assumptions and goals also find expression as *political values,* next among the fundamental building blocks of political thinking. In the case of liberalism—the system of thought that has dominated the American tradition—key values include individualism, natural rights (among which property rights have been paramount), freedom, and equality. Each of these values generates powerful loyalties, and together they may come to be viewed as inevitable or beyond question. Anarchists and conservatives hold sharply contrasting values, but they have found it very difficult to be heard in American history. Most of the arguments have been over what specific definitions to affix to the basic liberal values at various periods. Controversy has kept the definitions somewhat blurred, helping to allow change in at least some of their meanings over time. In some cases there have also been changes in the priorities among these values, notably in the rise of equality to challenge freedom. These types of changes are probably the most characteristic of the evolution of American political thought; certainly there have been no outright rejections of treasured values out of the past.

Armed with such insight, we can formulate some questions to ask of political thinkers in our tradition. Foremost is the nature of the thinker's basic assumptions and underlying values. What does he or she assume about human nature, the good society, the best forms of institutions and policies? Why? How do these premises and goals translate into definitions and priorities among political values and beliefs? Few thinkers describe the roots of their values and beliefs neatly, and some may not even state them clearly. That is where the analyst's job begins. From what thinkers advocate and the reasons they give for doing so, the analyst has to reconstruct the fundamental building blocks of their systems of thought in order to see their implications and compare them on grounds more substantial than mere issue positions. The starting point of the classic approach in the American context can only be liberalism.

LIBERALISM

The dominant system of thought in American political life has been one that sees the individual as a rational, self-interested person, entitled by nature to certain "rights" such as life, liberty, and property. Governments are created by contracts among such individuals to serve such rights and maintain order, and they are otherwise limited in their powers. Rights, contracts, and limits to government are all concepts that suggest a major role for law in organizing the society. An important unstated assumption is that private striving to fulfill needs provides the "best" means (i.e., least coercive and most related to talent and effort) of distributing economic and other rewards of social life.

This familiar litany of values and beliefs is known as liberalism. It has deep roots in Western thought, but it came together and took hold most powerfully in the American colonies in the eighteenth century in a process soon to be examined in detail. Its social base was initially the rising seventeenth-century middle class of artisans, merchants, financiers, and other small entrepreneurs. In Europe it served to defend their prerogatives and property against potential incursions from the land-based power of upper-class aristocrats and from the claims of the peasantry and proletariat. In the United States, where there was no comparable feudal residue to give rise to either a powerful aristocracy or a deprived peasantry of ex-serfs, the liberalism of the dominant middle-class merchants and financiers reigned virtually unchallenged.

Because there were no effective challenges to liberalism, some scholars have seen controversies in American political thought as taking place within an unrecognizedly narrow range.[1] By sharing so many similar commitments and by neither hearing nor perceiving other possibilities, Americans exaggerated differences in positions that were, on any absolute scale of potential viewpoints, not very far removed from each other. Other nonliberal arguments, such as classical conservatism on the right or anarchism or socialism on the left,[2] were either ignored or repressed as un-American.

The principal tension within the liberal tradition has been conflict over the assigning of priorities among the natural rights of individuals. To most liberals, property rights have been paramount, with resulting emphasis on law, contracts, procedural regularity, and stability. To some, human rights and equality in first political and then social and economic dimensions have been uppermost, with commensurately greater concern for participation, justice, and change. All liberals, of course, believe that property rights are important, but some are willing, in most circumstances, to reduce the priority assigned to property in favor of human rights. Much of the conflict in American political history has been over just this issue, and it has been bitter more often than not. That this conflict is real in the eyes of the contestants, however, should not obscure the fact that there is still a large body of agreement between them on other fundamental questions. We should admit the possibility that the American spectrum is relatively narrow, lacking a real conservative or radical alternative to the centrist liberal tradition. What looks to us like a wide range of political viewpoints in the United States may simply be our own failure to perceive the real range of possible alternatives.

It may be argued that the differences between American liberals who emphasize human rights and those who emphasize property rights are so great that it is not meaningful to characterize both groups as liberals. It seems to me that this is a question of what frame of reference we want to employ. If we are content to consider only what Americans have actually argued about in their politics, in a kind of culture-bound acceptance of self-imposed limitations, then the definition is indeed only a meaningless preliminary to decisive specifics. But if we wish to consider the entire range of possibilities and to see the implications for past and future of those very self-limitations, we must work with definitions that both provide such comparative dimensions and permit local subcategorization for what people have actually said in this context. I demonstrate the importance of defining liberalism this way and the extent to which liberalism has predominated in the United States by contrasting liberalism with a definition of conservatism drawn from its modern source, Edmund Burke, and somewhat modified to fit with Clinton Rossiter's *Conservatism in America*.[3]

---

1. Louis Hartz, *The Liberal Tradition in America* (New York: Harcourt, Brace and World, 1955).

2. The image of the familiar straight-line political spectrum here can be misleading. What is being measured from left to right is whatever is valued in the society—property, participation, and so on—with distribution wider and more equal on the left and progressively narrower, more limited, and unequal on the right. Simultaneously, conceptions of human nature and the resulting need for order are being arrayed: to the left, humankind is considered cooperative and good, with a minimum of governmentally secured order necessary; to the right, irrationality and emotionalism demand stringent order.

3. Clinton Rossiter, *Conservatism in America* (New York: Random House, 1955, 1962).

CONSERVATISM

Conservatism begins from quite a different focus, which leads to a different view of the relationship between people and their governments. Conservatism posits that society comes first—that it has an existence apart from the individuals who make it up. This independent entity is a continuing organism with a life of its own, progressing through centuries. The individuals who happen to make up its population at any given time are but transients, changing from day to day as deaths and births take place. People have no claims prior to those of society and no rights except those society gives them in furthering its own needs. Because people are emotional and frequently irrational, they need order; liberty is the product of an ordered society in which people are able to do what is right and desirable for them to do.

Conservatism does not deny the inevitability of change, but neither does it believe that change has merits for its own sake; the kind of change that is appropriate is what the society is ready for and what fits the established traditions of the society. If one imagines a long line moving from the past through the present and into the future, change that fits on the line is the appropriate kind: this same analogy may be used to connect generations—a partnership of the living with the dead and the unborn —and to suggest the relative consideration given to the needs of individuals and society. Government in this design cannot be either the creature or the servant of the people who happen to make up the society at any given moment, for it is an agent of the society.

Further, because of the inherent inequalities in distribution of talents, some people are better qualified than others to decide what government policies should be; therefore, either the franchise should be limited or other means should be devised to ensure that people

of talent predominate. Both political equality and majority rule are therefore considered illusory or undesirable. Only those with the requisite talent decide what government must do on behalf of the society, and individuals' lives are directed accordingly. Because one of the purposes for which the society exists is the betterment of the culture and the attainments of the society, individuals frequently derive very significant benefits and satisfactions from their lives within such a system; conservatives would argue that this is the only way, given the realities of human characteristics, that the amenities of life can ever be realized.

Does it not now appear that liberalism is a distinctive set of beliefs? And that we have indeed had few conservatives in the American political tradition? We do gain perspective on our past and present from comparison with a different pattern of beliefs. To view the main body of American thinkers as representing a wide range of opposing political positions is to miss the whole remaining spectrum of what might have been and, at least theoretically, could still be. And it is good to bear in mind that conservatism is only a moderately differing variant of liberalism in Western political ideas.

We *have* had a few conservatives in the United States, although they are sometimes not recognized as such. One reason for this is that, at any given moment, their views on particular issues (for example, how to reform Congress to make it perform more effectively as a representative institution) may coincide with those of liberals. Another reason may be that dominant liberalism has simply ignored or failed to understand conservatives' arguments. Or it may be that, in their efforts to conserve the hallowed traditions of the society, they look back and find nothing to conserve but elements of liberalism. Not only is this frustrating for conservative thinkers, but it confuses observers as well. Nevertheless, we shall try to point up those rare thinkers and positions throughout American political history who show signs of being conservative in character, if only to mark the boundaries and occasions where liberalism has not been uniformly endorsed.

RADICALISM

On the opposite side of liberalism from conservatism runs a small but frequently freshening stream of radicalism. Its impact has often exceeded its visible successes, for, while it has achieved real redistributive and participatory victories for numbers of people, it has done so in return for supporting liberalism. The American radical tradition can be understood only by recognizing that liberalism was not initially democratic and that what we know today as "democracy" is a special version powerfully affected by liberalism. As we see in several of the selections that follow, claims for wider participation and rights (for example, for women, blacks, immigrants, labor, the poor, and Indians) have continued from the earliest days of our history to the present. In almost every case, economic redistribution from the "haves" to the "have nots" has also been part of the challenge mounted in the name of democracy against the established economic, social, and political order of things. As capitalist industrialization began to rigidify social classes and exacerbate inequalities, various protests demanding greater equality arose. Gradually, the franchise was expanded, some redistributions were accomplished, and a sometimes precarious social unity maintained. In the process, liberalism came to wear the label of democracy in many people's minds; our system was democratic, and whatever the United States did defined *democratic*. But for some, true democracy still required greater equality (in social and economic matters, for example), fuller and more meaningful participation in public affairs, and other qualities in social and personal

relationships. It is these people who, generation after generation, have raised the radical banner.[4]

Radicalism means going to the roots of problems in search of causes and cures, and here it has been used in connection with egalitarianism—as a counterbalance on the left to conservatism on the right. Two criteria mark the ideas and thinkers who are *radical* in this sense. First, they emphasize the good qualities in human nature and the potential inherent in all people. Solely by the fact of their existence, people are entitled to a variety of human rights and opportunities. This will enable them to transcend selfish acquisitiveness and develop both a fraternal sense of community and satisfying interpersonal relations. Second, they believe that drastic reconstruction of the economy and society is necessary in order to achieve these goals. Government should be employed to create the conditions for realizing these goals and then reduced to minimal functions consistent therewith.

Dominant thinkers and other pragmatic and property-conscious Americans have impatiently rejected (or, even more devastatingly, ignored) such apparently "unrealistic" arguments. But the essence of the claim for greater equality, participation, and respect continues to rise in yet another form, decade after decade, and normally as a version of democracy. It has a continuing effect on liberalism, particularly when the conflict with the inequality fostered by liberalism's commitments to liberty and property rights becomes clear, as it recurrently does.

---

4. To be sure, some radicals have not been democrats using any definition of the term. Believing that circumstances required forcing others to be free, they have defended various coercive means. But most American radicals have proceeded from a version of what democracy could and should mean.

CHANGES IN LIBERALISM

One of the consequences of this tension has been the way liberalism has evolved over time. Imagine liberalism as having two parts: a central core of unchanging basic values and purposes and a penumbra of time-specific issue positions and tactically flexible orientations toward the use of government. In the central core of unchanging values are the key elements already described, such as individualism, limited government, natural rights (emphasizing property rights), and legalism. Also in this central core is the assumption that the individual is more important than government and that government exists for the purpose of permitting that individual to serve best his or her own needs and attain personal fulfillment. These values and commitments have remained essentially constant from the earliest days of the Republic to the present.

But there has been change in the surrounding issue positions and orientations toward the use of government. Indeed, these changes, made unconsciously (at least in some cases) in response to perceived changes in social, economic, and political conditions, have amounted to an almost complete reversal of the view of some liberals toward the propriety of the use of government. Most of the early liberals believed that the chief threat to individuals' capacities to develop themselves to the utmost lay in government action, and so they bound government with prohibitions on the one hand and practiced laissez-faire as a basic policy on the other. This position endured for at least the first hundred years, with some exceptions made by those who found government a convenient device for advancing their own interests. These people were able to rationalize that their use of government was necessitated by particular circumstances without raising questions about the basic general policy of laissez-faire.

Toward the end of the nineteenth century, however, two related developments led some liberals to question the desirability of following a nearly absolute policy of laissez-faire. One development was the rise of corporate and personal economic power to the point where it became clear to many that government was no longer the chief threat to individual attainment. The presence of accumulations of "private" power and the leverage that this power gave to some to direct and affect the lives of others led some liberals to feel that government could be used to redress the balance and restore for the individual some semblance of equal opportunity. Granger laws, rate regulations, and trust-busting are examples of such uses of government, and they are entirely consistent with the core values of seeking to promote the individual's capacity to serve his or her own ends and reach personal fulfillment.

The second development was the awakening of concern for human rights and social welfare as opposed to an exclusive emphasis on property rights. All liberals acknowledged the importance of property and economic rights —the rights of individuals to maximize the profit attainable from use of their property and the propriety of economic motivations generally. Classic economic liberalism of the Adam Smith brand had legitimated individual profit-seeking as the best way to advance the economy and ultimately to raise the standard of living for all. In addition, property had always been seen as the basis of individual political independence. The person who owned land would be dependent on no one else's favor and would be able to vote freely in elections; sufficient property would give individuals a stake in the society and lead them away from rash acts toward moderate and stable political behavior.

But toward the end of the nineteenth century the emphasis by some liberals on individual profiteering and self-aggrandizement, rationalized by the application of Darwinian natural selection analogies, produced a reaction from others not so exclusively devoted to property and economic rights. For one thing, the conditions of existence for many people were so marginal that action seemed necessary merely to preserve their existence. The byproducts of industrialization, urbanization, and monopoly control included impoverishment, unemployment, and severe practical limitations on economic opportunities. In addition, the pre–Civil War agitation over women's rights and the plight of blacks had contributed to a focus by some on the conditions of the less successful individuals within the society. For these reasons a split developed between the liberals who saw natural rights in terms of civil rights and human rights or social welfare and those who continued with a more exclusively property-rights view.

The first group began to see government as a useful tool for freeing individuals from the external forces that limited them from attaining their ends, and it has used government more and more for this purpose in the twentieth century. The second group, which has continued to place its priorities on economic rights—frequently due to the conviction that this remains the best way to advance the standard of living for all in the long run, not just to advance personal self-interest—have steadily resisted government "interference." Aside from the acknowledged difference in relative priority of economic and human rights, however, all remain steadfast in holding the core values of individualism, limited government, and so forth. Issue positions have shifted among the majority of liberals to produce an almost complete reversal in their view of the propriety of the use of government, but there has been little or no change in the core values or in the basic commitments to the individual and to the attempt to make self-devel-

opment possible. This is indicative of the flexibility inherent in liberal thought, on the one hand, and part of the explanation of the present confusion in the use of the terms *liberal* and *conservative,* on the other.

Liberal is often used to refer to the first group, those who accept the use of government to help people, and *conservative* to the second group, those who stress economic rights and noninterference by government. But both are liberal in their core values, and from outside the American context, their differences seem minor. For the sake of clarity, I propose to use the term "welfare state liberal" for the first, and "classical" or "1890s liberal" for the second, reserving the term "conservative" for the approach contrasted with liberalism above. Much conflict over political ideas and public policy among Americans occurs between the welfare state liberals and the classical liberals, but our analysis cannot be allowed to be that narrow; there are many other possibilities, and a wider perspective is essential.

This realization raises the question whether the straight-line spectrum, in which the two brands of liberalism are clustered at the middle and only a few thinkers scattered out to the left and right, is still a useful analytic tool. I think it has utility, if only because it is so traditional a means of talking about political ideas. But I acknowledge that the changing nature of some American ideas is also making that spectrum less appropriate and/or comprehensive every day. That is why I next tentatively offer an alternative to the classical approach.

The Four Themes Approach

The problems with the classical approach are inherent in its strengths—long usage and the distinctive but changing American context have muddied definitions and blurred analytical lines. Moreover, the complexity of recent thought and the new and often internal dimensions of concern that have surfaced (gender, place, participation, ecology, spirituality) appear to make the straight-line spectrum of the past seem out of date. One way of incorporating the internal and external aspects of these new dimensions and simultaneously simplifying the analytical task is by focusing on four concepts, or themes, that have been present throughout the evolution of American political thought. These are not exclusive—thinkers do not fit easily into one focus or another. Instead, the four themes imply continuing areas of interest and aspiration and serve to organize our understanding of what is happening in the evolution of American ideas over time. While this approach may be less demanding than the classical, it appears to be more flexible and accepting of new ways of grappling with the eternal questions. Some further explanation of each concept/theme now follows, and the reader is encouraged to choose the approach that seems most useful—or to employ both if preferred.

DIGNITY

The related notion of "equality" is more familiar, with its multiple and expanding definitions (legal equality, equality of opportunity, equality of condition) and tension with the notion of "freedom." The concept of dignity includes but is not limited to equality: it encompasses the same sense of aspiration and struggle against obstacles, often involving race, gender, class, or national origin. But it is more fluid, more internal, in the sense of being determined not by external measures but by the subjective feelings of the aspirants. Legal forms of equality and objective measures are much less important than how the aspirant group or individuals *feel* about their status—perhaps a more subtle way of understanding the roots of ideas and motivation in politics. We see many examples of the struggle for dignity in the selections that follow.

DEMOCRACY

Too often in American experience, "democracy" has been defined by the culture, structure, and practice of American politics—whatever *is* in the United States is automatically to be understood as democratic. This has meant that we can think and talk about only a strictly limited form of democracy, one in which liberal values (individual rights, particularly property), and by now the great inequalities produced by modern capitalism, come first and shape what "democracy" can become. Majoritarianism is in this view illegitimate —"the tyranny of the majority."

Here, we seek to free democracy of all such limits and see an ongoing struggle on the part of many diverse groups of people to achieve a full version of democracy. Expertise, whether scientific or legal, or distant bureaucracy, can be as important as property or inequality as barriers to genuine participation and control on the part of ordinary people. The goal of civic engagement, of sharing in the public life of the community and realizing personal development as a citizen, can now be accepted as a motivating factor in politics. So can the notion of legitimacy for the purposeful use of government on behalf of majoritarian goals. In short, the frame of reference for understanding what is going on in politics can be made much wider.

IDEOLOGY

The concept of ideology envisions a set of beliefs about how the world does and should work—beliefs that are grounded in underlying political values and affected by day-to-day perceptions of the "reality" of politics. Such beliefs are coherent with beliefs in ostensibly nonpolitical areas such as science, religion, morality, the understanding of "nature," psychological identity as a person, and notions of the good society. Ideology that explains and justifies the status quo can help to make even the disadvantaged members of the society more accepting of their lot, and thereby to stabilize the polity. At times, a new and different ideology can motivate serious challenges to that same status quo.

Therefore, there is always a major effort (sometimes unrecognized) on the part of the reigning social elements to shape and inculcate a dominant ideology that justifies the way things are: the social-class system, the truths of science and religion, what it means to be an American, the proper uses of nature, the pattern of inequality, and so forth. But it is not a simple or easy process. There are always challenges, and a focus on the ongoing struggle is a revealing way to understand what is happening in the evolution of a country's political thinking. For example, we shall see many instances in which notions of science are used to justify particular forms of inequality in American social life.

POWER

The final and most visible concept or theme is that of power, by which I mean the powers of institutions of government and the purposes that can or should be served by government. The principle of limited government (or laissez-faire—"leave alone," or "hands off"), for example, is intended to keep government from taking action, particularly in areas relating to the economy. Much of the continuing struggle over the powers of institutions and the purposes of government has to do with the question of whether and how much government should be doing with respect to the economy. Should slavery be allowed or protected by the

national government? Should economic distribution be shaped by the government in any way, and if so, what way?

These and many other issues have engaged the political thinkers and activists of our history and resulted in almost continuous revision of the Constitution, that fundamental allocation of powers between the nation and the states and between the institutions of the national government. The subtle and changing interpretations of the Supreme Court are too complex to be addressed in this book, except for the basic statement of the powers of the Court and the nature of the union, which are found in Part II. But the formal amendments to the Constitution tell a great deal about how the American consensus has evolved, both in terms of the powers added to the national government and those denied it. In every time period, therefore, we shall take note of such formal changes in the scope and character of government powers.

CONCLUSION

There is no magic to be found in these four concepts or themes. They do not lead in any single direction, nor do they offer a coherent interpretation of American political thought. But they do provide a focus on four of the most important ongoing lines of development of American political thought, and they do give a sense of what has been happening— what the struggles have been about, and who has won and lost. This is the essence of what we address in this book, and in American political thought: struggle, winners and losers, noninevitability, and never-ending choices about what is to be done. ❦

Part I

From Colony to Constitution: 1620–1800

Τ HE AMERICAN colonies began as distinctive fragments of English history, outposts of English society in a new and distant environment. But the English experience was not just the original source of colonial ideas and practices. It was also a continuing source, for events in England had more effect on colonial thought for decades after colonization began than did local American developments, and they retained substantial impact long after the Revolution. Gradually, however, distinctive conditions, experience, and interests gave greater autonomy to the forces that shaped American beliefs. By the 1760s, basic political concepts, definitions, and practices were different enough to enable an unlikely American coalition to provoke an inept British administration into actions that historically had caused Englishmen to resist, and the colonials were no exception. Thus the American republic was launched, a departure from the English tradition that billed itself as the renewal and extension of those very principles.

Tracing the process by which the American political mind became at once the regeneration and the rejection of the English is a task that has engaged generations of the best historians. We can only touch on the most salient highlights here; for a more thorough chronology of events and developments in England and America, readers may want to make use of one or more of the additional sources provided in the Selected General Bibliography. The vital point is to see the American and English experiences as inextricably linked. Although our focus is on the development of American political thought, of necessity we shall draw on the English sources in each of the four chronological periods discussed in this essay. We shall also look behind the ideas that emerged in search of the social and economic developments or political events that contributed to them.

Colonization and Commonwealth

The immediate origins of a distinctively American political thought lie in the sixteenth-century clash between a decaying Anglican feudalism and the spreading consequences of the English Reformation. The Anglican church was a vast hierarchy, dominated by its archbishops and their relations to the monarchy. Visibly opportunistic and often corrupt, it clung to familiar rituals and resisted change. In all these characteristics it resembled the feudal order it supported. A relatively few landed aristocrats administered their vast manors and the serfs and peasants, who had no alternative but to work the land, pay their taxes, and serve their lords. In this rigid social order, kings and queens succeeded in maintaining the fiction of the divine right of kings while in practice granting the concessions and favors necessary to preserve the loyalty of the majority of the nobles.

Both church and society were profoundly undermined by the individualism of the Reformation and its convergence with the interests of a growing middle class of merchants, tradespeople, professionals, and artisans. The moralistic, purifying urge of the Reformation found vulnerable targets throughout the domain of the established church, and the principle of "the priesthood of all believers" meant ready challenge by local ministers and laity alike to all efforts by the church to assert its authority. This new principle carried political potency as well, providing a wholly different basis for thinking about the nature of society. Instead of starting with the premise of an organic whole that assigned stations and obligations to people and demanded their loyalty and obedience, people would in time think of themselves as independent individuals with rights that came before the society—which was, after all, only a body of many similar individuals.

The rise of individualism would have been far less dynamic and powerful if it had not been for the momentum provided by economic interest. A whole new class was being generated by growing opportunities to produce and sell, to explore and trade, and to finance and facilitate all of these. These were activities undertaken individually or in joint ventures by contracting individuals, and they had no conceptual place in feudalism's simpler world. Moreover, these activities depended on a new kind of profit and property, and these had to be protected against king and aristocrats from above and serfs and peasants from below.

One of the early products of this long, slow, and largely unrecognized process was the development of a reform movement within the Anglican church known as Puritanism. Drawing support from those who wanted a more direct relationship between God and everyday life as Christians, Puritanism was critical of many aspects of church hierarchy, doctrine, and practice. The reform movement contained groups of varying views, ranging from those who merely sought limited reforms in the Anglican church, to those Separatists who felt that removal from the church was the only purifying remedy, and on to advocates of entirely new doctrines emphasizing even greater individual responsibility (for example, Seekers and Quakers).

A related product was the entrepreneurial spirit that led adventurers, financiers, and ultimately a variety of Puritan dissenters to join in forming fishing and trading companies that would establish settlements on the North American continent. The Plymouth Company began explorations in 1606, but Plymouth itself was founded by Separatists (Pilgrims) in 1620. A majority of the 101 persons on board the Mayflower were not Pilgrims, but the Pilgrim leaders ("saints") arranged for governance ashore on their covenant principle, and forty-one adults signed what is now known as the Mayflower Compact.

Other trading companies and individuals also received royal charters and grants for settlement and commercial development of various sectors of the lands claimed by England, but the next major emigration was that of the Massachusetts Bay Company in 1630. Their charter omitted mention of a place for holding the annual meeting, and the twelve orthodox Puritans who led the emigrating group seized on the oversight to convert the company into a self-governing commonwealth along the Massachusetts coast north of Plymouth. As the Anglican church, under the leadership of reactionary Bishop Laud, increased pressure to conform to its doctrines, life became difficult for Puritans in England. Between 1630 and

1640, about 20,000 of them resettled at Massachusetts Bay and the inland communities associated with it. With them came a diversity of theological viewpoints and the beginnings of the discord and intellectual innovation that made the New England colonies the primary source of new ideas on social and political organization on the continent.

By contrast with the aristocratic Anglican social order, the new Puritan commonwealth was middle-class and individualistic. But it was also a hierarchical system in which church and state were integrated and God's laws and expectations were administered by magistrates under the direction of an oligarchy of elders. Neither magistrates nor elders saw themselves as rulers in any arbitrary sense, however; they were the stewards of the society, chosen by God (and identified by worldly talents) to represent Him and work for the salvation of the souls entrusted to their care. The society they served was an organic community with a shared commitment to the establishment of a new kind of life involving mutual dependence and assistance in achieving the goals of Christianity. They were convinced that they were setting a standard of principles and practice that would be a model for the world, a self-conception that has long characterized American thought. The responsibility could be painful, as the experience of John Winthrop, the leading civil magistrate of the first two decades, clearly shows (see selection 1). Winthrop was constantly forced to defend himself and his office against the challenges of independently minded freeholders, but he accepted this as part of the struggle to do God's work on earth. In the process he articulated a defense of the necessity of rule by a few that stands out as a landmark of sincere conservatism.

The cohesion of the Puritan commonwealth began to be undermined almost from the beginning, in part because of its inherent individualism and in part because of decisions made by the Puritans themselves. A religious doctrine of individual salvation could not long support a church-state run entirely from above, despite the assertions of John Calvin and the Presbyterian organization. Martin Luther's "priesthood of all believers" gave too much responsibility to the lowest echelons, and there were too many issues on which conflicting views could arise. Moreover, the Puritans accepted the covenant principle in effect among the Separatists in Plymouth. This meant that each church was constituted by a new covenant among the freemen of its congregation, and as colonization spread, such decentralized units multiplied; in their isolation, doctrinal and other differences also increased. The Puritans also permitted land to be held and transferred by individuals, which gave an economic base to the independence already inherent in Puritan individualism and helped to spur the decentralization and covenanting in church governance that ultimately became known as Congregationalism.

Outspoken opposition to the Puritan orthodoxy came from those who held deviant religious doctrines and used the individualist and covenant principles in their defense, as well as from those who believed first in individual autonomy and rights to democratic self-government. The two stances often fused in the same thinkers and leaders, leading to sometimes bitter arguments and new settlements. Thomas Hooker, for example, left Massachusetts Bay in 1636 to found settlements in Connecticut that would be more fully grounded in control by individual free people.

The most creative of the outspoken opponents of the Puritan oligarchy, however, was Roger Williams, who argued for the utter freedom of the individual mind to seek and know God and was accordingly banished from Massachusetts Bay in 1636. Such freedom required religious toleration and individual rights of conscience and free speech, all of which became fundamental components of the communities that Williams and others established in Rhode Island. These basic rights were an essential part of the democratic political vision that Williams held, in which all people were to play an equal part in creating a self-governing community. For Williams, but for no others of the times, sovereignty lay with the people; they created the state to serve their needs and preserve their individual rights. The church was nothing more than a corporation granted existence by the entirely separate and superior state, and it had no claim to exercise authority over any but its freely consenting members. And Williams did not hesitate to press his subversive arguments on the resentful theocrats of Massachusetts Bay.

In England, 1641 to 1660 was the period of the "Long Parliament," the Civil Wars, and the Commonwealth under Cromwell. Puritan sympathies naturally lay with their counterpart thinkers who fought against the royalists, though not with the various independent sects that generated democratic and egalitarian ideas in the process. For Massachusetts Bay it meant an opportunity to declare its independence from British control and to redouble efforts to enforce religious conformity. When Charles II was restored to the throne, however, the New England colonies would become especially vulnerable.

The Commonwealth period, though apparently a political failure, nevertheless gave rise to some creative thinking about the nature of political and social order in England. Two thinkers in particular influenced current and future generations of Americans. One was Thomas Hobbes, whose *Leviathan* was published in 1651. Hobbes accounted for the rise of the state and the king not by the familiar divine-right theory but by positing an early "state of nature" in which unalterably self-interested individuals fought a "war of all

against all" and in which life was "nasty, brutish, and short." In these circumstances people welcomed a sovereign who could keep order and pledged him their obedience as long as he continued to do so. The immediate impression, and probably the intention, of the work was that it was an argument on behalf of royal absolutism. But the implication that the sovereign was owed loyalty only so long as he was able to enforce his will was troubling. Even more troubling as time went on was the fact that, instead of setting society as an organic whole ahead of the individual as had previously been common, Hobbes had accepted as the basis for society that individuals in a state of nature might effectively contract with other individuals to establish a sovereign. Finally, some Americans would use the unqualifiedly pessimistic Hobbesian view of human nature as a premise for designing political institutions. Hobbes's work thus helped to shift the focus of political thinking toward the individual and to make the question of the nature of such individuals a crucial dividing line between conservatives, liberals, and radical democrats.

The second major thinker of this period was James Harrington, whose ostensibly utopian *Commonwealth of Oceana* was published in 1656. Harrington's reputation was, in seventeenth-century America, second only to that of John Locke, for it was from Harrington that the colonists derived understanding of, among other things, the economic basis of political power, the nature of a written constitution, the importance of the secret ballot, and rotation of offices. Harrington, a thorough republican, dedicated *Oceana* to Cromwell in hopes that it would provide the basis for a lasting popular government. The work was an entire system of social, economic, and political order grounded in the principle of equality and thus was too advanced for Cromwell and his supporters. Needless to say, Harrington was imprisoned soon after the Restoration and spent the last sixteen years of his life in the Tower of London. But his approach to politics as a science and his principle of the "balance of property" necessary to maintain a stable state would later be carried forward by such careful students of his work as Alexander Hamilton and John Adams.

From the Restoration to the Great Awakening

By the time of the restoration of Charles II in 1660, the Massachusetts Bay Colony had been nearly independent politically for a full generation. The only continuing connections with England had been commercial, religious, and informal—with almost no attempt made by the mother country to assert governmental oversight. However, reports of religious discrimination and coercion, combined with the growing economic importance of New England, soon brought about a renewal of royal interest in the colonies. Orders were issued for religious toleration, and new commercial regulations soon followed. Royal investigators were dispatched to find out what was happening in the governments of New England. After protracted efforts to get Massachusetts Bay to comply with the Navigation Acts, accept royal standards of religious toleration, acknowledge appeals to the Privy Council, and take the oath of allegiance to the crown, the charter was finally annulled in 1684. Massachusetts was now to be governed as a royal colony and part of the Dominion of New England. Sir Edmund Andros was appointed governor in 1686 and swiftly proceeded to gather the reins of political and economic control within his administration. His actions were so grossly provocative that Bostonians, seizing the opportunity provided by the Glorious Revolution of 1688 in England, forcibly removed him from office and jailed him until their pleas resulted in his

official removal to London for trial. Subsequently, royal governors were more cautious, and, at least initially, more effective in gaining real political leverage in Massachusetts.

The Glorious Revolution was more than a shift from one line of kings to another; it marked the transfer of effective sovereign power from the monarchy to Parliament and necessarily served as a watershed in political thought. Parliament by this time included not only the large landholders and titled families of Britain but also some of the new gentry in the House of Commons. By assuming the power to force the Stuart kings from the throne and replace them with William of Orange, Parliament made clear its supremacy, at least at moments of crisis. Republicanism was not necessarily implied, for the aristocratic oligarchy held firmly to its postfeudal social order and prerogatives. But its actions contradicted the old idea of the divine right of kings and seemed to call for some new justification for the authority of the state.

In his *Second Treatise on Government*, published in 1690, John Locke provided a justification that later generations of Americans would find more congenial than English society ever did. Locke merged together Hobbes's premises of individualism and the state of nature with Harrington's emphasis on property and formal egalitarianism to form a complete vision of the origins and nature of government that has dominated American thinking to the present day. Slightly less pessimistic about human nature than Hobbes, Locke saw people as capable of knowing the rights (life, liberty, property) that were theirs by natural law through the exercise of their "right reason." In the original state of nature, however, enforcement of these rights would be inconvenient. Government was therefore instituted by a contract among all individuals (who were in these respects equal participants and thus equally obligated to obey) for the purpose of protecting the natural rights of all. When government failed to do so, people had the further right to replace it with a government that would; Locke limited this famous "right of revolution" with many conditions, however, in hopes of limiting its obvious subversive potential. Locke had no intention of endorsing any further shifts in authority after the Glorious Revolution.

What really engaged Locke's concern was establishing a means to protect property, and his solution was to combine making property holders the effective legislative power with limiting the powers of all governments by making them subject to the prior natural rights (including property rights) of individuals. The concept of property that Locke held was an inclusive one, starting with a person's body and the fruits of the labor of that body and reaching to the material things and money ultimately acquired through a person's efforts. Personal liberties and protections for material property were integrated in the single concept. Thus he was able to erect a network of defenses for the new middle class of merchants, financiers, artisans, and professionals that was already consolidating the gains made in the last decades. Quite naturally his system would seem far more appropriate and appealing on the American continent than it would to the still-dominant aristocratic rulers of England.

The idea of natural rights found in natural law and existing as a "higher law" prior to the power of governments was not new. It had always been appealed to whenever there was no other basis on which the actions of rulers could be constrained or impugned. But the alliance of kings who asserted their authority by means of divine right, with a church that claimed power to interpret the natural law (as God's law) and used it to concur in the king's entitlement, had reduced the potency of the idea in recent centuries. It had been kept alive chiefly in the writings of scholars of interna-

tional law, who needed some external source of the rules or practices that nations should follow in their relations with each other. Locke's writings were thus a leading, but not the only, means by which the concepts of higher law and natural rights reached the mainstream of American thought.

As evidence of this last point and as reaffirmation of the crucial shaping part played by the struggle over church government on the American continent, we turn to the writings of the Congregationalist minister John Wise. As minister of a rural church, Wise led town resistance to the taxes imposed by Governor Andros and was imprisoned, thus achieving general renown. His major writings, however, addressed the issue of how the churches were to be governed: by the decisions of the elders' oligarchy using the Presbyterian model or in decentralized, popularly controlled ways according to the Congregationalist model? In the early eighteenth century the leading Boston ministers Increase Mather and Cotton Mather led a campaign to restore central control of church doctrine and practices, much in the manner of the royal efforts to centralize management of the colonies. Although their campaign had already met with little success and had largely been discredited, Wise used the occasion to introduce a major political argument in the guise of a response. In his Vindication of the Government of the New England Churches (1717), Wise justified covenant Congregationalism by using the analogy of democratic civil government, which he interpreted from authoritative scripture as God's preferred form of government (see selection 2). Drawing on international law sources (in part because he apparently did not know Locke), Wise introduced the idea of natural rights on behalf of popularly controlled civil and church government. His work met with wide popular support at the time, so much so that it was reprinted in 1772 amidst the rising tempo of the prorevolutionary debates.

Clearly the Massachusetts Bay oligarchy was losing its power in the early eighteenth century and the level of argument dropped accordingly. New waves of immigration were assuring diversity in New England as in the rest of the nation. By the early 1750s, tens of thousands of new immigrants, mostly German and Scotch-Irish, would be clearing and settling the back country from Massachusetts and New York on down the Appalachians to the Carolinas. Relatively progressive governments had been established in Pennsylvania and New Jersey under Quaker auspices, and the plantation colonies were under firm local control. Political and religious controversies were eclipsed in this period by the rise of merchants and traders, whose entrepreneurial needs and efforts gave the times a comparative stability and quiet.

But even if the governance and toleration issues had been settled by the passage of time, the strength of religious motivations was not less. As a kind of preview of the role that moralistic and fundamentalist spirit would play throughout American history, the first "Great Awakening" occurred in the middle of the century. Revivalist ministers, many of them itinerants, called for restoration of personal and public morality, demanded purification of the church, and redoubled efforts toward individual salvation. They met with enthusiastic popular response, chiefly in the more rural back country, and several denominations experienced schisms or splits between rationalist conservatives and their more mystical and intuitive opponents. A general deepening of popular resistance to authority, particularly as associated with eastern urban centers, was the political result.

Another factor entering the evolving stream of colonial thought in this period was the growing cultural awareness of the Indian, and particularly for the northern colonies, the Iroquois governing practices. There were repeated diplomatic exchanges with the Iroquois confederacy with respect to trade, and consistent efforts to keep that nation from allying with the French. As a result, many colonial leaders were increasingly familiar with the Iroquois model of federal government (the "Six Nations") and were aware as well of the Indians' regular suggestions that the colonies unify enough to be able to make and enforce treaties. Benjamin Franklin was particularly conversant with Indian practices, and his Albany Plan of Union (see selection 3) was at least partially a result of that experience. How powerfully the Iroquois experience affected American ideas remains controversial, but it certainly was not an insignificant factor.

The Prerevolutionary Period

The relative calm of the first half of the eighteenth century also concealed some profound changes at the cultural level of politics. Values, concepts, and definitions were becoming more distinctive; American development was taking a separate course from that of England, or in Parrington's words, "an American mind had been created by the silent pressure of environment."[1]

When asked when the Revolution actually started, John Adams later put it similarly by replying that "the revolution was effected before the war commenced. The revolution was in the minds and hearts of the people."[2] Many of the sources of this process have already been identified; what remains is to see how the events and mutual provocations of the 1760s unveiled the transformation that had already occurred and brought matters to the boiling point of 1776.

---

1. Vernon L. Parrington, *Main Currents in American Thought* (New York: Harcourt, Brace, 1927), 1:180.

2. John Adams, letter to Mr. Niles, 14 January 1818.

The history of British efforts to get Americans to pay part of the costs of the French and Indian War and of British military defense and civil administration of the colonies is too well known to require recounting. Less well understood perhaps are the legal and constitutional arguments used by the colonists and their implications for subsequent American thinking.

The first appeal by Americans was to the British constitution, which Americans had endowed with special grandeur as the source and sustainer of the liberties of free people. The context was set by such 1764 policies as vigorous enforcement of customs collections and the effective annulment of colonial currency, which resulted in deflation and economic hardship. But the constitutional issue was joined with the issues raised by the Stamp Act of 1765, the first occasion when Parliament had ever directly taxed the colonies. The tax was imposed on all newspapers, pamphlets, legal documents, insurance policies, licenses, and playing cards and appeared to the colonists to be only the first of many such revenue-raising efforts. Although the act was later repealed, in part because of colonial remonstrance and refusal to import British goods, Parliament followed with a declaratory act asserting its power over the colonies "in all cases whatever" and with the Townshend Act, which taxed strategic imports.

The colonists argued first that Parliament had power to tax externally (trade, customs, etc.) but not internally within the colonies. The Townshend Act passed this new test and yet still imposed a burden the colonists considered excessive. John Dickinson then shifted the argument in his widely acclaimed Letters from a Farmer (1767–68). He argued that the British constitution when properly construed gave Parliament power to tax only for the regulation of trade and not for the purpose of raising revenue. The latter was improper because the colonists were not represented in Parliament and therefore could not grant their consent to taxes laid on them as the constitution required.

Dickinson's vigorous argument marked a crucial stage in relations between England and the colonies. He was a wealthy landholder and lawyer, a Whig in every way supportive of the British constitution, the King, Parliament, and its policies. But neither he nor others like him could tolerate the prospects of their property being made subject to taxation by that distant body or of their economic interests in trade being reduced. The radical democrats who were ready to confront British authority directly thus gained a major block of new allies, however narrow the grounds initially assumed. And the question of dividing powers between central and local governments began to be analyzed well in advance of the time when American federalism would be shaped by the constitutional convention of 1787.

The next stage of the argument dealt with whether Parliament had power over the colonies at all. It was still an argument over the proper meaning of the British constitution to which the Americans still expressed their loyalty. But it questioned Parliament's authority in the most basic manner on the grounds that at the time of settlement sovereignty lay with the English king and the transfer of the Glorious Revolution could not be operable with respect to the colonies. The debaters alleged that the only source of authority over the colonies was therefore the King of England, to whom they professed loyalty.

The situation in England was so clearly one of Parliamentary supremacy, however, that the argument simply made no sense in London. The final stage of protest thus used the most basic argument of all: the colonists insisted that their natural rights as embodied in natural or higher law were being violated. This argument was preferred by the more radical elements because it contained its own answer in the Lockean right of revolution. It was a peculiarly American argument in that it asserted a law higher than Parliament by which the latter was bound; if Parliament acted inconsistently with the colonists' natural rights, it was insisted, such actions were void and of no effect. In England no law or limit higher than Parliament was acknowledged, and once again the debate was at an impasse.

What was revealed in this escalating dialogue was partly conflict of economic and political interests but partly also a failure of communication resulting from the transformation in the meanings of key concepts that had occurred in the preceding decades. Bernard Bailyn, perhaps the most acute student of the prerevolutionary debates, identified the most fundamental changes occurring in the concepts of representation, constitutions and rights, and sovereignty.[3]

To the colonists, representation had come to mean direct representation in the legislative body by elected delegates who thereby conferred the consent of their constituents to legislation on a continuing, day-by-day basis. This accorded with the covenanting and participating experience of church congregations and town government alike. But even though the House of Commons was elected from geographic districts, Parliament held no such concept. Districts were not representative of population; some were "rotten boroughs" where few people lived. Seats in Parliament could be bought and sold openly, and members were not responsible to their electors. Parliament held to the concept of "virtual representation," in which every member represented all Englishmen, wherever they might be. Whenever

the issue of consent by the people was raised, Parliament's response was that such consent had been given at the time of the Glorious Revolution or some earlier point and that nothing further was required. The American concept thus had no counterpart in English experience and was readily denied.

The English concept of a constitution likewise stood in contrast to the evolved American view. Americans, with their experience under colonial charters and church covenants, understood a constitution as a written document embodying specific purposes and granting (or withholding) particular powers—all as the framers and signers of such documents had intended. Statutes or other acts of governments might be challenged on grounds that they violated the terms of the (higher) constitution. The British concept of a constitution was of the historical accumulation of traditions and ways of doing things expressed in the present form and practices of governing institutions. Parliament had the powers necessary and appropriate to governing; if an issue were raised between the historic rights of Englishmen and a statute enacted by Parliament, the matter would be resolved by appealing to Parliament for a decision. Whatever Parliament did became part of the constitution. With such a view Parliament could go no further in response to the colonists' arguments than to reconsider its policies and then enforce them.

Consistently, the two sides had contrasting ideas about the location of sovereignty. The experience of the colonists led them to understand sovereignty as located in the body of the people and always possessed by them in the ultimate sense. When great questions of the powers and forms of institutions had to be decided, only the people could do so. In the English view, on the other hand, sovereignty lay in Parliament. Whatever it did was binding on all. Most would have asserted that sovereignty existed never in the people of England but

---

3. Bernard Bailyn, *The Ideology of the American Revolution* (Cambridge, Mass.: Harvard University Press, 1967), chap. 5, passim. The remainder of this section depends heavily on his analysis.

rather in the king from whom Parliament acquired it. And in any event, the consent of the people for Parliament's exercise of sovereign power could be inferred from history.

What had come together for Americans was essentially a fusion of the English common law, the Enlightenment rationalism of Locke leavened by the ideas of the early eighteenth-century republicans such as Milton and Sidney, the Puritan heritage of covenanting and Congregationalism, and the independent self-reliance generated by the American environment. All these forces had worked underlying conceptual changes sufficient to give Americans a distinct political perspective. Economic interest to trade freely with countries other than England, to be free of duties and imposts, and to develop domestic manufacturing added more momentum toward independence.

But a third major factor was the image of corruption in English politics, a corruption that was undermining the still-revered British constitution. This image, amply justified by the vote-buying and other machinations of Parliamentary leaders, was supplemented by the growing conviction that there was developing in England a conspiracy against the traditional liberties of English people, particularly those in America. The colonists' cause thus became larger than themselves; the rights of free people, always before at their highest and best form in England, now had to be preserved by Americans. In Bailyn's words, this "gave a radical new meaning to their claims: it transformed them from constitutional arguments to expressions of a world regenerative creed."[4]

With this image of corruption and conspiracy against traditional liberties to work with, radical democrats such as Samuel Adams and later Tom Paine had increasing success in mobilizing support for independence. Adams

had been at work throughout the 1760s to impugn everything British and aristocratic; in Parrington's words, "The single purpose of his life was the organization of the rank and file to take over control of the political state."[5] But British policy soon gave the militants even more assistance: repeated economic constraints convinced reluctant Whigs that they had no property-protecting alternative to independence, and the Quebec Act destroyed the land claims and speculative prospects of a number of southern planters (Washington included). There remained only the need for the catalytic trigger of violence and bloodshed somewhere. That event was not long in coming.

Revolution to Constitution

The Declaration of Independence was almost an anticlimax. Militia had been training and mobilizing for war with Britain since 1774, and armed conflict with British regulars was almost constant in the northern colonies throughout 1775. In June of 1775, for example, the Continental Congress established a Continental army with Washington as its commander to go to the aid of the colonial militia then besieging Boston. By late 1775 a navy had been authorized, and fighting had spread to the southern colonies. January 1776 saw the publication and dramatic impact of Tom Paine's *Common Sense,* which for the first time attacked the much-revered British constitution itself and demanded a republican form of government. French aid for the war with England was assured in March 1776. The Congress moved steadily toward voting for independence as several states formally directed their delegates to seek such a declaration. To the last, however, there were delegates and prominent spokespeople who were opposed to it.

The Declaration was understood at the

---

4. Ibid., 138.

5. Parrington, 1:233.

time as a summary of the natural rights position and a recital of the colonists' grievances against the king. No mention in it is made of Parliament because the colonists' constitutional argument had by this time denied any relationship to that body. Nor is any plan of alternative government included. The intent of the Declaration was to produce the broadest possible majority in support of independence and to mobilize popular support behind that cause—hence the substitution of "happiness" for "property" as one of the "inalienable rights" with which all are endowed.

Still, the Declaration represents the high point of the radical democratic surge of the period, at least as far as formal documents are concerned. The Articles of Confederation, drafted shortly thereafter but not ratified for several years, created a league of states much in the jealously independent spirit of the Declaration, but they never gained the genuine support of leading politicians (or historians). State constitutions drafted in this period show modest egalitarian advances but were probably more noteworthy for the precedents they set for separating and balancing powers in the manner thought to have been done in the British constitution.

Much has been made of the Constitution of 1787 as a reaction against the spirit of the Declaration. It is certainly different in tone, with much attention to the powers necessary to maintaining political and economic stability. And it was more fully the product of the merchant and planter class; the radicals stayed home and opposed its ratification. But this is partly due to the difference in function between the two documents: mobilizing for sacrifice in war requires different language and substance from organizing a stable government.

However, how the conflicts of interest among sectors of the American social order were played out, what the intentions of the leading framers really were, and who won and who lost as a result are issues that must be explored and decided by readers themselves. This is the period in which the basic outlines of American liberalism (and shortly, liberal-capitalism) were being cast into institutions and practices. From that vantage point, these values and beliefs would reproduce themselves in the form of the political premises and values of future generations. The basic substance and range of agreement can only be grasped by the reader's direct engagement with original sources. The selections for this period are therefore more numerous, longer, and introduced by lengthier context-setting essays than are those for the other four periods covered in this book. They await analysis and will reward effort. ❦

1. John Winthrop

JOHN WINTHROP (1588–1649) was born to an established family in Suffolk, England, was educated at Cambridge and Gray's Inn, and practiced law in London. As a Puritan country squire facing declining economic status, he was drawn to the Massachusetts Bay Company project. His experience and leadership capabilities led to his election as its governor, and he sailed to Boston with the first large contingent of Puritan settlers in 1630. He served as governor or deputy governor of the colony almost every year until his death in 1649. Some of his stature derived from his status as an English gentleman of the period; he is reputed to have kept twenty male servants, some of them with families of their own, in the crude environment of early Boston. But much more was due to his integrity and hard work as "steward for the people." Conceding nothing to the preferences of the many, he nevertheless considered their welfare carefully as he administered the will of God as understood by the elders of the colony.

The excerpt here is drawn from Winthrop's journal, in which he recorded events and his reflections on them, regularly referring to himself in the third person. Winthrop's actions as deputy governor had been challenged by elected deputies from the towns but were upheld by the elders, who also fined and reprimanded the deputies for bringing the case. As the public session ended, Winthrop rose to deliver his celebrated "little speech," in which he reaffirms his basic position that government by the select few acting in God's name should not be subject to popular control, nor does it become arbitrary when so conducted. ∽

The Little Speech (1639)

... According to this agreement (5) (*July*) 3, presently after the lecture the magistrates and deputies took their places in the meeting house, and the people being come together, and the deputy governor placing himself within the bar, as at the time of the hearing, etc., the governor read the sentence of the court, without speaking any more, for the deputies had (by importunity) obtained a promise of silence from the magistrates. Then was the deputy governor desired by the court to go up and take his place again upon the bench, which he did accordingly, and the court being about to arise, he desired leave for a little speech, which was to this effect.

I suppose something may be expected from me, upon this charge that is befallen me, which moves me to speak now to you; yet I intend not to intermeddle in the proceedings of the court, or with any of the persons concerned therein. Only I bless God, that I see an issue of this troublesome business. I also acknowledge the justice of the court, and, for mine own part, I am well sat-

SOURCE: J.K. Hosmer, ed., *Winthrop's Journal* (New York: Scribner's, 1908), 2:237–41.

isfied, I was publicly charged, and I am publicly and legally acquitted, which is all I did expect or desire. And though this be sufficient for my justification before men, yet not so before the God, who hath seen so much amiss in my dispensations (and even in this affair) as calls me to be humble. For to be publicly and criminally charged in this court, is matter of humiliation, (and I desire to make a right use of it,) notwithstanding I be thus acquitted. If her father had spit in her face, (saith the Lord concerning Miriam,) should she not have been ashamed seven days? Shame had lien upon her, whatever the occasion had been. I am unwilling to stay you from your urgent affairs, yet give me leave (upon this special occasion) to speak a little more to this assembly. It may be of some good use, to inform and rectify the judgments of some of the people, and may prevent such distempers as have arisen amongst us. The great questions that have troubled the country, are about the authority of the magistrates and the liberty of the people. It is yourselves who have called us to this office, and being called by you, we have our authority from God, in way of an ordinance, such as hath the image of God eminently stamped upon it, the contempt and violation whereof hath been vindicated with examples of divine vengeance. I entreat you to consider, that when you choose magistrates, you take them from among yourselves, men subject to like passions as you are. Therefore when you see infirmities in us, you should reflect upon your own and that would make you bear the more with us, and not be severe censurers of the failings of your magistrates, when you have continual experience of the like infirmities in yourselves and others. We account him a good servant, who breaks not his covenant. The covenant between you and us is the oath you have taken of us, which is to this purpose, that we shall govern you and judge your causes by the rules of God's laws and our own, according to our best skill. When you agree with a workman to build you a ship or house, etc., he undertakes as well for his skill as for his faithfulness, for it is his profession, and you pay him for both. But when you call one to be a magistrate, he doth not profess nor undertake to have sufficient skill for that office, nor can you furnish him with gifts, etc., therefore you must run the hazard of his skill and ability. But if he fail in faithfulness, which by his oath he is bound unto, that he must answer for. If it fall out that the case be clear to common apprehension, and the rule clear also, if he transgress here, the error is not in the skill, but in the evil of the will: it must be required of him. But if the case be doubtful, or the rule doubtful, to men of such understanding and parts as your magistrates are, if your magistrates should err here, yourselves must bear it.

For the other point concerning liberty, I observe a great mistake in the country about that. There is a twofold liberty, natural (I mean as our nature is now corrupt) and civil or federal. The first is common to man with beasts and other creatures. By this, man, as he stands in relation to man simply, hath liberty to do what he lists; it is a liberty to evil as well as to good. This liberty is incompatible and inconsistent with authority, and cannot endure the least restraint of the most just authority. The exercise and maintaining of this liberty makes men grow more evil, and in time to be worse than brute beasts: *omnes sumus licentia deteriores*. This is that great enemy of truth and peace, that wild beast, which all the ordinances of God are bent against, to restrain and subdue it. The other kind of liberty I call civil or federal, it may also be termed moral, in reference to the covenant between God and man, in the moral law, and the politic covenants and constitutions, amongst men themselves. This liberty is the proper end and object of authority, and cannot subsist without it; and it is a liberty to that only which is good, just, and honest. This liberty you are to stand for, with the hazard (not only of your goods, but) of your lives, if need be. Whatsoever crosseth this, is not authority, but a distemper thereof. This liberty is maintained and exercised in a way of subjection to authority; it is of the same kind of liberty wherewith Christ hath made us free. The woman's own choice makes such a man her husband; yet being so chosen, he is her lord, and she is to be subject to him, yet in a way of liberty, not of bondage; and a true wife accounts her subjection her honor and freedom, and would not think her condition safe and free, but in her subjection to her husband's authority. Such is the liberty of the church under the authority of Christ, her king and husband; his yoke is so easy and sweet to her as a bride's ornaments; and if through forwardness or wantonness, etc., she shake it off, at any time, she is at no rest in her spirit, until she take it up again; and whether her lord smiles upon her, and embraceth her in his arms, or whether he frowns, or rebukes, or smites her, she apprehends the sweetness of his love in all, and is refreshed, supported, and instructed by every such dispensation of his authority over her. On the other side, ye know who they are that complain of this yoke and say, let us break their bands, etc., we will not have this man to rule over us. Even so, brethren, it will be between you and your magistrates. If you stand for your natural corrupt liberties, and will do what is good in your own eyes, you will not endure the least weight of authority, but will murmur, and oppose, and be always striving to shake off that yoke; but if you will be satisfied to enjoy such civil

and lawful liberties, such as Christ allows you, then you will quietly and cheerfully submit unto that authority which is set over you, in all the administrations of it, for your good. Wherein, if we fail at any time, we hope we shall be willing (by God's assistance) to hearken to good advice from any of you, or in any other way of God; so shall your liberties be preserved, in upholding the honor and power of authority amongst you.

The deputy governor having ended his speech, the court arose, and the magistrates and deputies retired to attend their other affairs. Many things were observable in the agitation and proceedings about this case. It may be of use to leave a memorial of some of the most material, that our posterity and others may behold the workings of Satan to ruin the colonies and churches of Christ in New England, and into what distempers a wise and godly people may fall in times of temptation; and when such have entertained some false and plausible principles, what deformed superstructures they will raise thereupon, and with what unreasonable obstinacy they will maintain them.

Some of the deputies had seriously conceived, that the magistrates affected an arbitrary government, and that they had (or sought to have) an unlimited power to do what they pleased without control, and that, for this end, they did strive so much to keep their negative power in the general court. This caused them to interpret all the magistrates' actions and speeches (not complying exactly with their own principles) as tending that way, by which occasions their fears and jealousies increased daily. For prevention whereof they judged it not unlawful to use even extrema remedia, as if salus populi had been now the transcendent rule to walk by, and that magistracy must be no other, in effect, than a ministerial office, and all authority, both legislative, consultative, and judicial, must be exercised by the people in their body representative. Hereupon they labored, *equis et velis*, to take away the negative vote. Failing of that, they pleaded that the magistrates had no power out of the general court, but what must be derived from the general court, and so they would have upon them commissions, for what was to be done in the vacancy of the general court, and some of themselves to be joined with the magistrates, and some of the magistrates left out. This not being yielded unto, recourse was had to the elders for advice, and the case stated, with incredible wariness; but the elders casting the cause against them, (as is before declared,) they yet believed, (or at least would that others should,) that the elders' advice was as much for them in their sense as for the magistrates, (and if it were, they had no cause to shun the advice of the elders, as they have seemed to do ever since). This project not prevailing, the next is, for such a body of laws, with prescript penalties in all cases, as nothing might be left to the discretion of the magistrates, (while in the mean time there is no fear of any danger in reserving a liberty for their own discretion in every case,) many laws are agreed upon, some are not assented unto by the magistrates not finding them just. Then is it given out, that the magistrates would have no laws, etc. This gave occasion to the deputy governor to write that treatise about arbitrary government, which he first tendered to the deputies in a model, and finding it approved by some, and silence in others, he drew it up more at large, and having advised with most of the magistrates and elders about it, he intended to have presented it orderly to the court. But to prevent that, the first day of the court the deputies had gotten a copy, which was presently read amongst them as a dangerous libel of some unknown author, and a committee was presently appointed to examine it, many false and dangerous things were collected out of it, all agreed and voted by them, and sent up to the magistrates for their assent, not seeming all this time to take any notice of the author, nor once moving to have his answer about it.... ◇

Primary Sources

Winthrop, John. *The History of New England from 1630 to 1649.* 2 vols. Boston: Little, Brown, 1853.

——. *Winthrop's Conclusions for the Plantation in New England.* Boston: Directors of Old South Work, 1896.

Secondary Sources

Dunn, Richard Slator. *John Winthrop, John Winthrop Jr., and the Problem of Colonial Dependency in New England, 1630–1676.* Princeton, N.J.: Princeton University Press, 1955.

Morgan, Edmund Sears. *The Puritan Dilemma: The Story of John Winthrop.* Boston: Little, Brown, 1958.

Moseley, James G. *John Winthrop's World: History as a Story, the Story as History.* Madison, Wisc.: University of Wisconsin Press, 1992.

Rutman, Darrett Bruce. *John Winthrop's Decision for America: 1629.* Philadelphia: Lippincott, 1975.

Winthrop, Robert Charles. *Life and Letters of John Winthrop.* New York: Da Capo Press, 1971.

2. John Wise

JOHN WISE (1652–1725) was born in Roxbury and was the son of a once-indentured servant. He graduated from Harvard in 1673 and served as minister to parishes in Connecticut and western Massachusetts before taking a new church at Ipswich near Boston. In 1687 he led the town's resistance against taxes levied by the arbitrary royal Governor Andros and was imprisoned. His writings argue explicitly for a democratic mode of church governance and against the efforts of Cotton Mather to tighten control from above. He based his argument on biblical sources, the principle of natural rights, and reason, but he was essentially defending the status quo of Congregational churches of the time rather than breaking new ground for church practice.

The selection here is from his *Vindication of the Government of the New England Churches* (1717), in which the democratic principle is most strongly espoused. This work stood out so clearly as the first major statement of the merits of democracy that it was reprinted during the prerevolutionary debates in 1772. ∾

"Democracy Is Founded in Scripture" (1717)

1. The forms of a regular state are three only, which forms arise from the proper and particular subject, in which the supreme power resides. As,

1. A democracy, which is when the sovereign power is lodged in a council consisting of all the members, and where every member has the privilege of a vote. This form of government, appears in the greatest part of the world to have been the most ancient. For that reason seems to show it to be most probable, that when men (being originally in a condition of natural freedom and equality) had thoughts of joining in a civil body, would without question be inclined to administer their common affairs, by their common judgment, and so much nec-

essarily, to gratify that inclination, establish a democracy; neither can it be rationally imagined that fathers of families being yet free and independent should in a moment or little time take off their long delight in governing their own affairs and devolve all upon some single sovereign Commander, for that it seems to have been thought more equitable that what belonged to all should be managed by all when all had entered by compact into one community. The original of our government, says Plato, (speaking of the Athenian Commonwealth) "was taken from the equality of our race. Other states there are composed of different blood, and of unequal lines, the consequence of which are disproportionable sovereignty, tyrannical or oligarchical sway; under which men live in such a manner, as to esteem themselves partly lords, and partly slaves to each other. But we and our countrymen, being all born brethren of the same mother, do not

SOURCE: John Wise, *Vindication of the Government of the New England Churches* (1717; reprint ed., Gainesville, Fla.: Scholar's Facsimiles and Reprints, 1935).

look upon ourselves, to stand under so hard a relation, as that of lords and slaves; but the parity of our descent incline us to keep up the like parity by our laws, and to yield the precedency to nothing but to superior virtue and wisdom." And moreover it seems very manifest that most civil communities arose at first from the union of families, that were nearly allied in race and blood. And though ancient story make frequent mention of kings, yet it appears that most of them were such that had an influence rather in persuading than in any power of commanding. So Justin describes that kind of government as the most primitive which Aristotle styles an heroical kingdom, viz., such as is no ways inconsistent with a democratical state.

A democracy is then erected when a number of free persons do assemble together in order to enter into a covenant for uniting themselves in a body: And such a preparative assembly has some appearance already of a democracy; it is a democracy in embryo, property in this respect, that every man has the privilege freely to deliver his opinion concerning *the* common affairs. Yet he who dissents from the vote of the majority is not in the least obliged by what they determine until by a second covenant a popular form be actually established, for not before then can we call it a democratical government, viz., till the right of determining all matters relating to the public safety is actually placed in a General Assembly of the whole people, or, by their own compact and mutual agreement, determine themselves the proper subject for the exercise of sovereign power. And to complete this state, and render it capable to exert its power to answer the end of a civil state, these conditions are necessary:

1. That a certain time and place be assigned for assembling;
2. That when the assembly be orderly met, as to time and place, that then the vote of the majority must pass for the vote of the whole body.
3. That magistrates be appointed to exercise the authority of the whole for the better dispatch of business, of everyday occurrence, who also may, with more mature diligence, search into more important affairs, and if in case anything happens of greater consequence, may report it to the assembly, and be peculiarly serviceable in putting all public decrees into execution. Because a large body of people is almost useless in respect of the last service, and of many others, as to the more particular application and exercise of power, therefore, it is most agreeable with the law of nature, that they institute their officers to act in their name and stead.

2. The second species of regular government is an aristocracy. And this is said then to be constituted when the people, or assembly united by a first covenant, and having thereby cast themselves into the first rudiments of a state, do then by common decree devolve the sovereign power on a council consisting of some select members, and these having accepted of the designation are then properly invested with sovereign command; and then an aristocracy is formed.

3. The third species of regular government is a monarchy, which is settled when the sovereign power is conferred on some one worthy person. It differs from the former because a monarch, who is but one person in natural as well as in moral account, and so is furnished with an immediate power of exercising sovereign command in all instances of government. But the forenamed must needs have particular time and place assigned, but the power and authority is equal in each.

2. Mixed governments, which are various and of diverse kinds (not now to be enumerated) yet possibly the fairest in the world is that which has a regular monarchy (in distinc-

tion as to what is despotic) settled upon a noble democracy as its basis. And each part of the government is so adjusted by pacts and laws that renders the whole constitution an Elysium. It is said of the British Empire, "That it is such a monarchy, as that by the necessary subordinate concurrence of the Lords and Commons, in the making and repealing all statutes or acts of Parliament; it has the main advantages of an aristocracy and of a democracy, and yet free from the disadvantages and evils of either. It is such a monarchy, as by most admirable temperament affords very much to the industry, liberty and happiness of the subject, and reserves enough for the majesty and prerogative of any King who will own his people as subjects, not as slaves. It is a Kingdom that, of all the kingdoms of the world, is most like to the Kingdom of Jesus Christ, whose yoke is easy, and burden light." Thus having drawn up this brief scheme concerning Man, and the nature of civil government he is become sole subject of, I shall next proceed to make improvements of the premises to accommodate the main subject under our consideration.

2. I shall now make some improvement of the foregoing principles of civil knowledge, fairly deduced from the Law of Nature. And, I shall peculiarly refer to ecclesiastical affairs, whereby we may, in probability, discover more clearly the kind and something of the nature of that government which Christ has placed in and over his Church. The learned debates of men and Divine Writ sometimes seem to cast such a grandeur on the Church and its officers as though they stood in peerage with civil empire. But all such expressions must needs be otherwise interpreted. God is the highest Cause that acts by Council, and it must needs be altogether repugnant to think he should forecast the state of this world by no better a scheme, than to order two sovereign powers in the same grand community, which would be

like placing two suns in the firmament, which would be to set the universe into a flame; that should such an error happen, one must needs be forthwith extinguished to bring the frame of nature into a just temper and keep it out of harm's way. But to proceed with my purpose, I shall go back upon the civil scheme and inquire after two things: first of rebellion against government in general and then in special; whether any of the aforesaid species of regular government can be predicable of the Church of God on earth.

1. In general concerning rebellion against government, for particular subjects to break in upon regular communities duly established, is from the premises to violate the Law of Nature, and is a high usurpation upon the first grand immunities of Mankind. Such rebels in states and usurpers in churches affront the world with a presumption that the best of the brotherhood are a company of fools and that themselves have fairly monopolized all the reason of Human Nature. Yea, they take upon them the boldness to assume a prerogative of trampling underfoot the natural original equality and liberty of their fellows, for to push the proprietors of settlements out of possession of their old, and impose new schemes upon them, is virtually to declare them in a state of vassalage, or that they were born to, and therefore will the usurper be so gracious as to insure them they shall not be sold at the next market. They must esteem it a favor, for by this time all the original prerogatives of man's nature are intentionally a victim smoking to satiate the usurper's ambition. It is a very tart observation on an English monarch, and where it may by proportion be applied to a subject, must need sink very deep and serve for evidence under this head. It is in the Secret History, says my author, "Where the constitution of a nation is such that the laws of the land are the measures both of the sovereign's command and the obedience of the subjects

whereby it is provided that, as the one are not to invade what by concessions and stipulations is granted to the ruler, for the other is not to deprive them of their lawful and determined rights and liberties; then the Prince who strives to subvert the fundamental laws of the society is the traitor and rebel, and not the people who endeavor to preserve and defend their own." It's very applicable to particular men in their rebellions or usurpations in Church or state.

2. In special I shall now proceed to inquire whether any of the aforesaid species of regular, unmixed governments can, with any good show of reason, be predicable of the Church of Christ on earth. If the Churches of Christ, as churches, are either the object or subject of a sovereign power entrusted in the hands of men, then most certainly one of the forecited schemes of a perfect government will be applicable to it.

Before I pursue the inquiry, it may not be improper to pause and make some caution here by distinguishing between that which may have some resemblance of civil power and the thing itself, and so the power of churches is but a faint resemblance of civil power, it comes in reality nothing near to the thing itself, for the one is truly coercive, the other persuasive, the one is sovereign power, the other is delegated and ministerial. But not to delay, I shall proceed with my inquiry and therein shall endeavor to humor the several great claimers of government in the Church of Christ. And

1. I shall begin with a monarchy. It's certain his Holiness, either by reasonable pleas or powerful cheats, has assumed an absolute and universal sovereignty; this fills his Cathedral Chair and is adorned with a Triple Crown, and in defense thereof does protest, "The Almighty has made him both Key-keeper of Heaven and Hell, with the adjacent territories of Purgatory, and vested in him an absolute sovereignty over the Christian world." And his right has so far prevailed, that princes and civil monarchs hold their crowns and donations as his dutiful sons and loyal subjects. He therefore decks himself with the spoils of the divine attributes, styling himself, "Our Lord God, Optimum, Maximum et supremum numen in Terris," a God on Earth, a visible Deity, and that his power is absolute and his wisdom infallible. And many of the great potentates of the earth have paid their fealty as though it was really so. One of them, clad in canvas, going barefoot in the depth of winter (in obedience to the decree stinting the penance in proportion to the wickedness of princes), has waited many days for absolution at the pious gates. Another has thrown himself down prostrate, a humble penitent, before him; he has placed his Holy Foot on the monarch's profane neck as crushing a vermine, crawling out of the stable of his sovereignty; and others frequently kiss his toes with very profound devotion. These and such like triumphant signals of his sovereign power does he wear. And indeed if he is the universal monarch of the Catholic Church, princes that are members of it must needs knock under, for that in one world there cannot possibly be two "Most Highs" any more than two "Infinities." Thus you see the clergy, or Gospel ministry of the Christian World, have so wisely handled business and managed the Gospel that they have fairly (as they avow) found a sovereign power bequeathed in it to the Ministry of Christ, and rummaging more warily and nicely, at last found a Spiritual Monarch very completely furnished with the keys of all sorts of power hanging at his girdle; and may we not pronounce the wiser they! seeing the world growing weary of religion, was willing to lull itself down to sleep, and leave them in sole trust with the whole interest of God's Kingdom. But the said inquiry is whether this sort of government has not plainly subverted the design of the Gospel, and the end for which Christ's government was ordained, viz., the moral,

spiritual, and eternal happiness of men?

But I have no occasion to pursue this remark with tedious demonstrations: It's very plain; it's written with blood in capital letters to be read at midnight by the flames of Smithfield, and other such like consecrated fires. That the government of this ecclesiastical monarch has instead of sanctifying, absolutely debauched the world, and subverted all good Christianity in it. So that without the least show of any vain presumption we may infer that God and wise Nature were never propitious to the birth of this monster.

An aristocracy which places the supreme power in a select company of choice persons. Here I freely acknowledge were the Gospel Ministry established the subject of this power, viz., to will and do in all Church affairs without control, etc., this government might do to support the Church in its most valuable rights, etc., if we could be assured they would make the Scripture and not their private will the rule of their personal and ministerial actions; and indeed, upon these terms, any species of government might serve the great design of Redemption; but considering how great an interest is imbarked, and how frail a bottom we trust, though we should rely upon the best of men, especially if we remember what is in the hearts of good men, (viz., much ignorance, abundance of small ends, many times cloaked with a high pretense in religion, pride skulking and often breeding revenge upon a small affront, and blown up by a pretended zeal, yet really and truly by nothing more divine than interest or ill nature), and also considering how very uncertain we are of the real goodness of those we esteem good men, and also how impossible it is to secure the entail of it to successors: And also if we remind how Christianity by the foresaid principle has been peeled, robbed, and spoiled already, it cannot consist with the light of Nature to venture again upon such perils, especially if we can find a later

way home. More distinctly.

It is very plain (allowing me to speak emblematically) the primitive constitution of the Churches was a democracy, as appears by the foregoing parallel. But after the Christian Churches were received into the favor of the Imperial Court, under the Dominion of Constantine the Great, there being many preliminaries which had furnished the ministers with a disposition thereunto, they quickly deprived the fraternities of their rights in the government of the churches, when they were once provided of a plentiful maintenance through the liberality of Constantine, that when Christianity was so luxuriantly treated as by his great bounty and noble settlement, it is said there was a Voice heard from Heaven, saying, "Now is poison poured into the Church." But the subversion of the constitution is a story too long now to tell. . . .

In a word, an aristocracy is a dangerous constitution in the Church of Christ as it possesses the Presbytery of all Church power: What has been observed sufficiently evinces it. And not only so but from the nature of the constitution, for it has no more barrier to it against the ambition, insults, and arbitrary measures of men than an absolute monarchy. But to abbreviate, it seems most agreeable with the Light of Nature that if there be any of the regular government settled in the Church of God it must needs be

3. A Democracy. This is a form of government which the Light of Nature does highly value and often directs to as most agreeable to the just and natural prerogatives of Human Beings. This was of great account in the early times of the world. And not only so, but upon the experience of several thousand years after the world had been tumbled and tossed from one species of government to another, at a great expense of blood and treasure, many of the wise nations of the world have sheltered them-

selves under it again, or at least have blended and balanced their governments with it.

It is certainly a great truth that man's original liberty, after it is resigned (yet under due restrictions), ought to be cherished in all wise governments; or otherwise a man, in making himself a subject, he alters himself from a freeman into a slave which to do is repugnant to the Law of Nature. Also the natural equality of men among men must be duly favored, in that government was never established by God or Nature to give one man a prerogative to insult over another; therefore in a civil, as well as in a natural, state of being, a just equality is to be indulged so far as that every man is bound to honor every man, which is agreeable both with Nature and Religion. The end of all good government is to cultivate humanity and promote the happiness of all and the good of every man in all his rights, his life, liberty, estate, honor, etc. without injury or abuse done to any. Then certainly it cannot easily be thought that a company of men that shall enter into a voluntary compact, to hold all power in their own hands, thereby to use and improve their united force, wisdom, riches and strength for the common and particular good of every member, as is the nature of a democracy; I say it cannot be that this sort of constitution will so readily furnish those in government with an appetite or disposition to prey upon each other or embezzle the common stock, as some particular persons may be apt to do when set off and entrusted with the same power. And, moreover, this appears very natural, that when the aforesaid government or power, settled in all, when they have elected certain capable persons to minister in their affairs, and the said ministers remain accountable to the Assembly, these officers must needs be under the influence of many wise cautions from their own thoughts (as well as under confinement by their commission) in their whole administration: And from thence it must needs follow that they will be more apt and inclined to steer right for the main point, viz., the peculiar good and benefit of the whole and every particular member fairly and sincerely. And why may not these stand for very rational pleas in Church order?

For certainly if Christ has settled any form of power in his Church he has done it for his Church's safety, and for the benefit of every member: Then he must needs be presumed to have made choice of that government as should least expose his people to hazard, either from the fraud or arbitrary measures of particular men. And it is as plain as daylight, there is no species of government like a democracy to attain this end. There is but about two steps from an aristocracy to a monarchy, and from thence but one to a tyranny. An able standing force and an ill-nature, *ipso facto,* turns an absolute monarch into a tyrant. This is obvious among the Roman Caesars and through the world. And all these direful transmutations are easier in Church affairs (from the different qualities of things) than in civil states. For what is it that cunning and learned men can't make the world swallow as an article of their creed if they are once invested with an uncontrollable power, and are to be the standing orators to mankind in matters of faith and obedience? ⟿

Primary Source

Wise, John. *The Churches Quarrel Espoused* (1713). Gainesville, Fla.: Scholar's Facsimiles and Reprints, 1966.

Secondary Source

Cook, George Allan. *John Wise: Early American Democrat.* New York: King's Crown Press, 1952.

3. Benjamin Franklin

BENJAMIN FRANKLIN (1706–90) was born in Puritan Boston. As a teenager, he was a printer's apprentice and journalist whose intellectual vigor and gift for polemics brought the restraint of the authorities down on him. As a result, he ran away to Philadelphia at age seventeen, and amid the diversity of sects and opportunities that characterized that rising city at the time soon became visible as a journalist and as the owner of a printing establishment. He published his own prolific writings (including the annual and profitable *Poor Richard's Almanack*) as well as many popular tracts, newspapers, and documents, not least of which were some major treaties with the Indians. He formed an intellectual, literary, and benevolent organization, the Junto, and from that base promoted such civic causes as a library, a hospital, and an educational system.

Barely forty, he retired from business with an adequate fortune to devote himself to scientific investigations and civic (eventually diplomatic) service to Pennsylvania and the colonies in general. He was the first and for decades the only American to enjoy international renown as a scientist and philosopher, and with that reputation he was able to gain ready access to the statesmen and philosophers of Europe. He served as Pennsylvania's representative in several negotiations with the Indians and was an early advocate of colonial union. Later, he carried out several diplomatic missions in London and Paris, ending his public career as an active member of the Constitutional Convention. Franklin was on a par with Washington in public visibility and respect, both in the new United States and globally.

The passages here focus particularly on Franklin's early advocacy of colonial union and on the part he played in bringing the lessons of the long-established (probably 200 or 300 years before the first English settlements) Iroquois Confederacy into mainstream American political discussions. The extent to which the Six Nations' federal system served as a model for the U.S. Constitution of 1787 is a matter of debate among historians today. Two younger historians, Bruce Johansen and Donald Grinde, have both individually and in a joint work produced a significant body of scholarship asserting that the Iroquois model was widely known and regularly drawn upon in the colonial discussions about union and federalism from 1744 until 1787 and beyond. It seems clear at least that there was much more open and regular cultural interchange between the English and the Iroquois than traditional historians have acknowledged, if only because the colonists needed the Iroquois on their side, first against the French in the 1750s and 1760s and then against the British in the 1770s. Franklin is central to this argument because he learned the Iroquois language and was present at so many councils with them in the 1740s and 1750s. Franklin not only provided his "Short Hints" but was the major architect of the premature Albany Plan of Union and of its eventual successor, the Articles of Confederation (see selection 7), and he remained a tireless advocate at the Convention of 1787. In many respects, his principles and polemics (e.g., the famous "Join or Die" cartoon showing a snake cut into pieces bearing the names of the separate colonies) can be seen as drawing on the Six Nations' experience.

The first selection shows Franklin's acuity as a political economist and his early commitment to an expansive nation. Written in 1751 to counter British colonial policy, he couched his nascent imperialism in terms of the eventual needs and goals of the British Empire, of which he expected the North American colonies to be a key part. The second presents some of the language of the *Great Law of Peace,* the effective constitution of the Six Nations (originally five, until the accession of the Tuscaroras in 1725). The principles of separation of powers, federalism, painstaking consensus building, and concern for public opinion can be seen at work here; one needs to remember that the Iroquois were a matrilineal

clan-based polity in which the "mothers" held power to nominate and recall the Lords, who exercised the people's delegated powers.

Franklin's "Short Hints" were written to a prospective delegate to the Albany Congress. The *Albany Plan of Union,* the extended version of his "Hints," was the final draft of the Congress's work, but accepted by no colony at the time. Nevertheless, all thoughtful men of the next twenty years knew of it and could not have been surprised when so much of it surfaced again (with Franklin's guidance) in the Articles of 1777. How much of Franklin's plan was directly based on the Iroquois model remains in dispute, but it is clear that he referred frequently to the Iroquois success in building a powerful confederation, as in his often quoted 1754 letter: "It would be a strange thing, if Six Nations of ignorant Savages should be capable of forming a union that has subsisted for ages, and yet a like union should be impracticable for ten or a dozen English colonies, to whom it is more necessary." ☙

Observations Concerning the Increase of Mankind, the Peopling of Countries, etc. (1751)

1. Tables of the Proportion of Marriages to Births, of Deaths to Births, of Marriages to the Numbers of Inhabitants, &c. form'd on Observations made upon the Bills of Mortality, Christnings, &c. of populous Cities, will not suit Countries; nor will Tables form'd on Observations made on full settled old Countries, as Europe, suit new Countries, as America.

2. For People increase in Proportion to the Number of Marriages, and that is greater in

SOURCE: Leonard W. Labaree, ed., *The Papers of Benjamin Franklin,* (New Haven: Yale University Press, 1961), 4:227–34.

Proportion to the Ease and Convenience of supporting a Family. When Families can be easily supported, more Persons marry, and earlier in Life.

3. In Cities, where all Trades, Occupations and Offices are full, many delay marrying, till they can see how to bear the Charges of a Family; which Charges are greater in Cities, as Luxury is more common: many live single during Life, and continue Servants to Families, Journeymen to Trades, &c. hence Cities do not by natural Generation supply themselves with Inhabitants; the Deaths are more than the Births.

4. In Countries full settled, the Case must be nearly the same; all Lands being occupied and improved to the Heighth: those who cannot get Land, must Labour for others that have it; when Labourers are plenty, their Wages will be low; by low Wages a Family is supported with Difficulty; this Difficulty deters many from Marriage, who therefore long continue Servants and single. Only as the Cities take Supplies of People from the Country, and thereby make a little more Room in the Country; Marriage is a little more incourag'd there, and the Births exceed the Deaths.

5. Europe is generally full settled with Husbandmen, Manufacturers, &c. and therefore cannot now much increase in People: America is chiefly occupied by Indians, who subsist mostly by Hunting. But as the Hunter, of all Men, requires the greatest Quantity of Land from whence to draw his Subsistence, (the Husbandman subsisting on much less, the Gardner on still less, and the Manufacturer requiring least of all), the Europeans found America as fully settled as it well could be by Hunters; yet these having large Tracks, were easily prevail'd on to part with Portions of Territory to the new Comers, who did not much interfere with the Natives in Hunting, and furnish'd them with many Things they wanted.

6. Land being thus plenty in America, and so cheap as that a labouring Man, that understands Husbandry, can in a short Time save Money enough to purchase a Piece of new Land sufficient for a Plantation, whereon he may subsist a Family; such are not afraid to marry; for if they even look far enough forward to consider how their Children when grown up are to be provided for, they see that more Land is to be had at Rates equally easy, all Circumstances considered.

7. Hence Marriages in America are more general, and more generally early, than in Europe. And if it is reckoned there, that there is but one Marriage per Annum among 100 Persons, perhaps we may here reckon two; and if in Europe they have but 4 Births to a Marriage (many of their Marriages being late) we may here reckon 8, of which if one half grow up, and our Marriages are made, reckoning one with another at 20 Years of Age, our People must at least be doubled every 20 Years.

8. But notwithstanding this Increase, so vast is the Territory of North-America, that it will require many Ages to settle it fully; and till it is fully settled, labour will never be cheap here, where no Man continues long a Labourer for others, but gets a Plantation of his own, no Man continues long a Journeyman to a Trade, but goes among those new Settlers, and sets up for himself, &c. Hence Labour is no cheaper now, in Pennsylvania, than it was 30 Years ago, tho' so many Thousand labouring People have been imported.

9. The Danger therefore of these Colonies interfering with their Mother Country in Trades that depend on Labour, Manufacturers, &c. is too remote to require the Attention of Great-Britain.

10. But in Proportion to the Increase of the Colonies, a vast Demand is growing for British Manufactures, a glorious Market wholly in the Power of Britain, in which Foreigners cannot interfere, which will increase in a short Time even beyond her Power of supplying, tho' her whole Trade should be to her Colonies: Therefore Britain should not too much restrain Manufactures in her Colonies. A wise and good Mother will not do it. To distress, is to weaken, and weakening the Children, weakens the whole Family.

11. Besides if the Manufactures of Britain (by Reason of the American Demands) should rise too high in Price, Foreigners who can sell cheaper will drive her Merchants out of Foreign Markets; Foreign Manufactures will thereby be encouraged and increased, and consequently foreign Nations, perhaps her Rivals

in Power, grow more populous and more powerful; while her own Colonies, kept too low, are unable to assist her, or add to her Strength.

12. 'Tis an ill-grounded Opinion that by the Labour of Slaves, America may possibly vie in Cheapness of Manufactures with Britain. The Labour of Slaves can never be so cheap here as the Labour of working Men is in Britain. Any one may compute it. Interest of Money is in the Colonies from 6 to 10 per Cent. Slaves one with another cost £30 Sterling per Head. Reckon then the Interest of the first Purchase of a Slave, the Insurance or Risque on his Life, his Cloathing and Diet, Expences in his Sickness and Loss of Time, Loss by his Neglect of Business (Neglect is natural to the Man who is not to be benefited by his own Care or Diligence), Expence of a Driver to keep him at Work, and his Pilfering from Time to Time, almost every Slave being *by Nature* a Thief, and compare the whole Amount with the Wages of a manufacturer of Iron or Wool in England, you will see that Labour is much cheaper there than it ever can be by Negroes here. Why then will Americans purchase Slaves? Because Slaves may be kept as long as a Man pleases, or has Occasion for their Labour; while hired Men are continually leaving their Master (often in the midst of his Business,) and setting up for themselves.

13. As the Increase of People depends on the Encouragement of Marriages, the following Things must diminish a Nation, viz. 1. The being conquered; for the Conquerors will engross as many Offices, and exact as much Tribute or Profit on the Labour of the conquered, as will maintain them in their new Establishment, and this diminishing the Subsistence of the Natives discourages their Marriages, and so gradually diminishes them, while the Foreigners increase. 2. Loss of Territory. Thus the Britons being driven into Wales, and crowded together in a barren Country insufficient to support such great Numbers, diminished 'till the People bore a Proportion to the Produce, while the Saxons increas'd on their abandoned Lands; 'till the Island became full of English. And were the English now driven into Wales by some foreign Nation, there would in a few Years be no more Englishmen in Britain, than there are now People in Wales. 3. Loss of Trade. Manufactures exported, draw Subsistence from Foreign Countries for Numbers; who are thereby enabled to marry and raise Families. If the Nation be deprived of any Branch of Trade, and no new Employment is found for the People occupy'd in that Branch, it will also be soon deprived of so many People. 4. Loss of Food. Suppose a Nation has a Fishery, which not only employs great Numbers, but makes the Food and Subsistence of the People cheaper; If another Nation becomes Master of the Seas, and prevents the Fishery, the People will diminish in Proportion as the Loss of Employ, and Dearness of Provision, makes it more difficult to subsist a Family. 5. Bad Government and insecure Property. People not only leave such a Country, and settling Abroad incorporate with other Nations, lose their native Language, and become Foreigners; but the Industry of those that remain being discourag'd, the Quantity of Subsistence in the Country is lessen'd, and the Support of a Family becomes more difficult. So heavy Taxes tend to diminish a People. 6. The Introduction of Slaves. The Negroes brought into the English Sugar Islands, have greatly diminish'd the Whites there; the Poor are by this Means depriv'd of Employment, while a few Families acquire vast Estates; which they spend on Foreign Luxuries, and educating their Children in the Habit of those Luxuries; the same Income is needed for the Support of one that might have maintain'd 100. The Whites who have Slaves, not labouring, are enfeebled, and therefore not so generally prolific; the Slaves being work'd too hard, and ill fed, their Constitutions are broken, and the Deaths

among them are more than the Births; so that a continual Supply is needed from Africa. The Northern Colonies having few Slaves increase in Whites. Slaves also pejorate the Families that use them; the white Children become proud, disgusted with Labour, and being educated in Idleness, are rendered unfit to get a Living by Industry.

14. Hence the Prince that acquires new Territory, if he finds it vacant, or removes the Natives to give his own People Room; the Legislator that makes effectual Laws for promoting of Trade, increasing Employment, improving Land by more or better Tillage; providing more Food by Fisheries; securing Property, or new Improvements in Husbandry, may be properly called *Fathers* of their Nation, as they are the Cause of the Generation of Multitudes, by the Encouragement they afford to Marriage.

15. As to Privileges granted to the married, (such as the *Jus trium Liberorum* among the Romans), they may hasten the filling of a Country that has been thinned by War or Pestilence, or that has otherwise vacant Territory; but cannot increase a People beyond the Means provided for their Subsistence.

16. Foreign Luxuries and needless Manufacturers imported and used in a Nation, do, by the same Reasoning, increase the People of a Nation that furnishes them, and diminish the People of the Nation that uses them. Laws therefore that prevent such Importations, and on the contrary promote the Exportation of Manufactures to be consumed in Foreign Countries, may be called (with Respect to the People that make them) *generative Laws,* as by increasing Subsistence they encourage Marriage. Such Laws likewise strengthen a Country, doubly, by increasing its own People and diminishing its Neighbours.

17. Some European Nations prudently refuse to consume the Manufactures of East-India. They should likewise forbid them to

their Colonies; for the Gain to the Merchant, is not to be compar'd with the Loss by this Means of People to the Nation.

18. Home Luxury in the Great, increases the Nation's Manufacturers employ'd by it, who are many, and only tends to diminish the Families that indulge in it, who are few. The greater the common fashionable Expence of any Rank of People, the more cautious they are of Marriage. Therefore Luxury should never be suffer'd to become common.

19. The great Increase of Offspring in particular Families, is not always owing to greater Fecundity of Nature, but sometimes to Examples of Industry in the Heads, and industrious Education; by which the Children are enabled to provide better for themselves, and their marrying early, is encouraged from the Prospect of good Subsistence.

20. If there be a Sect therefore, in our Nation, that regard Frugality and Industry as religious Duties, and educate their Children therein, more than others commonly do; such Sect must consequently increase more by natural Generation, than any other Sect in Britain.

21. The Importation of Foreigners into a Country that has as many Inhabitants as the present Employments and Provisions for Subsistence will bear; will be in the End no Increase of People; unless the New Comers have more Industry and Frugality than the Natives, and then they will provide more Subsistence, and increase in the Country; but they will gradually eat the Natives out. Nor is it necessary to bring in Foreigners to fill up any occasional Vacancy in a Country; for such Vacancy (if the Laws are good) will soon be filled by natural Generation. Who can now find the Vacancy made in Sweden, France or other Warlike Nations, by the Plague of Heroism 40 Years ago; in France, by the Expulsion of the Protestants; in England, by the Settlement of her Colonies; or in Guinea, by 100 Years Exportation of Slaves, that has blacken'd half

America? The thinness of Inhabitants in Spain is owing to National Pride and Idleness, and other Causes, rather than to the Expulsion of the Moors, or to the making of new Settlements.

22. There is in short, no Bound to the prolific Nature of Plants or Animals, but what is made by their crowding and interfering with each others Means of Subsistence. Was the Face of the Earth vacant of other Plants, it might be gradually sowed and overspread with one Kind only; as, for Instance, with Fennel; and were it empty of other Inhabitants, it might in a few Ages be replenish'd from one Nation only; as, for Instance, with Englishmen. Thus there are suppos'd to be now upwards of One Million English Souls in North-America, (tho' 'tis thought scarce 80,000 have been brought over Sea) and yet perhaps there is not one the fewer in Britain, but rather many more, on Account of the Employment the Colonies afford to Manufacturers at Home. This Million doubling, suppose but once in 25 Years, will in another Century be more than the People of England, and the greatest Number of Englishmen will be on this Side of the Water. What an Accession of Power to the British Empire by Sea as well as Land! What Increase of Trade and Navigation! What Numbers of Ships and Seamen! We have been here but little more than 100 Years, and yet the Force of our Privateers in the late War, united, was greater, both in Men and Guns, than that of the whole British Navy in Queen Elizabeth's Time. How important an Affair then to Britain, is the present Treaty for settling the Bounds between her Colonies and the French, and how careful should she be to secure Room enough, since on the Room depends so much the Increase of her People?

23. In fine, A Nation well regulated is like a Polypus; take away a Limb, its Place is soon supply'd; cut it in two, and each deficient Part shall speedily grow out of the Part remaining.

Thus if you have Room and Subsistence enough, as you may by dividing, make ten Polypes out of one, you may of one make ten Nations, equally populous and powerful; or rather, increase a Nation ten fold in Numbers and Strength.

And since Detachments of English from Britain sent to America, will have their Places at Home so soon supply'd and increase so largely here; why should the Palatine Boors be suffered to swarm into our Settlements, and by herding together establish their Language and Manners to the Exclusion of ours? Why should Pennsylvania, founded by the English, become a Colony of *Aliens,* who will shortly be so numerous as to Germanize us instead of our Anglifying them, and will never adopt our Language or Customs, any more than they can acquire our Complexion.

24. Which leads me to add one Remark: That the Number of purely white People in the World is proportionably very small. All Africa is black or tawny. Asia chiefly tawny. America (exclusive of the new Comers) wholly so. And in Europe, the Spaniards, Italians, French, Russians and Swedes, are generally of what we call a swarthy Complexion; as are the Germans also, the Saxons only excepted, who with the English, make the principal Body of White People on the Face of the Earth. I could wish their Numbers were increased. And while we are, as I may call it, *Scouring* our Planet, by clearing America of Woods, and so making this Side of our Globe reflect a brighter Light to the Eyes of inhabitants in Mars or Venus, why should we in the Sight of Superior Beings, darken its People? why increase the Sons of Africa, by Planting them in America, where we have so fair an Opportunity, by excluding all Blacks and Tawneys, of increasing the lovely White and Red? But perhaps I am partial to the Complexion of my Country, for such Kind of Partiality is natural to Mankind. ∼

Excerpts from the *Great Law of Peace of the Iroquois Nations*

RIGHTS, DUTIES, QUALIFICATIONS OF LORDS

26. It shall be the duty of all the Five Nations Confederate Lords, from time to time as occasion demands, to act as mentors and spiritual guides of their people and remind them of their Creator's will and words. They shall say:

"Hearken, that peace may continue unto future days!

"Always listen to the words of the Great Creator, for he has spoken.

"United People, let not evil find lodging in your minds.

"For the Great Creator has spoken and the cause of Peace shall not become old.

"The Cause of peace shall not die if you remember the Great Creator."

Every Confederate Lord shall speak words such as these to promote peace.

27. All Lords of the Five Nations Confederacy must be honest in all things. They must not idle or gossip, but be men possessing those honorable qualities that make true royaneh. It shall be a serious wrong for anyone to lead a Lord into trivial affairs, for the people must ever hold their Lords high in estimation out of respect to their honorable positions. 28. When a candidate Lord is to be installed he shall furnish four strings of shells (or wampum) one span in length bound together at one end. Such will constitute the evidence of his pledge to the Confederate Lords that he will live according to the constitution of the Great Peace and exercise justice in all affairs.

When the pledge is furnished the Speaker of the Council must hold the shell string in his hand and address the opposite side of the Council Fire and he shall commence his address saying: "Now behold him. He has now become a Confederate Lord. See how splendid he looks." An address may then follow. At the end of it he shall send the bunch of shell strings to the opposite side and they shall be received as evidence of the pledge. Then shall the opposite side say:

"We now do crown you with the sacred emblem of the deer's antlers, the emblem of your Lordship. You shall now become a mentor of the people of the Five Nations. The thickness of your skin shall be seven spans —which is to say that you shall be proof against anger, offensive actions and criticism. Your heart shall be filled with peace and good will and your mind filled with a yearning for the welfare of the people of the Confederacy. With endless patience you shall carry out your duty and your firmness shall be tempered with tenderness for your people. Neither anger nor fury shall find lodgment in your mind and all your words and actions shall be marked with calm deliberation. In all of your deliberations in the Confederate Council, in your efforts at law making, in all your official acts, self interest shall be cast into oblivion. Cast not over your shoulder behind you the warnings of the nephews and nieces should they chide you for any error or wrong you may do, but return to the way of the Great Law which is just and right. Look and listen for the welfare of the whole people and have always in view not only the present but also the coming generations, even those whose faces are yet beneath the surface of the ground—the unborn of the future Nation."

OFFICIAL SYMBOLISM

55. A larger bunch of shell strings, in the mak-

SOURCE: Donald A. Grinde Jr., *The Iroquois and the Founding of the American Nation* (Buffalo, N.Y.: Indian Historian Press, 1977), appendix A.

ing of which the Five Nations Confederate Lords have equally contributed, shall symbolize the completeness of the union and certify the pledge of the nations represented by the Confederate Lords of the Mohawk, the Oneida, the Onondaga, the Cayuga and the Seneca, that all are united and formed into one body or union called the Union of the Great Law, which they have established.

A bunch of shell strings is to be the symbol of the council fire of the Five Nations Confederacy. And the Lord whom the Council of Fire Keepers shall appoint to speak for them in opening the council shall hold the strands of shells in his hands when speaking. When he finishes speaking he shall deposit the strings on an elevated place (or pole) so that all the assembled Lords and the people may see it and know that the council is open and in progress.

When the council adjourns the Lord who has been appointed by his comrade Lords to close it shall take the strands of shells in his hands and address the assembled Lords. Thus will the council adjourn until such a time and place as appointed by the council. Then shall the shell strings be placed in a place for safekeeping.

Every five years the Five Nations Confederate Lords and the people shall assemble together and shall ask one another if their minds are still in the same spirit of unity for the Great Binding Law and if any of the Five Nations shall not pledge continuance and steadfastness to the pledge of unity then the Great Binding Law shall dissolve.

56. Five strings of shell tied together as one shall represent the Five Nations. Each string shall represent one territory and the whole a completely united territory known as the Five Nations Confederate Territory.

57. Five arrows shall be bound together very strong and each arrow shall represent one nation. As the five arrows are strongly bound this shall symbolize the complete union of the nations. Thus are the Five Nations united

completely and enfolded together, united into one head, one body and one mind. Therefore they shall labor, legislate and council together for the interest of future generations.

RIGHTS OF THE PEOPLE OF THE FIVE NATIONS

93. Whenever a specially important matter or a great emergency is presented before the Confederate Council and the nature of the matter affects the entire body of Five Nations threatening their utter ruin, then the Lords of the Confederacy must submit the matter to the decision of their people and the decision of the people shall affect the decision of the Confederate Council. This decision shall be a confirmation of the voice of the people.

94. The men of every clan of the Five Nations shall have a Council Fire ever burning in readiness for a council of the clan. When it seems necessary for a council to be held to discuss the welfare of the clans, then the men may gather about the fire. This council shall have the same rights as the council of the women.

95. The women of every clan of the Five Nations shall have a Council Fire ever burning in readiness for a council of the clan. When in their opinion it seems necessary for the interest of the people they shall hold a council and their decision and recommendation shall be introduced before the Council of Lords by the War Chief for its consideration.

96. All the Clan council fires of a nation or of the Five Nations may unite into one general council fire, or delegates from all the council fires may be appointed to unite in a general council for discussing the interests of the people. The people shall have the right to make appointments and to delegate their power to others of their number. When their council shall have come to a conclusion on any matter, their decision shall be reported to the Council of the Nation or to the Confederate Council (as the case may require) by the War

Chief or the War Chiefs.

97. Before the real people united their nations, each nation had its council fires. Before the Great Peace their councils were held. The Five Council Fires shall continue to burn as before and they are not quenched. The Lords of each nation in future shall settle their nations' affairs at this council fire governed always by the laws and rules of the council of the Confederacy and by the Great Peace. ✑

Short Hints towards a Scheme for Uniting the Northern Colonies (1754)

A GOVERNOUR GENERAL

To be appointed by the King.

To be a Military man.

To have a Salary from the Crown.

To have a negation on all acts of the Grand Council, and carry into execution what ever is agreed on by him and that Council.

A GRAND COUNCIL

One member to be chosen by the Assembly of each of the smaller Colonies and two or more by each of the larger, in proportion to the Sums they pay Yearly into the General Treasury.

MEMBERS PAY

—— Shillings sterling per Diem during their sitting and mileage for Travelling Expences.

PLACE AND TIME OF MEETING

To meet —— times in every Year, at the Capital of each Colony in Course, unless particular circumstances and emergencies require more frequent meetings and Alteration in the Course, of places. The Governour General to Judge of those circumstances &c. and call by his Writts.

GENERAL TREASURY

Its Fund, an Excise on Strong Liquors pretty equally drank in the Colonies or Duty on Liquor imported, or —— shillings on each Licence of Publick House or Excise on Superfluities as Tea &c. &c. all which would pay in some proportion to the present wealth of each Colony, and encrease as that wealth encreases, and prevent disputes about the Inequality of Quotas.

To be Collected in each Colony, and Lodged in their Treasury to be ready for the payment of Orders issuing from the Governour General and Grand council jointly.

DUTY AND POWER OF THE GOVERNOUR GENERAL AND GRAND COUNCIL

To order all Indian Treaties.

make all Indian purchases not within proprietary Grants

make and support new settlements by building Forts, raising and paying Soldiers to Garison the Forts, defend the frontiers and annoy the Ennemy.

equip Grand Vessels to scour the Coasts from Privateers in time of war, and protect the Trade and every thing that shall be found necessary for the defence and support of the Colonies in General, and encreasing and extending their settlements &c.

For the Expence they may draw on the fund in the Treasury of any Colony.

SOURCE: Leonard W. Labaree, ed., *The Papers of Benjamin Franklin* (New Haven: Yale University Press, 1961), 5:337–38.

MANNER OF FORMING THIS UNION

The scheme being first well considered cor-rected and improved by the Commissioners at Albany, to be sent home, and an Act of Parliament obtain'd for establishing it. ∽

The Albany Plan of Union (1754)

It is proposed that humble application be made for an act of Parliament of Great Britain, by virtue of which one general government may be formed in America, including all the said colonies, within and under which government each colony may retain its present constitution, except in the particulars wherein a change may be directed by the said act, as hereafter follows.

1. That the said general government be administered by a President-General, to be appointed and supported by the crown; and a Grand Council, to be chosen by the representatives of the people of the several Colonies met in their respective assemblies.

2. That within —— months after the passing such act, the House of Representatives that happen to be sitting within that time, or that shall be especially for that purpose convened, may and shall choose members for the Grand Council, in the following proportion, that is to say,

Massachusetts Bay	7
New Hampshire	2
Connecticut	5
Rhode Island	2
New York	4
New Jersey	3
Pennsylvania	6
Maryland	4
Virginia	7
North Carolina	4
South Carolina	4

3. —— who shall meet for the first time at the city of Philadelphia, being called by the President-General as soon as conveniently may be after his appointment.

4. That there shall be a new election of the members of the Grand Council every three years; and, on the death or resignation of any member, his place should be supplied by a new choice at the next sitting of the Assembly of the Colony he represented.

5. That after the first three years, when the proportion of money arising out of each Colony to the general treasury can be known, the number of members to be chosen for each Colony shall, from time to time, in all ensuing elections, be regulated by that proportion, yet so as that the number to be chosen by any one Province be not more than seven, nor less than two.

6. That the Grand Council shall meet once in every year, and oftener if occasion require, at such time and place as they shall adjourn to at the last preceding meeting, or as they shall be called to meet at by the President-General on any emergency; he having first obtained in writing the consent of seven of the members to such call, and sent duly and timely notice to the whole.

7. That the Grand Council have power to choose their speaker; and shall neither be dissolved, prorogued, nor continued sitting longer than six weeks at one time, without their own consent or the special command of the crown.

SOURCE: Henry Commager, ed., *Documents of American History* (New York: Appleton-Century-Crofts, 1973), 43–45.

8. That the members of the Grand Council shall be allowed for their service ten shillings sterling per diem, during their session and journey to and from the place of meeting; twenty miles to be reckoned a day's journey.

9. That the assent of the President-General be requisite to all acts of the Grand Council, and that it be his office and duty to cause them to be carried into execution.

10. That the President-General, with the advice of the Grand Council, hold or direct all Indian treaties, in which the general interests of the Colonies may be concerned; and make peace or declare war with Indian nations.

11. That they make such laws as they judge necessary for regulating all Indian trade.

12. That they make all purchases from Indians, for the crown, of lands not now within the bounds of particular Colonies, or that shall not be within their bounds when some of them are reduced to more convenient dimensions.

13. That they make new settlements on such purchases, by granting lands in the King's name, reserving a quitrent to the crown for the use of the general treasury.

14. That they make laws for regulating and governing such new settlements, till the crown shall think fit to form them into particular governments.

15. That they raise and pay soldiers and build forts for the defence of any of the Colonies, and equip vessels of force to guard the coasts and protect the trade on the ocean, lakes, or great rivers; but they shall not impress men in any Colony, without the consent of the Legislature.

16. That for these purposes they have power to make laws, and lay and levy such general duties, imposts, or taxes, as to them shall appear most equal and just (considering the ability and other circumstances of the inhabitants in the several Colonies), and such as may be collected with the least inconvenience to the people; rather discouraging luxury, than loading industry with unnecessary burdens.

17. That they may appoint a General Treasurer and Particular Treasurer in each government when necessary; and, from time to time, may order the sums in the treasuries of each government into the general treasury; or draw on them for special payments, as they find most convenient.

18. Yet no money to issue but by joint orders of the President-General and Grand Council; except where sums have been appropriated to particular purposes, and the President-General is previously empowered by an act to draw such sums.

19. That the general accounts shall be yearly settled and reported to the several Assemblies.

20. That a quorum of the Grand Council, empowered to act with the President-General, do consist of twenty-five members; among whom there shall be one or more from a majority of the Colonies.

21. That the laws made by them for the purposes aforesaid shall not be repugnant, but, as near as may be, agreeable to the laws of England, and shall be transmitted to the King in Council for approbation, as soon as may be after their passing; and if not disapproved within three years after presentation, to remain in force.

22. That, in the case of the death of the President-General, the Speaker of the Grand Council for the time being shall succeed, and be vested with the same powers and authorities, to continue till the King's pleasure be known.

23. That all military commission officers, whether for land or sea service, to act under this general constitution, shall be nominated by the President-General; but the approbation of the Grand Council is to be obtained, before they receive their commissions. And all civil officers are to be nominated by the Grand

Council, and to receive the President-General's approbation before they officiate.

24. But, in case of vacancy by death or removal of any officer, civil or military, under this constitution, the Governor of the Province in which such vacancy happens may appoint, till the pleasure of the President-General and Grand Council can be known.

25. That the particular military as well as civil establishments in each Colony remain in their present state, the general constitution notwithstanding; and that on sudden emergencies any Colony may defend itself, and lay the accounts of expense thence arising before the President-General and General Council, who may allow and order payment of the same, as far as they judge such accounts just and reasonable. ∾

Primary Sources

Labaree, Leonard W., ed. *The Papers of Benjamin Franklin*. Vols. 1–32. New Haven, Conn.: Yale University Press, 1960–67.

Van Doren, Carl, ed. *Benjamin Franklin's Autobiographical Writings*. New York: Vintage Press, 1945.

Secondary Sources

Clark, Ronald W. *Benjamin Franklin: A Biography*. New York: Random House, 1983.

Crane, Verner W. *Benjamin Franklin and a Rising People*. Boston: Little, Brown, 1954.

Grinde, Donald A. Jr. *The Iroquois and the Founding of the American Nation*. Buffalo, N.Y.: The Indian Historian Press, 1977.

Grinde, Donald A. Jr., and Bruce Johansen. *Exemplar of Liberty: Native America and the Evolution of Democracy*. Los Angeles: University of California Press, 1991.

Jennings, Francis. *Benjamin Franklin, Politician*. New York: Norton, 1996.

Johansen, Bruce E. *Forgotten Founders: Benjamin Franklin, the Iroquois, and the Rationale for the American Revolution*. Ipswich, Mass.: Gambit Publishers, 1982.

4. Samuel Adams

SAMUEL ADAMS (1722–1803) graduated from Harvard in 1740. Caring little about the family business, he became devoted to local and state politics and the twin causes of democracy and independence. He was a major organizer of opposition to the Sugar, Stamp, and Townshend Acts and a founder of the Non-Importation Association, the Sons of Liberty, and the Committees of Correspondence. He served in the Massachusetts legislature, the Continental Congress, the Massachusetts constitutional convention, and as governor. His numerous writings were always in the forefront of agitation and deliberate provocation, for Adams believed not only in liberty and independence but also in reconstruction of the society. He hated aristocracy and privilege and uncompromisingly sought to establish a thoroughly egalitarian and democratic social order.

The selection given here was produced in 1772 during a period of relative tranquility in which Adams sought to keep the colonists' resistance alive. Derived purely from Locke, it is a statement of the rights of the colonists drafted by Adams and passed by the town of Boston. ~

"The Rights of the Colonists" (1772)

Adopted by the Town of Boston,
November 20, 1772

The Committee appointed by the Town the second Instant "to State the Rights of the Colonists and of this Province in particular, as Men, as Christians, and as Subjects; to communicate and publish the same to the several Towns in this Province and to the World as the sense of this Town with the Infringements and Violations thereof that have been, or from Time to Time may be made. Also requesting of each Town a free Communication of their Sentiments Reported—

First, a State of the *Rights* of the Colonists and of this Province in particular.

Secondly, A List of the *Infringements,* and Violations of those Rights.

Thirdly, A Letter of Correspondence with the other Towns.

1st. Natural Rights of the Colonists as Men.—

Among the Natural Rights of the Colonists are these First: a Right to *Life;* Secondly to *Liberty;* thirdly to *Property;* together with the Right to support and defend them in the best manner they can—Those are evident Branches of, rather than deductions from the Duty of Self Preservation, commonly called the first Law of Nature—

All Men have a Right to remain in a State of Nature as long as they please: And in case of intollerable Oppression, Civil or Religious, to leave the Society they belong to, and enter into another.—

When Men enter into Society, it is by voluntary consent; and they have a right to de-

SOURCE: Harry Alonzo Cushing, *The Writings of Samuel Adams* (New York: Putnam's, 1906; reprint ed., New York: Octagon Books, 1968), 2:350–59, 369–74. Adams's footnotes have been omitted.

mand and insist upon the performance of such conditions, And previous limitations as form an equitable *original compact.* —

Every natural Right not expressly given up or from the nature of a Social Compact necessarily ceded remains. —

All positive and civil laws, should conform as far as possible, to the Law of natural reason and equity. —

As neither reason requires, nor religeon permits the contrary, every Man living in or out of a state of civil society, has a right peaceably and quietly to worship God according to the dictates of his conscience. —

"Just and true liberty, equal and impartial liberty" in matters spiritual and temporal, is a thing that all Men are clearly entitled to, by the eternal and immutable laws Of God and nature, as well as by the law of Nations, & all well grounded municipal laws, which must have their foundation in the former. —

In regard to Religeon, mutual tolleration in the different professions thereof, is what all good and candid minds in all ages have ever practiced; and both by precept and example inculcated on mankind: And it is now generally agreed among Christians that this spirit of toleration in the fullest extent consistent with the being of civil society "is the chief characteristical mark of the true church" & In so much that Mr. Lock[e] has asserted, and proved beyond the possibility of contradiction on any solid ground, that such toleration ought to be extended to all whose doctrines are not subversive of society. The only Sects which he thinks ought to be, and which by all wise laws are excluded from such toleration, are those who teach Doctrines subversive of the Civil Government under which they live. The Roman Catholicks or Papists are excluded by reason of such Doctrines as these "that Princes excommunicated may be deposed," and those they call *Hereticks* may be destroyed without mercy; besides their recognizing the

Pope in so absolute a manner, in subversion of Government, by introducing as far as possible into the states, under whose protection they enjoy life, liberty and property, that solecism in politicks, Imperium in imperio leading directly to the worst anarchy and confusion, civil discord, war and blood shed—

The natural liberty of Men by entring into society is abridg'd or restrained so far only as is necessary for the Great end of Society the best good of the whole—

In the state of nature, every man is under God, Judge and sole Judge, of his own rights and the injuries done him: By entering into society, he agrees to an Arbiter or indifferent Judge between him and his neighbours; but he no more renounces his original right, than by taking a cause out of the ordinary course of law, and leaving the decision to Referees or indifferent Arbitrations. In the last case he must pay the Referees for time and trouble; he should be also willing to pay his Just quota for the support of government, the law and constitution; the end of which is to furnish indifferent and impartial Judges in all cases that may happen, whether civil, ecclesiastical, marine or military. —

"The natural liberty of man is to be free from any superior power on earth, and not to be under the will or legislative authority of man; but only to have the law of nature for his rule." —

In the state of nature men may as the *Patriarchs* did, employ hired servants for the defence of their lives, liberty and property: and they should pay them reasonable wages. Government was instituted for the purposes of common defence; and those who hold the reins of government have an equitable natural right to an honourable support from the same principle "that the labourer is worthy of his hire" but then the same community which they serve, ought to be assessors of their pay: Governors have no right to seek what they please; by this, instead of being content with the station assigned them, that of honourable servants of the society, they would soon become Absolute masters, Despots, and Tyrants. Hence as a private man has a right to say, what wages he will give in his private affairs, so has a Community to determine what they will give and grant of their Substance, for the Administration of publick affairs. And in both cases more are ready generally to offer their Service at the proposed and stipulated price, than are able and willing to perform their duty.—

In short it is the greatest absurdity to suppose it in the power of one or any number of men at the entering into society, to renounce their essential natural rights, or the means of preserving those rights when the great end of civil government from the very nature of its institution is for the support, protection and defence of those very rights: the principal of which as is before observed, are life, liberty and property. If men through fear, fraud or mistake, should *in terms* renounce and give up any essential natural right, the eternal law of reason and the great end of society, would absolutely vacate such renunciation, the right to freedom being *the gift* of God Almighty, it is not in the power of Man to alienate this gift, and voluntarily become a slave—

2d. *The Rights of the Colonists as Christians —*

These may be best understood by reading—and carefully studying the institutes of the great Lawgiver and head of the Christian Church: which are to be found closely written and promulgated in the *New Testament —*

By the Act of the British Parliament commonly called the Toleration Act, every subject in England Except Papists &c was restored to, and re-established in, his natural right to worship God according to the dictates of his own conscience. And by the Charter of this Province it is granted ordained and established

(that it is declared as an original right) that there shall be liberty of conscience allowed in the worship of God, to all Christians except Papists, inhabiting or which shall inhabit or be resident within said Province or Territory. Magna Charta itself is in substance but a constrained Declaration, or proclamation, and promulgation in the name of King, Lord, and Commons of the sense the latter had of their original inherent, indefeasible natural Rights, as also those of free Citizens equally perdurable with the other. That great author, that great jurist, and even that Court writer Mr. Justice Blackstone holds that his recognition was justly obtained of King John sword in hand: and peradventure it must be one day sword in hand again rescued and preserved from total destruction and oblivion.—

3d. *The Rights of the Colonists as Subjects*

A Common Wealth or state is a body politick or civil society of men, united together to promote their mutual safety and prosperity, by means of their union.

The *absolute Rights* of Englishmen, and all freemen in or out of Civil society, are principally, *personal security, personal liberty* and *private property.*

All Persons born in the British American Colonies are by the laws of God and nature and by the Common law of England, *exclusive of all charters from the Crown,* well Entitled, and by the Acts of the British Parliament are declared to be entitled to all the natural essential, inherent & inseperable Rights Liberties and Privileges of Subjects born in Great Britain, or within the Realm. Among those Rights are the following; which no men or body of men, consistently with their own rights as men and citizens or members of society, can for themselves give up, or take away from others

First, "The first fundamental positive law of all Commonwealths or States, is the establishing the legislative power; as the first fundamental *natural* law also, which is to govern even the legislative power itself, is the preservation of the Society."

Secondly, The Legislative has no right to absolute arbitrary power over the lives and fortunes of the people: Nor can mortals assume a prerogative, not only too high for men, but for Angels, and therefore reserved for the exercise of the *Deity* alone.—

"The Legislative cannot Justly *assume* to itself a power to rule by extempore arbitrary decrees; but it is bound to see that Justice is dispensed, and that the rights of the subjects be decided, by promulgated, standing and known laws, and authorized *independent Judges;"* that is independent as far as possible of Prince or People. *"There shall be one rule of Justice for rich and poor; for the favorite in Court, and the Countryman at the Plough."*

Thirdly, The supreme court cannot Justly take from any man, any part of his property without his consent, in person or by his Representative.—

These are some of the first principles of natural law & Justice, and the great Barriers of all free states, and of the British Constitution in particular. It is utterly irreconcileable to these principles, and to many other fundamental maxims of the common law, common sense and reason that a British house of commons, should have a right, at pleasure, to give and grant the property of the Colonists. That these Colonists are well entitled to all the essential rights, liberties and privileges of men and freemen, born in Britain, is manifest not only from the Colony charter, in general, but acts of the British Parliament. The statute of the 13th of George 2.c.7. naturalizes even foreigners after seven years residence. The words of the Massachusetts Charter are these, "And further our will and pleasure is, and we do hereby for us, our heirs and successors, grant establish and ordain, that all and every of the subjects of us, our heirs and successors, which shall go to and inhabit within our said province or territory

and every of their children which shall happen to be born there or on the seas in going thither, or returning from thence shall have and enjoy, all liberties and immunities of free and natural subjects within any of the dominions of us, our heirs and successors, to all intents constructions & purposes whatsoever as if they and every of them were born within this our Realm of England." Now what liberty can there be, where property is taken away without consent? Can it be said with any colour of truth and Justice, that this Continent of three thousand miles in length, and of a breadth as yet unexplored, in which however, its supposed, there are five millions of people, has the least voice, vote or influence in the decisions of the British Parliament? Have they, all together, any more right or power to return a single number to that house of commons, who have not inadvertently, but deliberately assumed a power to dispose of their lives, Liberties and properties, then [than] to choose an Emperor of China! Had the Colonists a right to return members to the British Parliament it would only be hurtfull; as from their local situation and circumstances it is impossible they should be ever truly and properly represented there. The inhabitants of this country in all probability in a few years will be more numerous, than those of Great Britain and Ireland together; yet it is absurdly expected by the promoters of the present measures, that these, with their posterity to all generations, should be easy while their property, shall be disposed of by a house of commons at three thousand miles distant from them; and who cannot be supposed to have the least care or concern for their real interest: Who have not only no natural care for their interest, but must be *in effect* bribed against it; as every burden they lay on the colonists is so much saved or gained to themselves. Hitherto many of the Colonists have been free from Quit Rents; but if the breath of a British house of commons can originate an act for taking away all our money, our lands will go next or be subject to rack rents from haughty and relentless landlords who will ride at ease, while we are trodden in the dirt. The Colonists have been branded with the odious names of traitors and rebels, only for complaining of their grievances; How long such treatment will, or ought to be born is submitted. ∼

Primary Sources

Adams, Samuel. *Warren-Adams Letters, Being Chiefly a Correspondence among John Adams, Samuel Adams, and James Warren, 1743–1814.* 2 vols. Boston: Massachusetts Historical Society, 1917–25.

Cushing, Harry Alonzo. *The Writings of Samuel Adams.* New York: Octagon Books, 1968.

Lawson, Elizabeth, ed. *Samuel Adams: Selections from his Writings.* New York: International Publishers, 1946.

Secondary Sources

Beach, Stewart. *Samuel Adams: The Fateful Years, 1764–1776.* New York: Dodd, Mead, 1965.

Canfield, Cass. *Samuel Adams' Revolution, 1765–1776.* New York: Harper & Row, 1976.

Fowler, Lillian M. *Samuel Adams: Radical Puritan.* New York: Longman, 1997.

Miller, John Chester. *Sam Adams: Pioneer in Propaganda.* Stanford, Calif.: Stanford University Press, 1960.

Rich, Andrew L., and Arthur L. Smith, *Rhetoric of Revolution: Sam Adams, Emma Goldman, Malcolm X.* Durham, N.C.: Moore Publishing Co., 1970.

5. Thomas Paine

THOMAS PAINE (1737–1809) was born in England to a poor Quaker family. He had little education and worked at a variety of trades and occupations, developing a thorough dislike for the class system and bureaucracy of England before migrating to America in 1774. He settled in Philadelphia and began writing for local newspapers. In January 1776 he published *Common Sense,* an anonymous two-shilling pamphlet that sold 120,000 copies in three months and 500,000 copies overall. He joined the revolutionary army and later that year produced the first of his *Crisis* papers, a series that would rally popular support throughout the war.

Paine filled several government posts from 1777 to 1780. In 1781 he went to France for several months in search of financial aid for the Revolution. For the next five years he lived in New Jersey, writing and working on various inventions. In 1786 he published *Dissertations on Government, The Affairs of the Bank,* and *Paper Money.*

Paine's restless nature led him to return to Europe in 1787. Burke's condemnation of the French Revolution in 1790 prompted Paine to reply in early 1791 with his first part of the *Rights of Man.* The second part followed in 1792. That same year French citizenship was conferred on Paine by the French Assembly; by late 1793, however, the political scene had changed so much that Paine was arrested and imprisoned as a citizen of a country at war with France. During his imprisonment Paine composed part of *The Age of Reason.*

Released from prison in late 1794, Paine continued to live in Paris. During this period he published *Dissertation on First-Principles of Government* (1795), "Agrarian Justice" (1797), and *The Letter to George Washington* (1796).

In 1802 Paine returned to America. The last seven years of his life were spent in poverty, declining health, and social ostracism. He died in New York in June 1809.

Common Sense, excerpted here, was one of the first publications to attack the British constitution directly. All other American writers had viewed the British constitution as *the* model and source of liberty, which had unfortunately become corrupted over time by the actions of king and Parliament. Paine derided the whole idea of mixed government and monarchy, arguing for direct and simple government by the people. In his later *Crisis* papers he urged comprehensive social revolution to make a society of equals unprecedented in history; the first and last of these are given here. The later writings offer more detailed reflections on the basis of social order and the rights of people to shape a society to their own liking. ⌒

Common Sense (1776)

OF THE ORIGIN AND DESIGN OF GOVERNMENT IN GENERAL, WITH CONCISE REMARKS ON THE ENGLISH CONSTITUTION

Some writers have so confounded society with government as to leave little or no distinction between them, whereas they are not only different but have different origins. Society is produced by our wants, and government by our wickedness; the former promotes our happiness *positively* by uniting our affections, the latter *negatively* by restraining our vices. The one encourages intercourse, the other creates distinctions. The first is a patron, the last a punisher.

Society in every state is a blessing, but gov-

ernment even in its best state is but a necessary evil, in its worst state an intolerable one; for when we suffer or are exposed to the same miseries *by a government* which we might expect in a country *without government,* our calamity is heightened by reflecting that we furnish the means by which we suffer. Government, like dress, is the badge of lost innocence; the palaces of kings are built on the ruins of the bowers of paradise. For were the impulses of conscience clear, uniform, and irresistibly obeyed, man would need no other lawgiver; but that not being the case, he finds it necessary to surrender up a part of his property to furnish means for the protection of the rest, and this he is induced to do by the same prudence which in every other case advises him out of two evils to choose the least. Wherefore, security being the true design and end of government, it unanswerably follows that whatever form thereof appears most likely to ensure

SOURCE: All material in selection 5 may be found in *Thomas Paine: Common Sense and Other Writings,* ed. Nelson F. Adkins (New York: Liberal Arts Press, 1953).

it to us, with the least expense and greatest benefit, is preferable to all others.

In order to gain a clear and just idea of the design and end of government, let us suppose a small number of persons settled in some sequestered part of the earth unconnected with the rest; they will then represent the first peopling of any country, or of the world. In this state of natural liberty, society will be their first thought. A thousand motives will excite them thereto; the strength of one man is so unequal to his wants and his mind so unfitted for perpetual solitude that he is soon obliged to seek assistance and relief of another, who in his turn requires the same. Four or five united would be able to raise a tolerable dwelling in the midst of a wilderness, but one might labor out the common period of life without accomplishing anything; when he had felled his timber, he could not remove it, nor erect it after it was removed; hunger in the meantime would urge him from his work and every different want call him a different way. Disease, nay even misfortune, would be death; for though neither might be mortal, yet either would disable him from living and reduce him to a state in which he might rather be said to perish than to die.

Thus necessity, like a gravitating power, would soon form our newly arrived emigrants into society, the reciprocal blessings of which would supersede and render the obligations of law and government unnecessary while they remained perfectly just to each other, but as nothing but Heaven is impregnable to vice, it will unavoidably happen that in proportion as they surmount the first difficulties of emigration, which bound them together in a common cause, they will begin to relax in their duty and attachment to each other, and this remissness will point out the necessity of establishing some form of government to supply the defect of moral virtue.

Some convenient tree will afford them a statehouse, under the branch of which the whole colony may assemble to deliberate on public matters. It is more than probable that their first laws will have the title only of regulations and be enforced by no other penalty than public disesteem. In this first parliament every man by natural right will have a seat.

But as the colony increases, the public concerns will increase likewise, and the distance at which the members may be separated will render it too inconvenient for all of them to meet on every occasion as at first when their number was small, their habitations near, and the public concerns few and trifling. This will point out the convenience of their consenting to leave the legislative part to be managed by a select number chosen from the whole body, who are supposed to have the same concerns at stake which those have who appointed them and who will act in the same manner as the whole body would act were they present. If the colony continue increasing, it will become necessary to augment the number of representatives; and that the interest of every part of the colony may be attended to, it will be found best to divide the whole into convenient parts, each part sending its proper number; and that the *elected* might never form to themselves an interest separate from the *electors,* prudence will point out the propriety of having elections often, because as the elected might by that means return and mix again with the general body of the *electors* in a few months, their fidelity to the public will be secured by the prudent reflection of not making a rod for themselves. And as this frequent interchange will establish a common interest with every part of the community, they will mutually and naturally support each other, and on this (not on the unmeaning name of King) depends the *strength of government and the happiness of the governed.*

Here then is the origin and rise of government, namely, a mode rendered necessary by the inability of moral virtue to govern the world; here too is the design and end of government, viz., freedom and security. And however our eyes may be dazzled with show or our ears deceived by sound, however prejudice may warp our wills or interest darken our understanding, the simple voice of nature and reason will say it is right.

I draw my idea of the form of government from a principle in nature which no art can overturn, viz., that the more simple anything is, the less liable it is to be disordered and the easier repaired when disordered; and with this maxim in view I offer a few remarks on the so much boasted constitution of England. That it was noble for the dark and slavish times in which it was erected is granted. When the world was overrun with tyranny, the least remove therefrom was a glorious rescue. But that it is imperfect, subject to convulsions, and incapable of producing what it seems to promise is easily demonstrated.

Absolute governments (though the disgrace of human nature) have this advantage with them: that they are simple; if the people suffer, they know the head from which their suffering springs, know likewise the remedy, and are not bewildered by a variety of causes and cures. But the constitution of England is so exceedingly complex that the nation may suffer for years together without being able to discover in which part the fault lies; some will say in one and some in another, and every political physician will advise a different medicine.

I know it is difficult to get over local or longstanding prejudices; yet if we will suffer ourselves to examine the component parts of the English constitution, we shall find them to be the base remains of two ancient tyrannies, compounded with some new republican materials:

First, the remains of monarchical tyranny in the person of the king.

Secondly, the remains of aristocratical tyranny in the persons of the peers.

Thirdly, the new republican materials in the persons of the Commons, on whose virtue depends the freedom of England.

The two first, by being hereditary, are independent of the people; wherefore, in a *constitutional sense,* they contribute nothing toward the freedom of the state.

To say that the constitution of England is a *union* of three powers, reciprocally *checking* each other, is farcical; either the words have no meaning or they are flat contradictions.

To say that the Commons is a check upon the king presupposes two things:

First, that the king is not to be trusted without being looked after, or, in other words, that a thirst for absolute power is the natural disease of monarchy.

Secondly, that the Commons, by being appointed for that purpose, are either wiser or more worthy of confidence than the crown.

But as the same constitution which gives the Commons a power to check the king by withholding the supplies gives afterward the king a power to check the Commons by empowering him to reject their other bills, it again supposes that the king is wiser than those whom it has already supposed to be wiser than him. A mere absurdity!

There is something exceedingly ridiculous in the composition of monarchy; it first excludes a man from the means of information, yet empowers him to act in cases where the highest judgment is required. The state of a king shuts him from the world, yet the business of a king requires him to know it thoroughly; wherefore the different parts, by unnaturally opposing and destroying each other, prove the whole character to be absurd and useless....

OF MONARCHY AND HEREDITARY SUCCESSION

... To the evil of monarchy we have added that of hereditary succession; and as the first is a degradation and lessening of ourselves, so the second, claimed as a matter of right, is an insult and imposition on posterity. For all men being originally equals, no one by birth could have a right to set up his own family in perpetual preference to all others forever; and though himself might deserve some decent degree of honors of his co-contemporaries, yet his descendants might be far too unworthy to inherit them. One of the strongest natural proofs of the folly of hereditary right in kings is that nature disapproves it; otherwise she would not so frequently turn it into ridicule by giving mankind an *ass for a lion.*

Secondly, as no man at first could possess any other public honors than were bestowed upon him, so the givers of these honors could have no power to give away the right of posterity, and though they might say "We choose you for our head," they could not without manifest injustice to their children say "that your children and your children's children shall reign over ours forever." Because such an unwise, unjust, unnatural compact might (perhaps) in the next succession put them under the government of a rogue or a fool. Most wise men in their private sentiments have ever treated hereditary right with contempt; yet it is one of those evils which when once established is not easily removed; many submit from fear, others from superstition, and the more powerful part shares with the king the plunder of the rest.

This is supposing the present race of kings in the world to have had an honorable origin; whereas it is more than probable that, could we take off the dark covering of antiquity and trace them to their first rise, that we should find the first of them nothing better than the principal ruffian of some restless gang, whose savage manners or pre-eminence in subtilty obtained from the title of chief among plunderers and who, by increasing in power and extending his depredations, overawed the quiet and defenseless to purchase their safety by frequent contributions. Yet his electors could have no idea of giving hereditary right to his descendants, because such a perpetual exclusion of themselves was incompatible with the free and unrestrained principles they professed to live by. Wherefore hereditary succession in the early ages of monarchy could not take place as a matter of claim, but as something casual or complemental; but as few or no records were extant in those days, the traditionary history stuffed with fables, it was very easy, after the lapse of a few generations, to trump up some superstitious tale conveniently timed, Mahometlike, to cram hereditary right down the throats of the vulgar. Perhaps the disorders which threatened or seemed to threaten, on the decrease of a leader and the choice of a new one (for elections among ruffians could not be very orderly) induced many at first to favor hereditary pretensions; by which means it happened, as it has happened since, that what at first was submitted to as a convenience was afterward claimed as a right.
. . .

But it is not so much the absurdity as the evil of hereditary succession which concerns mankind. Did it insure a race of good and wise men, it would have the seal of divine authority, but as it opens a door to the *foolish* and *wicked,* and the *improper,* it has in it the nature of oppression. Men who look upon themselves born to reign and others to obey soon grow insolent. Selected from the rest of mankind, their minds are early poisoned by importance, and the world they act in differs so materially from the world at large that they have but little opportunity of knowing its true interests and, when they succeed to the government, are frequently the most ignorant and unfit of any throughout the dominions. . . .

If we inquire into the business of a king, we shall find that in some countries they have none; and after sauntering away their lives without pleasure to themselves or advantage to the nation, withdraw from the scene and leave their successors to tread the same idle round. In absolute monarchies the whole weight of business, civil and military, lies on the king, the children of Israel in their request for a king urged this plea, "that he may judge us, and go out before us and fight our battles." But in the countries where he is neither a judge nor a general, as in England, a man would be puzzled to know what *is* his business. . . .

In England a king has little more to do than to make war and give away places, which, in plain terms, is to impoverish the nation and set it together by the ears. A pretty business indeed for a man to be allowed eight hundred thousand sterling a year for, and worshipped into the bargain! Of more worth, is one honest man to society, and in the sight of God, than all the crowned ruffians that ever lived.

THOUGHTS OF THE PRESENT STATE OF AMERICAN AFFAIRS

In the following pages I offer nothing more than simple facts, plain arguments, and common sense; and have no other preliminaries to settle with the reader than that he will divest himself of prejudice and prepossession, and suffer his reason and his feelings to determine for themselves; that he will put on, or rather that he will not put off, the true character of a man, and generously enlarge his views beyond the present day.

Volumes have been written on the subject of the struggle between England and America. Men of all ranks have embarked in the controversy, from different motives and with various designs; but all have been ineffectual, and the period of debate is closed. Arms as the last resource decide the contest; the appeal was the choice of the king, and the continent has accepted the challenge. . . .

The sun never shined on a cause of greater worth. 'Tis not the affair of a city, a county, a province, or a kingdom, but of a continent—of at least one-eighth part of the habitable globe. 'Tis not the concern of a day, a year, or an age; posterity are virtually involved in the contest, and will be more or less affected even to the end time by the proceedings now. Now is the seedtime of continental union, faith, and honor. The least fracture now will be like a name engraved with the point of a pin on the tender rind of a young oak; the wound would enlarge with the tree, and posterity read it in full-grown characters.

By referring the matter from argument to arms, a new era for politics is struck—a new method of thinking has arisen. All plans, proposals, etc. prior to the nineteenth of April, i.e., to the commencement of hostilities, are like the almanacs of the last year, which, though proper then, are superseded and useless now. Whatever was advanced by the advocates on either side of the question then terminated in one and the same point, viz., a union with Great Britain; the only difference between the parties was the method of effecting it—the one proposing force, the other friendship; but it has so far happened that the first has failed, and the second has withdrawn her influence.

As much has been said of the advantages of reconciliation, which, like an agreeable dream, has passed away and left us as we were, it is but right that we should examine the contrary side of the argument and inquire into some of the many material injuries which these colonies sustain, and always will sustain, by being connected with and dependent on Great Britain. To examine that connection and dependence on the principles of nature and common sense; to see what we have to trust to, if separated, and what we are to expect, if dependent. . . .

I challenge the warmest advocate for reconciliation to show a single advantage that this continent can reap by being connected with Great Britain. I repeat the challenge; not a single advantage is derived. Our corn will fetch its price in any market in Europe, and our imported goods must be paid for, buy them where we will.

But the injuries and disadvantages we sustain by that connection are without number, and our duty to mankind at large, as well as to ourselves, instruct us to renounce the alliance; because any submission to or dependence on Great Britain tends directly to involve this continent in European wars and quarrels and sets us at variance with nations who would otherwise seek our friendship and against whom we have neither anger nor complaint. As Europe is our market for trade, we ought to form no partial connection with any part of it. It is the true interest of America to steer clear of European connections, which she never can do while, by her dependence on Britain, she is made the makeweight in the scale of British politics.

Europe is too thickly planted with kingdoms to be long at peace; and whenever a war breaks out between England and any foreign power, the trade of America goes to ruin *because of her connection with Britain*. The next war may not turn out like the last; and should it not, the advocates for reconciliation now will be wishing for separation then, because neutrality in that case would be a safer convoy than a man-of-war. Everything that is right or natural pleads for separation. The blood of the slain, the weeping voice of nature cries, " *'Tis time to part.*" ...

Men of passive tempers look somewhat lightly over the offenses of Great Britain and, still hoping for the best, are apt to call out, "Come, come, we shall be friends again for all this." But examine the passions and feelings of mankind, bring the doctrine of reconciliation to the touchstone of nature, and then tell me whether you can hereafter love, honor, and faithfully serve the power that has carried fire

and sword into your land? If you cannot do all these, then are you only deceiving yourselves, and by your delay bringing ruin upon posterity. Your future connection with Britain, whom you can neither love nor honor, will be forced and unnatural, and being formed only on the plan of present convenience will, in a little time, fall into a relapse more wretched than the first. But if you say you still can pass the violations over, then I ask, has your house been burned? Has your property been destroyed before your face? Are your wife and children destitute of a bed to lie on or bread to live on? Have you lost a parent or a child by their hands, and yourself the ruined and wretched survivor? If you have not, then are you not a judge of those who have. But if you have and can still shake hands with the murderers, then are you unworthy the name of husband, father, friend, or lover; and whatever may be your rank or title in life, you have the heart of a coward and the spirit of a sycophant.

This is not inflaming or exaggerating matters, but trying them by those feelings and affections which nature justifies and without which we should be incapable of discharging the social duties of life or enjoying the felicities of it. I mean not to exhibit horror for the purpose of provoking revenge, but to awaken us from fatal and unmanly slumbers, that we may pursue determinately some fixed object. It is not in the power of Britain or Europe to conquer America, if she does not conquer herself by delay and timidity. The present winter is worth an age if rightly employed, but if lost or neglected the whole continent will partake of the misfortune; and there is no punishment which that man will not deserve, be he who or what or where he will, that may be the means of sacrificing a season so precious and useful. ...

A government of our own is our natural right; and when a man seriously reflects on the precariousness of human affairs he will become convinced that it is infinitely wiser and safer to form a Constitution of our own in a cool, deliberate manner while we have it in our power than to trust such an interesting event to time and chance. If we omit it now, some Massanello may hereafter arise, who laying hold of popular disquietudes, may collect together the desperate and the discontented, and by assuming to themselves the powers of government may sweep away the liberties of the continent like a deluge. Should the government of America return again into the hands of Britain, the tottering situation of things will be a temptation for some desperate adventurer to try his fortune, and in such a case what relief can Britain give? Ere she could hear the news, the fatal business might be done, and ourselves suffering like the wretched Britons under the oppression of the conqueror. Ye that oppose independence now, ye know not what ye do; yet are opening a door to eternal tyranny by keeping vacant the seat of government. There are thousands and tens of thousands who would think it glorious to expel from the continent that barbarous and hellish power which has stirred up the Indians and Negroes to destroy us; the cruelty has a double guilt: it is dealing brutally by us and treacherously by them.

To talk of friendship with those in whom our reason forbids us to have faith and our affections, wounded through a thousand pores, instruct us to detest is madness and folly. Every day wears out the little remains of kindred between us and them; and can there be any reason to hope that, as the relationship expires, the affection will increase, or that we shall agree better when we have ten times more and greater concerns to quarrel over than ever?

Ye that tell us of harmony and reconciliation, can ye restore to us the time that is past? Can ye give to prostitution its former innocence? Neither can ye reconcile Britain and America. The last cord now is broken, the people of England are presenting addresses against us. There are injuries which nature cannot forgive; she would cease to be nature if she did. As well can the lover forgive the ravisher of his mistress as the continent forgive the murderers of Britain. The Almighty has implanted in us these unextinguishable feelings for good and wise purposes. They are the guardians of his image in our hearts. They distinguish us from the herd of common animals. The social compact would dissolve and justice be extirpated [from] the earth, or have only a casual existence, were we callous to the touches of affection. The robber and the murderer would often escape unpunished did not the injuries which our tempers sustain provoke us into justice.

O ye that love mankind! Ye that dare oppose not only the tyranny but the tyrant, stand forth! Every spot of the Old World is overrun with oppression. Freedom has been hunted round the globe. Asia and Africa have long expelled her. Europe regards her like a stranger, and England has given her warning to depart. O! receive the fugitive, and prepare in time an asylum for mankind. ⌇

The American Crisis I (1777)

These are the times that try men's souls. The summer soldier and the sunshine patriot will, in this crisis, shrink from the service of their country, but he that stands it *now* deserves the love and thanks of man and woman. Tyranny, like hell, is not easily conquered; yet we have this consolation with us that, the harder the conflict, the more glorious the triumph. What we obtain too cheap, we esteem too lightly; it is dearness only that gives everything its value. Heaven knows how to put a proper price upon its goods, and it would be strange indeed if so celestial an article as freedom should not be highly rated. Britain, with an army to enforce her tyranny, has declared that she has a right *(not only to tax)* but *to bind us in all cases whatsoever;* and if being *bound in that manner* is not slavery, then is there not such a thing as slavery upon earth. Even the expression is impious, for so unlimited a power can belong only to God.

Whether the independence of the continent was declared too soon or delayed too long I will not now enter into as an argument; my own simple opinion is that, had it been eight months earlier, it would have been much better. We did not make a proper use of last winter, neither could we while we were in a dependent state. However, the fault, if it were one, was all our own; we have none to blame but ourselves. But no great deal is lost yet. All that Howe has been doing for this month past is rather a ravage than a conquest, which the spirit of the Jerseys, a year ago, would have quickly repulsed, and which time and a little resolution will soon recover.

I have as little superstition in me as any man living, but my secret opinion has ever been and still is that God Almighty will not give up a people to military destruction or leave them unsupportedly to perish who have so earnestly and so repeatedly sought to avoid the calamities of war by every decent method which wisdom could invent. Neither have I so much of the infidel in me as to suppose that He has relinquished the government of the world and given us up to the care of devils, and as I do not I cannot see on what grounds the King of Britain can look up to heaven for help against us; a common murderer, a high-

wayman, or a housebreaker has as good a pretense as he....

... I turn with the warm ardor of a friend to those who have nobly stood and are yet determined to stand the matter out; I call not upon a few but upon all—not on *this* state or *that* state, but on *every* state—up and help us, lay your shoulders to the wheel, better have too much force than too little when so great an object is at stake. Let it be told to the future world that in the depth of winter, when nothing but hope and virtue could survive, that the city and the country, alarmed at one common danger, came forth to meet and to repulse it. Say not that thousands are gone, turn out your tens of thousands; throw not the burden of the day upon Providence, but "show your faith by your works," that God may bless you. It matters not where you live or what rank of life you hold, the evil or the blessing will reach you all. The far and the near, the home counties and the back, the rich and the poor will suffer or rejoice alike. The heart that feels not now is dead; the blood of his children will curse his cowardice who shrinks back at a time when a little might have saved the whole and made *them* happy. I love the man that can smile in trouble, that can gather strength from distress and grow brave by reflection. "Tis the business of little minds to shrink, but he whose heart is firm and whose conscience approves his conduct will pursue his principles unto death." My own line of reasoning is to myself as straight and clear as a ray of light. Not all the treasures of the world, so far as I believe, could have induced me to support an offensive war, for I think it murder; but if a thief breaks into my house, burns and destroys my property, and kills or threatens to kill me or those that are in it and to "bind me in all cases whatsoever" to his absolute will, am I to suffer it? What signifies it to me whether he who does it is a king or a common man, my countryman or not my countryman; whether it be done by an individual villain or an army of them? If we reason to the root of things, we shall find no difference; neither can any just cause be assigned why we should punish in the one case and pardon in the other. Let them call me rebel and welcome, I feel no concern from it; but I should suffer the misery of devils were I to make a whore of my soul by swearing allegiance to one whose character is that of a sottish, stupid, stubborn, worthless, brutish man. I conceive likewise a horrid idea in receiving mercy from a being who, at the last day, shall be shrieking to the rocks and mountains to cover him and fleeing with terror from the orphan, the widow, and the slain of America.

There are cases which cannot be overdone by language, and this is one. There are persons, too, who see not the full extent of the evil which threatens them; they solace themselves with hopes that the enemy, if he succeed, will be merciful. It is the madness of folly to expect mercy from those who have refused to do justice; and even mercy, where conquest is the object, is only a trick of war; the cunning of the fox is as murderous as the violence of the wolf, and we ought to guard equally against both. ◡

The American Crisis XIII (1783)

THOUGHTS ON THE PEACE AND THE PROBABLE ADVANTAGES THEREOF

"The times that tried men's souls" are over, and the greatest and completest revolution the world ever knew gloriously and happily accomplished.

But to pass from the extremes of danger to safety, from the tumult of war to the tranquility of peace, though sweet in contemplation, requires a gradual composure of the senses to receive it. Even calmness has the power of stunning, when it opens too instantly upon us. The long and raging hurricane that should cease in a moment would leave us in a state rather of wonder than enjoyment, and some moments of recollection must pass before we could be capable of tasting the felicity of repose. There are but few instances in which the mind is fitted for sudden transitions; it takes in its pleasures by reflection and comparison, and those must have time to act before the relish for new scenes is complete.

In the present case, the mighty magnitude of the object, the various uncertainties of fate it has undergone, the numerous and complicated dangers we have suffered or escaped, the eminence we now stand on, and the vast prospect before us must all conspire to impress us with contemplation.

To see it in our power to make a world happy, to teach mankind the art of being so, to exhibit on the theater of the universe a character hitherto unknown, and to have, as it were, a new creation entrusted to our hands are honors that command reflection and can neither be too highly estimated nor too gratefully received.

In this pause then of recollection, while the storm is ceasing and the long-agitated mind vibrating to a rest, let us look back on the scenes we have passed and learn from experience what is yet to be done.

Never, I say, had a country so many openings to happiness as this. Her setting out in life, like the rising of a fair morning, was unclouded and promising. Her cause was good. Her principles just and liberal. Her temper serene and firm. Her conduct regulated by the nicest steps, and everything about her wore the mark of honor. It is not every country (perhaps there is not another in the world) that can boast so fair an origin. Even the first settlement of America corresponds with the character of the revolution. Rome, once the proud mistress of the universe, was originally a band of ruffians. Plunder and rapine made her rich, and her oppression of millions made her great. But America need never be ashamed to tell her birth, nor relate the stages by which she rose to empire.

The remembrance, then, of what is past, if it operates rightly, must inspire her with the most laudable of all ambition, that of adding to the fair fame she began with. The world has seen her great in adversity; struggling, without a thought of yielding beneath accumulated difficulties, bravely, nay proudly, encountering distress; and rising in resolution as the storm increased. All this is justly due to her, for her fortitude has merited the character. Let then the world see that she can bear prosperity and that her honest virtue in time of peace is equal to the bravest virtue in time of war.

She is now descending to the scenes of quiet and domestic life. Not beneath the cypress shade of disappointment, but to enjoy in her own land and under her own vine the sweet of her labors and the reward of her toil. In this situation, may she never forget that a fair national reputation is of as much importance as independence. That it possesses a charm that wins upon the world and makes even enemies civil. That it gives a dignity which is often superior to power, and commands reverence where pomp and splendor fail.

It would be a circumstance ever to be lamented and never to be forgotten were a single blot, from any cause whatever, suffered to fall on a revolution which to the end of time must be an honor to the age that accomplished it, and which has contributed more to enlighten the world and diffuse a spirit of freedom and liberality among mankind than any human event (if this may be called one) that ever preceded it.

It is not among the least of the calamities of a long-continued war that it unhinges the mind from those nice sensations which at other times appear so amiable. The continual spectacle of woe blunts the finer feelings, and the necessity of bearing with the sight renders it familiar. In like manner are many of the moral obligations of society weakened, till the custom of acting by necessity becomes an apology where it is truly a crime. Yet let but a nation conceive rightly of its character, and it will be chastely just in protecting it. None ever began with a fairer than America and none can be under a greater obligation to preserve it. . . .

It is with confederated states as with individuals in society: something must be yielded up to make the whole secure. In this view of things we gain by what we give and draw an annual interest greater than the capital. I ever feel myself hurt when I hear the union, that great palladium of our liberty and safety, the least irreverently spoken of. It is the most sacred thing in the constitution of America and that which every man should be most proud and tender of. Our citizenship in the United States is our national character. Our citizenship in any particular state is only our local distinction. By the latter we are known at home, by the former to the world. Our great title is *Americans;* our inferior one varies with the place.

So far as my endeavors could go, they have all been directed to conciliate the affections, unite the interests, and draw and keep the mind of the country together; and the better to assist in this foundation work of the revolution, I have avoided all places of profit or office, either in the state I live in or in the United States, kept myself at a distance from all parties and party connections, and even disregarded all private and inferior concerns; and when we take into view the great work which we have gone through and feel, as we ought to feel, the just importance of it, we shall then see that the little wranglings and indecent contentions of personal parley are as dishonorable to our characters as they are injurious to our repose.

It was the cause of America that made me an author. The force with which it struck my mind and the dangerous condition the country appeared to be in, by courting an impossible and an unnatural reconciliation with those who were determined to reduce her, instead of striking out into the only line that could cement and save her—*a declaration of independence*—made it impossible for me, feeling as I did, to be silent; and if, in the course of more than seven years, I have rendered her any service, I have likewise added something to the reputation of literature by freely and disinterestedly employing it in the great cause of mankind and showing that there may be genius without prostitution.

Independence always appeared to me practicable and probable, provided the sentiment of the country could be formed and held to the object; and there is no instance in the world where a people so extended and wedded to former habits of thinking and under such a variety of circumstances were so instantly and effectually pervaded by a turn in politics as in the case of independence, and who supported their opinion, undiminished, through such a succession of good and ill fortune till they crowned it with success.

But as the scenes of war are closed and every man preparing for home and happier times, I therefore take my leave of the subject. I have most sincerely followed it from beginning to end and through all its turns and windings; and whatever country I may hereafter be in, I shall always feel an honest pride at the part I have taken and acted, and a gratitude to nature and providence for putting it in my power to be of some use to mankind. ⌖

Rights of Man — Part One (1791)

There never did, there never will, and there never can exist a Parliament, or any description of men, or any generation of men in any country, possessed of the right or the power of binding and controlling posterity to the "end of time," or of commanding forever how the world shall be governed or who shall govern it; and therefore all such clauses, acts, or declarations by which the makers of them attempt to do what they have neither the right nor the power to do, nor the power to execute, are in themselves null and void.

Every age and generation must be as free to act for itself, *in all cases,* as the ages and generation which preceded it. The vanity and

presumption of governing beyond the grave is the most ridiculous and insolent of all tyrannies.

Man has no property in man; neither has any generation a property in the generations which are to follow. The Parliament or the people of 1688, or of any other period, had no more right to dispose of the people of the present day, or to bind or to control them *in any shape whatever,* than the Parliament or the people of the present day have to dispose of, bind, or control those who are to live a hundred or a thousand years hence.

Every generation is and must be competent to all the purposes which its occasions require.

It is the living, and not the dead that are to be accommodated. When man ceases to be, his power and his wants cease with him; and having no longer any participation in the concerns of this world, he has no longer any authority in directing who shall be its governors, or how its government shall be organized or how administered.

I am not contending for nor against any form of government, nor for nor against any party here or elsewhere. That which a whole nation chooses to do it has a right to do. Mr. Burke says, No. Where then does the right exist? I am contending for the rights of the *living*, and against their being willed away and controlled and contracted for by the manuscript assumed authority of the dead; and Mr. Burke is contending for the authority of the dead over the rights and freedom of the living.

There was a time when kings disposed of their crowns by will upon their deathbeds and consigned the people, like beasts of the field, to whatever successor they appointed. This is now so exploded as scarcely to be remembered and so monstrous as hardly to be believed. But the parliamentary clauses upon which Mr. Burke builds his political church are of the same nature....

The error of those who reason by precedents drawn from antiquity, respecting the rights of man, is that they do not go far enough into antiquity. They do not go the whole way. They stop in some of the intermediate stages of a hundred or a thousand years and produce what was then done as a rule for the present day. This is no authority at all.

If we travel still further into antiquity, we shall find a directly contrary opinion and practice prevailing; and if antiquity is to be authority, a thousand such authorities may be produced, successively contradicting each other; but if we proceed on, we shall at least come out right; we shall come to the time when man came from the hand of his Maker. What was

he then? Man. Man was his high and only title, and a higher cannot be given him. But of titles I shall speak hereafter.

We have now arrived at the origin of man and at the origin of his rights. As to the manner in which the world has been governed from that day to this, it is no further any concern of ours than to make a proper use of the errors or the improvements which the history of it presents. Those who lived a hundred or a thousand years ago were then moderns as we are now. They had *their* ancients, and those ancients had others, and we also shall be ancients in our turn.

If the mere name of antiquity is to govern in the affairs of life, the people who are to live a hundred or a thousand years hence may as well take us for a precedent, as we make a precedent of those who lived a hundred or a thousand years ago.

The fact is that portions of antiquity, by proving everything, established nothing. It is authority against authority all the way, till we come to the divine origin of the rights of man at the creation. Here our inquiries find a resting place and our reason finds a home....

The illuminating and divine principle of the equal rights of man (for it has its origin from the Maker of man) relates not only to the living individuals, but to generations of men succeeding each other. Every generation is equal in rights to the generations which preceded it, by the same rule that every individual is born equal in rights with his contemporary.

Every history of the creation and every traditionary account, whether from the lettered or unlettered world, however they may vary in their opinion or belief of certain particulars, all agree in establishing one point, *the unity of man;* by which I mean that men are all of *one degree,* and consequently that all men are born equal and with equal natural rights, in the same manner as if posterity had been continued by *creation* instead of *generation,* the latter being only the mode by which the former is carried forward; and consequently every child born into the world must be considered as deriving its existence from God. The world is as new to him as it was to the first man that existed, and his natural right in it is of the same kind.... ∼

Primary Sources

The Complete Writings of Thomas Paine. Edited by Philip S. Foner. New York: Citadel Press, 1945.

Paine, Thomas. *The Age of Reason.* Paris, 1794.

———. *Agrarian Justice, Opposed to Agrarian Law, and to Agrarian Monopoly.* Paris, 1796.

———. *The American Crisis.* London, 1777.

———. *The Decline and Fall of the English System of Finance.* Paris, 1796.

———. *Dissertation on First-Principles of Government.* London, 1795.

———. *A Letter Addressed to the Abbe Raynal on the Affairs of North America; in which the Mistakes in the Abbe's Account of the Revolution of America Are Corrected and Cleared Up.* London, 1783.

———. *Miscellaneous Articles.* London, 1792.

Secondary Sources

Claeys, Gregory. *Thomas Paine: Social and Political Thought.* Boston: Unwin Hyman, 1989.

Clark, Harry Hayden. *Thomas Paine: Representative Selections.* New York: Hill, 1961.

Conway, Moncure Daniel. *The Life of Thomas Paine.* London: Watts, 1909.

Fruchtman, Jack, Jr. *Thomas Paine and the Religion of Nature.* Baltimore: Johns Hopkins University Press, 1993.

Merriam, C.E. "The Political Theories of Thomas Paine," *Political Science Quarterly* 14 (1899):389–404.

Penniman, Howard. "Thomas Paine—Democrat," *American Political Science Review* 37 (1943):244–62.

6. The Declaration of Independence

BY JUNE 1776 armed conflict had broken out in several colonies, and North Carolina and Virginia had both authorized their delegates in the Continental Congress to vote for independence. The doubts and reluctance many people felt regarding separation were being overcome, and the Congress authorized a committee to prepare a declaration of independence. Thomas Jefferson was the principal draftsperson, with John Adams and Benjamin Franklin making slight changes. Jefferson said he had "turned to no book or pamphlet" but merely expressed "the common sense of the matter" in his draft, which clearly follows the Lockean natural-rights doctrine. The document was submitted to the Congress on 28 June, and, after days of discussion in which the opposition of Pennsylvania, South Carolina, and Delaware were overcome, it passed unanimously (with New York abstaining) on 4 July 1776.

The Declaration marks the culmination of a democratic, egalitarian, and libertarian surge that colonists such as Samuel Adams and Thomas Paine had been urging on for years. Its first two paragraphs are at once an incisive summary of colonial beliefs and a rallying call to struggle and sacrifice for the best of causes.

The Articles of Confederation (selection 7) originated from the same egalitarian premises and should be read as a companion document.

As will be seen, the Declaration and the Articles stand together in contrast to the Constitution. Over time, however, the Declaration maintained visibility as a founding document while the Articles dropped from historical memory. Today, the Declaration and the Constitution are merged in the thinking of most Americans, and their substantive contrasts are often ignored. ∾

The Unanimous Declaration of the Thirteen United States of America (1776)

When in the Course of human events, it becomes necessary for one people to dissolve the political bands, which have connected them with another, and to assume among the powers of the earth, the separate and equal station to which the Laws of Nature and of Nature's God entitle them, a decent respect to the opinions of mankind requires that they should declare the causes which impel them to the separation.—We hold these truths to be self-evident, that all men are created equal, that they are endowed by their Creator with certain unalienable Rights, that among these are Life, Liberty and the pursuit of Happiness.—That to secure these rights, Governments are instituted among Men, deriving their just powers from the consent of the governed,—That whenever any Form of Government becomes destructive of these ends, it is the Right of the People to alter or to abolish it, and to institute new Government, laying its foundation on such principles and organizing its powers in such form, as to them shall seem most likely to effect their Safety and Happiness. Prudence, indeed, will dictate that Governments long established should not be changed for light and transient causes; and accordingly all experience hath shewn, that mankind are more disposed to suffer, while evils are sufferable, than

to right themselves by abolishing the forms to which they are accustomed. But when a long train of abuses and usurpations, pursuing invariably the same Object evinces a design to reduce them under absolute Despotism, it is their right, it is their duty, to throw off such Government, and to provide new Guards for their future security.—Such has been the patient sufferance of these Colonies; and such now the necessity which constrains them to alter their former Systems of Government. The history of the present King of Great Britain is a history of repeated injuries and usurpations, all having in direct object the establishment of an absolute Tyranny over these States. To prove this, let Facts be submitted to a candid world.—He has refused his Assent to Laws, the most wholesome and necessary for the public good.—He has forbidden his Governors to pass Laws of immediate and pressing importance, unless suspended in their operation till his Assent should be obtained, and when so suspended, he has utterly neglected to attend to them.—He has refused to pass other Laws for the accommodation of large districts of people, unless those people would relinquish the right of Representation in the Legislature, a right inestimable to them and formidable to tyrants only.—He has called together legislative bodies at places unusual, uncomfortable, and distant from the depository of their public Records, for the sole purpose of fatiguing them into compliance with his measures.—He has dissolved Representative Houses repeatedly for opposing with manly firmness his invasions on the rights of the people.—He has refused for a long time, after such dissolution, to cause others to be elected whereby the Legislative powers, incapable of Annihilation, have returned to the People at large for their exercise; the States remaining in the meantime exposed to all the dangers of invasion from without, and convulsions within.—He has endeavored to prevent the population of these States; for that purpose obstructing the Laws for Naturalization of Foreigners; refusing to pass others to encourage their migrations hither, and raising the conditions of new Appropriations of Lands.—He has obstructed the Administration of Justice, by refusing his Assent to Laws for establishing Judiciary powers.—He has made Judges dependent on his Will alone, for the tenure of their offices, and the amount and payment of their salaries.—He has erected a multitude of New Offices, and sent hither swarms of Officers to harass our people and eat out their substance.—He has kept among us, in times of peace, Standing Armies without the Consent of our legislatures.—He has affected to render the Military independent of and superior to the Civil power.—He has combined with others to subject us to a jurisdiction foreign to our constitution, and unacknowledged by our laws; giving his Assent to their Acts of pretended Legislation.—For quartering large bodies of armed troops among us:—For protecting them, by a mock Trial, from punishment for any Murders which they should commit on the Inhabitants of these States:—For cutting off our Trade with all parts of the world:—For imposing Taxes on us without our Consent:—For depriving us in many cases, of the benefits of Trial by Jury:—For transporting us beyond Seas to be tried for pretended offenses:—For abolishing the Free System of English Laws in a neighboring Province, establishing therein an Arbitrary government, and enlarging its Boundaries so as to render it at once an example and fit instrument for introducing the same absolute rule into these Colonies:—For taking away our Charters, abolishing our most valuable Laws, and altering fundamentally the Forms of our Governments:—For suspending our own Legislatures, and declaring themselves invested with power to legislate for us in all cases whatsoever.—He has abdicated Government here, by declaring us out of his Protection and waging War against us.—He has plundered our seas, ravaged our Coasts, burnt our towns, and destroyed the lives of our people.—He is at this time transporting large Armies of Foreign Mercenaries to compleat the works of death, desolation and tyranny, already begun with circumstances of Cruelty and perfidy, scarcely paralleled in the most barbarous ages, and totally unworthy the Head of a civilized nation.—He has constrained our fellow Citizens taken Captive on the high Seas to bear Arms against their Country, to become the executioners of their friends and Brethren, or to fall themselves by their hands.—He has excited domestic insurrections amongst us, and has endeavoured to bring on the inhabitants of our frontiers, the Merciless Indian Savages whose known rule of warfare, is an undistinguished destruction of all ages, sexes and conditions. In every stage of these Oppressions We have Petitioned for Redress in the most humble terms: Our repeated Petitions have been answered only by repeated injury. A Prince whose character is thus marked by every act which may define a Tyrant, is unfit to be the ruler of a free people. Nor have We been wanting in attentions to our British brethren. We have warned them from time to time of attempts by their legislature to extend an unwarrantable jurisdiction over us. We have reminded them of the circumstances of our emigration and settlement here. We have appealed to their native justice and magnanimity, and we have conjured them by the ties of our common kindred to disavow these usurpations, which would inevitably interrupt our connections and correspondence. They too have been deaf to the voice of justice and of consanguinity. We must, therefore, acquiesce in the necessity, which denounces our Separation, and hold them, as we hold the rest of mankind, Enemies in War, in Peace Friends.—

We, therefore, the Representatives of the United States of America, in General Congress, Assembled, appealing to the Supreme Judge of the world for the rectitude of our intentions do, in the Name, and by the Authority of the good People of these Colonies, solemnly publish and declare, That these United Colonies, are, and of Right ought to be Free and Independent States; that they are Absolved from all Allegiance to the British Crown, and that all political connection between them and the State of Great Britain, is and ought to be totally dissolved, and that as Free and Independent States, they have full Power to levy War, conclude Peace, contract Alliances, establish Commerce, and to do all other Acts and Things which Independent States may of right do.—And for the support of this Declaration, with a firm reliance on the protection of divine Providence, we mutually pledge to each other our Lives, our Fortunes and our sacred Honor. ✥

7. The Articles of Confederation

IN 1775 WAR was raging in the Boston area, and the Continental Congress appointed George Washington commander in chief of the fledgling army. But there was still a major faction in Congress and the country hoping for some kind of reconciliation. In July Franklin drafted and proposed to the Congress "Articles of Confederation and Perpetual Union," which amounted to a stronger, more unified version of his old Albany Plan of Union, complete with voting in proportion to the population of the various states. The clear call for independence involved, however, caused it to be ignored by the moderates still hoping for reconciliation. Nevertheless, when independence was finally voted in July 1776, the committee then charged with drafting a plan for confederation (chaired by Franklin's friend John Dickinson) began with the draft offered by Franklin the year before. What emerged was a document that maintained the equality of voting among the states of the Continental Congress but in other major respects conformed to the earlier draft. It was accepted by the Congress in 1777, but, although serving as the de facto governing "constitution," it was not finally ratified by all the states until 1781. ✑

Articles of Confederation (agreed by Congress, 15 November 1777; ratified and in force, 1 March 1781)

To all whom these Presents shall come, we the undersigned Delegates of the States affixed to our Names send greeting. Whereas the Delegates of the United States of America in Congress assembled did on the fifteenth day of November in the Year of our Lord One Thousand Seven Hundred and Seventy seven, and in the Second Year of the Independence of America agree to certain articles of Confederation and perpetual Union between the States of New-hampshire, Massachusetts-bay, Rhodeisland and Providence Plantations, Connecticut, New York, New Jersey, Pennsylvania, Delaware, Maryland, Virginia, North-Carolina, South-Carolina and Georgia in the Words following, viz. "Articles of Confederation and perpetual union between the states of Newhampshire, Massachusetts-bay, Rhodeisland and Providence Plantations, Connecticut, New York, New Jersey, Pennsylvania, Delaware, Maryland, Virginia, North-Carolina, South-Carolina and Georgia."

Art. I. The Stile of this confederacy shall be "The United States of America."

Art. II. Each state retains its sovereignty, freedom and independence, and every Power, Jurisdiction and right, which is not by this confederation expressly delegated to the United States, in Congress assembled.

Art. III. The said states hereby severally enter into a firm league of friendship with each other, for their common defence, the security of their Liberties, and their mutual and general welfare, binding themselves to assist each other, against all force offered to, or attacks made upon them, or any of them, on account

of religion, sovereignty, trade, or any other pretence whatever.

Art. IV. The better to secure and perpetuate mutual friendship and intercourse among the people of the different states in this union, the free inhabitants of each of these states, paupers, vagabonds and fugitives from Justice excepted, shall be entitled to all privileges and immunities of free citizens in the several states; and the people of each state shall have free ingress and regress to and from any other state, and shall enjoy therein all the privileges of trade and commerce, subject to the same duties, impositions and restrictions as the inhabitants thereof respectively, provided that such restriction shall not extend so far as to prevent the removal of property imported into any state, to any other state of which the Owner is an inhabitant; provided also that no imposition, duties or restriction shall be laid by any state, on the property of the united states, or either of them.

If any Person guilty of, or charged with treason, felony, or other high misdemeanor in any state, shall flee from Justice, and be found in any of the united states, he shall upon demand of the Governor or executive power, of the state from which he fled, be delivered up and removed to the state having jurisdiction of his offence.

Full faith and credit shall be given in each of these states to the records, acts and judicial proceedings of the courts and magistrates of every other state.

Art. V. For the more convenient management of the general interests of the united states, delegates shall be annually appointed in such manner as the legislature of each state shall direct, to meet in Congress on the first Monday in November, in every year, with a

SOURCE: Henry Commager, ed., *Documents of American History* (New York: Appleton-Century-Crofts, 1973), 111–15.

power reserved to each state, to recall its delegates, or any of them, at any time within the year, and to send other in their stead, for the remainder of the year.

No state shall be represented in Congress by less than two, nor by more than seven Members; and no person shall be capable of being a delegate for more than three years in any term of six years; nor shall any person, being a delegate, be capable of holding any office under the united states, for which he, or another for his benefit receives any salary, fees or emolument of any kind.

Each state shall maintain its own delegates in a meeting of the states, and while they act as members of the committee of the states.

In determining questions in the united states, in Congress assembled, each state shall have one vote.

Freedom of speech and debate in Congress shall not be impeached or questioned in any Court, or place out of Congress, and the members of congress shall be protected in their persons from arrests and imprisonments, during the time of their going to and from, and attendance on congress, except for treason, felony, or breach of the peace.

Art. VI. No state without the Consent of the united states in congress assembled, shall send any embassy to, or receive any embassy from, or enter into any conference, agreement, or alliance or treaty with any King, prince or state; nor shall any person holding any office of profit or trust under the united states, or any of them, accept of any present, emolument, office or title of any kind whatever from any king, prince or foreign state; nor shall the united states in congress assembled, or any of them, grant any title of nobility.

No two or more states shall enter into any treaty, confederation or alliance whatever between them, without the consent of the united states in congress assembled, specifying accurately the purposes for which the same is to be entered into, and how long it shall continue.

No state shall lay any imposts or duties, which may interfere with any stipulations in treaties, entered into by the united states in congress assembled, with any king, prince or state, in pursuance of any treaties already proposed by congress, to the courts of France and Spain.

No vessels of war shall be kept up in time of peace by any state, except such number only, as shall be deemed necessary by the united states in congress assembled, for the defence of such state, or its trade; nor shall any body of forces be kept up by any state, in time of peace, except such number only, as in the judgment of the united states, in congress assembled, shall be deemed requisite to garrison the forts necessary for the defence of such state; but every state shall always keep up a well regulated and disciplined militia, sufficiently armed and accoutred, and shall provide and constantly have ready for use, in public stores, a due number of field pieces and tents, and a proper quantity of arms, ammunition and camp equipage.

No state shall engage in any war without the consent of the united states in congress assembled, unless such state be actually invaded by enemies, or shall have received certain advice of a resolution being formed by some nation of Indians to invade such state, and the danger is so imminent as not to admit of a delay, till the united states in congress assembled can be consulted: nor shall any state grant commissions to any ships or vessels of war, nor letters of marque or reprisal, except it be after a declaration of war by the united states in congress assembled, and then only against the kingdom or state and the subjects thereof, against which war has been so declared, and under such regulations as shall be established by the united states in congress assembled, unless such state be infested by pirates, in which case vessels of war may be fitted out for that occasion, and kept so long as the danger shall continue, or until the united states in congress assembled shall determine otherwise.

Art. VII. When land-forces are raised by any state for the common defence, all officers of or under the rank of colonel, shall be appointed by the legislature of each state respectively by whom such forces shall be raised, or in such manner as such state shall direct, and all vacancies shall be filled up by the state which first made the appointment.

Art. VIII. All charges of war, and all other expences that shall be incurred for the common defence or general welfare, and allowed by the united states in congress assembled, shall be defrayed out of a common treasury, which shall be supplied by the several states, in proportion to the value of all land within each state, granted to or surveyed for any Person, as such land and the buildings and improvements thereon shall be estimated according to such mode as the united states in congress assembled, shall from time to time direct and appoint. The taxes for paying that proportion shall be laid and levied by the authority and direction of the legislatures of the several states within the time agreed upon by the united states in congress assembled.

Art. IX. The united states in congress assembled, shall have the sole and exclusive right and power of determining on peace and war, except in the cases mentioned in the sixth article—of sending and receiving ambassadors—entering into treaties and alliances, provided that no treaty of commerce shall be made whereby the legislative power of the respective states shall be restrained from imposing such imposts and duties on foreigners, as their own people are subjected to, or from prohibiting the exportation or importation of any species of goods or commodities whatsoever—of establishing rules for deciding in all cases, what captures on land or water shall be legal, and in what manner prizes taken by land or naval

forces in the service of the united states shall be divided or appropriated—of granting letters of marque and reprisal in times of peace—appointing courts for the trial of piracies and felonies committed on the high seas and establishing courts for receiving and determining finally appeals in all cases of captures, provided that no member of congress shall be appointed a judge of any of the said courts.

The united states in congress assembled shall also be the last resort on appeal in all disputes and differences now subsisting or that hereafter may arise between two or more states concerning boundary, jurisdiction or any other cause whatever; which authority shall always be exercised in the manner following. Whenever the legislative or executive authority or lawful agent of any state in controversy with another shall present a petition to congress, stating the matter in question and praying for a hearing, notice thereof shall be given the order of congress to the legislative or executive authority of the other state in controversy, and a day assigned for the appearance of the parties by their lawful agents, who shall then be directed to appoint by joint consent, commissioners or judge to constitute a court for hearing and determining the matter in question: but if they cannot agree, congress shall name three persons out of each of the united states, and from the list of such persons each party shall alternately strike out one, the petitioners beginning, until the number shall be reduced to thirteen; and from that number not less than seven, nor more than nine names as congress shall direct, shall in the presence of congress be drawn out by lot, and the persons whose names shall be so drawn or any five of them, shall be commissioners or judges, to hear and finally determine the controversy, so always as a major part of the judges who shall hear the cause shall agree in the determination: and if either party shall neglect to attend at the day appointed, without shewing reasons, which congress shall judge sufficient, or being present shall refuse to strike, the congress shall proceed to nominate three persons out of each state, and the secretary of congress shall strike in behalf of such party absent or refusing; and the judgment and sentence of the court to be appointed, in the manner before prescribed, shall be final and conclusive; and if any of the parties shall refuse to submit to the authority of such court, or to appear to defend their claim or cause, the court shall nevertheless proceed to pronounce sentence, or judgment, which shall in like manner be final and decisive, the judgment or sentence and other proceedings being in either case transmitted to congress, and lodged among the acts of congress for the security of the parties concerned: provided that every commissioner, before he sits in judgment, shall take an oath to be administered by one of the judges of the supreme or superior court of the state, where the cause shall be tried, "well and truly to hear and determine the matter in question, according to the best of his judgment, without favour, affection or hope of reward:" provided also that no state shall be deprived of territory for the benefit of the united states.

All controversies concerning the private right of soil claimed under different grants of two or more states, whose jurisdictions as they may respect such lands, and the states which passed such grants are adjusted, the said grants or either of them being at the same time claimed to have originated antecedent to such settlement of jurisdiction, shall on the petition of either party to the congress of the united states, be finally determined as near as may be in the same manner as is before prescribed for deciding disputes respecting territorial jurisdiction between different states.

The united states in congress assembled shall also have the sole and exclusive right and power of regulating the alloy and value of coin struck by their own authority, or by that of the respective states—fixing the standard of weights and measures throughout the united states—regulating the trade and managing all affairs with the Indians, not members of any of the states, provided that the legislative right of any state within its own limits be not infringed or violated—establishing and regulating post-offices from one state to another, throughout all the united states, and exacting such postage on the papers passing thro' the same as may be requisite to defray the expences of the said office—appointing all officers of the land forces, in the service of the united states, excepting regimental officers —appointing all the officers of the naval forces, and commissioning all officers whatever in the service of the united states—making rules for the government and regulation of the said land and naval forces, and directing their operations.

The united states in congress assembled shall have authority to appoint a committee, to sit in the recess of congress, to be denominated "A Committee of the States," and to consist of one delegate from each state; and to appoint such other committees and civil officers as may be necessary for managing the general affairs of the united states under their direction—to appoint one of their number to preside, provided that no person be allowed to serve in the office of president more than one year in any term of three years; to ascertain the necessary sums of Money to be raised for the service of the united states, and to appropriate and apply the same for defraying the public expences—to borrow money, or emit bills on the credit of the united states, transmitting every half year to the respective states an account of the sums of money so borrowed or emitted,—to build and equip a navy—to agree upon the number of land forces, and to make requisitions from each state for its quota, in proportion to the number of white inhabitants in such state; which requisition shall be binding, and thereupon the legislature of each state shall appoint the regimental officers, raise the men and cloath, arm and equip them in a soldier like manner, at the expence of the united states, and the officers and men so cloathed, armed and equipped shall march to the place appointed, and within the time agreed on by the united states in congress assembled: But if the united states in congress assembled shall, on consideration of circumstances judge proper that any state should not raise men, or should raise a smaller number than its quota, and that any other state should raise a greater number of men than the quota thereof, such extra number shall be raised, officered, cloathed, armed and equipped in the same manner as the quota of such state, unless the legislature of such state shall judge that such extra number cannot be safely spared out of the same, in which case they shall raise, officer, cloath, arm and equip as many of such extra number as they judge can be safely spared. And the officers and men so cloathed, armed and equipped, shall march to the place appointed, and within the time agreed on by the united states in congress assembled.

The united states in congress assembled shall never engage in a war, nor grant letters of marque and reprisal in time of peace, nor enter into any treaties or alliances, nor coin money, nor regulate the value thereof, nor ascertain the sums and expences necessary for the defence and welfare of the united states, or any of them, nor emit bills, nor borrow money on the credit of the united states, nor appropriate money, nor agree upon the number of vessels of war, to be built or purchased, or the number of land or sea forces to be raised, nor appoint a commander in chief of the army or navy, unless nine states assent to the same: nor shall a question on any other point, except for adjourning from day to day be determined, unless by the votes of a majority of the united states in congress assembled.

The congress of the united states shall have power to adjourn to any time within the year, and to any place within the united states, so that no period of adjournment be for a longer duration than the space of six Months, and shall publish the Journal of their proceedings monthly, except such parts thereof relating to treaties, alliances or military operations as in their judgment require secresy; and the yeas and nays of the delegates of each state on any question shall be entered on the Journal, when it is desired by any delegate; and the delegates of a state, or any of them, at his or their request shall be furnished with a transcript of the said Journal, except such parts as are above excepted, to lay before the legislatures of the several states.

Art. X. The committee of the states, or any nine of them, shall be authorised to execute, in the recess of congress such of the powers of congress as the united states in congress assembled, by the consent of nine states, shall from time to time think expedient to vest them with; provided that no power be delegated to the said committee, for the exercise of which, by the articles of confederation, the voice of nine states in the congress of the united states assembled is requisite.

Art. XI. Canada acceding to this confederation, and joining in the measures of the united states, shall be admitted into, and entitled to all the advantages of this union: but no other colony shall be admitted into the same, unless such admission be agreed to by nine states.

Art. XII. All bills of credit emitted, monies borrowed and debts contracted by, or under the authority of congress, before the assembling of the united states, in pursuance of the present confederation, shall be deemed and considered as a charge against the united states, for payment and satisfaction whereof the said united states, and the public faith are hereby solemnly pledged.

Art. XIII. Every state shall abide by the determinations of the united states in congress assembled, on all questions which by this confederation are submitted to them. And the Articles of this confederation shall be inviolably observed by every state, and the union shall be perpetual; nor shall any alteration at any time hereafter be made in any of them; unless such alteration be agreed to in a congress of the united states, and be afterwards confirmed by the legislatures of every state.

AND WHEREAS it hath pleased the Great Governor of the World to incline the heart of the legislatures we respectively represent in congress, to approve of, and to authorize us to ratify the said articles of confederation and perpetual union. KNOW YE that we the undersigned delegates, by virtue of the power and authority to us given for that purpose, do by these presents, in the name and in behalf of our respective constituents, fully and entirely ratify and confirm each and every of the said articles of confederation and perpetual union, and all and singular the matters and things therein contained: And we do further solemnly plight and engage the faith of our respective constituents, that they shall abide by the determinations of the united states in congress assembled, on all questions, which by the said confederation are submitted to them. And that the articles thereof shall be inviolably observed by the states we respectively represent, and that the union shall be perpetual. In Witness whereof we have hereunto set our hands in Congress. Done at Philadelphia in the state of Pennsylvania the ninth Day of July in the Year of our Lord one Thousand seven Hundred and Seventy-eight, and in the third year of the independence of America. ~

8. John Adams

JOHN ADAMS (1735–1826) graduated from Harvard in 1765 and began practicing law in 1768. He rose to prominence through essays attacking the Stamp Act of 1765 and was soon recognized as an authority on English and American individual rights and constitutionalism generally. He served in the Massachusetts legislature and the Continental Congresses and was principal author of the Massachusetts constitution of 1780. For several years thereafter he was minister to Great Britain, returning home in time to be elected as the first vice president in the new national government.

After serving throughout Washington's tenure, he was elected president in 1796 as the Federalist candidate. The bitter conflicts that developed during his years as president caused him to be defeated for reelection, however, and he lived the next twenty-five years in retirement. During the latter period he renewed his relationship with Jefferson, who, despite serving as vice president during Adams's presidency, had become his bitter critic and electoral opponent. The correspondence between the two after Jefferson left office revealed broad areas of agreement on essentially conservative principles. Both men died on 4 July 1826, the fiftieth anniversary of the Declaration of Independence they had worked so hard to have adopted.

Adams was a great admirer of the British constitution, which he saw as achieving the proper balance between the major sectors of society—the monarchy, the aristocracy, and the common people. With neither king nor aristocracy to provide the necessary limits on the common people, the problem Adams saw in America was to design a system that would fragment their potential power and allow the better class of people to exercise guidance. Adams's solution was the elaborate system of separation of powers and checks and balances that we know, plus reliance on an "empire of laws" that would be the province of the satisfyingly conservative legal profession.

Adams's writings on constitutionalism and his Massachusetts state constitution were widely circulated and read in the new nation. They served as guides and models for other states and were well known to those who framed the Constitution of 1787 while Adams

was in England. The first selection here is a cogent summary of his views at the time of independence, while the second defends the republicanism of those states that followed his prescriptions. In the latter, Adams responds to a monarchist's critique by tempering the conservatism he felt in the American context with a clear commitment to some "democratical branch" and to limitations on the national government's powers. The last selection reproduces an exchange of correspondence between Adams and his wife, Abigail, a spirited and independent woman who longed for a career of her own. Abigail's letter was written at a time when John was serving in the Continental Congress that, partly as a result of his effective floor management, would soon proclaim the Declaration of Independence. Her letter has become celebrated as one of the first statements of feminist demands for equality in American history. ∾

"Thoughts on Government" (1776)

My dear Sir: If I was equal to the task of forming a plan for the government of a colony, I should be flattered with your request and very happy to comply with it because, as the divine science of politics is the science of social happiness, and the blessings of society depend entirely on the constitutions of government, which are generally institutions that last for many generations, there can be no employment more agreeable to a benevolent mind than a research after the best.

Pope flattered tyrants too much when he said,

SOURCE: The first two selections in this chapter may be found in George A. Peck Jr., *The Political Writings of John Adams* (New York: Liberal Arts Press, 1954).

For forms of government let fools contest,
That which is best administered is best.
(*Essay on Man*)

Nothing can be more fallacious than this. But poets read history to collect flowers, not fruits; they attend to fanciful images not the effects of social institutions. Nothing is more certain from the history of nations and nature of man than that some forms of government are better fitted for being well administered than others.

We ought to consider what is the end of government before we determine which is the best form. Upon this point all speculative politicians will agree that the happiness of the individual is the end of man. From this principle it will follow that the form of government which communicates ease, comfort, security, or, in one word happiness, to the greatest number of persons and in the greatest degree is the best.

All sober inquirers after truth, ancient and modern, pagan and Christian, have declared that the happiness of man, as well as his dignity, consists in virtue. Confucius, Zoroaster, Socrates, Mahomet, not to mention authorities really sacred, have agreed in this.

If this is a form of government, then, whose principle and foundation is virtue, will not every sober man acknowledge it better calculated to promote the general happiness than any other form?

Fear is the foundation of most governments; but it is so sordid and brutal a passion and renders men in whose breasts it predominates so stupid and miserable that Americans will not be likely to approve of any political institution which is founded on it.

Honor is truly sacred but holds a lower rank in the scale of moral excellence than virtue. Indeed, the former is but a part of the latter and consequently has not equal pretensions to support a frame of government productive of human happiness.

The foundation of every government is some principle or passion in the minds of the people. The noblest principles and most generous affections in our nature, then, have the fairest chance to support the noblest and most generous models of government.

A man must be indifferent to the sneers of modern Englishmen to mention in their company the names of Sidney, Harrington, Locke, Milton, Nedham, Neville, Burnet, and Hoadly. No small fortitude is necessary to confess that one has read them. The wretched condition of this country, however, for ten or fifteen years past has frequently reminded me of their principles and reasonings. They will convince any candid mind that there is no good government but what is republican. That the only valuable part of the British constitution is so because the very definition of a republic is "an empire of

laws, and not of men." That, as a republic is the best of governments, so that particular arrangement of the powers of society or, in other words, that form of government which is best contrived to secure an impartial and exact execution of the laws is the best of republics.

Of republics there is an inexhaustible variety because the possible combinations of the powers of society are capable of innumerable variations.

As good government is an empire of laws, how shall your laws be made? In a large society inhabiting an extensive country, it is impossible that the whole should assemble to make laws. The first necessary step, then, is to depute power from the many to a few of the most wise and good. But by what rules shall you choose your representatives? Agree upon the number and qualifications of persons who shall have the benefit of choosing or annex this privilege to the inhabitants of a certain extent of ground.

The principal difficulty lies, and the greatest care should be employed, in constituting this representative assembly. It should be in miniature an exact portrait of the people at large. It should think, feel, reason, and act like them. That it may be the interest of this assembly to do strict justice at all times, it should be an equal representation, or, in other words, equal interests among the people should have equal interests in it. Great care should be taken to effect this and to prevent unfair, partial, and corrupt elections. Such regulations, however, may be better made in times of greater tranquility than the present; and they will spring up themselves naturally when all the powers of government come to be in the hands of the people's friends. At present, it will be safest to proceed in all established modes to which the people have been familiarized by habit.

A representation of the people in one assembly being obtained, a question arises whether all the powers of government—legislative, executive, and judicial—shall be left in this body? I think a people cannot be long free, nor ever happy, whose government is in one assembly. My reasons for this opinion are as follow:

1. A single assembly is liable to all the vices, follies, and frailties of an individual—subject to fits of humor, starts of passion, flights of enthusiasm, partialities, or prejudice—and consequently productive of hasty results and absurd judgments. And all these errors ought to be corrected and defects supplied by some controlling power.

2. A single assembly is apt to be avaricious and in time will not scruple to exempt itself from burdens which it will lay without compunction on its constituents.

3. A single assembly is apt to grow ambitious and after a time will not hesitate to vote itself perpetual. This was one fault of the Long Parliament, but more remarkably of Holland, whose assembly first voted themselves from annual to septennial, then for life, and after a course of years, that all vacancies happening by death or otherwise should be filled by themselves without any application to constituents at all.

4. A representative assembly, although extremely well qualified and absolutely necessary as a branch of the legislative, is unfit to exercise the executive power for want of two essential properties, secrecy and dispatch.

5. A representative assembly is still less qualified for the judicial power because it is too numerous, too slow, and too little skilled in the laws.

6. Because a single assembly, possessed of all the powers of government, would make arbitrary laws for their own interest, execute all laws arbitrarily for their own interest, and adjudge all controversies in their own favor.

But shall the whole power of legislation rest in one assembly? Most of the foregoing reasons apply equally to prove that the legislative power ought to be more complex, to which we may add that if the legislative power is wholly in one assembly and the executive in another or in a single person, these two powers will oppose and encroach upon each other until the contest shall end in war, and the whole power, legislative and executive, be usurped by the strongest.

The judicial power, in such case, could not mediate or hold the balance between the two contending powers because the legislative would undermine it. And this shows the necessity, too, of giving the executive power a negative upon the legislative; otherwise this will be continually encroaching upon that.

To avoid these dangers, let a distinct assembly be constituted as a mediator between the two extreme branches of the legislature, that which represents the people and that which is vested with the executive power.

Let the representative assembly then elect by ballot, from among themselves or their constituents or both, a distinct assembly which, for the sake of perspicuity, we will call a council. It may consist of any number you please, say twenty or thirty, and should have a free and independent exercise of its judgment and consequently a negative voice in the legislature.

These two bodies, thus constituted and made integral parts of the legislature, let them unite and by joint ballot choose a governor, who, after being stripped of most of those badges of domination called prerogatives, should have a free and independent exercise of his judgment and be made also an integral part of the legislature. This, I know, is liable to objections; and, if you please, you may make him only president of the council, as in Connecticut. But as the governor is to be invested with the executive power with consent of council, I think he ought to have a negative upon the legislative. If he is annually elective, as he ought to be, he will always have so much reverence and affection for the people, their representatives and counsellors, that, although you give him an independent exercise of his judgment, he will seldom use it in opposition to the two houses, except in cases the public utility of which would be conspicuous, and some such cases would happen.

In the present exigency of American affairs, when by an act of Parliament we are put out of the royal protection and consequently discharged from our allegiance, and it has become necessary to assume government for our immediate security the governor, lieutenant-governor, secretary, treasurer, commissary, attorney-general should be chosen by joint ballot of both houses. And these and all other elections, especially of representatives and counsellors, should be annual, there not being in the whole circle of the sciences a maxim more infallible than this, "where annual elections end, there slavery begins."

These great men, in this respect, should be once a year—

Like bubbles on the sea of matter borne,
They rise, they break, and to that sea
    return.

This will teach them the great political virtues of humility, patience, and moderation, without which every man in power becomes a ravenous beast of prey.

This mode of constituting the great offices of state will answer very well for the present; but if by experiment it should be found inconvenient, the legislature may at its leisure devise other methods of creating them; by elections of the people at large, as in Connecticut; or it may enlarge the term for which they shall be chosen to seven years, or three years, or for life, or make any other alterations which the society shall find productive of its ease, its

safety, its freedom, or, in one word, its happiness.

A rotation of all offices, as well as of representatives and counsellors, has many advocates and is contended for with many plausible arguments. It would be attended no doubt with many advantages; and if the society has a sufficient number of suitable characters to supply the great number of vacancies which would be made by such a rotation, I can see no objection to it. These persons may be allowed to serve for three years and then be excluded three years, or for any longer or shorter term.

Any seven or nine of the legislative council may be made a quorum for doing business as a privy council, to advise the governor in the exercise of the executive branch of power and in all acts of state.

The governor should have the command of the militia and of all your armies. The power of pardons should be with the governor and council.

Judges, justices, and all other officers civil and military, should be nominated and appointed by the governor with the advice and consent of council, unless you choose to have a government more popular; if you do, all officers, civil and military, may be chosen by joint ballot of both houses; or, in order to preserve the independence and importance of each house, by ballot of one house concurred in by the other. Sheriffs should be chosen by the freeholders of counties; so should registers of deeds and clerks of counties.

All officers should have commissions under the hand of the governor and seal of the colony.

The dignity and stability of government in all its branches, the morals of the people, and every blessing of society depend so much upon an upright and skillful administration of justice that the judicial power ought to be distinct from both the legislative and executive, and independent upon both, that so it may be a check upon both, as both should be checks upon that. The judges, therefore, should be always men of learning and experience in the laws, of exemplary morals, great patience, calmness, coolness, and attention. Their minds should not be distracted with jarring interests; they should not be dependent upon any man, or body of men. To these ends, they should hold estates for life in their offices; or, in other words, their commissions should be during good behavior and their salaries ascertained and established by law. For misbehavior the grand inquest of the colony, the house of representatives, should impeach them before the governor and council, where they should have time and opportunity to make their defense; but, if convicted, should be removed from their offices and subjected to such other punishment as shall be thought proper.

A militia law requiring all men, or with very few exceptions besides cases of conscience, to be provided with arms and ammunition, to be trained at certain seasons; and requiring counties, towns, or other small districts to be provided with public stocks of ammunition and entrenching utensils and with some settled plans for transporting provisions after the militia, when marched to defend their country against sudden invasions; and requiring certain districts to be provided with field-pieces, companies of matrosses, and perhaps some regiments of light-horse is always a wise institution, and in the present circumstances of our country indispensable.

Laws for the liberal education of youth, especially of the lower class of people, are so extremely wise and useful that to a humane and generous mind no expense for this purpose would be thought extravagant.

The very mention of sumptuary laws will excite a smile. Whether our countrymen have wisdom and virtue enough to submit to them, I know not; but the happiness of the people might be greatly promoted by them, and a revenue saved sufficient to carry on this war forever. Frugality is a great revenue, besides curing us of vanities, levities, and fopperies, which are real antidotes to all great, manly, and warlike virtues.

But must not all commissions run in the name of a king? No. Why may they not as well run thus, "The colony of _____ to A.B. greeting," and be tested by the governor?

Why may not writs, instead of running in the name of the king, run thus, "The colony of _____ to the sheriff," etc., and be tested by the chief justice?

Why may not indictments conclude, "against the peace of the colony of _____ and the dignity of the same?"

A constitution founded on these principles introduces knowledge among the people and inspires them with a conscious dignity becoming freemen; a general emulation takes place which causes good humor, sociability, good manners, and good morals to be general. That elevation of sentiment inspired by such a government makes the common people brave and enterprising. That ambition which is inspired by it makes them sober, industrious, and frugal. You will find among them some elegance, perhaps, but more solidity; a little pleasure, but a great deal of business; some politeness, but more civility. If you compare such a country with the regions of domination, whether monarchical or aristocratical, you will fancy yourself in Arcadia or Elysium.

If the colonies should assume governments separately, they should be left entirely to their own choice of the forms; and if a continental constitution should be formed, it should be a congress containing a fair and adequate representation of the colonies, and its authority should sacredly be confined to these cases, namely; war, trade, disputes between colony and colony, the post office, and the unappropriated lands of the crown, as they used to be called.

These colonies, under such forms of government and in such a union, would be unconquerable by all the monarchies of Europe.

You and I, my dear friend, have been sent into life at a time when the greatest lawgivers of antiquity would have wished to live. How few of the human race have ever enjoyed an opportunity of making an election of government—more than of air, soil, or climate—for themselves or their children! When, before the present epoch, had three millions of people full power and a fair opportunity to form and establish the wisest and happiest government that human wisdom can contrive? I hope you will avail yourself and your country of that extensive learning and indefatigable industry which you possess to assist her in the formation of the happiest governments and the best character of a great people. For myself, I must beg you to keep my name out of sight; for this feeble attempt, if it should be known to be mine, would oblige me to apply to myself those lines of the immortal John Milton in one of his sonnets:

> I did but prompt the age to quit their
>   clogs
> By the known rules of ancient liberty,
> When straight a barbarous noise environs
>   me
> Of owls and cuckoos, asses, apes, and
>   dogs.   ...~

"A Defense of the Constitutions of the United States" (1787)

It is become a kind of fashion among writers to admit, as a maxim, that if you could be always sure of a wise, active, and virtuous prince, monarchy would be the best of governments. But this is so far from being admissible that it will forever remain true that a free government has a great advantage over a simple monarchy. The best and wisest prince, by means of a freer communication with his people and the greater opportunities to collect the best advice from the best of his subjects, would have an immense advantage in a free state over a monarchy. A senate consisting of all that is most noble, wealthy, and able in the nation, with a right to counsel the crown at all times, is a check to ministers and a security against abuses such as a body of nobles who never meet and have no such right can never

SOURCE: John Adams, *A Defense of the Constitutions of the United States of America against the Attack of M. Turgot in His Letter to Dr. Price* (Philadelphia: Buddard Bartran, 1787).

supply. Another assembly composed of representatives chosen by the people in all parts gives free access to the whole nation and communicates all its wants, knowledge, projects, and wishes to government; it excites emulation among all classes, removes complaints, redresses grievances, affords opportunities of exertion to genius, though in obscurity, and gives full scope to all the faculties of man; it opens a passage for every speculation to the legislature to administration, and to the public; it gives a universal energy to the human character, in every part of the state, such as never can be obtained in a monarchy.

There is a third particular which deserves attention both from governments and people. In a simple monarchy the ministers of state can never know their friends from their enemies; secret cabals undermine their influence and blast their reputation. This occasions a jealousy, ever anxious and irritated, which never thinks the government safe without an encouragement of informers and spies throughout every part of the state, who interrupt the tranquility of private life, destroy the confidence of families in their own domestics and in one another, and poison freedom in its sweetest retirements. In a free government, on the contrary, the ministers can have no enemies of consequence but among the members of the great or little council, where every man is obliged to take his side and declare his opinions upon every question. This circumstance alone to every manly mind would be sufficient to decide the preference in favor of a free government. Even secrecy, where the executive is entire in one hand, is as easily and surely preserved in a free government as in a simple monarchy; and as to dispatch, all the simple monarchies of the whole universe may be defined to produce greater or more numerous examples of it than are to be found in English history. An Alexander or a Frederic, possessed of the prerogatives only of a king of England and leading his own armies, would never find himself embarrassed or delayed in any honest enterprise. He might be restrained, indeed, from running mad and from making conquests to the ruin of his nation merely for his own glory; but this is no argument against a free government.

There can be no free government without a democratical branch in the constitution. Monarchies and aristocracies are in possession of the voice and influence of every university and academy in Europe. Democracy, simple democracy, never had a patron among men of letters. Democratical mixtures in government have lost almost all the advocates they ever had out of England and America. Men of letters must have a great deal of praise and some of the necessaries, conveniences, and ornaments of life. Monarchies and aristocracies pay well and applaud liberally. The people have almost always expected to be served gratis and be paid for the honor of serving them; and their applauses and adorations are be-

stowed too often on artifices and tricks, on hypocrisy and superstition, on flattery, bribes, and largesses. It is no wonder then that democracies and democratical mixtures are annihilated all over Europe except on a barren rock, a paltry fen, an inaccessible mountain, or an impenetrable forest. The people of England, to their immortal honor, are hitherto an exception; but, to the humiliation of human nature, they show very often that they are like other men. The people in America have now the best opportunity and the greatest trust in their hands that Providence ever committed to so small a number since the transgression of the first pair; if they betray their trust, their guilt will merit even greater punishment than other nations have suffered and the indignation of Heaven. If there is one certain truth to be collected from the history of all ages, it is this: that the people's rights and liberties and the democratical mixture in a constitution can never be preserved without a strong executive, or, in other words, without separating the executive from the legislative power. If the executive power or any considerable part of it is left in the hands either of an aristocratical or a democratical assembly, it will corrupt the legislature as necessarily as rust corrupts iron or as arsenic poisons the human body; and when the legislature is corrupted, the people are undone.

The rich, the well-born, and the able require an influence among the people that will soon be too much for simple honesty and plain sense in a house of representatives. The most illustrious of them must, therefore, be separated from the mass and placed by themselves in a senate; this is, to all honest and useful intents, an ostracism. A member of a senate of immense wealth, the most respected birth, and transcendent abilities has no influence in the nation in comparison of what he would have in a single representative assembly. When a senate exists, the most powerful man in the state may be safely admitted into the house of representatives because the people have it in their power to remove him into the senate as soon as his influence becomes dangerous. The senate becomes the great object of ambition and the richest and the most sagacious wish to merit an advancement to it by services to the public in the house. When he has obtained the object of his wishes, you may still hope for the benefits of his exertions without dreading his passions; for the executive power being in other hands, he has lost much of his influence with the people and can govern very few votes more than his own among senators. . . .

The United States of America have exhibited, perhaps, the first example of governments erected on the simple principles of nature; and if men are not sufficiently enlightened to disabuse themselves of artifice, imposture, hypocrisy, and superstition, they will consider this event as an era in their history. Although the detail of the formation of the American governments is at present little known or regarded either in Europe or in America, it may hereafter become an object of curiosity. It will never be pretended that any persons employed in that service had interviews with the gods or were in any degree under the inspiration of Heaven, more than those at work upon ships or houses, or laboring in merchandise or agriculture; it will forever be acknowledged that these governments were contrived merely by the use of reason and the senses. . . . Neither the people nor their conventions, committees, or subcommittees considered legislation in any other light than an ordinary arts and sciences, only more important. Called without expectation, and compelled without previous inclination, though undoubtedly at the best period of time, both for England and America, suddenly to erect new systems of laws for their future government, they adopted the method of a wise architect in erecting a new palace for the

residence of his sovereign. They determined to consult Vitruvius, Palladio, and all other writers of reputation in the art; to examine the most celebrated buildings, whether they remain entire or in ruins; to compare these with the principles of writers, and to inquire how far both the theories and models were founded in nature or created by fancy; and when this was done, so far as their circumstances would allow, to adopt the advantages and reject the inconveniences of all. Unembarrassed by attachments to noble families, hereditary lines and successions, or any considerations of royal blood, even the pious mystery of holy oil had no more influence than that other one of holy water. The people were universally too enlightened to be imposed on by artifice; and their leaders, or more properly followers, were men of too much honor to attempt it. Thirteen governments thus founded on the natural authority of the people alone, without a pretense of miracle or mystery, and which are destined to spread over the northern part of that whole quarter of the globe, are a great point gained in favor of the rights of mankind. The experiment is made and has completely succeeded; it can no longer be called in question whether authority in magistrates and obedience of citizens can be grounded on reason, morality, and the Christian religion, without the monkery of priests or the knavery of politicians. As the writer was personally acquainted with most of the gentlemen in each of the states who had the principal share in the first draughts, the following work was really written to lay before the public a specimen of that kind of reading and reasoning which produced the American constitutions. . . .

M. Turgot is offended because the customs of England are imitated in most of the new constitutions in America without any particular motive. But if we suppose English customs to be neither good nor evil in themselves and merely indifferent, and the people by their birth, education, and habits were familiarly attached to them—would not this be a motive particular enough for their preservation rather than to endanger the public tranquility or unanimity by renouncing them? If those customs were wise, just, and good, and calculated to secure the liberty, property, and safety of the people as well or better than any other institutions, ancient or modern, would M. Turgot have advised the nation to reject them merely because it was at that time justly incensed against the English government? What English customs has it retained which may with any propriety be called evil? M. Turgot has instanced only one, namely, "that a body of representatives, a council, and a governor have been established because there is in England a house of commons, a house of lords, and a king." It was not so much because the legislature in England consisted of three branches, that such a division of power was adopted by the states, as because their own assemblies had ever been so constituted. It was not so much from attachment by habit to such a plan of power that it was continued as from conviction that it was founded in nature and reason.

M. Turgot seems to be of a different opinion and is for "collecting all authority into one center, the nation." It is easily understood how all authority may be collected into "one center" in a despot or monarch; but how it can be done when the center is to be the nation is more difficult to comprehend. Before we attempt to discuss the notions of an author, we should be careful to ascertain his meaning. It will not be easy, after the most anxious research, to discover the true sense of this extraordinary passage. If after the pains of "collecting all authority into one center," that center is to be the nation, we shall remain exactly where we began and no collection of authority at all will be made. The nation will be the authority, and the authority the nation. The center will be the circle, and the circle the center.

When a number of men, women, and children are simply congregated together there is no political authority among them; nor any natural authority but that of the parents over their children. To leave the women and children out of the question for the present, the men will all be equal, free, and independent of each other. Not one will have any authority over any other. The first "collection" of authority must be an unanimous agreement to form themselves into a *nation, people, community,* or *body politic* and to be governed by the majority of suffrages or voices. But even in this case, although the authority is collected into one center, that center is no longer the nation but the majority of the nation. Did M. Turgot mean that the people of Virginia, for example, half a million of souls scattered over a territory of two hundred leagues square, should stop here and have no other authority by which to make or execute a law or judge a cause but by a vote of the whole people and the decision of a majority! Where is the plain large enough to hold them; and what are the means, and how long would be the time, necessary to assembly them together?

A simple and perfect democracy never yet existed among men. If a village of half a mile square and one hundred families is capable of exercising all the legislative, executive, and judicial powers in public assemblies of the whole by unanimous votes or by majorities, it is more than has ever yet been proved in theory or experience. In such a democracy, for the most part, the moderator would be king, the town-clerk legislator and judge, and the constable sheriff; and upon more important occasions, committees would be only the counsellors of both the former and commanders of the latter.

Shall we suppose, then, that M. Turgot intended that an assembly of representatives should be chosen by the nation and vested with all the powers of government; and that this assembly should be the center in which all the authority was to be collected and should be virtually deemed the nation? After long reflection I have not been able to discover any other sense in his words, and this was probably his real meaning. . . .

As we have taken a cursory view of these countries in Europe where the government may be called, in any reasonable construction of the word, republican, let us now pause a few moments and reflect upon what we have seen. . . .

In every republic—in the smallest and most popular, in the larger and more aristocratical, as well as in the largest and most monarchical—we have observed a multitude of curious and ingenious inventions to balance, in their turn, all those powers, to check the passions peculiar to them, and to control them from rushing into those exorbitancies to which they are most addicted. The Americans will then be no longer censured for endeavoring to introduce an equilibrium which is much more profoundly mediated and much more effectual for the protection of the laws than any we have seen, except in England. We may even question whether that is an exception.

In every country we have found a variety of *orders* with very great distinctions. In America there are different orders of *offices,* but none of *men.* Out of office, all men are of the same species and of one blood; there is neither a greater nor a lesser nobility. Why, then, are the Americans accused of establishing different orders of men? To our inexpressible mortification we must have observed that the people have preserved a share of power of an existence in the government in no country out of England except upon the tops of a few inaccessible mountains, among rocks and precipices, in territories so narrow that you may span them with a hand's breadth, where, living unenvied, in extreme poverty, chiefly among pasturage, destitute of manufactures and commerce, they still exhibit the most charming picture of life and the most dignified character of human nature.

Wherever we have seen a territory somewhat larger, arts and sciences more cultivated, commerce flourishing, or even agriculture improved to any great degree, an aristocracy has risen up in the course of time, consisting of a few rich and honorable families who have united each other against both the people and the first magistrate, who have wrested from the former by art and by force all their participation in the government and have even inspired them with so mean an esteem of themselves and so deep a veneration and strong attachment to their rulers as to believe and confess them a superior order of beings.

We have seen these noble families, although necessitated to have a head, extremely jealous of his influence, anxious to reduce his power, and to constrain him to as near a level as possible with themselves, always endeavoring to establish a rotation by which they may all equally be entitled in turn to the preeminence, and likewise anxious to preserve to themselves as large a share as possible of power in the executive and judicial, as well as the legislative departments of the state.

These patrician families have also appeared in every instance to be equally jealous of each other and to have contrived by blending lot and choice, by mixing various bodies in the elections to the same offices, and even by a resort to the horrors of an inquisition, to guard against the sin that so easily besets them, of being wholly influenced and governed by a junto or oligarchy of a few among themselves.

We have seen no one government in which is a distinct separation of the legislative from the executive power and of the judicial from both, or in which any attempt has been made to balance these powers with one another, or to form an equilibrium between the one, the few, and the many, for the purpose of enacting and executing equal laws by common consent for the general interest, excepting in England.

Shall we conclude from these melancholy observations that human nature is incapable of liberty, that no honest equality can be preserved in society, and that such forcible causes are always at work as must reduce all men to a submission to despotism, monarchy, oligarchy, or aristocracy?

By no means. We have seen one of the first nations in Europe, possessed of ample and fertile territories at home and extensive dominions abroad, of a commerce with the whole world, immense wealth, and the greatest naval power which ever belonged to any nation, which has still preserved the power of the people by the equilibrium we are contending for, by the trial by jury, and by constantly refusing a standing army. The people of England alone, by preserving their share in the legislature at the expense of the blood of heroes and patriots, have enabled their king to curb the nobility without giving him a standing army.

After all, let us compare every constitution we have seen with those of the United States of America, and we shall have no reason to blush for our country. On the contrary, we shall feel the strongest motives to fall upon our knees in gratitude to heaven for having been graciously pleased to give us birth and education in that country and for having destined us to live under her laws! We shall have reason to exult if we make our comparison with England and the English constitution. Our people are undoubtedly sovereign; all the landed and other property is in the hands of the citizens; not only their representatives but their senators and governors are annually chosen; there are no hereditary titles, honors, offices, or distinctions; the legislative, executive, and judicial powers are carefully separated from each other; the powers of the one, the few, and the many are nicely balanced in the legislatures; trials by jury are preserved in all their glory,

and there is no standing army; the *habeas corpus* is in full force; the press is the most free in the world. Where all these circumstances take place, it is unnecessary to add that the laws alone can govern....

It is agreed that the people are the best keepers of their own liberties and the only keepers who can be always trusted, and therefore, the people's fair, full, and honest consent to every law, by their representatives, must be made an essential part of the constitution; but it is denied that they are the best keepers, or any keepers at all, of their own liberties when they hold, collectively or by representation, the executive and judicial power, or the whole and uncontrolled legislative; on the contrary, the experience of all ages has proved that they instantly give away their liberties into the hand of grandees or kings, idols of their own creation. The management of the executive and judicial powers together always corrupts them and throws the whole power into the hands of the most profligate and abandoned among themselves. The honest men are generally nearly equally divided in sentiment, and therefore, the vicious and unprincipled, by joining one party, carry the majority; and the vicious and unprincipled always follow the most profligate leader, him who bribes the highest and sets all decency and shame at defiance. It becomes more profitable, and reputable too, except with a very few, to be a party man than a public spirited one.

It is agreed that "the end of all government is the good and ease of the people in a secure enjoyment of their rights without oppression"; but it must be remembered that the rich are *people* as well as the poor; that they have rights as well as others, that they have as clear and as *sacred* right to their large property as others have to theirs which is smaller; that oppression to them is as possible and as wicked as to others; that stealing, robbing, cheating are the same crimes and sins, whether committed against them or others. The rich, therefore, ought to have an effectual barrier in the constitution against being robbed, plundered, and murdered, as well as the poor; and this can never be without an independent senate. The poor should have a bulwark against the same dangers and oppressions; and this can never be without a house of representatives of the people. But neither the rich nor the poor can be defended by their respective guardians in the constitution without an executive power, vested with a negative equal to either, to hold the balance even between them and decide when they cannot agree. If it is asked, When will this negative be used? it may be answered, Perhaps never. The known existence of it will prevent all occasion to exercise it; but if it has not a being, the want of it will be felt every day. If it has not been used in England for a long time past, it by no means follows that there have not been occasions when it might have been employed with propriety. But one thing is very certain, that there have been many occasions since the Revolution when the constitution would have been overturned if the negative had not been an indubitable prerogative of the crown.

It is agreed that the people are "most sensible of their own burdens, and being once put into a capacity and freedom of acting are the most likely to provide remedies for their own relief." For this reason they are an essential branch of the legislature and have a negative on all laws, an absolute control over every grant of money, and an unlimited right to accuse their enemies before an impartial tribunal. Thus far they are most sensible of their burdens and are most likely to provide remedies. But it is affirmed that they are not only incapable of managing the executive power but would be instantly corrupted by it in such numbers as would destroy the integrity of all elections. It is denied that the legislative power can be wholly entrusted in their hands with a moment's safety. The poor and the vicious would instantly rob the rich and virtuous, spend their plunder in debauchery or confer it upon some idol, who would become the despot; or, to speak more intelligibly if not more accurately, some of the rich, by debauching the vicious to their corrupt interest, would plunder the virtuous and become more rich until they acquired all the property, or a balance of property and of power, in their own hands and domineered as despots in an oligarchy. ◇

Correspondence with Abigail Adams (1776)

ABIGAIL ADAMS TO JOHN ADAMS

Braintree, March 31, 1776
—I long to hear that you have declared an independency—and by the way in the new Code

SOURCE: *The Adams Papers*, ed. L.H. Butterfield, Series II, *Adams Family Correspondence* (Cambridge, Mass.: Harvard University Press, 1963).

of Laws which I suppose it will be necessary for you to make I desire you would Remember the Ladies, and be more generous and favourable to them than your ancestors. Do not put such unlimited power into the hands of the Husbands. Remember all Men would be tyrants if they could. If perticuliar care and attention is not paid to the Laidies we are determined to foment a Rebelion, and will not hold ourselves bound by any Laws in which we have no voice, or Representation.

That your Sex are Naturally Tyrannical is a Truth so thoroughly established as to admit of no dispute, but such of you as wish to be happy willingly give up the harsh title of Master for the more tender and endearing one of Friend. Why then, not put it out of the power of the vicious and the Lawless to use us with cruelty and indignity with impunity. Men of Sense in all Ages abhor those customs which treat us only as the vassals of your Sex. Regard us then as Beings placed by providence under your protection and in immitation of the Supreem Being make use of that power only for our happiness.

John Adams to Abigail Adams

Ap. 14. 1776

As to Declarations of Independency, be patient. Read our Privateering Laws, and our Commercial Laws. What signifies a Word.

As to your extraordinary Code of Laws, I cannot but laugh. We have been told that our Struggle has loosened the bands of Government every where. That Children and Apprentices were disobedient—that schools and Colledges were grown turbulent—that Indians slighted their Guardians and Negroes grew insolent to their Masters. But your Letter was the first Intimation that another Tribe more numerous and powerfull than all the rest were grown discontented.—This is rather too coarse a Compliment but you are so saucy, I wont blot it out.

Depend upon it, We know better than to repeal our Masculine systems. Altho they are in full Force, you know they are little more than Theory. We dare not exert our Power in its full Latitude. We are obliged to go fair, and softly, and in Practice you know We are the subjects. We have only the Name of Masters, and rather than give up this, which would compleatly subject Us to the Despotism of the Peticoat, I hope General Washington, and all our brave Heroes would fight. I am sure every good Politician would plot, as long as he would against Despotism, Empire, Monarchy, Aristocracy, Oligarchy, or Ochlocracy. ∿

Primary Sources

Adams, John. *A Defense of the Constitutions of the United States of America against the Attack of M. Turgot in His Letter to Dr. Price.* 3 vols. Philadelphia: Buddard Bartran, 1787.

———. *Correspondence of the Late President Adams.* Boston: Everett and Munroe, 1809.

———. *The Political Writings of John Adams: Representative Selections.* Edited by George A. Peck Jr. New York: Liberal Arts Press, 1954.

Secondary Sources

Bowen, Catherine Drinker. *John Adams and the American Revolution.* Boston: Little, Brown, 1951.

Chinard, Gilbert. *Honest John Adams.* Boston: Little, Brown, 1933.

Dauer, Manning J. *The Adams Federalists.* Baltimore: Johns Hopkins Press, 1953.

Ferling, John. *John Adams: A Life.* Knoxville: University of Tennessee Press, 1992.

Handler, Edward. *America and Europe in the Political Thought of John Adams.* Cambridge, Mass.: Harvard University Press, 1964.

Haraszti, Zoltan. *John Adams and the Prophets of Progress.* Cambridge, Mass.: Harvard University Press, 1952.

9. The Constitution

THE YEARS OF the revolutionary war were a period of relative prosperity, with business expanding and prices rising as a result of deficit financing and of issuing a quantity of paper money. A banking crisis in England precipitated a sharp deflation in 1784, however; trade dropped sharply, prices and wages fell, and creditors began to press their debtors insistently—often foreclosing on farms and lands which the debtors had just cleared and improved. Debtors sought to have their states issue new paper money and require its acceptance in payment of debts and to have laws passed that would delay repayment or prevent foreclosures for a period of time. Some business interests sought to have their states enact protective legislation such as duties on imports or grants of monopoly rights over certain kinds of business. States refused to meet the financial quotas assigned them by Congress; under the Articles of Confederation there was no other way Congress could raise money to pay the bonds and other obligations of the United States, and so these obligations became practically worthless. People had helped Congress finance the revolutionary war by buying its bonds and paper money with their savings, only to find that they had little or no prospect of ever redeeming the investment.

Scholars are still debating how severe these years really were and which sectors of the economy were hit the hardest. But it is clear that leadership for doing something about these conditions lay with financiers and other creditors who feared what debtors might do, and with those economic interests that sought to do business on a national scale and feared mounting state protectionism. Virginia issued a call in 1786 for a convention to negotiate improvements in interstate commerce, but so few delegates actually appeared in Annapolis, Maryland, at the appointed time that nothing could be done. Alexander Hamilton, representing New York, nevertheless used the occasion to have the twelve delegates present issue a call to the states to send delegates to another convention to be held in Philadelphia in May 1787 to discuss *all* matters necessary "to render the constitution of the Federal Government adequate to the exigencies of the Union."

Almost simultaneously, debtors rose up in arms in western Massachusetts and forced the closing of courts. For several months armed forces under the command of a revolutionary-war captain named Daniel Shays prevented foreclosures and virtually controlled the region. With this threat in mind, several states appointed delegates to the Philadelphia convention, and Congress finally endorsed it in February 1787. The terms of the congressional endorsement were that the convention should meet "for the sole and express purpose of revising the Articles of Confederation and reporting to Congress and the several legislatures such alterations and provisions therein."

In all, fifty-five delegates attended the Philadelphia convention; more than half of them were college graduates and law-yers, and many of the leading public figures of the time were included. Not present, however, were several of those who had led the fight for the Declaration of Independence. John Ad-ams was in England, Jefferson in France —both on assignment from Congress. Samuel Adams, John Hancock, and Patrick Henry all remained at home. Alexander Hamilton, al-though a delegate from New York, was appar-ently too devoted to a plan for a limited Brit-ish-style monarchy to wield much influence. James Madison appears to have been a major figure, and most of what is known about the debates comes from the detailed notes he kept (which, however, were not published until 1840, four years after his death). One of the first acts of the assembled delegates was to agree to keep all their discussions secret. An-other was tacitly to accept the idea of writing an entirely new constitution rather than merely proposing revisions to the Articles as Congress had specified.

The convention lifted its secrecy code only on 17 September 1787, when it approved the final draft of the Constitution and forwarded it to Congress. The Constitution provided that ratification would be done by specially called conventions in each of the states and that it would go into effect when nine states had rati-fied. Congress officially sent the document to the states for their action on 28 September. In each case the state's legislature had to be called together to provide for the election of delegates to such conventions, the elections had to be held, the delegates had to be con-vened, and discussions had to be conducted before a ratification vote could be taken. And all of this had to be accomplished under the often-crude conditions of communication and transportation as fall turned into winter in 1787.

Nevertheless, the first state to ratify (Dela-ware) did so unanimously on 7 December

1787, and four others soon followed. The first extended debate occurred in Massachusetts, where opposition caused the Federalist propo-nents of the Constitution to agree to the addi-tion of a Bill of Rights as soon as the new con-gress met. At this point, a popular referendum in Rhode Island overwhelmingly rejected the document. By mid-June, however, eight states had ratified, but neither New York nor Vir-ginia, both essential to the new nation, had done so. Hamilton's delaying tactics prevented rejection in New York until after Madison gained a narrow victory in Virginia, overcom-ing determined opposition from Patrick Henry and others by agreeing to several conditions and revisions during more than three weeks of debates. (New Hampshire was actually the ninth state to ratify, but Virginia's ratification three days later was the decisive one.)

It has never been established whether a majority of the eligible voters of the times were in favor of ratification or not. More than half of the population, it is clear, was not even eligible to vote: women, slaves, and those who could not meet the various property require-ments of the states were all excluded. Many of those who were eligible did not know or care enough about the election of convention dele-gates to cast votes; moreover, the delegates acted as free agents in the conventions. The Federalists made a concerted effort to elect delegates favorable to the Constitution and were much stronger in the conventions than in the states generally. There was real and widespread opposition, however, manifested in conventions, in the press, and in the state legis-latures. Support essentially came from the longer-established financial and trading towns and cities along the eastern seaboard, and op-position came from the newer back-country areas where small farmers and debtors pre-dominated.

Why was there such opposition? Today it may be hard to appreciate the reasons. But in the context of the times there was the threat of the unknown, the makeup and secrecy of the convention, the speed with which the Federalists pressed for approval, and the volume of propaganda they generated—all of which served to alert a skeptical observer. Moreover, there was the substance of the document itself: a potentially powerful executive, a new court system, powers in the Congress to tax and regulate commerce, a standing army, and so forth. The debtor could find any number of provisions that seemed to favor creditors: exclusive power in the national government over the coining and value of money, prohibitions against state "impairment" of contractual obligations, and provisions for the enforcement of court judgments gained in other states on the debtor wherever he might move in search of a new start.

One way to analyze the Constitution is to read it carefully as a small farmer might have, who, deeply in debt to eastern banks, feared that continued low prices would prevent him from making payments, thus allowing the banks to foreclose his mortgage and take his newly built farm. Other ways to approach the Constitution would be from the viewpoint of a Baltimore merchant trying to sell imported goods in several states or of a revolutionary-war widow who held bonds issued by Congress that were currently worthless. The point is that the Constitution was *both* a plan of government reflecting underlying philosophical assumptions about human nature and the purposes of social order *and* a deeply personal allocation of immediate economic and political burdens and benefits. We are more in the habit of exploring the assumptions that lay behind the creation of a powerful executive or behind the complicated institutional system that gave significant power to lawyers and judges, particularly those on the Supreme Court. But we should also ask such basic questions as who won and who lost by means of the ratification of the document: who was obliged to sacrifice what for whose benefit? ∿

The Constitution of the United States of America (1787)

We the People of the United States, in Order to form a more perfect Union, establish Justice, insure domestic Tranquility, provide for the common defence, promote the general Welfare, and secure the Blessings of Liberty to ourselves and our Posterity, do ordain and establish this Constitution for the United States of America.

ARTICLE I

Section 1. All legislative Powers herein granted shall be vested in a Congress of the United States, which shall consist of a Senate and House of Representatives.

Section 2. The House of Representatives shall be composed of Members chosen every second Year by the People of the several States, and the Electors in each State shall have the Qualifications requisite for Electors of the most numerous Branch of the State Legislature.

No Person shall be a Representative who shall not have attained to the age of twenty five Years, and been seven Years a Citizen of the United States, and who shall not, when elected, be an Inhabitant of that State in which he shall be chosen.

Representatives and direct Taxes shall be

apportioned among the several States which may be included within this Union, *according to their respective Numbers, which shall be determined by adding to the whole Number of free Persons, including those bound to Service for a Term of Years,* and excluding Indians not taxed, *three fifths of all other persons.*[1] The actual Enumeration shall be made within three Years after the first Meeting of the Congress of the United States, and within every subsequent Term of ten Years, in such Manner as they shall by Law direct. The Number of Representatives shall not exceed one for every thirty Thousand, but each State shall have at Least one Representative; and until such enumeration shall be made, the State of New Hampshire shall be entitled to chuse three, Massachusetts eight, Rhode-Island and Providence Plantations one, Connecticut five, New-York six, New Jersey four, Pennsylvania eight, Delaware one, Maryland six, Virginia ten, North Carolina five, South Carolina five, and Georgia three.

When vacancies happen in the Representation from any State, the Executive Authority thereof shall issue Writs of Election to fill such Vacancies.

The House of Representatives shall chuse their Speaker and other Officers; and shall have the sole Power of Impeachment.

Section 3. The Senate of the United States shall be composed of two Senators from each State, *chosen by the Legislature thereof,*[2] for six Years; and each Senator shall have one Vote.

Immediately after they shall be assembled in Consequence of the first Election, they shall be divided as equally as may be into three Classes. The Seats of the Senators of the first Class shall be vacated at the Expiration of the second Year, of the second Class at the Expiration of the fourth Year, and of the third Class at the Expiration of the sixth Year, so that one third may be chosen every second Year; *and if Vacancies happen by Resignation, or otherwise, during the Recess of the Legislature of any State, the Executive thereof may take temporary Appointments until the next Meeting of the Legislature, which shall then fill such Vacancies.*[3]

No Person shall be a Senator who shall not have attained to the Age of thirty Years, and been nine Years a Citizen of the United States, and who shall not, when elected, be an Inhabitant of that State for which he shall be chosen.

The Vice President of the United States shall be President of the Senate, but shall have no Vote, unless they be equally divided.

The Senate shall chuse their other Officers, and also a President pro tempore, in the Absence of the Vice President, or when he shall exercise the Office of President of the United States.

The Senate shall have the sole Power to try all Impeachments. When sitting for that Purpose, they shall be on Oath or Affirmation. When the President of the United States is tried, the Chief Justice shall preside: And no Person shall be convicted without the Concurrence of two thirds of the Members present.

Judgment in Cases of Impeachment shall not extend further than to removal from Office, and disqualification to hold and enjoy any Office of honor, Trust or Profit under the United States: but the Party convicted shall nevertheless be liable and subject to Indictment, Trial, Judgment and Punishment, according to Law.

Section 4. The Times, Places and Manner of holding Elections for Senators and Repre-

---

1. Italics are used throughout to indicate passages that have been altered by subsequent amendments not included in this selection. In this case, see Amendment XIV.

2. See Amendment XVII.

---

3. Ibid.

sentatives, shall be prescribed in each State by the Legislature thereof; but the Congress may at any time by Law make or alter such Regulations, except as to the Places of chusing Senators.

The Congress shall assemble at least once in every Year, and such Meeting shall be on the first Monday in December, unless they shall by Law appoint a different Day.[4]

Section 5. Each House shall be the Judge of the Elections, Returns and Qualifications of its own Members, and a Majority of each shall constitute a Quorum to do Business; but a smaller Number may adjourn from day to day, and may be authorized to compel the Attendance of absent Members, in such Manner, and under such Penalties as each House may provide.

Each House may determine the Rules of its Proceedings, punish its Members for disorderly Behavior, and, with the Concurrence of two thirds, expel a Member.

Each House shall keep a journal of its Proceedings, and from time to time publish the same, excepting such Parts as may in their Judgment require Secrecy; and the Yeas and Nays of the Members of either House on any question shall, at the Desire of one fifth of those Present, be entered on the Journal.

Neither House, during the Session of Congress, shall, without the Consent of the other, adjourn for more than three days, nor to any other Place than that in which the two Houses shall be sitting.

Section 6. The Senators and Representatives shall receive a Compensation for their Services, to be ascertained by Law, and paid out of the Treasury of the United States. They shall in all Cases, except Treason, Felony and Breach of the Peace, be privileged from Arrest during their Attendance at the Session of their respective Houses, and in going to and return-

ing from the same; and for any Speech or Debate in either House, they shall not be questioned in any other Place.

No Senator or Representative shall, during the Time for which he was elected, be appointed to any civil Office under the Authority of the United States, which shall have been created, or the Emoluments whereof shall have been encreased during such time; and no Person holding any Office under the United States, shall be a Member of either House during his Continuance in Office.

Section 7. All Bills for raising Revenue shall originate in the House of Representatives; but the Senate may propose or concur with Amendments as on other Bills.

Every Bill which shall have passed the House of Representatives and the Senate, shall, before it become a Law, be presented to the President of the United States; if he approve he shall sign it, but if not he shall return it, with his Objections to that House in which it shall have originated, who shall enter the Objections at large on their Journal, and proceed to reconsider it. If after such Reconsideration two thirds of that House shall agree to pass the Bill, it shall be sent, together with the Objections, to the other House, by which it shall likewise be reconsidered, and if approved by two thirds of that House, it shall become a Law. But in all such Cases the Votes of both Houses shall be determined by Yeas and Nays, and the names of the Persons voting for and against the Bill shall be entered on the Journal of each House respectively. If any Bill shall not be returned by the President within ten Days (Sundays excepted) after it shall have been presented to him, the Same shall be a Law, in like Manner as if he had signed it, unless Congress by their Adjournment prevent its Return, in which Case it shall not be a Law.

Every Order, Resolution, or Vote to which the Concurrence of the Senate and House of Representatives may be necessary (except on a

---

4. See Amendment XX.

question of Adjournment) shall be presented to the President of the United States; and before the Same shall take Effect, shall be approved by him, or being disapproved by him, shall be repassed by two thirds of the Senate and House of Representatives, according to the Rules and Limitations presented in the Case of a Bill.

Section 8. The Congress shall have Power To lay and collect Taxes, Duties, Imposts and Excises, to pay the Debts and provide for the common Defence and general Welfare of the United States; but all Duties, Imposts and Excises shall be uniform throughout the United States;

To borrow Money on the credit of the United States;

To regulate Commerce with foreign Nations, and among the several States, and with the Indian Tribes;

To establish an uniform Rule of Naturalization, and uniform Laws on the subject of Bankruptcies throughout the United States;

To coin Money, regulate the Value thereof, and of foreign Coin, and fix the Standard of Weights and Measures;

To provide for the Punishment of counterfeiting the Securities and Current Coin of the United States;

To establish Post Offices and post Roads;

To promote the Progress of Science and useful Arts, by securing for limited Times to Authors and Inventors the exclusive Right to their respective Writings and Discoveries;

To constitute Tribunals inferior to the Supreme Court;

To define and punish Piracies and Felonies committed on the high Seas, and Offences against the Law of Nations;

To declare War, grant Letters of Marque and Reprisal, and make Rules concerning Captures on Land and Water;

To raise and support Armies, but no Appropriation of Money to that Use shall be for a longer Term than two Years;

To provide and maintain a Navy;

To make Rules for the Government and Regulation of the land and naval Forces;

To provide for calling forth the Militia to execute the Laws of the Union, suppress Insurrections and repel Invasions;

To provide for organizing, arming, and disciplining, the Militia, and for governing such Part of them as may be employed in the Service of the United States, reserving to the States respectively, the Appointment of the Officers, and the Authority of training the Militia according to the discipline prescribed by Congress;

To exercise exclusive Legislation in all Cases whatsoever, over such District (not exceeding ten Miles square) as may, by Cession of particular States, and the Acceptance of Congress, become the Seat of the Government of the United States, and to exercise like Authority over all Places purchased by the Consent of the Legislature of the State in which the Same shall be, for the Erection of Forts, Magazines, Arsenals, dock-Yards, and other needful Buildings;—And

To make all Laws which shall be necessary and proper for carrying into Execution the foregoing Powers, and all other Powers vested by this Constitution in the Government of the United States, or in any Department or Officer thereof.

Section 9. The Migration or Importation of such Persons as any of the states now existing shall think proper to admit, shall not be prohibited by the Congress prior to the Year one thousand eight hundred and eight, but a Tax or duty may be imposed on such Importation, not exceeding ten dollars for each Person.

The Privilege of the Writ of Habeas Corpus shall not be suspended, unless when in Cases of Rebellion or Invasion the public Safety may require it.

No Bill of Attainder or ex post facto Law

shall be passed.

No Capitation, or other direct, Tax shall be laid, unless in Proportion to the Census or Enumeration herein before directed to be taken.

No Tax or Duty shall be laid on Articles exported from any State.

No Preference shall be given by any Regulation of Commerce or Revenue to the Ports of one State over those of another: nor shall Vessels bound to, or from, one State, be obliged to enter, clear, or pay Duties in another.

No Money shall be drawn from the Treasury, but in Consequence of Appropriations made by Law; and a regular Statement and Account of the Receipts and Expenditures of all public Money shall be published from time to time.

No title of Nobility shall be granted by the United States: And no Person holding any Office of Profit or Trust under them, shall, without the Consent of the Congress, accept of any present, Emolument, Office, or Title, of any kind whatever, from any King, Prince, or foreign State.

Section 10. No State shall enter into any Treaty, Alliance, or Confederation; grant Letters of Marque and Reprisal; coin Money; emit Bills of Credit; make any Thing but gold and silver Coin a Tender in Payment of Debts; pass any Bill of Attainder, ex post facto Law, or Law impairing the Obligation of Contracts, or Grant any Title of Nobility.

No State shall, without the Consent of the Congress, lay any Imposts or Duties on Imports or Exports, except what may be absolutely necessary for executing its inspection Laws: and the net Produce of all Duties and Imposts, laid by any State on Imports or Exports, shall be for the Use of the Treasury of the United States; and all such Laws be subject to the Revision and Control of the Congress.

No State shall, without the Consent of Congress, lay any Duty of Tonnage, keep Troops, or Ships of War in time of Peace; enter into any Agreement or Compact with another State, or with a foreign Power, or engage in War, unless actually invaded, or in such imminent Danger as will not admit of delay.

ARTICLE II

Section 1. The executive Power shall be vested in a President of the United States of America. He shall hold his Office during the Term of four Years, and, together with the Vice President, chosen for the same Term be elected as follows:

Each State shall appoint, in such Manner as the Legislature thereof may direct, a Number of Electors, equal to the whole Number of Senators and Representatives to which the State may be entitled in the Congress: but no Senator or Representative, or Person holding an Office of Trust or Profit under the United States, shall be appointed an Elector.

The Electors shall meet in their respective States, and vote by Ballot for two Persons, of whom one at least shall not be an Inhabitant of the same State with themselves. And they shall make a List of all the Persons voted for, and of the Number of Votes for each; which List they shall sign and certify, and transmit sealed to the Seat of the Government of the United States directed to the President of the Senate. The President of the Senate shall, in the Presence of the Senate and House of Representatives, open all the Certificates, and the Votes shall then be counted. The Person having the greatest Number of Votes shall be the President, if such Number be a Majority of the whole Number of Electors appointed; and if there be more than one who have such Majority, and have an equal Number of Votes, then the House of Representatives shall immediately chuse by Ballot one of them for President; and if no Person have a Majority, then from the five highest on the List the said House shall in like Manner chuse the President. But in chusing the President, the votes shall be taken by States, the Representation from each State having one Vote; A quorum for this purpose shall consist of a Member or Members from two thirds of the States, and a Majority of all the States shall be necessary to a Choice. In every Case, after the Choice of the President, the Person having the Greatest Number of Votes of the Electors shall be the Vice President. But if there should remain two or more who have equal Votes, the Senate shall chuse from them by Ballot the Vice President.[5]

The Congress may determine the Time of chusing the Electors, and the Day on which they shall give their Votes; which Day shall be the same throughout the United States.

No Person except a natural born Citizen, or a Citizen of the United States, at the time of the Adoption of this Constitution, shall be eligible to the Office of President; neither shall any Person be eligible to that Office who shall not have attained to the Age of thirty five Years, and been fourteen Years a Resident within the United States.

The case of the Removal of the President from Office, or of his Death, Resignation, or Inability to discharge the Powers and Duties of the said Office, the Same shall devolve on the Vice President, and the Congress may by Law provide for the Case of Removal, Death, Resignation or Inability, both of the President and Vice President, declaring what Officer shall then act as President, and such Officer shall act accordingly, until the Disability be removed, or a President shall be elected.

The President shall, at stated Times, receive for his Services, a Compensation which shall neither be encreased nor diminished during the Period for which he shall have been elected, and he shall not receive within that Period any other Emolument from the United States, or any of them.

Before he enter on the Execution of his Of-

5. See Amendment XII.

fice, he shall take the following Oath or Affirmation:—"I do solemnly swear (or affirm) that I will faithfully execute the Office of President of the United States, and will to the best of my Ability, preserve, protect, and defend the Constitution of the United States."

Section 2. The President shall be Commander in Chief of the Army and Navy of the United States, and of the Militia of the several States, when called into the actual service of the United States; he may require the Opinion, in writing, of the principal Officer in each of the executive Departments, upon any Subject relating to the Duties of their respective Offices, and he shall have Power to grant Reprieves and Pardons for Offences against the United States, except in Case of Impeachment.

He shall have Power, by and with the Advice and Consent of the Senate, to make Treaties, provided two thirds of the Senators present concur; and he shall nominate, and by and with the Advice and Consent of the Senate, shall appoint Ambassadors, and other public Ministers and Consuls, Judges of the supreme Court, and all other Officers of the United States, whose Appointments are not herein otherwise provided for, and which shall be established by Law; but the Congress may by Law vest the Appointment of such inferior Officers, as they think proper, in the President alone, in the Courts of Law, or in the Heads of Departments.

The President shall have Power to fill up all Vacancies that may happen during the Recess of the Senate, by granting Commissions which shall expire at the End of their next Session.

Section 3. He shall from time to time give to the Congress Information of the State of the Union, and recommend to their Consideration such Measures as he shall judge necessary and expedient; he may, on extraordinary Occasions, convene both Houses, or either of them, and in Case of Disagreement between them, with Respect to the Time of Adjournment, he may adjourn them to such Time as he shall think proper; he shall receive Ambassadors and other public Ministers, he shall take Care that the Laws be faithfully executed, and shall Commission all the Officers of the United States.

Section 4. The President, Vice President, and all civil Officers of the United States, shall be removed from Office on Impeachment for, and Conviction of, Treason, Bribery, or other high Crimes and Misdemeanors.

ARTICLE III

Section 1. The judicial Power of the United States, shall be vested in one supreme Court and in such inferior Courts as the Congress may from time to time ordain and establish. The Judges, both of the supreme and inferior Courts, shall hold their Offices during good Behavior, and shall, at stated Times, receive for their Services, a Compensation, which shall not be diminished during their Continuance in Office.

Section 2. The Judicial Power shall extend to all Cases, in Law and Equity, arising under this Constitution, the Laws of the United States, and Treaties made, or which shall be made, under their Authority;—to all Cases affecting Ambassadors, other public Ministers and Consuls;—to all Cases of admiralty and maritime Jurisdiction;—to Controversies to which the United States shall be a Party;—to Controversies between two or more States; —*between a State and Citizens of another State;*[6]—between Citizens of different States; between Citizens of the same State claiming Lands under Grants of different states, *and between a State, or the Citizens thereof, and foreign States, Citizens, or Subjects.*[7]

In all cases affecting Ambassadors, other public Ministers and Consuls, and those in

which a State shall be Party, the supreme Court shall have original Jurisdiction. In all the other Cases before mentioned, the supreme Court shall have appellate Jurisdiction, both as to Law and Fact, with such Exceptions, and under such Regulations as the Congress shall make.

The Trial of all Crimes, except in Cases of Impeachment, shall be by Jury, and such Trial shall be held in the State where the said Crimes shall have been committed; but when not committed within any State, the Trial shall be at such Place or Places as the Congress may by Law have directed.

Section 3. Treason against the United States, shall consist only in levying War against them, or in adhering to their Enemies, giving them Aid and Comfort. No person shall be convicted of Treason unless on the Testimony of two Witnesses to the same overt Act, or on Confession in open Court.

The Congress shall have Power to declare the Punishment of Treason, but no Attainder of Treason shall work Corruption of Blood, or Forfeiture except during the Life of the Person attainted.

ARTICLE IV

Section 1. Full Faith and Credit shall be given in each State to the public Acts, Records, and judicial Proceedings of every other State. And the Congress may by general Laws prescribe the Manner in which such Acts, Records, and Proceedings shall be proved, and the Effect thereof.

Section 2. The Citizens of each State shall be entitled to all Privileges and Immunities of Citizens in the several States.

A Person charged in any State with Treason, Felony, or other Crime, who shall flee from Justice, and be found in another State, shall on Demand of the executive Authority of the State from which he fled, be delivered up, to be removed to the State having jurisdiction

---

6. See Amendment XI.
7. Ibid.

of the Crime.

No Person held to Service or Labour in one State, under the Laws thereof, escaping into another, shall, in Consequence of any Law or Regulation therein, be discharged from such Service or Labour, but shall be delivered up on Claim of the Party to whom such Service or Labour may be due.[8]

Section 3. New States may be admitted by the Congress into this Union; but no new State shall be formed or erected within the Jurisdiction of any other State; nor any State be formed by the Junction of two or more States, or Parts of States, without the Consent of the Legislatures of the States concerned as well as of the Congress.

The Congress shall have Power to dispose of and make all needful Rules and Regulations respecting the Territory or other Property belonging to the United States; and nothing in this Constitution shall be so construed as to Prejudice any claims of the United States, or of any particular State.

Section 4. The United States shall guarantee to every State in this Union a Republican Form of Government, and shall protect each of them against Invasion; and on Application of the Legislature, or of the Executive (when the Legislature cannot be convened) against domestic Violence.

ARTICLE V

The Congress, whenever two thirds of both Houses shall deem it necessary, shall propose Amendments to this Constitution, or, on the Application of the Legislatures of two thirds of the several States, shall call a Convention for proposing Amendments, which, in either Case, shall be valid to all Intents and Purposes, as Part of this Constitution, when ratified by the Legislatures of three fourths of the several States, or by Conventions in three

fourths thereof, as the one or the other Mode of Ratification may be proposed by the Congress; Provided that no Amendment which may be made prior to the Year One thousand eight hundred and eight shall in any Manner affect the first and fourth Clauses in the Ninth Section of the first Article; and that no State, without its Consent, shall be deprived of its equal Suffrage in the Senate.

ARTICLE VI

All Debts contracted and Engagements entered into, before the Adoption of this Constitution shall be as valid against the United States under this Constitution, as under the Confederation.

This Constitution, and the Laws of the United States which shall be made in Pursuance thereof, and all Treaties made, or which shall be made, under the Authority of the United States, shall be the supreme Law of the Land; and the Judges in every State shall be bound thereby, any Thing in the Constitution or Laws of any State to the Contrary notwithstanding.

The Senators and Representatives before mentioned, and the Members of the several State Legislatures, and all executive and judicial Officers, both of the United States and of the several States shall be bound by Oath or Affirmation, to support this Constitution; but no religious Test shall ever be required as a Qualification to any Office or public Trust under the United States.

ARTICLE VII

The Ratification of the Conventions of nine States, shall be sufficient for the Establishment of this Constitution between the States so ratifying the Same.

Done in Convention by the Unanimous Consent of the States present the Seventeenth Day of September in the year of our Lord one thousand seven hundred and eighty seven and

---

8. See Amendment XIII.

of the Independence of the United States of America the twelfth. In witness whereof We have hereunto subscribed our Names.

Articles in addition to, and amendment of, the Constitution of the United States of America, proposed by Congress, and ratified by the several States, pursuant to the Fifth Article of the original Constitution.

[*Ratification of the first ten amendments was completed 15 December 1791.*]

AMENDMENT I

Congress shall make no law respecting an establishment of religion, or prohibiting the free exercise thereof; or abridging the freedom of speech, or of the press; or the right of the people peaceably to assemble, and to petition the Government for a redress of grievances.

AMENDMENT II

A well regulated Militia, being necessary to the security of a free State, the right of the people to keep and bear Arms, shall not be infringed.

AMENDMENT III

No Soldier shall, in time of peace be quartered in any house, without the consent of the Owner, nor in time of war, but in a manner to be prescribed by law.

AMENDMENT IV

The right of the people to be secure in their persons, houses, papers, and effects, against unreasonable searches and seizures, shall not be violated, and no Warrants shall issue, but upon probable cause, supported by Oath or affirmation, and particularly describing the place to be searched, and the persons or things to be seized.

AMENDMENT V

No person shall be held to answer for a capital, or otherwise infamous crime, unless on a presentment or indictment of a Grand Jury, except in cases arising in the land or naval forces, or in the Militia, when an actual service in time of War or public danger; nor shall any person be subject for the same offence to be twice put in jeopardy of life or limb; nor shall be compelled in any criminal case to be a witness against himself, nor be deprived of life, liberty, or property, without due process of law; nor shall private property be taken for public use, without just compensation.

AMENDMENT VI

In all criminal prosecutions, the accused shall enjoy the right to a speedy and public trial, by an impartial Jury of the State and district wherein the crime shall have been committed, which district shall have been previously ascertained by law, and to be informed of the nature and cause of the accusation; to be confronted with the witness against him; to have compulsory process for obtaining witness in his favor, and to have the Assistance of Counsel for his defence.

AMENDMENT VII

In Suits at common law, where the value in controversy shall exceed twenty dollars, the right of trial by jury shall be preserved, and no fact tried by a jury, shall be otherwise re-examined in any Court of the United States, than according to the rules of the common law.

AMENDMENT VIII

Excessive bail shall not be required, nor excessive fines imposed, nor cruel and unusual punishments inflicted.

AMENDMENT IX

The enumeration in the Constitution, of certain rights, shall not be construed to deny or disparage others retained by the people.

AMENDMENT X

The powers not delegated to the United States by the Constitution, nor prohibited by it to the States, are reserved to the States respectively, or to the people. ∽

10. In Favor of Adoption of the Constitution

IN THE LONG winter of 1787–88, the Federalists were making every effort to get state legislatures to call ratifying conventions, to elect favorable convention delegates, and to build support nationally for the Constitution. As part of this campaign in the key but very reluctant state of New York, a series of essays signed by "Publius" appeared in New York newspapers. In the spring of 1788 they were published in book form as *The Federalist* and circulated widely. About fifty of the eighty-five essays were written by Hamilton, about thirty by Madison, and five by John Jay, a New York lawyer known for his expertise in foreign affairs.

Although intended as propaganda favoring the Constitution, *The Federalist* soon became the authoritative interpretation of both the intentions of the framers and the meaning of the Constitution itself. This remarkable evolution was due in part to the stature of the authors, in part to the absence of any other background work on the Constitution, but perhaps primarily to the level and quality of the arguments presented. Many scholars have hailed these essays as the high point of American political thinking, and they are generally accepted as expressing the basic liberal framework that has endured to this day.

JAMES MADISON (1751–1836) was born to a wealthy Virginia family and graduated from Princeton in 1772. In 1780 he became a delegate to the Continental Congress, a post he filled until the end of 1783. From 1784 to 1786 he was a member of the House of Delegates from Orange County, becoming a leader almost at once. He went to the Annapolis Convention of 1786 as a delegate from Virginia; he was also named as a delegate to the Philadelphia Convention. At the convention, Madison took a prominent part from the beginning and became one of the acknowledged leaders of the group favoring a strong central government; his influence on the convention's work was so great that he has been called the Father of the Constitution.

Madison was elected to the first session of the House of Representatives. During his term in Congress, as he became increasingly critical of Hamilton's financial policies, he became a recognized leader of the Jeffersonian party. In 1797 Madison voluntarily retired from public life, expecting to devote his time to farming.

With the election of Jefferson in 1800, Madison was brought again into a prominent public position when he was appointed secretary of state. He became the fourth president of the United States in 1808, but his term was marred by the mishandling of the War of 1812.

American thinkers are distinguishable not only by the relative exclusivity of their commitment to property rights but also by the ways in which they envision those values as being best served. Madison, for example, saw property rights in a context that also valued personal and civil rights, and he believed it possible for property to be served through the interplay of relatively gentle and subtle "natural" forces. In *The Federalist No. 10* he made clear that he considered property and economic motivations to be the principal sources and determinants of political activity, with the inevitable prospect of popular efforts at redistribution. The whole structure of separation of powers and checks and balances, together with the large size of the republic, was designed to moderate the anticipated popular thrust just enough to provide a sense of allowing the people's wishes without really endangering the basic pattern of property holding. This is Madison's famous principle of the "natural limits to numerical majorities," in which a republic of sufficient size would insure that the natural diversities of men and interests counteracted each other to prevent formation of a cohesive majority. He sought by this device to solve the "republican dilemma" by means of a "republican remedy." The dilemma was endemic to all popular governments: how to enable the people to take a substantial part and yet at the same time assure that the result would not be intolerable to vested interests. Madison's republican remedy consisted first of

large size, which would lead to countervailing elements sufficient to prevent single-minded majorities from forming and would also increase the probabilities that only well-tested citizens of uncommon moderation (and probably property) would rise to positions of leadership; his remedy consisted secondly of the additional tier of separation of powers and checks and balances. The latter provisions, by building in intra-elite conflict and potential deadlock, might be considered duplicative. One major critique of the Madisonian design concludes that these two provisions are inconsistent with each other and with the idea of wide popular participation and control. They demonstrate at least the extent of Madison's concern for the protection of property within the American system.

One conventional analysis of Madison has it that he was relatively close to Hamilton at the time of the writing of *The Federalist* but drifted away under the spell of Jefferson, shifting finally to become a thoroughgoing Republican party loyalist. The better argument seems to be that Madison was a property-conscious nationalist whose interests and personality led him to the scholar-activist's tasks of designing and explaining the instruments by which people might attain the goals they sought. He did not invest much time in speculation about human capacities, concentrating instead on the instrumental or institutional level after the fashion of a technician who accepts the assumptions of others and engineers the means for them to realize their goals. As balanced and moderate in values and temperament as the institutional arrangements he advocated, Madison was understandably more successful as scholar and subordinate than as president.

The other three *Federalist* essays by Madison included here (*Nos. 39, 48,* and *51*) are probably Madison's best-known efforts. They implement the design whose assumptions and goals are laid out in *No. 10*. One charge that

Madison seeks to refute is that of failure to keep the powers of the new government separated strictly enough. He argues that the distribution of powers in the hands of different institutions responsive to different electoral constituencies will better serve the cause of preventing unwise action. Adding this principle of checks and balances to that of separation of powers, of course, means that the government cannot act decisively except when all substantial interests are in agreement—and that is exactly what Madison intended.

ALEXANDER HAMILTON (1757–1804) was born on the island of Nevis in the British West Indies. Contradictory stories exist over his birthdate and parentage, but the accepted version is that his father was a Scottish merchant and his mother a French housekeeper. Hamilton's education was brief and desultory. At the age of twelve, Hamilton was placed in the office of a West Indian merchant; when he left this position, he was sent to New York to study with funds provided by relatives.

Once in New York, Hamilton soon became involved in the revolutionary activities of the day. Two pamphlets that he wrote, *A Full Vindication of the Measures of the Congress* and *The Farmer Refuted,* attracted immediate attention. Early in 1776 Hamilton was given command of a company of artillery, which he skillfully organized and disciplined. The company distinguished itself so well that Hamilton was invited to serve on Washington's staff. Hamilton accepted the offer and became indispensable to the general.

By the time of the Constitutional Convention, Hamilton had distinguished himself as a lawyer, married into a prominent New York family, and become active in New York politics. He was an admirer of the English mercantilist system and of the role played by the Bank of England in building national wealth and power. He quickly came to terms

with the Constitution as drafted, seeing in it the potential for using the new national government to play a role of development similar to the Bank of England. If the Constitution were adopted, there would be little doubt that Washington would be president or that Hamilton would again play a key part as his closest and most trusted assistant. Consequently, Hamilton threw himself into the writing of *The Federalist* and the management of the campaign for ratification with great energy.

At the outset of his essays, of which *Nos. 15* and *21* are typical, Hamilton laid out the many defects he saw in the Articles of Confederation. Running through these essays are some characteristic themes: the needs for power in the national government, for independence and stature among nations, and for development of the nation's potential wealth. Means to these ends include the supremacy of the nation over the states, the power to raise revenues, the application of national laws directly on citizens, and enforcement powers. Hamilton's strongest approval was reserved for the executive branch and the "energy" it implied. Elsewhere (*The Federalist No. 9*) he indicates that this energy might find its best use in crushing domestic insurrection, perhaps foreshadowing his excessive response to the Whiskey Rebellion. To the problems of faction that Madison had sought to ameliorate in such delicate fashion, Hamilton had a simpler answer: the power and majesty of the federal government would crush where it did not overawe and discourage.

Only slightly less vigorous approval was accorded to the new judiciary. Hamilton felt free to write his own aspirations for the new government into his defenses of its powers, as the famous *No. 78* shows. Here he boldly declares what the Constitution carefully leaves ambiguous, that the Supreme Court must have the power to declare acts of the other branches void if it believes them to be unauthorized by the Constitution. Throughout his essays, as well as in his later work as secretary of the treasury, there is a close connection between the role he has in mind for law and the legal system and the part to be played by a nationally managed financial system. The two are the twin pillars of national development, the basic means to the independent, industrialized political economy he envisioned.

Both executive and judicial agencies and powers were, in Hamilton's eyes, vital steps toward an energetic government. An associated principle for him was the institution of a direct relationship between the government and individual citizens. One of the principal defects of the Articles of Confederation in this view was their failure to provide any means by which the laws of the nation could be applied to individuals. Under the Articles, individuals were not bound by the enactment of Congress, which could only act in the form of imposing obligations on the states, which in their turn might or might not carry out the congressional purpose by enacting implementing statutes. A government that could only act on the states in their corporate capacities, of course, would encounter frequent uncooperativeness from those states when they disapproved of the ac-

tions decided on—and it would be a commensurately less powerful and efficacious government, which fit the purposes of the drafters of the Articles quite well. But to Hamilton a few years later, this appeared a serious obstacle. He insisted that the federal government must have the capacity to act directly on individuals to enable coercion to be realistically applied and the laws to be carried out efficiently. Under this arrangement every individual would be bound by federal laws and nothing required (or permitted) of the states as intermediaries. The individual who did not comply with the federal law would be immediately subject to enforcement by the combined executive and judicial agencies of the national government.

These well-approved innovations were means of making a government that would be energetic and useful. The further question remains, energetic and useful to what ends? Implicit throughout Hamilton's writings is the assumption that the maintenance of stability and order is itself a major accomplishment to be sought as a primary goal of government. But he had more specific purposes in mind, as we shall see in detail when we examine his program as secretary of the treasury (see selection 12). ∼

James Madison's *Federalist* Essays (1787–88)

The Federalist No. 10

To the People of the State of New York:

Among the numerous advantages promised by a well constructed Union, none deserves to be more accurately developed than its ten-

SOURCE: Available in many editions; one of the most useful complete versions in which all of these selections may be found is Clinton Rossiter, ed., *The Federalist Papers* (New York: New American Library, 1960).

dency to break and control the violence of faction. The friend of popular governments never finds himself so much alarmed for their character and fate, as when he contemplates their propensity to this dangerous vice. He will not fail, therefore, to set a due value on any plan which without violating the principles to which he is attached, provides a proper cure for it. The instability, injustice, and confusion introduced into the public councils, have, in truth, been the mortal diseases under which popular governments have everywhere perished; as they continue to be the favorite and fruitful topics from which the adversaries to liberty derive their most specious declamations. The valuable improvements made by the American constitutions on the popular models, both ancient and modern, cannot certainly be too much admired; but it would be an unwarrantable partiality, to contend that they have as effectually obviated the danger on this side, as was wished and expected. Complaints are everywhere heard from our most considerate and virtuous citizens, equally the friends of public and private faith, and of public and personal liberty, that our governments are too unstable, that the public good is disregarded in the conflicts of rival parties, and that measures are too often decided, not according to the rules of justice and the rights of the minor party, but by the superior force of an interested and overbearing majority. However anxiously we may wish that these complaints had no foundation, the evidence of known facts will not permit us to deny that they are in some degree true. It will be found, indeed, on a candid review of our situation, that some of the distresses under which we labor have been erroneously charged on the operation of our governments, but it will be found, at the same time, that other causes will not alone account for many of our heaviest misfortunes; and, particularly, for that prevailing and increasing distrust of public engagements, and alarm for private rights, which are echoed from one end of the continent to the other. These must be chiefly, if not wholly, effects of the unsteadiness and injustice with which a factious spirit has tainted our public administrations.

By a faction, I understand a number of citizens, whether amounting to a majority or minority of the whole, who are united and actuated by some common impulse of passion, or of interest, adverse to the rights of other citizens, or to the permanent and aggregate interests of the community.

There are two methods of curing the mischiefs of faction: the one, by removing its causes; the other, by controlling its effects.

There are again two methods of removing the causes of faction: the one, by destroying the liberty which is essential to its existence; the other, by giving to every citizen the same opinions, the same passions, and the same interests.

It could never be more truly said than of the first remedy, that it was worse than the disease. Liberty is to faction what air is to fire, an aliment without which it instantly expires. But it could not be less folly to abolish liberty, which is essential to political life, because it nourishes faction, than it would be to wish the annihilation of air, which is essential to animal life, because it imparts to fire its destructive agency.

The second expedient is as impracticable as the first would be unwise. As long as the reason of man continues fallible, and he is at liberty to exercise it, different opinions will be formed. As long as the connection subsists between his reason and his selflove, his opinions and his passions will have a reciprocal influence on each other; and the former will be objects to which the latter will attach themselves. The diversity in the faculties of men, from which the rights of property originate, is not less an insuperable obstacle to a uniformity of interests. The protection of these faculties is the first object of government. From the protection of different and unequal faculties of acquiring property, the possession of different degrees and kinds of property immediately results; and from the influence of these on the sentiments and views of the respective proprietors, ensues a division of the society into different interests and parties.

The latent causes of faction are thus sown in the nature of man, and we see them everywhere brought into different degrees of activity, according to the different circumstances of civil society. A zeal for different opinions concerning religion, concerning government, and many other points, as well of speculation as of practice; an attachment to different leaders ambitiously contending for pre-eminence and power; or to persons of other descriptions whose fortunes have been interesting to the human passions, have, in turn, divided mankind into parties, inflamed them with mutual animosity, and rendered them much more disposed to vex and oppress each other than to cooperate for their common good. So strong is this propensity of mankind to fall into mutual animosities that where no substantial occasion presents itself, the most frivolous and fanciful distinctions have been sufficient to kindle their unfriendly passions and excite their most violent conflicts. But the most common and durable source of factions has been the various and unequal distribution of property. Those who hold and those who are without property have ever formed distinct interests in society. Those who are creditors, and those who are debtors fall under a like discrimination. A landed interest, a manufacturing interest, a mercantile interest, a moneyed interest, with many lesser interests, grow up of necessity in civilized nations, and divide them into different classes, actuated by different sentiments and views. The regulation of these various and interfering interests forms the principal task of modern legislation, and involves the spirit of party and faction in the necessary and ordinary operations of the government.

No man is allowed to be a judge in his own cause, because his interest would certainly bias his judgment, and, not improbably, corrupt his integrity. With equal, nay with greater reason, a body of men are unfit to be both judges and parties at the same time; yet what are many of the most important acts of legislation, but so many judicial determinations,

not indeed concerning the rights of single persons, but concerning the rights of large bodies of citizens? And what are the different classes of legislators but advocates and parties to the causes which they determine? Is a law proposed concerning private debts? It is a question to which the creditors are parties on one side and the debtors on the other. Justice ought to hold the balance between them. Yet the parties are, and must be, themselves the judges; and the most numerous party, or, in other words, the most powerful faction must be expected to prevail. Shall domestic manufactures be encouraged, and in what degree, by restrictions on foreign manufactures? [These] are questions which would be differently decided by the landed and the manufacturing classes, and probably by neither with a sole regard to justice and the public good. The appointment of taxes on the various descriptions of property is an act which seems to require the most exact impartiality; yet there is, perhaps, no legislative act in which greater opportunity and temptation are given to a predominant party to trample on the rules of justice. Every shilling with which they overburden the inferior number, is a shilling saved to their own pockets.

It is in vain to say that enlightened statesmen will be able to adjust these clashing interests, and render them all subservient to the public good. Enlightened statesmen will not always be at the helm. Nor, in many cases, can such an adjustment be made at all without taking into view indirect and remote considerations, which will rarely prevail over the immediate interest which one party may find in disregarding the rights of another for the good of the whole.

The inference to which we are brought is, that the *causes* of faction cannot be removed, and that relief is only to be sought in the means of controlling its *effects*.

If a faction consists of less than a majority,

relief is supplied by the republican principle, which enables the majority to defeat its sinister views by regular vote. It may clog the administration, it may convulse the society; but it will be unable to execute and mask its violence under the forms of the Constitution. When a majority is included in a faction, the form of popular government, on the other hand, enables it to sacrifice to its ruling passion or interest both the public good and the rights of other citizens. To secure the public good and private rights against the danger of such a faction, and at the same time to preserve the spirit and the form of popular government, is then the great object to which our inquiries are directed. Let me add that it is the great desideratum by which this form of government can be rescued from the opprobrium under which it has so long labored, and be recommended to the esteem and adoption of mankind.

By what means is this object attainable? Evidently by one of two only. Either the existence of the same passion or interest in a majority at the same time must be prevented, or the majority, having such coexistent passion or interest, must be rendered, by their number and local situation, unable to concert and carry into effect schemes of oppression. If the impulse and the opportunity be suffered to coincide, we well know that neither moral nor religious motives can be relied on as an adequate control. They are not found to be such on the injustice and violence of individuals, and lose their efficacy in proportion to the number combined together, that is, in proportion as their efficacy becomes needful.

From this view of the subject it may be concluded that a pure democracy, by which I mean a society consisting of a small number of citizens, who assemble and administer the government in person, can admit of no cure for the mischiefs of faction. A common passion or interest will, in almost every case, be felt by a majority of the whole; a communication and concert result from the form of government itself; and there is nothing to check the inducements to sacrifice the weaker party or an obnoxious individual. Hence it is that such democracies have ever been spectacles of turbulence and contention; have ever been found incompatible with personal security or the rights of property; and have in general been as short in their lives as they have been violent in their deaths. Theoretic politicians, who have patronized this species of government, have erroneously supposed that by reducing mankind to a perfect equality in their political rights, they would, at the same time, be perfectly equalized and assimilated in their possessions, their opinions, and their passions.

A republic, by which I mean a government in which the scheme of representation takes place, opens a different prospect, and promises the cure for which we are seeking. Let us examine the points in which it varies from pure democracy, and we shall comprehend both the nature of the cure and the efficacy which it must derive from the Union.

The two great points of difference between a democracy and a republic are: first, the delegation of the government, in the latter, to a small number of citizens elected by the rest; secondly, the greater number of citizens, and greater sphere of country, over which the latter may be extended.

The effect of the first difference is, on the one hand, to refine and enlarge the public views, by passing them through the medium of a chosen body of citizens, whose wisdom may best discern the true interest of their country, and whose patriotism and love of justice will be least likely to sacrifice it to temporary or partial considerations. Under such a regulation, it may well happen that the public voice, pronounced by the representatives of the people, will be more consonant to the public good than if pronounced by the people themselves, convened for the purpose. On the other hand, the effect may be inverted. Men of factious tempers, of local prejudices, or of sinister designs, may, by intrigue, by corruption, or by other means, first obtain the suffrages, and then betray the interests, of the people. The question resulting is, whether small or extensive republics are more favorable to the election of proper guardians of the public weal; and it is clearly decided in favor of the latter by two obvious considerations:

In the first place, it is to be remarked that, however small the republic may be, the representatives must be raised to a certain number, in order to guard against the cabals of a few; and that, however large it may be, they must be limited to a certain number, in order to guard against the confusion of a multitude. Hence, the number of representatives in the two cases not being in proportion to that of the two constituents, and being proportionally greater in the small republic, it follows that, if the proportion of fit characters be not less in the large than in the small republic, the former will present a greater option, and consequently a greater probability of a fit choice.

In the next place, as each representative will be chosen by a greater number of citizens in the large than in the small republic, it will be more difficult for unworthy candidates to practice with success the vicious arts by which elections are too often carried; and the suffrages of the people being more free, will be more likely to centre in men who possess the most attractive merit and the most diffusive and established characters.

It must be confessed that in this, as in most other cases, there is a mean, on both sides of which inconveniences will be found to lie. By enlarging too much the number of electors, you render the representative too little acquainted with all their local circumstances and lesser interests; as by reducing it too much, you render him unduly attached to these, and

too little fit to comprehend and pursue great and national objects. The federal Constitution forms a happy combination in this respect; the great and aggregate interests being referred to the national, the local and particular to the State legislatures.

The other point of difference is, the greater number of citizens and extent of territory which may be brought within the compass of republican than of democratic government; and it is this circumstance principally which renders factious combinations less to be dreaded in the former than in the latter. The smaller the society, the fewer probably will be the distinct parties and interests composing it; the fewer the distinct parties and interests, the more frequently will a majority be found of the same party; and the smaller the number of individuals composing a majority, and the smaller the compass within which they are placed, the more easily will they concert and execute their plans of oppression. Extend the sphere and you take in a greater variety of parties and interests; you make it less probable that a majority of the whole will have a common motive to invade the rights of other citizens; or if such a common motive exists, it will be more difficult for all who feel it to discover their own strength, and to act in unison with each other. Besides other impediments, it may be remarked that, where there is a consciousness of unjust or dishonorable purposes, communication is always checked by distrust in proportion to the number whose concurrence is necessary.

Hence, it clearly appears, that the same advantage which a republic has over a democracy, in controlling the effects of faction, is enjoyed by a large over a small republic,—is enjoyed by the Union over the States composing it. Does the advantage consist in the substitution of representatives whose enlightened views and virtuous sentiments render them superior to local prejudices and to schemes of injustice? It will not be denied that the representation of the Union will be most likely to possess these requisite endowments. Does it consist in the greater security afforded by a greater variety of parties, against the event of any one party being able to outnumber and oppress the rest? In an equal degree does the increased variety of parties comprised within the Union, increase this security? Does it, in fine, consist in the greater obstacles opposed to the concert and accomplishment of the secret wishes of an unjust and interested majority? Here, again, the extent of the Union gives it the most palpable advantage.

The influence of factious leaders may kindle a flame within their particular States, but will be unable to spread a general conflagration through the other States. A religious sect may degenerate into a political faction in a part of the Confederacy; but the variety of sects dispersed over the entire face of it must secure the national councils against any danger from that source. A rage for paper money, for an abolition of debts, for an equal division of property, or for any other improper or wicked project, will be less apt to pervade the whole body of the Union than a particular member of it; in the same proportion as such a malady is more likely to taint a particular county or district, than an entire State.

In the extent and proper structure of the Union, therefore, we behold a republican remedy for the diseases most incident to republican government. And according to the degree of pleasure and pride we feel in being republicans ought to be our zeal in cherishing the spirit and supporting the character of Federalist.

Publius

The Federalist No. 39

To the People of the State of New York:
The last paper having concluded the observations which were meant to introduce a candid survey of the plan of government reported by the convention, we now proceed to the execution of that part of our undertaking.

The first question that offers itself is, whether the general form and aspect of the government be strictly republican. It is evident that no other form would be reconcilable with the genius of the people of America; with the fundamental principles of the Revolution; or with that honorable determination which animates every votary of freedom, to rest all our political experiments on the capacity of mankind for self-government. If the plan of the convention, therefore, be found to depart from the republican character, its advocates must abandon it as no longer defensible.

What, then, are the distinctive characters of the republican form? Were an answer to this question to be sought, not by recurring to principles, but in the application of the term by political writers, to the constitutions of different States, no satisfactory one would ever be found. Holland, in which no particle of the supreme authority is derived from the people, has passed almost universally under the denomination of a republic. The same title has been bestowed on Venice, where absolute power over the great body of the people is exercised, in the most absolute manner, by a small body of hereditary nobles. Poland, which is a mixture of aristocracy and of monarchy in their worst forms, has been dignified with the same appellation. The government of England, which has one republican branch only, combined with an hereditary aristocracy and monarchy, has, with equal impropriety, been frequently placed on the list of republics. These examples, which are nearly as dissimilar to each other as to a genuine republic, show the extreme inaccuracy with which the term has been used in political disquisitions.

If we resort for a criterion to the different principles on which different forms of government are established, we may define a republic to be, or at least may bestow that name on, a government which derives all its powers directly or indirectly from the great body of the people, and is administered by persons holding their offices during pleasure, for a limited period, or during good behavior. It is *essential* to such a government that it be derived from the great body of the society, not from an inconsiderable proportion, or a favored class of it; otherwise a handful of tyrannical nobles, exercising their oppressions by a delegation of their powers, might aspire to the rank of republicans, and claim for their government the honorable title of republic. It is *sufficient* for such a government that the persons administering it be appointed, either directly or indirectly, by the people, and that they hold their appointments by either of the tenures just specified; otherwise every government in the United States, as well as every other popular government that has been or can be well organized or well executed, would be degraded from the republican character. According to the constitution of every State in the Union, some or other of the officers of government are appointed indirectly only by the people. According to most of them, the chief magistrate himself is so appointed. And according to one, this mode of appointment is extended to one of the coordinate branches of the legislature. According to all the constitutions, also, the tenure of the highest offices is extended to a definite period, and in many instances, both within the legislative and executive departments, to a period of years. According to the provisions of most of the constitutions, again, as well as according to the most respectable and received opinions on the subject, the members of the judiciary department are to retain their offices by the firm tenure of good behavior.

On comparing the Constitution planned by the convention with the standard here fixed, we perceive at once that it is, in the most rigid sense, conformable to it. The House of Representatives, like that of one branch at least of all the State legislatures, is elected immediately by the great body of the people. The Senate, like the present Congress, and the Senate of Maryland, derives its appointment indirectly from the people. The President's is indirectly derived from the choice of the people, according to the example in most of the States. Even the judges with all officers of the Union, will, as in the several States, be the choice, though a remote choice, of the people themselves. The duration of the appointments is equally conformable to the republican standard, and to the model of State constitutions. The House of Representatives is periodically elective, as in all the States; and for the period of two years, as in the State of South Carolina. The Senate is elective, for the period of six years; which is but one year more than the period of the Senate of Maryland, and but two more than that of the Senates of New York and Virginia. The President is to continue in office for the period of four years; as in New York and Delaware the chief magistrate is elected for three years, and in South Carolina for two years. In the other States the election is annual. In several of the States, however, no constitutional provision is made for the impeachment of the chief magistrate. And in Delaware and Virginia he is not impeachable till out of office. The President of the United States is impeachable at any time during his continuance in office. The tenure by which the judges are to hold their places, is, as it unquestionably ought to be, that of good behavior. The tenure of the ministerial offices generally, will be a subject of legal regulation, conformably to the reason of the case and the example of the State constitutions.

Could any further proof be required of the republican complexion of this system, the most decisive one might be found in its absolute prohibition of titles of nobility, both under the federal and the State governments; and in its express guaranty of the republican form to each of the latter.

"But it was not sufficient," say the adversaries of the proposed Constitution "for the convention to adhere to the republican form. They ought, with equal care, to have preserved the *federal* form, which regards the Union as a *Confederacy* of sovereign states; instead of which, they have framed a *national* government, which regards the Union as a *consolidation* of the States." And it is asked by what authority this bold and radical innovation was undertaken? The handle which has been made of this objection requires that it should be examined with some precision.

Without inquiring into the accuracy of the distinction on which the objection is founded, it will be necessary to a just estimate of its force, first, to ascertain the real character of the government in question; secondly, to inquire how far the convention were authorized to propose such a government; and thirdly, how far the duty they owed to their country could supply any defect of regular authority.

First — In order to ascertain the real character of the government, it may be considered in relation to the foundation on which it is to be established; to the sources from which its ordinary powers are to be drawn; to the operation of those powers; to the extent of them; and to the authority by which future changes in the government are to be introduced.

On examining the first relation, it appears, on one hand, that the Constitution is to be founded on the assent and ratification of the people of America, given by deputies elected for the special purpose; but, on the other, that this assent and ratification is to be given by the people, not as individuals composing one entire nation, but as composing the distinct and independent States to which they respectively belong. It is to be the assent and ratification of the several States, derived from the supreme authority in each State,—the authority of the

people themselves. The act, therefore, establishing the Constitution, will not be a *national,* but a *federal* act.

That it will be a federal and not a national act, as these terms are understood by the objectors; the act of the people, as forming so many independent States, not as forming one aggregate nation, is obvious from this single consideration, that it is to result neither from the decision of the *majority* of the people of the Union, nor from that of *majority* of the States, It must result from the *unanimous* assent of the several States that are parties to it, differing no otherwise from their ordinary assent than in its being expressed, not by the legislative authority, but by that of the people themselves. Were the people regarded in this transaction as forming one nation, the will of the majority of the whole people of the United States would bind the minority, in the same manner as the majority in each State must bind the minority; and the will of the majority must be determined either by a comparison of the individual votes, or by considering the will of the majority, of the States as evidence of the will of a majority of the people of the United States. Neither of these rules has been adopted. Each State, in ratifying the Constitution, is considered as a sovereign body, independent of all others, and only to be bound by its own voluntary act. In this relation, then, the new Constitution will, if established, be a *federal,* and not a *national* constitution.

The next relation is, to the sources from which the ordinary powers of government are to be derived. The House of Representatives will derive its powers from the people of America; and the people will be represented in the same proportion, and on the same principle, as they are in the legislature of a particular State. So far the government is *national,* not *federal*. The Senate, on the other hand, will derive its powers from the States, as political and coequal societies; and these will be represented on the principle of equality in the Senate, as they now are in the existing Congress. So far the government is *federal,* not *national.* The executive power will be derived from a very compound source. The immediate election of the President is to be made by the States in their political characters. The votes allotted to them are in a compound ratio, which considers them partly as unequal members of the same society. The eventual election, again, is to be made by that branch of the legislature which consists of the national representatives; but in this particular act they are to be thrown into the form of individual delegations, from so many distinct and coequal bodies politic. From this aspect of the government, it appears to be of a mixed character, presenting at least as many *federal* as *national* features.

The difference between a federal and national government, as it relates to the *operation* of the *government,* is supposed to consist in this, that in the former the powers operate on the political bodies composing the Confederacy, in their political capacities; in the latter, on the individual citizens composing the nation, in their individual capacities. On trying the Constitution by this criterion, it falls under the *national,* not the *federal* character; though perhaps not so completely as has been understood. In several cases, and particularly in the trial of controversies to which States may be parties, they must be viewed and proceeded against in their collective and political capacities only. So far the national countenance of the government on this side seems to be disfigured by a few federal features. But this blemish is perhaps unavoidable in any plan; and the operation of the government on the people, in their individual capacities, in its ordinary and most essential proceedings, may, on the whole, designate it, in this relation, a *national* government.

But if the government be national with re-gard to the *operation* of its powers, it changes its aspect again when we contemplate it in relation to the extent of its powers. The idea of a national government involves in it, not only an authority over the individual citizens, but an indefinite supremacy over all persons and things, so far as they are objects of lawful government. Among a people consolidated into one nation, this supremacy is completely vested in the national legislature. Among communities united for particular purposes, it is vested partly in the general and partly in the municipal legislatures. In the former case, the local authorities are subordinate to the supreme; and may be controlled, directed, or abolished by it at pleasure. In the latter, the local or municipal authorities form distinct and independent portions of the supremacy, no more subject, within their respective spheres, to the general authority, than the general authority is subject to them, within its own sphere. In this relation, then, the proposed government cannot be deemed a *national* one; since its jurisdiction extends to certain enumerated objects only, and leaves to the several States a residuary and inviolable sovereignty over all other objects. It is true that in controversies relating to the boundary between the two jurisdictions, the tribunal which is ultimately to decide, is to be established under the general government. But this does not change the principle of the case. The decision is to be impartially made, according to the rules of the Constitution; and all the usual and most effectual precautions are taken to secure this impartiality. Some such tribunal is clearly essential to prevent an appeal to the sword and a dissolution of the compact; and that it ought to be established under the general rather than under the local governments, or to speak more properly, that it could be safely established under the first alone, is a position not likely to be combated.

If we try the Constitution by its last relation to the authority by which amendments are to be made, we find it neither wholly *national* nor wholly *federal.* Were it wholly national, the supreme and ultimate authority would reside in the *majority* of the people of the Union; and this authority would be competent at all times, like that of a majority of every national society, to alter or abolish its established government. Were it wholly federal, on the other hand, the concurrence of each State in the Union would be essential to every alteration that would be binding on all. The mode provided by the plan of the convention is not founded on either of these principles. In requiring more than a majority, and particularly in computing the proportion by *States,* not by *citizens,* it departs from the *national* and advances towards the *federal* character; in rendering the concurrence of less than the whole number of States sufficient, it loses again the *federal* and partakes of the *national* character.

The proposed Constitution, therefore, is, in strictness, neither a national nor a federal Constitution, but a composition of both. In its foundation it is federal, not national; in the sources from which the ordinary powers of the government are drawn, it is partly federal and partly national; in the operation of these powers, it is national, not federal; in the extent of them, again, it is federal, not national; and, finally, in the authoritative mode of introducing amendments, it is neither wholly federal nor wholly national.

Publius
From the New York Packet
Friday, February 1, 1788

The Federalist No. 48

To the People of the State of New York:

It was shown in the last paper that the political apothegm there examined does not require that the legislative, executive, and judiciary departments should be wholly unconnected with each other. I shall undertake, in the next place, to show that unless these departments be so far connected and blended as to give to each a constitutional control over the others, the degree of separation which the maxim requires, as essential to a free government, can never in practice be duly maintained.

It is agreed on all sides, that the powers properly belonging to one of the departments ought not to be directly and completely administered by either of the other departments. It is equally evident, that none of them ought to possess, directly or indirectly, an overruling influence over the others, in the administration of their respective powers. It will not be denied, that power is of an encroaching nature, and that it ought to be effectually restrained from passing the limits assigned to it. After discriminating, therefore, in theory, the several classes of power, as they may in their nature be legislative, executive, or judiciary, the next and most difficult task is to provide some practical security for each, against the invasion of the others. What this security ought to be, is the great problem to be solved.

Will it be sufficient to mark, with precision, the boundaries of these departments in the constitution of the government, and to trust to these parchment barriers against the encroaching spirit of power? This is the security which appears to have been principally relied on by the compilers of most of the American constitutions. But experience assures us, that the efficacy of the provision has been greatly overrated; and that some more adequate defence is indispensably necessary for the more feeble, against the more powerful, members of the government. The legislative department is everywhere extending the sphere of its activity, and drawing all power into its impetuous vortex.

The founders of our republics have so much merit for the wisdom which they have displayed, that no task can be less pleasing than that of pointing out the errors into which they have fallen. A respect for truth, however, obliges us to remark, that they seem never for a moment to have turned their eyes from the danger to liberty from the overgrown and all grasping prerogative of an hereditary magistrate, supported and fortified by an hereditary branch of the legislative authority. They seem never to have recollected the danger from legislative usurpations, which, by assembling all power in the same hands, must lead to the same tyranny as is threatened by executive usurpations.

In a government where numerous and extensive prerogatives are placed in the hands of an hereditary monarch, the executive department is very justly regarded as the source of danger, and watched with all the jealousy which a zeal for liberty ought to inspire. In a democracy, where a multitude of people exercise in person the legislative functions, and are continually exposed, by their incapacity for regular deliberation and concerted measures, to the ambitious intrigues of their executive magistrates, tyranny may well be apprehended, on some favorable emergency, to start up in the same quarter. But in a representative republic, where the executive magistracy is carefully limited both in the extent and the duration of its power; and where the legislative power is exercised by an assembly, which is inspired, by a supposed influence over the people, with an intrepid confidence in its own strength; which is sufficiently numerous to feel all the passions which actuate a multitude, yet not so numerous as to be incapable of pursuing the objects of its passions, by means which reason prescribes; it is against the enterprising ambition of this department that the people ought to indulge all their jealousy and exhaust all their precautions.

The legislative department derives a superiority in our governments from other circumstances. Its constitutional powers being at once more extensive, and less susceptible of

precise limits, it can, with the greater facility, mask, under complicated and indirect measures, the encroachments which it makes on the coordinate departments. It is not unfrequently a question of real nicety in legislative bodies, whether the operation of a particular measure will, or will not, extend beyond the legislative sphere. On the other side, the executive power being restrained within a narrower compass, and being more simple in its nature, and the judiciary being described by landmarks still less uncertain, projects of usurpation by either of these departments would immediately betray and defeat themselves. Nor is this all: as the legislative department alone has access to the pockets of the people, and has in some constitutions full discretion, and in all a prevailing influence, over the pecuniary rewards of those who fill the other departments, a dependence is thus created in the latter, which gives still greater facility to encroachments of the former.

I have appealed to our own experience for the truth of what I advance on this subject. Were it necessary to verify this experience by particular proofs, they might be multiplied without end. I might find a witness in every citizen who has shared in, or been attentive to, the course of public administrations. I might collect vouchers in abundance from the records and archives of every State in the Union. But as a more concise, and at the same time equally satisfactory, evidence, I will refer to the example of two States, attested by two unexceptionable authorities.

The first example is that of Virginia, a State which, as we have seen, has expressly declared in its constitution, that the three great departments ought not to be intermixed. The authority in support of it is Mr. Jefferson, who, besides his other advantages for remarking the operation of the government, was himself the chief magistrate of it. In order to convey fully the ideas with which his experience had impressed him on this subject, it will be necessary to quote a passage of some length from his very interesting "Notes on the State of Virginia," p. 195.

All the powers of government, legislative, executive, and judiciary, result to the legislative body. The concentrating these in the same hands, is precisely the definition of despotic government. It will be no alleviation, that these powers will be exercised by a plurality of hands, and not by a single one. One hundred and seventy three despots would surely be as oppressive as one. Let those who doubt it, turn their eyes on the republic of Venice. As little will it avail us, that they are chosen by ourselves. An *elective despotism* was not the government we fought for; but one which should not only be founded on free principles, but in which the powers of government should be so divided and balanced among several bodies of magistracy, as that no one could transcend their legal limits, without being effectively checked and restrained by the others. For this reason, that convention which passed the ordnance of government, laid its foundation on this basis, that the legislative, executive, and judiciary departments should be separate and distinct, so that no person should exercise the powers of more than one of them at the same time. *But no barrier was provided between these several powers.* The judiciary and the executive members were left dependent on the legislative for their subsistence in office, and some of them for their continuance in it. If, therefore, the legislature assumes executive and judiciary powers, no opposition is likely to be made; nor, if made, can be effectual; because in that case they may put their proceedings into the form of acts of Assembly, which will render them obligatory on the other branches. They have accordingly, *in many*

instances, decided rights which should have been left to *judiciary controversy,* and *the direction of the executive, during the whole time of their session, is becoming habitual and familiar.*

The other State which I shall take for an example is Pennsylvania; and the other authority, the Council of Censors, which assembled in the years 1783 and 1784. A part of the duty of this body, as marked out by the constitution, was "to inquire whether the constitution had been preserved inviolate in every part; and whether the legislative and executive branches of government had performed their duty as guardians of the people, or assumed to themselves, or exercised, other or greater powers than they are entitled to by the constitution." In the execution of this trust, the council were necessarily led to a comparison of both the legislative and executive proceedings, with the constitutional powers of these departments; and from the facts enumerated, and to the truth of most of which both sides in the council subscribed, it appears that the constitution had been flagrantly violated, by the legislature in a variety of important instances.

A great number of laws had been passed, violating, without any apparent necessity, the rule requiring that all bills of a public nature shall be previously printed for the consideration of the people; although this is one of the precautions chiefly relied on by the constitution against improper acts of the legislature.

The constitutional trial by jury had been violated, and powers assumed which had not been delegated by the constitution.

Executive powers had been usurped.

The salaries of the judges, which the constitution expressly requires to be fixed, had been occasionally varied; and cases belonging to the judiciary department frequently drawn within legislative cognizance and determination.

Those who wish to see the several particulars falling under each of these heads, may consult the journals of the council, which are in print. Some of them, it will be found, may be imputable to peculiar circumstances connected with the war; but the greater part of them may be considered as the spontaneous shoots of an ill-constituted government.

It appears, also, that the executive department had not been innocent of frequent breaches of the constitution. There are three observations, however, which ought to be made on this head: *first,* a great proportion of the instances were either immediately produced by the necessities of the war, or recommended by Congress or the commander-in-chief; *secondly,* in most of the other instances, they conformed either to the declared or the known sentiments of the legislative department; *thirdly,* the executive department of Pennsylvania is distinguished from that of the other States by the number of members composing it. In this respect, it has as much affinity to a legislative assembly as to an executive council. And being at once exempt from the restraint of an individual responsibility for the acts of the body, and deriving confidence from mutual example and joint influence, unauthorized measures would, of course, be more freely hazarded, than where the executive department is administered by a single hand, or by a few hands.

Publius

The Federalist No. 51

To the People of the State of New York:

To what expedient, then, shall we finally resort, for maintaining in practice the necessary partition of power among the several departments, as laid down in the Constitution? The only answer that can be given is, that as all these exterior provisions are found to be inadequate, the defect must be supplied, by so contriving the interior structure of the government as that its several constituent parts may, by their mutual relations, be the means of keeping each other in their proper places. Without presuming to undertake a full development of this important idea, I will hazard a few general observations, which may perhaps place it in a clearer light, and enable us to form a more correct judgment of the principles and structure of the government planned by the convention.

In order to lay a due foundation for that separate and distinct exercise of the different powers of government, which to a certain extent is admitted on all hands to be essential to the preservation of liberty, it is evident that each department should have a will of its own; and consequently should be so constituted that the members of each should have as little agency as possible in the appointment of the members of the others. Were this principle rigorously adhered to, it would require that all the appointments for the supreme executive, legislative, and judiciary magistracies should be drawn from the same fountain of authority, the people, through channels having no communication whatever with one another. Perhaps such a plan of constructing the several departments would be less difficult in practice than it may in contemplation appear. Some difficulties, however, and some additional expense would attend the execution of it. Some deviations, therefore, from the principle must be admitted. In the constitution of the judiciary department in particular, it might be inexpedient to insist rigorously on the principle; first, because peculiar qualifications being essential in the members, the primary consideration ought to be to select that mode of choice which best secures these qualifications; secondly, because the permanent tenure by which the appointments are held in that department, must soon destroy all sense of dependence on the authority conferring them.

It is equally evident, that the members of

each department should be as little dependent as possible on those of the others, for the emoluments annexed to their offices. Were the executive magistrate, or the judges, not independent of the legislature in this particular, their independence in every other would be merely nominal.

But the great security against a gradual concentration of the several powers in the same department, consists of giving to those who administer each department the necessary constitutional means and personal motives to resist encroachments of the others. The provision for defence must in this, as in all other cases, be made commensurate to the danger of attack. Ambition must be made to counteract ambition. The interest of the man must be connected with the constitutional rights of the place. It may be a reflection on human nature, that such devices should be necessary to control the abuses of government. But what is government itself, but the greatest of all reflections on human nature? If men were angels, no government would be necessary. If angels were to govern men, neither external nor internal controls on government would be necessary. In framing a government which is to be administered by men over men, the great difficulty lies in this: you must first enable the government to control the governed; and in the next place oblige it to control itself. A dependence on the people is, no doubt, the primary control on the government; but experience has taught mankind the necessity of auxiliary precautions.

This policy of supplying, by opposite and rival interests, the defect of better motives, might be traced through the whole system of human affairs, private as well as public. We see it particularly displayed in all the subordinate distributions of power, where the constant aim is to divide and arrange the several offices in such a manner as that each may be a check on the other—that the private interest of every individual may be a sentinel over the public rights. These inventions of prudence cannot be less requisite in the distribution of the supreme powers of the State.

But it is not possible to give to each department an equal power of self-defence. In republican government, the legislative authority necessarily predominates. The remedy for this inconvenience is to divide the legislature into different branches; and to render them, by different modes of election and different principles of action, as little connected with each other as the nature of their common functions and their common dependence on the society will admit. It may even be necessary to guard against dangerous encroachments by still further precautions. As the weight of the legislative authority requires that it should be thus divided, the weakness of the executive may require, on the other hand, that it should be fortified. An absolute negative on the legislature appears, at first view, to be the natural defence with which the executive magistrate should be armed. But perhaps it would be neither altogether safe nor alone sufficient. On ordinary occasions it might not be exerted with the requisite firmness, and on extraordinary occasions it might be perfidiously abused. May not this defect of an absolute negative be supplied by some qualified connection between this weaker department and the weaker branch of the stronger department, by which the latter may be led to support the constitutional rights of the former, without being too much detached from the rights of its own department?

If the principles on which these observations are founded be just, as I persuade myself they are, and they be applied as a criterion to the several State constitutions, and to the federal Constitution, it will be found that if the latter does not perfectly correspond with them, the former are infinitely less able to bear such a test.

There are, moreover, two considerations

particularly applicable to the federal system of America, which place that system in a very interesting point of view.

First. In a single republic, all power surrendered by the people is submitted to the administration of a single government; and the usurpations are guarded against by a division of the government into distinct and separate departments. In the compound republic of America, the power surrendered by the people is first divided between two distinct governments, and then the portion allotted to each subdivided among distinct and separate departments. Hence a double security arises to the rights of the people. The different governments will control each other, at the same time that each will be controlled by itself.

Second. It is of great importance in a republic not only to guard the society against the oppression of its rulers, but to guard one part of the society against the injustice of the other part. Different interests necessarily exist in different classes of citizens. If a majority be united by a common interest, the rights of the minority will be insecure. There are but two methods of providing against this evil: the one by creating a will in the community independent of the majority—that is, of the society itself; the other, by comprehending in the society so many separate descriptions of citizens as will render an unjust combination of a majority of the whole very improbable, if not impracticable. The first method prevails in all governments possessing an hereditary or self-appointed authority. This, at best, is but a precarious security; because a power independent of the society may as well espouse the unjust views of the major, as the rightful interests of the minor party, and may possibly be turned against both parties. The second method will be exemplified in the federal republic of the United States. Whilst all authority in it will be derived from and dependent on the society, the society itself will be broken into so many

parts, interests and classes of citizens, that the rights of individuals, or of the minority, will be in little danger from interested combinations of the majority. In a free government the security for civil rights must be the same as that for religious rights. It consists in the one case in the multiplicity of interests, and in the other in the multiplicity of sects. The degree of security in both cases will depend on the number of interests and sects; and this may be presumed to depend on the extent of country and number of people comprehended under the same government. This view of the subject must particularly recommend a proper federal system to all the sincere and considerate friends of republican government, since it shows that in exact proportion as the territory of the Union may be formed into more circumscribed Confederacies, or States, oppressive combinations of a majority will be facilitated; the best security, under the republican forms, for the rights of every class of citizens, will be diminished; and consequently the stability and independence of some member of the government, the only other security, must be proportionally increased. Justice is the end of government. It is the end of civil society. It ever has been and ever will be pursued until it be obtained, or until liberty be lost in the pursuit. In a society under the forms of which the stronger faction can readily unite and oppress the weaker, anarchy may as truly be said to reign as in a state of nature, where the weaker individual is not secured against the violence of the stronger; and as, in the latter state, even the stronger individuals are prompted, by the uncertainty of their condition, to submit to a government which may protect the weak as well as themselves; so, in the former state, will the more powerful factions or parties be gradually induced, by a like motive, to wish for a government which will protect all parties, the weaker as well as the more powerful. It can be little doubted that if the State of Rhode Island was separated from the Confederacy and left to itself, the insecurity of rights under the popular form of government within such narrow limits would be displayed by such reiterated oppressions of factious majorities that some power altogether independent of the people would soon be called for by the voice of the very factions whose misrule had proved the necessity of it. In the extended republic of the United States, and among the great variety of interests, parties, and sects which it embraces, a coalition of a majority of the whole society could seldom take place on any other principles than those of justice and the general good; whilst there being thus less danger to a minor from the will of a major party, there must be less pretext, also, to provide for the security of the former, by introducing into the government a will not dependent on the latter, or, in other words, a will independent of the society itself. It is no less certain than it is important, notwithstanding the contrary opinions which have been entertained, that the larger the society, provided it lie within a practical sphere, the more duly capable it will be of self-government. And happily for the *republican cause,* the practicable sphere may be carried to a very great extent, by a judicious modification and mixture of the federal principle.

Publius ∼

Alexander Hamilton's *Federalist* Essays (1787–88)

The Federalist No. 15

To the People of the State of New York:

In the course of the preceding papers, I have endeavored, my fellow-citizens, to place before you, in a clear and convincing light, the importance of Union to your political safety and happiness. I have unfolded to you a complication of dangers, to which you would be exposed, should you permit that sacred knot which binds the people of America together to be severed or dissolved by ambition or by avarice, by jealousy or by misrepresentation. In the sequel of the inquiry through which I propose to accompany you, the truths intended to be inculcated will receive further confirmation from facts and arguments hitherto unnoticed. If the road over which you will still have to pass should in some places appear to you tedious or irksome you will recollect that you are in quest of information on a subject the most momentous which can engage the attention of a free people, that the field through which you have to travel is in itself spacious, and that the difficulties of the journey have been unnecessarily increased by the mazes with which sophistry has beset the way. It will be my aim to remove the obstacles from your progress in as compendious a manner as it can be done, without sacrificing utility to despatch.

In pursuance of the plan which I have laid down for the discussion of the subject, the point next in order to be examined in the "insufficiency of the present Confederation to the preservation of the Union." It may perhaps be asked what need there is of reasoning or proof to illustrate a position which is not either controverted or doubted, to which the understandings and feelings of all classes of men assent, and which in substance is admitted by the opponents as well as by the friends of the new Constitution. It must in truth be acknowledged that, however these may differ in other respects, they in general appear to harmonize in this sentiment, at least, that there are material imperfections in our national system, and that something is necessary to be done to rescue us from impending anarchy. The facts that support this opinion are no longer objects of speculation. They have forced themselves upon the sensibility of the people at large, and have at length extorted from those whose mistaken policy has had the principal share in precipitating the extremity at which we are arrived, a reluctant confession of the reality of those defects in the scheme of our federal government, which have been long pointed out and regretted by the intelligent friends of the Union.

We may indeed with propriety be said to have reached almost the last stage of national humiliation. There is scarcely any thing that can wound the pride or degrade the character of an independent nation which we do not experience. Are there engagements to the performance of which we are held by every tie respectable among men? These are the subjects of constant and unblushing violation. Do we owe debts to foreigners and to our own citizens contracted in a time of imminent peril for the preservation of our political existence? These remain without any proper or satisfactory provision for their discharge. Have we valuable territories and important posts in the possession of a foreign power which, by express stipulations, ought long since to have been surrendered? These are still retained, to the prejudice of our interests, not less than of our rights. Are we in a condition to resent or repel the aggression? We have neither troops, nor treasury, nor government. Are we even in a condition to remonstrate with dignity? The just imputations on our own faith, in respect to the same treaty, ought first to be removed. Are we entitled by nature and compact to a free participation in the navigation of the Mississippi? Spain excludes us from it. Is public credit an indispensable resource in time of public danger? We seem to have abandoned its cause as desperate and irretrievable. Is commerce of importance to national wealth? Ours is at the lowest point of declension. Is respectability in the eyes of foreign powers a safeguard against foreign encroachments? The imbecility of our government even forbids them to treat with us. Our ambassadors abroad are the mere pageants of mimic sovereignty. Is a violent and unnatural decreace in the value of land a symptom of national distress? The price of improved land in most parts of the country is much lower than can be accounted for by the quantity of waste land at market, and can only be fully explained by that want of private and public confidence, which are so alarmingly prevalent among all ranks, and which have a direct tendency to depreciate property of every kind. Is private credit the friend and patron of industry? That most useful kind which relates to borrowing and lending is reduced within the narrowest limits, and this still more from an opinion of insecurity than from the scarcity of money. To shorten an enumeration of particulars which can afford neither pleasure nor instruction, it may in general be demanded, what indication is there of national disorder, poverty, and insignificance that could befall a community so peculiarly blessed with natural advantages as we are, which does not form a part of the dark catalogue of our public misfortunes.

This is the melancholy situation to which we have been brought by those very maxims and councils which would now deter us from adopting the proposed Constitution; and which, not content with having conducted us to the brink of a precipice, seem resolved to plunge us into the abyss that awaits us below. Here, my countrymen, impelled by every motive that ought to influence an enlightened people, let us make a firm stand for our safety, our tranquillity, our dignity, our reputation. Let us at last break the fatal charm which has too long seduced us from the paths of felicity and prosperity.

It is true, as has been before observed; that facts, too stubborn to be resisted, have produced a species of general assent to the abstract proposition that there exist material defects in our national system; but the usefulness of the concession, on the part of the old adversaries of federal measures, is destroyed by a strenuous opposition to a remedy, upon the only principles that can give it a chance of success. While they admit that the government of the United States is destitute of energy, they contend against conferring upon it those powers which are requisite to supply that energy. They seem still to aim at things repugnant and irreconcilable; at an augmentation of federal authority, without a diminution of State authority; at sovereignty in the Union, and complete independence in the members. They still, in fine, seem to cherish with blind devotion the political monster of an *imperium in imperio.* This renders a full display of the principal defects of the Confederation necessary, in order to show that the evils we experience do not proceed from minute or partial imperfections, but from fundamental errors in the structure of the building, which cannot be amended otherwise than by an alteration in the first principles and main pillars of the fabric.

The great and radical vice in the construction of the existing Confederation is in the principle of LEGISLATION for STATES or GOVERNMENTS, in their CORPORATE or COLLECTIVE CAPACITIES, and as contradistinguished from the INDIVIDUALS of which they consist. Though this principle does not run through all the powers delegated to the Union, yet it pervades and governs those on which the efficacy of the rest depends. Except as to the rule of apportionment, the United States has an indefinite discretion to make requisitions for men and money; but they have no authority to raise either, by regulations extending to the individual citizens of America. The consequence of this is, that

though in theory their resolutions concerning those objects are laws, constitutionally binding on the members of the Union, yet in practice they are mere recommendations which the States observe or disregard at their option.

It is a singular instance of the capriciousness of the human mind, that after all the admonitions we have had from experience on this head, there should still be found men who object to the new Constitution, for deviating from a principle which has been found the bane of the old, and which is in itself evidently incompatible with the idea of Government; a principle, in short, which, if it is to be executed at all, must substitute the violent and sanguinary agency of the sword to the mild influence of the magistracy.

There is nothing absurd or impracticable in the idea of a league or alliance between independent nations for certain defined purposes precisely stated in a treaty regulating all the details of time, place, circumstance, and quantity; leaving nothing to future discretion; and depending for its execution on the good faith of the parties. Compacts of this kind exist among all civilized nations, subject to the usual vicissitudes of peace and war, of observance and nonobservance, as the interests or passions of the contracting powers dictate. In the early part of the present century there was an epidemical rage in Europe for this species of compacts, from which the politicians of the times fondly hoped for benefits which were never realized. With a view to establishing the equilibrium of power and the peace of that part of the world, all the resources of negotiations were exhausted, and triple and quadruple alliances were formed; but they were scarcely formed before they were broken, giving an instructive but afflicting lesson to mankind, how little dependence is to be placed on treaties which have no other sanction than the obligations of good faith, and which oppose general considerations of peace and justice to the impulse of any immediate interest or passion.

If the particular States in this country are disposed to stand in a similar relation to each other, and to drop the project of a general DISCRETIONARY SUPERINTENDENCE, the scheme would indeed be pernicious, and would entail upon us all the mischiefs which have been enumerated under the first head; but it would have the merit of being, at least, consistent and practicable. Abandoning all views towards a confederate government, this would bring us to a simple alliance offensive and defensive; and would place us in a situation to be alternate friends and enemies of each other, as our mutual jealousies and rivalships, nourished by the intrigues of foreign nations, should prescribe to us.

But if we are unwilling to be placed in this perilous situation; if we still will adhere to the design of a national government, or, which is the same thing, of a superintending power, under the direction of a common council, we must resolve to incorporate into our plan those ingredients which may be considered as forming the characteristic difference between a league and a government; we must extend the authority of the Union to the persons of the citizens—the only proper objects of government.

Government implies the power of making laws. It is essential to the idea of a law, that it be attended with a sanction; or, in other words, a penalty or punishment for disobedience. If there be no penalty annexed to disobedience, the resolutions or commands which pretend to be laws will, in fact, amount to nothing more than advice or recommendation. This penalty, whatever it may be, can only be inflicted in two ways; by the agency of the courts and ministers of justice, or by military force; by the COERCION of the magistracy, or by the coercion of arms. The first kind can evidently apply only to men; the last kind

must of necessity, be employed against bodies politic, or communities, or States. It is evident that there is no process of a court by which the observance of the laws can, in the last resort, be enforced. Sentences may be denounced against them for violations of their duty; but these sentences can only be carried into execution by the sword. In an association where the general authority is confined to the collective bodies of the communities that compose it, every breach of the laws must involve a state of war; and military execution must become the only instrument of civil disobedience. Such a state of things can certainly not deserve the name of government, nor would any prudent man choose to commit his happiness to it.

There was a time when we were told that breaches, by the States, of the regulations of the federal authority were not to be expected; that a sense of common interest would preside over the conduct of the respective members, and would beget a full compliance with all the constitutional requisitions of the Union. This language, at the present day, would appear as wild as a great part of what we now hear from the same quarter will be thought, when we shall have received further lessons from that best oracle of wisdom, experience. It at all times betrayed an ignorance of the true springs by which human conduct is actuated, and belied the original inducements to the establishment of civil power. Why has government been instituted at all? Because the passions of men will not conform to the dictates of reason and justice, without constraint. Has it been found that bodies of men act with more rectitude or greater disinterestedness than individuals? The contrary of this has been inferred by all accurate observers of the conduct of mankind; and the inference is founded upon obvious reasons. Regard to reputation has a less active influence when the infamy of a bad action is to be divided among a number than when it is to fall singly upon one. A spirit of faction, which is apt to mingle its poison in the deliberations of all bodies of men, will often hurry the persons of whom they are composed into improprieties and excesses, for which they would blush in a private capacity.

In addition to all this, there is, in the nature of sovereign power, an impatience of control, that disposes those who are invested with the exercise of it, to look with an evil eye upon all external attempts to restrain or direct its operations. From this spirit it happens, that in every political association which is formed upon the principle of uniting in a common interest a number of lesser sovereignties, there will be found a kind of eccentric tendency in the subordinate or inferior orbs, by the operation of which there will be a perpetual effort in each to fly off from the common centre. This tendency is not difficult to be accounted for. It has its origin in the love of power. Power controlled or abridged is almost always the rival and enemy of that power by which it is controlled or abridged. This simple proposition will teach us, how little reason there is to expect, that the persons intrusted with the administration of the affairs of the particular members of a confederacy will at all times be ready, with perfect, good humor, and an unbiased regard to the public weal, to execute the resolutions or decrees of the general authority. The reverse of this results from the constitution of human nature.

If, therefore, the measures of the Confederacy cannot be executed without the intervention of the particular administrations, there will be little prospect of their being executed at all. The rulers of the respective members, whether they have a constitutional right to do it or not, will undertake to judge of the propriety of the measures themselves. They will consider the conformity of the thing proposed or required to their immediate interests or aims; the momentary conveniences or inconveniences that would attend its adoption. All this

will be done; and in a spirit of interested and suspicious scrutiny, without that knowledge of national circumstances and reasons of state, which is essential to a right judgment, and with that strong predilection in favor of local objects which can hardly fail to mislead the decision. The same process must be repeated in every member of which the body is constituted; and the execution of the plans, framed by the councils of the whole, will always fluctuate on the discretion of the ill-informed and prejudiced opinion of every part. Those who have been conversant in the proceedings of popular assemblies; who have seen how difficult it often is, where there is no exterior pressure of circumstances, to bring them to harmonious resolutions on important points, will readily conceive how impossible it must be to induce a number of such assemblies, deliberating at a distance from each other, at different times, and under different impressions, long to cooperate in the same views and pursuits.

In our case, the concurrence of thirteen distinct sovereign wills is requisite, under the Confederation, to the complete execution of every important measure that proceeds from the Union. It has happened as was to have been foreseen. The measures of the Union have not been executed; the delinquencies of the States have, step by step matured themselves to an extreme, which has, at length, arrested all the wheels of the national government; and brought them to an awful stand. Congress at this time scarcely possess the means of keeping up the forms of administration, till the States can have time to agree upon a more substantial substitute for the present shadow of a federal government. Things did not come to this desperate extremity at once. The causes which have been specified produced at first only unequal and disproportionate degrees of compliance with the requisitions of the Union. The greater deficiencies of some States furnished the pretext of example and the temptation of

interest to the complying, or to the least delinquent States. Why should we do more in proportion than those who are embarked with us
in the same political voyage? Why should we
consent to bear more than our proper share of
the common burden? These were suggestions
which human selfishness could not withstand,
and which even speculative men, who looked
forward to remote consequences, could not,
without hesitation, combat. Each State, yielding to the persuasive voice of immediate interest or convenience, has successively withdrawn
its support till the frail and tottering edifice
seem ready to fall upon our heads, and to
crush us beneath its ruins.

Publius

The Federalist No. 21

To the People of the State of New York:

Having in the three last numbers taken a
summary review of the principal circumstances
and events which have depicted the genius and
fate of other confederate governments, I shall
now proceed in the enumeration of the most
important of those defects which have hitherto
disappointed our hopes from the system established among ourselves. To form a safe and
satisfactory judgment of the proper remedy, it
is absolutely necessary that we should be well
acquainted with the extent and malignity of
the disease.

The next most palpable defect of the subsisting Confederation is the total want of a
SANCTION to its laws. The United States, as
now composed, have no powers to exact obedience, or punish disobedience to their resolutions, either by pecuniary mulcts, by a suspension or divesture of privileges, or by any other
constitutional mode. There is no express delegation of authority to them to use force
against delinquent members; and if such a
right should be ascribed to the federal head, as
resulting from the nature of the social compact

between the States, it must be by inference and
construction, in the face of that part of the
second article, by which it is declared, "that
each State shall retain every power, jurisdiction and right, not *expressly* delegated to the
United States in Congress assembled." There
is, doubtless, a striking absurdity in supposing
that a right of this kind does not exist, but we
are reduced to the dilemma either by embracing that supposition, preposterous as it may
seem, or of contravening or explaining away a
provision, which has been of late a repeated
theme of the eulogies of those who oppose the
new Constitution, and the want of which, in
that plan, has been the subject of much plausible animadversion, and severe criticism. If we
are unwilling to impair the force of this applauded provision, we shall be obliged to
conclude, that the United States afford the extraordinary spectacle of a government destitute even of the shadow of constitutional
power to enforce the execution of its own
laws. It will appear, from the specimens which
have been cited, that the American Confederacy, in this particular, stands discriminated
from every other institution of a similar kind,
and exhibits a new and unexampled phenomenon in the political world.

The want of a mutual guaranty of the State
government is another capital imperfection in
the federal plan. There is nothing of this kind
declared in the articles that compose it; and to
imply a tacit guaranty from considerations of
utility, would be a still more flagrant departure
from the clause which has been mentioned,
than to imply a tacit power of coercion from
the like considerations. The want of a guaranty, though it might in its consequences endanger the Union, does not so immediately
attack its existence as the want of a constitutional sanction of its laws.

Without a guaranty the assistance to be derived from the Union in repelling those domestic dangers which may sometimes threaten the

existence of the State constitutions, must be renounced. Usurpation may rear its crest in each State, and trample upon the liberties of the people while the national government could legally do nothing more than behold its encroachments with indignation and regret. A successful faction may erect a tyranny on the ruins of order and law, while no succor could constitutionally be afforded by the Union to the friends and supporters of the government. The tempestuous situation from which Massachusetts has scarcely emerged, evinces that dangers of this kind are not merely speculative. Who can determine what might have been the issue of her late convulsions, if the malcontents had been headed by a Caesar or by a Cromwell? Who can predict what effect a despotism, established in Massachusetts, would have upon the liberties of New Hampshire or Rhode Island, of Connecticut or New York?

The inordinate pride of State importance has suggested to some minds an objection to the principle of a guaranty in the federal government, as involving an officious interference in the domestic concerns of the members. A scruple of this kind would deprive us of one of the principal advantages to be expected from unions, and can only flow from a misapprehension of the nature of the provision itself. It could be no impediment to reforms of the State constitutions by a majority of the people in a legal and peaceable mode. This right would remain undiminished. The guaranty could only operate against changes to be effected by violence. Towards the preventions of calamities of this kind, too many checks cannot be provided. The peace of society and the stability of government depend absolutely on the efficacy of the precautions adopted on this head. Where the whole power of the government is in the hands of the people, there is the less pretence for the use of violent remedies in partial or occasional distempers of the State. The natural cure for an ill administration, in a popular or representative constitution, is a change of men. A guaranty by the national authority would be as much levelled against the usurpations of rulers as against the ferments and outrages of faction and sedition in the community.

The principle of regulating the contributions of the States to the common treasury by QUOTAS is another fundamental error in the Confederation. Its repugnancy to an adequate supply of the national exigencies has been already pointed out, and has sufficiently appeared from the trial which has been made of it. I speak of it now solely with a view to equality among the States. Those who have been accustomed to contemplate the circumstances which produce and constitute national wealth, must be satisfied that there is no common standard or barometer by which the degrees of it can be ascertained. Neither the value of lands, nor the numbers of the people, which have been successively proposed as the rule of State contributions, has any pretension to being a just representative. If we compare the wealth of the United Netherlands with that of Russia or Germany, or even of France, and if we at the same time compare the total value of the lands and the aggregate population of that contracted district with the total value of the aggregate population of the immense regions of either of the three last-mentioned countries, we shall at once discover that there is no comparison between the proportion of either of these two objects and that of the relative wealth of those nations. If the like parallel were to be run between several of the American States, it would furnish a like result. Let Virginia be contrasted with North Carolina, Pennsylvania with Connecticut, or Maryland with New Jersey, and we shall be convinced that the respective abilities of those States, in relation to revenue, bear little or no analogy to their comparative stock in lands or to their comparative population. The position may be

equally illustrated by a similar process between the counties of the same State. No man
who is acquainted with the State of New York
will doubt that the active wealth of King's
County bears a much greater proportion to
that of Montgomery than it would appear to
be if we should take either the total value of
the lands or the total number of the people as
a criterion!

The wealth of nations depends upon an infinite variety of causes. Situation, soil, climate,
the nature of the productions, the nature of
the government, the genius of the citizens, the
degree of information they possess, the state of
commerce, of arts, of industry,—these circumstances and many more, too complex, minute,
or adventitious to admit of a particular specification, occasion differences hardly conceivable
in the relative opulence and riches of different
countries. The consequence clearly is that
there can be no common measure of national
wealth, and, of course, no general or station-
ary rule by which the ability of a state to pay
taxes can be determined. The attempt, therefore, to regulate the contributions of the members of a confederacy by any such rule, cannot
fail to be productive of glaring inequality and
extreme oppression.

This inequality would of itself be sufficient
in America to work the eventual destruction of
the Union, if any mode of enforcing a compliance with its requisitions could be devised.
The suffering States would not long consent to
remain associated upon a principle which dis-
tributes the public burdens with so unequal a
hand, and which was calculated to impoverish
and oppress the citizens of some States, while
those of others would scarcely be conscious of
the small proportion of the weight they were
required to sustain. This, however, is an evil
inseparable from the principle of quotas and
requisitions.

There is no method of steering clear of this
inconvenience, but by authorizing the national
government to raise its own revenues in its
own way. Imposts, excises, and, in general, all
duties upon articles of consumption, may be
compared to a fluid, which will, in time, find
its level with the means of paying them. The
amount to be contributed by each citizen will
in a degree be at his own option, and can be
regulated by an attention to his resources. The
rich may be extravagant, the poor can be frugal; and private oppression may always be
avoided by a judicious selection of objects
proper for such impositions. If inequalities
should arise in some States from duties on particular objects, these will, in all probability, be
counterbalanced by proportional inequalities
in other States, from the duties on other objects. In the course of time and things, an equilibrium, as far as it is attainable in so complicated a subject, will be established everywhere.
Or, if inequalities should still exist, they would
neither be so great in their degree, so uniform
in their operation, nor so odious in their appearance, as those which would necessarily
spring from quotas, upon any scale that can
possibly be devised.

It is a signal advantage of taxes on articles
of consumption, that they contain in their own
nature a security against excess. They prescribe their own limit; which cannot be exceeded without defeating the end proposed,
—that is, an extension of the revenue. When
applied to this object, the saying is as just as it
is witty, that, "in political arithmetic, two and
two do not always make four." If duties are
too high, they lessen the consumption; the collection is eluded; and the product to the treasury is not so great as when they are confined
within proper and moderate bounds. This
forms a complete barrier against any material
oppression of the citizens by taxes of this class,
and is itself a natural limitation of the power
of imposing them.

Impositions of this kind usually fall under
the denomination of indirect taxes, and must

for a long time constitute the chief part of the revenue raised in this country. Those of the direct kind, which principally relate to land and buildings, may admit of a rule of apportionment. Either the value of land, or the number of the people, may serve as a standard. The state of agriculture and the populousness of a country have been considered as nearly connected with each other. And, as a rule, for the purpose intended, numbers, in the view of simplicity and certainty, are entitled to the preference. In every country it is a herculean task to obtain a valuation of the land; in a country imperfectly settled and progressive in improvement, the difficulties are increased almost to impracticability. The expense of an accurate valuation is, in all situations, a formidable objection. In a branch of taxation where no limits to the discretion of the government are to be found in the nature of things, the establishment of a fixed rule, not incompatible with the end, may be attended with fewer inconveniences than to leave that discretion altogether at large.

Publius

The Federalist No. 23

To the People of the State of New York:

The necessity of a Constitution, at least equally energetic with the one proposed, to the preservation of the Union, is the point at the examination of which we are now arrived.

This inquiry will naturally divide itself into three branches—the objects to be provided for by the federal government, the quantity of power necessary to the accomplishment of those objects, the persons upon whom that power ought to operate. Its distribution and organization will more properly claim our attention under the succeeding head.

The principal purposes to be answered by union are these—the common defence of the members; the preservation of the public peace, as well against internal convulsions as external attacks; the regulation of commerce with other nations and between the States; the superintendence of our intercourse, political and commercial, with foreign countries.

The authorities essential to the common defence are these: to raise armies; to build and equip fleets; to prescribe rules for the government of both; to direct their operations; to provide for their support. These powers ought to exist without limitation, *because it is impossible to foresee or define the extent and variety of national exigencies, or the correspondent extent and variety of the means which may be necessary to satisfy them*. The circumstances that endanger the safety of nations are infinite, and for this reason no constitutional shackles can wisely be imposed on the power to which the care of it is committed. This power ought to be coextensive with all the possible combinations of such circumstances; and ought to be under the direction of the same councils which are appointed to preside over the common defence.

This is one of those truths which, to a correct and unprejudiced mind, carries its own evidence along with it; and may be obscured, but cannot be made plainer by argument or reasoning. It rests upon axioms as simple as they are universal; the *means* ought to be proportioned to the *end*; the persons, from whose agency the attainment of any *end* is expected, ought to possess the *means* by which it is to be attained.

Whether there ought to be a federal government intrusted with the care of the common defence, is a question in the first instance, open for discussion; but the moment it is decided in the affirmative, it will follow, that the government ought to be clothed with all the powers requisite to complete execution of its trust. And unless it can be shown that the circumstances which may affect the public safety are reducible within certain determinate limits;

unless the contrary of this position can be fairly and rationally disputed, it must be admitted, as a necessary consequence that there can be no limitation of that authority which is to provide for the defence and protection of the community, in any matter essential to its efficacy—that is, in any matter essential to the *formation, direction* or *support* of the NATIONAL FORCES.

Defective as the present Confederation has been proved to be, this principle appears to have been fully recognized by the framers of it; though they have not made proper or adequate provision for its exercise. Congress have an unlimited discretion to make requisitions of men and money; to govern the army and the navy to direct their operations. As their requisitions are made constitutionally binding upon the States, who are in fact under the most solemn obligations to furnish the supplies required of them, the intention evidently was, that the United States should command whatever resources were by them judged requisite to the "common defence and general welfare." It was presumed that a sense of their true interests, and a regard to the dictates of good faith, would be found sufficient pledges for the punctual performance of the duty of the members to the federal head.

The experiment has, however, demonstrated that this expectation was ill-founded and illusory; and the observations, made under the last head, will, I imagine, have sufficed to convince the impartial and discerning, that there is an absolute necessity for an entire change in the first principles of the system; that if we are in earnest about giving the Union energy and duration, we must abandon the vain project of legislating upon the States in their collective capacities; we must extent the laws of the federal government to the individual citizens of America; we must discard the fallacious scheme of quotas and requisitions, as equally impracticable and unjust. The

result from all this is that the Union ought to be invested with full power to levy troops; to build and equip fleets; and to raise the revenues which will be required for the formation and support of an army and navy, in the customary and ordinary modes practiced in other governments.

If the circumstances of our country are such as to demand a compound instead of a simple, a confederate instead of a sole, government, the essential point which will remain to be adjusted will be to discriminate the OBJECTS, as far as it can be done, which shall appertain to the different provinces or departments of power; allowing to each the most ample authority for fulfilling the objects committed to its charge. Shall the Union be constituted the guardian of the common safety? Are fleets and armies the guardian of the common safety? Are fleets and armies and revenues necessary to this purpose? The government of the Union must be empowered to pass all laws, and to make all regulations which have relation to them. The same must be the case in respect to commerce, and to every other matter to which its jurisdiction is permitted to extend. Is the administration of justice between the citizens of the same State the proper department of the local governments? These must possess all the authorities which are connected with this object, and with every other that may be allotted to their particular cognizance and direction. Not to confer in each case a degree of power commensurate to the end, would be to violate the most obvious rules of prudence and propriety, and improvidently to trust the great interests of the nation to hands which are disabled from managing them with vigor and success.

Who so likely to make suitable provisions for the public defence, as that body to which the guardianship of the public safety is confided; which, as the centre of information, will best understand the extent and urgency of the dangers that threaten; as the representative of the WHOLE, will feel itself most deeply interested in the preservation of every part; which, from the responsibility implied in the duty assigned to it, will be most sensibly impressed with the necessity of proper exertions; and which, by the extension of its authority throughout the States, can alone establish uniformity and concert in the plans and measures by which the common safety is to be secured? Is there not a manifest inconsistency in devolving upon the federal government the care of the general defense, and leaving in the State governments the *effective* powers by which it is to be provided for? Is not a want of cooperation the infallible consequence of such a system? And will not weakness, disorder, and undue distribution of the burdens and calamities of war, an unnecessary and intolerable increase of expense, be its natural and inevitable concomitants? Have we not had unequivocal experience of its effects in the course of the revolution which we have just accomplished?

Every view we may take of the subject, as candid inquirers after truth, will serve to convince us, that it is both unwise and dangerous to deny the federal government an unconfined authority, as to all those objects which are intrusted to its management. It will indeed deserve the most vigilant and careful attention of the people, to see that it be modelled in such a manner as to admit of its being safely vested with the requisite powers. If any plan which has been, or may be, offered to our consideration, should not, upon a dispassionate inspection, be found to answer this description, it ought to be rejected. A government, the constitution of which renders it unfit to be trusted with all the powers which a free people *ought to delegate to any government,* would be an unsafe and improper depositary of the NATIONAL INTERESTS. Wherever THESE can with propriety be confided, the coincident powers may safely accompany them. This is

the true result of all just reasoning upon the subject. And the adversaries of the plan promulgated by the convention ought to have confined themselves to showing, that the internal structure of the proposed government was such as to render it unworthy of the confidence of the people. They ought not to have wandered into inflamatory declamations and unmeaning cavils about the extent of the powers. The POWERS are not too extensive for the OBJECTS of federal administration, or, in other words, for the management of our NATIONAL INTERESTS; nor can any satisfactory argument be framed to show that they are chargeable with such an excess. If it be true, as has been insinuated by some of the writers on the other side, that the difficulty arises from the nature of the thing, and that the extent of the country will not permit us to form a government in which such ample powers can safely be reposed, it would prove that we ought to contract our views, and resort to the expedient of separate confederacies, which will move within more practicable spheres. For the absurdity must continually stare us in the face of confiding to a government the direction of the most essential national interests, without daring to trust it to the authorities which are indispensable to their proper and efficient management. Let us not attempt to reconcile contradictions, but firmly embrace a rational alternative.

I trust, however, that the impracticability of one general system cannot be shown. I am greatly mistaken, if any thing of weight has yet been advanced of this tendency; and I flatter myself that the observations which have been made in the course of these papers have served to place the reverse of that position in as clear a light as any matter still in the womb of time and experience can be susceptible of. This, at all events, must be evident, that the very difficulty itself, drawn from the extent of the country, is the strongest argument in favor of an energetic government; for any other can certainly never preserve the Union of so large an empire. If we embrace the tenets of those who oppose the adoption of the proposed Constitution, as the standard of our political creed, we cannot fail to verify the gloomy doctrines which predict the impracticability of a national system pervading entire limits of the present Confederacy.

Publius

The Federalist No. 78

To the People of the State of New York:

We proceed now to an examination of the judiciary department of the proposed government.

In unfolding the defects of the existing Confederation, the utility and necessity of a federal judicature have been clearly pointed out. It is the less necessary to recapitulate the considerations there urged, as the propriety of the institution in the abstract is not disputed; the only questions which have been raised being relative to the manner of constituting it, and to its extent. To these points, therefore, our observations shall be confined.

The manner of constituting it seems to embrace these several objects: First, the mode of appointing the judges. Second, the tenure by which they are to hold their places. Third, the partition of the judiciary authority between different courts, and their relations to each other.

First. As to the mode of appointing the judges; this is the same with that of appointing the officers of the Union in general, and has been so fully discussed in the two last numbers, that nothing can be said here which would not be useless repetition.

Second. As to the tenure by which the judges are to hold their places; this chiefly concerns their duration in office; the provisions for their support; the precautions for their responsibility.

According to the plan of the convention, all judges who may be appointed by the United States are to hold their offices *during good behavior;* which is conformable to the most approved of the State constitutions, and among the rest, to that of this State. Its propriety having been drawn into question by the adversaries of that plan, is no light symptom of the rage for objection, which disorders their imaginations and judgments. The standard of good behavior for the continuance in office of the judicial magistracy, is certainly one of the most valuable of the modern improvements in the practice of government. In a monarchy it is an excellent barrier to the despotism of the prince; in a republic it is no less excellent barrier to the encroachments and oppressions of the representative body. And it is the best expedient which can be devised in any government, to secure a steady, upright, and impartial administration of the laws.

Whoever attentively considers the different departments of power must perceive, that, in a government in which they are separated from each other, the judiciary, from the nature of its functions, will always be the least dangerous to the political rights of the Constitution; because it will be least in a capacity to annoy or injure them. The Executive not only dispenses the honors, but holds the sword of the community. The legislature not only commands the purse, but prescribes the rules by which the duties and rights of every citizen are to be regulated. The judiciary, on the contrary, has no influence over either the sword or the purse; no direction either of the strength or of the wealth of the society; and can take no active resolution whatever. It may truly be said to have neither FORCE nor WILL, but merely judgment; and must ultimately depend upon the aid of the executive arm even for the efficacy of its judgments.

This simple view of the matter suggests several important consequences. It proves incontestably, that the judiciary is beyond comparison the weakest of the three departments of power; that it can never attack with success either of the other two; and that all possible care is requisite to enable it to defend itself against their attacks. It equally proves, that though individual oppression may now and then proceed from the courts of justice, the general liberty of the people can never be endangered from that quarter; I mean so long as the judiciary remains truly distinct from both the legislature and the Executive. For I agree, that "there is no liberty if the power of judging be not separated from the legislative and executive powers." And it proves, in the last place, that as liberty can have nothing to fear from the judiciary alone, but would have every thing to fear from its union with either of the other departments; that as all the effects of such a union must ensue from a dependence of the former on the latter, notwithstanding a nominal and apparent separation; that as, from the natural feebleness of the judiciary, it is in continual jeopardy of being overpowered, awed, or influenced by its coordinate branches; and that as nothing can contribute so much to its firmness and independence as permanency in office, this quality may therefore be justly regarded as an indispensable ingredient in its constitution, and, in a great measure, as the citadel of the public justice and the public security.

The complete independence of the courts of justice is peculiarly essential in a limited Constitution. By a limited Constitution, I understand one which contains certain specified exceptions to the legislative authority; such, for instance, as that it shall pass no bills of attainder, no *ex-post-facto* laws, and the like. Limitations of this kind can be preserved in practice no other way than through the medium of courts of justice, whose duty it must be to declare all acts contrary to the manifest tenor of the Constitution void. Without this, all the reservations of particular rights or privileges would amount to nothing.

Some perplexity respecting the rights of the courts to pronounce legislative acts void, because contrary to the constitution, has arisen from an imagination that the doctrine would imply a superiority of the judiciary to the legislative power. It is urged that the authority which can declare the acts of another void, must necessarily be superior to the one whose acts may be declared void. As this doctrine is of great importance in all the American constitutions, a brief discussion of the ground on which it rests cannot be unacceptable.

There is no position which depends on clearer principles, than that every act of a delegated authority, contrary to the tenor of the commission under which it is exercised, is void. No legislative act, therefore, contrary to the Constitution, can be valid. To deny this, would be to affirm, that the deputy is greater than his principal; that the servant is above his master; that the representatives of the people are superior to the people themselves; that men acting by virtue of powers, may do not only what their powers do not authorize, but what they forbid.

If it be said that the legislative body are themselves the constitutional judges of their own powers, and that the construction they put upon them is conclusive upon the other departments, it may be answered that this cannot be the natural presumption, where it is not to be collected from any particular provisions in the Constitution. It is not otherwise to be supposed, that the Constitution could intend to enable the representatives of the people to substitute their *will* to that of their constituents. It is far more rational to suppose, that the courts were designed to be an intermediate body between the people and the legislature, in order, among other things, to keep the latter within the limits assigned to their authority. The interpretation of the laws is the proper and peculiar province of the courts. A constitution is, in fact, and must be regarded by the judges, as a fundamental law. It therefore belongs to them to ascertain its meaning, as well as the meaning of any particular act proceeding from the legislative body. If there should happen to be an irreconcilable variance between the two, that which has the superior obligation and validity ought, of course, to be preferred; or, in other words, the Constitution ought to be preferred to the statute, the intention of the people to the intention of their agents.

Nor does this conclusion by any means suppose a superiority of the judicial to the legislative power. It only supposes that the power of the people is superior to both; and that where the will of the legislature, declared in its statutes, stands in opposition to that of the people, declared in the Constitution, the judges ought to be governed by the latter rather than the former. They ought to regulate their decisions by the fundamental laws, rather than by those which are not fundamental.

This exercise of judicial discretion, in determining between two contradictory laws, is exemplified in a familiar instance. It not uncommonly happens, that there are two statutes existing at one time, clashing in whole or in part with each other, and neither of them containing any repealing clause or expression. In such a case, it is the province of the courts to liquidate and fix their meaning and operation. So far as they can, by any fair construction, be reconciled to each other, reason and law conspire to dictate that this should be done; where this is impracticable, it becomes a matter of necessity to give effect to one, in exclusion of the other. The rule which has obtained in the courts for determining their relative validity is, that the last in order of time shall be preferred to the first. But this is a mere rule of construction, not derived from any positive law, but from the nature and reason of the thing. It is a

rule not enjoined upon the courts by legislative provision, but adopted by themselves, as consonant to truth and propriety, for the direction of their conduct as interpreters of the law. They thought it reasonable, that between the interfering acts of an *equal* authority, that which was the last indication of its will should have the preference.

But in regard to the interfering acts of a superior and subordinate authority, of an original and derivative power, the nature and reason of the thing indicate the converse of that rule as proper to be followed. They teach us that the prior act of a superior ought to be preferred to the subsequent act of an inferior and subordinate authority; and that accordingly, whenever a particular statute contravenes the Constitution, it will be the duty of the judicial tribunals to adhere to the latter and disregard the former.

It can be of no weight to say that the courts, on the presence of a repugnancy, may substitute their own pleasure to the constitutional intentions of the legislature. This might as well happen in the case of two contradictory statutes; or it might as well happen in every adjudication upon any single statute. The courts must declare the sense of the law; and if they should be disposed to exercise WILL instead of JUDGMENT, the consequence would equally be the substitution of their pleasure to that of the legislative body. The observation, if it prove any thing, would prove that there ought to be no judges distinct from that body.

If, then, the courts of justice are to be considered as the bulwarks of a limited Constitution against legislative encroachments, this consideration will afford a strong argument for the permanent tenure of judicial offices, since nothing will contribute so much as this to that independent spirit in the judges which must be essential to the faithful performance of so arduous a duty.

This independence of the judges is equally requisite to guard the Constitution and the rights of individuals from the effects of those ill humors, which the arts of designing men or the influence of particular conjectures, sometimes disseminate among the people themselves, and which, though they speedily give place to better information, and more deliberate reflection, have a tendency, in the meantime, to occasion dangerous innovations in the government, and serious oppressions of the minor party in the community. Though I trust the friends of the proposed Constitution will never concur with its enemies, in questioning that fundamental principle of republican government, which admits the rights of the people to alter or abolish the established Constitution, whenever they find it inconsistent with their happiness, yet it is not to be inferred from this principle, that the representatives of the people, whenever a momentary inclination happens to lay hold of a majority of their constituents, incompatible with the provisions in the existing Constitution, would, on that account, be justifiable, in a violation of those provisions; or that the courts would be under a greater obligation to connive at infractions in this shape, than when they had proceeded wholly from the cabals of the representative body. Until the people have, by some solemn and authoritative act, annulled or changed the established form, it is binding upon themselves collectively, as well as individually; and no presumption or, even knowledge, of their sentiments, can warrant their representatives in a departure from it, prior to such an act. But it is easy to see, that it would require an uncommon portion of fortitude in the judges to do their duty as faithful guardians of the Constitution, where legislative invasions of it had been instigated by the major voice of the community.

But it is not with a view to infractions of the Constitution only, that the independence of the judges may be an essential safeguard against the effects of occasional ill humors in the society. These sometimes extend no farther than to the injury of the private rights of particular classes of citizens, by unjust and partial laws. Here also the firmness of the judicial magistracy is of vast importance in mitigating the severity and confining the operation of such laws. It not only serves to moderate the immediate mischiefs of those which may have been passed but it operates as a check upon the legislative body in passing them; who, perceiving that obstacles to the success of iniquitous intention are to be expected from the scruples of the courts, are in a manner compelled by the very motives of the injustices they mediate to qualify their attempts. This is a circumstance calculated to have more influence upon the character of our governments, than but few may be aware of. The benefits of the integrity and moderation of the judiciary have already been felt in more States than one; and though they may have displeased those whose sinister expectations they may have disappointed, they must have commanded the esteem and applause of all the virtuous and disinterested. Considerate men, of every description, ought to prize whatever will tend to beget or fortify that temper in the courts; as no man can be sure that he may not be tomorrow the victim of a spirit of injustice, by which he may be a gainer today. And every man must now feel, that the inevitable tendency of such a spirit is to sap the foundations of public and private confidence, and to introduce in its stead universal distrust and distress.

That inflexible and uniform adherence to the rights of the Constitution, and of individuals, which we perceive to be indispensable in the courts of justice, can certainly not be expected from judges who hold their offices by a temporary commission. Periodical appointments, however regulated, or by whomsoever made would, in some way or other, be fatal to their necessary independence. If the power of making them was committed either to the Executive or legislature, there would be danger of an improper complaisance to the branch which possessed it; if to both, there would be an unwillingness to hazard the displeasure of either; if to the people, or to persons chosen by them for the special purpose, there would be too great a disposition to consult popularity, to justify a reliance that nothing would be consulted but the Constitution and the laws.

There is yet a further and a weightier reason for the permanency of the judicial offices, which is deducible from the nature of the qualifications they require. It has been frequently remarked, with great propriety, that a voluminous code of laws is one of the inconveniences necessarily connected with the advantages of a free government. To avoid an arbitrary discretion in the courts, it is indispensable that they should be bound down by strict rules and precedents, which serve to define and point out their duty in every particular case that comes before them; and it will readily be conceived from the variety of controversies which grow out of the folly and wickedness of mankind, that the records of those precedents must unavoidably swell to a very considerable bulk, and must demand long and laborious study to acquire a competent knowledge of them. Hence, it is, that there can be but few men in the society who will have sufficient skill in the laws to qualify them for the stations of judges.

And making the proper deductions for the ordinary depravity of human nature, the number must be still smaller of those who unite the requisite integrity with the requisite knowledge. These considerations apprise us, that the government can have no great option between fit character; and that a temporary duration in office, which would naturally discourage such characters from quitting a lucrative line of practice to accept a seat on the bench, would have a tendency to throw the administration of justice into hands less able, and less well qualified, to conduct it with utility and dignity. In the present circumstances of this country, and in those in which it is likely to be for a long time to come, the disadvantages on this score would be greater than they may at first sight appear; but it must be confessed, that they are far inferior to those which present themselves under the other aspects of the subject.

Upon the whole, there can be no room to doubt that the convention acted wisely in copying from the models of those constitutions which have established *good behavior* as the tenure of their judicial offices, in point of duration; and that so far from being blameable on this account, their plan would have been inexcusably defective, if it had wanted this important feature of good government. The experience of Great Britain affords an illustrious comment on the excellence of the institution.

Publius ∽

Primary Sources (James Madison)

Journal of the Federal Convention. Edited by E.H. Scott. Chicago: Albert, Scott, and Co., 1893.

Madison, James. *A Discourse on the Death of General Washington.* Richmond: John Martin and Co., 1844.

The Papers of James Madison. Edited by Henry D. Gilpin. 3 vols. Washington, D.C.: Lang and O'Sullivan, 1840.

The Writings of James Madison. Edited by Gaillard Hunt. 9 vols. New York: Putnam's, 1900.

Secondary Sources (James Madison)

Brant, Irving. *James Madison.* 6 vols. New York: Bobbs-Merrill, 1950.

Burns, Edward McNall. *James Madison: Philosopher of the Constitution.* New Brunswick, N.J.: Rutgers University Press, 1938.

Hunt, Gaillard. *The Life of James Madison.* New York: Doubleday, 1902.

Koch, Adrienne. *Jefferson and Madison.* New York: Knopf, 1950.

Rutland, Robert A. *James Madison: The Founding Father.* New York: Macmillan, 1987.

Primary Sources (Alexander Hamilton)

Hamilton, Alexander. "Defense of Mr. Jay's Treaty," vols. 1, 2, and 3 of *American Remembrances.* Edited by Matthew Carey. Philadelphia: H. Tuckniss, 1795.

———. *Letters of Pacificus.* Philadelphia: Samuel E. Smith, 1796.

———. *Observations on Certain Documents Contained in No. V and VI of "The History of the United States for the Year 1796" in which the Charge of Speculation against Alexander Hamilton, Late Secretary of the Treasury, Is Fully Refuted.* Philadelphia: John Bioren, 1797.

The Works of Alexander Hamilton. Edited by Henry Cabot Lodge. New York: Putnam's, 1904.

Secondary Sources (Alexander Hamilton)

Charles, Joseph. "Hamilton and Washington: The Origins of the American Party System," *William and Mary Quarterly* 12 (no. 2, 1955):218–67.

Emery, Noemie. *Alexander Hamilton: An Intimate Portrait.* New York: Putnam, 1982.

Frisch, Morton J. *Alexander Hamilton and the Political Order.* Lanham, Md.: University Press of America, 1991.

Hacker, Louis M. *Alexander Hamilton in the American Tradition.* New York: McGraw-Hill, 1957.

Lodge, Henry Cabot. *Alexander Hamilton.* Boston: Houghton Mifflin, 1882.

Mitchell, Broadus. *Heritage from Hamilton.* New York: Columbia University Press, 1957.

Schachner, Nathan. *Alexander Hamilton.* New York: Appleton-Century, 1946.

Stourzh, Gerald. *Alexander Hamilton and the Idea of Republican Government.* Stanford, Calif.: Stanford University Press, 1970.

11. Against Adoption of the Constitution

THE OPPOSITION TO the Constitution came from several sources, although its core lay in the poorer and more democratically inclined sectors of the population. In New York, for example, considerable opposition came from wealthy and conservative landowners who feared the Constitution's republicanism and from those who savored the revenues drawn from goods arriving in New York's harbor and intended for eventual consumers in New Jersey and Connecticut. Many simply feared that the creation of a powerful central government would threaten individual liberties much in the manner of the British authorities, whose rule had so recently been terminated. Others felt that the Federalists sought to gain economically from the institution of the new government; charges were made then and later that speculators were purchasing the worthless revolutionary-war bonds and other obligations at deflated prices in hopes that they would be redeemed in full by the government under the Constitution.[1]

The three selections included here reflect this range of opposition. The statement of dissent by the minority at the Pennsylvania ratifying convention reviews many of the widely shared resentments against the high-pressure Federalist campaign and adds some special ones unique to the Pennsylvania situation. The dissenters were accurate in their allegation that anti-Federalist members of the legislature had been physically dragged to their seats to make up the necessary quorum for setting up the ratifying convention. Some of their fears about the new Constitution, on the other hand, were clearly exaggerated.

Samuel Adams, whose efforts on behalf of individual rights and independence were reviewed previously, was concerned about citizen's potential loss of local control and about the rise of a new aristocracy. The principle of decentralized power is integral to democratic self-government, and Adams clearly thought he saw the beginnings of another aristocratic social order in the proposed centralization of power.

Richard Henry Lee (1732–94) was born in Virginia and educated in England. He served in the Virginia House of Burgesses, in the Continental Congress, and as president of the Congress under the Articles of Confederation. With Thomas Jefferson and Patrick Henry he helped organize the intercolonial Committees of Correspondence. In the Continental Congress he was a close friend and ally of Samuel Adams. He introduced the resolution in June 1776 calling for a declaration of independence. But he refused to serve as a delegate to the constitutional convention.

The first five *Letters from the Federal Farmer* were written by Lee between 8 and 15 October 1787, when the Constitution had barely made its appearance. They were printed as a pamphlet by the opposition party in New York and sold several thousand copies. In December 1787 and January 1788 Lee wrote another pamphlet of thirteen letters expressing his reservations in much greater detail. The final passage in this selection consists of excerpts from the second pamphlet that give his argument for a bill of rights. ∾

---

1. See Charles Beard, *An Economic Interpretation of the Constitution of the United States* (New York: Free Press, 1935).

Dissent of the Pennsylvania Minority (1787)

It was not until after the termination of the late glorious contest, which made the people

---

SOURCE: "The Address and Reasons of Dissent of the Minority of the Convention of the State of Pennsylvania to Their Constituents," *Pennsylvania Packet and Daily Advertiser*, 18 December 1787. Footnotes are the authors'.

of the United States an independent nation, that any defect was discovered in the present confederation. It was formed by some of the ablest patriots in America. It carried us successfully through the war, and the virtue and patriotism of the people, with their disposition to promote the common cause, supplied the want of power in Congress.

The Continental Convention met in the city of Philadelphia at the time appointed. It was composed of some men of excellent character; of others who were more remarkable for their ambition and cunning than their patriotism, and of some who had been opponents to the independence of the United States. The delegates from Pennsylvania were, six of them, uniform and decided opponents to the Constitution of this commonwealth. The convention sat upwards of four months. The doors were kept shut, and the members brought under the most solemn engagements of secrecy.[1] Some of those who opposed their going so far beyond their powers, retired, hopeless, from the convention; others had the firmness to refuse signing the plan altogether; and many who did sign it, did it not as a system they wholly approved, but as the best that could be then obtained, and notwithstanding the time spent on this subject, it is agreed on all hands to be a work of haste and accommodation.

Whilst the gilded chains were forging in the secret conclave, the meaner instruments of the despotism without were busily employed in alarming the fears of the people with dangers which did not exist, and exciting their hopes of greater advantages from the expected plan than even the best government on earth could produce. The proposed plan had not many hours issued forth from the womb of suspicious secrecy, until such as were prepared for the purpose, were carrying about petitions for people to sign, signifying their approbation of the system, and requesting the legislature to call a convention. While every measure was taken to intimidate the people against opposing it, the public papers teemed with the most violent threats against those who should dare to think for themselves, and *tar and feathers* were liberally promised to all those who would

not immediately join in supporting the proposed government, be it what it would. Under such circumstances petitions in favor of calling a Convention were signed by great numbers in and about the city, before they had leisure to read and examine the system, many of whom —now they are better acquainted with it, and have had time to investigate its principles— are heartily opposed to it. The petitions were speedily handed in to the legislature.

Affairs were in this situation, when on the 28th of September last, a resolution was proposed to the assembly by a member of the house, who had been also a member of the federal convention, for calling a State convention to be elected within *ten* days for the purpose of examining and adopting the proposed Constitution of the United States, though at this time the house had not received it from Congress. This attempt was opposed by a minority, who after offering every argument in their power to prevent the precipitate measure, without effect, absented themselves from the house as the only alternative left them, to prevent the measures taking place previous to their constituents being acquainted with the business. That violence and outrage which had been so often threatened was now practiced; some of the members were seized the next day by a mob collected for the purpose, and forcibly dragged to the house, and there detained by force whilst the quorum of the legislature *so formed,* completed their resolution. We shall dwell no longer on this subject: the people of Pennsylvania have been already acquainted therewith. We would only further observe that every member of the legislature, previously to taking his seat, by solemn oath or affirmation, declares "that he will not do or consent to any act or thing whatever, that will have a tendency to lessen or abridge their rights and privileges, as declared in the constitution of this State." And that constitution which they are so solemnly sworn to support, cannot le-

---

1. The Journals of the conclave are still concealed.

gally be altered but by a recommendation of the council of censors, who alone are authorized to propose alterations and amendments, and even these must be published at least *six months* for the consideration of the people. The proposed system of government for the United States, if adopted, will alter and may annihilate the constitution of Pennsylvania, and therefore the legislature had no authority whatever to recommend the calling a convention for that purpose. This proceeding could not be considered as binding on the people of this commonwealth. The house was formed by violence, some of the members composing it were detained there by force, which alone would have vitiated any proceedings to which they were otherwise competent; but had the legislature been legally formed, this business was absolutely without their power.

In this situation of affairs were the subscribers elected members of the Convention of Pennsylvania—a Convention called by a legislature in direct violation of their duty, and composed in part of members who were compelled to attend for that purpose, to consider of a Constitution proposed by a Convention of the United States, who were not appointed for the purpose of framing a new form of government, but whose powers were expressly confined to altering and amending the present articles of confederation. Therefore the members of the continental Convention in proposing the plan acted as individuals, and not as deputies from Pennsylvania.[2] The assembly who called the State Convention acted as individuals, and not as the legislature of Pennsylvania; nor could they or the Convention chosen on their recommendation have authority to do any act or thing that can alter or annihilate the Constitution of Pennsylvania (both of which will be done by the new Constitution), nor are their proceedings, in our opinion, at all binding on the people.

The election for members of the Convention was held at so early a period, and the want of information was so great, that some of us did not know of it until after it was over, and we have reason to believe that great numbers of the people of Pennsylvania have not yet had an opportunity of sufficiently examining the proposed Constitution. We apprehend that no change can take place that will affect the internal government or Constitution of this commonwealth, unless a majority of the people should evidence a wish for such a change; but on examining the number of votes given for members of the present State Convention, we find that of upwards of *seventy thousand* freemen who are entitled to vote in Pennsylvania, the whole convention has been elected by about *thirteen thousand* votes, and though *two-thirds* of the members of the Convention have thought proper to ratify the proposed Constitution, yet those *two-thirds* were elected by the votes of only *six thousand and eight hundred* freemen.

In the city of Philadelphia and some of the eastern counties the junto that took the lead in the business agreed to vote for none but such as would solemnly promise to adopt the system *in toto,* without exercising their judgment. In many of the counties the people did not attend the elections, as they had not an opportunity of judging of the plan. Others did not

---

2. The continental Convention, in direct violation of the 13th article of the confederation, have declared "that the ratification of nine States shall be sufficient for the establishment of this Constitution, between the States so ratifying the same." Thus has the plighted faith of the States been sported with! They had solemnly engaged that the confederation now subsisting should be inviolably preserved by each of them, and the Union thereby formed should be perpetual, unless the same should be altered by mutual consent.

consider themselves bound by the call of a set of men who assembled at the State-house in Philadelphia and assumed the name of the legislature of Pennsylvania; and some were prevented from voting by the violence of the party who were determined at all events to force down the measure. To such lengths did the tools of despotism carry their outrage, that on the night of the election for members of convention, in the city of Philadelphia, several of the subscribers (being then in the city to transact your business) were grossly abused, illtreated and insulted while they were quiet in their lodging, though they did not interfere nor had anything to do with the said election, but, as they apprehend, because they were supposed to be adverse to the proposed constitution, and would not tamely surrender those sacred rights which you had committed to their charge.

The convention met, and the same disposition was soon manifested in considering the proposed constitution, that had been exhibited in every other stage of the business. We were prohibited by an express vote of the convention from taking any questions on the separate articles of the plan, and reduced to the necessity of adopting or rejecting *in toto*. 'Tis true the majority permitted us to debate on each article, but restrained us from proposing amendments. They also determined not to permit us to enter on the minutes our reasons of dissent against any of the articles, nor even on the final question our reasons of dissent against the whole. Thus situated we entered on the examination of the proposed system of government, and found it to be such as we could not adopt, without, as we conceived, surrendering up your dearest rights. We offered our objections to the convention, and opposed those parts of the plan which, in our opinion, would be injurious to you, in the best manner we were able; and closed our arguments by offering the following propositions to the convention.

1. The right of conscience shall be held inviolable; and neither the legislative, executive nor judicial powers of the United States shall have authority to alter, abrogate or infringe any part of the constitution of the several States, which provide for the preservation of liberty in matters of religion.

2. That in controversies respecting property, and in suits between man and man, trial by jury shall remain as heretofore, as well in the federal courts as in those of the several States.

3. That in all capital and criminal prosecutions, a man has a right to demand the cause and nature of his accusation, as well in the federal courts as in those of the several States; to be heard by himself and his counsel; to be confronted with the accusers and witnesses; to call for evidence in his favor, and a speedy trial by an impartial jury of his vicinage, without whose unanimous consent he cannot be found guilty, nor can he be compelled to give evidence against himself, and, that no man be deprived of his liberty, except by the law of the land or the judgment of his peers.

4. That excessive bail ought not to be required, nor excessive fines imposed, nor cruel nor unusual punishments inflicted.

5. That warrants unsupported by evidence, whereby any officer or messenger may be commanded or required to search suspected places; or to seize any person or persons, his or their property not particularly described, are grievous and oppressive, and shall not be granted either by the magistrates of the federal government or others.

6. That the people have a right to the freedom of speech, of writing and publishing their sentiments; therefore the freedom of the press shall not be restrained by any law of the United States.

7. That the people have a right to bear arms for the defence of themselves and their own State or the United States, or for the pur-

pose of killing game; and no law shall be passed for disarming the people or any of them unless for crimes committed, or real danger of public injury from individuals; and as standing armies in the time of peace are dangerous to liberty, they ought not to be kept up; and that the military shall be kept under strict subordination to, and be governed by the civil powers.

8. The inhabitants of the several States shall have liberty to fowl and hunt in seasonable time on the lands they hold, and on all other lands in the United States not inclosed, and in like manner to fish in all navigable waters, and others not private property, without being restrained therein by any laws to be passed by the legislature of the United States.

9. That no law shall be passed to restrain the legislatures of the several States from enacting laws for imposing taxes, except imposts and duties on goods imported or exported, and that no taxes, except imposts and duties upon goods imported and exported, and postage on letters, shall be levied by the authority of Congress.

10. That the house of representatives be properly increased in number; that elections shall remain free; that the several States shall have power to regulate the elections for senators and representatives without being controlled either directly or indirectly by any interference on the part of the Congress; and that the elections of representatives be annual.

11. That the power of organizing, arming and disciplining the militia (the manner of disciplining the militia to be prescribed by Congress), remain with the individual States, and that Congress shall not have authority to call or march any of the militia out of their own State, without the consent of such State, and for such length of time only as such State shall agree.

That the sovereignty, freedom and independency of the several States shall be retained, and every power, jurisdiction and right which is not by this Constitution expressly delegated to the United States in Congress assembled.

12. That the legislature, executive and judicial powers be kept separate; and to this end that a constitutional council be appointed to advise and assist the President, who shall be responsible for the advice they give—hereby the senators would be relieved from almost constant attendance; and also that the judges be made completely independent.

13. That no treaty which shall be directly opposed to the existing laws of the United States in Congress assembled, shall be valid until such laws shall be repealed or made conformable to such treaty; neither shall any treaties be valid which are in contradiction to the Constitution of the United States, or the constitution of the several States.

14. That the judiciary power of the United States shall be confined to cases affecting ambassadors, other public ministers and consuls, to cases of admiralty and maritime jurisdiction; to controversies to which the United States shall be a party; to controversies between two or more States—between a State and citizens of different States—between citizens claiming lands under grants of different States, and between a State or the citizens thereof and foreign States; and in criminal cases to such only as are expressly enumerated in the constitution; and that the United States in Congress assembled shall not have power to enact laws which shall alter the laws of descent and distribution of the effects of deceased persons, the titles of lands or goods, or the regulation of contracts in the individual States.

After reading these propositions, we declared our willingness to agree to the plan, provided it was so amended as to meet those propositions or something similar to them, and finally moved the convention to adjourn, to give the people of Pennsylvania time to consider the subject and determine for themselves; but these were all rejected and the final vote taken, when our duty to you induced us to vote against the proposed plan and to decline signing the ratification of the same.

During the discussion we met with many insults and some personal abuse. We were not even treated with decency, during the sitting of the convention, by the persons in the gallery of the house. However, we flatter ourselves that in contending for the preservation of those invaluable rights you have thought proper to commit to our charge, we acted with a spirit becoming freemen; and being desirous that you might know the principles which actuated our conduct, and being prohibited from inserting our reasons of dissent on the minutes of the convention, we have subjoined them for your consideration, as to you alone we are accountable. It remains with you whether you will think those inestimable privileges, which you have so ably contended for, should be sacrificed at the shrine of despotism, or whether you mean to contend for them with the same spirit that has so often baffled the attempts of an aristocratic faction to rivet the shackles of slavery on you and your unborn posterity.

Our objections are comprised under three general heads of dissent, viz.:

We dissent, first, because it is the opinion of the most celebrated writers on government, and confirmed by uniform experience, that a very extensive territory cannot be governed on the principles of freedom, otherwise than by a confederation of republics, possessing all the powers of internal government, but united in the management of their general and foreign concerns.

If any doubt could have been entertained of the truth of the foregoing principle, it has been fully removed by the concession of *Mr. Wilson,* one of the majority on this question, and who was one of the deputies in the late general convention. In justice to him, we will give his own words; they are as follows, viz.: "The extent of country for which the new constitution was required, produced another difficulty in the business of the federal convention. It is the opinion of some celebrated writers, that to a small territory, the democratical; to a middling territory (as Montesquieu has termed it), the monarchical; and to an extensive territory, the despotic form of government is best adapted. Regarding then the wide and almost unbounded jurisdiction of the United States, at first view, the hand of despotism seemed necessary to control, connect and protect it; and hence the chief embarrassment rose. For we know that although our constituents would cheerfully submit to the legislative restraints of a free government, they would spurn at every attempt to shackle them with despotic power." And again, in another part of his speech, he continues: "Is it probable that the dissolution of the State governments, and the establishment of one *consolidated empire* would be eligible in its nature, and satisfactory to the people in its administration? I think not, as I have given reasons to show that so extensive a territory could not be governed, connected and preserved, but by the *supremacy of despotic power.* All the exertions of the most potent emperors of Rome were not capable of keeping that empire together, which in extent was far inferior to the dominion of America."

We dissent, secondly, because the powers vested in Congress by this constitution, must necessarily annihilate and absorb the legislative, executive, and judicial powers of the several States, and produce from their ruins one consolidated government, which from the nature of things will be *an iron handed despotism,* as nothing short of the supremacy of despotic sway could connect and govern these United States under one government....

3. We dissent, thirdly, because if it were practicable to govern so extensive a territory

as these United States include, on the plan of a consolidated government, consistent with the principles of liberty and the happiness of the people, yet the construction of this Constitution is not calculated to attain the object; for independent of the nature of the case, it would of itself necessarily produce a despotism, and that not by the usual gradations, but with the celerity that has hitherto only attended revolutions effected by the sword.... ∽

Letter from Samuel Adams to Richard Henry Lee (1787)

3 December 1787

My dear Sir

... I confess, as I enter the Building I stumble at the Threshold. I meet with a National Government, instead of a Federal Union of Sovereign States. I am not able to conceive why the Wisdom of the Convention led them to give the Preference to the former before the latter. If the several States in the Union are to become one entire Nation, under one Legislature, the Powers of which shall extend to every Subject of Legislation, and its Laws be supreme & controul the whole, the Idea of Sovereignty in these States must be lost. Indeed I think, upon such a Supposition, those Sovereignties ought to be eradicated from the Mind; for they would be Imperia in Imperio justly deemd a Solecism in Politicks, & they would be highly dangerous, and destructive of the Peace Union and Safety of the Nation. And can this National Legislature be competent to make Laws for the *free* internal Government of one People, living in Climates so remote and whose "Habits & particular Interests" are and probably always will be so different. Is it to be expected that General Laws can be adapted to the Feelings of the more Eastern and the more Southern Parts of so extensive a Nation? It appears to me difficult if practicable. Hence then may we not look for Discontent, Mistrust, Disaffection to Government and frequent Insurrections, which will require standing Armies to suppress them in one Place & another where they may happen to arise. Or if Laws could be made, adapted to the local Habits, Feelings, Views & Interests of those distant Parts, would they not cause Jealousies of Partiality in Government which would excite Envy and other malignant Passions productive of Wars and fighting. But should we continue distinct sovereign States, confederated for the Purposes of mutual Safety and Happiness, each contributing to the federal Head such a Part of its Sovereignty as would render the Government fully adequate to those Purposes and *no more,* the People would govern themselves more easily, the Laws of each State being well adapted to its own Genius & Circumstances, and the Liberties of the United States would be more secure than they can be, as I humbly conceive, under the proposed new Constitution. You are sensible, Sir, that the Seeds of Aristocracy began to spring even before the Conclusion of our Struggle for the natural Rights of Men, Seeds which like a Canker Worm lie at the Root of free Governments. So great is the Wickedness of some Men, & the stupid Servility of others, that one would be almost inclined to conclude that Communities cannot be free. The few haughty Families, think *They* must govern. The Body of the People tamely consent & submit to be their Slaves. This unravels the Mystery of Millions being enslaved by the few! ... ∽

SOURCE: Harry Alonzo Cushing, *The Writings of Samuel Adams* (New York: Putnam's, 1906), 4:323–25.

Richard Henry Lee, *Letters from a Federal Farmer* (1787–88)

LETTER I

... To have a just idea of the government before us, and to show that a consolidated one is the object in view, it is necessary not only to examine the plan, but also its history, and the politics of its particular friends.

The confederation was formed when great confidence was placed in the voluntary exertions of individuals, and of the respective states; and the framers of it, to guard against usurpations, so limited and checked the powers, that, in many respects, they are inadequate to the exigencies of the union. We find, therefore, members of congress urging alterations in the federal system almost as soon as it was adopted. It was early proposed to vest congress with powers to levy an impost, to regulate trade, etc. but such was known to be the caution of the states in parting with power, that the vestment, even of these, was proposed to be under several checks and limitations. During the war, the general confusion, and the introduction of paper money, infused in the minds of people vague ideas respecting government and credit. We expected too much from the return of peace, and of course we have been disappointed. Our government has been new and unsettled; and several legislatures, by making tender, suspension, and paper money laws, have given just cause of uneasiness to creditors. By these and other causes, several orders of men in the community have been prepared, by degrees, for a change of government; and this very abuse of power in the legislatures, which, in some cases, has been charged upon the democratic part of the community, has furnished aristocratical men with those very weapons, and those very means, with which, in great measure, they are rapidly effecting their favorite object. And should an oppressive government be the consequence of the proposed change, posterity may reproach not only a few overbearing unprincipled men, but those parties in the states which have misused their powers.

The conduct of several legislatures, touching paper money, and tender laws, has prepared many honest men for changes in government, which otherwise they would not have thought of—when by the evils, on the one hand, and by the secret instigations of artful men, on the other, the minds of men became sufficiently uneasy, a bold step was taken, which is usually followed by a revolution, or a civil war. A general convention for mere commercial purposes was moved for—the authors of this measure saw that the people's attention was turned solely to the amendment of the federal system; and that, had the idea of a total change been started, probably no state would have appointed members to the convention. The idea of destroying, ultimately, the state government, and forming one consolidated system, could not have been admitted—a convention, therefore, merely for vesting in congress power to regulate trade was proposed. This was pleasing to the commercial towns: and the landed people had little or no concern about it. September, 1786, a few men from the middle states met at Annapolis, and hastily proposed a convention to be held in May, 1787, for the purpose, generally, of amending the confederation—this was done before the delegates of Massachusetts, and of the other states arrived—still not a word was said about destroying the old constitution, and making a new one—The States still unsuspect-

SOURCE: *Letters from a Federal Farmer* (Letters I, IV, V, XVI). In Forrest McDonald, ed., *Empire and Nation* (Englewood Cliffs, N.J.: Prentice-Hall, 1962).

ing, and not aware that they were passing the Rubicon, appointed members to the new convention, for the sole and express purpose of revising and amending the confederation—and, probably, not one man in ten thousand in the United States, till within these ten or twelve days, had an idea that the old ship was to be destroyed, and he put to the alternative of embarking in the new ship presented, or of being left in danger of sinking—The States, I believe, universally supposed the convention would report alterations in the confederation, which would pass an examination in congress, and after being agreed to there, would be confirmed by all the legislatures, or be rejected. Virginia made a very respectable appointment, and placed at the head of it the first man in America: In this appointment there was a mixture of political characters; but Pennsylvania appointed principally those men who are esteemed aristocratical. Here the favorite moment for changing the government was evidently discerned by a few men, who seized it with address. Ten other states appointed, and tho' they chose men principally connected with commerce and the judicial department yet they appointed many good republican characters—had they all attended we should now see, I am persuaded a better system presented. The non-attendance of eight or nine men, who were appointed members of the convention, I shall ever consider as a very unfortunate event to the United States.—Had they attended I am pretty clear that the result of the convention would not have had that strong tendency to aristocracy now discernible in every part of the plan. There would not have been so great an accumulation of powers, especially as to the internal police of the country, in a few hands, as the constitution reported proposes to vest in them—the young visionary men, and the consolidating aristocracy, would have been more restrained than they have been. Eleven states met in the con-

vention, and after four months close attention presented the new constitution, to be adopted or rejected by the people. The uneasy and fickle part of the community may be prepared to receive any form of government; but, I presume, the enlightened and substantial part will give any constitution presented for their adoption a candid and thorough examination; and silence those designing or empty men, who weakly and rashly attempt to precipitate the adoption of a system of so much importance—We shall view the convention with proper respect—and, at the same time, that we reflect there were men of abilities and integrity in it, we must recollect how disproportionately the democratic and aristocratic parts of the community were represented.—Perhaps the judicious friends and opposers of the new constitution will agree, that it is best to let it rest solely on its own merits, or be condemned for its own defects.

In the first place, I shall premise, that the plan proposed is a plan of accommodation—and that it is in this way only, and by giving up a part of our opinions, that we can ever expect to obtain a government founded in freedom and compact. This circumstance candid men will always keep in view, in the discussion of this subject.

The plan proposed appears to be partly federal, but principally however, calculated ultimately to make the states one consolidated government.

The first interesting question, therefore suggested, is, how far the states can be consolidated into one entire government on free principles. In considering this question extensive objects are to be taken into view, and important changes in the forms of government to be carefully attended to in all their consequences. The happiness of the people at large must be the great object to this point. If we are so situated as a people, as not to be able to enjoy equal happiness and advantage under one government, the consolidation of the states cannot be admitted.

There are three different forms of free government under which the United States may exist as one nation; and now is, perhaps, the time to determine to which we will direct our views. 1. Distinct republics connected under a federal head. In this case the respective state governments must be the principal guardians of the peoples rights, and exclusively regulate their internal police: in them must rest the balance of government. The congress of the states, or federal head must consist of delegates amenable to, and removable by the respective states: This congress must have general directing powers; powers to require men and monies of the states; to make treaties: peace and war: to direct the operations of armies, etc. Under this federal modification of government, the powers of congress would be rather advisory or recommendatory than coercive. 2. We may do away with the several state governments, and form or consolidate all the states into one entire government, with one executive, one judiciary, and one legislature, consisting of senators and representatives collected from all parts of the union: In this case there would be a complete consolidation of the states. 3. We may consolidate the states as to certain national objects, and leave them severally distinct independent republics, as to internal police generally. Let the general government consist of an executive, a judiciary and balanced legislature, and its powers extend exclusively to all foreign concerns, causes arising on the seas to commerce, imports, armies, navies, Indian affairs, peace and war, and to a few internal concerns of the community; to the coin, post offices, weights and measures, a general plan for the militia, to naturalization, *and, perhaps to bankruptcies,* leaving the internal police of the community, in other re-

spects, exclusively to the state governments; as the administration of justice in all causes arising internally, the laying and collecting of internal taxes, and the forming of the militia according to a general plan prescribed. In this case there would be a complete consolidation, *quoad* certain objects only.

Touching the first, or federal plan, I do not think much can be said in its favor: The sovereignty of the nation, without coercive and efficient powers to collect the strength of it, cannot always be depended on to answer the purposes of government and in a congress of representatives of sovereign states, there must necessarily be an unreasonable mixture of powers in the same hands.

As to the second, or complete consolidating plan, it deserves to be carefully considered at this time, by every American: If it be impracticable, it is a fatal error to model our governments directing our views ultimately to it.

The third plan, or partial consolidation, is, in my opinion, the only one that can secure the freedom and happiness of this people. I once had some general ideas that the second plan was practicable, but from long attention, and the proceedings of the convention, I am fully satisfied, that this third plan is the only one we can with safety and propriety proceed upon. Making this the standard to point out, with candor and fairness, the parts of the new constitution which appear to be improper, is my object. The convention appears to have proposed the partial consolidation evidently with a view to collect all powers ultimately, in the United States into one entire government; and from its views in this respect, and from the tenacity of the small states to have an equal vote in the senate, probably originated the greatest defects in the proposed plan....

LETTER IV

... It is true, we are not disposed to differ much, at present, about religion; but when we are making a constitution, it is to be hoped, for ages and millions yet unborn, why not establish the free exercise of religion, as a part of the national compact. There are other essential rights, which we have justly understood to be the rights of freemen; as freedom from hasty and unreasonable search warrants, warrants not founded on oath, and not issued with due caution, for searching and seizing men's papers, property, and persons. The trials by jury in civil causes, it is said, varies so much in the several states, that no words could be found for the uniform establishment of it. If so, the federal legislation will not be able to establish it by any general laws. I confess I am of opinion it may be established, but not in that beneficial manner in which we may enjoy it, for the reasons beforementioned. When I speak of the jury trial of the vicinage, or the trial of the fact in the neighborhood,—I do not lay so much stress upon the circumstance of our being tried by our neighbors: in this enlightened country men may be probably impartially tried by those who do not live very near them: but the trial of facts in the neighborhood is of great importance in other respects. Nothing can be more essential than the cross examining of witnesses, and generally before the triers of the facts in question. The common people can establish facts with much more ease with oral than written evidence; when trials of facts are removed to a distance from the homes of the parties and witnesses, oral evidence becomes intolerably expensive, and the parties must depend on written evidence, which to the common people is expensive and almost useless; it must be frequently taken *ex parte,* and but very seldom leads to the proper discovery of truth.

The trial by jury is very important in another point of view. It is essential in every free country, that common people should have a part and share of influence, in the judicial as well as in the legislative department. To hold open to them the offices of senators, judges, and offices to fill which an expensive education is required, cannot answer any valuable purposes for them; they are not in a situation to be brought forward and to fill those offices; these, and most other offices of any considerable importance, will be occupied by the few. The few, the well born, etc. as Mr. Adams calls them, in judicial decisions as well as in legislation, are generally disposed, and very naturally too, to favor those of their own description.

The trial by jury in the judicial department, and the collection of the people by their representatives in the legislature, are those fortunate inventions which have procured for them, in this country, their true proportion of influence, and the wisest and most fit means of protecting themselves in the community. Their situation, as jurors and representatives, enables them to acquire information and knowledge in the affairs and government of the society; and to come forward, in turn, as the sentinels and guardians of each other. I am very sorry that even a few of our countrymen should consider jurors and representatives in a different point of view, as ignorant troublesome bodies, which ought not to have any share in the concerns of government.

I confess I do not see in what cases the congress can, with any pretense of right, make a law to suppress the freedom of the press; though I am not clear, that congress is restrained from laying any duties whatever on printing, and from laying duties particularly heavy on certain pieces printed, and perhaps congress may require large bonds for the payment of these duties. Should the printer say, the freedom of the press was secured by the constitution of the state in which he lived, congress might, and perhaps, with great propriety, answer, that the federal constitution is the only compact existing between them and the people; in this compact the people have named no others, and therefore congress in exercising the powers assigned them, and in making laws to carry them into execution, are restrained by nothing beside the federal constitution, any more than a state legislature is restrained by a compact between the magistrates and people of a county, city, or town of which the people, in forming the state constitution, have taken no notice.

It is not my object to enumerate rights of inconsiderable importance; but there are others, no doubt, which ought to be established as a fundamental part of the national system. . . .

LETTER V

... This subject of consolidating the states is new; and because forty or fifty men have agreed in a system, to suppose the good sense of this country, an enlightened nation, must adopt it without examination, and though in a state of profound peace, without endeavoring to amend those parts they perceive are defective, dangerous to freedom, and destructive of the valuable principles of republican government—is truly humiliating. It is true there may be danger in delay; but there is danger in adopting the system in its present form; and I see the danger in either case will arise principally from the conduct and views of two very unprincipled parties in the United States—two fires, between which the honest and substantial people have long found themselves situated. One party is composed of little insurgents, men in debt, who want no law, and who want a share of the property of others; these are called levellers, Shayites, etc. The other party is composed of a few, but more dangerous men, with their servile dependents; these avariciously grasp at all power and property; you may discover in all the actions of these men, an evident dislike to free and equal government, and they will go systematically to work to change, essentially, the forms of government in this country; these are called aristocrats, m—ites, etc. etc. Between these two parties is the weight of the community; the men of middling property, men not in debt on the one hand, and men, on the other, content with republican governments, and not aiming at immense fortunes, offices, and power. In 1786, the little insurgents, the levellers, came forth, invaded the rights of others, and attempted to establish governments according to their wills. Their movements evidently gave encouragement to the other party, which, in 1787, has taken the political field, and with its fashionable dependents, and the tongue and the pen, is endeavouring to establish, in great haste, a politer kind of government. These two parties, which will probably be opposed or united as it may suit their interests and views, are really insignificant, compared with the solid, free, and independent part of the community. It is not my intention to suggest, that either of these parties, and the real friends of the proposed constitution, are the same men. The fact is, these aristocrats support and hasten the adoption of the proposed constitution, merely because they think it is a stepping stone to their favorite object. I think I am well founded in this idea; I think the general politics of these men support it, as well as the common observation among them, That the proffered plan is the best that can be got at present, it will do for a few years and lead to something better. The sensible and judicious part of the community will carefully weigh all these circumstances; they will view the late convention as a respectable assembly of men —America probably never will see an assembly of men of a like number, more respectable. But the members of the convention met without knowing the sentiments of one man in ten thousand in these states, respecting the new ground taken. Their doings are but the first attempts in the most important scene ever opened. Though each individual in the late conventions will not, probably, be so respectable as each individual in the federal convention, yet as the state conventions will probably consist of fifteen hundred or two thousand men of abilities, and versed in the science of governments, collected from all parts of the community and from all orders of men, it must be acknowledged that the weight of respectability will be in them—In them will be collected the solid sense and the real political character of the country. Being revisers of the subject, they will possess peculiar advantages. To say that these conventions ought not to attempt, coolly and deliberately, the revision of the system, or that they cannot amend it, is very foolish or very assuming. If these conventions, after examining the system, adopt it, I shall be perfectly satisfied, and wish to see men make the administration of the government an equal blessing to all orders of men. I believe the great body of our people to be virtuous and friendly to good government, to the protection of liberty and property; and it is the duty of all good men, especially of those who are placed as sentinels to guard their rights—it is their duty to examine into the prevailing politics of parties, and to disclose them—while they avoid exciting undue suspicions, to lay facts before the people, which will enable them to form a proper judgment. Men who wish the people of this country to determine for themselves, and deliberately to fit the government to their situation, must feel some degree of indignation at those attempts to hurry the adoption of a system, and to shut the door against examination. The very attempts create suspicions, that those who make them have secret

views, or see some defects in the system, which in the hurry of affairs, they expect will escape the eye of a free people.

What can be the views of those gentlemen in Pennsylvania, who precipitated decisions on this subject? What can be the views of those gentlemen in Boston, who countenanced the Printers in shutting up the press against a fair and free investigation of this important system in the usual way? The members of the convention have done their duty—why should some of them fly to their states—almost forget a propriety of behavior, and precipitate measures for the adoption of a system of their own making? I confess candidly, when I consider these circumstances in connection with the unguarded parts of the system I have mentioned, I feel disposed to proceed with very great caution, and to pay more attention than usual to the conduct of particular characters. If the constitution presented be a good one, it will stand the test with a well informed people; all are agreed there shall be state conventions to examine it; and we must believe it will be adopted, unless we suppose it is a bad one, or that those conventions will make false divisions respecting it. I admit if proper measures are taken against the adoption of the system as well as for it—all who object to the plan proposed ought to point out the defects objected to, and to propose those amendments with which they can accept it, or to propose some other system of government, that the public mind may be known, and that we may be brought to agree in some system of government, to strengthen and execute the present, or to provide a substitute. I consider the field of enquiry just opened, and that we are to look to the state conventions for ultimate decisions on the subject before us; it is not to be presumed, that they will differ about small amendments, and lose a system when they shall have made it substantially good; but touching the essential amendments, it is to be presumed the several conventions will pursue the most rational measures to agree in and obtain them; and such defects as they shall discover and not remove, they will probably notice, keep them in view as the groundwork of future amendments, and in the firm and manly language which every free people ought to use, will suggest to those who may hereafter administer the government, that it is their expectation, that the system will be so organized by legislative acts, and the government so administered, as to render those defects as little injurious as possible. Our countrymen are entitled to an honest and faithful government; to a government of laws and not of men; and also to one of their choosing—as a citizen of the country, I wish to see these objects secured, and licentious, assuming, and overbearing men restrained; if the constitution or social compact be vague and unguarded, then we depend wholly upon the prudence, wisdom and mod-eration of those who manage the affairs of government; or on what, probably, is equally uncertain and precarious, the success of the people oppressed by the abuse of government, in receiving it from the hands of those who abuse it, and placing it in the hands of those who will use it well.

In every point of view, therefore, in which I have been able, as yet, to contemplate this subject, I can discern but one rational mode of proceeding relative to it: and that is to examine it with freedom and candor, to have state conventions some months hence, which shall examine coolly every article, clause, and word in the system proposed, and to adopt it with such amendments as they shall think fit. How far the state conventions ought to pursue the mode prescribed by the federal convention of adopting or rejecting the plan *in toto,* I leave it to them to determine.... ∼

Primary Sources

Ford, Paul Leicester, ed. *Pamphlets on the Constitution.* 1894. Reprint, New York: B. Franklin, 1971.

McDonald, Forrest, ed. *Empire and Nation.* Englewood Cliffs, N.J.: Prentice-Hall, 1962.

Secondary Source

Chitwood, Oliver P. *Richard Henry Lee, Statesman of the Revolution.* Morgantown: West Virginia University Library, 1967.

12. Alexander Hamilton's Program

So FAR WE have seen Alexander Hamilton as military leader, loyal ally of Washington, and eager proponent of energy in the national government. With his appointment as the first secretary of the treasury, Alexander Hamilton emerged as the architect of national wealth, power, and grandeur. More than any other of the great people of his times, Hamilton had a vision of a powerful and independent industrialized political economy of the future and a clear program for the stages of development that would attain it.

The three major writings excerpted below contain the essence of his thought and program. The *Report on Credit* proposed "funding" the existing national debt and paying back the current holders of bonds and other obligations at the full face value of their holdings. "Funding" involved explicitly committing certain national revenues (duties on imports and excise taxes on tobacco and whiskey were suggested) to periodic payments of principal and interest, and it had the effect of assuring the nation's creditors that they would be repaid. With such a restoration of the nation's creditworthiness, the government could even borrow new money to start making payments immediately. A second proposal in the *Report on Credit* was to assume the debts of the states and pay them back, using the same procedures. A third was to establish a national bank run by private bankers to manage the government's money.

While all believed that the credit of the new government should be established, these were highly controversial proposals. First, the new taxes appeared to be laid disproportionately on tea and other widely used consumer items and on activities carried on only by back-country farmers, such as making whiskey out of whatever surplus grain they could not transport to eastern markets. Second, the current holders of revolutionary-war bonds and other obligations were speculators and financiers who had avidly bought at very low prices; to pay them back at full value would result in enormous profits for them and nothing for the people who had actually provided the money in patriotic response to the urgent call of the Congress. Madison led the fight in the House of Representatives to pay the original purchasers at least some proportion of their investment, but Hamilton's argument prevailed. This issue precipitated the first in the series of internal conflicts that soon resulted in Madison and Jefferson forming a political party to oppose the Federalists. Third, some states had already paid back their wartime debts, and their representatives objected to contributing further revenues to pay the un-

paid debts of other states. Fourth, a national bank would overshadow state banks and give its wealthy investors additional power and profit and did not appear within the Constitution's grant of powers to Congress.

The second paper responds to the last point. Faced with a bill passed by Congress to create such a banking corporation, Washington asked his attorney general (Edmund Randolph) and his secretary of state (Thomas Jefferson) if it were constitutional and appropriate for him to sign it. Both men were strict constructionists who believed that the new national government should have only those powers explicitly granted and narrowly construed by the Constitution so as to reserve as many powers as possible for the states. Both held the bank to be unconstitutional and recommended not signing the bill. Washington immediately asked Hamilton for his opinion and followed his advice by signing the bill. Hamilton argued for a broad construction of national powers, particularly those implied as "necessary and proper" to execute other powers already granted. This is the view that has prevailed, with certain exceptions, to the present.

The third paper, Hamilton's *Report on Manufactures,* contained proposals not implemented until after the War of 1812 demonstrated the need for relying less on goods produced abroad. But the report shows Hamilton's vision most clearly, as well as his determination to use the national government to foster purposefully the kind of economy he sought. Throughout his life, Hamilton was an ardent devotee of manufacturing and new machinery for various forms of production. He belonged to societies for the promotion of manufacturing and invested heavily in several inventions that never became profitable. The report also demonstrates the detail in which Hamilton grasped the conditions and possibilities of the nation.

Hamilton believed, in his own words, that

"money is the vital principle of the body politic." A successful economy would produce sufficient revenue for the government to discharge its obligations, maintain order, and foster the expansion of commerce. The reciprocity and mutuality of vested interests here make it difficult to identify which was primary for Hamilton. His initiative in the Annapolis Convention of 1786 was for the purpose of proposing arrangements that would improve commerce between the states, but he went on record as attacking the weakness of the Articles of Confederation for raising revenues, even before they had been ratified by all the states. Throughout the *Federalist Papers* he speaks of commerce and revenue together, and it seems clear that he envisioned a partnership between business and government in which risks, opportunities, and rewards were essentially inseparable. This union of government with business and finance is distinctly Hamiltonian and distinctly at odds with the limited-government and laissez-faire views of almost all of his major contemporaries. Hamilton stood ready to make conscious and deliberate use of government wherever it could be a useful instrument for advancing commerce and, perhaps not incidentally, for serving the interests of the business people, financiers, and incipient manufacturers whose success Hamilton so desired.

In so employing government, Hamilton was boldly seeking to bring about conditions that would be strikingly different from those that then obtained in the new nation. Financial and commercial considerations dominated his thinking. Clinton Rossiter aptly terms Hamilton as having been of the right but not conservative.[1] This captures the essence of Hamilton: the exclusiveness of his business and property-rights orientation, coupled with his decisive use of government to bring about change to a specific set of economic conditions in which commerce would be greatly facilitated. He cannot be understood as a conservative, using our definition, for he did not begin with a conception of society as an organism prior to the individual interests with it; he avidly sought change of a totally antitraditional sort, and his motivations were exclusively economic at the cost of concern for the natural aristocracy of those whose talent might be more appropriate for the many facets of governing. A better way of interpreting Hamilton would be to see him as a liberal who understood natural rights in terms nearly exclusively of property rights, who saw the furtherance of the material goals of property holders as paramount and as an appropriate purpose to which government might be devoted.

A visionary with such a commitment to business and finance and such a controversial program could not fail to spark vigorous opposition. Hamilton's program and Hamilton himself came under increasing attack by Jefferson and the growing Democratic-Republican party. Hamilton was charged with mismanagement of the treasury, conflict of interest, and participation in a bank that collapsed in scandal, but none of these allegations proved accurate. Nevertheless, he resigned in 1795 (having outlasted Jefferson by a year) despite Washington's continued support. Defeated in his attempt to block the more traditionally conservative John Adams from the presidency in 1796, he retired to New York and resumed the lucrative practice of law. He returned to the national scene briefly in 1801 when he used his influence to help select Jefferson for president over Aaron Burr. After Hamilton in 1804 again prevented Burr from attaining office, this time as governor of New York, a duel ensued between them and Hamilton was killed. ⤳

---

1. Clinton Rossiter, *Conservatism in America* (New York: Random House, 1955), 108.

Report on Credit (1790)

The Secretary of the Treasury, in obedience to the resolution of the House of Representatives, on the twenty-first day of September last, has, during the recess of Congress, applied himself to the consideration of a proper plan for the support of the public Credit, with all the attention which was due to the authority of the House, and to the magnitude of the object.

In the discharge of this duty, he has felt, in no small degree, the anxieties which naturally flow from a just estimate of the difficulty of the task, from a well-founded diffidence of his own qualifications for executing it with success, and from a deep and solemn conviction of the momentous nature of the truth contained in the resolution under which his investigations have been conducted, "That an *adequate* provision for the support of the Public Credit, is a matter of high importance to the honor and prosperity of the United States."

With an ardent desire that his well-meant endeavors may be conducive to the real advantage of the nation, and with the utmost deference to the superior judgment of the House, he now respectfully submits the result of his enquiries and reflections, to their indulgent construction.

In the opinion of the Secretary, the wisdom of the House, in giving their explicit sanction to the proposition which has been stated, cannot but be applauded by all, who will seriously consider, and trace through their obvious consequences, these plain and undeniable truths.

That exigencies are to be expected to occur, in the affairs of nations, in which there will be a necessity for borrowing.

That loans in times of public danger, especially from foreign war, are found an indispensable resource, even to the wealthiest of them.

And that in a country, which, like this, is possessed of little active wealth, or in other words, little monied capital, the necessity for the resource, must, in such emergencies, be proportionately urgent.

And as on the one hand, the necessity for borrowing in particular emergencies cannot be doubted, so on the other, it is equally evident, that to be able to borrow upon *good terms,* it is essential that the credit of a nation should be well established.

For when the credit of a country is in any degree questionable, it never fails to give an extravagant premium in one shape or another, upon all the loans it has occasion to make. Nor does the evil end here; the same disadvantage must be sustained upon whatever is to be bought on terms of future payment.

From this constant necessity of *borrowing* and *buying dear,* it is easy to conceive how immensely the expences of a nation, in a course of time, will be augmented by an unsound state of the public credit.

To attempt to enumerate the complicated variety of mischiefs in the whole system of the social economy, which proceed from a neglect of the maxims that uphold public credit, and justify the solicitude manifested by the House on this point, would be an improper intrusion on their time and patience.

In so strong a light nevertheless do they appear to the Secretary, that on their due observance at the present critical juncture, materially depends, in his judgment, the individual and aggregate prosperity of the citizens of the United States; their relief from the embarrassments they now experience; their character as a People; the cause of good government.

SOURCE: All selections in this chapter may be found in Samuel McKee Jr., ed., *Papers on Public Credit, Commerce and Finance* (Indianapolis: Bobbs-Merrill, 1957).

If the maintenance of public credit, then, be truly so important, the next enquiry which suggests itself is, by what means it is to be effected? The ready answer to which question is, by good faith, by punctual performance of contracts. States, like individuals, who observe their engagements, are respected and trusted: while the reverse is the fate of those, who pursue an opposite conduct. . . .

While the observance of that good faith, which is the basis of public credit, is recommended by the strongest inducements of political expediency, it is enforced by considerations of still greater authority. There are arguments for it, which rest on the immutable principles of moral obligation. And in proportion as the mind is disposed to contemplate, in the order of Providence, as intimate connection between public virtue and public happiness, will be its repugnancy to a violation of those principles.

This reflection derives additional strength from the nature of the debt of the United States. It was the price of liberty. The faith of America has been repeatedly pledged for it, and with solemnities, that give peculiar force to the obligation. There is indeed reason to regret that it has not hitherto been kept; that the necessities of the war, conspiring with inexperience in the subjects of finance, produced direct infractions; and that the subsequent period has been a continued scene of negative violation, or non-compliance. But a diminution of this regret arises from the reflection, that the last seven years have exhibited an earnest and uniform effort, on the part of the government of the union, to retrieve the national credit, by doing justice to the creditors of the nation; and that the embarrassments of a defective constitution, which defeated this laudable effort, have ceased.

From this evidence of a favorable disposition, given by the former government, the institution of a new one, cloathed with powers competent to calling forth the resources of the community, has excited correspondent expectations. A general belief, accordingly, prevails, that the credit of the United States will quickly be established on the firm foundation of an effectual provision for the existing debt. The influence, which this has had at home, is witnessed by the rapid increase, that has taken place in the market value of the public securities. From January to November, they rose thirty-three and a third per cent, and from that period to this time, they have risen fifty per cent more. And the intelligence from abroad announces effects proportionably favourable to our national credit and consequence.

It cannot but merit particular attention, that among ourselves the most enlightened friends of good government are those, whose expectations are the highest.

To justify and preserve their confidence; to promote the increasing respectability of the American name; to answer the calls of justice; to restore landed property to its due value; to furnish new resources both to agriculture and commerce, to cement more closely the union of the states; to add to their security against foreign attack; to establish public order on the basis of an upright and liberal policy. These are the great and invaluable ends to be secured, by a proper and adequate provision, at the present period, for the support of public credit. . . .

Having now taken a concise view of the inducements to a proper provision for the public debt, the next enquiry which presents itself is, what ought to be the nature of such a provision? This requires some preliminary discussions.

It is agreed on all hands, that the part of the debt which has been contracted abroad, and is denominated the foreign debt, ought to be provided for, according to the precise terms of the contracts relating to it. The discussions, which can arise, therefore, will have reference essentially to the domestic part of it, or to that which has been contracted at home. It is to be regretted, that there is not the same unanimity of sentiment on this part as on the other.

The Secretary has too much deference for the opinions of every part of the community, not to have observed one, which has, more than once, made its appearance in the public prints, and which is occasionally to be met with in conversation. It involves this question, whether a discrimination ought not be made between original holders of the public securities, and present possessors, by purchase. Those who advocate a discrimination are for making a full provision for the securities of the former, at their nominal value; but contend, that the latter ought to receive no more than the cost to them, and the interest: And the idea is sometimes suggested of making good the difference to the primitive possessor.

In favor of this scheme, it is alledged, that it would be unreasonable to pay twenty shillings in the pound, to one who had not given more for it than three or four. And it is added, that it would be hard to aggravate the misfortune of the first owner, who, probably through necessity, parted with his property at so great a loss, by obliging him to contribute to the profit of the person, who had speculated on his distresses.

The Secretary, after the most mature reflection on the force of this argument, is induced to reject the doctrine it contains as equally unjust and impolitic, as highly injurious, even to the original holders of public securities; as ruinous to public credit.

It is inconsistent with justice, because in the first place, it is a breach of contract; in violation of the rights of a fair purchaser.

The nature of the contract in its origin, is, that the public will pay the sum expressed in the security, to the first holder, or his *assignee*. The *intent*, in making the security assignable, is, that the proprietor may be able to make use of his property, by selling it for as much as it *may be worth in the market*, and that the buyer may be *safe* in the purchase.

Every buyer therefore stands exactly in the place of the seller, has the same rights with him to the identical sum expressed in the security, and having acquired that right, by fair purchase, and in conformity to the original *agreement* and *intention* of the government, his claim cannot be disputed, without manifest injustice.

That he is to be considered as a fair purchaser, results from this: Whatever necessity the seller may have been under, was occasioned by the government, in not making a proper provision for its debts. The buyer had no agency in it, and therefore ought not to suffer. He is not even chargeable with having taken an undue advantage. He paid what the commodity was worth in the market, and took the risks of reimbursement upon himself. He of course, gave a fair equivalent, and ought to reap the benefit of his hazard; a hazard which was far from inconsiderable, and which, perhaps, turned on little less than a revolution in government.

That the case of those, who parted with their securities from necessity, is a hard one, cannot be denied. But whatever complaint of injury, or claim of redress, they may have, respects the government solely. They have not only nothing to object to the persons who relieved their necessities, by giving them the current price of their property, but they are even under an implied condition to contribute to the reimbursement of those persons. They knew, that by the terms of the contract with themselves, the public were bound to pay to those, to whom they should convey their title, the sums stipulated to be paid to them; and, that as citizens of the United States, they were to bear their proportion of the contribution for that purpose. This, by the act of assignment, they tacitly engage to do; and if they had an option, they could not, with integrity or good faith, refuse to do it, without the consent of those to whom they sold.

But though many of the original holders sold from necessity, it does not follow, that this was the case with all of them. It may well be supposed, that some of them did it either through want of confidence in an eventual provision, or from the allurements of some profitable speculation. How shall it be ascertained, in any case, that the money, which the original holder obtained for his security, was not more beneficial to him, than if he had held it to the present time, to avail himself of the provision which shall be made? How shall it be known, whether if the purchaser had employed his money in some other way, he would not be in a better situation, than by having applied it in the purchase of securities, though he should now receive their full amount? And if neither of these things can be known, how shall it be determined whether a discrimination, independent of the breach of contract, would not do a real injury to purchasers; and if it included a compensation to the primitive proprietors, would not give them an advantage, to which they had no equitable pretension.

It may well be imagined, also, that there are not wanting instances, in which individuals, urged by a present necessity parted with the securities received by them from the public, and shortly after replaced them with others, as an indemnity for their first loss. Shall they be deprived of the indemnity which they have endeavoured to secure by so provident an arrangement?

Questions of this sort, on a close inspection, multiply themselves without end, and demonstrate the injustices of a discrimination, even on the most subtile calculations of equity, abstracted from the obligation of contract.

The difficulties too of regulating the details of a plan for that purpose, which would have even the semblance of equity, would be found immense. It may well be doubted whether they would not be insurmountable, and replete with such absurd, as well as inequitable consequences, as to disgust even the proposers of the measure. . . .

But there is still a point in view in which it will appear perhaps even more exceptionable, than in either of the former. It would be repugnant to an express provision of the Constitution of the United States. This provision is, that "all debts contracted and engagements entered into before the adoption of that Constitution shall be as valid against the United States under it, as under the confederation," which amounts to a constitutional ratification of the contracts respecting the debt, in the state in which they existed under the confederation. And resorting to that standard, there can be no doubt, that the rights of assignees and original holders, must be considered as equal. . . .

The Secretary concluding, that a discrimination, between the different classes of creditors of the United States, cannot with propriety be *made,* proceeds to examine whether a difference ought to be permitted to *remain* between them, and another description of public creditors—those of the states individually.

The Secretary, after mature reflection on this point, entertains a full conviction, that an assumption of the debts of the particular states by the union, and a like provision for them, as for those of the union, will be a measure of sound policy and substantial justice.

It would, in the opinion of the Secretary, contribute, in an eminent degree, to an orderly, stable and satisfactory arrangement of the national finances.

Admitting, as ought to be the case, that a provision must be made in some way or other, for the entire debt; it will follow, that no greater revenues will be required, whether that provision be made wholly by the United States, or partly by them, and partly by the states separately.

The principal question then must be, whether such a provision cannot be more conveniently and effectually made, by one general plan issuing from one authority, than by different plans or originating in different authorities....

If all the public creditors receive their dues from one source, distributed with an equal hand, their interest will be the same. And having the same interests, they will unite in the support of the fiscal arrangements of the government: As these, too, can be made with more convenience, where there is no competition: These circumstances combined will insure to the revenue laws a more ready and more satisfactory execution.

If on the contrary there are distinct provisions, there will be distinct interests, drawing different ways. That union and concert of views, among the creditors, which in every government is of great importance to their security, and to that of public credit, will not only not exist, but will be likely to give place to mutual jealousy and opposition. And from this cause, the operation of the systems which may be adopted, both by the particular states, and by the union, with relation to their respective debts, will be in danger of being counteracted.

There are several reasons, which render it probable, that the situation of the state creditors would be worse, than that of the creditors of the union, if there be not a national assumption of the state debts. Of these it will be sufficient to mention two; one, that a principal branch of revenue is exclusively vested in the union; the other, that a state must always be checked in the imposition of taxes on articles of consumption, from the want of power to extend the same regulation to the other states, and from the tendency of partial duties to injure its industry and commerce. Should the state creditors stand upon a less eligible footing than the others, it is unnatural to expect they would see with pleasure a provision for them. The influence which their dissatisfaction might have, could not but operate injuriously, both for the creditors, and the credit, of the United States....

This sum may, in the opinion of the Secretary, be obtained from the present duties on imports and tonnage, with the additions, which without any possible disadvantages either to trade, or agriculture, may be made on wines, spirits, including those distilled within the United States, tea and coffee.

The Secretary conceives, that it will be sound policy, to carry the duties upon articles of this kind, as high as will be consistent with the practicability of a safe collection. This will lessen the necessity, both of having recourse to direct taxation, and of accumulating duties where they would be more inconvenient to trade, and upon objects, which are more to be regarded as necessaries of life.

That the articles which have been enumerated, will, better than most others, bear high duties, can hardly be a question. They are all of them, in reality—luxuries—the greatest part of them foreign luxuries; some of them, in the excess in which they are used, pernicious luxuries. And there is, perhaps, none of them, which is not consumed in so great abundance, as may, justly, denominate it, a source of national extravagance and impoverishment. The consumption of ardent spirits particularly, no doubt very much on account of their cheapness, is carried to an extreme, which is truly to be regretted, as well in regard to the health and the morals, as to the economy of the community.

Should the increase of duties tend to a decrease of the consumption of those articles, the effect would be, in every respect desirable. The saving which it would occasion, would leave individuals more at their ease, and promote a more favorable balance of trade. As far as this decrease might be applicable to distilled spirits, it would encourage the substitution of cyder and malt liquors, benefit agriculture, and open a new and productive source of revenue.

It is not however, probable, that this decrease would be in a degree, which would frustrate the expected benefit to the revenue from raising the duties. Experience has shewn, that luxuries of every kind, lay the strongest hold on the attachments of mankind, which, especially when confirmed by habit, are not easily alienated from them. . . .

Deeply impressed, as the Secretary is, with a full and deliberate conviction, that the establishment of public credit, upon the basis of a satisfactory provision, for the public debt is, under the present circumstances of this country, the true desideratum towards relief from individual and national embarrassments will be likely to press still more severely upon the community—He cannot but indulge an anxious wish, that an effectual plan for that purpose may, during the present session, be the result of the united wisdom of the legislature. ⌖

Opinion on the Constitutionality of the Bank (1791)

The Secretary of the Treasury having perused with attention the papers containing the opinions of the Secretary of State and Attorney General concerning the constitutionality of the bill for establishing a National Bank proceeds according to the order of the President to submit the reasons which have induced him to entertain a different opinion.

It will naturally have been anticipated that, in performing this task he would feel uncommon solicitude. Personal considerations alone arising from the reflection that the measure originated with him would be sufficient to produce it. The sense which he has manifested of the great importance of such an institution to the successful administration of the department under his particular care, and an expectation of serious ill consequences to result from a failure of the measure, do not permit him to be without anxiety on public accounts. But the chief solicitude arises from a firm persuasion, that principles of construction like those espoused by the Secretary of State and the Attorney General would be fatal to the just and indispensable authority of the United States.

In entering upon the argument it ought to be premised, that the objections of the Secretary of State and Attorney General are founded on a great denial of the authority of the United States to erect corporations. The latter indeed expressly admits, that if there be anything in the bill which is not warranted by the constitution, it is the clause of incorporation.

Now it appears to the Secretary of the Treasury, that this *general principle* is *inherent* in the very *definition* of *Government* and *essential* to every step of the progress to be made by that of the United States, namely—that every power vested in a Government is in its nature *sovereign*, and includes by *force* of the *term*, a right to employ all the *means* requisite, and fairly *applicable* to the attainment of the *ends* of such power; and which are not precluded by restrictions and exceptions specified in the constitution, or not immoral, or not contrary to the essential ends of political society. . . .

This general and indisputable principle puts at once an end to the *abstract* question. Whether the United States have power to *erect a corporation?* that is to say, to give a *legal* or *artificial* capacity to one or more persons, distinct from the natural. For it is unquestionably incident to *sovereign power* to erect corporations, and consequently to *that* of the United States in *relation to the objects* intrusted to the management of the government. The difference is this—where the authority of the government is general, it can create corporations in *all cases;* where it is confined to certain branches of legislation, it can create corporations only in those cases.

Here then as far as concerns the reasonings of the Secretary of State and the Attorney General, the affirmative of the constitutionality of the bill might be permitted to rest. It will occur to the President that the principle here advanced has been untouched by either of them. . . .

It is objected that none but *necessary* and proper means are to be employed, and the Secretary of State maintains, that no means are to be considered as *necessary* but those without which the grant of the power would be *nugatory.* . . .

It is essential to the being of the National government, that so erroneous a conception of the meaning of the word *necessary,* should be explored.

It is certain, that neither the grammatical nor popular sense of the term requires that construction. According to both, *necessary* often means no more than *needful, requisite, incidental, useful,* or *conducive to.* It is a common mode of expression to say, that it is *necessary* for a government or a person to do this thing or that thing, when nothing more is intended or understood, than that the interests of the government or person require, or will be promoted, by the doing of this or that thing. The imagination can be at no loss for exemplifications of the use of the word in this sense.

And it is the true one in which it is to be understood as used in the constitution. The whole turn of the clause containing it indicates, that it was the intent of the convention, by that clause to give a liberal latitude to the exercise of the specified powers. The expressions have peculiar comprehensiveness. They are, "to make *all laws,* necessary and proper for *carrying into execution* the foregoing powers and *all other powers* vested by the constitution in the *government* of the United States, or in any *department* or *officer* thereof." To understand the word as the Secretary of State does, would be to depart from its obvious and popular sense, and to give it a *restrictive* operation, an idea never before entertained. It would be to give it the same force as if the word *absolutely* or *indispensably* had been prefixed to it.

Such a construction would beget endless uncertainty and embarrassment. The cases must be palpable and extreme in which it could be pronounced with certainty that a measure was absolutely necessary, or one without which the exercise of a given power would be nugatory. There are few measures of any government, which would stand so severe a test. To insist upon it, would be to make the criterion of the exercise of any implied power *a case of extreme necessity;* which is rather a rule to justify the overleaping of the bounds of constitutional authority, than to govern the ordinary exercise of it.

The *degree* in which a measure is necessary, can never be a test of the *legal* right to adopt it. That must be a matter of opinion; and can only be a test of expediency. The *relation* between the *measure* and the *end,* between the *nature of the mean* employed towards the execution of a power and the object of that power, must be the criterion of constitutionality not the more or less of *necessity* or *utility.* . . .

The doctrine which is contended for . . . leaves therefore a criterion of what is constitutional, and of what is not so. This criterion is the *end,* to which the measure relates as a *mean.* If the end can be clearly comprehended within any of the specified powers, and if the measure has an obvious relation to that end, and is not forbidden by any particular provision of the constitution—it may safely be deemed to come within the compass of the national authority. There is also this further criterion which may materially assist the decision: Does the proposed measure abridge a pre-existing right of any State, or of any individual? If it does not, there is a strong presumption in favour of its constitutionality; and slighter relations to any declared object of the constitution may be permitted to turn the scale....

It is presumed to have been satisfactorily shewn in the course of the preceding observations

1. That the power of the government, *as to* the objects intrusted to its management, is in its nature sovereign.
2. That the right of erecting corporations is one, inherent in and inseparable from the idea of sovereign power.
3. That the position, that the government of the United States can exercise no power but such as is delegated to it by its constitution does not militate against this principle.
4. That the word *necessary* in the general clause can have no *restrictive* operation, derogating from the force of this principle; indeed, that the degree in which a measure is, or is not necessary, cannot be *a test of constitutional right,* but of expediency only.
5. That the power to erect corporations is not to be considered as an *independent* or *substantive* power but as an *incidental* and *auxiliary* one; and was therefore more properly left to implication, than

expressly granted.
6. That the principle in question does not extend the power of the government beyond the prescribed limits, because it only affirms a power to *incorporate* for *purposes within the sphere of the specified powers.*
7. And lastly that the right to exercise such a power, in certain cases, is unequivocally granted in the most *positive* and *comprehensive* terms.

To all which it only remains to be added that such a power has actually been exercised in two very imminent instances: namely in the erection of two governments, one, northwest of the river Ohio, and the other southwest —the *last, independent of any antecedent compact.* And there results a full and complete demonstration, that the Secretary of State and Attorney General are mistaken, when they deny generally the power of the National government to erect corporations.

It shall now be endeavoured to be shewn that there is a power to erect one of the kind proposed by the bill. This will be done, by tracing a natural and obvious relation between the institution of a bank, and the objects of several of the enumerated powers of the government; and by strewing that, *politically* speaking, it is necessary to the effectual execution of one or more of those powers. In the course of this investigation, various instances will be stated, by way of illustration of a right to erect corporation under those powers....

A Bank relates to the collection of taxes in two ways; *indirectly,* by increasing the quantity of circulating medium and quickening circulation, which facilitates the means of paying —*directly,* by creating a *convenient species* of *medium* in which they are to be paid....

A Bank has a direct relation to the power of borrowing money, because it is an usual and in sudden emergencies an essential instrument in the obtaining of loans to government.

A nation is threatened with war. Large sums are wanted, on a sudden, to make the requisite preparations. Taxes are laid for the purpose, but it requires time to obtain the benefit of them. Anticipation is indispensable. If there be a bank, the supply can, at once be had; if there be none loans from Individuals must be sought. The progress of these is often too slow for the exigency; in some situations they are not practicable at all. Frequently when they are, it is of great consequence to be able to anticipate the product of them by advances from a bank.

The essentiality of such an institution as an instrument of loans is exemplified at this very moment. An Indian expedition is to be prosecuted. The only fund out of which the money can arise consistently with the public engagements, is a tax which will only begin to be collected in July next. The preparations, however, are instantly to be made. The money must therefore be borrowed. And of whom could it be borrowed, if there were no public banks? . . .

The institution of a bank has also a natural relation to the regulation of trade between the States: in so far as it is conducive to the creation of a convenient medium of *exchange* between them, and to the keeping up a full circulation by preventing the frequent displacement of the metals in reciprocal remittances. Money is the very hinge on which commerce turns. And this does not mean merely gold and silver, many other things have served the purpose with different degrees of utility. Paper has been extensively employed. . . .

The very general power of laying and collecting taxes and appropriating their proceeds —that of borrowing money indefinitely—that of coining money and regulating foreign coins—that of making all needful rules and regulations respecting the property of the United States—these powers combined, as well as the reason and nature of the thing speak strongly this language: That it is the manifest design and scope of the constitution to vest in Congress all the powers requisite to the effectual administration of the finances of the United States. As far as concerns this object, there appears to be no parsimony of power. ∿

Report on Manufactures (1791)

The Secretary of the Treasury, in obedience to the order of ye House of Representatives, of the 15th day of January, 1790, has applied his attention, at as early a period as his other duties would permit, to the subject of Manufactures; and particularly to the means of promoting such as will tend to render the United States, independent of foreign nations for military and other essential supplies. And he thereupon respectfully submits the following Report.

The expedience of encouraging manufactures in the United States, which was not long since deemed very questionable, appears at this time to be pretty generally admitted. The embarrassments, which have obstructed the progress of our external trade, have led to serious reflections on the necessity of enlarging the sphere of our domestic commerce: the restrictive regulations, which in foreign markets abridge the vent of the increasing surplus of our Agricultural produce, serve to beget an earnest desire, that a more extensive demand for that surplus may be created at home: And the complete success, which has rewarded manufacturing enterprise, in some valuable branches, conspiring with the promising symptoms, which attend some less mature essays, in others, justify a hope, that the obstacles to the growth of this species of industry are less formidable than they were apprehended to be, and that it is not difficult to find, in its further extension a full indemnification for any external disadvantages, which are or may be experienced, as well as an accession of resources, favorable to national independence and safety.

There still are, nevertheless, respectable patrons of opinions, unfriendly to the encouragement of manufactures. The following are, substantially, the arguments, by which these opinions are defended.

In every country (say those who entertain them) Agriculture is the most beneficial and *productive* object of human industry. This position, generally, if not universally true, applies with peculiar emphasis to the United States, on account of their immense tracts of fertile territory, uninhabited and unimproved. Nothing can afford so advantageous an employment for capital and labour, as the conversion of this extensive wilderness into cultivated farms. Nothing equally with this, can contribute to the population, strength and real riches of the country.

To endeavor, by the extraordinary patronage of Government, to accelerate the growth of manufactures, is, in fact, to endeavor, by force and art, to transfer the natural current of industry from a more, to a less beneficial channel. Whatever has such a tendency must necessarily be unwise. Indeed it can hardly ever be wise in a government, to attempt to give a direction to the industry of its citizens. This under the quicksighted guidance of private interest, will, if left to itself, infallibly find its own way to the most profitable employment: and 'tis by such employment, that the public prosperity will be most effectually prompted. To leave industry to itself, therefore, is, in almost every case, the soundest as well as the simplest policy.

This policy is, not only recommended to the United States, by considerations which affect all nations it is, in a manner, dictated to them by the imperious force of a very peculiar situation. The smallness of their population compared with their territory—the constant allurements to emigration from the settled to the unsettled parts of the country—the facility, with which the less independent condition of an artisan can be exchanged for the more independent condition of a farmer—these, and similar causes conspire to produce, and, for a length of time must continue to occasion, a scarcity of hands for manufacturing occupation, and dearness of labor generally. To these disadvantages for the prosecution of manufactures, a deficiency of pecuniary capital being added, the prospect of a successful competition with the manufactures of Europe must be regarded as little less than desperate. Extensive manufactures can only be the offspring of a redundant, at least of a full population. Till the latter shall characterize the situation of this country, 'tis vain to hope for the former.

If contrary to the natural course of things, an unseasonable and premature spring can be given to certain fabrics, by heavy duties, prohibitions, bounties, or by other forced expedients; this will only be to sacrifice the interests of the community to those of particular classes. Besides the misdirection of labor, a virtual monopoly will be given to the persons employed on such fabrics; and an enhancement of price, the inevitable consequence of every monopoly, must be defrayed at the expense of the other parts of the society. It is far preferable, that those persons should be engaged in the cultivation of the earth, and that we should procure, in exchange for its productions, the commodities, with which foreigners are able to supply us in greater perfection, and upon better terms.

This mode of reasoning is founded upon facts and principles, which have certainly respectable pretensions. If it had governed the conduct of nations more generally, than it has done, there is room to suppose, that it might have carried them faster to prosperity and greatness, than they have attained, by the pursuit of maxims too widely opposite. Most general theories, however, admit of numerous exceptions, and there are few, if any, of the political kind, which do not blend a considerable portion of error, with the truths they inculcate.

In order to [reach] an accurate judgment how far that which has been just stated ought to be deemed liable to a similar inputation, it is necessary to advert carefully to the considerations, which plead in favour of manufactures, and which appear to recommend the special and positive encouragement of them; in certain cases, and under certain reasonable limitations.

It ought readily to be conceded that the cultivation of the earth—as the primary and most certain source of national supply—as the immediate and chief source of subsistence to man—as the principal source of those materials which constitute the nutriment of other kinds of labor—as including a state most favourable to the freedom and independence of the human mind—one, perhaps, most conducive to the multiplication of the human species—has *intrinsically a strong claim to pre-eminence over every other kind of industry.*

But that it has a title to any thing like an exclusive predilection, in any country, ought to be admitted with great caution. That it is even more productive than every other branch of Industry requires more evidence than has yet been given in support of the position. That its real interests, precious and important as without the help of exaggeration, they truly are, will be advanced, rather than injured by the due encouragement of manufactures, may, it is believed, be satisfactorily demonstrated. And it is also believed that the expedience of such encouragement in a general view may be shown to be recommended by the most cogent and persuasive motives of national policy....

It is now proper to proceed a step further, and to enumerate the principal circumstances, from which it may be inferred—that manufacturing establishments not only occasion a positive augmentation of the Produce and Revenue of the Society, but that they contribute essentially to rendering them greater than they could possibly be, without such establishments. These circumstances are—

1. The division of labour.
2. An extension of the use of Machinery.
3. Additional employment to classes of the community not ordinarily engaged in the business.
4. The promoting of emigration from foreign Countries.
5. The furnishing greater scope for the diversity of talents and dispositions which discriminate men from each other.
6. The affording a more ample and various field for enterprize.
7. The creating in some instances a new and securing in all, a more certain and steady demand for the surplus produce of the soil.

Each of these circumstances has a considerable influence upon the total mass of industrious effort in a community: Together, they add to it a degree of energy and effect, which are not easily conceived. Some comments upon each of them, in the order in which they have been stated, may serve to explain their importance....

In order to [form] a better judgment of the Means proper to be resorted to by the United States, it will be of use to Advert to those which have been employed with success in other Countries. The principal of these are—

I. Protecting duties—or duties on those foreign articles which are the rivals of the domestic ones intended to be encouraged. . . .
II. Prohibitions of rival articles, or duties equivalent to prohibitions. . . .
III. Prohibitions of the exportation of the materials and manufactures. . . .
IV. Pecuniary bounties.

[The last of these] has been one of the most efficacious means of encouraging manufactures, and, is in some views, the best. Though it has not yet been practiced upon by the Government of the United States (unless the allowance on the exportation of dried and pickled Fish and salted meat could be considered a bounty), and though it is less favored by Public Opinion than some other modes. Its advantages are these—

1. It is a species of encouragement more positive and direct than any other, and for that very reason, has a more immediate tendency to stimulate and uphold new enterprises, increasing the chances of profit, and diminishing the risks of loss, in the first attempts.
2. It avoids the inconvenience of a temporary augmentation of price, which is incident to some other modes, or it produces it to a less degree, either by making no addition to the charges on the rival foreign article, as in the Case of protecting duties, or by making a smaller addition. . . .
3. Bounties have not, like high protecting duties, a tendency to produce scarcity. . . .
4. Bounties are sometimes not only the best, but the only proper expedient for uniting the encouragement of a new object of agriculture, with that of a new object of manufacture. It is the Interest of the farmer to have the production of the raw material promoted, by counteracting the interference of the foreign material of the same kind. It is the Interest of the manufacturer to have the material abundant and cheap. If prior to the domestic production of the Material, in sufficient quantity, to supply the manufacturer on good terms, a duty be laid upon the importation of it from abroad, with a view to promote the raising of it at home, the Interests both of the Farmer and Manufacturer will be disserved. By either destroying the requisite supply, or raising the price of the article beyond what can be afforded to be given for it, by the Conductor of an infant manufacture, it is abandoned or fails; and there being no domestic manufactories to create a demand for the raw material, which is raised by the farmer, it is in vain, that the Competition of the like foreign article may have been destroyed.

It cannot escape notice, that the duty upon the importation of an article can not otherwise aid the domestic production of it, than by giving the latter greater advantages in the home market. It can have no influence upon the advantageous sale of the article produced in foreign markets; no tendency, therefore, to promote its exportation.

The true way to conciliate these two interests is to lay a duty on foreign *manufactures* of the material, the growth of which is desired to be encouraged, and to apply the produce of that duty, by way of bounty, either upon the production of the material itself or upon its manufacture at home, or upon both. In this disposition of the thing, the Manufacturer commences his enterprise under every advantage which is attainable, as to quantity or price of the raw material: And the Farmer, if the bounty be immediately to him, is enabled by it to enter into a successful competition with the foreign material; if the bounty be to the manufacturer on so much of the domestic material as he consumes, the operation is nearly the same; he has a motive of interest to prefer the domestic Commodity, if of equal quality, even at a higher price than the foreign, so long as the difference of prices is any thing short of the bounty which is allowed upon the article.

A Question has been made concerning the Constitutional right of the Government of the United States to apply this species of encouragement, but there is certainly no good foundation for such a question. The National Legislature has express authority "To lay and Collect taxes, duties, imposts, and excises, to pay the Debts, and provide for the *Common defence* and *general welfare*" with no other qualifications than that "all duties, imposts, and excises shall be *uniform* throughout the United States, and that no capitation or other direct tax shall be laid unless in proportion to numbers ascertained by a census or enumeration taken on the principles prescribed in the Constitution," and that "no tax or duty shall be laid on articles exported from any States."

These three qualifications excepted the power to *raise money* is plenary and *indefinite,* and the objects to which it may be *appropriated* are no less comprehensive than the payment of the Public debts, and the providing for the common defence and *general Welfare.* The terms *"general Welfare"* were doubtless intended to signify more than was expressed or imported in those which Preceded; otherwise, numerous exigencies incident to the affairs of a nation would have been left without a provision. The phrase is as comprehensive as any that could have been used, because it was not fit that the constitutional authority of the Union to appropriate its revenues should have been restricted within narrower limits than the "General Welfare" and because this necessarily

embraces a vast variety of particulars, which are susceptible neither of specification or of definition.

It is therefore of necessity left to the discretion of the National Legislature, to pronounce upon the objects, which concern the general Welfare, and for which under that description, an appropriation of money is requisite and proper. And there seems to be no room for a doubt that whatever concerns the general interests of *Learning,* of *Agriculture,* of *Manufactures,* and of *Commerce,* are within the sphere of the national Councils, *as far as regards an application of money.*

The only qualification of the generality of the Phrase in question, which seems to be admissible, is this—That the object to which an appropriation of money is to be made be *General,* and not *local;* its operation extending in fact, or by possibility, throughout the Union, and not being confined to a particular spot.

No objection ought to arise to this construction from a supposition that it would imply a power to do whatever else should appear to Congress conducive to the General Welfare. A power to appropriate money with this lattitude which is granted too *in express terms* would not carry a power to do any other thing not authorized in the constitution, either expressly or by fair implication.

In countries where there is great private wealth, much may be effected by the voluntary contributions of patriotic individuals, but in a community situated like that of the United States the public purse must supply the deficiency of private resource. In what can it be so useful, as in prompting and improving the efforts of industry?

All which is humbly submitted.

Alexander Hamilton,
Secy of the Treasury

～

For references, see the end of selection 10.

13. Thomas Jefferson: Principles and Program

THOMAS JEFFERSON (1743–1826) was born to a wealthy Virginia family, graduated from the College of William and Mary, and practiced law until he entered public life in 1769. He served in the Virginia House of Burgesses and in the Continental Congress, during which time he drafted the Declaration of Independence. Back in Virginia during the war, he drafted the constitutional provisions and legislation that would establish a truly republican government with assured civil and religious liberty, public education, and so forth. He also served as governor of Virginia before returning to Congress, where he drafted the Northwest Ordinance of 1784, the model for later organization of United States territories. After four years as minister to France, he was appointed by George Washington as the first secretary of state.

Jefferson initially cooperated with Hamilton but soon came to oppose his fiscal policies and centralization of power. Jefferson saw Hamilton's policies as enriching the wealthy through paper profits and speculation rather than through productive effort. He feared that an urban mass of impoverished and unstable workers would be created should Hamilton's goal of establishing manufacturing succeed. And he adamantly opposed the expansion of national powers at the cost of state and local responsibilities. In 1793 he resigned from the Cabinet and began with Madison to build the Democratic-Republican party as the means of opposing Hamilton and the Federalists.

Jefferson came close to winning the presidential election of 1796, which meant that he had to serve as vice president under the Federalist John Adams. He was sympathetic to the French Revolution and welcomed the representatives of the new regime. Federalists sided with England and thoroughly disapproved of the spread in the United States of the egalitarian ideas generated in France. The Federalist Congress passed the Alien and Sedition Acts in 1798 to prevent agitation by agents and sympathizers of France, many of whom were journalists and members of Jefferson's Democratic-Republican party. These statutes made it a crime to criticize the government, extended the period of residency required for naturalization as a citizen, and gave the president power summarily to deport aliens considered dangerous. These statutes not only were severely repressive but also were administered in a partisan manner to silence political opposition to the Federalist administration.

Despite serving as part of that administration, Jefferson felt obliged to act against it. He secretly drafted the Kentucky Resolutions of November 1798, which Madison carried to the Kentucky legislature for adoption. Madison then drafted a very similar resolution, which shortly thereafter became the Virginia Resolutions of December 1798. These resolutions express in unequivocal terms

Jefferson's views on the nature of the union and on the proper remedy for unconstitutional acts by the national government. They declare the union to be a compact of states in which each state retains the right to judge whether the national government has exceeded the powers granted it. Where the government has done so, Jefferson's draft suggests, a state may declare such action void within its jurisdiction and call a convention of the other states to resolve the issue. Jefferson noted carefully that only extreme provocation would warrant such a declaration, but he went on to show in detail how the intrusion of the Alien and Sedition Laws on basic political freedoms was just such a violation of the Constitution.

The Kentucky and Virginia Resolutions were a major rallying point for the Democratic-Republican party and sparked equivalent resentment from the Federalists. Their theory of the union, their view that the states rather than the federal judiciary should judge whether Congress had exceeded its powers, and their defense of freedom of speech and the press in this instance came under heavy attack from Federalist journalists and state legislatures. To refute these charges and to keep the mobilizing effect of the resolutions alive, the Virginia legislature appointed Madison chairman of a committee to consider the allegations made. Working closely with Jefferson, Madison produced a lengthy document in 1799 incorporating all the positions taken in the earlier resolutions, defended them historically and prudentially, and called for all to rally around the defense of civil liberties (and by implication, of the Democratic-Republican party). The first selection given here consists of excerpts from this last document.

Partly as a result of reaction against the Alien and Sedition Laws and the prosecutions undertaken to carry them out, the Democratic-Republicans won the election of 1800. With Hamilton's help, Jefferson was chosen president over Aaron Burr, with whom he had been tied in the electoral-college balloting. As president, Jefferson practiced a simple economy but left the Hamiltonian structure and policies essentially untouched. He was committed to decentralization and agrarianism and opposed to speculation and urbanization. His belief in strictly limited national powers was suspended, however, when the opportunity arose to acquire the vast Louisiana Purchase. His correspondence and his efforts in founding the University of Virginia provide some of the clearest insights into his basic principles. Because he never wrote a comprehensive statement of his beliefs, we must turn for understanding to a selection of his addresses, letters, and drafts of legislation. Excerpts of these follow the first selection.

Jefferson was forever the Lockean—stressing the independence that land ownership yields to the stalwart yeoman, emphasizing the limits that property imposes on the scope of government action, and consistently including ownership of property among the sources of virtue. He also remained steadfast, however, in insisting on government by the living, in the sense of people having the right to change their governments or interpretations of their constitutions at least once per generation —powers that in the eyes of many constituted distinct threats to property. His major principle was, in his words, to "cherish the people"; this was to be done through their maximum participation in the decisions of government. This principle lies behind his strict constructionist view of the Constitution, his opposition to judicial review, his support for interpretation by the states, and his decentralization ideas. Whatever could be decided by the people should be, and at the lowest possible level.

To some extent, Jefferson's commitment to popular decision making was a relative matter, generated out of his greater fear for what might happen if decisions were made exclusively by elites with various self-serving inclinations. But it was also a matter of principle: he saw in the people innate capacities to make at least some forms of decision, he was optimistic in general about their trustworthiness, and he cared about individual growth and fulfillment. This did not prevent him from "covering his bet" somewhat: he carefully prescribed the books to be employed in the curriculum of his University of Virginia so that Republican (as opposed to exclusively Federalist) views would predominate, and in his letters, particularly to John Adams, he showed his enduring judgment that a natural aristocracy of talent was a vital component of good government. This was not a lately acquired view or one offered for Adams's benefit. A concern for the proper aristocracy lay behind his insistence on a role for the people in all forms of candidate selection and election. He believed that choice by the people was the best way of recognizing appropriate talents and of installing them in positions of governmental responsibility—much to be preferred to the risks of self-appointed leadership or aristocracies of wealth.

It seems clear that Jefferson was far from the radical that some of his Federalist opponents thought him. He was convinced that there were limits beyond which popular capacity was exhausted and should not be trusted. Men of talent (and like most of his era, he excluded women from consideration) were the proper leaders and governors. Where he differed from his detractors was in how to define talent and how to identify those who had it. These are important, perhaps vital, differences, but he still subscribed to government by individuals quite distinct from the common person and did not hesitate to declare it. We have noted his enduring concern for property, both as the basis of political independence and as an educator towards good citizenship. In the context of the times, he was perceived by nervous Federalists as a populist demagogue, which he was not. The confusion was neither the first nor the last occasion on which property-oriented liberals perceived human or civil-rights liberals as radical redistributors of property. On the evidence, Jefferson was very much of the center, and Federalist perceptions were more a testimony to the capacity of those who are well-off to imagine depredations on their property than to any inherent intentions of Thomas Jefferson. ∽

"Madison's Report to the Virginia General Assembly" (1800)

... The third resolution is in the words following:

> That this Assembly doth explicitly and peremptorily declare, that it views the powers of the Federal Government, as resulting from the compact, to which the States are parties, as limited by the plain sense and intention of the instrument constituting that compact; as no farther valid than they are authorized by the grants enumerated in that compact; and that in case of a *deliberate, palpable* and *dangerous* exercise of other powers not granted by the said compact, the states who are parties thereto, have the right, and are in duty bound, to interpose, for arresting the progress of the evil, and for maintaining within their respective limits, the authorities, rights and liberties appertaining to them.

It appears to your committee to be a plain principle, founded in common sense, illustrated by common practice, and essential to the nature of compacts; that where resort can be had to no tribunal superior to the authority of the parties the parties themselves must be the rightful judges in the last resort, whether the bargain made, has been pursued or violated. The Constitution of the United States was formed by the sanction of the States, given by each in its sovereign capacity. It adds to the stability and dignity, as well as to the authority of the Constitution, that it rests on this legitimate and solid foundation. The States then being the parties to the constitutional compact, and in their sovereign capacity, it follows of necessity, that there can be no tribunal above their authority, to decide in the last resort, whether the compact made by them be violated; and consequently that as the parties to it, they must themselves decide in the last resort, such questions as may be of sufficient magnitude to require their interposition.

It does not follow, however, that because the States as sovereign parties to their constitutional compact, must ultimately decide whether it has been violated, that such a decision ought to be interposed either in a hasty manner, or on doubtful and inferior occasions. Even in the case of ordinary conventions between different nations, where, by the strict rule of interpretation, a breach of a part may be deemed a condition of every other part, and of the whole, it is always laid down that the breach must be both wilful and material to justify an application of the rule. But in the case of an intimate and constitutional union, like that of the United States, it is evident that the inter-

SOURCE: "Madison's Report to the Virginia General Assembly, January 1800 (Relevant to the Responses of the Other States to the Virginia Resolution of 1798)," *The Kentucky-Virginia Resolutions and Mr. Madison's Report of 1799* (Richmond, Va.: Virginia Commission on Constitutional Government, 1960).

position of the parties, in their sovereign capacity, can be called for by occasions only deeply and essentially affecting the vital principles of their political system. . . .

But it is objected that the judicial authority is to be regarded as the sole expositor of the Constitution, in the last resort; and it may be asked for what reason, the declaration by the General Assembly, supposing it to be theoretically true, could be required at the present day and in so solemn a manner.

On this objection it might be observed *first,* that there may be instances of usurped power, which the forms of the Constitution would never draw within the control of the Judicial Department: *secondly,* that if the decision of the judiciary be raised above the authority of the sovereign parties to the Constitution, the decisions of the other departments, not carried by the forms of the Constitution before the judiciary, must be equally authoritative and final with the decisions of that department. But the proper answer to the objection is, that the resolution of the General Assembly relates to those great and extraordinary cases, in which all the forms of the Constitution may prove ineffectual against infractions dangerous to the essential rights of the parties to it. The resolution supposes that dangerous powers not delegated, may not only be usurped and executed by the other departments, but that the Judicial Department also may exercise or sanction dangerous powers beyond the grant of the Constitution, and consequently that the ultimate right of the parties to the Constitution, to judge whether the compact has been dangerously violated, must extend to violations by one delegated authority, as well as by another; by the judiciary, as well as by the executive, or the legislature.

However true therefore it may be that the Judicial Department is, in all questions submitted to it by the forms of the Constitution, to decide in the last resort, this resort must necessarily be deemed the last in relations to the authorities of the other departments of the government; not in relation to the rights of the parties to the constitutional compact, from which the judicial as well as the other departments hold their delegated trusts. On any other hypothesis, the delegation of judicial power, would annul the authority delegating it; and the concurrence, of this department with the others in usurped powers, might subvert forever, and beyond the possible reach of any rightful remedy, the very Constitution, which all were instituted to preserve....

The resolution next in order, is contained in the following terms:

That the General Assembly doth particularly protest against the palpable, and alarming infractions of the Constitution, in the two late cases of the "Alien and Sedition acts," passed at the last session of Congress; the first of which, exercises a power no where delegated to the Federal government; and which by winning legislative and judicial powers to those of executive, subverts the general principles of a free government, as well as the particular organization, and positive provisions of the Federal Constitution; and the other of which acts, exercises in like manner, a power not delegated by the Constitution, but on the contrary, expressly and positively forbidden by one of the amendments thereto;—a power, which more than any other, ought to produce universal alarm; because it is leveled against that right of freely examining public characters and measures, and of free communication among the people thereon, which has ever been justly deemed the only effectual guardian of every other right....

In the administration of preventive justice, the following principles have been held sacred;

that some probable ground of suspicion be exhibited before some judicial authority; that it be supported by oath or affirmation; that the party may avoid being thrown into confinement, by finding pledges or sureties for his legal conduct sufficient in the judgment of some judicial authority; that he may have the benefit of a writ of habeas corpus, and thus obtain his release, if wrongfully confined, and that he may at any time be discharged from his recognizance, or his confinement, and restored to his former liberty and rights, on the order of the proper judicial authority; if it shall see sufficient cause.

All these principles of the only preventive justice known to American jurisprudence, are violated by the Alien Act. The ground of suspicion is to be judged of, not by any judicial authority, but by the executive magistrate alone; no oath or affirmation is required; if the suspicion be held reasonable by the President, he may order the suspected alien to depart the territory of the United States, without the opportunity of avoiding the sentence, by finding pledges for his future good conduct; as the President may limit the time of departure as he pleases, the benefit of the writ of habeas corpus, may be suspended with respect to the party, although the Constitution ordains, that it shall not be suspended, unless when the public safety may require it in case of rebellion or invasion, neither of which existed at the passage of the act: And the party being, under the sentence of the President, either removed from the United States, or being punished by imprisonment, or disqualification ever to become a citizen on conviction of not obeying the order of removal, he cannot be discharged from the proceedings against him, and restored to the benefits of his former situation, although the *highest judicial authority* should see the most sufficient cause for it.

But, in the last place, it can never be admitted, that the removal of aliens, authorized by the act; is to be considered, not as punishment for an offence; but as a measure of precaution and prevention. If the banishment of an alien from a country into which he has been invited, as the asylum most auspicious to his happiness; a country, where he may have formed the most tender of connections, where he may have vested his entire property, and acquired property of the real and permanent, as well as the moveable and temporary kind; where he enjoys under the laws, a greater share of the blessings of personal security and personal liberty, than he can elsewhere hope for, and where he may have nearly compleated his probationary title to citizenship; if moreover, in the execution of the sentence against him, he is to be exposed, not only to the ordinary dangers of the sea, but to the peculiar casualties incident to a crisis of war, and of unusual licentiousness on that element and possibly to vindictive purposes which his emigration itself may have provoked; if a banishment of this sort be not a punishment, and among the severest of punishments, it will be difficult to imagine a doom to which the name can be applied. And if it be a punishment, it will remain to be enquired, whether it can be constitutionally inflicted, on mere suspicion, by the single will of the executive magistrate, on persons convicted of no personal offence against the laws of the land, nor involved in any offence against the law of nations, charged on the foreign state of which they are members. . . .

The *second* object against which the resolution protests is the Sedition Act.

Of this act it is affirmed (1) that it exercises in like manner a power not delegated by the Constitution; (2) that the power, on the contrary, is expressly and positively forbidden by one of the amendments to the Constitution; (3) that this is a power, which more than any other ought to produce universal alarm; because it is leveled against that right of freely examining public characters and measures,

and of free communication thereon; which has ever been justly deemed the only effectual guardian of every other right.

I. That it exercises a power not delegated by the Constitution.

Here, again it will be proper to recollect, that the Federal Government being composed of powers specifically granted, with a reservation of all others to the States or to the people, the positive authority under which the Sedition Act could be passed must be produced by those who assert its constitutionality. In what part of the Constitution then is this authority to be found?

Several attempts have been made to answer this question, which will be examined in their order. The committee will begin with one, which has filled them with equal astonishment and apprehension; and which, they cannot but persuade themselves, must have the same effect on all, who will consider it with coolness and impartiality, and with a reverence for our Constitution, in the true character in which it issued from the sovereign authority of the people. The committee refer to the doctrine lately advanced as a sanction to the Sedition Act: "that the common or unwritten law," a law of vast extent and complexity, and embracing almost every possible subject of legislation, both civil and criminal, "makes a part of the law of these States; in their united and national capacity."

The novelty, and in the judgment of the committee, the extravagance of this pretension, would have consigned it to the silence, in which they have passed by other arguments, which an extraordinary zeal for the act has drawn into the discussion. But the auspices, under which this innovation presents itself, have constrained the committee to bestow on it an attention, which other considerations might have forbidden.

In executing the task, it may be of use, to look back to the colonial state of this country, prior to the revolution; to trace the effect of the revolution which converted the colonies into independent States; to enquire into the import of the articles of confederation, the first instrument by which the union of the States was regularly established; and finally to consult the Constitution of 1788, which is the oracle that must decide the important question.

In the State prior to the revolution, it is certain that the common law under different limitations, made a part of the colonial codes. But whether it be understood that the original colonists brought the law with them, or made it their law by adoption; it is equally certain that it was the separate law of each colony within its respective limits, and was unknown to them, as a law pervading and operating through the whole, as one society.

It could not possibly be otherwise. The common law was not the same in any two of the colonies; in some, the modifications were materially and extensively different. There was no common legislature, by which a common will, could be expressed in the form of a law; nor any common magistracy, by which such a law could be carried into practice. The will of each colony alone and separately, had its organs for these purposes.

This stage of our political history, furnishes no foothold for the patrons of this new doctrine.

Did then, the principle or operation of the great event which made the colonies, independent states, imply or introduce the common law, as a law of the union?

The fundamental principle of the revolution was, that the colonies were coordinate members with each other, and with Great Britain; of an Empire, united by a common Executive Sovereign, but not united by any common Legislative Sovereign. The Legislative power was maintained to be as complete in each American Parliament, as in the British Parliament....

Such being the ground of our revolution, no support nor colour can be drawn from it, for the doctrines that the common law is binding on these States as one society. The doctrine on the contrary, is evidently repugnant to the fundamental principle of the revolution.

The articles of confederation, are the next source of information on this subject.

In the interval between the commencement of the revolution, and the final ratification of these articles, the nature and extent of the union was determined by the circumstances of the crisis, rather than by any accurate delineation of the general authority. It will not be alleged that the "common law," could have had any legitimate birth as a law of the United States, during that state of things. If it came as such, into existence at all, the charter of confederation must have been its parent.

Here again, however, its pretensions are absolutely destitute of foundation. This instrument does not contain a sentence or syllable, that can be tortured into a countenance of the idea, that the parties to it were with respect to the objects of the common law, to form one community. No such law is named or implied, or alluded to, as being in force or as brought into force by that compact. No provision is made by which such a law could be carried into operation; whilst on the other hand, every such inference or pretext is absolutely precluded, by article 2d, which declares "that each State retains its sovereignty, freedom and independence, and every power, jurisdiction and right, which is not by this confederation expressly delegated to the United States, in Congress assembled."

Thus far it appears, that not a vestige of this extraordinary doctrine can be found, in the origin or progress of American institutions. The evidence against it, has, on the contrary, grown stronger at every step; till it has amounted to a formal and positive exclusion, by written articles of compact among the parties concerned.

II. The next point which the resolution requires to be proved is, that the power over the press exercised by the Sedition Act, is positively forbidden by one of the amendments to the Constitution. . . .

The amendment stands in these words— "Congress shall make no law respecting the establishment of religion, or prohibiting the free exercise thereof, *or abridging the freedom of speech or of the press;* or the right of the people peaceably to assemble and to petition the government for a redress of grievances." . . .

. . . Some degree of abuse is inseparable from the proper use of every thing; and in no instance is this more true, than in that of the press. It has accordingly been decided by the practice of the States, that it is better to leave a few of its noxious branches, to their luxuriant growth, than by pruning them away, to injure the vigor of those yielding the proper fruits. And can the wisdom of this policy be doubted by any who reflect, that to the press alone, chequered as it is with abuses, the world is indebted for all the triumphs which have been gained by reason and humanity, over error and oppression; who reflect that to the same beneficient source, the United States owe much of the lights which conducted them to the rank of a free and independent nation; and which have improved their political system, into a shape so auspicious to their happiness. Had "sedition acts," forbidding every publication that might bring the constituted agents into contempt or disrepute, or that might excite the hatred of the people against the authors of unjust or pernicious measures, been uniformly enforced against the press; might not the United States have been languishing at this day, under the infirmities of a sickly confederation? Might they not possibly be miserable colonies, groaning under a foreign yoke? . . .

When the Constitution was under the discussions which preceded its ratification, it is well known, that great apprehensions were expressed by many, lest the omission of some positive exception from the powers delegated, of certain rights, and of the freedom of the press particularly, might expose them to the danger of being drawn by construction within some of the powers vested in Congress; more especially of the power to make all laws necessary and proper, for carrying their own powers into execution. . . .

. . . In most of the States, the ratifications were followed by propositions, and instructions for rendering the Constitution more explicit, and more safe to the rights, not meant to be delegated by it. Among those rights, the freedom of the press, in most instances, is particularly and emphatically mentioned.

In pursuance of the wishes thus expressed, the first Congress that assembled under the constitution, proposed certain amendments which have since, by the necessary ratifications, been made a part of it; among which amendments is the article containing, among other prohibitions on the Congress, an express declaration that they should make no law abridging the freedom of the press.

Without tracing farther the evidence on this subject, it would seem scarcely possible to doubt, that no power whatever over the press, was supposed to be delegated by the Constitution, as it originally stood; and that the amendment was intended as a positive and absolute reservation of it. . . .

III. And in the opinion of the committee well may it be said, as the resolution concludes with saying, that the unconstitutional power exercised over the press by the "Sedition Act," ought "more than any other, to produce universal alarm because it is leveled against that right of freely examining public characters and measures, and of free communication among the people thereon, which has ever been justly deemed the only effectual guardian of every other right."

Without scrutinizing minutely into all the provisions of the "Sedition Act," it will be sufficient to cite so much of section 2. as follows: "And be it further enacted, that if any person shall write, print, utter, or publish, or shall cause or procure to be written, printed, uttered or published, or shall knowingly and willingly assist or aid in writing, printing, uttering or publishing any false, scandalous, and malicious writing or writings against the government of the United States, or either house of the Congress of the United States or the President of the United States, *with an intent to defame the said government, or either house of the said Congress, or the President, or to bring them, or either of them, into contempt or disrepute; or to excite against them, or either, or any of them, the hatred of the good people of the United States, &c. Then such person being thereof convicted before any court of the United States, having jurisdiction thereof, shall be punished by a fine not exceeding two thousand dollars, and by imprisonment not exceeding two years."* ...

May it not be asked of every intelligent friend to the liberties of his country whether, the power exercised in such an act as this, ought not to produce great and universal alarm?

Whether a rigid execution of such an act, in time past, would not have repressed that information and communication among the people, which is indispensable to the just exercise of their electoral rights? And whether such an act, if made perpetual, and enforced with rigor, would not, in time to come, either destroy our free system of government, or prepare a convulsion that might prove equally fatal to it.

The extensive view of the subject thus taken by the committee, has led them to report to the house, as the result of the whole, the following resolution.

Resolved, That the General Assembly, having carefully and respectfully attended to the proceedings of a number of the States, in answer to their resolutions of December 21, 1798, and having accurately and fully re-examined and reconsidered the latter, find it to be their indispensable duty to adhere to the same, as founded in the truth, as consonant with the Constitution, and as conducive to its preservation; and more especially to be their duty, to renew, as they do hereby renew, their protest against "the Alien and Sedition Acts," as palpable and alarming infractions of the Constitution. ～

Notes on Virginia (1785)

The error seems not sufficiently eradicated that the operations of the mind, as well as the acts of the body, are subject to the coercion of the laws. But our rulers can have authority over

SOURCE: Remaining passages in this selection may be found in Edward Dumbauld, ed., *Jefferson: His Political Writings* (Indianapolis: Bobbs-Merrill, 1955).

such natural rights only as we have submitted to them. The rights of conscience we never submitted, we could not submit. We are answerable for them to our God. The legitimate powers of government extend to such acts only as are injurious to others. But it does me no injury for my neighbor to say there are twenty gods or no God. It neither picks my pocket nor breaks my leg. If it be said his testimony in a court of justice cannot be relied on, reject it then, and be the stigma on him. Constraint may make him worse by making him a hypocrite, but it will never make him a truer man. It may fix him obstinately in his errors but will not cure them. Reason and free inquiry are the only effectual agents against error. Give a loose rein to them, they will support the true religion by bringing every false one to their tribunal, to the test of their investigation. They are the natural enemies of error, and of error only. Had not the Roman government permitted free inquiry, Christianity could never have been introduced. Had not free inquiry been indulged at the era of the Reformation, the corruptions of Christianity could not have been purged away. If it be restrained now, the present corruptions will be protected and new ones encouraged. Were the government to prescribe to us our medicine and diet, our bodies would be in such keeping as our souls are now. Thus in France the emetic was once forbidden as a medicine, and the potato as an article of food. Government is just as infallible, too, when it fixes systems in physics. Galileo was sent to the Inquisition for affirming that the earth was a sphere; the government had declared it to be as flat as a trencher, and Galileo was obliged to abjure his error. This error, however, at length prevailed; the earth became a globe, and Descartes declared it was whirled round its axis by a vortex. The government in which he lived was wise enough to see that this was no question of civil jurisdiction, or we should all have been involved by authority in vortices. In fact, the vortices have been exploded, and the Newtonian principle of gravitation is now more firmly established, on the basis of reason, than it would be were the government to step in and to make it an article of necessary faith. Reason and experiment have been indulged, and error has fled before them. It is error alone which needs the support of government. Truth can stand by

itself. Subject opinion to coercion: whom will you make your inquisitors? Fallible men; men governed by bad passions, by private as well as public reasons. And why subject it to coercion? To produce uniformity. But is uniformity of opinion desirable? No more than of face and stature. Introduce the bed of Procrustes then; and, as there is danger that the large men may beat the small, make us all of a size by lopping the former and stretching the latter. Difference of opinion is advantageous in religion. The several sects perform the office of *censor morum* over each other. Is uniformity attainable? Millions of innocent men, women, and children, since the introduction of Christianity, have been burned, tortured, fined, imprisoned; yet we have not advanced one inch toward uniformity. What has been the effect of coercion? To make one half the world fools and the other half hypocrites; to support roguery and error all over the earth. Let us reflect that it is inhabited by a thousand millions of people; that these profess probably a thousand different systems of religion; that ours is but one of that thousand; that if there be but one right, and ours that one, we should wish to see the nine hundred and ninety-nine wandering sects gathered into the fold of truth. But against such a majority we cannot effect this by force. Reason and persuasion are the only practicable instruments. To make way for these, free inquiry must be indulged; and how can we wish others to indulge it while we refuse it ourselves? But every state, says an inquisitor, has established some religion. No two, say I, have established the same. Is this a proof of the infallibility of establishments? Our sister States of Pennsylvania and New York, however, have long subsisted without any establishment at all. The experiment was new and doubtful when they made it. It has answered beyond conception. They flourish infinitely. Religion is well supported; of various kinds, indeed, but all good enough; all sufficient to preserve peace and order; or if a sect arises whose tenets would subvert morals, good sense has fair play, and reasons and laughs it out of doors without suffering the state to be troubled with it. They do not hang more malefactors than we do. They are not more disturbed with religious dissensions. On the contrary, their harmony is unparalleled and can be ascribed to nothing but their unbounded tolerance, because there is no other circumstance in which they differ from every nation on earth. They have made the happy discovery that the way to silence religious disputes is to take no notice of them. Let us too give this experiment fair play and get rid, while we may, of those tyrannical laws. It is true we are as yet secured against them by the spirit of the times. I doubt whether the people of this country would suffer an execution for heresy, or a three years' imprisonment for not comprehending the mysteries of the Trinity. But is the spirit of the people an infallible, a permanent reliance? Is it government? Is this the kind of protection we receive in return for the rights we give up? Besides, the spirit of the times may alter, will alter. Our rulers will become corrupt, our people careless. A single zealot may commence persecution, and better men be his victims. It can never be too often repeated that the time for fixing every essential right on a legal basis is while our rulers are honest and ourselves united. From the conclusion of this war we shall be going downhill. It will not then be necessary to resort every moment to the people for support. They will be forgotten, therefore, and their rights disregarded. They will forget themselves but in the sole faculty of making money, and will never think of uniting to effect a due respect for their rights. The shackles, therefore, which shall not be knocked off at the conclusion of this war will remain on us long, will be made heavier and heavier, till our rights shall revive or expire in a convulsion. ∼

First Inaugural Address (1801)

Friends and Fellow Citizens: Called upon to undertake the duties of the first executive office of our country, I avail myself of the presence of that portion of my fellow citizens which is here assembled, to express my grateful thanks for the favor with which they have been pleased to look toward me, to declare a sincere consciousness that the task is above my talents, and that I approach it with those anxious and awful presentiments which the greatness of the charge and the weakness of my powers so justly inspire. A rising nation, spread over a wide and fruitful land, traversing all the seas with the rich productions of their industry, engaged in commerce with nations who feel power and forget right, advancing rapidly to destinies beyond the reach of mortal eye—when I contemplate these transcendent objects, and see the honor, the happiness, and the hopes of this beloved country committed to the issue and the auspices of this day, I shrink from the contemplation, and humble myself before the magnitude of the undertaking. Utterly indeed, should I despair, did not the presence of many whom I here see remind me, that in the other high authorities provided by our constitution, I shall find resources of wisdom, of virtue, and of zeal, on which to rely under all difficulties. To you, then, gentlemen, who are charged with the sovereign functions of legislation, and to those associated with you, I look with encouragement for that guidance and support which may enable us to steer with safety the vessel in which we are all embarked amid the conflicting elements of a troubled world.

During the contest of opinion through which we have passed, the animation of discussion and of exertions has sometimes worn an aspect which might impose on strangers unused to think freely and to speak and to write what they think; but this being now decided by the voice of the nation, announced according to the rules of the constitution, all will, of course, arrange themselves under the will of the law, and unite in common efforts for the common good. All, too, will bear in mind this sacred principle, that though the will of the majority is in all cases to prevail, that will, to be rightful, must be reasonable; that the minority possess their equal rights, which equal laws must protect, and to violate which would be oppression. Let us, then, fellow-citizens, unite with one heart and one mind. Let us restore to social intercourse that harmony and affection without which liberty and even life itself are but dreary things. And let us reflect that having banished from our land that religious intolerance under which mankind so long bled and suffered, we have yet gained little if we countenance a political intolerance as despotic, as wicked, and capable of as bitter and bloody persecutions. During the throes and convulsions of the ancient world, during the agonizing spasms of infuriated man, seeking through blood and slaughter his long-lost liberty, it was not wonderful that the agitation of the billows should reach even this distant and peaceful shore; that this should be more felt and feared by some and less by others; that this should divine opinions as to measures of safety. But every difference of opinion is not a difference of principle. We have called by different names brethren of the same principle. We are all republicans—we are federalists. If there be any among us who would wish to dis-

solve this Union or to change its republican form, let them stand undisturbed as monuments of the safety with which error of opinion may be tolerated where reason is left free to combat it. I know, indeed, that some honest men fear that a republican government cannot be strong; that this government is not strong enough. But would the honest patriot, in the full tide of successful experiment abandon a government which has so far kept us free and firm, on the theoretic and visionary fear that this government, the world's best hope, may by possibility want energy to preserve itself? I trust not. I believe this, on the contrary, the strongest government on earth. I believe it is the only one where every man, at the call of the laws, would fly to the standard of the law, and would meet invasions of the public order as his own personal concern. Sometimes it is said that man cannot be trusted with the government of himself. Can he, then, be trusted with the government of others? Or have we found angels in the forms of kings to govern him? Let history answer this question.

Let us, then, with courage and confidence pursue our own federal and republican principles, our attachment to our union and representative government. Kindly separated by nature and a wide ocean from the exterminating havoc of one quarter of the globe; too high-minded to endure the degradations of the others; possessing a chosen country, with room enough for our descendants to the hundredth and thousandth generation; entertaining a due sense of our equal right to the use of our own faculties, to the acquisitions of our industry, to honor and confidence from our fellow citizens, resulting not from birth but from our actions and their sense of them; enlightened by a benign religion, professed, indeed, and practiced in various forms, yet all of them including honesty, truth, temperance, gratitude, and the love of man; acknowledging and adoring an overruling Providence, which by all its dispensations proves that it delights in the happiness of man here and his greater happiness hereafter; with all these blessings, what more is necessary to make us a happy and prosperous people? Still one thing more, fellow citizens —a wise and frugal government, which shall restrain men from injuring one another, which shall leave them otherwise free to regulate their own pursuits of industry and improvement, and shall not take from the mouth of labor the bread it has earned. This is the sum of good government, and this is necessary to close the circle of our felicities.

About to enter, fellow citizens, on the exercise of duties which comprehend everything dear and valuable to you, it is proper that you should understand what I deem the essential principles of our government, and consequently those which ought to shape its administration. I will compress them within the narrowest compass they will bear, stating the general principle, but not all its limitations. Equal and exact justice to all men, of whatever state or persuasion, religious or political; peace, commerce, and honest friendship with all nations—entangling alliances with none; the support of the State governments in all their rights, as the most competent administrations for our domestic concerns and the surest bulwarks against anti-republican tendencies; the preservation of the general government in its whole constitutional vigor, as the sheet anchor of our peace at home and safety abroad; a jealous care of the right of election by the people —a mild and safe corrective of abuses which are lopped by the sword of the revolution where peaceable remedies are unprovided; absolute acquiescence in the decisions of the majority—the vital principle of republics, from which there is no appeal but to force, the vital principle and immediate parent of despotism; a well-disciplined militia—our best reliance in peace and for the first moments of war, till regulars may relieve them; the supremacy of

the civil over the military authority; economy in the public expense, that labor may be lightly burdened; the honest payment of our debts and sacred preservation of the public faith; encouragement of agriculture, and of commerce as its handmaid; the diffusion of information and the arraignment of all abuses at the bar of public reason; freedom of religion; freedom of the press; freedom of person under the protection of the *habeas corpus;* and trial by juries impartially selected—these principles form the bright constellation which has gone before us, and guided our steps through an age of revolution and reformation. The wisdom of our sages and the blood of our heroes have been devoted to their attainment. They should be the creed of our political faith—the text of civil instruction—the touchstone by which to try the services of those we trust; and should we wander from them in moments of error or alarm, let us hasten to retrace our steps and to regain the road which alone leads into peace, liberty, and safety.

I repair, then, fellow citizens, to the post you have assigned me. With experience enough in subordinate offices to have seen the difficulties of this, the greatest of all, I have learned to expect that it will rarely fall to the lot of imperfect man to retire from this station with the reputation and the favor which bring him into it. Without pretensions to that high confidence reposed in our first and great revolutionary character, whose preeminent services had entitled him to the first place in his country's love, and destined for him the fairest page in the volume of faithful history, I ask so much confidence only as may give firmness and effect to the legal administration of your affairs. I shall often go wrong through defect of judgment. When right, I shall often be thought wrong by those whose positions will not command a view of the whole ground. I ask your indulgence for my own errors, which will never be intentional; and your support against the errors of others, who may condemn what they would not if seen in all its parts. The approbation implied by your suffrage is a consolation to me for the past; and my future solicitude will be to retain the good opinion of those who have bestowed it in advance, to conciliate that of others by doing them all the good in my power, and to be instrumental to the happiness and freedom of all.

Relying, then, on the patronage of your good will, I advance with obedience to the work, ready to retire from it whenever you become sensible how much better choice it is in your power to make. And may that Infinite Power which rules the destinies of the universe, lead our councils to what is best, and give them a favorable issue for your peace and prosperity. ⌒

Selected Letters (1787–1823)

LETTER TO WILLIAM S. SMITH (1787)

November 1787

God forbid we should ever be twenty years without such a rebellion [Shays's Rebellion]. The people cannot be all, and always, well-informed. The part which is wrong will be discontented in proportion to the importance of the facts they misconceive. If they remain quiet under such misconceptions, it is a lethargy, the forerunner of death to the public liberty. We have had thirteen States independent for eleven years. There has been one rebellion. That comes to one rebellion in a century and a half for each State. What country before ever existed a century and a half without a rebellion? And what country can preserve its liberties if its rulers are not warned from time to time that this people preserve the spirit of resistance? Let them take arms. The remedy is to set them right as to facts, pardon and pacify them. What signify a few lives lost in a century or two? The tree of liberty must be refreshed from time to time with the blood of patriots and tyrants. It is its natural manure. Our convention has been too much impressed by the insurrection of Massachusetts, and on the spur of the moment they are setting up a kite to keep the hen yard in order.

LETTER TO JAMES MADISON (1787)

Paris, December 1787

Dear Sir, ... The season admitting only of operations in the Cabinet, and these being in a great measure secret, I have little to fill a letter. I will therefore make up the deficiency by adding a few words on the Constitution proposed by our Convention. I like much the general idea of framing a government which should go on of itself peaceably, without needing continual recurrence to the state legislatures. I like the organization of the government into Legislative, Judiciary and Executive. I like the power given the Legislature to levy taxes, and for that reason solely approve of the greater house being chosen by the people directly. For tho' I think a house chosen by them will be very illy qualified to legislate for the Union, for foreign nations etc. yet this evil does not weigh against the good of preserving inviolate the fundamental principle that the people are not to be taxed but by representatives chosen immediately by themselves. I am captivated by the compromise of the opposite claims of the great and little states, of the latter to equal, and the former to proportional influence. I am much pleased too with the substitution of the method of voting by persons, instead of that of voting by states: and I like the negative given to the Executive with a third of either house though I should have liked it better had the Judiciary been associated for that purpose, or invested with a similar and separate power. There are other good things of less moment. I will now add what I do not like. First the omission of a bill of rights providing clearly and without the aid of sophisms for freedom of religion, freedom of the press, protection against standing armies, restriction against monopolies, the eternal and unremitting force of the habeas corpus laws, and trials by jury in all matters of fact triable by the laws of the land and not by the law of nations. To say, as Mr. Wilson does, that a bill of rights was not necessary because all is reserved in the case of the general government which is not given, while the particular ones all is given which is not reserved, might do for the audience to whom it was addressed, but is surely a *gratis dictum,* opposed by strong inferences from the body of the instrument, as well as from the omission of the clause of our present confederation which had declared that in express terms. It was a hard conclusion to say because there has been no uniformity among the states as to the cases triable by jury, because some have been so incautious as to abandon this mode of trial, therefore the more prudent states shall be reduced to the same level of calamity. It would have been much more just and wise to have concluded the other way that as most of the states had judiciously preserved this palladium, those who had wandered should be brought back to it, and to have established general right instead of general wrong. Let me add that a bill of rights is what the people are entitled to against every government on earth, general or particular, and what no just government should refuse, or rest on inferences. The second feature I dislike, and

greatly dislike, is the abandonment in every instance of the necessity of rotation in office, and most particularly in the case of the President. Experience concurs with reason in concluding that the first magistrate will always be reelected if the Constitution permits it. He is then an officer for life. This once observed, it becomes of so much consequence to certain nations to have a friend or a foe at the head of our affairs that they will interfere with money and with arms. A Galloman or an Angloman will be supported by the nation he befriends. If once elected, and at a second or third election out voted by one or two votes, he will pretend false votes, foul play, hold possession of the reins of government, be supported by the States voting for him, especially if they are the central ones lying in a compact body themselves and separating their opponents: and they will be aided by one nation of Europe, while the majority are aided by another. The election of a President of America some years hence will be much more interesting to certain nations of Europe than ever the election of a king of Poland was. Reflect on all the instances in history ancient and modern, of elective monarchies, and say if they do not give foundation for my fears. The Roman emperors, the popes, while they were of any importance, the German emperors till they became hereditary in practice, the kings of Poland, the Deys of the Ottoman dependences. It may be said that if elections are to be attended with these disorders, the seldomer they are renewed the better. But experience shows that the only way to prevent disorder is to render them uninteresting by frequent changes. An incapacity to be elected a second time would have been the only effectual preventative. The power of removing him every fourth year by the vote of the people is a power which will not be exercised. The king of Poland is removable every day by the Diet, yet he is never removed. —Smaller objections are the Appeal in fact as well as law, and the binding all persons Legislative Executive and Judiciary by oath to maintain that constitution. I do not pretend to decide what would be the best method of procuring the establishment of the manifold good things in this constitution, and of getting rid of the bad. Whether by adopting it in hopes of future amendment, or, after it has been duly weighed and canvassed by the people, after seeing the parts they generally dislike, and those they generally approve, to say to them "We see now what you wish. Send together your deputies again, let them frame a constitution for you omitting what you have condemned, and establishing the powers you approve. Even these will be a great addition to the energy of your government."—At all events I hope you will not be discouraged from other trials, if the present one should fail of its full effect.—I have thus told you freely what I like and dislike: merely as a matter of curiosity, for I know your own judgment has been formed on all these points after having heard everything which could be urged on them. I own I am not a friend to a very energetic government. It is always oppressive. The late rebellion in Massachusetts has given more alarm than I think it should have done. Calculate that one rebellion in 13 states in the course of 11 years, is but one for each state in a century and a half. No country should be so long without one. Nor will any degree of power in the hands of government prevent insurrections. France, with all its despotism, and two or three hundred thousand men always in arms has had three insurrections in the three years I have been here in every one of which greater numbers were engaged than in Massachusetts and a great deal more blood was spilt.

In Turkey, which Montesquieu supposes more despotic, insurrections are the events of every day. In England, where the hand of power is lighter than here, but heavier than with us they happen every half dozen years. Compare again the ferocious depredations of their insurgents with the order, the moderation and the almost self extinguishment of ours.—After all, it is my principle that the will of the majority should always prevail. If they approve the proposed Convention in all its parts, I shall concur in it cheerfully, in hopes that they will amend it whenever they shall find it work wrong. I think our governments will remain virtuous for many centuries; as long as they are chiefly agricultural; and this will be as long as there shall be vacant lands in any part of America. When they get piled upon one another in large cities, as in Europe, they will become corrupt as in Europe. Above all things I hope the education of the common people will be attended to; convinced that on their good sense we may rely with the most security for the preservation of a due degree of liberty. I have tired you by this time with my disquisitions and will therefore only add assurances of the sincerity of those sentiments of esteem and attachment with which I am Dear Sir your affectionate friend and servant.

P.S. The instability of our laws is really an immense evil. I think it would be well to provide in our constitutions that there shall always be a twelve-month between the ingrossing a bill and passing it: that it should then be offered to its passage without changing a word: and that if circumstances should be thought to require a speedier passage, it should take two thirds of both houses instead of a bare majority.

LETTER TO THE ABBÉ ARNOUX (1789)

Paris, July 1789

We think, in America, that it is necessary to introduce the people into every department of government as far as they are capable of exercising it, and that is the only way to insure a long continued and honest administration of its powers.

1. They are not qualified to exercise themselves the executive department, but they are qualified to name the person who shall exercise it. 2. They are not qualified to legislate. With us, therefore, they only choose the legislators. 3. They are not qualified to judge questions of *law,* but they are capable of judging questions of *fact.* In the form of juries, therefore, they determine all matters of fact, leaving to the permanent judges to decide the law resulting from those facts. But we all know that permanent judges acquire an *esprit de corps;* that, being known, they are liable to be tempted by bribery; that they are misled by favor, by relationship, by a spirit of party, by a devotion to the executive or legislative power; that it is better to leave a cause to the decision of cross and pile than to that of a judge biased to one side; and that the opinion of twelve honest jurymen gives still a better hope of right than cross and pile does. It is left, therefore, to the juries, if they think the permanent judges are under any bias whatever in any cause, to take on themselves to judge the law as well as the fact. They never exercise this power but when they suspect partiality in the judges, and by the exercise of this power they have been the firmest bulwarks of English liberty. Were I called upon to decide whether the people had best be omitted in the legislative or judiciary department, I would say it is better to leave them out of the legislature. The execution of the laws is more important than the making of them. However, it is best to have the people in all the three departments, where that is possible.

LETTER TO JOHN ADAMS (1813)

October 1813

... For I agree with you that there is a natural aristocracy among men. The grounds of this are virtue and talents. Formerly, bodily powers gave place among the *aristoi.* But since the invention of gunpowder has armed the weak as well as the strong with missile death, bodily strength, like beauty, good humor, politeness and other accomplishments, has become but an auxiliary ground of distinction.

There is also an artificial aristocracy, founded on wealth and birth, without either virtue or talents; for with these it would belong to the first class. The natural aristocracy I consider as the most precious gift of nature, for the instruction, the thrusts, and government of society. And indeed, it would have been inconsistent in creation to have formed man for the social state, and not to have provided virtue and wisdom enough to manage the concerns of the society. May we not even say, that the form of government is the best, which provides the most effectually for a pure selection of these natural aristoi into the offices of government? The artificial aristocracy is a mischievous ingredient in government, and provision should be made to prevent its ascendancy. On the question what is the best provision, you and I differ, but we differ as rational friends, using the free exercise of our own reason, and mutually indulging its errors. You think it best to put the pseudo-aristoi into a separate chamber of legislation, where they may be hindered from doing mischief by their coordinate branches, and where, also, they may be a protection to wealth against the Agrarian and plundering enterprises of the majority of the people. I think that to give them power in order to prevent them from doing mischief, is arming them for it, and increasing instead of remedying the evil. For if the co-ordinate branches can arrest their action, so may they that of the co-ordinates. Mischief may be done negatively as well as positively. Of this, a cabal in the Senate of the United States, has furnished many proofs. Nor do I believe them necessary to protect the wealthy; because enough of these will find their way into every branch of the legislation, to protect themselves. From fifteen to twenty legislatures of our own, in action for thirty years past, have proved that no fears of an equalization of property are to be apprehended from them. I think the best remedy is exactly that provided by all our constitutions, to leave to the citizens the free election and separation of the aristoi from the pseudo-aristoi, of the wheat from the chaff. In general they will elect the really good and wise. In some instances, wealth may corrupt, and birth blind them; but not in sufficient degree to endanger the society.

It is probable that our difference of opinion may, in some measure, be produced by a difference of character in those among whom we live. From what I have seen of Massachusetts and Connecticut myself, and still more from what I have heard, and the character given of the former by yourself, who know them so much better, there seems to be in those two States a traditionary reverence for certain families, which has rendered the offices of the government nearly hereditary in those families. I presume that from an early period of your history, members of those families happening to possess virtue and talents, have honestly exercised them for the good of the people, and by their services have endeared their names to them. In coupling Connecticut with you, I mean it politically only, not morally. For having made the Bible the common law of their land, they seem to have modeled their morality on the story of Jacob and Laban. But although this hereditary succession to office with you, may, in some degree, be founded in real family merit, yet in a much higher degree, it has proceeded from your strict alliance of Church and State. These families are canonised in the eyes of the people on common principles, "you tickle me, and I will

tickle you." In Virginia we have nothing of this. Our clergy, before the revolution, having been secured against rivalship by fixed salaries, did not give themselves the trouble of acquiring influence over the people. Of wealth, there were great accumulations in particular families, handed down from generation to generation, under the English law of entails. But the only object of ambition for the wealthy was a seat in the King's Council. All their court then was paid to the crown and its creatures; and they Philipised in all collisions between the King and the people. Hence they were unpopular; and that unpopularity continues attached to their names. A Randolph, a Carter, or a Burwell must have great personal superiority over a common competitor to be elected by the people even at this day. At the first session of our legislature after the Declaration of Independence, we passed a law abolishing entails. And this was followed by one abolishing the privilege primogeniture, and dividing the lands of intestates equally among all their children, or other representatives. These laws, drawn by myself, laid the axe to the foot of pseudo-aristocracy. And had another which I prepared been adopted by the legislature, our work would have been complete. It was a bill for the more general diffusion of learning. This proposed to divide every county into wards of five or six miles square, like your townships; to establish in each ward a free school for reading, writing and common arithmetic; to provide for the annual selection of the best subjects from these schools, who might receive, at the public expense, a higher degree of education at a district school; and from these district schools to select a certain number of the most promising subjects, to be completed at an University, where all the useful sciences should be taught. Worth and genius would thus have been sought out from every condition of life, and completely prepared by education for defeating the competition of wealth and birth for public trusts. My proposition had, for a further object, to impart to these wards those portions of self-government for which they are best qualified, by confiding to them the care of their poor, their roads, police, elections, the nomination of jurors, administration of justice in small cases, elementary exercises of militia; in short, to have made them little republics, with a warden at the head of each, for all those concerns which, being under their eye, they would better manage than the larger republics of the county or State. A general call of ward meetings by their wardens on the same day through the State, would at any time produce the genuine sense of the people on any required point, and would enable the State to act in mass, as your people have so often done, and with so much effect by their town meetings. The law for religious freedom, which made a part of this system, having put down the aristocracy of the clergy, and restored to the citizen the freedom of the mind, and those of entails and descents nurturing an equality of condition among them, this on education would have raised the mass of the people to the high ground of moral respectability necessary to their own safety, and to orderly government; and would have completed the great object of qualifying them to select the veritable aristoi, for the trusts of government, to the exclusion of the pseudalists.... Although this law has not yet been acted on but in a small and inefficient degree, it is still considered as before the legislature, with other bills of the revised code, not yet taken up, and I have great hope that some patriotic spirit will, at a favorable moment, call it up, and make it the keystone of the arch of our government.

With respect to aristocracy, we should further consider, that before the establishment of the American States, nothing was known to history but the man of the old world, crowded within limits either small or overcharged, and steeped in the vices which that situation gener-

ates. A government adapted to such men would be one thing; but a very different one, that for the man of these States. Here everyone may have land to labor for himself, if he chooses; or, preferring the exercise of any other industry, may exact for it such compensation as not only to afford a comfortable subsistence, but wherewith to provide for a cessation from labor in old age. Everyone, by his property, or by his satisfactory situation, is interested in the support of law and order. And such men may safely and advantageously reserve to themselves a wholesome control over their public affairs, and a degree of freedom, which, in the hands of the *canaille* of the cities of Europe, would be instantly perverted to the demolition and destruction of everything public and private. The history of the last twenty-five years of France, and of the last forty years in America, nay of its last two hundred years, proves the truth of both parts of this observation.

But even in Europe a change has sensibly taken place in the mind of man. Science had liberated the ideas of those who read and reflect, and the American example had kindled feelings of right in the people. An insurrection has consequently begun, of science, talents, and courage, against rank and birth, which have fallen into contempt. It has failed in its first effort, because the mobs of the cities, the instrument used for its accomplishment, debased by ignorance, poverty, and vice, could not be restrained to rational action. But the world will recover from the panic of this first catastrophe. Science is progressive, and talents and enterprise on the alert. Resort may be had to the people of the country, a more governable power from their principles and subordination; and rank, and birth, and tinsel-aristocracy will finally shrink into insignificance, even there. This, however, we have no right to meddle with. It suffices for us, if the moral and physical condition of our own citizens qualifies them to select the able and good for the direction of their government, with a recurrence of elections at such short periods as will enable them to displace an unfaithful servant, before the mischief he meditates may be irremediable.

I have thus stated my opinion on a point on which we differ, not with a view to controversy, for we are both too old to change opinions which are the result of a long life of inquiry and reflection; but on the suggestions of a former letter of yours, that we ought not to die before we have explained ourselves to each other. We acted in perfect harmony, through a long and perilous contest for our liberty and independence. A constitution has been acquired, which, though neither of us thinks perfect, yet both consider as competent to render our fellow citizens the happiest and the securest on whom the sun has ever shone. If we do not think exactly alike as to its imperfections, it matters little to our country, which, after devoting to it long lives of disinterested labor, we have delivered over to our successors in life, who will be able to take care of it and of themselves. . . .

LETTER TO PIERRE SAMUEL DuPONT DE NEMOURS (1816)

Poplar Forest, April 1816

I received, my dear friend, your letter covering the constitution for your Equinoctial republics. . . . I suppose it well-formed for those for whom it was intended, and the excellence of every government is its adaptation to the state of those to be governed by it. For us it would not do. Distinguishing between the structure of the government and the moral principles on which you prescribe its administration, with the latter we concur cordially, with the former we should not. We of the United States, you know, are constitutionally and conscientiously democrats. We consider society as one of the natural wants with which man has been created; that he has been endowed with faculties and qualities to effect its satisfaction by concurrence of others having the same want; that when, by the exercise of these faculties, he has procured a state of society, it is one of his acquisitions which he has a right to regulate and control, jointly indeed with all those who have concurred in the procurement, whom he cannot exclude from its use or direction more than they him. We think experience has proved it safer, for the mass of individuals composing the society, to reserve to themselves personally the exercise of all rightful powers to which they are competent, and to delegate those to which they are not competent to deputies named, and removable for unfaithful conduct by themselves immediately. Hence, with us, the people (by which is meant the mass of individuals composing the society) being competent to judge of the facts occurring in ordinary life, they have retained the functions of judges of facts under the name of jurors; but being unqualified for the management of affairs requiring intelligence above the common level, yet competent judges of human character, they chose, for their management, representatives, some by themselves immediately, others by electors chosen by themselves. . . .

But when we come to the moral principles on which the government is to be administered, we come to what is proper for all conditions of society. I meet you there in all the benevolence and rectitude of your native character, and I love myself always most where I concur most with you. Liberty, truth, probity, honor are declared to be the four cardinal principles of your society. I believe with you that morality, compassion, generosity are innate elements of the human constitution; that there exists a right independent of force; that a right to property is founded in our natural wants, in the means with which we are endowed to satisfy these wants, and the right to what we acquire by those means without violating the similar rights of other sensible beings, that no one has a right to obstruct another exercising his faculties innocently for the relief of sensibilities made a part of his nature; that justice is the fundamental law of society; that the majority, oppressing an individual, is guilty of a crime, abuses its strength, and by acting on the law of the strongest breaks up the foundations of society; that action by the citizens in person, in affairs within their reach and competence, and in all others by representatives, chosen immediately and removable by themselves, constitutes the essence of a republic; that all governments are more or less republican in proportion as this principle enters more or less into their composition; and that a government by representation is capable of extension over a great surface of country than one of any other form. These, my friend, are the essentials in which you and I agree; however, in our zeal for their maintenance we may be perplexed and divaricate as to the structure of society most likely to secure them.

In the constitution of Spain, as proposed by the late Cortes, there was a principle entirely new to me and not noticed in yours, that no person born after that day should ever acquire the rights of citizenship until he could read and write. It is impossible sufficiently to estimate the wisdom of this provision. Of all those which have been thought of for securing fidelity in the administration of the government, constant ralliance to the principles of the constitution, and progressive amendments with the progressive advances of the human mind or changes in human affairs, it is the most effectual. Enlighten the people generally, and tyranny and oppressions of body and mind will vanish like evil spirits at the dawn of day. Although I do not with some enthusiasts believe that the human condition will ever advance to such a state of perfection as that there shall no longer be pain or vice in the world, yet I believe it susceptible of much improvement, and most of all in matters of government and religion, and that the diffusion of knowledge among the people is to be the instrument by which it is to be effected.

LETTER TO JOHN TAYLOR (1816)

Monticello, May 1816

... Besides much other good matter (in your *Enquiry into the Principles of Our Government*), it settles unanswerably the right of instructing representatives and their duty to obey. The system of banking we have both equally and ever reprobated. I contemplate it as a blot left in all our constitutions, which, if not covered, will end in their destruction, which is already hit by the gamblers in corruption and is sweeping away in its progress the fortunes and morals of our citizens. Funding I consider as limited, rightfully, to a redemption of the debt within the lives of a majority of the generation contracting it; every generation coming equally, by the laws of the Creator of the world, to the free possession of the earth He made for their subsistence, unencumbered by their predecessors, who, like them, were but tenants for life. You have successfully and completely pulverized Mr. Adams' system of orders and his opening the mantle of republicanism to every government of laws, whether consistent or not with natural right. Indeed, it must be acknowledged that the term "republic" is of very vague application in every language. Witness the self-styled republics of Holland, Switzerland, Genoa, Venice, Poland. Were I to assign to this term a precise and definite idea, I would say purely and simply it means a government by its citizens in mass, acting directly and personally, according to rules established by the majority, and that every other government is more or less republican in proportion as it has in its composition more or less of this ingredient of the direct action of the citizens. Such a government is evidently restrained to very narrow limits of space and population. I doubt if it would be practicable beyond the extent of a New England township.... Other shades of republicanism may be found in other forms of government where the executive, judiciary, and legislative functions, and the different branches of the latter, are chosen by the people more or less directly for longer terms of years, or for life, or made hereditary, or where there are mixtures of authorities, some dependent on, and others independent of, the people. The further the departure from direct and constant control by the citizens, the less has the government of the ingredient of republicanism; evidently none where the authorities are hereditary, as in France, Venice, etc., or self-chosen, as in Holland, and little, where for life, in proportion as the life continues in being after the act of election.

The purest republican feature in the government of our own State is the House of Representatives. The Senate is equally so the first year, less the second, and so on. The Executive still less, because not chosen by the people directly. The Judiciary seriously anti-republican, because for life, and the national arm wielded, as you observe, by military leaders irresponsible but to themselves. Add to this the vicious constitution of our county courts (to whom the justice, the executive administration, the taxation, police, the military appointments of the county, and nearly all our daily concerns are confided), self-appointed, self-continued, holding their authorities for life, and with an impossibility of breaking in on the perpetual succession of any faction once possessed of the bench. They are in truth the executive, the ju-

diciary, and the military of their respective counties, and the sum of the counties makes the State. And add also that one half of our brethren who fight and pay taxes are excluded like helots from the rights of representation, as if society were instituted for the soil and not for the men inhabiting it, or one half of these could dispose of the rights and the will of the other half without their consent.

What constitutes a State?
Not high-raised battlements, or labor'd
    mound,
  Thick wall, or moated gate;
Not cities proud, with spires and turrets
    crown'd;
  No! men, high-minded men;
  Men, who their duties know;
But know their rights; and knowing, dare
    maintain;
  These constitute a State.

In the General Government, the House of Representatives is mainly republican; the Senate scarcely so at all, as not elected by the people directly and so long secured even against those who do elect them; the Executive more republican than the Senate, from its shorter term, its election by the people in *practice*, (for they vote for A only on an assurance that he will vote for B), and because, *in practice also,* a principle of rotation seems to be in a course of establishment; the judiciary independent of the nation, their coercion by impeachment being found nugatory.

If, then, the control of the people over the organs of their government be the measure of its republicanism, and I confess I know no other measure, it must be agreed that our governments have much less of republicanism than ought to have been expected; in other words, that the people have less regular control over their agents than their rights and their interests require. And this I ascribe, not to any want of republican dispositions in those who formed these constitutions, but to a submission of true principle to European authorities, to speculators on government, whose fears of the people have been inspired by the populace of their own great cities and were unjustly entertained against the independent, the happy, and therefore orderly citizens of the United States....

On this view of the import of the term "republic," instead of saying, as has been said, "that it may mean anything or nothing," we may say with truth and meaning that governments are more or less republican as they have more or less of the element of popular election and control in their composition; and believing as I do that the mass of the citizens is the safest despository of their own rights, and especially that the evils flowing from the duperies of the people are less injurious than those from the egoism of their agents, I am a friend to that composition of government which has in it the most of this ingredient. And I sincerely believe with you that banking establishments are more dangerous than standing armies, and that the principle of spending money to be paid by posterity, under the name of funding, is but swindling futurity on a large scale.

LETTER TO SAMUEL KERCHEVAL (1816)

Monticello, July 1816

... At the birth of our republic, I committed that opinion to the world, in the draught of a constitution annexed to the *Notes on Virginia,* in which a provision was inserted for a representation permanently equal. The infancy of the subject at that moment, and our inexperience of self-government, occasioned gross departures in that draught from genuine republican canons. In truth, the abuses of monarchy had so much filled all the space of political contemplation, that we imagined everything republican which not monarchy. We had not yet penetrated to the mother principle, that "governments are republican only in proportion as they embody the will of their people, and execute it." Hence, our first constitutions had really no leading principles in them. But experience and reflection have but more and more confirmed me in the particular importance of the equal representation then proposed. On that point, then, I am entirely in sentiment with your letters; and only lament that a copy-right of your pamphlet prevents their appearance in the newspapers, where alone they would be generally read, and pro-duce general effect. The present vacancy, too, of other matter, would give them place in every paper, and bring the question home to every man's conscience.

But inequality of representation in both Houses of our legislature, is not the only republican heresy in this first essay of our revolutionary patriots at forming a constitution. For let it be agreed that a government is republican in proportion as every member composing it has his equal voice in the direction of its concerns (not indeed in person, which would be impracticable beyond the limits of a city, or small township, but) by representatives chosen by himself, and responsible to him at short periods, and let us bring to the test of this canon every branch of our constitution.

In the legislature, the House of Representatives is chosen by less than half the people, and not at all in proportion to those who do choose. The Senate are still more disproportionate, and for long terms of irresponsibility. In the Executive, the Governor is entirely independent of the choice of the people, and of their control; his Council equally so, and at best but a fifth wheel to a wagon. In the Judiciary, the judges of the highest courts are dependent on none but themselves. In England, where judges were named and removable at the will of an hereditary executive, from which branch most misrule was feared, and has flowed, it was a great point gained, by fixing them for life, to make them independent of that executive. But in a government founded on the public will, this principle operates in an opposite direction, and against that will. There, too, they were still removable on a concurrence of the executive and legislative branches. But we have made them independent of the nation itself. They are irremovable, but by their own body, for any depravities of conduct, and even by their own body for the imbecilities of dotage. The justices of the inferior courts are self-chosen, are for life, and perpetuate their own body in succession forever, so that a faction once possessing themselves of the bench of a county, can never be broken up, but hold their county in chains, forever indissoluble. Yet these justices are the real executive as well as judiciary, in all our minor and most ordinary concerns. They tax us at will; fill the office of sheriff, the most important of all the executive officers of the county; name nearly all our military leaders, which leaders, once named, are removable but by themselves. The juries, our judges of all fact, and of law when they choose it, are not selected by the people, nor amenable to them. They are chosen by an officer named by the court and executive. Chosen, did I say? Picked up by the sheriff from the loungings of the court yard, after everything respectable has retired from it. Where then is our republicanism to be found? Not in our constitution certainly but merely in the spirit of our people. That would oblige even a despot to govern us republicanly. Owing to this spirit, and to nothing in the form of our constitution, all things have gone well. But this fact, so triumphantly misquoted by the enemies of reformation, is not the fruit of our constitution, but has prevailed in spite of it.

Our functionaries have done well, because generally honest men. If any were not so, they feared to show it.

But it will be said, it is easier to find faults than to amend them. I do not think their amendment so difficult as is pretended. Only lay down true principles, and adhere to them inflexibly. Do not be frightened into their surrender by the alarms of the timid, or the creakings of wealth against the ascendancy of the people. If experience be called for, appeal to that of our fifteen or twenty governments for forty years, and show me where the people have done half the mischief in these forty years, that a single despot would have done in a single year; or show half the riots and rebellions, the crimes and the punishments, which have taken place in any single nation, under kingly government, during the same period. The true foundation of republican government is the equal right of every citizen, in his person and property, and in their management. Try by this, as a tally, every provision of our constitution, and see if it hangs directly on the will of the people. Reduce your legislature to a convenient number for full, but orderly discussion. Let every man who fights or pays, exercise his just and equal right in their election. Submit them to approbation or rejection at short intervals. Let the executive be chosen in the same way, and for the same term, by those whose agent he is to be, and leave no screen of a council behind which to skulk from responsibility. It has been thought that the people are not competent electors of judges *learned in the law.* But I do know that this is true, and, if doubtful, we should follow principle. In this, as in many other elections, they would be guided by reputation, which would not err oftener, perhaps, than the present mode of appointment. In one State of the Union, at least, it has long been tried, and with the most satisfactory success. The judges of Connecticut have been chosen by the people every six months, for nearly two centuries, and I believe there has hardly ever been an instance of change, so powerful is the curb of incessant responsibility. If prejudice, however, derived from a monarchical institution, is still to prevail against the vital elective principle of our own, and if the existing example among ourselves of periodical election of judges by the people be still mistrusted, let us at least not adopt the evil, and reject the good, of the English precedent; let us retain amovability on the concurrence of the executive and legislative branches, and nomination by the executive alone. Nomination to office is an executive function. To give it to the legislature, as we do, is a violation of the principle of the separation of powers. It swerves the members from correctness, by temptations to intrigue for office themselves, and to a corrupt barter of votes; and destroys responsibility by dividing it among a multitude. By leaving nomination in its proper place, among executive functions, the principle of the distribution of power is preserved, and responsibility weighs with its heaviest force on a single head.

The organization of our county administrations may be thought more difficult. But follow principle, and the knot unties itself. Divide the counties into wards of such size as that every citizen can attend, when called on, and act in person. Ascribe to them the government of their wards in all things relating to themselves exclusively. A justice, chosen by themselves, in each, a constable, a military company, a patrol, a school, the care of their own poor, their own portion of the public roads, the choice of one or more jurors to serve in some court, and the delivery, within their own wards, of their own votes for all elective officers of higher sphere, will relieve the county administration of nearly all its business, will have it better done, and by making every citizen an acting member of the government, and in the offices nearest and most

interesting to him, will attach him by his strongest feelings to the independence of his country, and its republican constitution. The justices thus chosen by every ward, would constitute the county court, would do its judiciary business, direct roads and bridges, levy county and poor rates, and administer all the matters of common interest of the whole country. These wards, called townships in New England, are the vital principles of their governments, and have proved themselves the wisest invention ever devised by the wit of man for the perfect exercise of self-government, and for its preservation. We should thus marshal our government into (1) the general federal republic, for all concerns foreign and federal; (2) that of the State, for what related to our own citizens exclusively; (3) the county republics, for the duties and concerns of the county; and (4) the ward republics, for the small, and yet numerous and interesting concerns of the neighborhood; and in government, as well as in every other business of life, it is by division and subdivision of duties alone, that all matters, great and small, can be managed to perfection. And the whole is cemented by giving to every citizen, personally, a part in the administration of the public affairs.

The sum of these amendments is (1) General suffrage, (2) equal representation in the legislature, (3) an executive chosen by the people, (4) judges elective or amovable, (5) justices, jurors, and sheriffs elective, (6) ward divisions, and (7) periodical amendments of the constitution.

I have thrown out these as loose heads of amendment, for consideration and correction; and their object is to secure self-government by the republicanism of our constitution, as well as by the spirit of the people; and to nourish and perpetuate that spirit. I am not among those who fear the people. They, and not the rich, are our dependence for continued freedom. And to preserve their independence, we must not let our rulers load us with perpetual debt. We must make our election between *economy and liberty,* or *profusion and servitude.* If we run into such debts, as that we must be taxed in our meat and in our drink, in our necessaries and our comforts, in our labors and our amusements, for our callings and our creeds, as the people of England are, our people, like them, must come to labor sixteen hours in the twenty-four, give the earnings of fifteen of these to the government for their debts and daily expenses; and the sixteenth being insufficient to afford us bread, we must live, as they now do, on oatmeal and potatoes; have no time to think, no means of calling the mismanagers to account; but be glad to obtain subsistence by hiring ourselves to rivet their chains on the necks of our fellow-sufferers. Our landholders, too, like theirs, retaining indeed the title and stewardship of estates called theirs, but held really in trust for the treasury, must wander, like theirs, in foreign countries, and be contented with penury, obscurity, exile, and the glory of the nation. This example reads to us the salutary lesson, that private fortunes are destroyed by public as well as by private extravagance. And this is the tendency of all human governments. A departure from principle in one instance becomes a precedent for a second; that second for a third; and so on, till the bulk of the society be reduced to be mere automatons of misery, and to have no sensibilities left but for sinning and suffering. Then begins, indeed, the *bellum omnium in omnia,* which some philosophers observing to be so general in this world, have mistaken it for the natural, instead of the abusive state of man. And the fore horse of this frightful team is public debt. Taxation follows that, and in its train wretchedness and oppression.

Some men look at constitutions with sanctimonious reverence, and deem them like the arc of the covenant, too sacred to be touched. They ascribe to the men of the preceding age a wisdom more than human, and suppose what they did to be beyond amendment. I knew that age well; I belonged to it, and labored with it. It deserved well of its country. It was very like the present, but without the experience of the present; and forty years of experience in government is worth a century of bookreading; and this they would say themselves, were they to rise from the dead. I am certainly not an advocate for frequent and untried changes in laws and constitutions. I think moderate imperfections had better be borne with; because, when once known, we accommodate ourselves to them, and find practical means of correcting their ill effects. But I know also, that laws and institutions must go hand in hand with the progress of the human mind. As that becomes more developed, more enlightened, as new discoveries are made, new truths disclosed, and manners and opinions change with the change of circumstances, institutions must advance also, and keep pace with the times. We might as well require a man to wear still the coat which fitted him when a boy, as civilized society to remain ever under the regimen of their barbarous ancestors. It is this preposterous idea which has lately deluged Europe in blood. Their monarchs, instead of wisely yielding to the gradual change of circumstances, of favoring progressive accommodation to progressive improvement, have clung to old abuses, entrenched themselves behind steady habits, and obliged their subjects to seek through blood and violence rash and ruinous innovations, which, had they been referred to the peaceful deliberations and collected wisdom of the nation, would have been put into acceptable and salutary forms. Let us follow no such examples, nor weakly believe that one generation is not as capable as another of taking care of itself, and of ordering its own affairs. Let us, as our sister States have done, avail ourselves of our reason and experience, to correct the crude essays of our first and unexperienced, although wise, virtuous, and well-meaning councils. And lastly, let us provide in our constitution for its revision at stated periods. What these periods should be, nature herself indicates. By the European tables of mortality, of the adults living at any one moment of time, a majority will be dead in about nineteen years. At the end of that period, then, a new majority is come into place; or, in other words, a new generation. Each generation is as independent as the one preceding, as that was of all which had gone before. It has then, like them, a right to choose for itself the form of government it believes most promotive of its own happiness; consequently, to accommodate to the circumstances in which it finds itself, that received from its predecessors; and it is for the peace and good of mankind that a solemn opportunity of doing this every nineteen or twenty years, should be provided by the constitution; so that it may be handed on, with periodical repairs, from generation to generation, to the end of time, if anything human can so long endure. It is now forty years since the constitution of Virginia was formed. The same tables inform us, that, within that period, two-thirds of the adults then living are now dead. Have then the remaining third, even if they had the wish, the right to hold in obedience to their will, and to laws heretofore made by them, the other two-thirds, who, with themselves compose the present mass of adults? If they have not, who has? The dead? But the dead have no rights. They are nothing; and nothing cannot own something. Where there is no substance, there can be no accident. This corporeal globe, and everything upon it, belong to its present corporeal inhabitants, during their generation. They alone have a right to direct what is the concern of themselves, alone, and to declare the law of that direction; and this declaration can only be made by their majority. That majority, then, has a right to depute representatives to a convention, and to make the constitution what they think will be the best for themselves. But how collect their voice? This is the real difficulty. If invited by private authority, or county or district meetings, these divisions are so large that few will attend; and their voice will be imperfectly, or falsely pronounced. Here then, would be one of the advantages of the ward divisions I have proposed. The mayor of every ward, on a question like the present, would call his ward together, take the simple yea or nay of its members, convey these to the county court, who would hand on those of all its wards to the proper general authority; and the voice of the whole people would be thus fairly, fully, and peaceably expressed, discussed, and decided by the common reason of the society. If this avenue be shut to the call of suffrance, it will make itself heard through that of force, and we shall go on, as other nations are doing, in the endless circle of oppression, rebellion, reformation; and oppression, rebellion, reformation, again; and so on forever.

These, Sir, are my opinions of the governments we see among men, and of the principles by which alone we may prevent our own from falling into the same dreadful track. I have given them at greater length than your letter called for. But I cannot say things by halves; and I confide them to your honor, so to use them as to preserve me from the gridiron of the public papers. If you shall approve and enforce them, as you have done that of equal representation, they may do some good. If not, keep them to yourself as the effusions of withered age and useless time. I shall, with not the less truth, assure you of my great respect and consideration.

LETTER TO SAMUEL KERCHEVAL (1816)

Monticello, September 1816

... The article, however, nearest my heart is the division of counties into wards. These will be pure and elementary republics, the sum of all which taken together composes the State, and will make of the whole a true democracy as to the business of the wards, which is that of nearest and daily concern. The affairs of the larger sections: of counties, of States, and of the Union, not admitting personal transaction by the people, will be delegated to agents elected by themselves, and representation will thus be substituted where personal action becomes impracticable. Yet, even over these representative organs, should they become corrupt and perverted, the division into wards, constituting the people in their wards a regularly organized power, enables them by that organization to crush, regularly and peaceably, the usurpations of their unfaithful agents, and rescues them from the dreadful necessity of doing it insurrectionally. In this way we shall be as republican as a large society can be and secure the continuance of purity in our government by the salutary, peaceable, and regular control of the people. No other depositories of power have ever yet been found which did not end in converting to their own profit the earnings of those committed to their charge....

... I have been told that on the question of equal representation, our fellow citizens in some sections of the State claim peremptorily a right of representation for their slaves. Principle will, in this as in most other cases, open the way for us to correct conclusion. Were our State a pure democracy in which all its inhabitants should meet together to transact all their business, there would yet be excluded from their deliberations: (1) infants, until arrived at years of discretion; (2) women, who, to prevent depravation of morals and ambiguity of issue, could not mix promiscuously in the public meetings of men; (3) slaves, from whom the unfortunate state of things with us takes away the rights of will and of property. Those then who have no will could be permitted to exercise none in the popular assembly, and, of course, could delegate none to an agent in a representative assembly.

LETTER TO WILLIAM JOHNSON (1823)

Monticello, June 1823

You request me confidentially, to examine the question, whether the Supreme Court has advanced beyond its constitutional limits, and trespassed on those of the State authorities? I do not undertake, my dear Sir, because I am unable. Age and the wane of mind consequent on it, had disqualified me from investigations so severe, and researches so laborious. And it is the less necessary in this case, as having been already done by others with a logic and learning to which I could add nothing. On the decision of the case of Cohen vs. The State of Virginia, in the Supreme Court of the United States, in March, 1821, Judge Roane, under the signature of Algernon Sidney, wrote for the Enquirer a series of papers on the law of that case. I considered these papers maturely as they came out, and confess that they appeared to me to pulverize every word which had been delivered by Judge Marshall, of the extra-judicial part of his opinion; and all was extra-judicial, except the decision that the act of Congress had not purported to give to the corporation of Washington the authority claimed by their lottery law, of controlling the laws of the States within the States themselves. But unable to claim that case, he could not let it go entirely, but went on gratuitously to prove, that notwithstanding the eleventh amendment of the constitution, a State *could* be brought as a defendant, to the bar of his court; and again, that Congress might authorize a corporation of its territory to exercise legislation within a State, and paramount to the laws of that State.

I cite the sum and result only of his doctrines, according to the impression made on my mind at the time, and still remaining. If not strictly accurate in circumstances, it is so in substance. This doctrine was so completely refuted by Roane, that if he can be answered, I surrender human reason as a vain and useless faculty, given to bewilder, and not to guide us. And I mention this particular case as one only of several, because it gave occasion to that thorough examination of the constitutional limits between the General and State jurisdictions, which you have asked for. There were two other writers in the same paper, under the signatures of Fletcher of Saltoun, and Somers, who, in a few essays, presented some very luminous and striking view of the question. And there was a particular paper which recapitulated all the cases in which it was thought the federal court had usurped on the State jurisdictions. These essays will be found in the Enquirers of 1821, from May the 10th to July the 13th. It is not in my present power to send them to you, but if Ritchie can furnish them, I will procure and forward them. If they had been read in the other States, as they were here, I think they would have left, there as here, no dissentients from their doctrine. The subject was taken up by our legislature of 1821–1822, and two draughts of remonstrances were prepared and discussed. As well as I remember, there was no difference of opinion as to the matter of right; but there was as to the expediency of a remonstrance at that time, the general mind of the States being then under extraordinary excitement by the Missouri question, and it was dropped on that consideration. But this case is not dead, it only sleepeth. The Indian chief said he did not go to war for every petty injury by itself, but put it

into his pouch, and when that was full, he then made war. Thank Heaven, we have provided a more peaceable and rational mode of redress.

This practice of Judge Marshall, of travelling out of his case to prescribe what the law would be in a moot case not before the court, is very irregular and very censurable. I recollect another instance, and the more particularly, perhaps, because it in some measure bore on myself. Among the midnight appointments of Mr. Adams, were commissions to some federal justices of the peace for Alexandria. These were signed and sealed by him, but not delivered. I found them on the table of the department of State, on my entrance into office, and forbade their delivery. Marbury, named in one of them, applied to the Supreme Court for a mandamus to the Secretary of State (Mr. Madison) to deliver the commission intended for him. The court determined at once, that being an original process, they had no cognizance of it; and therefore the question before them was ended. But the Chief Justice went on to lay down what the law would be, had they jurisdiction of the case, to wit: that they should command the delivery. The object was clearly to instruct any other court having the jurisdiction, what they should do if Marbury should apply to them. Besides the impropriety of this gratuitous interference, could anything exceed the perversion of law? For if there is any principle of law never yet contradicted it is that delivery is one of the essentials to the validity of the deed. Although signed and sealed, yet as long as it remains in the hands of the party himself, it is in *fieri* only, it is not a deed, and can be made so only by its delivery. In the hands of a third person it may be made an escrow. But whatever is in the executive offices is certainly deemed to be in the hands of the President; and in this case, was actually in my hands, because, when I countermanded them, there was as yet no Secretary of State. Yet this case of Marbury and Madison is continually cited by bench and bar, as if it were settled law, without any animadversion on its being merely an *obiter* dissertation of the Chief Justice.

It may be impracticable to lay down any general formula of words which shall decide at once, and with precision, in every case, this limit of jurisdiction. But there are two canons which will guide us safely in most of the cases. First, the capital and leading object of the constitution was to leave with the States all authorities which respected their own citizens only, and to transfer to the United States those which respected citizens of foreign or other States: to make us several as to ourselves, but one as to all others. In the latter case, then constructions should lean to the general jurisdiction, if the words will bear it; and in favor of the States in the former, if possible to be so construed. And indeed, between citizens and citizens of the same State, and under their own laws, I know but a single case in which a jurisdiction is given to the General Government. That is, where anything but gold or silver is made a lawful tender, or the obligation of contracts is any otherwise impaired. The separate legislatures had so often abused that power, that the citizens themselves chose to trust it to the general, rather than to their own special authorities. Second, on every question of construction, carry ourselves back to the time when the constitution was adopted, recollect the spirit manifested in the debates, and instead of trying what meaning may be squeezed out of the text, or invented against it, conform to the probable one in which it was passed. Let us try Cohen's case by these canons only, referring always, however, for full argument, to the essays before cited.

1. It was between a citizen and his own State, and under a law of his State. It was a domestic case, therefore, and not a foreign one.

2. Can it be believed, that under the jealousies prevailing against the General Government, at the adoption of the constitution, the States meant to surrender the authority of preserving order, of enforcing moral duties and restraining vice, within their own territory? And this is the present case, that of Cohen being under the ancient and general law of gaming. Can any good be effected by taking from the States the moral rule of their citizens, and subordinating it to the general authority, or to one of their corporations, which may justify forcing the meaning of words, hunting after possible constructions, and hanging inference on inference, from heaven to earth, like Jacob's ladder? Such an intention was impossible, and such a licentiousness of construction and inference, if exercised by both governments, as may be done with equal right, would equally authorize both to claim all power, general and particular, and break up the foundations of the Union. Laws are made for men of ordinary understanding, and should, therefore, be construed only by the ordinary rules of common sense. Their meaning is not to be sought for in metaphysical subtleties, which may make anything mean everything or nothing, at pleasure. It should be left to the sophisms of advocates, whose trade it is, to prove that a defendant is a plaintiff, though dragged into court, *torto collo,* like Bonaparte's volunteers, into the field in chains, or that a power has been given, because it ought to have been given, *et alia talia.* The States supposed that by their tenth amendment, they had secured themselves against constructive powers. They were not lessened yet by Cohen's case, nor aware of the slipperiness of the eels of the law. I ask for no straining of words against the General Government, nor yet against the States. I believe the States can best govern our home concerns, and the General Government our foreign ones. I wish, therefore, to see maintained that wholesome distri-

bution of powers established by the constitution for the limitation of both, and never to see all offices transferred to Washington, where, further withdrawn from the eyes of the people, they may more secretly be bought and sold as at market.

But the Chief Justice says, "there must be an ultimate arbiter somewhere." True, there must; but does that prove it is either party?

The ultimate arbiter is the people of the Union, assembled by their deputies in convention, at the call of Congress, or of two-thirds of the States. Let them decide to which they mean to give an authority claimed by two of their organs. And it has been the peculiar wisdom and felicity of our constitution, to have provided this peaceable appeal, where that of other nations is at once to force. ∾

Primary Sources

Jefferson, Thomas. *Autobiography of Thomas Jefferson*. New York: Capricorn, 1959.

———. *History of the Expedition under the Command of Captains Lewis and Clarke*. Dublin: J. Christie, 1817.

———. *The Life and Morals of Jesus of Nazareth*. Washington, D.C.: Government Printing Office, 1904.

———. *A Summary View of the Rights of British America*. New York: Scholar's Facsimiles and Reprints, 1943.

The Jeffersonian Cyclopedia. Edited by J.P. Foley. New York: Funk and Wagnalls, 1900.

Memoir, Correspondence, and Miscellanies, from the Papers of Thomas Jefferson. Edited by Thomas Jefferson Randolph. Boston: Gray and Bowen, 1830.

The Writings of Thomas Jefferson. Edited by Andrew A. Libscomb, under the auspices of the Thomas Jefferson Memorial Association. Washington, D.C., 1904.

Secondary Sources

Boorstin, Daniel J. *The Lost World of Thomas Jefferson*. New York: Henry Holt, 1948.

Koch, Adrienne. *The Philosophy of Thomas Jefferson*. New York: Columbia University Press, 1943.

Koch, Adrienne, and William Peden. *The Life and Selected Writings of Thomas Jefferson*. New York: Random House, 1944.

Lerner, Max. *Thomas Jefferson: America's Philosopher King*. Edited and with an introduction by Robert Schmuhl. New Brunswick, N.J.: Transaction Publishers, 1996.

Padover, Saul K. *Jefferson*. New York: Harcourt, Brace and World, 1942.

Randall, Willard S. *Thomas Jefferson: A Life*. New York: Henry Holt, 1993.

Wills, Garry. *Inventing America: Jefferson's Declaration of Independence*. New York: Vintage, 1978.

Wiltse, Charles M. "Jeffersonian Democracy; a Dual Tradition," *American Political Science Review* 28 (1934):838–51.

Part II

Development and Democracy: 1800–1865

THE EARLY decades of the nineteenth century were dominated by two loosely related processes. One was economic development of the new nation roughly along the lines of the Hamiltonian model. The other was democratization within the now-established liberal framework. In reaction to one or both or as an extension of the latter, several social movements arose to inject new ideas into the evolving mainstream. By the 1840s and 1850s, however, the slavery issue had become the focus for practically all thought and action in the country. We shall touch briefly on each of these events and then summarize their implications.

Hamiltonian Development under Jeffersonian Government

The conflicts in the late 1790s over the nature of the union, the powers of the national government, and the Alien and Sedition Acts led to the defeat of the Federalist party in the election of 1800. But Jefferson and Burr received an equal number of votes in the electoral college, and the election of the president became the responsibility of the outgoing Federalist-dominated House of Representatives. Here Hamilton employed his influence on behalf of Jefferson, who in Hamilton's eyes was the lesser evil; this act contributed to the bitterness between Hamilton and Burr that ultimately led to Hamilton's death in their 1804 duel.

Hamilton's judgment was vindicated by Jefferson's performance in office, to the pleased surprise of anxious Federalists and the chagrin of Jefferson's more radical followers. To be sure, Jefferson saw to it that the Alien and Sedition Acts were no longer enforced, and he pardoned those convicted under them. But he made none of the leveling moves that Federalists feared and expected, maintained Hamilton's revenue and bond-redemption system, and, most important, refrained from attacking the National Bank. The essence of the Hamiltonian program remained intact, although the official policy of the administration was laissez-faire and agrarian.

The chief conflict between the legacy of Hamilton and the principles of Jefferson arose over the role that the law, particularly the powers of the United States Supreme Court, would play in the developing nation. Hamilton's vision called for a governing role for law and lawyers and for a strong federal judiciary capped by a Supreme Court with the power of *judicial review,* the power to declare acts of the other branches of government unconstitutional and therefore void. He was convinced that the conservative character of the law and lawyers would provide a major bulwark against popular majorities, and thus he made judicial power a fundamental part of his program. In this way Hamilton enlisted the great majority of lawyers into perhaps the most effective force possible for supporting his version of national development.

The issue of judicial review arose in 1803 when Chief Justice John Marshall, a devoted Hamiltonian, exercised the power by declaring a section of the Judiciary Act of 1789 unconstitutional and thus void (see selection 14). Whether the Supreme Court should have such power is a basic political question that carries great importance for the nature of our system. Although it has now been decided in the Hamiltonian affirmative and generally accepted, it is important to recapture a sense of what democratic Jeffersonian principles were lost in the process.[1] The question turns on two issues: What is the nature of the choice to be made when there is an alleged conflict between a statute and the Constitution? And who should make such a choice? Hamilton argued in *The Federalist No. 78* that the choice was a purely mechanical one involving only the clear standards of law (which the Constitution declared itself to embody). Therefore, it was properly the sole responsibility of the highest judges. He denied that this would give the Supreme Court more than coequal status with the other branches because the justices would merely be doing what the higher law required.

Jefferson insisted that the choice involved was not a mechanical one for which "law" provided clear answers. Rather, it was one of

---

1. This point is made without reference to the content or consequences of any particular decision, which might well be made in the direction of expanding democracy; it refers to the undemocratic character of the *institution* and its powers, in which a few judges appointed for life terms can overrule the acts of the people's elected representatives.

value preferences where interests, goals, and underlying philosophies might lead reasonable people in different directions. In such cases popular majorities or their elected representatives should be responsible for making the decisions. In Jefferson's words, it was after all "the people's Constitution," not that of the lawyers. He would have implemented his views by having questions of the scope of the Constitution's powers referred to conventions in the states or by trusting elected legislatures. Both routes would have kept this vital power closer to the people.

Marshall's success in establishing, however tenuously at the time, the power of judicial review in the midst of Jefferson's presidency thus amounted to a major Hamiltonian victory, one destined to bear its most significant fruit at the close of the century. But this was not the only way in which Hamilton's principles were implemented through judges' interpretations of law. In a series of Supreme Court decisions, Marshall asserted extensive national powers over commerce and national precedence over state laws, enforced the contract clause's limitations on state powers, defended the National Bank, and made broad construction of the powers of the national government a part of constitutional law. At local courts around the nation, judges were steadily asserting common-law powers and shaping the substance of the law so as to provide the legal infrastructure for capitalist economic development. Despite their opposition to expansion of national power at the expense of the states and to the lawmaking of judges and the resultant reduction in the scope of popularly elected officials' powers, the Jeffersonians could do little to block either process.

The embarrassing experiences of the War of 1812 lent further impetus to portions of Hamilton's program. Federal development of transportation systems and other internal improvements, use of a protective tariff to spur domestic manufacturing, and renewal of the National Bank all came about in major part because of wartime failures.

Democratization within the Liberal Framework

Jefferson's critique of Federalist policy had always stressed the rights and needs of ordinary small farmers over those of the financiers, merchants, and unproductive speculators he saw clustered around Hamilton and Adams. Defense of the French Revolution and opposition to the repressive Alien and Sedition Acts mounted by his Democratic-Republican party had added to his reputation as a champion of the people. Loud denunciations of Jefferson as a flaming radical by the Federalist party helped confirm this image for many. Jefferson's election and eight-year incumbency thus brought significant popular support to the new national government and to its Constitution. The term *democracy* began to lose its pejorative character and, domesticated by Jefferson's middle-of-the-road administration, gradually became acceptable as a description of the national government.

Not all of Jefferson's followers were satisfied with his policies, and some voiced complaints regularly. His old ally John Taylor, of Caroline County, Virginia, charged him with acquiescing in the manipulations, supposedly emanating from the Bank, of credit and currency values. For many agrarians the National Bank was both substance and symbol. It was the manifestation of finance capital and speculation, creating unearned profits for a few at the expense of the many small farmers and leading ultimately to immigration, urbanization, panics, and depression. Jefferson's failure to destroy the Bank cost him much support from those further to the left than he but probably gained him more support from centrists and old Federalists.

Democratization was not limited to the new popular base brought to the national government by Jefferson and his party. In many states, new constitutions were being drafted by specially elected conventions. In nearly every case, though often after much controversy, property requirements for the right (of white men, that is) to vote were eliminated. Concessions were often made to the radical Democratic-Republicans who sought shorter terms for officeholders, elected judges, and other democratic reforms. The opening up of the West, the organization of new governments there, and eventually the admission of such territories as states—all helped to generate a new surge of egalitarianism in the country. In a society still basically agrarian in character, particularly in its newer regions, a rough equality seemed to prevail. That all could become property holders and that most sought and were encouraged to do so, lent powerful support for a general commitment to property rights as the foundation of a good society and government.

The last expression of Jeffersonian, agrarian democracy occurred with the election of Andrew Jackson in 1828. The Northeast was already dotted with mills, factories, and railroads, but the hero of New Orleans was able to win enough votes from slaveholders, western agrarians, and New Yorkers to win the election. In office his prominent nationalism and attack on the financial interests represented in the second National Bank succeeded in holding his fragile coalition together. But then sectional economic interests and the contradiction of having slavery in an egalitarian, natural-rights society prevailed. When their reign ended, a wholly new political economy would be in existence—and with it commensurate need for new understandings of what democracy could and should mean in the United States.

Development and Democratization: Reactions and Extensions

The parallel processes of capitalist development and democratization gave rise to four major movements, each of which brought new dimensions into American political thought. In chronological order, these were abolitionism, Transcendentalism, middle-class utopian socialism combined with working-class radicalism (both pre Marxian), and feminism. Finally, the pro-slavery position was forced to articulate a comprehensive conservative argument, which it did principally through the work of Calhoun.

Abolitionism began with Quaker agitation before the Revolution and ran parallel with other efforts to free slaves and prohibit the slave trade after the Constitution was adopted. Several Northern states formally abolished slavery before 1800. As late as the mid–1820s, most antislavery societies were to be found in Southern states. Many supported solving the problem by returning slaves to Africa, deporting them elsewhere, or colonizing Caribbean islands. But militant Northern abolitionism, based on the moral right of all to the equality enshrined in the Declaration of Independence, began in the late 1820s. From the 1830s on, the lectures and writings of William Ellery Channing, William Lloyd Garrison, and others began to force the issue onto the national agenda. Partly in reaction to the abolitionists, partly in reaction to slave insurrections, but primarily because the cotton gin and other economic conditions had made slavery more profitable, the Southern states began to tighten restrictions on slaves and to use their power in the national government to protect their system. Pro-abolitionist agitation and organizations spread rapidly to the Middle West. Some urged outright action to free the slaves—as opposed to the Garrisonian arguments for appealing to people's moral sense and withdraw-

ing from association with slaveholders. Initially, all varieties of abolitionists met with opposition, often violent, throughout the North. Several newspapers were destroyed, and some abolitionists were killed, injured, or thrown out of town before they could begin agitating. Frederick Douglass, an escaped slave, was one of the most effective of all abolitionists (selection 19), partly because in speaking for his own race he was not guilty of exhibiting the paternalism and naive racism that characterized many abolitionists. The most explosive single document in the cause, however, was Harriet Beecher Stowe's *Uncle Tom's Cabin* (1852), followed by the Supreme Court's 1857 decision in *Dred Scott* v. *Sanford*. In *Dred Scott* the Court held that slaves were not citizens and went on to void the famous congressional Missouri Compromise Act of 1820, thereby undermining any possibility of legislating a solution for the slavery issue. Increasingly, the question began to be seen simply as one of equality—and the meaning of which, as understood in the Declaration of Independence, was seen to be at odds with the fact of slavery.

Transcendentalism was an individualistic, elitist (in the sense of cultured intellectualism) reaction to materialism and egalitarianism. Its New England adherents, all persons of literary bent, were repelled by the growing factory system and the character and conditions of the work force generated by it and the railroads then under construction. Nearly all Unitarians, they turned to individual self-development through exploration of the mysteries of the relationship between mankind and nature to counterbalance what they saw as a self-aggrandizing and collectivizing system supported by a pervertedly "rational" way of thinking. They stressed the responsibility of the individual for independence and self-reliance and of intellectuals to provide the cultural identity to make those ideals possible. When the individual was properly autonomous, of course, he would often have to take moral stands against governments and other sources of power in the society. Ralph Waldo Emerson and Henry David Thoreau (selections 15 and 16) were leading members of this school of thought, but their direct influence was limited to intellectual and other elite levels.

Middle-class utopian socialism and working-class radicalism originated separately but soon influenced each other. No real power developed behind a joint movement, however, partly because practical politics and bitterness toward the wage-slavery system (and possibly shared American racist beliefs) led many in the working-class movement to give slavery only secondary priority. The middle-class socialists sought to moderate the harshness of the factory system, eliminate the dulling and destructive consequences work had for people, and make individuals whole again by restoring cooperative communities. One branch of the movement centered around the wealthy Robert Owen, whose visibility was such that when he arrived from England he was invited to address Congress in 1825. He founded an experimental cooperative community at New Harmony, Indiana, in 1825. It lasted for five years before disintegrating under the pressures of the still-powerful individualism of its members and the hostility of the larger society.

Another early effort at forming a new kind of community where people would not be dominated by machines and the profit system was made by Frances Wright at Nashoba, Tennessee, in 1825. Wright sought to include in the project the education and gradual freeing of slaves as a model for the entire South. She was also one of the first strong advocates of women's rights, an advocate of free love, and an atheist. The combination was more than sufficient to generate hostility from all sides. Like New Harmony, Nashoba too survived only until 1830.

The intellectual ferment surrounding these early socialist experiments soon found other outlets in workers' political parties in particular and labor reform in general. Labor parties formed in several eastern cities from 1828 to 1834, seeking the ten-hour day, abolition of imprisonment for debt, and universal education, among other reforms. By the late 1830s, independent labor parties had dissolved into radical factions of the major parties, particularly the Jacksonian Democratic party (where they were known as the Loco-Focos). Orestes Brownson (selection 17) is typical of the middle-class intellectual leadership engaged in support of the working-class movement. His antipathy to organized religion, his support for the Democratic party as the best vehicle for social reform, and his efforts to put the evils of wage slavery before those of chattel slavery are also representative of the views of this movement.

Feminism can be traced back to Abigail Adams's famous correspondence with her husband and certainly to the efforts of Frances Wright and other antislavery orators such as Southerners Sarah and Angelina Grimke. As an organized movement, however, it began in 1848 at Seneca Falls, New York, where a declaration and several resolutions passed by a convention of men and women achieved national notice. The convention was called by Elizabeth Cady Stanton and aided by Lucretia Mott and others. As with many others before and since, Stanton's declaration was closely modeled on the Declaration of Independence —from the emphasis on natural rights and equality to the bill of particular wrongs that required righting.

Feminism and the abolitionist movement were closely connected, in part because equality is an indivisible concept. Also, many of the early abolitionist agitators were women who had had to overcome hostility directed at them for speaking in public, as well as deal with resentments audiences felt for their subject matter. The cause of equality for blacks soon became for many abolitionists, both male and female, the cause of equality for women as well. So it was in the case of Stanton and Mott, who had been refused accreditation at an antislavery convention in London because of their gender. After the Seneca Falls convention, women's rights became the first priority for most of the women involved. Stanton, soon joined by Susan B. Anthony in what was to be a lifelong collaboration, was particularly active in pressing for reform of the many state legislative provisions that made women subordinate in status. As the antislavery effort began to dominate the national agenda and the Civil War approached, however, the cause of women's rights was increasingly forced into the background.

Proslavery and Conservative Reaction

The growing strength of the abolitionist movement and particularly the grounding of its claims in the natural right of equality began by the 1850s to put serious strain on the Southern planter–Northern merchant alliance. The South was no longer vital as a market, for the railroads had made the West accessible. And the South could no longer count on enough Northern support to continue controlling the national government. Two forms of argument developed in an effort to preserve the South's status. One was an outright defense of the slave system as more humane than and culturally superior to the wage slavery and profit orientation of Northern capitalism. One proponent of this position was George Fitzhugh, whose views are well described by the titles of his major works: *Sociology for the South; or, the Failure of Free Society* (1854) and *Cannibals All! or, Slaves without Masters* (1857). For this argument, see selection 21.

The other product of the South's necessity was a proposal for institutional change proceeding from the truly conservative thought of John C. Calhoun. Calhoun had once been an ardent nationalist, but sectional interests eventually made him a states-rights advocate and then a nullifier. The centerpiece of his proposal was a dual executive system, offered as a means of implementing his "concurrent majority" principle, which was designed to prevent simple majorities from working their will (see selection 20).

What made Calhoun conservative was his explicit concept of the organic relationship between society and government, his severe pessimism about the nature of man, and his continual seeking for a means of providing the order that constitutes liberty and permits progress for the civilization it serves. He envisioned no lessening of suffering for those elements of the society who were at its lower levels, and indeed he considered this "mud-sill" a prerequisite for progress: they were (as always) available to do the labor, and only their service would enable others to move ahead and release some to have sufficient leisure to assure cultural as well as material progress.

Calhoun's inconsistencies occurred when as a conservative thinker he looked backward and endorsed the thoroughly liberal principles of the Declaration of Independence. In the Jeffersonian tradition, as Calhoun was, it was impossible for him to avoid the Declaration, but having endorsed it, neither could he avoid its implications—that all people are created equal with natural rights prior to those of society or government. Calhoun did assert that people's rights came from their society and were not inherent in them—a conservative position—but he had no audience for such an argument. In seeking to put himself in the line of established traditions, he was obliged to accept the Declaration and suffer the consequences of trying to reason toward conservative means and ends from liberal premises. This meant that he could not wholly deny the entitlement of slaves to some status, and, having granted some, it was difficult to explain denying them more. Acceptance of the Declaration and the Jeffersonian tradition also led him to laissez-faire and limited government positions, which resulted in inconsistent views of government's availability to serve conservative purposes.

The problem for Calhoun was that the South had both national and local interests that were themselves inconsistent. The South needed sufficient power at the national level to assure that it would not be outvoted in order to protect slavery and its precarious economic posture. But the very values and practices that rationalized slavery rendered economic conditions more precarious and made it more difficult to secure support from Northern states or from the newly developing territories. The abortive effort to provide a semifeudal rationale for slavery could only succeed in putting the South further behind in a country whose ideology was exclusively Lockean and Jeffersonian, and in opening a gap that was too great to permit Southern attainment of minimum national goals. Calhoun's best work was his evolution of the "concurrent majority principle," by which he sought to make it possible for two quite distinctive interests to maintain a tenuous coalition. He attempted, through frank acknowledgment of fundamental difference and the granting of veto powers to each major interest, to assure each that it could never be threatened by the other. In the course of this argument he made an appeal to Northern capitalists by arguing that class interests should unite them with the plantation South against the threat of a rising proletariat. The effort earned him the revealing characterization of "the Marx of the master class" from a modern historian, Richard Hofstadter, but little reception from his immediate audience. The "concurrent majority principle," to the

extent that it can be considered a real issue at all and not just an artifact of the slavery controversy, suffers from the unlikely premise that there will always be two major interests and that they will be permanent and cohesive (and apparently geographically defined). If this were not the case, the principle would be totally unworkable. Perhaps it is to be taken as a symbolic admonition that no dominant group should seek to press its perhaps temporary dominance beyond the limits of others' endurance. This is apparently what is meant by some contemporary commentators who suggest that Calhoun's concurrent majority has found operational significance at the present time.

Summary

Liberalism had always been strongly represented in the minds of all Americans through the concepts of individualism, natural rights, and property. In the early decades of the republic, property became more widely everyone's right and possession and an indelible building block of social thought. In the same period the institutional mechanisms implementing liberal beliefs gained broad popular support through the incumbency of Jefferson and the succeeding Democratic-Republicans Madison and Monroe. The label *democracy* began to be applied to the national government and the Constitution despite the latter's clear antimajoritarian bias. In the process, the latter was in fact democratized. The dominant view of the proper role of government was strict laissez-faire, which was consistent with the belief that private striving would result in a self-regulating, harmonious, and progressive economy.

In this respect the deliberate use of the national government to build a self-sufficient and powerful American political economy (and incidentally to serve financial and manufacturing interests) is an exception to the liberal creed.

Hamilton *was* out of step with the laissez-faire principle in his modern mercantilist program, but his policies served as the bridge between capitalism and liberalism and indeed constituted the beginnings of the positive state we know today. No doubt the advent of the capitalist Industrial Revolution was inexorable, but the Hamiltonian tax, credit, and banking systems—to say nothing of the inducements and support provided by a truly national market, protective tariffs, and internal improvements—greatly aided this development. Moreover, it made clear, at least to some, that business and government were indispensable partners in building the "free enterprise" system.

No exception to liberalism's beliefs and practices was the central role played by law and lawyers in these early decades. Hamilton's arguments only carried the natural functions of law and lawyers to their full extent more rapidly and explicitly than might otherwise have occurred. Liberalism's primary commitments to property rights, limited government, and contractual bases for both business and governmental transactions required expression in laws and legal procedures. Lawyers were more than ready to claim a governing role, even in the face of a democratic surge that sought to deny them their special status.

The religious component of American political thought in this period was expressed in two ways. One paralleled the East-West sectionalism in the early decades and fused with the democratic egalitarianism of the western agrarians. Originating with the Second Great Awakening in 1800, it was an evangelistic, fundamentalist call for Protestant morality and salvation. Faith and hard work on the land were posed against rationalist doctrines and established wealth on the eastern seaboard.

Nativism and anti-Catholicism were often parts of the same pattern of beliefs, all of which helped set parameters for American political thought and action.

The other part played by religion occurred in the social-reform movements of the times. A high proportion of the leaders of the abolitionist, Transcendental, socialist, and working-class movements were initially ministers brought to their causes by Christian principles of social justice. But in almost every case they were forced to criticize and in some cases reject the organized churches for willingly supporting the status quo. These people often became religious radicals who stressed the need for a personal relationship with God that would be evidenced in part by efforts to better the lives of all through social reform. Calls for political action in the American experience thus have often been cast in the form of religious obligation.

Little has yet been said of the American fascination with science, invention, and machinery in general. The rapid spread of industrialization, with all its profound implications, could not have occurred had there not been a ready receptivity. From Benjamin Franklin's wide interests, to Jefferson's inventiveness, to Hamilton's lifelong fascination with developing manufacturing in all its forms, the cultural ground was being prepared for a century of romance with the machine. The assumption that progress was inherent in new devices for doing work was widespread. Fame and profit seemed to await everyone's ingenious efforts at finding ways to put nature to work for humanity. That the factory system and other forms of industrialization also threatened republican values was recognized by some, but their efforts to raise the issue met with only limited success. ❧

14. Chief Justice John Marshall

CHIEF JUSTICE JOHN MARSHALL (1756–1835) served in the Revolution under General Washington and later wrote a major biography of his hero. In the 1780s he began almost simultaneously to practice law in Virginia and to serve in its state assembly. He was also a member of the constitutional ratifying convention of 1788. He was a Federalist congressman, secretary of state (1800–1801), and the third chief justice of the United States (1801–35), serving longer in the last position than any other chief justice in American history.

Marshall was both a strong Federalist and an ardent admirer of Hamilton. He is credited with authoritatively establishing in constitutional law such major components of Hamilton's program as the Court's power of judicial review, a uniform national market, enforcement of contracts, the supremacy of the national government over the states, and a "broad constructionist" approach to the scope of national powers. In the two cases excerpted here, Marshall follows Hamilton closely in asserting the power of judicial review (drawing on *The Federalist No. 78*) and the power of the national government to create banking corporations (drawing on Hamilton's analysis of the "necessary and proper" clause in his opinion on the constitutionality of the Bank).

Marbury v. *Madison* was a suit brought against James Madison, Jefferson's secretary of state, by one of the "midnight judges," so-called because the outgoing Federalist Congress created several new judgeships on the eve of Jefferson's inauguration in 1801. When he had assumed office, Madison had found Marbury's commission to serve as a justice of the peace in the District of Columbia undelivered; believing with Jefferson that all these new judgeships were both unnecessary and also a Federalist political maneuver to embarrass Republicans, Madison refused to deliver it. The outgoing secretary of state who had failed to deliver the commission was John Marshall, serving also as chief justice in the last days of the Adams administration. Marshall, though an intimately involved party, nevertheless sat with the Court to hear and decide the case.

The dilemma facing Marshall was politically very serious. If the Court ordered Madison (and Jefferson) to deliver the commission, they would probably refuse on the grounds that each coordinate branch should be the final authority over its acts. The power of the Court and its capacity to protect Federalist interests would then appear greatly reduced, and the claims made for it by Hamilton in *The Federalist No. 78* undermined. But if the Court refused to order Madison to deliver the commission, it would appear to be unable to defend legitimate Federalist claims against the expected leveling intentions of the Jeffersonian Republicans—and again its power and prestige would decline. Marshall solved this dilemma and simultaneously established the precedent of judicial review first by declaring Marbury's right to his commission and then, in what seemed to many to be a tortured interpretation, by finding that the congressional statute authorizing the Court to grant orders in a case of this kind was unconstitutional and therefore void. Because the party limited by the Court's decision was the Court itself, this first exercise of the power of judicial review was obeyed and the precedent fully established. Despite being president, Jefferson could do nothing to prevent this major component of the Hamiltonian system from becoming part of the body of constitutional law.

McCulloch v. *Maryland* involved an effort by the state of Maryland to tax the National Bank so heavily as to prohibit its operation within that state. The first issue the case presented was whether the nature of the Union was national or federal—in other words, whether the Constitution was an act of all the people of the United States or merely a compact among sovereign states. Marshall firmly declared the national status of the founding agreement. The next issue was the scope of national power under the "necessary and proper" clause (Article I, Section 8), and Marshall came down squarely for the Hamiltonian view. Finally, he voided Maryland's tax on the grounds of national supremacy, leaving states-rights advocates empty-handed. ᐳ

Marbury v. *Madison* (1803)

The following opinion of the court was delivered by the Chief Justice [Marshall]....

The first object of inquiry is—Has the applicant a right to the commission he demands? ... [The court finds that as Marbury's appointment was complete he has a right to the commission.]

2. This brings us to the second inquiry; which is: If he has a right, and that right has been violated, do the laws of this country afford him a remedy?... [The court finds that they do.]

3. It remains to be inquired whether he is entitled to the remedy for which he applies? This depends on 1st. The nature of the writ applied for; and 2d. The power of this court.

1st. The nature of the writ.... This, then, is a plain case for a *mandamus,* either to deliver the commission, or a copy of it from the record; and it only remains to be inquired, whether it can issue from this court.

[2d. The power of this court.] The act to

establish the judicial courts of the United States authorizes the supreme court "to issue writs of *mandamus,* in cases warranted by the principles and usages of law, to any courts appointed, or persons holding office, under the authority of the United States." ... The constitution vests the whole judicial power of the United States in one supreme court, and such inferior courts as congress shall, from time to time, ordain and establish. This power is expressly extended to all cases arising under the laws of the United States; and consequently, in some form, may be exercised over the present case; because the right claimed is given by a law of the United States.

In the distribution of this power, it is declared, that "the supreme court shall have original jurisdiction, in all cases affecting ambassadors, other public ministers and consuls, and those in which a state shall be a party. In all other cases, the supreme court shall have appellate jurisdiction." ... If it had been intended to leave it in the discretion of the legislature, to apportion the judicial power be-

SOURCE: 1 Cranch, 137, 2 L.Ed. 60 (1803).

tween the supreme and inferior courts, according to the will of that body, it would certainly have been useless to have proceeded further than to have defined the judicial power, and the tribunals in which it should be vested. The subsequent part of the section is mere surplusage—is entirely without meaning, if such is to be the construction. If congress remains at liberty to give this court appellate jurisdiction, where the constitution has declared their jurisdiction shall be original; and original jurisdiction where the constitution has declared it shall be appellate; the distribution of jurisdiction, made in the constitution, is form without substance.... To enable this court, then, to issue a *mandamus,* it must be shown to be an exercise of appellate jurisdiction, or to be necessary to enable them to exercise appellate jurisdiction.... It is the essential criterion of appellate jurisdiction, that it revises and corrects the proceedings in a cause already instituted, and does not create that cause. Although, therefore, a *mandamus* may be directed to courts, yet to issue such a writ to an officer, for the delivery of a paper, is, in effect, the same as to sustain an original action for that paper, and therefore seems not to belong to appellate, but to original jurisdiction. Neither is it necessary in such a case as this, to enable the court to exercise its appellate jurisdiction. The authority, therefore, given to the supreme court, by the act establishing the judicial courts of the United States, to issue writs of *mandamus* to public officers, appears not to be warranted by the constitution; and it becomes necessary to inquire whether a jurisdiction so conferred can be exercised.

The question, whether an act, repugnant to the constitution, can become the law of the land, is a question deeply interesting to the United States: but, happily, not of an intricacy proportioned to its interest. It seems only necessary to recognize certain principles, supposed to have been long and well established, to decide it. That the people have an original right to establish, for their future government, such principles as, in their opinion, shall most conduce to their own happiness, is the basis on which the whole American fabric has been erected. The exercise of this original right is a very great exertion; nor can it, nor ought it, to be frequently repeated. The principles, therefore, so established, are deemed fundamental: and as the authority from which they proceed is supreme, and can seldom act, they are designed to be permanent.

This original and supreme will organizes the government, and assigns to different departments their respective powers. It may either stop here, or establish certain limits not to be transcended by those departments. The government of the United States is of the latter description. The powers of the legislature are defined and limited; and that those limits may not be mistaken, or forgotten, the constitution is written. To what purpose are powers limited, and to what purpose is that limitation committed to writing, if these limits may, at any time, be passed by those intended to be restrained? The distinction between a government with limited and unlimited powers is abolished, if those limits do not confine the persons on whom they are imposed, and if acts prohibited and acts allowed, are of equal obligation. It is a proposition too plain to be contested, that the constitution controls any legislative act repugnant to it; or, that the legislature may alter the constitution by an ordinary act.

Between these alternatives, there is no middle ground. The constitution is either a superior paramount law, unchangeable by ordinary means, or it is on a level with ordinary legislative acts, and, like other acts, is alterable when the legislature shall please to alter it. If the former part of the alternative be true, then a legislative act, contrary to the constitution, is not law; if the latter part be true, then written constitutions are absurd attempts, on the part of the people, to limit a power, in its own nature, illimitable.

Certainly, all those who have framed written constitutions contemplate them as forming the fundamental and paramount law of the nation, and consequently, the theory of every such government must be, that an act of the legislature, repugnant to the constitution, is void. This theory is essentially attached to a written constitution, and is, consequently, to be considered, by this court, as one of the fundamental principles of our society. It is not, therefore, to be lost sight of, in the further consideration of this subject.

If an act of the legislature, repugnant to the constitution, is void, does it, notwithstanding its invalidity, bind the courts, and oblige them to give it effect? Or, in other words, though it be not law, does it constitute a rule as operative as if it was a law? This would be to overthrow, in fact, what was established in theory; and would seem, at first view, an absurdity too gross to be insisted on. It shall, however, receive a more attentive consideration.

It is, emphatically, the province and duty of the judicial department, to say what the law is. Those who apply the rule to particular cases, must of necessity expound and interpret that rule. If two laws conflict with each other, the courts must decide on the operation of each. So, if a law be in opposition to the constitution; if both the law and the constitution apply to a particular case, so that the court must either decide that case, conformably to the law, disregarding the constitution; or conformably to the constitution, disregarding the law; the court must determine which of these conflicting rules governs the case: this is of the very essence of judicial duty. If then, the courts are to regard the constitution, and the constitution is superior to any ordinary act of the legislature, the constitution, and not such ordinary act, must govern the case to which they

both apply.

Those, then, who controvert the principle, that the constitution is to be considered, in court, as a paramount law, are reduced to the necessity of maintaining that courts must close their eyes on the constitution, and see only the law. This doctrine would subvert the very foundation of all written constitutions. It would declare that an act which, according to the principles and theory of our government, is entirely void, is yet, in practice, completely obligatory. It would declare, that if the legislature shall do what is expressly forbidden, such act, notwithstanding the express prohibition, is in reality effectual. It would be giving to the legislature a practical and real omnipotence, with the same breath which professes to restrict their powers within narrow limits. It is prescribing limits, and declaring that those limits may be passed at pleasure. That it thus reduces to nothing, what we have deemed the greatest improvement on political institutions, a written constitution, would, of itself, be sufficient, in America, where written constitutions have been viewed with so much reverence, for rejecting the construction. But the peculiar expressions of the constitution of the United States furnish additional arguments in favor of its rejection. The judicial power of the United States is extended to all cases arising under the constitution. Could it be the intention of those who gave this power, to say, that in using it, the constitution should not be looked into? That a case arising under the constitution should be decided, without examining the instrument under which it arises? This is too extravagant to be maintained. In some cases, then, the constitution must be looked into by the judges. And if they can open it at all, what part of it are they forbidden to read or to obey?

There are many other parts of the constitution which serve to illustrate this subject. It is declared, that "no tax or duty shall be laid on articles exported from any state." Suppose, a duty on the export of cotton, of tobacco, or of flour; and a suit instituted to recover it. Ought judgment to be rendered in such a case? Ought the judges to close their eyes on the constitution, and only see the laws?

The constitution declares "that no bill of attainder or *ex post facto* law shall be passed." If, however, such a bill should be passed, and a person should be prosecuted under it; must the court condemn to death those victims whom the constitution endeavors to preserve?

"No person," says the constitution, "shall be convicted of treason, unless on the testimony of two witnesses to the same overt act, or on confession in open court." Here, the language of the constitution is addressed especially to the courts. It prescribes, directly for them, a rule of evidence not to be departed from. If the legislature should change that rule, and declare one witness, or a confession out of court, sufficient for conviction, must the constitutional principle yield to the legislative act?

From these, and many other selections which might be made, it is apparent, that the framers of the constitution contemplated that instrument as a rule for the government of courts, as well as of the legislature. Why otherwise does it direct the judges to take an oath to support it? This oath certainly applies, in an especial manner, to their conduct in their official character. How immoral to impose it on them, if they were to be used as the instruments, and the knowing instruments, for violating what they swear to support!

The oath of office, too, imposed by the legislature, is completely demonstrative of the legislative opinion on this subject. It is in these words: "I do solemnly swear, that I will administer justice, without respect to persons, and do equal right to the poor and to the rich; and that I will faithfully and impartially discharge all the duties incumbent on me as _____, according to the best of my abilities and understanding, agreeable to the constitution and laws of the United States." Why does a judge swear to discharge his duties agreeably to the constitution of the United States, if that constitution forms no rule for his government? If it is closed upon him, and cannot be inspected by him? If such be the real state of things, this is worse than solemn mockery. To prescribe, or to take this oath, becomes equally a crime.

It is also not entirely unworthy of observation, that in declaring what shall be the supreme law of the land, the constitution itself is first mentioned; and not the laws of the United States, generally, but those only which shall be made in pursuance of the constitution, have that rank.

Thus, the particular phraseology of the constitution of the United States confirms and strengthens the principle, supposed to be essential to all written constitutions, that a law repugnant to the constitution is void; and that courts, as well as other departments, are bound by that instrument.

The rule must be discharged. ⁓

McCulloch v. Maryland (1819)

Marshall, Chief Justice, delivered the opinion of the court.

In the case now to be determined, the de-

<hr/>

SOURCE: 4 Wheat. 316, 4 L.Ed. 579 (1819).

fendant, a sovereign state, denies the obligation of a law enacted by the legislature of the Union; and the plaintiff, on his part, contests the validity of an act which has been passed by the legislature of that state. The constitution of our country, in its most interesting and vital parts, is to be considered; the conflicting powers of the government of the Union and of its members, as marked in that constitution, are to be discussed; and an opinion given, which may essentially influence the great operations of the government. No tribunal can approach such a question without a deep sense of its importance, and of the awful responsibility involved in its decision. But it must be decided peacefully, or remain a source of hostile legislation, perhaps of hostility of a still more serious nature; and if it is to be so decided, by this tribunal alone can the decision be made. On the supreme court of the United States has the constitution of our country devolved this important duty.

The first question made in the cause is, has congress power to incorporate a bank? It has been truly said, that this can scarcely be considered as an open question, entirely unprejudiced by the former proceedings of the nation respecting it. The principle now contested was introduced at a very early period of our history, has been recognized by many successive legislatures, and has been acted upon by the judicial department, in cases of peculiar delicacy, as a law of undoubted obligation. . . .

The power now contested was exercised by the first congress elected under the present constitution. The bill for incorporating the Bank of the United States did not steal upon an unsuspecting legislature, and pass unobserved. Its principle was completely understood, and was opposed with equal zeal and ability. After being resisted, first in the fair and open field of debate, and afterwards in the executive cabinet, with as much persevering talent as any measure has ever experienced, and being supported by arguments which convinced minds as pure and as intelligent as this country can boast, it became a law. The original act was permitted to expire; but a short experience of the embarrassments to which the

refusal to revive it exposed the government, convinced those who were most prejudiced against the measure of its necessity, and induced the passage of the present law. It would require no ordinary share of intrepidity to assert, that a measure adopted under these circumstances, was a bold and plain usurpation, to which the constitution gave no countenance. These observations belong to the cause: but they are not made under the impression that, were the question entirely new, the law would be found irreconcilable with the constitution.

In discussing this question, the counsel for the state of Maryland have deemed it of some importance, in the construction of the constitution, to consider that instrument not as emanating from the people, but as the act of sovereign and independent states. The powers of the general government, it has been said, are delegated by the states, who alone are truly sovereign; and must be exercised in subordination to the states, who alone possess supreme dominion. It would be difficult to sustain this proposition. The convention which framed the constitution was, indeed, elected by the state legislatures. But the instrument, when it came from their hands, was a mere proposal, without obligation, or pretensions to it. It was reported to the then existing congress of the United States, with a request that it might "be submitted to a convention of delegates, chosen in each state by the people thereof, under the recommendation of its legislature, for their assent and ratification." This mode of proceeding was adopted; and by the convention, by congress, and by the state legislatures, the instrument was submitted to the *people*. They acted upon it, in the only manner in which they can act safely, effectively, and wisely, on such a subject by assembling in convention. It is true, they assembled in their several states; and where else should they have assembled? No political dreamer was ever wild enough to think of breaking down the lines which separate the states, and of compounding the American people into one common mass. Of consequence, when they act, they act in their states. But the measures they adopt do not, on that account, cease to be the measures of the people themselves, or become the measures of the state governments.

From these conventions the constitution derives its whole authority. The government proceeds directly from the people; is "ordained and established" in the name of the people; and is declared to be ordained, "in order to form a more perfect union, establish justice, insure domestic tranquillity, and secure the blessings of liberty, to themselves and to their posterity." The assent of the States, in their sovereign capacity, is implied in calling a convention, and thus submitting that instrument to the people. But the people were at perfect liberty to accept or reject it; and their act was final. It required not the affirmance, and could not be negatived, by the state governments. The constitution, when thus adopted, was of complete obligation, and bound the state sovereignties. . . .

It has been said that the people had already surrendered all their powers to the State sovereignties, and had nothing more to give. But, surely, the question whether they may resume and modify the powers granted to government, does not remain to be settled in this country. Much more might the legitimacy of the general government be doubted, had it been created by the States. The powers delegated to the State sovereignties were to be exercised by themselves, not by a distinct and independent sovereignty, created by themselves. To the formation of a league, such as was the confederation, the State sovereignties were certainly competent. But when "in order to form a more perfect union," it was deemed necessary to change this alliance into an effective government, possessing great and sovereign

powers, and acting directly on the people, the necessity of referring it to the people, and of deriving its powers directly from them, was felt and acknowledged by all.

The government of the Union, then (whatever may be the influence of this fact on the case), is emphatically and truly a government of the people. In form and in substance it emanates from them, its powers are granted by them, and are to be exercised directly on them, and for their benefit.

This government is acknowledged by all to be one of enumerated powers. The principle, that it can exercise only the powers granted to it, would seem too apparent, to have required to be enforced by all those arguments, which its enlightened friends, while it was depending before the people, found it necessary to urge; that principle is now universally admitted. But the question respecting the extent of the powers actually granted, is perpetually arising, and will probably continue to rise, as long as our system shall exist. In discussing these questions, the conflicting powers of the general and state governments must be brought into view, and the supremacy of their respective laws, when they are in opposition, must be settled.

If any one proposition could command the universal assent of mankind, we might expect that it would be this—that the government of the Union, though limited in its powers, is supreme within its sphere of action. This would seem to result, necessarily, from its nature. It is the government of all; its powers are delegated by all; it represents all, and acts for all. Though any one state may be willing to control its operations, no state is willing to allow others to control them. The nation, on those subjects on which it can act, must necessarily bind its component parts. But this question is not left to mere reason: the people have, in express terms, decided it, by saying, "this constitution, and the laws of the United States, which shall be made in pursuance thereof," "shall be the supreme law of the land," and by requiring that the members of the state legislatures, and the officers of the executive and judicial departments of the states, shall take the oath of fidelity to it. The government of the United States, then, though limited in its powers, is supreme; and its laws, when made in pursuance of the constitution, form the supreme law of the land, "anything in the constitution or laws of any state, to the contrary notwithstanding."

Among the enumerated powers, we do not find that of establishing a bank or creating a corporation. But there is no phrase in the instrument which, like the articles of confederation, excludes incidental or implied powers; and which requires that everything granted shall be expressly and minutely described. Even the 10th amendment, which was framed for the purpose of quieting the excessive jealousies which had been excited, omits the word "expressly," and declares only that the powers "not delegated to the United States, nor prohibited to the states, are reserved to the states or to the people"; thus leaving the question, whether the particular power which may become the subject of contest, has been delegated to the one government, or prohibited to the other, to depend on a fair construction of the whole instrument. The men who drew and adopted this amendment had experienced the embarrassments resulting from the insertion of this word in the articles of confederation, and probably omitted it, to avoid those embarrassments. A constitution, to contain an accurate detail of all the subdivisions of which its great powers will admit, and of all the means by which they may be carried into execution, would partake of the prolixity of a legal code, and could scarcely be embraced by the human mind. It would, probably, never be understood by the public. Its nature, therefore, requires, that only its great outlines should be marked, its important objects designated, and the mi-

nor ingredients which compose those objects, be deduced from the nature of the objects themselves. That this idea was entertained by the framers of the American constitution, is not only to be inferred from the nature of the instrument, but from the language. Why else were some of the limitations, found in the 9th section of the 1st article, introduced? It is also, in some degree, warranted, by their having omitted to use any restrictive term which might prevent its receiving a fair and just interpretation. In considering this question, then, we must never forget, that it is a *constitution* we are expounding.

Although, among the enumerated powers of government, we do not find the word "bank," or "incorporation," we find the great powers, to lay and collect taxes; to borrow money; to regulate commerce; to declare and conduct war; and to raise and support armies and navies. The sword and the purse, all the external relations, and no inconsiderable portion of the industry of the nation, are intrusted to its government. It can never be pretended, that these vast powers draw after them others of inferior importance, merely because they are inferior. Such an idea can never be advanced. But it may with great reason be contended, that a government, intrusted with such ample powers, on the due execution of which the happiness and prosperity of the nation so vitally depends, must also be intrusted with ample means for their execution. The power being given, it is the interest of the nation to facilitate its execution. It can never be their interest, and cannot be presumed to have been their intention, to clog and embarrass its execution, by withholding the most appropriate means. Throughout this vast republic, from the St. Croix to the Gulf of Mexico, from the Atlantic to the Pacific, revenue is to be collected and expended, armies are to be marched and supported. The exigencies of the nation may require, that the treasure raised in the north should be transported to the south, that raised in the east, conveyed to the west, or that this order should be reversed. Is that construction of the constitution to be preferred, which would render these operations difficult, hazardous, and expensive? Can we adopt that construction (unless the words imperiously require it), which would impute to the framers of that instrument, when granting these powers for the public good, the intention of impeding their exercise by withholding a choice of means? If, indeed, such be the mandate of the constitution, we have only to obey; but that instrument does not profess to enumerate the means by which the powers it confers may be executed; nor does it prohibit the creation of a corporation, if the existence of such a being be essential to the beneficial exercise of those powers. It is, then, the subject of fair inquiry, how far such means may be employed.

It is not denied, that the powers given to the government imply the ordinary means of execution. That, for example, of raising revenue, and applying it to national purposes, is admitted to imply the power of conveying money from place to place, as the exigencies of the nation may require, and of employing the usual means of conveyance. But it is denied, that the government has its choice of means, or, that it may employ the most convenient means, if, to employ them, it be necessary to erect a corporation. On what foundation does this argument rest? On this alone: the power of creating a corporation, is one appertaining to sovereignty, and is not expressly conferred on congress. This is true. But all legislative powers appertain to sovereignty. The original power of giving the law on any subject whatever, is a sovereign power; and if the government of the Union is restrained from creating a corporation, as a means for performing its functions, on the single reason that the creation of a corporation is an act of sovereignty; if the sufficiency of this reason be acknowl-

edged, there would be some difficulty in sustaining the authority of congress to pass other laws for the accomplishment of the same objects. The government which has a right to do an act, and has imposed on it, the duty of performing that act, must, according to the dictates of reason, be allowed to select the means; and those who contend that it may not select any appropriate means, that one particular mode of effecting the object is expected, take upon themselves the burden of establishing that exception. . . .

. . . The power of creating a corporation, though appertaining to sovereignty, is not, like the power of making war, or levying taxes, or of regulating commerce, a great substantive and independent power, which cannot be implied as incidental to other powers, or used as a means of executing them. It is never the end for which other powers are exercised, but a means by which other objects are accomplished. No contributions are made to charity, for the sake of an incorporation, but a corporation is created to administer the charity; no seminary of learning is instituted, in order to be incorporated, but the corporate character is conferred to subserve the purposes of education. No city was ever built, with the sole object of being incorporated, but is incorporated as affording the best means of being well governed. The power of creating a corporation is never used for its own sake, but for the purpose of effecting something else. No sufficient reason is, therefore, perceived, why it may not pass as incidental to those powers which are expressly given, if it be a direct mode of executing them.

But the constitution of the United States has not left the right of congress to employ the necessary means, for the execution of the powers conferred on the government, to general reasoning. To its enumeration of powers is added, that of making "all laws which shall be necessary and proper, for carrying into execution the foregoing powers, and all other powers vested by this constitution, in the government of the United States, or in any department thereof." The counsel for the state of Maryland have urged various arguments, to prove that this clause, though, in terms, a grant of power, is not so in effect; but is really restrictive of the general right, which might otherwise be implied, of selecting means for executing the enumerated powers. In support of this proposition, they have found it necessary to contend, that this clause was inserted for the purpose of conferring on congress the power of making laws. That, without it, doubts might be entertained whether congress could exercise its powers in the form of legislation.

But could this be the object for which it was inserted? ... Could it be necessary to say, that a legislature should exercise legislative powers, in the shape of legislation? After allowing each house to prescribe its own course of proceeding, after describing the manner in which a bill should become a law, would it have entered into the mind of a single member of the convention, that an express power to make laws was necessary to enable the legislature to make them? That a legislature, endowed with legislative powers, can legislate, is a proposition too self-evident to have been questioned.

But the argument on which most reliance is placed, is drawn from the peculiar language of this clause. Congress is not empowered by it to make all laws, which may have relation to the powers conferred on the government, but only such as may be "necessary and proper" for carrying them into execution. The word "necessary" is considered as controlling the whole sentence, and as limiting the right to pass laws for the execution of the granted powers, to such as are indispensable, and without which the power would be nugatory. That it excludes the choice of means, and leaves to congress, in

each case, that only which is most direct and simple.

Is it true, that this is the sense in which the word "necessary" is always used? Does it always import an absolute physical necessity, so strong, that one thing, to which another may be termed necessary, cannot exist without that other? We think it does not. If reference be had to its use, in the common affairs of the world, or in approved authors, we find that it frequently imports no more than that one thing is convenient, or useful, or essential to another. ...

We admit, as all must admit, that the powers of the government are limited, and that its limits are not to be transcended. But we think the sound construction of the constitution must allow to the national legislature that discretion, with respect to the means by which the powers it confers are to be carried into execution, which will enable that body to perform the high duties assigned to it, in the manner most beneficial to the people. Let the end be legitimate, let it be within the scope of the constitution, and all means which are appropriate, which are plainly adapted to that end, which are not prohibited, but consistent with the letter and spirit of the constitution, are constitutional. ...

It being the opinion of the court, that the act incorporating the bank is constitutional, and that the power of establishing a branch in the state of Maryland might be properly exercised by the bank itself, we proceed to inquire—

Whether the state of Maryland may, without violating the constitution, tax that branch? That the power of taxation is one of vital importance; that it is retained by the states; that it is not abridged by the grant of a similar power to the government of the Union; that it is to be concurrently exercised by the two governments are truths which have never been denied. But such is the paramount character of the constitution, that its capacity to withdraw any subject from the action of even this power, is admitted. The states are expressly forbidden to lay any duties on imports or exports, except what may be absolutely necessary for executing their inspection laws. If the obligation of this prohibition must be conceded—if it may restrain a state from the exercising of its taxing power on imports and exports the same paramount character would seem to restrain, as it certainly may restrain, a state from such other exercise of this power, as is in its nature incompatible with, and repugnant to, the constitutional laws of the Union. A law, absolutely repugnant to another, as entirely repeals that other as if express terms of repeal were used.

On this ground, the counsel for the bank place its claim to be exempted from the power of a state to tax its operations. There is no express provision for the case, but the claim has been sustained on a principle which so entirely pervades the constitution, is so intermixed with the materials which compose it, so interwoven with its web, so blended with its texture, as to be incapable of being separated from it, without rending it into shreds. This great principle is, that the constitution and the laws made in pursuance thereof are supreme; that they control the constitution and laws of the respective states, and cannot be controlled by them. From this, which may be almost termed an axiom, other propositions are deduced as corollaries, on the truth or error of which, and on their application to this case, the cause has been supposed to depend. These

are, 1st: That a power to create implies a power to preserve: 2d. That a power to destroy, if wielded by a different hand, is hostile to, and incompatible with, these powers to create and preserve: 3d. That where this repugnancy exists, that authority which is supreme must control, not yield to that over which it is supreme. . . .

The court has bestowed on this subject its most deliberate consideration. The result is a conviction that the states have no power, by taxation or otherwise, to retard, impede, burden, or in any manner control, the operations of the constitutional laws enacted by congress to carry into execution the powers vested in the general government. This is, we think, the unavoidable consequence of that supremacy which the constitution has declared. We are unanimously of opinion, that the law passed by the legislature of Maryland, imposing a tax on the Bank of the United States, is unconstitutional and void.

This opinion does not deprive the states of any resources which they originally possessed. It does not extend to a tax paid by the real property of the bank, in common with the other real property within the state, nor to a tax imposed on the interest which the citizens of Maryland may hold in this institution, in common with other property of the same description throughout the state. But this is a tax on the operations of the bank, and is, consequently, a tax on the operation of an instrument employed by the government of the Union to carry its powers into execution. Such a tax must be unconstitutional. ∿

Secondary Sources

Konefsky, Samuel J. *John Marshall and Alexander Hamilton: Architects of the American Constitution.* New York: Macmillan, 1964.

Smith, Jean E. *John Marshall: Definer of a Nation.* New York: Henry Holt, 1996.

15. Ralph Waldo Emerson

RALPH WALDO EMERSON (1803–82) was born in Boston, the son of a minister. He graduated from Harvard College and Harvard Divinity School, teaching to support himself along the way, and was ordained minister of Boston's Second Church in 1829. By 1832 he had resigned his position out of conscience and begun the career as a lecturer and essayist for which he is best known. Initially supported by an inheritance, he soon developed a rewarding and international role as a provocative thinker, often delivering dozens of major addresses in a year and periodically publishing these and other reflections in collections of essays. He was more interested in encouraging others to think freshly for themselves than in providing consistent answers, but for two generations of Americans he served as a (sometimes controversial) intellectual gadfly—with shaping effects on the nineteenth century's cultural understanding of nature, science, progress, and individualism. His concerns included the relationship of nature to the human spirit, the obligations of the intuitional self in the world, slavery, and the place of religion and ethics in social life.

The selections here include, first, an excerpt from the controversial Divinity School Address of 1838, which caused Emerson to be excluded from Harvard for thirty years. In it, he draws on Eastern sources and argues to the graduating class of ministerial students that only the individual can know truth and wisdom, and only from his or her own intuition and higher self. Second is an excerpt from his mystical "The Over-Soul" (1847), in which he explores the human soul's potential unity ("the eternal ONE") with the universe and time. The final excerpt is from what is perhaps his most famous essay, "Self-Reliance" (1847), in which he makes the case for skepticism, individualism, and nonconformity. ❧

The Divinity School Address (1838)

... The intuition of the moral sentiment is an insight of the perfection of the laws of the soul. These laws execute themselves. They are out of time, out of space, and not subject to circumstance. Thus; in the soul of man there is a justice whose retributions are instant and

SOURCE: Richard Poirier, ed., *Ralph Waldo Emerson* (New York: Oxford University Press, 1990), 53–67, 131ff, 152.

entire. He who does a good deed, is instantly ennobled. He who does a mean dead, is by the action itself contracted. He who puts off impurity, thereby puts on purity. If a man is at heart just, then in so far is he God; the safety of God, the immortality of God, the majesty of God do enter into that man with justice. If a man dissemble, deceive, he deceives himself, and goes out of acquaintance with his own being. A man in the view of absolute goodness, adores, with total humility. Every step so downward, is a step upward. The man who renounces himself, comes to himself.

See how this rapid intrinsic energy worketh everywhere, righting wrongs, correcting appearances, and bringing up facts to a harmony with thoughts. Its operation in life, though slow to the senses, is, at last, as sure as in the soul. By it, a man is made the Providence to himself, dispensing good to his goodness, and evil to his sin. Character is always known. Thefts never enrich; alms never impoverish; murder will speak out of stone walls. The least admixture of a lie,—for example, the taint of vanity, the least attempt to make a good impression, a favorable appearance,—will instantly vitiate the effect. But speak the truth, and all nature and all spirits help you with unexpected furtherance. Speak the truth, and all things alive or brute are vouchers, and the very roots of the grass underground there, do seem to stir and move to bear you witness. See again the perfection of the Law as it applies itself to the affections, and becomes the law of society. As we are, so we associate. The good, by affinity, seek the good; the vile, by affinity, the vile. Thus of their own volition, souls proceed into heaven, into hell.

These facts have always suggested to man the sublime creed, that the world is not the product of manifold power, but of one will, of one mind; and that one mind is everywhere active, in each ray of the star, in each wavelet of the pool; and whatever opposes that will, is everywhere balked and baffled, because things are made so, and not otherwise. Good is positive. Evil is merely privative, not absolute: it is like cold, which is the privation of heat. All evil is so much death or nonentity. Benevolence is absolute and real. So much benevolence as a man hath, so much life hath he. For all things proceed out of his same spirit, which is differently named love, justice, temperance, in its different applications, just as the ocean receives different names on the several shores which it washes. All things proceed out of the same spirit, and all things conspire with it. Whilst a man seeks good ends, he is strong by the whole strength of nature. In so far as he roves from these ends, he bereaves himself of power, of auxiliaries; his being shrinks out of all remote channels, he becomes less and less, a mote, a point, until absolute badness is absolute death.

The perception of this law of laws awakens in the mind a sentiment which we call the religious sentiment, and which makes our highest happiness. Wonderful is its power to charm and to command. It is a mountain air. It is the embalmer of the world. It is myrrh and storax, and chlorine and rosemary. It makes the sky and the hills sublime, and the silent song of the stars is it. By it, is the universe made safe and habitable, not by science or power. Thought may work cold and intransitive in things, and find no end or unity; but the dawn of the sentiment of virtue on the heart, gives and is the assurance that Law is sovereign over all natures; and the worlds, time, space, eternity, do seem to break out into joy.

This sentiment is divine and deifying. It is the beatitude of man. It makes him illimitable. Through it, the soul first knows itself. It corrects the capital mistake of the infant man, who seeks to be great by following the great, and hopes to derive advantages *from another,*—by showing the fountain of all good to be in himself, and that he, equally with every man, is an inlet into the deeps of Reason. When he says, "I ought"; when love warms him; when he chooses, warned from on high, the good and great deed; then, deep melodies wander through his soul from Supreme Wisdom. Then he can worship, and be enlarged by his worship; for he can never go behind this sentiment. In the sublimest flights of the soul, rectitude is never surmounted, love is never outgrown.

This sentiment lies at the foundation of society, and successively creates all forms of worship. The principle of veneration never dies out. Man fallen into superstition, into sensuality, is never quite without the visions of the moral sentiment. In like manner, all the expressions of this sentiment are sacred and permanent in proportion to their purity. The expressions of this sentiment affect us more than all other compositions. The sentences of the oldest time, which ejaculate this piety, are still fresh and fragrant. This thought dwelled always deepest in the minds of men in the devout and contemplative East; not alone in Palestine, where it reached its purest expression, but in Egypt, in Persia, in India, in China. Europe has always owed to oriental genius, its divine impulses. What these holy bards said, all sane men found agreeable and true. And the unique impression of Jesus upon mankind, whose name is not so much written as ploughed into the history of this world, is proof of the subtle virtue of this infusion.

Meantime, whilst the doors of the temple stand open, night and day, before every man, and the oracles of this truth cease never, it is guarded by one stern condition; this, namely; it is an intuition. It cannot be received at second hand. Truly speaking, it is not instruction, but provocation, that I can receive from another soul. What he announces, I must find true in me, or wholly reject; and on his word, or as his second, be he who he may, I can accept nothing. On the contrary, the absence of this primary faith is the presence of degradation. As is the flood so is the ebb. Let this faith depart, and the very words it spake, and the things it made, become false and hurtful. Then falls the church, the state, art, letters, life. The doctrine of the divine nature being forgotten, a sickness infects and dwarfs the constitution. Once man was all; now he is an appendage, a nuisance. And because the indwelling Supreme Spirit cannot wholly be got rid of, the doctrine of it suffers this perversion, that the divine nature is attributed to one or two persons, and denied to all the rest, and denied with fury. The doctrine of inspiration is lost; the base doctrine of the majority of voices, usurps the place of the doctrine of the soul. Miracles, prophecy, poetry; the ideal life, the holy life, exist as ancient history merely; they are not in the belief, not in the aspiration of society; but, when suggested, seem ridiculous. Life is comic or pitiful, as soon as the high ends of being fade out of sight, and man becomes near-sighted, and can only attend to what addresses the senses. ∾

The Over-Soul (1847)

... The Supreme Critic on the errors of the past and the present, and the only prophet of that which must be, is that great nature in which we rest, as the earth lies in the soft arms of the atmosphere; that Unity, that Over-soul, within which every man's particular being is contained and made one with all other; that common heart, of which all sincere conversation is the worship, to which all right action is submission; that overpowering reality which confutes our tricks and talents, and constrains every one to pass for what he is, and to speak from his character, and not from his tongue, and which evermore tends to pass into our thought and hand, and become wisdom, and virtue, and power, and beauty. We live in succession, in division, in parts, in particles. Meantime within man is the soul of the whole; the wise silence; the universal beauty, to which every part and particle is equally related; the eternal ONE. And this deep power in which we exist, and whose beatitude is all accessible to us, is not only self-sufficing and perfect in every hour, but the act of seeing and the thing seen, the seer and the spectacle, the subject and the object, are one. We see the world piece by piece, as the sun, the moon, the animal, the tree; but the whole, of which these are the shining parts, is the soul. Only by the vision of that Wisdom can the horoscope of the ages be read, and by falling back on our better thoughts, by yielding to the spirit of prophecy which is innate in every many, we can know what it saith. Every man's words, who speaks from that life, must sound vain to those who do not dwell in the same thought on their own part. I dare not speak for it. My words do not carry its august sense; they fall short and cold. Only itself can inspire whom it will, and behold! their speech shall be lyrical, and sweet, and universal as the rising of the wind. Yet I desire, even by profane words, if I may not use sacred, to indicate the heaven of this deity, and to report what hints I have collected of the transcendent simplicity and energy of the Highest Law.

If we consider what happens in conversation, in reveries, in remorse, in times of passion, in surprises, in the instructions of dreams, wherein often we see ourselves in masquerade,—the droll disguises only magnifying and enhancing a real element, and forcing it on our distinct notice,—we shall catch many hints that will broaden and lighten into knowledge of the secret of nature. All goes to show that the soul in man is not an organ, but animates and exercises all the organs; is not a function, like the power of memory, of calculation, of compassion, but uses these as hands and feet; is not a faculty, but a light; is not the intellect or the will, but the master of the intellect and the will; is the background of our being, in which they lie,—an immensity not possessed and that cannot be possessed. From within or

from behind, a light shines through us upon things, and makes us aware that we are nothing, but the light is all. A man is the façade of a temple wherein all wisdom and all good abide. What we commonly call man, the eating, drinking, planting, counting man, does not, as we know him, represent himself, but misrepresents himself. Him we do not respect, but the soul, whose organ he is, would he let it appear through his action, would make our knees bend. When it breathes through his intellect, it is genius; when it breathes through his will, it is virtue; when it flows through his affection, it is love. And the blindness of the intellect begins, when it would be something of itself. The weakness of the will begins, when the individual would be something of himself. All reform aims, in some one particular, to let the soul have its way through us; in other words, to engage us to obey.

Of this pure nature every man is at some time sensible. Language cannot paint it with his colors. It is too subtile. It is undefinable, unmeasurable, but we know that it pervades and contains us. We know that all spiritual being is in man. A wise old proverb says, 'God comes to see us without bell'; that is, as there is no screen or ceiling between our heads and the infinite heavens, so is there no bar or wall in the soul where man, the effect, ceases, and God, the cause, begins. The walls are taken away. We lie open on one side to the deeps of spiritual nature, to the attributes of God. Justice we see and know, Love, Freedom, Power. These natures no man ever got above, but they tower over us, and most in the moment when our interest tempt us to wound them.

The sovereignty of this nature whereof we speak is made known by its independency of those limitations which circumscribe us on every hand. The soul circumscribes all things. As I have said, it contradicts all experience. In like manner it abolishes time and space. The influence of the senses has, in most men, overpowered the mind to that degree, that the walls of time and space have come to look real and insurmountable; and to speak with levity of these limits is, in the world, the sign of insanity. Yet time and space are but inverse measures of the force of the soul. The spirit sports with time,—

> 'Can crowd eternity into an hour,
> Or stretch an hour to eternity.'

We are often made to feel that there is another youth and age than that which is measured from the year of our natural birth. Some thoughts always find us young, and keep us so. Such a thought is the love of the universal and eternal beauty. Every man parts from that contemplation with the feeling that it rather belongs to ages than to mortal life. The least activity of the intellectual powers redeems us in a degree from the conditions of time. In sickness, in languor, give us a strain of poetry, or a profound sentence, and we are refreshed; or produce a volume of Plato, or Shakspeare, or remind us of their names, and instantly we come into a feeling of longevity. See how deep divine thought reduces centuries, and millenniums, and makes itself present through all ages. Is the teaching of Christ less effective now than it was when first his mouth was opened? The emphasis of facts and persons in my thought has nothing to do with time. And so, always, the soul's scale is one; the scale of the senses and the understanding is another. Before the revelations of the soul, Time, Space, and Nature shrink away. In common speech, we refer all things to time, as we habitually refer the immensely sundered stars to one concave sphere. And so we say that the Judgment is distant or near, that the Millennium approaches, that a day of certain political, moral, social reforms is at hand, and the like, when we mean, that, in the nature of things, one of the facts we contemplate is external and fugitive, and the other is permanent and connate

with the the soul. The things we now esteem fixed shall, one by one, detach themselves, like ripe fruit, from our experience, and fall. The wind shall blow them none knows whither. The landscape, the figures, Boston, London, are facts as fugitive as any institution past, or any whiff of mist or smoke, and so is society, and so is the world. The soul looketh steadily forwards, creating a world before her, leaving worlds behind her. She has no dates, nor rites, nor persons, nor specialties, nor men. The soul knows only the soul; the web of events is the flowing robe in which she is clothed.

After its own law and not by arithmetic is the rate of its progress to be computed. The soul's advances are not made by gradation, such as can be represented by motion in a straight line; but rather by ascension of state, such as can be represented by metamorphosis,—from the egg to the worm, from the worm to the fly. The growths of genius are of a certain *total* character, that does not advance the elect individual first over John, then Adam, then Richard, and give to each the pain of discovered inferiority, but by every throe of growth the man expands there where he works, passing, at each pulsation, classes, populations, of men. With each divine impulse the mind rends the thin rinds of the visible and finite, and comes out into eternity, and inspires and expires its air. It converses with truths that have always been spoken in the world, and becomes conscious of a closer sympathy with Zeno and Arrian, than with persons in the house.

This is the law of moral and mental gain. The simple rise as by specific levity, not into a particular virtue, but into the region of all the virtues. They are in the spirit which contains them all. The soul requires purity, but purity is not it; requires justice, but justice is not that; requires beneficence, but is somewhat better; so that there is a kind of descent and accommodation felt when we leave speaking of moral nature, to urge a virtue which it enjoins. To the well-born child, all the virtues are natural, and not painfully acquired. Speak to his heart, and the man becomes suddenly virtuous.

Within the same sentiment is the germ of intellectual growth, which obeys the same law. Those who are capable of humility, of justice, of love, of aspiration, stand already on a platform that commands the sciences and arts, speech and poetry, action and grace. For whoso dwells in this moral beatitude already anticipates those special powers which men prize so highly. The lover has no talent, no skill, which passes for quite nothing with his enamoured maiden, however little she may possess of related faculty; and the heart which abandons itself to the Supreme Mind finds itself related to all its works, and will travel a royal road to particular knowledges and powers. In ascending to this primary and aboriginal sentiment, we have come from our remote station on the circumference instantaneously to the centre of the world, where, as in the closet of God, we see causes, and anticipate the universe, which is but a slow effect.

One mode of the divine teaching is the incarnation of the spirit in a form,—in forms, like my own. I live in society; with persons who answer to thoughts in my own mind, or express a certain obedience to the great instincts to which I live. I see its presence to them. I am certified of a common nature; and these other souls, these separated selves, draw me as nothing else can. They stir in me the new emotions we call passion; of love, hatred, fear, admiration, pity; thence comes conversation, competition, persuasion, cities, and war. Persons are supplementary to the primary teaching of the soul. In youth we are mad for persons. Childhood and youth see all the world in them. But the larger experience of man discovers the identical nature appearing through them all. Persons themselves acquaint

us with the impersonal. In all conversation between two persons, tacit reference is made, as to a third party, to a common nature. That third party or common nature is not social; it is impersonal; is God. And so in groups where debate is earnest, and especially on high questions, the company become aware that the thought rises to an equal level in all bosoms, that all have a spiritual property in what was said, as well as the sayer. They all become wiser than they were. It arches over them like a temple, this unity of thought, in which every heart beats with nobler sense of power and duty, and thinks and acts with unusual solemnity. All are conscious of attaining to a higher self-possession. It shines for all. There is a certain wisdom of humanity which is common to the greatest men with the lowest, and which our ordinary education often labors to silence and obstruct. The mind is one, and the best minds, who love truth for its own sake, think much less of property in truth. They accept it thankfully everywhere, and do not label or stamp it with any man's name, for it is theirs long beforehand, and from eternity. The learned and the studious of thought have no monopoly of wisdom. Their violence of direction in some degree disqualifies them to think truly. We owe many valuable observations to people who are not very acute or profound, and who say the thing without effort, which we want and have long been hunting in vain. The action of the soul is oftener in that which is felt and left unsaid, than in that which is said in any conversation. It broods over every society, and they unconsciously seek for it in each other. We know better than we do. We do not yet possess ourselves, and we know at the same time that we are much more. I feel the same truth how often in my trivial conversation with my neighbours, that somewhat higher in each of us overlooks this by-play, and Jove nods to Jove from behind each of us. . . .

Self-Reliance (1847)

I read the other day some verses written by an eminent painter which were original and not conventional. The soul always hears an admonition in such lines, let the subject be what it may. The sentiment they instil is of more value than any thought they may contain. To believe your own thought, to believe that what is true for you in your private heart is true for all men,—that is genius. Speak your latent conviction, and it shall be the universal sense; for the inmost in due time becomes the outmost,—and our first thought is rendered back to us by the trumpets of the Last Judgment. Familiar as the voice of the mind is to each, the highest merit we ascribe to Moses, Plato, and Milton is, that they set at naught books and traditions, and spoke not what men but what they thought. A man should learn to detect and watch that gleam of light which flashes across his mind from within, more than the lustre of the firmament of bards and sages. Yet he dismisses without notice his thought, because it is his. In every work of genius we recognize our own rejected thoughts; they come back to us with a certain alienated majesty. Great works of art have no more affecting lesson for us than this. They teach us to abide by our spontaneous impression with good-humored inflexibility then most when the whole cry of voices is on the other side. Else, tomorrow a stranger will say with masterly good sense precisely what we have thought and felt all the time, and we shall be forced to take with shame our own opinion from another.

There is a time in every man's education when he arrives at the conviction that envy is ignorance; that imitation is suicide; that he must take himself for better, for worse, as his portion; that though the wide universe is full of good, no kernel of nourishing corn can come to him but through his toil bestowed on that plot of ground which is given to him to till. The power which resides in him is new in nature, and none but he knows what that is which he can do, nor does he know until he has tried. Not for nothing one face, one character, one fact, makes much impression on him, and another none. This sculpture in the memory is not without preëstablished harmony. The eye was placed where one ray should fall, that it might testify of that particular ray. We but half express ourselves, and are ashamed of that divine idea which each of us represents. It may be safely trusted as proportionate and of good issues, so it be faithfully imparted, but God will not have his work made manifest by cowards. A man is relieved and gay when he has put his heart into his work and done his best; but what he has said or done otherwise, shall give him no peace. It is a deliverance which does not deliver. In the attempt his genius deserts him; no muse befriends; no invention, no hope.

Trust thyself: every heart vibrates to that iron string. Accept the place the divine providence has found for you, the society of your contemporaries, the connection of events. Great men have always done so, and confided themselves childlike to the genius of their age, betraying their perception that the absolutely trustworthy was seated at their heart, working through their hands, predominating in all their being. And we are now men, and must accept in the highest mind the same transcendent destiny; and not minors and invalids in a protected corner, nor cowards fleeing before a revolution, but guides, redeemers, and benefactors, obeying the Almighty effort, and advancing on Chaos and the Dark. . . .

Whoso would be a man must be a nonconformist. He who would gather immortal palms must not be hindered by the name of goodness, but must explore if it be goodness. Nothing is at last sacred but the integrity of your own mind. Absolve you to yourself, and you shall have the suffrage of the world. I remember an answer which when quite young I was prompted to make to a valued adviser, who was wont to importune me with the dear old doctrines of the church. On my saying, What have I to do with the sacredness of traditions, if I live wholly from within? my friend suggested,—'But these impulses may be from below, not from above.' I replied, 'They do not seem to me to be such; but if I am the Devil's child, I will live then from the Devil.' No law can be sacred to me but that of my nature. Good and bad are but names very readily transferable to that or this; the only right is what is after my constitution, the only wrong what is against it. A man is to carry himself in the presence of all opposition, as if every thing were titular and ephemeral but he. I am ashamed to think how easily we capitulate to badges and names, to large societies and dead institutions. Every decent and well-spoken individual affects and sways me more than is right. I ought to go upright and vital, and speak the rude truth in all ways. If malice and vanity wear the coat of philanthropy, shall that pass? If an angry bigot assumes this bountiful cause of Abolition, and comes to me with his last news from Barbadoes, why should I not say to him, 'Go love thy infant; love thy wood-chopper: be good-natured and modest: have that grace; and never varnish your hard, uncharitable ambition with this incredible tenderness for black folk a thousand miles off. Thy love afar is spite at home.' Rough and graceless world be such greeting, but truth is handsomer than the affectation of love. Your goodness must have some edge to it,—else it is none. The doctrine of hatred must be preached as the counteraction of the doctrine of love when that pules and whines. I shun father and mother and wife and brother, when my genius

calls me. I would write on the lintels of the door-post, *Whim*. I hope it is somewhat better than whim at last, but we cannot spend the day in explanation. Expect me not to show cause why I seek or why I exclude company. Then, again, do not tell me, as a good man did to-day, of my obligation to put all poor men in good situations. Are they *my* poor? I tell thee, thou foolish philanthropist, that I grudge the dollar, the dime, the cent, I give to such men as do not belong to me and to whom I do not belong. There is a class of persons to whom by all spiritual affinity I am bought and sold; for them I will go to prison, if need be; but your miscellaneous popular charities; the education at college of fools; the building of meeting-houses to the vain end to which many now stand; alms to sots; and the thousandfold Relief Societies;—though I confess with shame I sometimes succumb and give the dollar, it is a wicked dollar which by and by I shall have the manhood to withhold.

Virtues are, in the popular estimate, rather the exception than the rule. There is the man *and* his virtues. Men do what is called a good action, as some piece of courage or charity, much as they would pay a fine in expiation of daily non-appearance on parade. Their works are done as an apology or extenuation of their living in the world,—as invalids and the insane pay a high board. Their virtues are penances. I do not wish to expiate, but to live. My life is for itself and not for a spectacle. I much prefer that it should be of a lower strain, so it be genuine and equal, than that it should be glittering and unsteady. I wish it to be sound and sweet, and not to need diet and bleeding. I ask primary evidence that you are a man, and refuse this appeal from the man to his actions. I know that for myself it makes no difference whether I do or forbear those actions which are reckoned excellent. I cannot consent to pay for a privilege where I have intrinsic right. Few and mean as my gifts may be, I actually am, and do not need for my own assurance or the assurance of my fellows any secondary testimony.

What I must do is all that concerns me, not what the people think. This rule, equally arduous in actual and in intellectual life, may serve for the whole distinction between greatness and meanness. It is the harder, because you will always find those who think they know what is your duty better than you know it. It is easy in the world to live after the world's opinion; it is easy in solitude to live after our own; but the great man is he who in the midst of the crowd keeps with perfect sweetness the independence of solitude.

The objection to conforming to usages that have become dead to you is, that it scatters your force. It loses your time and blurs the impression of your character. If you maintain a dead church, contribute to a dead Bible-society, vote with a great party either for the government or against it, spread your table like base housekeepers,—under all these screens I have difficulty to detect the precise man you are. And, of course, so much force is withdrawn from your proper life. But do your work, and I shall know you. Do your work, and you shall reinforce yourself. A man must consider what a blindman's-bluff is this game of conformity. If I know your sect, I anticipate your argument. I hear a preacher announce for his text and topic the expediency of one of the institutions of his church. Do I not know before hand that not possibly can he say a new and spontaneous word? Do I not know that, with all this ostentation of examining the grounds of the institution, he will do no such thing? Do I not know that he is pledged to himself not to look but at one side,—the permitted side, not as a man, but as a parish minister? He is a retained attorney, and these airs of the bench are the emptiest affectation. Well, most men have bound their yes with one or another handkerchief, and attached themselves to some one of these communities of opinion.

This conformity makes them not false in a few particulars, authors of a few lies, but false in all particulars. Their every truth is not quite true. Their two is not the real two, their four not the real four; so that every word they say chagrins us, and we know not where to begin to set them right. Meantime nature is not slow to equip us in the prison-uniform of the party to which we adhere. We come to wear one cut of face and figure, and acquire by degrees the gentlest asinine expression. There is a mortifying experience in particular, which does not fail to wreak itself also in the general history; I mean 'the foolish face of praise,' the forced smile which we put on in company where we do not feel at ease in answer to conversation which does not interest us. The muscles, not spontaneously moved, but moved by a low usurping wilfulness, grow tight about the outline of the face with the most disagreeable sensation.

For nonconformity the world whips you with its displeasure. And therefore a man must know how to estimate a sour face. The bystanders look askance on him in the public street or in the friend's parlour. If this aversation had its origin in contempt and resistance like his own, he might well go home with a sad countenance; but the sour faces of the multitude, like their sweet faces, have no deep cause, but are put on and off as the wind blows and a newspaper directs. Yet is the discontent of the multitude more formidable than that of the senate and the college. It is easy enough for a firm man who knows the world to brook the rage of the cultivated classes. Their rage is decorous and prudent, for they are timid as being very vulnerable themselves. But when to their feminine rage the indignation of the people is added, when the ignorant and the poor are aroused, when the unintelligent brute force that lies at the bottom of society is made to growl and mow, it needs the habit of magnanimity and religion to treat it godlike as a trifle of no concernment.

The other terror that scares us from self-trust is our consistency; a reverence for our past act or word, because the eyes of others have no other data for computing our orbit than our past acts, and we are loath to disappoint them.

But why should you keep your head over your shoulder? Why drag about this corpse of your memory, lest you contradict somewhat you have stated in this or that public place? Suppose you should contradict yourself; what then? It seems to be a rule of wisdom never to rely on your memory alone, scarcely even in acts of pure memory, but to bring the past for judgment into the thousand-eyed present, and live ever in a new day. In your metaphysics you have denied personality to the Deity: yet when the devout mentions of the soul come, yield to them heart and life, though they should clothe God with shape and color. Leave your theory, as Joseph his coat in the hand of the harlot, and flee.

A foolish consistency is the hobgoblin of little minds, adored by little statesmen and philosophers and divines. With consistency a great soul has simply nothing to do. He may as well concern himself with his shadow on the wall. Speak what you think now in hard words, and to-morrow speak what to-morrow thinks in hard words again, though it contradict every thing you said to-day.—'Ah, so you shall be sure to be misunderstood.'—Is it so bad, then, to be misunderstood? Pythagoras was misunderstood, and Socrates, and Jesus, and Luther, and Copernicus, and Galileo, and Newton, and every pure and wise spirit that ever took flesh. To be great is to be misunderstood. . . .

The relations of the soul to the divine spirit are so pure, that it is profane to seek to interpose helps. It must be that when God speaketh he should communicate, not one thing, but all things; should fill the world with his voice; should scatter forth light, nature, time, souls,

from the centre of the present thought; and new date and new create the whole. Whenever a mind is simple, and receives a divine wisdom, old things pass away,—means, teachers, texts, temples fall; it lives now, and absorbs past and future into the present hour. All things are made sacred by relation to it,—one as much as another. All things are dissolved to their centre by their cause, and, in the universal miracle, petty and particular miracles disappear. If, therefore, a man claims to know and speak of God, and carries you backward to the phraseology of some old mouldered nation in another country, in another world, believe him not. Is the acorn better than the oak which is its fulness and completion? Is the parent better than the child into whom he has cast his ripened being? Whence, then, this worship of the past? The centuries are conspirators against the sanity and authority of the soul. Time and space are but physiological colors which the eye makes, but the soul is light; where it is, is day; where it was, is night; and history is an impertinence and an injury, if it be any thing more than a cheerful apologue or parable of my being and becoming.

Man is timid and apologetic; he is no longer upright; he dares not say 'I think,' 'I am,' but quotes some saint or sage. He is ashamed before the blade of grass or the blowing rose. These roses under my window make no reference to former roses or to better ones; they are for what they are; they exist with God to-day. There is no time to them. There is simply the rose; it is perfect in every moment of its existence. Before a leaf-bud has burst, its whole life acts; in the full-blown flower there is no more; in the leafless root there is no less. Its nature is satisfied, and it satisfies nature, in all moments alike. But man postpones or remembers; he does not live in the present, but with reverted eye laments the past, or heedless of the riches that surround him, stands on tiptoe to foresee the future. He cannot be happy and strong until he too lives with nature in the present, above time.

This should be plain enough. Yet see what strong intellects dare not yet hear God himself, unless he speak the phraseology of I know not what David, or Jeremiah, or Paul. We shall not always set so great a price on a few texts, on a few lives. We are like children who repeat by rote the sentences of grandames and tutors, and, as they grow older, of the men of talents and character they chance to see,—painfully recollecting the exact words they spoke; afterwards, when they come into the point of view which those had who uttered these sayings, they understand them, and are willing to let the words go; for, at any time, they can use words as good when occasion comes. If we live truly, we shall see truly. It as easy for the strong man to be strong, as it is for the weak to be weak. When we have new perception, we shall gladly disburden the memory of its hoarded treasures as old rubbish. When a man lives with God, his voice shall be as sweet as the murmur of the brook and the rustle of the corn.

And now at last the highest truth on this subject remains unsaid; probably cannot be said; for all that we say is the far-off remembering of the intuition. That thought, by what I can now nearest approach to say it, is this. When good is near you, when you have life in yourself, it is not by any known or accustomed way; you shall not discern the footprints of any other; you shall not see the face of man; you shall not hear any name;—the way, the thought, the good, shall be wholly strange and new. It shall exclude example and experience. You take the way from man, not to man. All persons that ever existed are its forgotten ministers. Fear and hope are alike beneath it. There is somewhat low even in hope. In the hour of vision, there is nothing that can be called gratitude, nor properly joy. The soul raised over passion beholds identity and eternal causation, perceives the self-existence of Truth and Right, and calms itself with knowing that all things go well. Vast spaces of nature, the Atlantic Ocean, the South Sea,—long intervals of time, years, centuries,—are of no account. This which I think and feel underlay every former state of life and circumstances, as it does underlie my present, and what is called life, and what is called death.

Life only avails, not the having lived. Power ceases in the instant of repose; it resides in the moment of transition from a past to a new state, in the shooting of the gulf, in the darting to an aim. This one fact the world hates, that the soul *becomes;* for that for ever degrades the past, turns all riches to poverty, all reputation to a shame, confounds the saint with the rogue, shoves Jesus and Judas equally aside. Why, then, do we prate of self-reliance? Inasmuch as the soul is present, there will be power not confident but agent. To talk of reliance is a poor external way of speaking. Speak rather of that which relies, because it works and is. Who has more obedience than I masters me, though he should not raise his finger. Round him I must revolve by the gravitation of spirits. We fancy it rhetoric, when we speak of eminent virtue. We do not yet see that virtue is Height, and that a man or a company of men, plastic and permeable to principles, by the law of nature must overpower and ride all cities, nations, kings, rich men, poets, who are not.

This is the ultimate fact which we so quickly reach on this, as on every topic, the resolution of all into the ever-blessed ONE. Self-existence is the attribute of the Supreme Cause, and it constitutes the measure of good by the degree in which it enters into all lower forms. All things real are so by so much virtue as they contain. Commerce, husbandry, hunting, whaling, war eloquence, personal weight, are somewhat, and engage my respect as examples of its presence and impure action. I see the same law working in nature for conservation and growth. Power is in nature the essential measure of right. Nature suffers nothing to remain in her kingdoms which cannot help itself. The genesis and maturation of a planet, its poise and orbit, the bended tree recovering itself from the strong wind, the vital resources of every animal and vegetable, are demonstrations of the self-suffering, and therefore self-relying soul.

Thus all concentrates: let us not rove; let us sit at home with the cause. Let us stun and astonish the intruding rabble of men and books and institutions, by a simple declaration of the divine fact. Bid the invaders take the shoes from off their feet, for God is here within. Let our simplicity judge them, and our docility to our own law demonstrate the poverty of nature and fortune beside our native riches.

But now we are a mob. Man does not stand in awe of man, nor is his genius admonished to stay at home, to put itself in communication with the internal ocean, but it goes abroad to beg a cup of water of the urns of other men. We must go alone. I like the silent church before the service begin, better than any preaching. How far off, how cool, how chaste the persons look, begirt each one with a precinct or sanctuary! So let us always sit. Why should we assume the faults of our friend, or wife, or father, or child, because they sit around our hearth, or are said to have the same blood? All men have my blood, and I have all men's. Not for that will I adopt their petulance or folly, even to the extent of being ashamed of it. But your isolation must not be mechanical, but spiritual, that is, must be elevation. At times the whole world seems to be in conspiracy to importune you with emphatic trifles. Friend, client, child, sickness, fear, want, charity, all knock at once at thy closet door, and say,—'Come out unto us.' But keep thy state; come not into their confusion. The power men possess to annoy me, I give them by a weak cu-

riosity. No man can come near me but through my act. 'What we love that we have, but by desire we bereave ourselves of the love.'

If we cannot at once rise to the sanctities of obedience and faith, let us at least resist our temptations; let us enter into the state of war, and wake Thor and Woden, courage and constancy, in our Saxon breasts. This is to be done in our smooth times by speaking the truth. Check this lying hospitality and lying affection. Live no longer to the expectation of these deceived and deceiving people with whom we converse. Say to them, O father, O mother, O wife, O brother, O friend, I have lived with you after appearances hitherto. Henceforward I am the truth's. Be it known unto you that hencefoward I obey no laws less than the eternal law. I will have no covenants but proximities. I shall endeavour to nourish my parents, to support my family, to be the chaste husband of one wife,—but these relations I must fill after a new and unprecedented way. I appeal from your customs. I must be myself. I cannot break myself any longer for you, or you. If you can love me for what I am, we shall be the happier. If you cannot, I will still seek to deserve that you should. I will not hide my tastes or aversions. I will so trust that what is deep is holy, that I will do strongly before the sun and moon whatever inly rejoices me, and the heart appoints. If you are noble, I will love you; if you are not, I will not hurt you and myself by hypocritical attentions. If you are true, but not in the same truth with me, cleave to your companions; I will seek my own. I do this not selfishly, but humbly and truly. It is alike your interest, and mine, and all men's, however long we have dwelt in lies, to live in truth. Does this sound harsh to-day? You will soon love what is dictated by your nature as well as mine, and, if we follow the truth, it will bring us out safe at last.—But so you may give these friends pain. Yes, but I cannot sell my liberty and my power, to save their sensibility. Besides, all persons have their moments of reason, when they look out into the region of absolute truth; then will they justify me, and do the same thing.

The populace think that your rejection of popular standards is a rejection of all standard, and mere antinomianism; and the bold sensualist will use the name of philosophy to gild his crimes. But the law of consciousness abides. There are two confessionals, in one or the other of which we must be shriven. You may fulfil your round of duties by clearing yourself in the *direct,* or in the *reflex* way. Consider whether you have satisfied your relations to father, mother, cousin, neighbour, town, cat, and dog; whether any of these can upbraid you. But I may also neglect this reflex standard, and absolve me to myself. I have my own stern claims and perfect circle. It denies the name of duty to many offices that are called duties. But if I can discharge its debts, it enables me to dispense with the popular code. If any one imagines that this law is lax, let him keep its commandment one day.

And truly it demands something godlike in him who has cast off the common motives of humanity, and has ventured to trust himself for a taskmaster. High be his heart, faithful his will, clear his sight, that he may in good earnest be doctrine, society, law, to himself, that a simple purpose may be to him as strong as iron necessity is to others!

If any man consider the present aspects of what is called by distinction *society,* he will see the need of these ethics. The sinew and heart of man seem to be drawn out, and we are become timorous, desponding whimperers. We are afraid of truth, afraid of fortune, afraid of death, and afraid of each other. Our age yields no great and perfect persons. We want men and women who shall renovate life and our social state, but we see that most natures are insolvent, cannot satisfy their own wants, have an ambition out of all proportion to their practical force, and do lean and beg day and night continually. Our housekeeping is mendicant, our arts, our occupations, our marriages, our religion, we have not chosen, but society has chosen for us. We are parlour soldiers. We shun the rugged battle of fate, where strength is born. . . .

So use all that is called Fortune. Most men gamble with her, and gain all, and lose all, as her wheel rolls. But do thou leave as unlawful these winnings, and deal with Cause and Effect, the chancellors of God. In the Will work and acquire, and thou hast chained the wheel of Chance, and shalt sit hereafter out of fear from her rotations. A political victory, a rise of rents, the recovery of your sick, or the return of your absent friend, or some other favorable event, raises your spirits, and you think good days are preparing for you. Do not believe it. Nothing can bring you peace but yourself. Nothing can bring you peace but the triumph of principles. . . . ⌒

Primary Sources

Poirier, Richard, ed. *Ralph Waldo Emerson.* New York: Oxford University Press, 1990.

Spiller, Robert, Joseph Slater, et al., eds. *The Collected Works of Ralph Waldo Emerson.* 6 vols. Cambridge, Mass.: The Belknap Press of Harvard University, 1971– .

Secondary Sources

Baker, Carlos. *Emerson among the Eccentrics: A Group Portrait.* New York: Viking Press, 1996.

Cavell, Stanley. *The Quest of the Ordinary.* Chicago: University of Chicago Press, 1988.

McAleer, John. *Ralph Waldo Emerson: Days of Encounter.* Boston: Little, Brown, 1984.

Packer, Barbara. *Emerson's Fall: A New Interpretation of the Major Essays.* New York: Continuum, 1982.

16. Henry David Thoreau

HENRY DAVID THOREAU (1817–62) graduated from Harvard and taught school in Concord until 1841, when he went to live in Emerson's home and encountered the leaders of Transcendentalism. In 1845 he built a cabin on Emerson's property at Walden Pond and lived there until 1847 as a living example of his own critiques. This sojourn enabled him to develop the philosophy of nature expressed in *Walden* and led to a continuing interest in the study of the natural environment and man's relation to it.

Thoreau was not only a strongly committed and consistent Transcendentalist but an outspoken critic of slavery. Acting on such principles, he refused to pay taxes on the grounds that the government was using its revenues to promote the cause of slavery by fighting the Mexican War. His arrest in 1845 led to his writing the famous essay on civil disobedience, reproduced in its entirety here—an eloquent statement that remains in American history as perhaps the leading expression of morality and individual conscience against government coercion. ᴄᴧ

"Civil Disobedience" (1848)

I heartily accept the motto, "That government is best which governs least;" and I should like to see it acted up to more rapidly and systematically. Carried out, it finally amounts to this, which also I believe—"That government is best which governs not at all"; and when men are prepared for it, that will be the kind of government which they will have. Government is at best but an expedient; but most governments are usually, and all governments are sometimes, inexpedient. The objections which have been brought against a standing army, and they are many and weighty, and deserve to prevail, may also at last be brought against a standing government. The standing army is only an arm of the standing government. The government itself, which is only the mode which the people have chosen to execute their

will, is equally liable to be abused and perverted before the people can act through it. Witness the present Mexican war, the work of comparatively a few individuals using the standing government as their tool; for, in the outset, the people would not have consented to this measure.

This American government—what is it but a tradition, though a recent one, endeavoring to transmit itself unimpaired to posterity, but each instant losing some of its integrity? It has not the vitality and force of a single living man; for a single man can bend it to his will. It is a sort of wooden gun to the people themselves. But it is not the less necessary for this; for the people must have some complicated machinery or other, and hear its din, to satisfy that idea of government which they have. Governments show thus how successfully men can be imposed on, even impose on themselves, for their own advantage. It is excellent, we must all allow. Yet this government never

SOURCE: Perry Miller, ed., *Walden, with Civil Disobedience* (New York: New American Library, 1960).

of itself furthered any enterprise, but by the alacrity with which it got out of its way. It does not keep the country free. It does not settle the West. It does not educate. The character inherent in the American people has done all that has been accomplished, and it would have done somewhat more, if the government had not sometimes got in its way. For government is an expedient by which men would fain succeed in letting one another alone; and, as has been said, when it is most expedient, the governed are most let alone by it. Trade and commerce, if they were not made of india-rubber, would never manage to bounce over the obstacles which legislators are continually putting in their way; and, if one were to judge these men wholly by the effects of their actions and not partly by their intentions, they would deserve to be classed and punished with those mischievous persons who put obstructions on the railroads.

But, to speak practically and as a citizen unlike those who call themselves no-government men, I ask for, not at once no government, but *at once* a better government. Let every man make known what kind of government would command his respect, and that will be one step toward obtaining it.

After all, the practical reason why, when the power is once in the hands of the people, a majority are permitted, and for a long period continue, to rule is not because they are most likely to be in the right, nor because this seems fairest to the minority, but because they are physically the stronger. But a government in which the majority rule in all cases cannot be based on justice, even as far as men understand it. Can there not be a government in which majorities do not virtually decide right and wrong, but conscience?—in which majorities decide only those questions to which the rule of expediency is applicable? Must the citizen ever for a moment, or in the least degree, resign his conscience to the legislator? Why

has every man a conscience, then? I think that we should be men first, and subjects afterward. It is not desirable to cultivate a respect for the law, so much as for the right. The only obligation which I have a right to assume is to do at any time what I think right. It is truly enough said that a corporation has no conscience; but a corporation of conscientious men is a corporation with a conscience. Law never made men a whit more just; and, by means of their respect for it, even the well-disposed are daily made the agents of injustice. A common and natural result of an undue respect for law is, that you may see a file of soldiers, colonel, captain, corporal, privates, powder-monkeys, and all, marching in admirable order over hill and dale to the wars, against their wills, ay, against their common sense and consciences, which makes it very steep marching indeed, and produces a palpitation of the heart. They have no doubt that it is a damnable business in which they are concerned; they are all peaceably inclined. Now, what are they? Men at all? or small movable forts and magazines, at the service of some unscrupulous man in power? Visit the Navy-Yard, and behold a marine, such a man as an American government can make, or such as it can make a man with its black arts—a mere shadow and reminiscence of humanity, a man laid out alive and standing, and already, as one may say, buried, under arms with funeral accompaniments, though it may be,

Not a drum was heard, not a funeral note,
  As his corpse to the rampart we hurried;
Not a soldier discharged his farewell shot
  O'er the grave where our hero we buried.

The mass of men serve the state thus, not as men mainly, but as machines, with their bodies. They are the standing army; and the militia, jailers, constables, *posse comitatus,* etc. In most cases there is no free exercise whatever of the judgment or of the moral sense; but they put themselves on a level with wood and earth and stones; and wooden men can perhaps be manufactured that will serve the purpose as well. Such command no more respect than men of straw or a lump of dirt. They have the same sort of worth only as horses and dogs. Yet such as these even are commonly esteemed good citizens. Others—as most legislators, politicians, lawyers, ministers, and office-holders—serve the state chiefly with their heads; and, as they rarely make any moral distinctions, they are as likely to serve the devil, without *intending* it, as God. A very few—as heroes, patriots, martyrs, reformers in the great *sense,* and *men*—serve the state with their consciences also, and so necessarily resist it for the most part; and they are commonly treated as enemies by it. A wise man will only be useful as a man, and will not submit to be "clay," and "stop a hole to keep the wind away," but leave that office to his dust at least:

I am too high-born to be propertied,
To be a secondary at control,
Or useful serving-man and instrument
To any sovereign state throughout the
    world.

He who gives himself entirely to his fellow-men appears to them useless and selfish; but he who gives himself partially to them is pronounced a benefactor and philanthropist.

How does it become a man to behave toward this American government today? I answer, that he cannot without disgrace be associated with it. I cannot for an instant recognize that political organization as *my* government which is the *slave's* government also.

All men recognize the right of revolution; that is, the right to refuse allegiance to, and to resist the government, when its tyranny or its inefficiency are great and unendurable. But almost all say that such is not the case now. But such was the case, they think, in the Revolution of '75. If one were to tell me that this was

a bad government because it taxed certain foreign commodities brought to its ports, it is most probable that I should not make an ado about it, for I can do without them. All machines have their friction; and possibly this does enough good to counterbalance the evil. At any rate, it is a great evil to make a stir about it. But when the friction comes to have its machine, and oppression and robbery are organized, I say, let us not have such a machine any longer. In other words, when a sixth of the population of a nation which has undertaken to be the refuge of liberty are slaves, and a whole country is unjustly overrun and conquered by a foreign army, and subjected to military law, I think that it is not too soon for honest men to rebel and revolutionize. What makes this duty the more urgent is the fact that the country so overrun is not our own, but ours is the invading army.

Paley, a common authority with many on moral questions, in his chapter on the "Duty of Submission to Civil Government," resolves all civil obligation into expediency; and he proceeds to say that "so long as the interest of the whole society requires it, that is, so long as the established government cannot be resisted or changed without public inconvenience, it is the will of God . . . that the established government be obeyed—and no longer. This principle being admitted, the justice of every particular case of resistance is reduced to a computation of the quantity of the danger and grievance on the one side, and of the probability and expense of redressing it on the other." Of this, he says, every man shall judge for himself. But Paley appears never to have contemplated those cases to which the rule of expedience does not apply, in which a people, as well as an individual, must do justice, cost what it may. If I have unjustly wrested a plank from a drowning man, I must restore it to him though I drown myself. This, according to Paley, would be inconvenient. But he that would save his life, in such a case, shall lose it. This people must cease to hold slaves, and to make war on Mexico, though it cost them their existence as a people.

In practice, nations agree with Paley; but does any one think that Massachusetts does exactly what is right at the present crisis?

A drab of state, a cloth-o'-silver slut,
To have her train borne up, and her soul
trail in the dirt.

Practically speaking, the opponents to a reform in Massachusetts are not a hundred thousand politicians at the South, but a hundred thousand merchants and farmers here, who are more interested in commerce and agriculture than they are in humanity, and are not prepared to do justice to the slave and to Mexico, *cost what it may.* I quarrel not with far-off foes, but with those who, near at home, cooperate with, and do the bidding of, those far away, and without whom the latter would be harmless. We are accustomed to say, that the mass of men are unprepared; but improvement is slow, because the few are not materially wiser or better than the many. It is not so important that many should be as good as you, as that there be some absolute goodness somewhere, for that will leaven the whole lump. There are thousands who are in *opinion* opposed to slavery and to the war, who yet in effect do nothing to put an end to them, who, esteeming themselves children of Washington and Franklin, sit down with their hands in their pockets, and say that they know not what to do, and do nothing; who even postpone the question of freedom to the question of free trade, and quietly read the prices—current along with the latest advices from Mexico, after dinner, and, it may be, fall asleep over them both. What is the price-current of an honest man and patriot today? They hesitate, and they regret, and sometimes they petition; but they do nothing in earnest and with effect. They will wait, well disposed, for others to remedy the evil, that they may no longer have it to regret. At most, they give only a cheap vote, and a feeble countenance and God-speed, to the right, as it goes by them. There are nine hundred and ninety-nine patrons of virtue to one virtuous man. But it is easier to deal with the real possessor of a thing than with the temporary guardian of it.

All voting is a sort of gaming, like checkers or backgammon, with a slight moral tinge to it, playing with right and wrong, with moral questions; and betting naturally accompanies it. The character of the voters is not staked. I cast my vote, perchance, as I think right; but I am not vitally concerned that that right should prevail. I am willing to leave it to the majority. Its obligation, therefore, never exceeds that of expedience. Even voting *for the right* is *doing* nothing for it. It is only expressing to men feebly your desire that it should prevail. A wise man will not leave the right to the mercy of chance, nor wish it to prevail through the power of the majority. There is but little virtue in the action of masses of men. When the majority shall at length vote for the abolition of slavery, it will be because they are indifferent to slavery, or because there is but little slavery left to be abolished by their vote. *They* will then be the only slaves. Only *his* vote can hasten the abolition of slavery who asserts his own freedom by his vote.

I hear of a convention to be held at Baltimore, or elsewhere, for the selection of a candidate for the Presidency, made up chiefly of editors, and men who are politicians by profession; but I think, what is it to any independent, intelligent, and respectable man what decision they may come to? Shall we not have the advantage of his wisdom and honesty, nevertheless? Can we not count upon some independent votes? Are there not many individuals in the country who do not attend conventions? But no: I find that the respectable man, so called, has immediately drifted from his position, and despairs of his country, when his country has more reason to despair of him. He forthwith adopts one of the candidates thus selected as the only *available* one, thus proving that he is of no more worth than that of any unprincipled foreigner or hireling native, who may have been bought. O for a man who is a *man,* and, as my neighbor says, has a bone in his back which you cannot pass your hand through! Our statistics are at fault: the population has been returned too large. How many men are there to a square thousand miles in this country? Hardly one. Does not America offer any inducement for men to settle here? The American has dwindled into an Odd Fellow—one who may be known by the development of his organ of gregariousness, and a manifest lack of intellect and cheerful self-reliance; whose first and chief concern, on coming into the world, is to see that the almshouses are in good repair; and, before yet he has lawfully donned the virile garb, to collect a fund for the support of the widows and orphans that may be; who, in short, ventures to live only by the aid of the Mutual Insurance company, which has promised to bury him decently.

It is not a man's duty, as a matter of course, to devote himself to the eradication of any, even the most enormous, wrong; he may still properly have other concerns to engage him; but it is his duty, at least, to wash his hands of it, and, if he gives it no thought longer, not to give it practically his support. If I devote myself to other pursuits and contemplations, I must first see, at least, that I do not pursue them sitting upon another man's shoulders. I must get off him first, that he may pursue his contemplations too. See what gross inconsistency is tolerated. I have heard some of my townsmen say, "I should like to have them order me out to help put down an insurrection of the slaves, or to march to Mexico;—see if I

would go"; and yet these very men have each, directly by their allegiance, and so indirectly, at least, by their money, furnished a substitute. The soldier is applauded who refuses to serve in an unjust war by those who do not refuse to sustain the unjust government which makes the war; is applauded by those whose own act and authority he disregards and sets at naught; as if the state were penitent to that degree that it hired one to scourge it while it sinned, but not to that degree that it left off sinning for a moment. Thus, under the name of Order and Civil Government, we are all made at last to pay homage to and support our own meanness. After the first blush of sin comes its indifference; and from immoral it becomes, as it were, *un*moral, and not quite unnecessary to that life which we have made.

The broadest and most prevalent error requires the most disinterested virtue to sustain it. The slight reproach to which the virtue of patriotism is commonly liable, the noble are most likely to incur. Those who, while they disapprove of the character and measures of a government, yield to it their allegiance and support are undoubtedly its most conscientious supporters, and so frequently the most serious obstacles to reform. Some are petitioning the State to dissolve the Union, to disregard the requisitions of the President. Why do they not dissolve it themselves—the union between themselves and the State—and refuse to pay their quota into its treasury? Do not they stand in the same relation to the State that the State does to the Union? And have not the same reasons prevented the State from resisting the Union which have prevented them from resisting the State?

How can a man be satisfied to entertain an opinion merely, and enjoy *it?* Is there any enjoyment in it, if his opinion is that he is aggrieved? If you are cheated out of a single dollar by your neighbor, you do not rest satisfied with knowing that you are cheated, or with saying that you are cheated, or even with petitioning him to pay you your due; but you take effectual steps at once to obtain the full amount, and see that you are never cheated again. Action from principle, the perception and the performance of right, changes things and relations; it is essentially revolutionary, and does not consist wholly with anything which was. It not only divides States and churches, it divided families; ay, it divides the *individual,* separating the diabolical in him from the divine.

Unjust laws exist: shall we be content to obey them, or shall we endeavor to amend them, and obey them until we have succeeded, or shall we transgress them at once? Men generally, under such a government as this, think that they ought to wait until they have persuaded the majority to alter them. They think that, if they should resist, the remedy would be worse than the evil. But it is the fault of the government itself that the remedy *is* worse than the evil. *It* makes it worse. Why is it not more apt to anticipate and provide for reform? Why does it not cherish its wise minority? Why does it cry and resist before it is hurt? Why does it not encourage its citizens to be on the alert to point out its faults, and *do* better than it would have them? Why does it always crucify Christ and excommunicate Copernicus and Luther, and pronounce Washington and Franklin rebels?

One would think, that a deliberate and practical denial of its authority was the only offence never contemplated by government; else, why has it not assigned its definite, its suitable and proportionate, penalty? If a man who has no property refuses but once to earn nine shillings for the State, he is put in prison for a period unlimited by any law that I know, and determined only by the discretion of those who placed him there; but if he should steal ninety times nine shillings from the State, he is soon permitted to go at large again.

If the unjustice is part of the necessary friction of the machine of government, let it go, let it go: perchance it will wear smooth—certainly the machine will wear out. If the unjustice has a spring, or a pulley, or a rope, or a crank, exclusively for itself, then perhaps you may consider whether the remedy will not be worse than the evil; but if it is of such a nature that it requires you to be the agent of unjustice to another, then, I say, break the law. Let your life be a counterfriction to stop the machine. What I have to do is to see, at any rate, that I do not lend myself to the wrong which I condemn.

As for adopting the ways which the State has provided for remedying the evil, I know not of such ways. They take too much time, and a man's life will be gone. I have other affairs to attend to. I came into this world, not chiefly to make this a good place to live in, but to live in it, be it good or bad. A man has not everything to do, but something; and because he cannot do *everything,* it is not necessary that he should do *something* wrong. It is not my business to be petitioning the Governor or the Legislature any more than it is theirs to petition me; and if they should not hear my petition, what should I do then? But in this case the State has provided no way: its very Constitution is the evil. This may seem to be harsh and stubborn and unconciliatory; but it is to treat with the utmost kindness and consideration the only spirit that can appreciate or deserve it. So is all change for the better, like birth and death, which convulse the body.

I do not hesitate to say, that those who call themselves Abolitionists should at once effectually withdraw their support, both in person and property, from the government of Massachusetts, and not wait till they constitute a majority of one, before they suffer the right to prevail through them. I think that it is enough if they have God on their side, without waiting for that other one. Moreover, any man more right than his neighbors constitutes a majority of one already.

I meet this American government, or its representative, the State government, directly, and face to face, once a year—no more—in the person of its tax-gatherer; this is the only mode in which a man situated as I am necessarily meets it; and it then says distinctly, Recognize me, and the simplest, the most effectual, and, in the present posture of affairs, the indispensablest mode of treating with it on this head, of expressing your little satisfaction with and love for it, is to deny it then. My civil neighbor, the tax-gatherer, is the very man I have to deal with—for it is, after all, with men and not with parchment that I quarrel—and he has voluntarily chosen to be an agent of the government. How shall he ever know well what he is and does as an officer of the government, or as a man, until he is obliged to consider whether he shall treat me, his neighbor, for whom he has respect, as a neighbor and well-disposed man, or as a maniac and disturber of the peace, and see if he can get over this obstruction to his neighborliness without a ruder and more impetuous thought or speech corresponding with his action. I know this well, that if one thousand, if one hundred, if ten men whom I could name—if ten *honest* men only—ay, if *one* HONEST man, in this State of Massachusetts, *ceasing to hold slaves,* were actually to withdraw from this copartnership, and be locked up in the county jail therefor, it would be the abolition of slavery in America. For it matters not how small the beginning may seem to be: what is once well done is done forever. But we love better to talk about it: that we say is our mission. Reform keeps many scores of newspapers in its service, but not one man. If my esteemed neighbor, the State's ambassador, who will devote his days to the settlement of the question of human rights in the Council Chamber, instead of being threatened with the prisons of

Carolina, were to sit down the prisoner of Massachusetts, that State which is so anxious to foist the sin of slavery upon her sister—though at present she can discover only an act of inhospitality to be the ground of a quarrel with her—the Legislature would not wholly waive the subject the following winter.

Under a government which imprisons any unjustly, the true place for a just man is also a prison. The proper place today, the only place which Massachusetts has provided for her freer and less desponding spirits, is in her prisons, to be put out and locked out of the State by her own act, as they have already put themselves out by their principles. It is there that the fugitive slave, and the Mexican prisoner on parole, and the Indian come to plead the wrongs of his race should find them; on that separate, but more free and honorable, ground, where the State places those who are not *with* her, but *against* her—the only house in a slave State in which a free man can abide with honor. If any think that their influence would be lost there, and their voices no longer afflict the ear of the State, that they would not be as an enemy within its walls, they do not know by how much truth is stronger than error, nor how much more eloquently and effectively he can combat injustice who has experienced a little in his own person. Cast your whole vote, not a strip of paper merely, but your whole influence. A minority is powerless while it conforms to the majority; it is not even a minority then; but it is irresistible when it clogs by its whole weight. If the alternative is to keep all just men in prison, or give up war and slavery, the State will not hesitate which to choose. If a thousand men were not to pay their tax-bills this year, that would not be a violent and bloody measure, as it would be to pay them, and enable the State to commit violence and shed innocent blood. This is, in fact, the definition of a peaceable revolution, if any such is possible. If the tax-gatherer, or any other public officer, asks me, as one has done, "But what shall I do?" my answer is, "If you really wish to do anything, resign your office." When the subject has refused allegiance, and the officer has resigned his office, then the revolution is accomplished. But even suppose blood should flow. Is there not a sort of blood shed when the conscience is wounded? Through this would a man's real manhood and immortality flow out, and he bleeds to an everlasting death. I see his blood flowing now.

I have contemplated the imprisonment of the offender, rather than the seizure of his goods—though both will serve the same purpose—because they who assert the purest right, and consequently are most dangerous to a corrupt State, commonly have not spent much time in accumulating property. To such the State renders comparatively small service, and a slight tax is wont to appear exorbitant, particularly if they are obliged to earn it by special labor with their hands. If there were one who lived wholly without the use of money, the State itself would hesitate to demand it of him. But the rich man—not to make any invidious comparison—is always sold to the institution which makes him rich. Absolutely speaking, the more money, the less virtue; for money comes between a man and his objects, and obtains them for him; and it was certainly no great virtue to obtain it. It puts to rest many questions which he would otherwise be taxed to answer; while the only new question which it puts is the hard but superfluous one, how to spend it. Thus his moral ground is taken from under his feet. The opportunities of living are diminished in proportion as what are called the "means" are increased. The best thing a man can do for his culture when he is rich is to endeavor to carry out those schemes which he entertained when he was poor. Christ answered the Herodians according to their condition. "Show me the tribute-money," said he;—and one took a penny out of his pocket;—if you use money which has the image of Caesar on it, and which he has made current and valuable, that is, *if you are men of the State,* and gladly enjoy the advantages of Caesar's government, then pay him back some of his own when he demands it. "Render therefore to Caesar that which is Caesar's, and to God those things which are God's"—leaving them no wiser than before to which was which; for they did not wish to know.

When I converse with the freest of my neighbors, I perceive that, whatever they may say about the magnitude and seriousness of the question, and their regard for the public tranquility, the long and the short of the matter is, that they cannot spare the protection of the existing government, and they dread the consequences to their property and families of disobedience to it. For my own part, I should not like to think that I ever rely on the protection of the State. But, if I deny the authority of the State when it presents its tax-bill, it will soon take and waste all my property, and so harass me and my children without end. This is hard. This makes it impossible for a man to live honestly, and at the same time comfortably, in outward respects. It will not be worth the while to accumulate property; that would be sure to go again. You must hire or squat somewhere, and raise but a small crop, and eat that soon. You must live within yourself, and depend upon yourself always tucked up and ready for a start, and not have many affairs. A man may grow rich in Turkey even, if he will be in all respects a good subject of the Turkish government. Confucius said: "If a state is governed by the principles of reason, poverty and misery are subjects of shame; if a state is not governed by the principles of reason, riches and honors are the subjects of shame." No: until I want the protection of Massachusetts to be extended to me in some distant Southern port, where my liberty is endangered, or until I am bent solely on building up an estate at home by peaceful enterprise, I can afford to refuse allegiance to Massachusetts, and her right to my property and life. It costs me less in every sense to incur the penalty of disobedience to the State than it would to obey. I should feel as if I were worth less in that case.

Some years ago, the State met me in behalf of the Church, and commanded me to pay a certain sum toward the support of a clergyman whose preaching my father attended, but never I myself. "Pay," it said, "or be locked up in the jail." I declined to pay. But, unfortunately, another man saw fit to pay it. I did not see why the schoolmaster should be taxed to support the priest, and not the priest the schoolmaster, for I was not the State's schoolmaster, but I supported myself by voluntary subscription. I did not see why the lyceum should not present its tax-bill, and have the State to back its demand, as well as the Church. However, at the request of the selectmen, I condescended to make some such statement as this in writing: —"Know all men by these presents, that I, Henry Thoreau, do not wish to be regarded as a member of any incorporated society which I have not joined." This I gave to the town clerk; and he has it. The State, having thus learned that I did not wish to be regarded as member of that church, has never made a like demand on me since; though it said that it must adhere to its original presumption that time. If I had known how to name them, I should then have signed off in detail from all the societies which I never signed on to; but I did not know where to find a complete list.

I have paid no poll tax for six years. I was put into a jail once on this account, for one night; and, as I stood considering the walls of solid stone, two or three feet thick, the door of wood and iron, a foot thick, and the iron grating which strained the light, I could not help being struck with the foolishness of that institution which treated me as if I were mere flesh

and blood and bones, to be locked up. I wondered that it should have concluded at length that this was the best use it could put me to, and had never thought to avail itself of my services in some way. I saw that, if there was a wall of stone between me and my townsmen, there was a still more difficult one to climb or break through before they could get to be as free as I was. I did not for a moment feel confined, and the walls seemed a great waste of stone and mortar. I felt as if I alone of all my townsmen had paid my tax. They plainly did not know how to treat me, but behaved like persons who are underbred. In every threat and in every compliment there was a blunder; for they thought that my chief desire was to stand the other side of stone wall. I could not but smile to see how industriously they locked the door on my meditations, which followed them out again without let or hindrance, and *they* were really all that was dangerous. As they could not reach me, they had resolved to punish my body, just as boys, if they cannot come at some person against whom they have a spite, will abuse his dog. I saw that the State was half-witted, that it was timid as a lone woman with her silver spoons, and that it did not know its friends from its foes, and I lost all my remaining respect for it, and pitied it.

Thus the State never intentionally confronts a man's sense, intellectual or moral, but only his body, his senses. It is not armed with superior wit or honesty, but with superior physical strength. I was not born to be forced. I will breathe after my own fashion. Let us see who is the strongest. What force has a multitude? They only can force me who obey a higher law than I. They force me to become like themselves. I do not hear of *men* being *forced* to live this way or that by masses of men. What sort of life were that to live? When I meet a government which says to me, "Your money or your life," why should I be in haste to give it my money? It may be in a great strait, and not know what to do: I cannot help that. It must help itself; do as I do. It is not worth the while to snivel about it. I am not responsible for the successful working of the machinery of society. I am not the son of the engineer. I perceive that, when an acorn and a chestnut fall side by side, the one does not remain inert to make way for the other, but both obey their own laws, and spring and grow and flourish as best they can, till one, perchance, overshadows and destroys the other. If a plant cannot live according to its nature, it dies; and so a man.

The night in prison was novel and interesting enough. The prisoners in their shirt-sleeves were enjoying a chat and the evening air in the doorway, when I entered. But the jailer said, "Come, boys, it is time to lock up"; and so they dispersed, and I heard the sound of their steps returning into the hollow apartments. My room-mate was introduced to me by the jailer as "a first-rate fellow and a clever man." When the door was locked, he showed me where to hang my hat, and how he managed matters there. The rooms were whitewashed once a month; and this one, at least, was the whitest, most simply furnished, and probably the neatest apartment in the town. He naturally wanted to know where I came from, and what brought me there; and, when I had told him, I asked him in my turn how he came there, presuming him to be an honest man, of course; and, as the world goes, I believe he was. "Why" said he, "they accuse me of burning a barn; but I never did it." As near as I could discover, he had probably gone to bed in a barn when drunk, and smoked his pipe there; and so a barn was burnt. He had the reputation of being a clever man, had been there some three months waiting for his trial to come on, and would have to wait as much longer; but he was quite domesticated and contented, since he got his board for nothing, and thought that he was well treated.

He occupied one window, and I the other; and I saw that if one stayed there long, his principal business would be to look out the window. I had soon read all the tracts that were left there, and examined where former prisoners had broken out, and where a grate had been sawed off, and heard the history of the various occupants of that room; for I found that even here there was a history and a gossip which never circulated beyond the walls of the jail. Probably this is the only house in the town where verses are composed, which are afterward printed in a circular form, but not published. I was shown quite a long list of verses which were composed by some young men who had been detected in an attempt to escape, who avenged themselves by singing them.

I pumped my fellow-prisoner as dry as I could, for fear I should never see him again; but at length he showed me which was my bed, and left me to blow out the lamp.

It was like traveling into a far country, such as I had never expected to behold, to lie there for one night. It seemed to me that I never had heard the town clock strike before, nor the evening sounds of the village; for we slept with the windows open, which were inside the grating. It was to see my native village in the light of the Middle Ages, and our Concord was turned into a Rhine stream, and visions of knights and castles passed before me. They were the voices of old burghers that I heard in the streets. I was an involuntary spectator and auditor of whatever was done and said in the kitchen of the adjacent village inn—a wholly new and rare experience to me. It was a closer view of my native town. I was fairly inside of it. I never had seen its institutions before. This is one of its peculiar institutions; for it is a shire town. I began to comprehend what its inhabitants were about.

In the morning, our breakfasts were put through the hole in the door, in small oblong-square tin pans, made to fit, and holding a pint of chocolate, with brown bread, and an iron spoon. When they called for the vessels again, I was green enough to return what bread I had left; but my comrade seized it, and said that I should lay that up for lunch or dinner. Soon after he was let out to work at haying in a neighboring field, whither he went every day, and would not be back till noon; so he bade me goodday, saying that he doubted if he should see me again.

When I came out of prison—for some one interfered, and paid that tax—I did not perceive that great changes had taken place on the common, such as he observed who went in a youth and emerged a tottering and gray-headed man, and yet a change had to my eyes come over the scene—the town, and State, and country—greater than any that mere time could effect. I saw yet more distinctly the State in which I lived. I saw to what extent the people among whom I lived could be trusted as good neighbors and friends; that their friendship was for summer weather only; that they did not greatly propose to do right; that they were a distinct race from me by their prejudices and superstitions, as the Chinamen and Malays are; that in their sacrifices to humanity they ran no risks, not even to their property; that after all they were not so noble but they treated the thief as he had treated them, and hoped, by a certain outward observance and a few prayers, and by walking in a particular straight though useless path from time to time, to save their souls. This may be to judge my neighbors harshly; but I believe that many of them are not aware that they have such an institution as the jail in their village.

It was formerly the custom in our village, when a poor debtor came out of jail, for his acquaintances to salute him, looking through their fingers, which were crossed to represent the grating of a jail window, "How do ye do?" My neighbors did not thus salute me, but first looked at me, and then at one another, as if I had returned from a long journey. I was put into jail as I was going to the shoemaker's to get a shoe which was mended. When I was let out the next morning, I proceeded to finish my errand, and, having put on my mended shoe, joined a huckleberry party, who were impatient to put themselves under my conduct; and in half an hour—for the horse was soon tackled—was in the midst of a huckleberry field, on one of our highest hills, two miles off, and then the State was nowhere to be seen.

This is the whole history of "My Prisons."

I have never declined paying the highway tax, because I am as desirous of being a good neighbor as I am of being a bad subject; and as for supporting schools, I am doing my part to educate my fellow-countrymen now. It is for no particular item in the tax-bill that I refuse to pay it. I simply wish to refuse allegiance to the State, to withdraw and stand aloof from it effectually. I do not care to trace the course of my dollar, if I could, till it buys a man or a musket to shoot one with—the dollar is innocent—but I am concerned to trace the effects of my allegiance. In fact, I quietly declare war with the State, after my fashion, though I will still make what use and get what advantage of her I can, as is usual in such cases.

If others pay the tax which is demanded of me, from a sympathy with the State, they do but what they have already done in their own case, or rather they abet injustice to a greater extent than the State requires. If they pay the tax from a mistaken interest in the individual taxed, to save his property, or prevent his going to jail, it is because they have not considered wisely how far they let their private feelings interfere with the public good.

This, then, is my position at present. But one cannot be too much on his guard in such a case, lest his action be biased by obstinacy or an undue regard for the opinions of men. Let him see that he does only what belongs to himself and to the hour.

I think sometimes, Why, this people mean well, they are only ignorant; they would do better if they knew how: why give your neighbors this pain to treat you as they are not inclined to? But I think again, This is no reason why I should do as they do, or permit others to suffer much greater pain of a different kind. Again, I sometimes say to myself, When many millions of men, without heat, without ill will, without personal feelings of any kind, demand of you a few shillings only, without the possibility, such is their constitution, of retracting or altering their present demand, and without the possibility, on your side, of appeal to any other millions, why expose yourself to this overwhelming brute force? You do not resist cold and hunger, the winds and the waves, thus obstinately; you quietly submit to a thousand similar necessities. You do not put your head into the fire. But just in proportion as I regard this as not wholly a brute force, but partly a human force, and consider that I have relations to those millions as to so many millions of men, and not of mere brute or inanimate things, I see that appeal is possible, first and instantaneously, from them to the Maker of them, and, secondly, from them to themselves. But if I put my head deliberately into the fire, there is no appeal to fire or to the Maker of fire, and I have only myself to blame. If I could convince myself that I have any right to be satisfied with men as they are, and to treat them accordingly, and not according, in some respects, to my requisitions and expectations of what they and I ought to be, then, like a good Musselman and fatalist, I should endeavor to be satisfied with things as they are, and say it is the will of God. And, above all, there is this difference between resisting this and a purely brute or natural force, that I can resist this with some effect; but I

cannot expect, like Orpheus, to change the nature of the rocks and trees and beasts.

I do not wish to quarrel with any man or nation. I do not wish to split hairs, to make fine distinctions, or set myself up as better than my neighbors. I seek rather, I may say, even an excuse for conforming to the laws of the land. I am but too ready to conform to them. Indeed, I have reason to suspect myself on this head; and each year, as the taxgatherer comes round, I find myself disposed to review the acts and position of the general and State governments, and the spirit of the people, to discover a pretext for conformity.

> We must affect our country as our
>   parents,
> And if at any time we alienate
> Our love or industry from doing it honor,
> We must respect effects and teach the soul
> Matter of conscience and religion,
> And not desire of rule or benefit.

I believe that the State will soon be able to take all my work of this sort out of my hands, and then I shall be no better a patriot than my fellow-countrymen. Seen from a lower point of view, the Constitution, with all its faults, is very good; the law and the courts are very respectable; even this State and this American government, are, in many respects, very admirable, and rare things, to be thankful for, such as a great many have described them; but seen from a point of view a little higher, they are what I have described them; seen from a higher still, and the highest, who shall say what they are, or that they are worth looking at or thinking of at all?

However, the government does not concern me much, and I shall bestow the fewest possible thoughts on it. It is not many moments that I live under a government, even in this world. If a man is thought-free, fancy-free, imagination-free, that which *is not* never for a long time appearing *to be* to him, unwise rulers or reformers cannot fatally interrupt him.

I know that most men think differently from myself; but those whose lives are by profession devoted to the study of these or kindred subjects content me as little as any. Statesmen and legislators, standing so completely within the institution, never distinctly and nakedly behold it. They speak of moving society, but have no resting-place without it. They may be men of a certain experience and discrimination, and have no doubt invented ingenious and even useful systems, for which we sincerely thank them; but all their wit and usefulness lie within certain not very wide limits. They are wont to forget that the world is not governed by policy and expediency. Webster never goes behind government, and so cannot speak with authority about it. His words are wisdom to those legislators who contemplate no essential reform in the existing government; but for thinkers, and those who legislate for all time, he never once glances at the subject. I know of those whose serene and wise speculations on this theme would soon reveal the limits of his mind's range and hospitality. Yet, compared with the cheap professions of most reformers, and the still cheaper wisdom and eloquence of politicians in general, his are almost the only sensible and valuable words, and we thank Heaven for him. Comparatively, he is always strong, original, and, above all, practical. Still, his quality is not wisdom, but prudence. The lawyer's truth is not Truth, but consistency or a consistent expediency. Truth is always in harmony with herself, and is not concerned chiefly to reveal the justice that may consist with wrong-doing. He well deserves to be called, as he has been called, the Defender of the Constitution. There are really no blows to be given by him but defensive ones. He is not a leader, but a follower. His leaders are the men of '87. "I have never made an effort," he says, "and never propose to make an effort; I have never countenanced an effort, and never mean to countenance an effort, to disturb the arrangement as originally made, by which the various States came into the Union." Still thinking of the sanction which the Constitution gives to slavery, he says, "Because it was a part of the original compact—let it stand." Notwithstanding his special acuteness and ability, he is unable to take a fact out of its merely political relations, and behold it as it lies absolutely to be disposed of by the intellect—what, for instance, it behooves a man to do here in America today with regard to slavery—but ventures, or is driven, to make some such desperate answer as the following, while professing to speak absolutely, and as a private man—from which what new and singular code of social duties might be inferred? "The manner," says he, "in which the governments of those States where slavery exists are to regulate it is for their own consideration, under their responsibility to their constituents, to the general laws of propriety, humanity, and justice, and to God. Associations formed elsewhere, springing from a feeling of humanity, or any other cause, having nothing whatever to do with it. They have never received any encouragement from me, and they never will." (*Note.* These extracts have been inserted since the lecture was read.)

They who know of no purer sources of truth, who have traced up its stream no higher, stand, and wisely stand, by the Bible and the Constitution, and drink at it there with reverence and humility; but they who behold where it comes trickling into this lake or that pool, gird up their loins once more, and continue their pilgrimage toward its fountainhead.

No man with a genius for legislation has appeared in America. They are rare in the history of the world. There are orators, politicians, and eloquent men, by the thousand; but the speaker has not yet opened his mouth to speak who is capable of settling the much-vexed questions of the day. We love eloquence for its own sake, and not for any truth which it may utter, or any heroism it may inspire. Our legislators have not yet learned the comparative value of free trade and of Freedom, of union, and of rectitude, to a nation. They have no genius or talent for comparatively humble questions of taxation and finance, commerce and manufactures and agriculture. If we were left solely to the wordy wit of legislators in Congress for our guidance, uncorrected by the reasonable experience and the effectual complaints of the people, America would not long retain her rank among the nations. For eighteen hundred years, though perchance I have no right to say it, the New Testament has been written; yet where is the legislator who has wisdom and practical talent enough to avail himself of the light which it sheds on the science of legislation?

The authority of government, even such as I am willing to submit to—for I will cheerfully obey those who know and can do better than I, and in many things even those who neither know nor can do so well—is still an impure one: to be strictly just, it must have the sanction and consent of the governed. It can have no pure right over my person and property but what I concede to it. The progress from an absolute to a limited monarchy, from a limited monarchy to a democracy, is a progress toward a true respect for the individual. Even the Chinese philosopher was wise enough to regard the individual as the basis of the empire. Is a democracy, such as we know it, the last improvement possible in government? Is it not possible to take a step further towards recognizing and organizing the rights of man? There will never be a really free and enlightened State until the State comes to recognize the individual as a higher and independent power, from which all its own power and authority are derived, and treats him accordingly. I please myself with imagining a State at least which can afford to be just to all men, and to treat the individual with respect as a neighbor, which even would not think it inconsistent with its own repose if a few were to live aloof from it, not meddling with it, nor embraced by it, who fulfilled all the duties of neighbors and fellow-men. A State which bore this kind of fruit, and suffered it to drop off as fast as it ripened, would prepare the way for a still more perfect and glorious State, which also I have imagined, but not yet anywhere seen. ∽

Primary Sources

The Heart of Thoreau's Journals. Edited by Odell Shepard. Boston: Houghton Mifflin, 1927.

The Journal of Henry D. Thoreau. Edited by Bradford Terrey and Francis H. Allen. 14 vols. Boston: Houghton Mifflin, 1906.

Thoreau, Henry D. *Walden.* 2 vols. Boston: Houghton Mifflin, 1854.

———. *A Week on the Concord and Merrimack Rivers.* Boston: Houghton Mifflin, 1867.

Secondary Sources

Burbick, Joan. *Thoreau's Alternative History: Changing Perspectives on Nature, Culture, and Language.* Philadelphia: University of Pennsylvania Press, 1987.

Derleth, August. *Concord Rebel.* Philadelphia: Chilton, 1962.

Mackaye, James, ed. *Thoreau: Philosopher of Freedom.* New York: Vanguard, 1930.

Van Doren, Mark. *Henry David Thoreau: A Critical Study.* New York: Russell, 1961.

17. Orestes Brownson

ORESTES BROWNSON (1803–76) was a self-educated resident of upstate New York whose early career was shaped by rationalist rebellion against Calvinist theology. He became a Universalist minister and editor of the church newspaper and other local papers, attaining visibility as a critic of established church orthodoxies. Turning to social concerns, he used his editorial positions to advocate Owenite (early socialist) solutions for the poor condition of working people. Moving to New Hampshire as a Unitarian minister, he soon became engaged in the intellectual ferment around Boston. Eventually he moved there and initiated his own journal, the *Boston Quarterly Review,* which later became *Brownson's Quarterly Review.* In the latter's pages, almost all of which he wrote himself, he articulated a critique of developing capitalism from the perspective of working people that had clear similarities to the critique that Karl Marx (who was unknown to Brownson) was making in Europe. For Brownson the real enemy was capitalism. The Southern planter was a necessary ally, and chattel slavery a more humane system than wage slavery in any event, so he actively opposed abolition.

The essay excerpted here was written in 1840, when the consequences of the Panic of 1837 were still calling the future of the economic order into question. Earlier, Brownson had called for political action within the Jacksonian Democratic party and suspension of antislavery agitation. "The Laboring Classes" extends this argument and includes some of his best efforts on behalf of workers. ﹏

"The Laboring Classes" (1840)

... What we would ask is, throughout the Christian world, the actual condition of the laboring classes, viewed simply and exclusively in their capacity of laborers? They constitute at least a moiety of the human race. We exclude the nobility, we exclude also the middle class, and include only actual laborers, who are laborers and not proprietors, owners of none of the funds of production, neither houses, shops, nor lands, nor implements of labor, being therefore solely dependent on

SOURCE: *Boston Quarterly Review* 3 (no. 3, July 1840):367–95.

their hands. We have no means of ascertaining their precise proportion to the whole number of the race; but we think we may estimate them at one half. In any contest they will be as two to one, because the large class of proprietors who are not employers, but laborers on their own lands or in their own shops, will make common cause with them.

Now we will not so belie our acquaintance with political economy, as to allege that these alone perform all that is necessary to the production of wealth. We are not ignorant of the fact, that the merchant, who is literally the common carrier and exchange dealer, performs a useful service, and is therefore entitled to a portion of the proceeds of labor. But make all necessary deductions on his account, and then ask what portion of the remainder is retained, either in kind or in its equivalent, in the hands of the original producer, the workingman? All over the world this fact stares us in the face, the workingman is poor and depressed, while a large portion of the nonworkingmen, in the sense we now use the term, are wealthy. It may be laid down as a general rule, with but few exceptions, that men are rewarded in an inverse ratio to the amount of actual service they perform. Under every government on earth the largest salaries are annexed to those offices, which demand of their incumbents the least amount of actual labor either mental or manual. And this is in perfect harmony with the whole system of repartition of the fruits of industry, which obtains in every department of society. Now here is the system which prevails, and here is its result. The whole class of simple laborers are poor, and in general unable to procure anything beyond the bare necessaries of life.

In regard to labor two systems obtain; one that of slave labor, the other that of free labor. Of the two, the first is, in our judgment, except so far as the feelings are concerned, decidedly the least oppressive. If the slave has never been a free man, we think, as a general rule, his sufferings are less than those of the free laborer at wages. As to actual freedom one has just about as much as the other. The laborer at wages has all the disadvantages of freedom and none of its blessings, while the slave, if denied the blessings, is freed from the disadvantages. We are no advocates of slavery, we are as heartily opposed to it as any modern abolitionist can be; but we say frankly that, if there must always be a laboring population distinct from proprietors and employers, we regard the slave system as decidedly preferable to the system at wages. It is no pleasant thing to go days

without food, to lie idle for weeks, seeking work and finding none, to rise in the morning with a wife and children you love, and know not where to procure them a breakfast, and to see constantly before you no brighter prospect than the almshouse. Yet these are no unfrequent incidents in the lives of our laboring population. Even in seasons of general prosperity, when there was only the ordinary cry of "hard times," we have seen hundreds of people in a not very populous village, in a wealthy portion of our common country, suffering for the want of the necessaries of life, willing to work, and yet finding no work to do. Many and many is the application of a poor man for work, merely for his food, we have seen rejected. These things are little thought of, for the applicants are poor; they fill no conspicuous place in society, and they have no biographers. But their wrongs are chronicled in heaven. It is said there is no want in this country. There may be less than in some other countries. But death by actual starvation in this country is, we apprehend, no uncommon occurrence. The sufferings of a quiet, unassuming but useful class of females in our cities, in general sempstresses, too proud to beg or to apply to the alms-house, are not easily told. They are industrious; they do all that they can find to do; but yet the little there is for them to do; and the miserable pittance they receive for it, is hardly sufficient to keep soul and body together. And yet there is a man who employs them to make shirts, trousers, &c., and grows rich on their labors. He is one of our respectable citizens, perhaps is praised in the newspapers for his liberal donations to some charitable institution. He passes among us as a pattern of morality, and is honored as a worthy Christian. And why should he not be, since our *Christian* community is made up of such as he, and since our clergy would not dare question his piety, lest they should incur the reproach of infidelity, and lose their standing, and their salaries? Nay, since our clergy are raised up, educated, fashioned, and sustained by such as he? Not a few of our churches rest on Mammon for their foundation. The basement is a trader's shop.

We pass through our manufacturing villages, most of them appear neat and flourishing. The operatives are well dressed, and we are told, well paid. They are said to be healthy, contented, and happy. This is the fair side of the picture; the side exhibited to distinguished visitors. There is a dark side, moral as well as physical. Of the common operatives, few, if any, by their wages, acquire a competence. A few of what Carlyle terms not inaptly the *body-servants* are well paid, and now and then an agent or an overseer rides in his coach. But the great mass wear out their health, spirits, and morals, without becoming one whit better off than when they commenced labor. The bills of mortality in these factory villages are not striking, we admit, for the poor girls when they can toil no longer go home to die. The average life, working life we mean, of the girls that come to Lowell, for instance, from Maine, New Hampshire, and Vermont, we have been assured, is only about three years. What becomes of them then? Few of them ever marry; fewer still ever return to their native places with reputations unimpaired. "She has worked in a Factory," is almost enough to damn to infamy the most worthy and virtuous girl. We know no sadder sight on earth than one of our factory villages presents, when the bell at break of day, or at the hour of breakfast, or dinner, calls out its hundreds or thousands of operatives. We stand and look at these hard working men and women hurrying in all directions, and ask ourselves, where go the proceeds of their labors? The man who employs them, and for whom they are toiling as so many slaves, is one of our city nabobs, revelling in luxury; or he is a member of our legislature, enacting laws to put money in his own

pocket; or he is a member of Congress, contending for a high Tariff to tax the poor for the benefit of the rich; or in these times he is shedding crocodile tears over the deplorable condition of the poor laborer, while he docks his wages twenty-five percent; building miniature log cabins, shouting Harrison and "hard cider." And this man too would fain pass for a Christian and a republican. He shouts for liberty, stickles for equality, and is horrified at a Southern planter who keeps slaves.

One thing is certain; that of the amount actually produced by the operative, he retains a less proportion than it costs the master to feed, clothe, and lodge his slave. Wages is a cunning device of the devil, for the benefit of tender consciences, who would retain all the advantages of the slave system, without the expense, trouble, and odium of being slave-holders. . . .

Now the great work for this age and the coming, is to raise up the laborer, and to realize in our own social arrangements and in the actual condition of all men, that equality between man and man, which God has established between the rights of one and those of another. In other words, our business is to emancipate the proletaries, as the past has emancipated the slaves. This is our work. There must be no class of our fellow men doomed to toil through life as mere workmen at wages. If wages are tolerated it must be, in the case of the individual operative, only under such conditions that by the time he is of a proper age to settle in life, he shall have accumulated enough to be an independent laborer on his own capital,—on his own farm or in his own shop. Here is our work. How is it to be done?

Reformers in general answer this question, or what they deem its equivalent, in a manner which we cannot but regard as very unsatisfactory. They would have all men wise, good, and happy; but in order to make them so, they tell us that we want not external changes, but internal, and therefore instead of declaiming against society and seeking to disturb existing social arrangements, we should confine ourselves to the individual reason and conscience; seek merely to lead the individual to repentance, and to reformation of life; make the individual a practical, a truly religious man, and all evils will either disappear, or be sanctified to the spiritual growth of the soul.

This is doubtless a capital theory, and has the advantage that kings, hierarchies, nobilities,—in a word, all who fatten on the toil and blood of their fellows, will feel no difficulty in supporting it. Nicholas of Russia, the Grand Turk, his Holiness the Pope, will hold us their especial friends for advocating a theory, which secures to them the odor of sanctity even while they are sustaining by their anathemas or their armed legions, a system of things of which the great mass are and must be the victims. If you will only allow me to keep thousands toiling for my pleasure or my profit, I will even aid you in your pious efforts to convert their souls. I am not cruel; I do not wish either to cause, or to see suffering; I am therefore disposed to encourage your labors for the souls of the workingman, providing you will secure to me the products of his bodily toil. So far as the salvation of his soul will not interfere with my income, I hold it worthy of being sought; and if a few thousand dollars will aid you, Mr. Priest, in reconciling him to God, and making fair weather for him hereafter, they are at your service. I shall not want him to work for me in the world to come, and I can indemnify myself for what your salary costs me, by paying him less wages. A capital theory this, which one may advocate without incurring the reproach of a disorganizer, a jacobin, a leveller, and without losing the Friendship of the rankest aristocrat in the land.

This theory, however, is exposed to one slight objection, that of being condemned by something like six thousand years' experience. For six thousand years its beauty has been extolled, its praises sung, and its blessings sought, under every advantage which learning, fashion, wealth, and power can secure; and yet under its practical operations, we are assured, that mankind, though totally depraved at first, have been growing worse and worse ever since.

For our part, we yield to none in our reverence for science and religion; but we confess that we look not for the regeneration of the race from priests and pedagogues. They have had a fair trial. They cannot construct the temple of God. They cannot conceive its plan, and they know not how to build. They daub with untempered mortar, and the walls they erect tumble down if so much as a fox attempt to go up thereon. In a word they always league with the people's masters, and seek to reform without disturbing the social arrangements which render reform necessary. They would change the consequents without changing the antecedents, secure to men the rewards of holiness, while they continue their allegiance to the devil. We have no faith in priests and pedagogues. They merely cry peace, peace, and that too when there is no peace, and can be none. . . .

. . . Make all your rich men good Christians, and you have lessened not the evils of existing inequality in wealth. The mischievous effects of this inequality do not result from the personal characters of either rich or poor, but from itself, and they will continue, just so long as there are rich men and poor men in the same community. You must abolish the system or accept its consequences. No man can serve both God and Mammon. If you will serve the devil, you must look to the devil for your wages; we know no other way. . . .

The evil we have pointed out, we have said, is not of individual creation, and it is not to be removed by individual effort, saving so far as individual effort induces the combined effort of the mass. But whence has this evil originated? How comes it that all over the world the working classes are depressed, are the low and vulgar, and virtually the slaves of the nonworking classes? This is an inquiry which has not yet received the attention it deserves....

The cause of the inequality, we speak of, must be sought in history, and be regarded as having its root in Providence, or in human nature, only in that sense in which all historical facts have their origin in these....

[At this point the author draws on historical examples to assert that the organized church has been both a primary cause and legitimator of this inequality.]

We may offend in what we say, but we cannot help that. We insist upon it, that the complete and final destruction of the priestly order, in every practical sense of the word priest, is the first step to be taken towards elevating the laboring classes. Priests are, in their capacity of priests, necessarily enemies to freedom and equality. All reasoning demonstrates this, and all history proves it. There must be no class of men set apart and authorized, either by law or fashion, to speak to us in the name of God, or to be the interpreters of the word of God....

The next step in this work of elevating the working classes will be to resuscitate the Christianity of Christ. The Christianity of the Church has done its work. We have had enough of that Christianity. It is powerless for good, but by no means powerless for evil. It now unmans us and hinders the growth of God's kingdom. The moral energy which is awakened it misdirects, and makes its deluded disciples believe that they have done their duty to God when they have joined the church, offered a prayer, sung a psalm, and contributed

of their means to send out a missionary to preach unintelligible dogmas to the poor heathen, who, God knows, have unintelligible dogmas enough already, and more than enough. All this must be abandoned, and Christianity, as it came from Christ, be taken up, and preached, and preached in simplicity and in power....

We speak strongly and pointedly on this subject, because we are desirous of arresting attention. We would draw the public attention to the striking contrast which actually exists between the Christianity of Christ, and the Christianity of the Church. That moral and intellectual energy which exists in our country, indeed throughout Christendom, and which would, if rightly directed, transform this wilderness world into a blooming paradise of God, is now by the pseudo-gospel, which is preached, rendered wholly inefficient, by being wasted on that which, even if effected, would leave all the crying evils of the times untouched. Under the influence of the Church, our efforts are not directed to the reorganization of society, to the introduction of equality between man and man, to the removal of the corruptions of the rich, and the wretchedness of the poor....

Having, by breaking down the power of the priesthood and the Christianity of the priests, obtained an open field and freedom for our operations, and by preaching the true Gospel of Jesus, directed all minds to the great social reform needed, and quickened in all souls the moral power to live for it or to die for it; our next resort must be to government, to legislative enactments. Government is instituted to be the agent of society, or more properly the organ through which society may perform its legitimate functions. It is not the master of society; its business is not to control society, but to be the organ through which society effects its will. Society has never to petition government; government is its servant, and subject to its commands.

Now the evils of which we have complained are of a social nature. That is, they have their root in the constitution of society as it is, and they have attained to their present growth by means of social influences, the action of government, or laws, and of systems and institutions upheld by society, and of which individuals are the slaves. This being the case, it is evident that they are to be removed only by the action of society, that is, by government, for the action of society is government.

But what shall government do? Its first doing must be an undoing. There has been thus far quite too much government, as well as government of the wrong kind. The first act of government we want, is a still further limitation of itself. It must begin by circumscribing within narrower limits its powers. And then it must proceed to repeal all laws which bear against the laboring classes, and then to enact such laws as are necessary to enable them to maintain their equality. We have no faith in those systems of elevating the working classes, which propose to elevate them without calling in the aid of the government. We must have government, and legislation expressly directed to this end.

But again what legislation do we want so far as this country is concerned? We want first the legislation which shall free the government, whether State or Federal, from the control of the Banks. The Banks represent the interest of the employer, and therefore of necessity interests adverse to those of the employed; that is, they represent the interests of the business community in opposition to the laboring community. So long as the government remains under the control of the Banks, so long it must be in the hands of the natural enemies of the laboring classes, and may be made, nay, will be made, an instrument of depressing them yet lower. It is obvious then

that, if our object be the elevation of the laboring classes, we must destroy the power of the Banks over the government, and place the government in the hands of the laboring classes themselves, or in the hands of those, if such there be, who have an identity of interest with them. But this cannot be done so long as the Banks exist. Such is the subtle influence of credit, and such the power of capital, that a banking system like ours, if sustained, necessarily and inevitably becomes the real and efficient government of the country. We have been struggling for ten years in this country against the power of the banks, struggling to free merely the Federal government from their grasp, but with humiliating success. At this moment, the contest is almost doubtful,—not indeed in our mind, but in the minds of a no small portion of our countrymen. The partizans of the Banks count on certain victory. The Banks discount freely to build "log cabins," to purchase "hard cider," and to defray the expense of manufacturing enthusiasm for a cause which is at war with the interests of the people. That they will succeed, we do not for one moment believe; but that they could maintain the struggle so long, and be as strong as they now are, at the end of ten years' constant hostility, proves but all too well the power of the Banks, and their fatal influence on the political action of the community. The present character, standing, and resources of the Bank party, prove to a demonstration that the Banks must be destroyed, or the laborer not elevated. Uncompromising hostility to the whole banking system should therefore be the motto of every working man, and of every friend of Humanity. The system must be destroyed. On this point [there] must be no misgiving, no subterfuge, no palliation. The system is at war with the rights and interest of labor, and it must go. Every friend of the system must be marked as an enemy to his race, to his country, and especially to the laborer. No matter who he is, in what party he is found, or what name he bears, he is, in our judgment, no true democrat, as he can be no true Christian.

Following the distraction of the Banks, must come that of all monopolies, of all *privilege*. There are many of these. We cannot specify them all; we therefore select only one, the greatest of them all, the privilege which some have of being born rich while others are born poor. It will be seen at once that we allude to the hereditary descent of property, an anomaly in our American system, which must be removed, or the system itself will be destroyed. We cannot now go into a discussion of this subject, but we promise to resume it at our earliest opportunity. We only say now, that as we have abolished hereditary monarchy and hereditary nobility, we must complete the work by abolishing hereditary property.* A

---

* I am aware that I broach in this place a delicate subject, though I by no means advance a novel doctrine. In justice to those friends with whom I am in the habit of thinking and acting on most subjects, as well as to the political party with which I am publicly connected, I feel bound to say, that my doctrine, on the hereditary descent of property, is put forth by myself alone, and on my own responsibility. There are to my knowledge, none of my friends who entertain the doctrine, and who would not, had I consulted them, have labored to convince me of its unsoundness. Whatever then may be the measure of condemnation the community in its wisdom may judge it proper to mete out for its promulgation, that condemnation should fall on my head alone. I hold not myself responsible for others' opinions, and I wish not others to be held responsible for mine.

I cannot be supposed to be ignorant of the startling nature of the proposition I have made, nor can I, if I regard myself of the least note in the commonwealth, expect to be able to put forth such propositions, and go scathless. Because I advance singular doctrines, it is not necessary to suppose that I am ignorant of public

man shall have all he honestly acquires, so long as he himself belongs to the world in which he acquires it. But his power over his property must cease with his life, and his property must then become the property of the state, to be disposed of by some equitable law for the use of the generation which takes his place. Here is the principle without any of its details, and this is the grand legislative measure to which we look forward. We see no means of elevating the laboring classes which can be effectual without this. And is this a measure to be easily carried? Not at all. It will cost infinitely more than it cost to abolish either hereditary monarchy or hereditary nobility. It is a great measure, and a startling [one]. The rich, the business community, will never voluntarily consent to it, and we think we know too much of human nature to believe that it will ever be effected peaceably. It will be

---

opinion, or that I need to be informed as to the manner in which my doctrines are likely to be received. I have made the proposition, which I have, deliberately, with what I regard a tolerably clear view of its essential bearings, and after having meditated it and been satisfied of its soundness, for many years. I make it then with my eyes open, if the reader please, "with malice prepense." I am then entitled to no favor, and I ask as I expect none. But I am not quite so unfortunate as to be wholly without friends in this world. There are those to whom I am linked by the closest ties of affection, and whose approbation and encouragement, I have ever found an ample reward for all the labors I could perform. Their reputations are dear to me. For their sake I add this note, that they may not be in the least censured for the fact, that one whom they have honored with their friendship, and in a journal which, in its general character, they have not hesitated to commend, has seen proper to put forth a doctrine, which, to say the least, for long years to come must be condemned almost unanimously.

O.A.B.

effected only by the strong arm of physical force. It will come, if it ever come at all, only at the conclusion of war, the like of which the world as yet has never witnessed, and from which, however inevitable it may seem to the eye of philosophy, the heart of Humanity recoils with horror.

We are not ready for this measure yet. There is much previous work to be done, and we should be the last to bring it before the legislature. The time, however, has come for its free and full discussion. It must be canvassed in the public mind, and society prepared for acting on it. No doubt they who broach it, and especially they who support it, will experience a due share of contumely and abuse. They will be regarded by the part of the community they oppose, or may be thought to oppose, as "graceless varlets," against whom every man of substance should set his face. But this is not, after all, a thing to disturb a wise man, nor to deter a true man from telling, his whole thought. He who is worthy of the name of man, speaks what he honestly believes the interests of his race demand, and seldom disquiets himself about what may be the consequences to himself. Men have, for what they believed the cause of God or man, endured the dungeon, the scaffold, the stake, the cross, and they can do it again, if need be. This subject must be freely, boldly, and fully discussed, whatever may be the fate of those who discuss it. ∿

Primary Sources

Brownson, Henry F., ed. *The Works of Orestes Augustus Brownson.* New York: AMS Press, 1966.

Brownson, Orestes A. *Essays and Reviews, Chiefly on Theology, Politics and Socialism.* New York: D.L.J. Sadlier, 1852.

Secondary Sources

Roemer, Lawrence. *Brownson on Democracy and the Trend Toward Socialism.* New York: Philosophical Library, 1953.

Schlesinger, Arthur M., Jr. *Orestes A. Brownson: A Pilgrim's Progress.* New York: Octagon Books, 1939.

18. Elizabeth Cady Stanton

ELIZABETH CADY STANTON (1815–1902) graduated from Troy Female Seminary in New York and first became active in the antislavery movement. After six years of marriage, however, her own life experience shifted her focus to the condition of women. She became the driving force behind the American feminist movement of the mid-nineteenth century. With others she sponsored the first major feminist convention at Seneca Falls, New York, in 1848 and drafted the "Declaration of Sentiments and Resolutions" ultimately adopted there. The claims made on behalf of women involved many different rights, but the most controversial at the time was the right to vote. With the advance commitment and effective floor support of her friend Frederick Douglass, however, Stanton succeeded in winning convention support by a narrow margin for the demand that would dominate the women's movement for the next century.

The Seneca Falls "Declaration of Sentiments and Resolutions" is presented here in its entirety, together with excerpts from an ad-

dress Stanton made to the New York state legislature. The latter, written in conjunction with Stanton's lifelong collaborator, Susan B. Anthony, was one in a long series of efforts to change the many state laws that effectively subjugated women. ∽

Declaration of Sentiments and Resolutions (1848)

When, in the course of human events, it becomes necessary for one portion of the family of man to assume among the people of the earth a position different from that which they have hitherto occupied, but one to which the laws of nature and of nature's God entitle them, a decent respect to the opinions of mankind requires that they should declare the causes that impel them to such a course.

We hold these truths to be self-evident: that all men and women are created equal; that they are endowed by their Creator with certain inalienable rights; that among these are life, liberty, and the pursuit of happiness; that to secure these rights governments are instituted, deriving their just powers from the consent of the governed. Whenever any form of government becomes destructive of these ends, it is the right of those who suffer from it to refuse allegiance to it, and to insist upon the institution of a new government, laying its foundation on such principles, and organizing its powers in such form, as to them shall seem most likely to effect their safety and happiness. Prudence, indeed, will dictate that govern-

ments long established should not be changed for light and transient causes; and accordingly all experience hath shown that mankind are more disposed to suffer, while evils are sufferable, than to right themselves by abolishing the forms to which they were accustomed. But when a long train of abuses and usurpations, pursuing invariably the same object, evinces a design to reduce them under absolute despotism, it is their duty to throw off such government, and to provide new guards for their future security. Such has been the patient sufferance of the women under this government, and such is now the necessity which constrains them to demand the equal station to which they are entitled.

The history of mankind is a history of repeated injuries and usurpations on the part of man toward woman, having in direct object the establishment of an absolute tyranny over her. To prove this, let facts be submitted to a candid world.

He has never permitted her to exercise her inalienable right to the elective franchise.

He has compelled her to submit to laws, in the formation of which she had no voice.

He has withheld from her rights which are given to the most ignorant and degraded men—both natives and foreigners.

Having deprived her of this first right of a citizen, the elective franchise, thereby leaving her without representation in the halls of legis-

SOURCE: Both excerpts in this selection may be found in Elizabeth Cady Stanton, Susan B. Anthony, and Matilda Joslyn Gage, eds., *History of Woman Suffrage*, 4 vols. (New York: Fowler & Wells, 1881–1922; reprinted, New York: Arno Press, 1969).

lation, he has oppressed her on all sides.

He has made her, if married, in the eye of the law, civilly dead.

He has taken from her all right in property, even to the wages she earns.

He has made her, morally, an irresponsible being, as she can commit many crimes with impunity, provided they be done in the presence of her husband. In the covenant of marriage, she is compelled to promise obedience to her husband, he becoming, to all intents and purposes, her master—the law giving him power to deprive her of her liberty, and to administer chastisement.

He has so framed the laws of divorce, as to what shall be the proper causes, and in case of separation, to whom the guardianship of the children shall be given, as to be wholly regardless of the happiness of women—the law, in all cases, going upon a false supposition of the supremacy of man, and giving all power into his hands.

After depriving her of all rights as a married woman, if single, and the owner of property, he has taxed her to support a government which recognizes her only when her property can be made profitable to it.

He has monopolized nearly all the profitable employments, and from those she is permitted to follow, she receives but a scanty remuneration. He closes against her all the avenues to wealth and distinction which he considers most honorable to himself. As a teacher of theology, medicine, or law, she is not known.

He has denied her the facilities for obtaining a thorough education, all colleges being closed against her.

He allows her in Church, as well as State, but a subordinate position, claiming Apostolic authority for her exclusion from the ministry, and, with some exceptions, from any public participation in the affairs of the Church.

He has created a false public sentiment by giving to the world a different code of morals for men and women, by which moral delinquencies which exclude women from society, are not only tolerated, but deemed of little account in man.

He has usurped the prerogative of Jehovah himself, claiming it as his right to assign for her a sphere of action, when that belongs to her conscience and to her God.

He has endeavored, in every way that he could, to destroy her confidence in her own powers, to lessen her self-respect, and to make her willing to lead a dependent and abject life.

Now, in view of this entire disfranchisement of one-half the people of this country, their social and religious degradation—in view of the unjust laws above mentioned, and because women do feel themselves aggrieved, oppressed, and fraudulently deprived of their most sacred rights, we insist that they have immediate admission to all the rights and privileges which belong to them as citizens of the United States.

In entering upon the great work before us, we anticipate no small amount of misconception, misrepresentation, and ridicule; but we shall use every instrumentality within our power to effect our object. We shall employ agents, circulate tracts, petition the State and National legislatures, and endeavor to enlist the pulpit and the press in our behalf. We hope this Convention will be followed by a series of Conventions embracing every part of the country.

RESOLUTIONS

WHEREAS, The great precept of nature is conceded to be, that "man shall pursue his own true and substantial happiness." Blackstone in his Commentaries remarks, that this law of Nature being coeval with mankind, and dictated by God himself, is of course superior in obligation to any other. It is binding over all the globe, in all countries and at all times, no human laws are of any validity if contrary to this, and such of them as are valid, derive all their force, and all their validity, and all their authority, mediately and immediately, from this original; therefore,

Resolved, That such laws as conflict, in any way, with the true and substantial happiness of woman, are contrary to the great precept of nature and of no validity, for this is "superior in obligation to any other."

Resolved, That all laws which prevent woman from occupying such a station in society as her conscience shall dictate, or which place her in a position inferior to that of man, are contrary to the great precept of nature, and therefore of no force or authority.

Resolved, That woman is man's equal—was intended to be so by the Creator, and the highest good of the race demands that she should be recognized as such.

Resolved, That the women of this country ought to be enlightened in regard to the laws under which they live, that they may no longer publish their degradation by declaring themselves satisfied with their present position, nor their ignorance, by asserting that they have all the rights they want.

Resolved, That inasmuch as man, while claiming for himself intellectual superiority, does accord to woman moral superiority, it is pre-eminently his duty to encourage her to speak and teach, as she has an opportunity, in all religious assemblies.

Resolved, That the same amount of virtue, delicacy, and refinement of behavior that is required of woman in the social state, should also be required of man, and the same transgressions should be visited with equal severity on both man and woman.

Resolved, That the objection of indelicacy and impropriety, which is so often brought against woman when she addresses a public audience, comes with a very ill-grace from those who encourage, by their attendance, her appearance on the stage, in the concert, or in feats of the circus.

Resolved, That woman has too long rested satisfied in the circumscribed limits which corrupt customs and a perverted application of the Scriptures have marked out for her, and that it is time she should move in the enlarged sphere which her great Creator has assigned her.

Resolved, That it is the duty of the women of this country to secure to themselves their sacred right to the elective franchise.

Resolved, That the equality of human rights results necessarily from the fact of the identity of the race in capabilities and responsibilities.

Resolved, therefore, That, being invested by the Creator with the same capabilities, and the same consciousness of responsibility for their exercise, it is demonstrably the right and duty of woman, equally with man, to promote every righteous cause by every righteous means; and especially in regard to the great subjects of morals and religion, it is self-evidently her right to participate with her brother in teaching them, both in private and in public, by writing and by speaking, by any instrumentalities proper to be used, and in any assemblies proper to be held; and this being a self-evident truth growing out of the divinely implanted principles of human nature, any custom or authority adverse to it, whether modern or wearing the hoary sanction of antiquity, is to be regarded as a self-evident falsehood, and at war with mankind. ∽

Address to the New York State Legislature (1860)

You who had read the history of nations, from Moses down to our last election, where have you ever seen one class looking after the interests of another? Any of you can readily see the defects in other governments, and pronounce sentence against those who have sacrificed the masses to themselves; but when we come to our own case, we are blinded by custom and self-interest. Some of you who have no capital can see the injustice which the laborer suffers; some of you who have no slaves, can see the cruelty of his oppression; but who of you appreciate the galling humiliation, the refinements of degradation, to which women (the mothers, wives, sisters, and daughters of freemen) are subject, in this the last half of the nineteenth century? How many of you have ever read even the laws concerning them that now disgrace your statute-books? In cruelty and tyranny, they are not surpassed by any slaveholding code in the Southern States; in fact they are worse, by just so far as woman, from her social position, refinement, and education, is on a more equal ground with the oppressor.

Allow me just here to call the attention of that party now so much interested in the slave of the Carolinas, to the similarity in his condition and that of the mothers, wives, and daughters of the Empire State. The negro has no name. He is Cuffy Douglas or Cuffy Brooks, just whose Cuffy he may chance to be. The woman has no name. She is Mrs. Richard Roe or Mrs. John Doe, just whose Mrs. she may chance to be. Cuffy has no right to his earnings; he can not buy or sell, or lay up anything that he can call his own. Mrs. Roe has no right to her earnings; she can neither buy nor sell, make contracts, nor lay up anything that she can call her own. Cuffy has no right to his children; they can be sold from him at any time. Mrs. Roe has no right to her children; they may be bound out to cancel a father's debts of honor. The unborn child, even, by the last will of the father, may be placed under the guardianship of a stranger and a foreigner. Cuffy has no legal existence; he is subject to restraint and moderate chastisement. Mrs. Roe has no legal existence; she has not the best right to her own person. The husband has the power to restrain, and administer moderate chastisement.

Blackstone [author of *Commentaries on the Laws of England*] declares that the husband and wife are one, and learned commentators have decided that that one is the husband. In all civil codes, you will find them classified as one. Certain rights and immunities, such and such privileges are to be secured to white male citizens. What have women and negroes to do with rights? What know they of government, war, or glory?

The prejudice against color, of which we hear so much, is no stronger than that against sex. It is produced by the same cause, and manifested very much in the same way. The negro's skin and the woman's sex are both *prima facie* evidence that they were intended to be in subjection to the white Saxon man. The few social privileges which the man gives the woman, he makes up to the negro in civil rights. The woman may sit at the same table and eat with the white man; the free negro may hold property and vote. The woman may sit in the same pew with the white man in church; the free negro may enter the pulpit and preach. Now, with the black man's right to suffrage, the right unquestioned, even by Paul, to minister at the altar, it is evident that the prejudice against sex is more deeply rooted and more unreasonably maintained than that against color....

Just imagine an inhabitant of another planet entertaining himself some pleasant evening in searching over our great national compact, our Declaration of Independence, our Constitutions, or some of our statute-books; what would he think of those "women and negroes" that must be so fenced in, so guarded against? Why, he would certainly suppose we were monsters, like those fabulous giants or Brobdingnagians of olden times, so dangerous to civilized man, from our size, ferocity, and power. Then let him take up our poets, from Pope down to Dana; let him listen to our Fourth of July toasts, and some of the sentimental adulations of social life, and no logic could convince him that this creature of the law, and this angel of the family altar, could be one and the same being. Man is in such a labyrinth of contradictions with his marital and property rights; he is so befogged on the whole question of maidens, wives, and mothers, that from pure benevolence we should relieve him from this troublesome branch of legislation. We should vote, and make laws for ourselves. Do not be alarmed, dear ladies! You need spend no time reading Grotius, Coke, Puffendorf, Blackstone, Bentham, Kent, and Story to find out what you need. We may safely trust the shrewd selfishness of the white man, and consent to live under the same broad code where he has so comfortably ensconced himself. Any legislation that will do for man, we may abide by most cheerfully. . . .

Now do not think, gentlemen, we wish you to do a great many troublesome things for us. We do not ask our legislators to spend a whole session in fixing up a code of laws to satisfy a class of most unreasonable women. We ask no more than the poor devils in the Scripture asked, "Let us alone." In mercy, let us take care of ourselves, our property, our children, and our homes. True, we are not so strong, so wise, so crafty as you are, but if any kind friend leaves us a little money, or we can by great industry earn fifty cents a day, we would rather buy bread and clothes for our children than cigars and champagne for our legal protectors. There has been a great deal written and said about protection. We, as a class, are tired of one kind of protection, that which leaves us everything to do, to dare, and to suffer, and strips us of all means for its accomplishment. We would not tax man to take care of us. No, the Great Father has endowed all his creatures with the necessary powers for self-support, self-defense, and protection. We do not ask man to represent us; it is hard enough in times like these for man to carry backbone enough to represent himself. So long as the mass of men spend most of their time on the fence, not knowing which way to jump, they are surely in no condition to tell us where we had better stand. In pity for man, we would no longer hang like a mill-stone round his neck. Undo what man did for us in the dark ages, and strike out all special legislation for us; strike the words "white male" from all your constitutions, and then, with fair sailing, let us sink or swim, live or die, survive or perish together. ∽

Primary Sources

Buhle, MariJo, and Paul Buhle, eds. *The Concise History of Women Suffrage: Selections from the Classic Work of Stanton, Anthony, Gage and Harper.* Urbana: University of Illinois Press, 1978.

Stanton, Elizabeth Cady. *Eighty Years and More (1815–1897): Reminiscences of Elizabeth Cady Stanton.* New York: Source Book Press, 1970.

———. *The Woman's Bible: The Original Feminist Attack on the Bible.* New York: Arno Press, 1974.

Stanton, Elizabeth Cady, Susan B. Anthony, and Matilda Joslyn Gage. *History of Woman Suffrage.* 6 vols. New York: Arno Press, 1969.

Secondary Sources

Banner, Lois W. *Elizabeth Cady Stanton: A Radical for Woman's Rights.* Boston: Little, Brown, 1980.

Flexner, Eleanor. *Century of Struggle: The* *Women's Rights Movement in the U.S.* Cambridge, Mass.: Harvard University Press, Belknap Press, 1975.

Oakley, Mary Ann B. *Elizabeth Cady Stanton.* Old Westbury, N.Y.: Feminist Press, 1972.

19. Frederick Douglass

FREDERICK DOUGLASS (1817–95) was born a slave on the eastern shore of Maryland. As a child he taught himself to read and write, despite the objections of his master. By the time he was seventeen he had experienced firsthand the bitter degradation of slave life. Because he was spirited he had been turned over to a "slave breaker." He finally turned on the man and put an end to his torture, thereby deriving the confidence to gain his freedom entirely. In 1838 he escaped to New York and then to New Bedford, Massachusetts. By 1841 he had become involved with abolitionist efforts, in which he was initially profoundly influenced by William Lloyd Garrison. Moving to Rochester, New York, in 1847, he started a newspaper (*The North Star*) and wrote and lectured widely for the abolitionist cause. Later he broke with Garrison because Garrison disavowed political action, preferring withdrawal from a "union with slaveholders" to ending slavery affirmatively. Douglass was an early supporter of women's rights, arguing, together with the leaders of the feminist movement, that the issues of equality applied equally to women and blacks. By the start of the Civil War he was recognized as the leading spokesperson for blacks in their own cause.

The materials excerpted here include a representative antislavery lecture (1848), with its forceful depiction of life under slavery, and a later summary of antislavery positions (1855) that contrasts Douglass's views with those of other abolitionists. Also included are examples of his attitudes on black self-improvement and on the rights of women. ⌒

Speech at the Anti-Slavery Association (1848)

I would like to hold up to you a picture, not drawn by an American pen or pencil, but by a foreigner. I want to show you how you look abroad in the delectable business of kidnapping and slavedriving. Some time since—I think it was in the December number of "Punch"—I saw an excellent pictorial description of America. What think you it was? It was entitled, "Brother Jonathan." It was a long, lean, gaunt, shrivelled-looking creature,

---

SOURCE: *The North Star,* 2 June 1848.

stretched out on two chairs, and his legs resting on the prostrate bust of Washington: projecting from behind was a cat o' nine tails knotted at the ends; around his person he wore a belt, in which were stuck those truly American implements, a bowie-knife, dirk, and revolving pistol: behind him was a whipping-post, with a naked woman tied to it, and a strong-armed American citizen in the act of scourging her livid flesh with a cowskin. At his feet was another group;—a sale going on of human cattle, and around the auctioneer's table were gathered the *respectability*—the religion represented in the person of the clergy —of America, buying them for export to the goodly city of New Orleans. Little further on, there was a scene of branding—a small group of slaves tied hand and foot, while their patriotic and philanthropic masters were burning their name into their quivering flesh. Further on, there was a drove of slaves, driven before the lash to a ship moored out in the stream, bound for New Orleans. Above these and several other scenes illustrative of the character of our institutions, waved the star-spangled banner.—Still further back in the distance was the picture of the achievements of our gallant army in Mexico, shooting, stabbing, hanging, destroying property, and massacreing the innocent with the innocent, not with the guilty, and over all this was a picture of the devil himself, looking down with satanic satisfaction on passing events. Here I conceive to be a true picture of America, and I hesitate not to say but this description falls far short of the real facts and of the aspect we bear to the world around us. . . .

. . . Sir, I would like to go bring more vividly before this audience, the wrongs of my down-trodden countrymen. I have no disposition to look at this matter in any sentimental light, but to bring before you stern facts, and keep forever before the American people the damning and disgraceful fact that three mil-

lions of people are in chains to-day; that while we are here speaking in their behalf, saying noble words and doing noble deeds, they are under the yoke, smarting beneath the lash, sundered from each other, trafficked in and brutally treated; and that the American nation, to keep them in their present condition, stands ready with its ten thousand bayonets, to plunge them into their hearts, if they attempt to strike for their freedom. I want every man north of Mason and Dixon's line, whenever they attend an antislavery meeting, to remember that it is the Northern arm that does this; that you are not only guilty of withholding your influence, but that you are the positive enemies of the slave, the positive holders of the slave, and that in your right arm rests the physical power that keeps him under the yoke. I want you to feel that I am addressing slaveholders, speaking to men who have entered into a solemn league and covenant with the slaveholders of the country, that in any emergency, if at any time the spirit of freedom finds a lodgment in the bosom of the American slave, and they shall be moved to throw up barricades against their tyrants, as the French did in the streets of Paris, that you, every man of you that swears to support the Constitution, is sworn to pour leaden death in their hearts. I am speaking to slaveholders; and if I speak plainly, set it not down to impudence, but to oppression, to slavery. For God's sake, let a man speak when he cannot do anything else; when fetters are on his limbs, let him have this small right of making his wrongs known; at least, let it be done in New York. I am glad to see there is a disposition to let it be done here—to allow him to tell what is in him, with regard to his own personal wrongs at any rate.

Sir, I have been frequently denounced because I have dared to speak against the American nation, against the church, the northern churches, especially, charging them with being the slaveholders of the country. I desire to say here as elsewhere, that I am not at all ambitious of the ill opinions of my countrymen, nor do I desire their hatred; but I must say, as I have said, that I want no man's friendship, no matter how high he may stand in church or state, I want no man's sympathies or approbation who is not ready to strike the chains from the limbs of my brethren. I do not ask the esteem and friendship of any minister or any man, no matter how high his standing, nor do I wish to shake any man's hand who stands indifferent to the wrongs of any brethren. Some have boasted that when Fred. Douglass has been at their houses, he has been treated kindly, but as soon as he got into their pulpits he began to abuse them—that as soon as the advantage is given to him, he takes it to stab those who befriend him.—Friends, I wish to stab no man, but if you stand on the side of the slaveholder, and cry out "the Union as it is," "the Constitution as it is," "the Church as it is," you may expect that the heart that throbs beneath this bosom, will give utterance against you. I am bound to speak, and whenever there is an opportunity to do so, I *will* speak against slavery. . . .

. . . I will just say, however, that we have had some advice given us lately, from very high authority; I allude to Henry Clay, who, in his last speech before the Colonization Society, at Washington, advised the free colored people of the United States that they had better go to Africa.

He says he does not wish to coerce us, but thinks we had better go! What right has he to tell us to go? We have as much right to stay here as he has. I don't care if you did throw up your caps for him when he came to this city—I don't care if he did give you "his heart on the outside of the City Hall and his hand on the inside." I have as much right to stay here as he has! And I want to say to our white friends that we, colored folks, have had the subject

under careful consideration, and have decided to stay! I want to say to any colonization friends here, that they may give their minds no further uneasiness on our account, for our minds are made up. I think this is about the best argument on that subject.

Now there is one thing about us colored folks; it is this, that under all these most adverse circumstances, we live, and move and have our being, and that too in peace, and we are almost persuaded that there is a providence in our staying here. I do not know but the United States would rot in this tyranny if there were not some Negroes in this land—some to clink their chains in the ear of listening humanity, and from whose prostrate forms the lessons of liberty can be taught to the whites. It is through us now that you are learning that your own rights are stricken down. At this time it is the abolitionist that holds up the lamp that shows the political parties of the north their fetters and chains. A little while ago, and the northern men were bound in the strange fanatic delusion that they had something to do with making of presidents of the U. States; that is about given up now. No one now of common sense, or common reading, imagines for a moment that New York has anything to do with deciding who the President shall be. They are allowed to vote, but what is the amount of this privilege? It is to vote for the slaveholder, or whom the slaveholder select? No men that are now accounted sane think of any other than of a slaveholder or assassin, or both, who shall hold the destinies of the nation, and the reason is because the people are convinced that they belong—as they used to say—to the colored boys of the south, to the party. They used sometimes to ask me, "Boy, who do you belong to?" and I used to answer, "to Captain Thomas Auld, of St. Michael's, a classleader in the Methodist Episcopal church; and now," I would ask, "who do you belong to?" I will tell you. You belong to the Democratic party, to the Whig party, and these parties belong to the slaveholder, and the slaveholder rules the country. As the boy said about ruling England—"I rule mamma, and mamma rules papa, and papa rules the people, and the people rule England." To be sure you have the right to vote, which is like what I once heard of a certain boy, who said he was going to live with his Uncle Robert, and when I go there, said he, I am going to do just as I please—if Uncle Robert will let me! The Northern people are going to do just as they please—if the slaveholders will let them! The little bit of opposition that has manifested itself in that little protuberance on American politics—the Wilmot Proviso—which our friend Clay has fully described as a tempest in a teapot, has now quite flattened down. The Whigs, who said, We will stand by it at all hazards, have fairly backed out; they got afraid of the Union. In Ohio, I heard men, striking their [fists] to-gether, saying they would stand by at all hazards, and after a little while the Ohio State Legislature came to the conclusion, after having carefully considered the matter, that "to press the question of no more slave territory, must be disastrous to our American Union." New York came out expressly in favor of the Proviso, and it has since seen that the Union will be periled by adherence to that principle. And all over the North there is this fainting away before that power which was before undefined, as has been so eloquently touched upon by my friend Phillips; for while men hold up their hands in favor of the Union and the Constitution, there is a moral conflict in their hearts, for, as was so beautifully expressed by Mr. Parker, of Boston, men cannot fight slavery under the Constitution; the Constitution soils the armor about them: we cannot strike slavery while we have it on us: there is no other way but to throw it off.... ∾

"The Various Phases of Anti-Slavery" (1855)

All men desire Liberty. They desire to possess this inalienable birthright themselves, if they are not concerned about others being the recipients of its countless blessings. They instinctively shrink from the idea of having their Intellectual, their Moral, and their Physical organism, subjugated to the entire control of Tyranny, clothed in the vesture of assumed superiority. This love of their own identity is inseparably connected with their desire and hope of immortality. And even those who attack the citadel of man's personality, and seek to reduce him to a thing, are jealous of any invasion of their own Rights, and will resist to the death any encroachment upon the sacred domain of their own personal liberty. They are Abolitionists, as they seek to abolish any system of Oppression *which has them* for its victims, even though they trample their own principles in the dust, when the Rights of others are invaded. This is neither just nor generous. No man should crave the possession of that which he assiduously endeavors to withhold from another.

Again, we maintain that no man has a Right to make any concession to Tyranny, which he would refuse to make if *he* were the

---

SOURCE: *Frederick Douglass' Paper*, 16 November 1855.

victim.—He has no Right to make any compromise of contract in reference to the "Institution" of slavery, as it is falsely called, which he would be unwilling to make, were he, himself, the slave. He should place himself, as it were, in the position of the slave, and advocate those principles and measures, which, judging from his stand-point, he would deem just and advisable. Now, we hold that there is but one class of men and women in the land, who stand upon the slave's platform, and advocate the principles and measures which he would advocate, had he the opportunity. Abolitionism in this country is a sort of heterogeneous compound. It is composed, too, of certain elements, some of which are totally dissimilar. They have no affinity, in some respects, the one for the other; and the lack of homogeneousness must, in some way, be supplied, before a perfect fusion, or commingling of the elements can be effected.

We have the Free Soil, or Republican Party, as the representative of Principles and Measures which are themselves totally distinct, and diverse from those which are advocated with so much zeal and ability by those who rejoice in the cognomen of Garrison Abolitionists. Then we have the Radical Abolitionists, who profess to believe the Principles and Measures adverted to, unsound, unjust, impracticable, and, of course, wholly intenable.

What, then, are the distinctive features of these respective organizations? Wherein do they differ? What do they propose to accomplish? Let us briefly examine them. This is the Age of Inquiry, of deep, sober, rational Investigation. All systems, and opinions, and creeds, and Institutions, which cannot withstand the ordeal of the most rigid Investigation, cannot, at this crisis, find a lodgment in the popular heart; they cannot receive the approving smiles of the popular conscience.

First, then we have the Free Soil, or Republican Party. This is a powerful Party, so far as numbers and influence is concerned, and is sweeping over the country with restless efficacy. What are its characteristics? The Principle which imparts vitality to the Republican organization, is, simply, the *Non-Extension of Slavery.* Its motto is, "No Slavery Outside the Slave States." It proposes to restrict Slavery, and keep it within what is called its *constitutional limits.* It does not propose to interfere with Slavery where it already exists, but seeks to prevent the spread of the infectious malady. It virtually concedes to slaveholders, the constitutional right of plundering their helpless victims and plundering them as long as they are able, *provided they do so in a certain locality.* In a word, it proceeds upon the gratuitous assumption of the legality and constitutionality of Slavery, and, at the same time, seeks to relieve the Federal Government from all responsibility for its existence or continuance. It thunders in the ear of the Government, the declaration that "Slavery is Sectional; Liberty, National." Not one of its leading advocates, so far as we have any knowledge, has ever intimated a desire in public, to abolish Slavery, by Legislation; thus to strike off the fetters of the three millions and a half of men, women, and children, *who are the present victims of the insatiate rapacity of American Despotism.* To intimate such an intention would place them in advance of the party with which they are identified. They, indeed, hate Slavery, and affirm, that by surrounding the slave States with a girdle of Freedom, Slavery will eventually die, for lack of room and air in which to breathe. This, we believe, is a fair and impartial statement of the position of the Free Soil, or Republican Party. If we have erred in stating its true position, we have done so unintentionally, and stand ready to be corrected.

Secondly, we have another body of Anti-Slavery men in the country, who style themselves Garrison Abolitionists. These, too, are powerful, if not in numbers, in the array of

talent, wealth, and energy, at their command.
—The motto of the Garrison party, is "no union with slaveholders." They affirm the Constitution of the United States to be pro-Slavery in its character, and therefore denounce it, as "an agreement with Death and a covenant with Hell." They are opposed to *political action, for the Abolition of Slavery,* and refuse to vote for the officers of the Government, because of the alleged pro-Slavery character of the Constitution, by which it professes to be guided in its administration. Its disunion sentiments were thus distinctly stated at an annual meeting of the Pennsylvania Anti-Slavery Society, convened in the city of Philadelphia, Oct. 25th, '52:

> *Resolved.* That, independent of all questions as to the meaning of particular clauses of the Constitution, and whether it be admitted or denied that it contains certain guarantees for the benefit of slavery, the effort to establish a union between States that are slaveholding and States that are free must in the nature of things be abortive, since the legislation demanded by the former is diametrically opposed to that required by the latter; and therefore we reiterate the doctrine of the American Anti-Slavery Society, 'No Union with Slaveholders.'

At the same meeting W. Lloyd Garrison thus stated the position of those who occupy the Platform of the American Anti-Slavery Society. Said he:

> The position of this Society upon the Constitution is well known. We hold that it contains certain wicked compromises of the rights of the Slave. It gives the Slaveholders a political representation for their slaves, thus bribing them to hold and multiply their human chattels. I cannot swear to give such power to Slaveholders. Does our Declaration of Sentiment require

me to do it? On the contrary, the principles and spirit forbid such an oath.—So of the obligation to put down a slave insurrection and return fugitive slaves. To be faithful to the principles of that Declaration, I must stand outside of the government organized upon pledges to do such acts. So if I find that the church of which I am a member, is pro-slavery, as I recognize its Christian character by that membership, I must stand outside the church.

So much then, for the position of the Garrison Abolitionists. They are *in* the country, but at the same time, they profess to stand outside of the Government. But this is not all. The Free Soil or Republican Party says, "Let *Slavery* take care of its own interests." The Garrison Party, through one of the most eloquent exponents of its theory, virtually tells the Slave to take care of *himself.* This may seem to be an unjust and ungenerous assertion. But what says one of the most able advocates of the disunion movement. Hear him:

> All the slaves ask of us, is to stand out of the way, withdraw our pledge to keep the peace on the plantation; withdraw our pledge to return him, withdraw that representation which the Constitution gives in proportion to the number of slaves, and without any agitation here, without any individual virtue, which the times have eaten out of us, God will vindicate the oppressed, by the laws of justice which he has founded, Trample under foot your own unjust pledges, break in pieces your compact with hell by which you become the abettors of oppression. Stand alone, and let no cement of the Union bind the slave, and he will right himself.

The idea of the slave righting himself, presupposes his ability to do so, unaided by

Northern interference. O no! the slave *cannot* "right himself" any more than an infant can grapple with a giant. He must receive the effective aid of those who, at the North, are, despite their denial, the members of the confederacy, and, as such, "verily guilty concerning their brother."

But we have another Anti-Slavery or Abolition Party, the Liberty Party, or Radical Abolitionists. Who are they? What do they propose to effect?

They deny that Slavery can be legalized, and, therefore, affirm that all slaveholding enactments are illegal. They also deny that the Constitution of the United States is a pro-slavery instrument, and affirm that it is, legitimately, susceptible only, of an Anti-Slavery interpretation. They regard it as having been established for the express purpose of establishing justice, &c., and of securing the blessings of Liberty to all the people of the Confederacy, not merely one class of People, but the whole, *we*, the people, as well as *you*, or *they*, the People. Radical Abolitionism asserts, that if the various provisions of the Constitution, (right of trial by Jury, *habeas corpus*, and others,) were faithfully executed, it would instantly free every Slave in the land. All they ask, is, that the present Constitution, imperfect as it is, shall receive a righteous, a correct interpretation, that its manifold provisions be executed, and Slavery will find no refuge under it.

Radical Abolitionism lays the axe at the root of the tree. It proposes not only to hew down the Upas Tree, but to tear it up root and branch. It believes that the Federal Government has the power to abolish Slavery everywhere in the United States, and that such is the duty of the Government. They are opposed to a dissolution of the Union, *unless a Southern Confederacy could be organized in which there would be no abolitionists, white or black, and a Northern Confederacy, in which there would be no apologists for Slavery.* By withdrawing from the Slave States, we withdraw from nearly four millions of Abolitionists, black and white. And on the other hand, we retain in our midst some of the most influential supporters of the traffic in human flesh. These are some of the leading views entertained by Radical Abolitionists. We believe them to be just, tenable, and practicable; and thus believing, can conscientiously give our adhesion and our support to no other.—Of their ultimate triumph, we have not the shadow of a doubt. We know they are regarded as impracticable. But those who assume their impracticability, pronounced, a few years ago, the same judgment upon the views they now cherish so ardently, and promulgated with so much zeal and ability. They even deprecated the idea of any agitation, whatever, upon the subject. And we do not despair of yet congratulating them upon their admission into the ranks of Radical Abolitionists. We shall, therefore, contribute our mite toward effecting this desirable consummation. ∽

Primary Sources

Douglass, Frederick. *Life and Times of Frederick Douglass: His Early Life as a Slave, His Escape from Bondage, and His Complete History, Written by Himself.* New York: Collier Books, 1962.

———. *My Bondage and My Freedom.* Chicago: Johnson Publishing, 1970.

———. *Narrative of the Life of Frederick Douglass, an American Slave, Written by Himself.* Edited by Benjamin Quarles. Cambridge, Mass.: Harvard University Press, Belknap Press, 1960.

Foner, Philip, ed. *Frederick Douglass, Selections from His Writings.* New York: International Publishers, 1965.

Ritchie, Barbara. *The Mind and Heart of Frederick Douglass: Excerpts from Speeches of the Great Negro Orator.* New York: T.Y. Crowell, 1968.

Secondary Sources

Bontemps, Anna Wendell. *Free at Last: The Life of Frederick Douglass.* New York: Dodd, Mead, 1971.

Burke, Ronald K. *Frederick Douglass: Crusading Orator for Human Rights.* New York: Garland Publishers, 1996.

DuBois, Shirley Graham. *There Was Once a Slave: The Heroic Story of Frederick Douglass.* New York: J. Messner, 1947.

Foner, Philip. *Frederick Douglass: A Biography.* New York: Citadel Press, 1964.

———. *Frederick Douglass on Women's Rights.* Westport, Conn.: Greenwood Press, 1976.

———. *The Life and Writings of Frederick Douglass.* 5 vols. New York: International Publishers, 1950–75.

20. John C. Calhoun

JOHN C. CALHOUN (1782–1850) was born to a prosperous South Carolina family and graduated from Yale in 1804. In 1807 he was admitted to the bar and in the following year entered the South Carolina legislature.

Calhoun entered Congress in 1811 and soon rose to national attention for his outspoken support of the war with Great Britain. In 1817 President Monroe asked Calhoun to be secretary of war, a position in which he served for seven and a half years.

In 1824 Calhoun ran for vice president on both the John Quincy Adams and Andrew Jackson tickets. In 1828 Calhoun was elected for a second term as vice president, this time serving with Jackson. Calhoun and Jackson soon clashed over political, social, and personal questions, however, and Jackson turned to Martin Van Buren for his presidential successor.

Returning to the Senate at the beginning of 1833, Calhoun came to be regarded as the main source of arguments, plans, and inspiration for the Southern bloc over the slavery question. In early 1844 President Tyler's secretary of state died and Calhoun was asked to fill the vacancy. Calhoun accepted the position, but he was not asked to remain in President Polk's cabinet. In the last years of his life Calhoun wrote two major works: A *Discourse on the Constitution and Government of the United States* and A *Disquisition on Government,* the second of which is excerpted here. ◆

A Disquisition on Government (1848)

THE NATURE OF MAN AND THE ORIGIN OF GOVERNMENT

In order to have a clear and just conception of the nature and object of government, it is indispensable to understand correctly what that constitution or law of our nature is in which government originates, or to express it more fully and accurately—that law without which government would not and with which it must necessarily exist. Without this, it is as impossible to lay any solid foundation for the science of government as it would be to lay one for that of astronomy without a like understanding of that constitution or law of the material world according to which the several bodies composing the solar system mutually act on each other and by which they are kept in their respective spheres. The first question, accordingly, to be considered, What is that constitution or law of our nature without which government would not exist and with which its existence is necessary?

In considering this, I assume as an incontestable fact that man is so constituted as to be a social being. His inclinations and wants, physical and moral, irresistibly impel him to associate with his kind; and he has, accordingly, never been found, in any age or country, in any state other than the social. In no other, indeed, could he exist, and in no other—were it possible for him to exist—could he attain to a full development of his moral and intellectual faculties or raise himself, in the scale of being, much above the level of the brute creation.

I next assume also as a fact not less incontestable that, while man is so constituted as to

SOURCE: *John C. Calhoun: A Disquisition on Government*, ed. Richard K. Cralle (New York: P. Smith, 1963).

make the social state necessary to his existence and the full development of his faculties, this state itself cannot exist without government. The assumption rests on universal experience. In no age or country has any society or community ever been found, whether enlightened or savage, without government of some description.

Having assumed these as unquestionable phenomena of our nature, I shall, without further remark, proceed to the investigation of the primary and important question, What is that constitution of our nature which, while it impels man to associate with his kind, renders it impossible for society to exist without government?

The answer will be found in the fact (not less contestable than either of the others) that, while man is created for the social state and is accordingly so formed as to feel what affects others as well as what affects himself, he is, at the same time, so constituted as to feel more intensely what affects him directly than what affects him indirectly through others, or, to express it differently, he is so constituted that his direct or individual affections are stronger than his sympathetic or social feelings. I intentionally avoid the expression *"selfish* feelings" as applicable to the former, because, as commonly used, it implies an unusual excess of the individual over the social feelings in the person to whom it is applied and, consequently, something depraved and vicious. My object is to exclude such inference and to restrict the inquiry exclusively to facts in their bearings on the subject under consideration, viewed as mere phenomena appertaining to our nature—constituted as it is; and which are as unquestionable as is that of gravitation or any other phenomenon of the material world.

In asserting that our individual are stronger

than our social feelings, it is not intended to deny that there are instances, growing out of peculiar relations—as that of a mother and her infant—or resulting from the force of education and habit over peculiar constitutions, in which the latter have overpowered the former; but these instances are few and always regarded as something extraordinary. The deep impression they make, whenever they occur, is the strongest proof that they are regarded as exceptions to some general and well-understood law of our nature, just as some of the minor powers of the material world are apparently to gravitation. . . .

It follows, then, that man is so constituted that government is necessary to the existence of society, and society to his existence and the perfection of his faculties. It follows also that government has its origin in this two-fold constitution of his nature: the sympathetic or social feelings constituting the remote, and the individual or direct the proximate, cause.

If man had been differently constituted in either particular—if, instead of being social in his nature, he had been created without sympathy for his kind and independent of others for his safety and existence; or if, on the other hand, he had been so created as to feel more intensely what affected others than what affected himself (if that were possible) or even had this supposed interest been equal—it is manifest that in either case there would have been no necessity for government, and that none would ever have existed. But although society and government are thus intimately connected with and dependent on each other —of the two society is the greater. It is the first in the order of things and in the dignity of its object; that of society being primary—to preserve and perfect our race—and that of government secondary and subordinate—to preserve and perfect society. Both are, however, necessary to the existence and well-being of our race and equally of divine ordination. . . .

But government, although intended to protect and preserve society, has itself a strong tendency to disorder and abuse of its powers, as all experience and almost every page of history testify. The cause is to be found in the same constitution of our nature which makes government indispensable. The powers which it is necessary for government to possess in order to repress violence and preserve order cannot execute themselves. They must be administered by men in whom, like others, the individual are stronger than the social feelings. And hence the powers vested in them to prevent injustice and oppression on the part of others will, if left unguarded, be by them converted into instruments to oppress the rest of the community. That by which this is prevented, by whatever name called, is what is meant by *constitution,* in its most comprehensive sense, when applied to *government.*

Having its origin in the same principle of our nature, *constitution* stands to *government* as *government* stands to *society;* and as the end for which society is ordained would be defeated without government, so that for which government is ordained would, in a great measure, be defeated without constitution. But they differ in this striking particular. There is no difficulty in forming government. It is not even a matter of choice whether there shall be one or not. Like breathing, it is not permitted to depend on our volition. Necessity will force it on all communities in some one form or another. Very different is the case as to constitution. Instead of a matter of necessity, it is one of the most difficult tasks imposed on man to form a constitution worthy of the name, while to form a perfect one—one that would completely counteract the tendency of government to oppression and abuse and hold it strictly to the great ends for which it is ordained—has thus far exceeded human wisdom, and possibly ever will. From this another striking difference results. Constitution is the contrivance of man, while government is of divine ordination. Man is left to perfect what the wisdom of the Infinite ordained as necessary to preserve the race.

With these remarks I proceed to the consideration of the important and difficult question, How is this tendency of government to be counteracted? Or, to express it more fully, How can those who are invested with the powers of government be prevented from employing them as the means of aggrandizing themselves instead of using them to protect and preserve society? ...

There is but one way in which this can possibly be done, and that is by such an organism as will furnish the ruled with the means of resisting successfully this tendency on the part of the rulers to oppression and abuse. Power can only be resisted by power—and tendency by tendency. Those who exercise power and those subject to its exercise—the rulers and the ruled—stand in antagonistic relations to each other. The same constitution of our nature which leads rulers to oppress the ruled —regardless of the object for which government is ordained—will, with equal strength, lead the ruled to resist when possessed of the means of making peaceable and effective resistance. Such an organism, then, as will furnish the means by which resistance may be systematically and peaceably made on the part of the ruled to oppression and abuse of power on the part of the rulers is the first and indispensable step toward *forming* a constitutional government. And as this can only be effected by or through the right of suffrage—the right on the part of the ruled to choose their rulers at proper intervals and to hold them thereby responsible for their conduct—the responsibility of the rulers to the ruled, through the right of suffrage, is the indispensable and primary principle in the *foundation* of a constitutional government. When this right is properly guarded, and the people sufficiently enlight-

ened to understand their own rights and the interests of the community and duly to appreciate the motives and conduct of those appointed to make and execute the laws, it is all-sufficient to give to those who elect effective control over those they have elected.

I call the right of suffrage the indispensable and primary principle, for it would be a great and dangerous mistake to suppose, as many do, that it is, of itself, sufficient to form constitutional governments. ...

The right of suffrage, of itself, can do no more than give complete control to those who elect over the conduct of those they have elected. ... The sum total, then, of its effects, when most successful, is to make those elected the true and faithful representatives of those who elected them—instead of irresponsible rulers, as they would be without it; and thus, by converting it into an agency, and the rulers into agents, to divest government of all claims to sovereignty and to retain it unimpaired to the community. But it is manifest that the right of suffrage in making these changes transfers, in reality, the actual control over the government from those who make and execute the laws to the body of the community and thereby places the powers of the government fully in the mass of the community as they would be if they, in fact, had assembled, made, and executed the laws themselves without the intervention of representatives or agents. The more perfectly it does this, the more perfectly it accomplishes its ends; but in doing so, it only changes the seat of authority without counteracting, in the least, the tendency of the government to oppression and abuse of its powers.

If the whole community had the same interests so that the interests of each and every portion would be so affected by the action of the government that the laws which oppressed or impoverished one portion would necessarily oppress and impoverish all others—or the reverse—then the right of suffrage, of itself, would be all-sufficient to counteract the tendency of the government to oppression and abuse of its powers, and, of course, would form, of itself, a perfect constitutional government. The interest of all being the same, by supposition, as far as the action of the government was concerned, all would have like interests as to what laws should be made and how they should be executed. All strife and struggle would cease as to who should be elected to make and execute them. The only question would be, who was most fit, who the wisest and most capable of understanding the common interest of the whole. This decided, the election would pass off quietly and without party discord, as no one portion could advance its own peculiar interest without regard to the rest by electing a favorite candidate.

But such is not the case. On the contrary, nothing is more difficult than to equalize the action of the government in reference to the various and diversified interests of the community; and nothing more easy than to pervert its powers into instruments to aggrandize and enrich one or more interests by oppressing and impoverishing the others; and this, too, under the operation of laws couched in general terms and which, on their face, appear fair and equal. Nor is this the case in some particular communities only. It is so in all—the small and the great, the poor and the rich—irrespective of pursuits, productions, or degrees of civilization; with, however, this difference, that the more extensive and populous the country, the more diversified the condition and pursuits of its population; and the richer, more luxurious, and dissimilar the people, the more difficult it is to equalize the action of the government, and the more easy for one portion of the community to pervert its powers to oppress and plunder the other.

Such being the case, it necessarily results that the right of suffrage, by placing the con-

trol of the government in the community, must, from the same constitution of our nature which makes government necessary to preserve society, lead to conflict among its different interests—each striving to obtain possession of its powers as the means of protecting itself against the others or of advancing its respective interests regardless of the interests of others. For this purpose, a struggle will take place between the various interests to obtain a majority in order to control the government. If no one interest be strong enough, of itself, to obtain it, a combination will be formed between those whose interests are most alike —each conceding something to the others until a sufficient number is obtained to make a majority. The process may be slow and much time may be required before a compact, organized majority can be thus formed, but formed it will be in time, even without preconcert or design, by the sure workings of that principle or constitution of our nature in which government itself originates. When once formed, the community will be divided into two great parties—a major and minor—between which there will be incessant struggles on the one side to retain, and on the other to obtain the majority and, thereby, the control of the government and the advantages it confers.

So deeply seated, indeed, is this tendency to conflict between the different interests or portions of the community that it would result from the action of the government itself, even though it were possible to find a community where the people were all of the same pursuits, placed in the same condition of life, and in every respect so situated as to be without inequality of condition or diversity of interests. The advantages of possessing the control of the powers of the government, and thereby of its honors and emoluments, are, of themselves, exclusive of all other considerations, ample to divide even such a community into two great hostile parties.

In order to form a just estimate of the full force of these advantages, without reference to any other consideration, it must be remembered that government—to fulfill the ends for which it is ordained, and more especially that of protection against external dangers—must in the present condition of the world be clothed with powers sufficient to call forth the resources of the community and be prepared at all times to command them promptly in every emergency which may possibly arise. For this purpose large establishments are necessary, both civil and military (including naval, where, from situation, that description of force may be required), with all the means necessary for prompt and effective action, such as fortifications, fleets, armories, arsenals, magazines, arms of all descriptions, with well-trained forces in sufficient numbers to wield them with skill and energy whenever the occasion requires it. The administration and management of a government with such vast establishments must necessarily require a host of employees, agents, and officers—of whom many must be vested with high and responsible trusts and occupy exalted stations accompanied with much influence and patronage. To meet the necessary expenses, large sums must be collected and disbursed, and for this purpose heavy taxes must be imposed, requiring a multitude of officers for their collection and disbursement. The whole united must necessarily place under the control of government an amount of honors and emoluments sufficient to excite profoundly the ambition of the aspiring and the cupidity of the avaricious, and to lead to the formation of hostile parties and violent party conflicts and struggles to obtain the control of the government. And what makes this evil remediless through the right of suffrage of itself, however modified or carefully guarded or however enlightened the people, is the fact that, as far as the honors and emoluments of the government and its fiscal action are concerned, it is impossible to equalize it. The reason is obvious. Its honors and emoluments, however great, can fall to the lot of but a few, compared to the entire number of the community and the multitude who will seek to participate in them. But without this there is a reason which renders it impossible to equalize the action of the government so far as its fiscal operation extends—which I shall next explain....

Some one portion of the community must pay in taxes more than it receives back in disbursements, while another receives in disbursements more than it pays in taxes. It is, then, manifest, taking the whole process together, that taxes must be, in effect, bounties to that portion of the community which receives more in disbursements than it pays in taxes, while to the other which pays in taxes more than it receives in disbursements they are taxes in reality—burthens instead of bounties. This consequence is unavoidable. It results from the nature of the process, be the taxes ever so equally laid and the disbursements ever so fairly made in reference to the public service....

The necessary result, then, of the unequal fiscal action of the government is to divide the community into two great classes: one consisting of those who, in reality, pay the taxes and, of course, bear exclusively the burthen of supporting the government and the other, of those who are the recipients of their proceeds through disbursements, and who are, in fact, supported by the government; or, in fewer words, to divide it into tax-payers and tax-consumers.

But the effect of this is to place them in antagonistic relations in reference to the fiscal action of the government and the entire course of policy therewith connected. For the greater the taxes and disbursements, the greater the gain of the one and the loss of the other, and vice versa; and consequently, the more the policy of the government is calculated to increase taxes and disbursements, the more it will be favored by the one and opposed by the other.

The effect, then, of every increase is to enrich and strengthen the one, and impoverish and weaken the other. This, indeed, may be carried to such an extent that one class or portion of the community may be elevated to wealth and power, and the other depressed to abject poverty and dependence, simply by the fiscal action of the government; and this too through disbursements only—even under a system of equal taxes imposed for revenue only. If such may be the effect of taxes and disbursements when confined to their legitimate objects—that of raising revenue for the public service—some conception may be formed how one portion of the community may be crushed, and another elevated on its ruins, by systematically perverting the power of taxation and disbursement for the purpose of aggrandizing and building up one portion of the community at the expense of the other. That it *will* be so used, unless prevented, is, from the constitution of man, just as certain as that it *can* be so used, and that, if not prevented, it must give rise to two parties and to violent conflicts and struggles between them to obtain the control of the government, is, for the same reason, not less certain.

Nor is it less certain, from the operation of all these causes, that the dominant majority, for the time, would have the same tendency to oppression and abuse of power which, without the right of suffrage, irresponsible rulers would have. No reason, indeed, can be assigned why the latter would abuse their power, which would not apply, with equal force, to the former. The dominant majority, for the time, would in reality, through the right of suffrage, be the rulers—the controlling, governing, and irresponsible power; and those who make and execute the laws would, for the time, be in reality but *their* representatives and

agents. . . .

As, then, the right of suffrage, without some other provision, cannot counteract the tendency of government, the next question for consideration is, What is that other provision? This demands the most serious consideration, for of all the questions embraced in the science of government it involves a principle, the most important and the least understood, and when understood, the most difficult of application in practice. It is, indeed, emphatically that principle which *makes* the constitution, in its strict and limited sense.

From what has been said, it is manifest that this provision must be of a character calculated to prevent any one interest or combination of interests from using the powers of government to aggrandize itself at the expense of the others. Here lies the evil; and just in proportion as it shall prevent, or fail to prevent it, in the same degree it will effect, or fail to effect, the end intended to be accomplished. There is but one certain mode in which this result can be secured, and that is by the adoption of some restriction or limitation, which shall so effectually prevent any one interest or combination of interests from obtaining the exclusive control of the government as to render hopeless all attempts direct to that end. There is, again, but one mode in which this can be effected, and that is by taking the sense of each interest or portion of the community which may be unequally and injuriously affected by the action of the government separately, through its own majority or in some other way by which its voice may be fairly expressed, and to require the consent of each interest either to put or to keep the government in action. This, too, can be accomplished only in one way, and that is by such an organism of the government—and, if necessary for the purpose of the community also—as will, by dividing and distributing the powers of government, give to each division or interest, through its appropriate organ, either a concurrent voice in making and executing the laws or a veto on their execution. It is only by such an organism that the assent of each can be made necessary to put the government in motion, or the power made effectual to arrest its action when put in motion; and it is only by the one or the other that the different interests, orders, classes, or portions into which the community may be divided can be protected, and all conflict and struggle between them prevented—by rendering it impossible to put or to keep it in action without the concurrent consent of all.

Such an organism as this, combined with the right of suffrage, constitutes, in fact, the elements of constitutional government. The one, by rendering those who make and execute the laws responsible to those on whom they operate, prevents the rulers from oppressing the ruled; and the other, by making it impossible for any one interest or combination of interests, or class, or order, or portion of the community to obtain exclusive control, prevents any one of them from oppressing the other. It is clear that oppression and abuse of power must come, if at all, from the one or the other quarter. From no other can they come. It follows that the two, suffrage and proper organism combined, are sufficient to counteract the tendency of government to oppression and abuse of power and to restrict it to the fulfillment of the great ends for which it is ordained....

It may be readily inferred, from what has been stated, that the effect of organism is neither to supersede nor diminish the importance of the right of suffrage, but to aid and perfect it. The object of the latter is to collect the sense of the community. The more fully and perfectly it accomplishes this, the more fully and perfectly it fulfills its end. But the most it can do, of itself, is to collect the sense of the greater number; that is, of the stronger interests or combination of interests, and to assume

this to be the sense of the community. It is only when aided by a proper organism that it can collect the sense of the entire community, of each and all its interests—of each, through its appropriate organ, and of the whole through all of them united. This would truly be the sense of the entire community, for whatever diversity each interest might have within itself—as all would have the same interest in reference to the action of the government—the individuals composing each would be fully and truly represented by its own majority or appropriate organ, regarded in reference to the other interests. In brief, every individual of every interest might trust, with confidence, its majority or appropriate organ against that of every other interest.

THE NUMERICAL VERSUS THE CONCURRENT MAJORITY

It results, from what has been said, that there are two different modes in which the sense of the community may be taken: one, simply by the right of suffrage, unaided; the other, by the right through a proper organism. Each collects the sense of the majority. But one regards numbers only and considers the whole community as a unit having but one common interest throughout, and collects the sense of the greater number of the whole as that of the community. The other, on the contrary, regards interests as well as numbers—considering the community as made up of different and conflicting interests, as far as the action of the government is concerned—and takes the sense of each through its majority or appropriate organ, and the united sense of all as the sense of the entire community. The former of these I shall call the numerical or absolute majority, and the latter, the concurrent or constitutional majority. I call it the constitutional majority because it is an essential element in every constitutional government, be its form what it may. So great is the difference, politically speaking, between the two majorities that they cannot be confounded without leading to great and fatal errors; and yet the distinction between them has been so entirely overlooked that when the term "majority" is used in political discussions, it is applied exclusively to designate the numerical—as if there were no other. Until this distinction is recognized and better understood, there will continue to be great liability to error in properly constructing constitutional governments, especially of the popular form, and of preserving them when properly constructed. Until then, the latter will have a strong tendency to slide, first, into the government of the numerical majority, and finally, into absolute government of some other form. To show that such must be the case, and at the same time to mark more strongly the difference between the two in order to guard against the danger of overlooking it, I propose to consider the subject more at length.

THE NUMERICAL MAJORITY NOT THE PEOPLE

The first and leading error which naturally arises from overlooking the distinction referred to is to confound the numerical majority with the people, and this so completely as to regard them as identical. This is a consequence that necessarily results from considering the numerical as the only majority. All admit that a proper government, or democracy, is the government of the people, for the terms imply this. A perfect government of the kind would be one which would embrace the consent of every citizen or member of the community, but as this is impracticable in the opinion of those who regard the numerical as the only majority and who can perceive no other way by which the sense of the people can be taken, they are compelled to adopt this as the only true basis of popular government, in contradistinction to governments of the aristocratical or monarchial form. Being thus constrained,

they are, in the next place, forced to regard the numerical majority as in effect the entire people; that is, the greater part as the whole, and the government of the greater part as the government of the whole. It is thus the two come to be confounded and a part made identical with the whole. And it is thus also that all the rights, powers, and immunities of the whole people come to be attributed to the numerical majority—and, among others, the supreme, sovereign authority of establishing and abolishing governments at pleasure.

This radical error, the consequence of confounding the two and of regarding the numerical as the only majority, has contributed more than any other cause to prevent the formation of popular constitutional governments and to destroy them even when they have been formed. It leads to the conclusion that in their formation and establishment nothing more is necessary than the right of suffrage and the allotment to each division of the community a representation in the government in proportion to numbers. If the numerical majority were really the people, and if to take its sense truly were to take the sense of the people truly, a government so constituted would be a true and perfect model of a popular constitutional government; and every departure from it would detract from its excellence. But as such is not the case, as the numerical majority, instead of being the people, is only a portion of them, such a government, instead of being a true and perfect model of the people's government, that is, a people self-governed, is but the government of a part over a part—the major over the minor portion.

But this misconception of the true elements of constitutional government does not stop here. It leads to others equally false and fatal, in reference to the best means of preserving and perpetuating them, when, from some fortunate combination of circumstances, they are correctly formed. For they who fall into these errors regard the restrictions which organism imposes on the will of the numerical majority as restrictions on the will of the people and, therefore, as not only useless but wrongful and mischievous. And hence they endeavor to destroy organism under the delusive hope of making government more democratic. . . .

Having now explained the reasons why it is so difficult to form and preserve popular constitutional government so long as the distinction between the two majorities is overlooked and the opinion prevails that a written constitution, with suitable restrictions and a proper division of its powers, is sufficient to counteract the tendency of the numerical majority to the abuse of its power—I shall next proceed to explain, more fully, why the concurrent majority is an indispensable element in forming constitutional governments, and why the numerical majority, of itself, must, in all cases, make governments absolute.

The necessary consequences of taking the sense of the community by the concurrent majority is, as has been explained, to give to each interest or portion of the community a negative on the others. It is this mutual negative among its various conflicting interests which invests each with the power of protecting itself, and places the rights and safety of each where only they can be securely placed, under its own guardianship. Without this there can be no systematic, peaceful, or effective resistance to the natural tendency of each to come into conflict with the others; and without this there can be no constitution. It is this negative power—the power of preventing or arresting the action of the government, be it called by what term it may, veto, interposition, nullification, check, or balance of power—which in fact forms the constitution. They are all but different names for the negative power. In all its forms, and under all its names, it results from the concurrent majority. Without this there can be no negative, and without a nega-

tive, no constitution. The assertion is true in reference to all constitutional governments, be their forms what they may. It is, indeed, the *negative* power which makes the constitution, and the *positive* which makes the government. The one is the power of acting, and the other the power of preventing or arresting action. The two, combined, make constitutional governments. . . .

Constitutional governments, of whatever form, are, indeed, much more similar to each other in their structure and character than they are, respectively, to the absolute governments, even of their own class. All constitutional governments, of whatever class they may be, take the sense of the community by its parts—each through its appropriate organ—and regard the sense of all its parts as the sense of the whole. They all rest on the right of suffrage and the responsibility of rulers, directly or indirectly. On the contrary, all absolute governments, of whatever form, concentrate power in one uncontrolled and irresponsible individual or body whose will is regarded as the sense of the community. And hence the great and broad distinction between governments is not that of the one, the few, or the many, but of the constitutional and the absolute.

From this there results another distinction which, although secondary in its character, very strongly marks the difference between these forms of government. I refer to their respective conservative principle—that is, the principle by which they are upheld and preserved. This principle in constitutional government is *compromise;* and in absolute governments is *force,* as will be next explained.

It has been already shown that the same constitution of man which leads those who govern to oppress the governed, if not prevented, will, with equal force and certainty, lead the latter to resist oppression when possessed of the means of doing so peaceably and successfully. But absolute governments, of all forms, exclude all other means of resistance to their authority than that of force, and, of course, leave no other alternative to the governed but to acquiesce in oppression, however great it may be, or to resort to force to put down the government. But the dread of such a resort must necessarily lead the government to prepare to meet force in order to protect itself, and hence, of necessity, force becomes the conservative principle of all such governments.

On the contrary, the government of the concurrent majority, where the organism is perfect, excludes the possibility of oppression by giving to each interest, or portion, or order—where there are established classes—the means of protecting itself by its negative against all measures calculated to advance the peculiar interests of others at its expense. Its effect, then, is to cause the different interests, portions, or orders, as the case may be, to desist from attempting to adopt any measure calculated to promote the prosperity of one, or more, by sacrificing that of others: and thus to force them to unite in such measures only as would promote the prosperity of all, as the only means to prevent the suspension of the action of the government, and thereby, to avoid anarchy, the greatest of all evils. It is by means of such authorized and effectual resistance that oppression is prevented and the necessity of resorting to force superseded in governments of the concurrent majority; and hence compromise, instead of force, becomes their conservative principle. . . .

In another particular, governments of concurrent majority have greatly the advantage. I allude to the difference in their respective tendency in reference to dividing or uniting the community, let its interests be ever so diversified or opposed, while that of the numerical is to divide it into two conflicting portions, let its interests be naturally ever so united and identified.

That the numerical majority will divide the community, let it be ever so homogeneous, into two great parties, which will be engaged in perpetual struggles to obtain the control of the government has already been established. The great importance of the object at stake must necessarily form strong party attachments and party antipathies—attachments on the part of the members of each to their respective parties through whose efforts they hope to accomplish an object dear to all; and antipathies to the opposite party, as presenting the only obstacle to success. . . .

The concurrent majority, on the other hand, tends to unite the most opposite and conflicting interests and to blend the whole in one common attachment to the country. By giving to each interest, or portion, the power of self-protection, all strife and struggle between them for ascendancy is prevented, and thereby not only every feeling calculated to weaken the attachment to the whole is suppressed, but the individual and the social feelings are made to unite in one common devotion to country. Each sees and feels that it can best promote its own prosperity by conciliating the good will and promoting the prosperity of the others. And hence there will be diffused throughout the whole community kind feelings between its different portions and, instead of antipathy, a rivalry amongst them to promote the interests of each other, as far as this can be done consistently with the interest of all. . . .

If the two to be compared in reference to the ends for which government is ordained, the superiority of the government of the concurrent majority will not be less striking. These, as has been stated, are twofold: to protect and to perfect society. But to preserve society, it is necessary to guard the community against injustice, violence, and anarchy within, and against attacks from without. If it fail in either, it would fail in the primary end of government and would not deserve the name.

To perfect society, it is necessary to develop the faculties, intellectual and moral, with which man is endowed. But the mainspring to their development and civilization, with all their blessings, is the desire of individuals to better their condition. For this purpose liberty and security are indispensable. Liberty leaves each free to pursue the course he may deem best to promote his interest and happiness, as far as it may be compatible with the primary end for which government is ordained, while security gives assurance to each that he shall not be deprived of the fruits of his exertions to better his condition. These combined give to this desire the strongest impulse of which it is susceptible. For to extend liberty beyond the limits assigned would be to weaken the government and to render it incompetent to fulfill its primary end—the protection of society against dangers, internal and external. The effect of this would be insecurity; and of insecurity, to weaken the impulse of individuals to better their condition and thereby retard progress and improvement. On the other hand, to extend the powers of the government so as to contract the sphere assigned to liberty would have the same effect, by disabling individuals in their efforts to better their condition.

Herein is to be found the principle which assigns to power and liberty their proper spheres and reconciles each to the other under all circumstances. For if power be necessary to secure to liberty the fruits of its exertions, liberty, in turn, repays power with interest—by increased population, wealth and other advantages which progress and improvement bestow on the community. By thus assigning to each its appropriate sphere, all conflicts between them cease, and each is made to cooperate with and assist the other in fulfilling the great ends for which government is ordained.

But the principle, applied to different communities, will assign to them different limits. It will assign a larger sphere to power and a more contracted one to liberty, or the reverse,

according to circumstances. To the former, there must ever be allotted, under all circumstances, a sphere sufficiently large to protect the community against danger from without and violence and anarchy within. The residuum belongs to liberty. More cannot be safely or rightly allotted to it.

But some communities require a far greater amount of power than others to protect them against anarchy and external dangers; and, of course, the sphere of liberty in such must be proportionally contracted. The causes calculated to enlarge the one and contract the other are numerous and various. Some are physical—such as open and exposed frontiers surrounded by powerful and hostile neighbors. Others are moral—such as the different degrees of intelligence, patriotism, and virtue among the mass of the community, and their experience and proficiency in the art of self-government. Of these, the moral are by far the most influential. A community may possess all the necessary moral qualifications in so high a degree as to be capable of self-government under the most adverse circumstances, while, on the other hand, another may be so sunk in ignorance and vice as to be incapable of forming a conception of liberty or of living, even when most favored by circumstances, under any other than an absolute and despotic government.

The principle in all communities, according to these numerous and various causes, assigns to power and liberty their spheres. To allow to liberty, in any case, a sphere of action more extended than this assigns would lead to anarchy, and this, probably, in the end to a contraction instead of an enlargement of its sphere. Liberty, then, when forced on a people unfit for it, would, instead of a blessing, be a curse, as it would in its reaction lead directly to anarchy—the greatest of all curses. No people, indeed, can long enjoy more liberty than that to which their situation and advanced intelligence and morals fairly entitle them. If more than this be allowed, they must soon fall into confusion and disorder—to be followed, if not by anarchy and despotism, by a change to a form of government more simple and absolute, and therefore better suited to their condition. And hence, although it may be true that a people may not have as much liberty as they are fairly entitled to and are capable of enjoying, yet the reverse is unquestionably true—that no people can long possess more than they are fairly entitled to.

Liberty, indeed, though among the greatest of blessings, is not so great as that of protection, inasmuch as the end of the former is the progress and improvement of the race, while that of the latter is its preservation and perpetuation. And hence, when the two come into conflict, liberty must, and ever ought, to yield to protection, as the existence of the race is of greater moment than its improvement.

It follows, from what has been stated, that it is a great and dangerous error to suppose that all people are equally entitled to liberty. It is a reward to be earned, not a blessing to be gratuitously lavished on all alike—a reward reserved for the intelligent, the patriotic, the virtuous and deserving, and not a boon to be bestowed on a people too ignorant, degraded and vicious to be capable either of appreciating or of enjoying it. Nor is it any disparagement to liberty that such is and ought to be the case. On the contrary, its greatest praise—its proudest distinction is that an all-wise Providence has reserved it as the noblest and highest reward for the development of our faculties, moral and intellectual. A reward more appropriate than liberty could not be conferred on the deserving, nor a punishment inflicted on the undeserving more just than to be subject to lawless and despotic rule. This dispensation seems to be the result of some fixed law; and every effort to disturb or defeat it, by attempting to elevate a people in the scale of liberty

above the point to which they are entitled to rise, must ever prove abortive, and end in disappointment. The progress of a people rising from a lower to a higher point in the scale of liberty is necessarily slow; and by attempting to precipitate, we either retard or permanently defeat it.

LIBERTY AND EQUALITY

There is another error, not less great and dangerous, usually associated with the one which has just been considered. I refer to the opinion that liberty and equality are so intimately united that liberty cannot be perfect without perfect equality.

That they are united to a certain extent, and that equality of citizens, in the eyes of the law, is essential to liberty in a popular government is conceded. But to go further and make equality of *condition* essential to liberty would be to destroy both liberty and progress. The reason is that inequality of condition, while it is a necessary consequence of liberty, is at the same time indispensable to progress. In order to understand why this is so, it is necessary to bear in mind that the mainspring to progress is the desire of individuals to better their condition, and that the strongest impulse which can be given to it is to leave individuals free to exert themselves in the manner they may deem best for that purpose, as far at least as it can be done consistently with the ends for which government is ordained, and to secure to all the fruits of their exertions. Now, as individuals differ greatly from each other in intelligence, sagacity, energy, perseverance, skill, habits of industry and economy, physical power, position and opportunity—the necessary effect of leaving all free to exert themselves to better their condition must be a corresponding inequality between those who may possess these qualities and advantages in a high degree and those who may be deficient in them. The only means by which this result can be prevented are either to impose such restrictions on the exertions of those who may possess them in a high degree as will place them on a level with those who do not, or to deprive them of the fruits of their exertions. But to impose such restrictions on them would be destructive of liberty, while to deprive them of the fruits of their exertions would be to destroy the desire of bettering their condition. It is, indeed, this inequality of condition between the front and rear ranks, in the march of progress, which gives so strong an impulse to the former to maintain their position, and to the latter to press forward into their files. This gives to progress its greatest impulse. To force the front rank back to the rear or to attempt to push forward the rear into line with the front, by the interposition of the government, would put an end to the impulse and effectually arrest the march of progress.

THE "STATE OF NATURE" PURELY HYPOTHETICAL

These great and dangerous errors have their origin in the prevalent opinion that all men are born free and equal—than which nothing can be more unfounded and false. It rests upon the assumption of a fact which is contrary to universal observation, in whatever light it may be regarded. It is, indeed, difficult to explain how an opinion so destitute of all sound reason ever could have been so extensively entertained unless we regard it as being confounded with another which has some semblance of truth, but which, when properly understood, is not less false and dangerous. I refer to the assertion that all men are equal in the state of nature, meaning by a state of nature a state of individuality supposed to have existed prior to the social and political state, and in which men lived apart and independent of each other. If such a state ever did exist, all men would have been, indeed, free and equal in it; that is, free to do as they pleased and exempt from the authority of control of others—as, by supposition, it existed anterior to society and government. But such a state is purely hypothetical. It never did nor can exist, as it is inconsistent with the preservation and perpetuation of the race. It is, therefore, a great misnomer to call it "the state of nature." Instead of being the natural state of man, it is, of all conceivable states, the most opposed to his nature—most repugnant to his feelings and most incompatible with his wants. His natural state is the social and political—the one for which his Creator made him, and the only one in which he can preserve and perfect his race. As, then, there never was such a state as the so-called state of nature, and never can be, it follows that men, instead of being born in it, are born in the social and political state; and of course, instead of being born free and equal, are born subject, not only to parental authority, but to the laws and institutions of the country where born and under whose protection they draw their first breath. . . .

Such are the many and striking advantages of the concurrent over the numerical majority. Against the former but two objections can be made. The one is that it is difficult of construction, which has already been sufficiently noticed; and the other that it would be impracticable to obtain the concurrence of conflicting interests where they were numerous and diversified, or, if not, that the process for this purpose would be too tardy to meet with sufficient promptness the many and dangerous emergencies to which all communities are exposed. This objection is plausible and deserves a fuller notice than it has yet received.

The diversity of opinion is usually so great on almost all questions of policy that it is not surprising, on a slight view of the subject, it should be thought impracticable to bring the various conflicting interests of a community to unite on any one line of policy, or that a government founded on such a principle would be too slow in its movements and too weak in its foundation to succeed in practice. But plausible as it may seem at the first glance, a more deliberate view will show that this opinion is erroneous. It is true that, when there is no urgent necessity, it is difficult to bring those who differ to agree on any one line of action. Each will naturally insist on taking the course he may think best, and, from pride of opinion, will be unwilling to yield to others. But the case is different when there is an urgent necessity to unite on some common course of action, as reason and experience both prove. When something *must* be done—and when it can be done only by the united consent of all—the necessity of the case will force to a compromise, be the case of that necessity what it may. On all questions of acting, necessity, where it exists, is the overruling motive; and where, in such cases, compromise among the parties is an indispensable condition to acting, it exerts an overruling influence in predisposing them to acquiesce in some one opinion or course of action. . . .

But to form a juster estimate of the full force of this impulse to compromise, there must be added that in governments of the concurrent majority each portion, in order to advance its own peculiar interests, would have to conciliate all others by showing a disposition to advance theirs; and for this purpose each would select those to represent it whose wisdom, patriotism, and weight of character would command the confidence of the others. Under its influence—and with representatives so well qualified to accomplish the object for which they were selected—the prevailing desire would be to promote the common interests of the whole; and hence the competition would be, not which should yield the least to promote the common good, but which should yield the most. It is thus that concession would cease to be considered a sacrifice—would become a free-will offering on the altar of the

country and lose the name of compromise. And herein is to be found that feature which distinguishes governments of the concurrent majority so strikingly from those of the numerical. In the latter, each faction, in the struggle to obtain the control of the government, elevates to power the designing, the artful, and unscrupulous who in their devotion to party—instead of aiming at the good of the whole—aim exclusively at securing the ascendancy of party.

When traced to its source, this difference will be found to originate in the fact that in governments of the concurrent majority individual feelings are, from its organism, necessarily enlisted on the side of the social, and made to unite with them in promoting the interests of the whole as the best way of promoting the separate interests of each, while in those of the numerical majority the social are necessarily enlisted on the side of the individual and made to contribute to the interest of parties regardless of that of the whole. To effect the former—to enlist the individual on the side of the social feelings to promote the good of the whole—is the greatest possible achievement of the science of government, while to enlist the social on the side of the individual to promote the interest of parties at the expense of the good of the whole is the greatest blunder which ignorance can possibly commit.

To this also may be referred the greater solidity of foundation on which governments of the concurrent majority repose. Both ultimately rest on necessity, for force, by which those of the numerical majority are upheld, is only acquiesced in from necessity—in a necessity not more imperious, however, than that which compels the different portions in governments of the concurrent majority to acquiesce in compromise. There is, however, a great difference in the motive, the feeling, the aim which characterize the act in the two cases. In the one, it is done with that reluctance and hostility ever incident to enforced submission to what is regarded as injustice and oppression, accompanied by the desire and purpose to seize on the first favorable opportunity for resistance; but in the other, willingly and cheerfully, under the impulse of an exalted patriotism, impelling all to acquiesce in whatever the common good requires. ∾

Primary Sources

Calhoun: Basic Documents. Edited by John M. Anderson. Carroltown, Penn.: Bald Eagle Press, 1952.

The Papers of John C. Calhoun. Edited by Robert L. Meriwether. Columbia: University of South Carolina Press, 1959.

The Works of John C. Calhoun. Edited by Richard K. Cralle. 6 vols. New York: D. Appleton and Co., 1859.

Secondary Sources

Bartlett, Irving H. *John C. Calhoun: A Biography.* New York: Norton, 1993.

Heckscher, Gunnar. "Calhoun's Idea of 'Concurrent Majority,'" *American Political Science Review* 31 (August 1939): 555–90.

Hunt, Gaillard. *John C. Calhoun.* Philadelphia: Jacobs, 1907.

Spain, August O. *The Political Theory of John C. Calhoun.* New York: Bookman, 1951.

Styron, Arthur. *The Cast Iron Man.* New York: Longmans, 1935.

Wiltse, Charles M. *John C. Calhoun, Nationalist.* Indianapolis: Bobbs-Merrill, 1944.

21. George Fitzhugh

GEORGE FITZHUGH (1806–81) was born to a Virginia family of fading gentility and was essentially self-educated (though very well) in the classics, economics, and law. He wrote for several Southern newspapers and journals, effectively defending slavery by attacking "free society" for being an individualistic, anarchic world created by capitalism. Fitzhugh is distinguished among all American conservatives for being utterly consistent and fundamental in his critique of liberal society. He attacks not only the Reformation and Locke, for their pernicious emphasis on individualism, contract, and being self-serving, but also Jefferson and his followers.

Fitzhugh's first book was *Sociology for the South; or, the Failure of Free Society* (1854). There he set upon Adam Smith, laissez-faire, and the idea that social well-being could flow from individuals pursuing their self-interest. Instead he called for purposeful government planning, development, and control. *Cannibals All! or, Slaves without Masters* (1857), excerpted here, was a sharper and more focused attack on Northern thought and practice. Agreeing with the socialist critique of the "wage-slavery" system, he found the solution for it in a system so conservative that it had precedents only in pre-Reformation English feudal society. ∾

Cannibals All! (1857)

We are all, North and South, engaged in the White Slave Trade, and he who succeeds best is esteemed most respectable. It is far more cruel than the Black Slave Trade, because it exacts more of its slaves, and neither protects nor governs them. We boast that it exacts more when we say, "that the *profits* made from employing free labor are greater than those from slave labor." The profits, made from free labor, are the amount of the products of such labor, which the employer, by means of the command which capital or skill gives him, takes away, exacts, or "exploitates" from the free laborer. The profits of slave labor are that portion of the products of such labor which the power of the master enables him to appropriate. These profits are less, because the master allows the slave to retain a larger share of the results of his own labor than do the employers of free labor. But we not only boast that the White Slave Trade is more exacting and fraudulent (in fact, though not in intention) than Black Slavery; but we also boast that it is more cruel, in leaving the laborer to take care of himself and family out of the pittance which skill or capital have allowed him to retain. When the day's labor is ended, he is free, but is overburdened with the cares of family and household, which make his freedom an empty and delusive mockery. But his employer is really free, and may enjoy the profits made by others' labor, without a care, or a trouble, as to their well-being. The negro slave is free, too, when the labors of the day are over, and free in mind as well as body; for the master provides food, raiment, house,

fuel, and everything else necessary to the physical well-being of himself and family. The master's labors commence just when the slave's end. No wonder men should prefer white slavery to capital, to negro slavery, since it is more profitable, and is free from all the cares and labors of black slave-holding.

Now, reader, if you wish to know yourself—to "descant on your own deformity" —read on. But if you would cherish self-conceit, self-esteem, or self-appreciation, throw down our book; for we will dispel illusions which have promoted your happiness, and show you that what you have considered and practiced as virtue is little better than moral Cannibalism. But you will find yourself in numerous and respectable company; for all good and respectable people are "Cannibals all" who do not labor, or who are successfully trying to live without labor, on the unrequited labor of other people:—Whilst low, bad, and disreputable people, are those who labor to support themselves, and to support said respectable people besides. Throwing the negro slaves out of the account, and society is divided in Christendom into four classes: the rich, or independent respectable people, who live well and labor not at all; the professional and skillful respectable people, who do a little light work, for enormous wages; the poor hard-working people, who support everybody, and starve themselves; and the poor thieves, swindlers, and sturdy beggars, who live like gentlemen, without labor, on the labor of other people. The gentlemen exploitate, which being done on a large scale and requiring a great many victims, is highly respectable —whilst the rogues and beggars take so little from others that they fare little better than those who labor.

But, reader, we do not wish to fire into the

SOURCE: George Fitzhugh, *Cannibals All! or, Slaves without Masters,* ed. C. Vann Woodward (Cambridge, Mass.: Harvard University Press, 1960), passim. The footnotes are Fitzhugh's.

flock. "Thou art the man!" You are a Cannibal! and if a successful one, pride yourself on the number of your victims quite as much as any Fiji chieftain, who breakfasts, dines, and sups on human flesh—and your conscience smites you, if you have failed to succeed, quite as much as his, when he returns from an unsuccessful foray.

Probably, you are a lawyer, or a merchant, or a doctor, who has made by your business fifty thousand dollars, and retired to live on your capital. But, mark! not to spend your capital. That would be vulgar, disreputable, criminal. That would be, to live by your own labor; for your capital is your amassed labor. That would be to do as common working men do; for they take the pittance which their employers leave them to live on. They live by labor; for they exchange the results of their own labor for the products of other people's labor. It is, no doubt, an honest, vulgar way of living, but not at all a respectable way. The respectable way of living is to make other people work for you, and to pay them nothing for so doing—and to have no concern about them after their work is done. Hence, white slaveholding is much more respectable than negro slavery—for the master works nearly as hard for the negro as he for the master. But you, my virtuous, respectable leader, exact three thousand dollars per annum from white labor (for your income is the product of white labor) and make not one cent of return in any form. You retain your capital, and never labor, and yet live in luxury on the labor of others. Capital commands labor, as the master does the slave. Neither pays for labor; but the master permits the slave to retain a larger allowance from the proceeds of his own labor, and hence "free labor is cheaper than slave labor." You, with the command over labor which your capital gives you, are a slave owner—a master, without the obligations of a master. They who work for you, who create your income, are slaves, without the rights of slaves. Slaves without a master! Whilst you were engaged in amassing your capital, in seeking to become independent, you were in the White Slave Trade. To become independent is to be able to make other people support you, without being obliged to labor for *them.* Now, what man in society is not seeking to attain this situation? He who attains it is a slave owner, in the worst sense. He who is in pursuit of it is engaged in the slave trade. You, reader, belong to the one or other class. The men without property, in free society, are theoretically in a worse condition than slaves. Practically, their condition corresponds with this theory, as history and statistics everywhere demonstrate. The capitalists, in free society, live in ten times the luxury and show that Southern masters do, because the slaves to capital work harder and cost less than negro slaves.

The negro slaves of the South are the happiest, and, in some sense, the freest people in the world. The children and the aged and infirm work not at all, and yet have all the comforts and necessaries of life provided for them. They enjoy liberty, because they are oppressed neither by care nor labor. The women do little hard work, and are protected from the despotism of their husbands by their masters. The negro man and stout boys work, on the average, in good weather, not more than nine hours a day. The balance of their time is spent in perfect abandon. Besides, they have their Sabbaths and holidays. White men, with so much of license and liberty, would die of ennui; but negroes luxuriate in corporeal and mental repose. With their faces upturned to the sun, they can sleep at any hour; and quiet sleep is the greatest of human enjoyments. "Blessed be the man who invented sleep." 'Tis happiness in itself—and results from contentment with the present, and confident assurance of the future. We do not know whether free laborers ever sleep. They are fools to do so; for, whilst they sleep, the wily and watchful capitalist is devising means to ensnare and exploitate them. The free laborer must work or starve. He is more of a slave than the negro, because he works longer and harder for less allowance than the slave, and has no holiday, because the cares of life with him begin when its labors end. He has no liberty, and not a single right. We know, 'tis often said, air and water are common property, which all have equal right to participate and enjoy; but this is utterly false. The appropriation of the lands carries with it the appropriation of all on or above the lands, *usque ad coelum, aut ad inferos.*[1] A man cannot breathe the air without a place to breathe it from, and all places are appropriated. All water is private property "to the middle of the stream," except the ocean, and that is not fit to drink.

Free laborers have not a thousandth part of the rights and liberties of negro slaves. Indeed, they have not a single liberty, unless it be the right or liberty to die. But the reader may think that he and other capitalists and employers are freer than negro slaves. Your capital would soon vanish, if you dared indulge in the liberty and abandon of negroes. You hold your wealth and position by the tenure of constant watchfulness, care, and circumspection. You never labor; but you are never free.

Where a few own the soil, they have unlimited power over the balance of society, until domestic slavery comes in to compel them to permit this balance of society to draw a sufficient and comfortable living from *terra mater.* Free society asserts the right of a few to the earth—slavery maintains that it belongs, in different degrees, to all.

But, reader, well may you follow the slave trade. It is the only trade worth following, and slaves the only property worth owning. All other is worthless, a mere *caput mortuum,*[2] except in so far as it vests the owner with the power to command the labors of others—to enslave them. Give you a palace, ten thousand acres of land, sumptuous clothes, equipage, and every other luxury; and with your artificial wants you are poorer than Robinson Crusoe, or the lowest working man, if you have no slaves to capital, or domestic slaves. Your capital will not bring you an income of a cent, nor supply one of your wants, without labor. Labor is indispensable to give value to property, and if you owned every thing else, and did not own labor, you would be poor. But fifty thousand dollars means, and is, fifty thousand dollars worth of slaves. You can command, without touching on that capital, three thousand dollars' worth of labor per annum. You could do no more were you to buy slaves with it, and then you would be cumbered with the cares of governing and providing for them. You are a slaveholder now, to the amount of fifty thousand dollars, with all the advantages, and none of the cares and responsibilities of a master.

"Property in man" is what all are struggling to obtain. Why should they not be obliged to take care of man, their property, as they do of their horses and their hounds, their cattle and their sheep. Now, under the delusive name of liberty, you work him "from morn to dewy eve"—from infancy to old age—then turn him out to starve. You treat your horses and hounds better. Capital is a cruel master. The free slave trade, the commonest, yet the cruellest of trades....

Mobs, secret associations, insurance companies, and social and communistic experiments are striking features and characteristics of our day, outside of slave society. They are all at-

---

1. "Even to heaven or to hell."

2. "Worthless residue."

tempting to supply the defects of regular governments, which have carried the Let Alone practice so far that one-third of mankind are let alone to indulge in such criminal immoralities as they please, and another third to starve. Mobs (*vide* California) supply the deficiencies of a defective police, and insurance companies and voluntary unions and associations afford that security and protection which government, under the lead of political economy, has ceased to render.

A lady remarked to us, a few days since, "that society was like an army, in which the inferior officers were as necessary as the commander-in-chief. Demoralization and insubordination ensue if you dispense with sergeants and corporals in an army, and the same effects result from dispensing with guardians, masters, and heads of families in society." We don't know whether she included the ladies in her ideas of the heads of families; protesting against such construction of her language, we accept and thank her for her illustration. Rev'd Nehemiah Adams has a similar thought in his admirable work, *A Southside View of Slavery,* which we regret is not before us. On some public occasion in Charleston, he was struck with the good order and absence of all dissipation, and very naively asked where was their mob. He was informed that "they were at work." He immediately perceived that slavery was an admirable police institution, and moralizes very wisely on the occasion. Slavery is an indispensable police institution—especially so to check the cruelty and tyranny of vicious and depraved husbands and parents. Husbands and parents have, in theory and practice, a power over their subjects more despotic than kings; and the ignorant and vicious exercise their power more oppressively than kings. Every man is not fit to be king, yet all must have wives and children. Put a master over them to check their power, and we need not resort to the unnatural remedies of woman's rights, limited marriages, voluntary divorces, and free love, as proposed by the abolitionists....

We may be doing Mr. Jefferson injustice in assuming that his "fundamental principles" and Mr. Seward's "higher law" mean the same thing; but the injustice can be very little, as they both mean just nothing at all, unless it be a determination to inaugurate anarchy, and to do all sorts of mischief. We refer the reader to the chapter on the Declaration of Independence, &c., in our *Sociology* for a further dissertation on the fundamental powder-cask abstractions, on which our glorious institutions *affect* to repose. We say *affect,* because we are sure neither their repose nor their permanence would be disturbed by the removal of the counterfeit foundation.

The true greatness of Mr. Jefferson was his fitness for revolution. He was the genius of innovation, the architect of ruin, the inaugurator of anarchy. His mission was to pull down, not to build up. He thought everything false as well in the physical as in the moral world. He fed his horses on potatoes, and defended harbors with gunboats, because it was contrary to human experience with human opinion. He proposed to govern boys without the authority of masters or the control of religion, supplying their places with Laissez Faire philosophy, and morality from the pages of Lawrence Sterne. His character, like his philosophy, is exceptional—invaluable in urging on revolution, but useless, if not dangerous, in quiet times.

We would not restrict, control, or take away a single human right or liberty which experience showed was already sufficiently governed and restricted by public opinion. But we do believe that the slaveholding South is the only country on the globe that can safely tolerate the rights and liberties which we have discussed.

The annals of revolutionary Virginia were

illustrated by three great and useful men. The mighty mind of Jefferson, fitted to pull down; the plastic hand of Madison to build up; and the powerful arm of Washington to defend, sustain, and conserve.

We are the friend of popular government, but only so long as conservatism is the interest of the governing class. At the South, the interests and feelings of many non-property holders, are identified with those of a comparatively few property holders. It is not necessary to the security of property, that a majority of voters should own property; but where the pauper majority becomes so large as to disconnect the mass of them in feeling and interest from the property holding class, revolution and agrarianism are inevitable. We will not undertake to say that events are tending this way at the North. The absence of laws of entail and primogeniture may prevent it; yet we fear the worst, for, despite the laws of equal inheritance and distribution, wealth is accumulating in few hands, and pauperism is increasing. We shall attempt hereafter to show that a system of very small entails might correct this tendency....

All modern philosophy converges to a single point—the overthrow of all government, the substitution of the untrammelled "Sovereignty of the Individual" for the Sovereignty of Society, and the inauguration of anarchy. First domestic slavery, next religious institutions, then separate property, then political government, and, finally, family government and family relations, are to be swept away. This is the distinctly avowed programme of all able abolitionists and socialists; and towards this end the doctrines and the practices of the weakest and most timid among them tend. Proudhon, and the French socialists generally, avow this purpose in France, and Stephen Pearl Andrews re-echoes it from America. The more numerous and timid class are represented by Mr.

Greeley and the *Tribune,* who would not "at once rush," like French revolutionists, "with the explosive force of escapement, point blank to the bull's eye of its final destiny," but would inaugurate social conditions that would gradually bring about that result. Mr. Greeley does not propose to do away at once with marriage, religion, private property, political government and parental authority, but adopts the philosophy and the practices of Fourier, which promise gradually to purify human nature, and fit it, in a few generations, for that social millennium into which the bolder and more consistent Andrews urges society at once to plunge.

The Christian socialists are beautifully and energetically collaborating with the infidel socialists and abolitionists to bring about this millennium. They also are divided into two parties. The one would wait upon Providence —only help it a little, like Mr. Greeley—and permit our poor old effete world to pass out of existence by gentle euthanasia. The other and bolder party feel themselves "called" as special instruments to give at once the coup de grace to the old world, and to usher in the new golden age of free love and free lands, of free women and free negroes, of free children and free men.

We like the Northern socialist theoretical abolitionists—read their speeches, essays, lectures, and books, because they agree with us that their own form of society is a humbug and a failure; and in their efforts, speculation and schemes to reorganize it, afford the most beautiful perfect and complete specimen of the *reductio ad absurdum.* A lecture from Mr. Andrews on No-government, an Oneida den of incest, a Greeley phalanstery, or a New York free love saloon afford equally good instances of this mode of demonstration by the absurdities which they exhibit, and equally good proofs of the naturalness and necessity of slavery, since such horrid abuses are everywhere the approved and practiced outgrowth of free society. As all our thoughts, arguments, proofs and demonstrations are suggested by or borrowed from the abolitionists, it seems to us we ought to dedicate to them. The *Tribune* very properly remarked that our *Sociology* was the first attempt of the kind at the South. It ridiculed our ignorance, too, severely. It should have recollected that were there no sickness there would be no physicians. We assure the *Tribune* we are quite a prodigy in these matters for a Southern man. We have no social diseases, and therefore no social doctors to write about them or cure them. Such diseases have been rare; for Aristotle complains that there are no terms to express the relations of husband and wife, or parent and child. These relations have worked so smoothly in slave society to this day that we in writing have felt the same want of language of which Aristotle, more than two thousand years ago, complained. You should invent such terms at the North, if it be true, as Mr. Andrews states in italics, that there are ten fugitives from Northern matrimony to one from Southern slavery—from which he seems to infer very logically that the necessity of abolishing the family at the North is ten times as great as that for abolishing slavery at the South. He and you are experts, and we know it is presumptuous in us to dispute what you say about your own society. Still we are dead against your phalansteries and his love saloons. Gentlemen and scholars, generally at the South, would as soon be caught studying or practicing the black art, as in reading Owen or Fourier, or in building phalansteries. For ourselves like the Bastard in *King John,* we learn things, "not to deceive, but to avoid deceit." We have whole files of infidel and abolition papers, like the *Tribune, the Liberator* and *Investigator*. Fanny Wright, the Devil's Pulpit and the Devil's Parson, Tom Paine, Owen, Voltaire, et *id genus omne*, are our daily companions. Good people give our office a wide berth as they pass it, and even the hens who loiter about it, have caught the infection of Woman's Rights, for we saw but a few days ago a Shanghai cock under its eaves hovering a brood of twenty chickens, whilst madam hen was strutting about in as large a liberty as any Bloomer or wise woman of the North.

Love and veneration for the family is with us not only a principle, but probably a prejudice and a weakness. We were never two weeks at a time from under the family roof, until we had passed middle life, and now that our years almost number half a century, we have never been from home for an interval of two months. And our historical reading, as well as our habits of life, may have unfitted us to appreciate the communist and fusion theories of Fanny Wright, Owen and Mr. Greeley. In attempting to vindicate and justify the ways of God and Nature, against the progressiveness of Black Republicanism in America, and Red Republicanism in Europe, we would forewarn the reader that we are a prejudiced witness. We are the enthusiastic admirer of the social relations exhibited in the histories of Abraham, Isaac and Jacob. The social relations established in Deuteronomy, and 25th chapter Leviticus, and as practiced by the Jews to this day, elicit our unfeigned admiration and approval. Moses is with us the Prince of Legislators, and the twenty-fifth Leviticus the best of political platforms. The purity of the family seems to be his paramount object. . . .

We do not agree with the authors of the Declaration of Independence, that governments "derive their just powers from the consent of the governed." [None of] the women, the children, the negroes, and but few of the non-property holders were consulted, or consented to the Revolution, or the governments that ensued from its success. As to these, the new governments were self-elected despotisms, and the governing class self-elected despots. Those governments originated in force, and have been continued by force. All governments must originate in force, and be continued by force. The very term, government, implies that it is carried on against the consent of the governed. Fathers do not derive their authority, as heads of families, from the consent of wife and children, nor do they govern their families by their consent. They never take the vote of the family as to the labors to be performed, the moneys to be expended, or as to anything else. Masters dare not take the vote of slaves as to their government. If they did, constant holiday, dissipation, and extravagance would be the result. Captains of ships are not appointed by the consent of the crew, and never take their vote, even in "doubling Cape Horn." If they did, the crew would generally vote to get drunk, and the ship would never weather the cape. Not even in the most democratic countries are soldiers governed by their consent, nor is their vote taken on the eve of battle. They have some how lost (or never had) the "inalienable rights of life, liberty, and the pursuit of happiness," and, whether Americans or Russians, are forced into battle without and often against their consent. The ancient republics were governed by a small class of adult male citizens who assumed and exercised the government without the consent of the governed. The South is governed just as those ancient republics were. In the county in which we live, there are eighteen thousand souls, and only twelve hundred voters. But we twelve hundred, the governors, never asked and never intend to ask the consent of the sixteen thousand eight hundred whom we govern. Were we to do so, we should soon have an "organized anarchy." The governments of Europe could not exist a week without the positive force of standing armies.

They are all governments of force, not of consent. Even in our North, the women, children, and free negroes, constitute four-fifths of the population; and they are all governed without their consent. But they mean to correct this gross and glaring iniquity at the North. They hold that all men, women, and negroes, and smart children are equals, and entitled to equal rights. The widows and free negroes begin to vote in some of those States, and they will have to let all colors and sexes and ages vote soon, or give up the glorious principles of human equality and universal emancipation.

The experiment which they will make, we fear, is absurd in theory, and the symptoms of approaching anarchy and agrarianism among them leave no doubt that its practical operation will be no better than its theory. Antirentism, "vote-myself-a-farm-ism," and all the other Isms, are but the spattering drops that precede a social deluge.

Abolition ultimates in "Consent Government"; Consent Government in Anarchy, Free Love, Agrarianism, &c., &c., and "Self-elected Despotism" winds up the play.

If the interests of the governors, or governing class, be not conservative, they certainly will not conserve institutions injurious to their interests. There never was and never can be an old society, in which the immediate interests of a majority of human souls do not conflict with all established order, all right of property, and all existing institutions. Immediate interest is all the mass look to; and they would be sure to revolutionize government, as often as the situation of the majority was worse than that of the minority. Divide all property to-day, and a year hence the inequalities of property would provoke a re-division.

In the South, the interest of the governing class is eminently conservative, and the South is fast becoming the most conservative of nations.

Already, at the North, government vibrates and oscillates between Radicalism and Conservatism; at present, Radicalism or Black Republicanism is in the ascendant.

The number of paupers is rapidly increasing; radical and agrarian doctrines are spreading; the women and the children, and the negroes, will soon be let in to vote; and then they will try the experiment of "Consent Government and Constituted Anarchy."

It is falsely said, that revolutions never go backwards. They always go backwards, and generally farther back than where they started. The Social Revolution now going on at the North, must some day go backwards. Shall it do so now, ere it has perpetrated an infinitude of mischief, shed oceans of blood, and occasioned endless human misery; or will the Conservatives of the North let it run the length of its leather, inflict all these evils, and then rectify itself by issuing into military despotism? We think that by a kind of alliance, offensive and defensive, with the South, Northern Conservatism may now arrest and turn back the tide of Radicalism and Agrarianism. We will not presume to point out the whole means and *modus operandi*. They on the field of action will best see what is necessary to be done.

Whilst we hold that all government is a matter of force, we yet think the governing class should be numerous enough to understand, and so situated as to represent fairly, all interests. The Greek and Roman masters were thus situated; so were the old Barons of England, and so are the white citizens of the South. If not all masters, like Greek and Roman citizens, they all belong to the master race, have exclusive rights and privileges of citizenship, and an interest not to see this right of citizenship extended, disturbed, and rendered worthless and contemptible.

Whilst the governments of Europe are more obviously kept alive and conducted by force than at any other period, yet are they all, from necessity, watchful and regardful of Public Opinion. Opinion now rules the world, but not as expressed through the ballot-box. Governments become more popular as they become more forcible. A large governing class is not apt to mistake or disregard opinion; and, therefore, Republican institutions are best adapted to the times. Under Monarchical forms, the governments of Europe are daily becoming more Republican. The fatal error committed in Western Europe is the wielding of government by a class who govern, but do not represent, the masses. Their interests and those of the masses are antagonistic, whilst those of masters and slaves are identical.

Looking to theory, to the examples of the Ancient Republics, and to England under the Plantagenets, we shall find that Southern institutions are far the best now existing in the world.

We think speculations as to constructing governments are little worth; for all government is the gradual accretion of Nature, time and circumstances. Yet these theories have occurred to us, and, as they are conservative, we will suggest them. In slaveholding countries all freemen should vote and govern, because their interests are conservative. In free states, the government should be in the hands of the landowners, who are also conservative. A system of primogeniture, and entails of small parcels of land, might, in a great measure, identify the interests of all; or, at least, those who held no lands would generally be the children and kinsmen of those who did, and be taken care of by them. The frequent accumulation of large fortunes, and consequent pauperism of the masses, is the greatest evil of modern society. Would not small entails prevent this? All cannot own lands, but as many should own them as is consistent with good farming and advanced civilization. The social institutions of the Jews, as established by Moses and Joshua, most nearly fulfill our ideas of perfect government.

A word, at parting, to Northern Conservatives. A like danger threatens North and

South, proceeding from the same source. Abolitionism is maturing what Political Economy began. With inexorable sequence Let Alone is made to usher in No-Government. North and South our danger is the same, and our remedies, though differing in degree, must in character be the same. Let Alone must be repudiated, if we would have any Government. We must, in all sections, act upon the principle that the world is "too little governed." You of the North need not institute negro slavery, far less reduce white men to the state of negro slavery. But the masses require more of protection, and the masses and philosophers equally require more of control. . . . ∾

Primary Source

Fitzhugh, George. *Sociology for the South.* Richmond, Va.: DeBow, 1854.

Secondary Sources

Genovese, Eugene D. *The World the Slaveholders Made.* New York: Vintage, 1971.

Wish, Harvey. *George Fitzhugh, Propagandist of the Old South.* Gloucester, Mass.: Peter Smith, 1962.

22. Abraham Lincoln

ABRAHAM LINCOLN (1809–65) was born in Kentucky and moved to Indiana, then to Illinois. He had little formal education but was admitted to the bar in 1836. He served as a state legislator and member of Congress from 1847 to 1849 but did not run for reelection. His first truly national visibility occurred in 1854 with the Peoria speech, in which he denounced the Kansas-Nebraska Act. The new Republican party nominated him for the Senate in 1858, a nomination which he accepted with a speech made famous by its inclusion of the statement, "A house divided against itself cannot stand . . . this government cannot endure permanently, half slave and half free." Although he lost the election to Democrat Stephen A. Douglas, his debates with Douglas gained him substantial national support. Because his position on slavery was rather conservative and his commitment to the Declaration of Independence and the Union so strong, his views spanned most of the political spectrum of the times.

Elected president in 1860, he first sought to prevent secession and then to end slavery with compromise and compensation. His program for reconstruction was far more moderate than that of other Republicans. Had he not been assassinated in April 1865, it is possible that the effects of the Civil War would have been much shorter-lived. The excerpts given here emphasize the scope and substance of Lincoln's views as they are articulated in his major speeches, for he wrote no books. ∾

Speech on the Dred Scott Decision (1857)

... There is a natural disgust in the minds of nearly all white people, to the idea of an indiscriminate amalgamation of the white and black races; and Judge Douglas evidently is basing his chief hope, upon the chances of being able to appropriate the benefit of this disgust to himself. If he can, by much drumming and repeating, fasten the odium of that idea upon his adversaries, he thinks he can struggle through the storm. He therefore clings to this hope, as a drowning man to the last plank. He makes an occasion for lugging it in from the opposition to the Dred Scott decision. He finds the Republicans insisting that the Declaration of Independence includes *all* men, black as well as white; and forthwith he boldly denies that it includes negroes at all, and proceeds to argue gravely that all who contend it does, do so only because they want to vote, and eat, and sleep, and marry with negroes! He will have it that they cannot be consistent else. Now I protest against that counterfeit logic which concludes that, because I do not want a black woman for a *slave* I must necessarily want her for a *wife*. I need not have her for either, I can just leave her alone. In some respects she certainly is not my equal; but in her natural right to eat the bread she earns with her own hands without asking leave of any one else, she is my equal, and the equal of all others.

Chief Justice Taney, in his opinion in the Dred Scott case, admits that the language of the Declaration is broad enough to include the whole human family, but he and Judge Douglas argue that the authors of that instrument did not intend to include negroes, by the fact that they did not at once, actually place them on an equality with the whites. Now this grave argument comes to just nothing at all, by the other fact, that they did not at once, *or ever afterwards,* actually place all white people on an equality with one or another. And this is the staple argument of both the Chief Justice and the Senator, for doing this obvious violence to the plain unmistakable language of the Declaration. I think the authors of that notable instrument intended to include *all* men, but they did not intend to declare all men equal *in all respects.* They did not mean to say all were equal in color, size, intellect, moral developments, or social capacity. They defined with tolerable distinctness, in what respects they did consider all men created equal—equal in "certain inalienable rights, among which are life, liberty, and the pursuit of happiness." This they said, and this meant. They did not mean to assert the obvious untruth, that all were then actually enjoying that equality, nor yet, that they were about to confer it immediately upon them. In fact they had no power to confer such a boon. They meant simply to declare the *right,* so that the *enforcement* of it might follow as fast as circumstances should permit. They meant to set up a standard maxim for free society, which should be familiar to all, and revered by all; constantly looked to, constantly labored for, and even though never perfectly attained, constantly approximated, and thereby constantly spreading and deepening its influence, and augmenting the happiness and value of life to all people of all colors everywhere. The assertion that "all men are created equal" was of no practical use in effecting our separation from Great Britain; and it was placed in the Declaration, not for that, but for future use. Its authors meant it to

---

SOURCE: All selections in this chapter may be found in Richard N. Current, ed., *The Political Thought of Abraham Lincoln* (Indianapolis: Bobbs-Merrill, 1967).

be, thank God, it is now proving itself, a stumbling block to those who in after times might seek to turn a free people back into the hateful paths of despotism. They knew the proneness of prosperity to breed tyrants, and they meant when such should re-appear in this fair land and commence their vocation they should find left for them at least one hard nut to crack.

I have now briefly expressed my view of the *meaning* and *objects* of that part of the Declaration of Independence which declares that "all men are created equal."

Now let us hear Judge Douglas' view of the same subject, as I find it in the printed report of his late speech. Here it is:

"No man can vindicate the character, motives and conduct of the signers of the Declaration of Independence, except upon the hypothesis that they referred to the white race alone, and not to the African, when they declared all men to have been created equal—that they were speaking of British subjects on this continent being equal to British subjects born and residing in Great Britain—that they were entitled to the same inalienable rights, and among them were enumerated life, liberty and the pursuit of happiness. The Declaration was adopted for the purpose of justifying the colonists in the eyes of the civilized world in withdrawing their allegiance from the British crown, and dissolving their connection with the mother country."

My good friends, read that carefully over some leisure hour, and ponder well upon it —see what a mere wreck—mangled ruin—it makes of our once glorious Declaration.

"They were speaking of British subjects on this continent being equal to British subjects born and residing in Great Britain!" Why, according to this, not only negroes but white people outside of Great Britain and America are not spoken of in that instrument. The English, Irish and Scotch, along with white Americans, were included to be sure, but the French, Germans and other white people of the world are all gone to pot along with the Judge's inferior races.

I had thought the Declaration promised something better than the condition of British subjects; but no, it only meant that we should be *equal* to them in their own oppressed and *unequal* condition. According to that, it gave no promise that having kicked off the King and Lords of Great Britain, we should not at once be saddled with a King and Lords of our own.

I had thought the Declaration contemplated the progressive improvement in the condition of all men everywhere; but no, it merely "was adopted for the purpose of justifying the colonists in the eyes of the civilized world in withdrawing their allegiance from the British crown, and dissolving their connection with the mother country." Why, that object having been effected some eighty years ago, the Declaration is of no practical use now—mere rubbish—old wadding left to rot on the battlefield after the victory is won.

I understand you are preparing to celebrate the "Fourth," tomorrow week. What for? The doings of that day had no reference to the present; and quite half of you are not even descendants of those who were referred to at that day. But I suppose you will celebrate; and will even go so far as to read the Declaration. Suppose after you read it once in the old fashioned way, you read it once more with Justice Douglas' version. It will then run thus: "We hold these truths to be self-evident that all British subjects who were on this continent eighty-one years ago, were created equal to all British subjects born and *then* residing in Great Britain."

And now I appeal to all—to Democrats as well as others,—are you really willing that the Declaration shall be thus frittered away?— thus left no more at most, than an interesting memorial of the dead past? thus shorn of its vitality, and practical value; and left without the *germ* or even the *suggestion* of the individual rights of man in it?

But Judge Douglas is especially horrified at the thought of the mixing blood by the white and black races: agreed for once—a thousand times agreed. There are white men enough to marry all the white women, and black men enough to marry all the black women; and so let them be married. On this point we fully agree with the Judge; and when he shall show that his policy is better adapted to prevent amalgamation than ours we shall drops ours, and adopt his. Let us see. In 1850 there were in the United States, 405,751 mulattoes. Very few of these are the offspring of whites and *free* blacks; nearly all have sprung from black *slaves* and white masters. A separation of the races is the only perfect preventive of amalgamation but as an immediate separation is impossible the next best thing is to *keep* them apart *where* they are not already together. If white and black people never get together in Kansas, they will never mix blood in Kansas. That is at least one self-evident truth. A few free colored persons may get into the free States, in any event, but their number is too insignificant to amount to much in the way of mixing blood. In 1850 there were in the free states, 56,649 mulattoes; but for the most part they were not born there—they came from the slave States, ready made up. In the same year the slave States had 348,874 mulattoes all of home production. The proportion of free mulattoes to free blacks—the only colored classes in the free states—is much greater in the slave than in the free states. It is worthy of note too, that among the free states those which make the colored man the nearest to equal the white, have, proportionably the fewest mulattoes the least of amalgamation. In New Hampshire, the State which goes farthest towards equality between the races, there are just 184 Mulattoes while there are in Virginia—how many do you

think? 79,775, being 23,126 more than in all the free States together.

These statistics show that slavery is the greatest source of amalgamation; and next to it, not the elevation, but the degeneration of the free blacks. Yet Judge Douglas dreads the slightest restraints on the spread of slavery, and the slightest human recognition of the negro, as tending horribly to amalgamation.

This very Dred Scott case affords a strong test as to which party most favors amalgamation, the Republican or the dear Union-saving Democracy. Dred Scott, his wife and two daughters were all involved in the suit. We desired the court to have held that they were citizens so far at least as to entitle them to a hearing as to whether they were free or not; and then, also, that they were in fact and in law really free. Could we have had our way, the chances of these black girls, ever mixing their blood with that of white people, would have been diminished at least to the extent that it could not have been without their consent. But Judge Douglas is delighted to have them decided to be slaves, and not human enough to have a hearing, even if they were free, and thus left subject to the forced concubinage of their masters, and liable to become the mothers of mulattoes in spite of themselves—the very state of case that produces nine tenths of all the mulattoes—all the mixing of blood in the nation.

Of course, I state this case as an illustration only, not meaning to say or intimate that the master of Dred Scott and his family, or any more than a per centage of masters generally, are inclined to exercise this particular power which they hold over their female slaves.

I have said that the separation of the races is the only perfect preventive of amalgamation. I have no right to say all the members of the Republican party are in favor of this, nor to say that as a party they are in favor of it. There is nothing in their platform directly on the subject. But I can say a very large proportion of its members are for it, and that the chief plank in their platform—opposition to the spread of slavery—is most favorable to that separation.

Such separation, if ever effected at all, must be effected by colonization; and no political party, as such, is now doing anything directly for colonization. Party operations at present only favor or retard colonization incidentally. The enterprise is a difficult one; but "when there is a will there is a way;" and what colonization needs most is a hearty will. Will springs from the two elements of moral sense and self-interest. Let us be brought to believe it is morally right, and, at the same time, favorable to, or, at least, not against, our interest, to transfer the African to his native clime, and we shall find a way to do it, however great the task may be. The children of Israel, to such numbers as to include four hundred thousand fighting men, went out of Egyptian bondage in a body.

How differently the respective courses of the Democratic and Republican parties incidentally bear on the question of forming a will—a public sentiment—for colonization, is easy to see. The Republicans inculcate, with whatever of ability they can, that the negro is a man; that his bondage is cruelly wrong, and that the field of his oppression ought not to be enlarged. The Democrats deny his manhood; deny, or dwarf to insignificance, the wrong of his bondage: so far as possible, crush all sympathy for him, and cultivate and excite hatred and disgust against him; compliment themselves as Union-savers for doing so; and call the indefinite outspreading of his bondage "a sacred right of self-government.". . . ∾

Letter to Boston Republicans (1859)

Gentlemen

Your kind note inviting me to attend a Festival in Boston, on the 13th. Inst. in honor of the birth-day of Thomas Jefferson, was duly received. My engagements are such that I can not attend.

Bearing in mind that about seventy years ago, two great political parties were first formed in this country, that Thomas Jefferson was the head of one of them, and Boston the headquarters of the other, it is both curious and interesting that those supposed to descend politically from the party opposed to Jefferson, should now be celebrating his birth-day in their own original seat of empire, while those claiming political descent from him have nearly ceased to breathe his name everywhere.

Remembering too, that the Jefferson party were formed upon their supposed superior devotion to the *personal* rights of men, holding the rights of *property* to be secondary only, and greatly inferior, and then assuming that the so-called democracy of to-day, are the Jefferson, and their opponents, the anti-Jefferson parties, it will be equally interesting to note how completely the two have changed hands as to the principle upon which they were originally supposed to be divided.

The democracy of to-day hold the *liberty* of one man to be absolutely nothing, when in conflict with another man's right of *property*. Republicans, on the contrary, are for both the *man* and the *dollar*; but in cases of conflict, the man *before* the dollar.

I remember once being much amused at seeing two partially intoxicated men engage in a fight with their great-coats on, which fight, after a long, and rather harmless contest, ended in each having fought himself *out* of his own coat, and *into* that of the other. If the two leading parties of this day are really identical with the two in the days of Jefferson and Adams, they have performed about the same feat as the two drunken men. But soberly, it is now no child's play to save the principles of Jefferson from total overthrow in this nation.

One would start with great confidence that he could convince any sane child that the simpler propositions of Euclid are true; but, nevertheless, he would fail, utterly, with one who should deny the definitions and axioms. The principles of Jefferson are the definitions and axioms of free society. And yet they are denied, and evaded, with no small show of success. One dashingly calls them "glittering generalities"; another bluntly calls them "self evident lies"; and still others insidiously argue that they apply only to "superior races."

These expressions, differing in form, are identical in object and effect—the supplanting the principles of free government, and restoring those of classification, caste, and legitimacy. They would delight a convocation of crowned heads, plotting against the people. They are the vanguard—the miners, and sappers—of returning despotism. We must repulse them, or they will subjugate us.

This is a world of compensations; and he who would *be* no slave, must consent to *have* no slave. Those who deny freedom to others, deserve it not for themselves; and, under a just God, can not long retain it.

All honor to Jefferson—to the man who, in the concrete pressure of a struggle for national independence by a single people, had the coolness, forecast, and capacity to introduce into a merely revolutionary document, an abstract truth, applicable to all men and all times, and so to embalm it there, that to-day, and in all coming days, it shall be a rebuke and a stumbling-block to the very harbingers of re-appearing tyranny and oppression. ∾

Cooper Union Address (1860)

... Some of you delight to flaunt in our faces the warning against sectional parties given by Washington in his Farewell Address. Less than eight years before Washington gave that warning, he had, as President of the United States, approved and signed an act of Congress, enforcing the prohibition of slavery in the Northwestern Territory, which act embodied the policy of the Government upon that subject up to and at the very moment he penned that warning, and about one year after he penned it, he wrote La Fayette that he considered that prohibition a wise measure, expressing in the same connection his hope that we should at some time have a confederacy of free States.

Bearing this in mind, and seeing that sectionalism has since arisen upon this same subject, is that warning a weapon in your hands against us, or in our hands against you? Could Washington himself speak, would he cast the blame of that sectionalism upon us, who sustain his policy, or upon you who repudiate it? We respect that warning of Washington, and we commend it to you, together with his example pointing to the right application of it.

But you say you are conservative—eminently conservative—while we are revolutionary, destructive, or something of the sort. What is conservatism? Is it not adherence to the old and tried, against the new and untried? We stick to, contend for, the identical old policy on the point in controversy which was adopted by "our fathers who framed the Government under which we live;" while you with one accord reject, and scout, and spit upon that old policy, and insist upon substituting something new. True, you disagree among yourselves as to what that substitute shall be. You are divided on new propositions and plans, but you are unanimous in rejecting and denouncing the old policy of the fathers. Some of you are for reviving the foreign slave trade; some for a Congressional Slave-Code for the Territories; some for Congress forbidding the Territories to prohibit Slavery within their limits; some for maintaining Slavery in the Territories through the judiciary; some for the "gur-reat pur-rinciple" that "if one man would enslave another, no third man should object," fantastically called "Popular Sovereignty;" but never a man among you in favor of federal prohibition of slavery in federal territories, according to the practice of "our fathers who framed the Government under which we live." Not one of all your various plans can show a precedent or an advocate in the century within which our Government originated. Consider, then, whether your claim of conservatism for yourselves, and your charge of destructiveness against us, are based on the most clear and stable foundations.

Again, you say we have made the slavery question more prominent than it formerly was. We deny it. We admit that it is more prominent, but we deny that we made it so. It was not we, but you, who discarded the old policy of the fathers. We resisted, we still resist, your innovation; and thence comes the greater prominence of the question. Would you have that question reduced to its former proportions? Go back to that old policy. What has been will be again, under the same conditions. If you would have the peace of the old times, readopt the precepts and policy of the old times.... ∾

First Inaugural Address (1861)

Fellow-citizens of the United States:
In compliance with a custom as old as the government itself, I appear before you to address you briefly, and to take in your presence the oath prescribed by the Constitution of the United States to be taken by the President "before he enters on the execution of his office."

I do not consider it necessary at present for me to discuss those matters of administration about which there is no special anxiety or excitement.

Apprehension seems to exist among the people of the Southern States that by the accession of a Republican administration their property and their peace and personal security are to be endangered. There has never been any reasonable cause for such apprehension. Indeed, the most ample evidence to the contrary has all the while existed and been open to their inspection. It is found in nearly all the published speeches of him who now addresses you. I do but quote from one of those speeches when I declare that "I have no purpose, directly or indirectly, to interfere with the institution of slavery in the States where it exists. I believe I have no lawful right to do so, and I have no inclination to do so." Those who nominated and elected me did so with full knowledge that I had made this and many similar declarations, and had never recanted them. And, more than this, they placed in the platform for my acceptance, and as a law to themselves and to me, the clear and emphatic resolution which I now read:—

"*Resolved,* That the maintenance inviolate of the rights of the States, and especially the right of each State to order and control its own domestic institutions according to its own judgment exclusively, is essential to that balance of power on which the perfection and endurance of our political fabric depend, and we denounce the lawless invasion by armed force of the soil of any State or Territory, no matter under what pretext, as among the gravest of crimes." I now reiterate these sentiments; and, in doing so, I only press upon the public attention the most conclusive evidence of which the case is susceptible, that the property, peace, and security of no section are to be in any wise endangered by the now incoming administration. I add, too, that all the protection which, consistently with the Constitution and the laws, can be given, will be cheerfully given to all the States when lawfully demanded, for whatever cause—as cheerfully to one section as to another.

There is much controversy about the delivering up of fugitives from service or labor. The clause I now read is as plainly written in the Constitution as any other of its provisions:—

"No person held to service or labour in one State, under the laws thereof, escaping into another, shall in consequence of any law or regulation therein, be discharged from such service or labour, but shall be delivered up on claim of the party to whom such service or labour may be due."

It is scarcely questioned that this provision was intended by those who made it for the reclaiming of what we call fugitive slaves; and the intention of the lawgiver is the law. All members of Congress swear their support to the whole Constitution—to this provision as much as to any other. To the proposition, then, that slaves whose cases come within the terms of this clause "shall be delivered up,"

their oaths are unanimous. Now, if they would make the effort in good temper, could they not with nearly equal unanimity frame and pass a law by means of which to keep good that unanimous oath?

There is some difference of opinion whether this clause should be enforced by national or by State authority; but surely that difference is not a very material one. If the slave is to be surrendered, it can be of but little consequence to him or to others by which authority it is done. And should any one in any case be content that his oath shall go unkept on a merely unsubstantial controversy as to how it shall be kept?

Again, in any law upon this subject, ought not all the safeguards of liberty known in civilized and humane jurisprudence to be introduced, so that a free man be not, in any case, surrendered as a slave? And might it not be well at the same time to provide by law for the enforcement of that clause in the Constitution which guarantees that "the citizens of each State shall be entitled to all privileges and immunities of citizens in the several States"?

I take the official oath to-day with no mental reservations, and with no purpose to construe the Constitution or laws by any hypercritical rules. And while I do not choose now to specify particular acts of Congress as proper to be enforced, I do suggest that it will be much safer for all, both in official and private stations, to conform to and abide by all those acts which stand unrepealed, than to violate any of them, trusting to find impunity in having them held to be unconstitutional.

It is seventy-two years since the first inauguration of a President under our National Constitution. During that period fifteen different and greatly distinguished citizens have, in succession, administered the executive branch of the government. They have conducted it through many perils, and generally with great success. Yet, with all this scope of precedent, I now enter upon the same task for the brief constitutional term of four years under great and peculiar difficulty. A disruption of the Federal Union, heretofore only menaced, is now formidably attempted.

I hold that, in contemplation of universal law and of the Constitution, the Union of these States is perpetual. Perpetuity is implied, if not expressed, in the fundamental law of all national governments. It is safe to assert that no government proper ever had a provision in its organic law for its own termination. Continue to execute all the express provisions of our National Constitution, and the Union will endure forever—it being impossible to destroy it except by some action not provided for in the instrument itself.

Again, if the United States be not a government proper, but an association of States in the nature of contract merely, can it, as a contract, be peaceably unmade by less than all the parties who made it? One party to a contract may violate it—break it, so to speak; but does it not require all to lawfully rescind it?

Descending from these general principles, we find the proposition that in legal contemplation the Union is perpetual confirmed by the history of the Union itself. The Union is much older than the Constitution. It was formed, in fact, by the Articles of Association in 1774. It was matured and continued by the Declaration of Independence in 1776. It was further matured, and the faith of all the then thirteen States expressly plighted and engaged that it should be perpetual, by the Articles of Confederation in 1778. And, finally, in 1787, one of the declared objects for ordaining and establishing the Constitution was "to form a more perfect Union."

But if the destruction of the Union by one or by a part only of the States be lawfully possible, the Union is less perfect than before the Constitution, having lost the vital element of perpetuity.

It follows from these views that no State upon its own mere motion can lawfully get out of the Union: that resolves and ordinances to that effect are legally void; and that acts of violence, within any State or States, against the authority of the United States, are insurrectionary or revolutionary, according to circumstances.

I therefore consider that, in view of the Constitution and the laws, the Union is unbroken; and to the extent of my ability I shall take care, as the Constitution itself expressly enjoins upon me, that the laws of the Union be faithfully executed in all the States. Doing this I deem to be only a simple duty on my part; and I shall perform it so far as practicable, unless my rightful masters, the American people, shall withhold the requisite means, or in some authoritative manner direct the contrary. I trust this will not be regarded as a menace, but only as the declared purpose of the Union that it will constitutionally defend and maintain itself.

In doing this there needs to be no bloodshed or violence; and there shall be none, unless it be forced upon the national authority. The power confided to me will be used to hold, occupy, and possess the property and places belonging to the government, and to collect the duties and imposts; but beyond what may be necessary for these objects, there will be no invasion, no using of force against or among the people anywhere. Where hostility to the United States, in any interior locality, shall be so great and universal as to prevent competent resident citizens from holding the Federal offices, there will be no attempt to force obnoxious strangers among the people for that object. While the strict legal right may exist in the government to enforce the exercise of these officers, the attempt to do so would be so irritating, and so nearly impracticable withal, that I deem it better to forego for the time the uses of such officers.

The mails, unless repelled, will continue to be furnished in all parts of the Union. So far as possible, the people everywhere shall have that sense of perfect security which is most favorable to calm thought and reflection. The course here indicated will be followed unless current events and experience shall show a modification or change to be proper, and in every case and exigency my best discretion will be exercised according to circumstances actually existing, and with a view and a hope of a peaceful solution of the national troubles and the restoration of fraternal sympathies and affections.

That there are persons in one section or another who seek to destroy the Union at all events, and are glad of any pretext to do it, I will neither affirm nor deny; but if there be such, I need address no word to them. To those, however, who really love the Union may I not speak?

Before entering upon so great a matter as the destruction of our national fabric, with all its benefits, its memories, and its hopes, would it not be wise to ascertain precisely why we do it? Will you hazard so desperate a step while there is any possibility that any portion of the ills you fly from have no real existence? Will you, while the certain ills you fly to are greater than all the real ones you fly from—will you risk the commission of so fearful a mistake?

All profess to be content in the Union if all constitutional rights can be maintained. It is true, then, that any right, plainly written in the Constitution, has been denied? I think not. Happily the human mind is so constituted that no party can reach to the audacity of doing this. Think, if you can, of a single instance in which a plainly written provision of the Constitution has ever been denied. If by the mere force of numbers a majority should deprive a minority of any clearly written constitutional right, it might, in a moral point of view, justify revolution—certainly would if such a right were a vital one. But such is not our case. All the vital rights of minorities and of individuals are so plainly assured to them by affirmations and negations, guaranties and prohibitions, in the Constitution, that controversies never arise concerning them. But no organic law can ever be framed with a provision specifically applicable to every question which may occur in practical administration. No foresight can anticipate, nor any document of reasonable length contain, express provisions for all possible questions. Shall fugitives from labor be surrendered by national or by State authority? The Constitution does not expressly say. *May* Congress prohibit slavery in the Territories? The Constitution does not expressly say. *Must* Congress protect slavery in the Territories? The Constitution does not expressly say.

From questions of this class spring all our constitutional controversies and we divide upon them into majorities and minorities. If the minority will not acquiesce, the majority must, or the government must cease. There is no other alternative; for continuing the government is acquiescence on one side or the other.

If a minority in such case will secede rather than acquiesce, they make a precedent which in turn will divide and ruin them; for a minority of their own will secede from them whenever a majority refuses to be controlled by such minority. For instance, why may not any portion of a new confederacy a year or two hence arbitrarily secede again, precisely as portions of the present Union now claim to secede from it? All who cherish disunion sentiments are now being educated to the exact temper of doing this.

Is there such a perfect identity of interest among the States to compose a new Union, as to produce harmony only, and prevent renewed secession?

Plainly, the central idea of secession is the essence of anarchy. A majority held in restraint by constitutional checks and limitations, and always changing easily with deliberate changes of popular opinions and sentiments, is the only true sovereign of a free people. Whoever rejects it does, of necessity, fly to anarchy or to despotism. Unanimity is impossible; the rule of a minority, as a permanent arrangement, is wholly inadmissible; so that, rejecting the majority principle, anarchy or despotism in some form is all that is left.

I do not forget the position, assumed by some, that constitutional questions are to be decided by the Supreme Court; nor do I deny that such decisions must be binding, in any case, upon the parties to a suit, as to the object of that suit, while they are also entitled to very high respect and consideration in all parallel cases by all other departments of the government. And while it is obviously possible that such decision may be erroneous in any given case, still the evil effect following it, being limited to that particular case, with the chance that it may be overruled and never become a precedent for other cases, can better be borne than could the evils of a different practice. At the same time, the candid citizen must confess that if the policy of the government, upon vital questions affecting the whole people, is to be irrevocably fixed by decisions of the Supreme Court, the instant they are made, in ordinary litigation between parties in personal actions, the people will have ceased to be their own rulers, having to that extent practically resigned their government into the hands of that eminent tribunal. Nor is there in this view any assault upon the court or the judges. It is a duty from which they may not shrink to decide cases properly brought before them and it is no fault of theirs if others seek to turn their decisions to political purposes.

One section of our country believes slavery is right, and ought to be extended, while the other believes it is wrong, and ought not to be extended. This is the only substantial dispute.

The fugitive-slave clause of the Constitution, and the law for the suppression of the foreign slave trade, are each as well enforced, perhaps, as any law can ever be in a community where the moral sense of the people imperfectly supports the law itself. The great body of the people abide by the dry legal obligation in both cases, and a few break over in each. This, I think, cannot be perfectly cured; and it would be worse in both cases after the separation of the sections than before. The foreign slave trade, now imperfectly suppressed, would be ultimately revived, without restriction, in one section, while fugitive slaves, now only partially surrendered, would not be surrendered at all by the other.

Physically speaking, we cannot separate. We cannot remove our respective sections from each other, nor build an impassable wall between them. A husband and wife may be divorced, and go out of the presence and beyond the reach of each other; but the different parts of our country cannot do this. They cannot but remain face to face, and intercourse, either amicable or hostile, must continue between them. It is possible, then, to make that intercourse more advantageous or more satisfactory after separation than before? Can aliens make treaties easier than friends can make laws? Can treaties be more faithfully enforced between aliens than laws can among friends? Suppose you go to war, you cannot fight always; and when, after much loss on both sides, and no gain on either, you cease fighting, the identical old questions as to terms of intercourse are again upon you.

This country, with its institutions, belongs to the people who inhabit it. Whenever they shall grow weary of the existing government, they can exercise their constitutional right of amending it, or their revolutionary right to dismember or overthrow it. I cannot be ignorant of the fact that many worthy and patriotic citizens are desirous of having the National Constitution amended. While I make no recommendation of amendments, I full recognize the rightful authority of the people over the whole subject, to be exercised in either of the modes prescribed in the instrument itself; and I should, under existing circumstances, favor rather than oppose a fair opportunity being afforded the people to act upon it. I will venture to add that to me the convention mode seems preferable, in that it allows amendments to originate with the people themselves, instead of only permitting them to take or reject propositions originated by others not especially chosen for the purpose, and which might not be precisely such as they would wish to either accept or refuse. I understand a proposed amendment to the Constitution—which amendment, however, I have not seen—has passed Congress, to the effect that the Federal Government shall never interfere with the domestic institutions of the States, including that of persons held to service. To avoid misconstruction of what I have said, I depart from my purpose not to speak of particular amendments so far as to say that, holding such a provision to now be implied constitutional law, I have no objection to its being made express and irrevocable.

The chief magistrate derives all his authority from the people, and they have conferred none upon him to fix terms for the separation of the States. The people themselves can do this also if they choose; but the Executive, as such, has nothing to do with it. His duty is to administer the present government, as it came to his hands, and to transmit it, unimpaired by him, to his successor.

Why should there not be a patient confidence in the ultimate justice of the people? Is there any better or equal hope in the world? In our present differences, is either party without faith of being in the right? If the Almighty Ruler of Nations, with His eternal truth and justice, be on your side of the North, or on yours of the South, that truth and that Justice will surely prevail by the judgment of this great tribunal of the American people.

By the frame of the government under which we live, this same people have wisely given their public servants but little power for mischief; and have, with equal wisdom, provided for the return of that little to their own hands at very short intervals. While the people retain their virtue and vigilance, no administration, by any extreme of wickedness or folly, can very seriously injure the government in the short space of four years.

My countrymen, one and all, think calmly and well upon this whole subject. Nothing valuable can be lost by taking time. If there be an object to hurry any of you in hot haste to a step which you would never take deliberately, that object will be frustrated by taking time; but no good object can be frustrated by it. Such of you as are now dissatisfied still have the old Constitution unimpaired, and, on the sensitive point, the laws of your own framing under it; while the new administration will have no immediate power, if it would, to change either. If it were admitted that you who are dissatisfied hold the right side in the dispute, there still is no single good reason for precipitate action. Intelligence, patriotism, Christianity, and a firm reliance on Him who has never yet forsaken this favored land, are still competent to adjust in the best way all our present difficulty.

In your hands, my dissatisfied fellow-countrymen, and not in mine, is the momentous issue of civil war. The government will not assail you. You can have no conflict without being yourselves the aggressors. You have no oath registered in heaven to destroy the government, while I shall have the most solemn one to "preserve, protect, and defend it."

I am loath to close. We are not enemies, but friends. We must not be enemies. Though passion may have strained, it must not break our bonds of affection. The mystic chords of memory, stretching from every battlefield and patriot grave to every living heart and hearthstone all over the broad land, will yet swell the chorus of the Union when again touched, as surely they will be, by the better angels of our nature. ⌒

Second Annual Message to Congress (1862)

... On the twenty-second day of September last a proclamation was issued by the Executive, a copy of which is herewith submitted.

In accordance with the purpose expressed in the second paragraph of that paper, I now respectfully recall your attention to what may be called "compensated emancipation.". . .

In this view, I recommend the adoption of the following resolution and articles amendatory to the Constitution of the United States:

Resolved by the Senate and House of Representatives of the United States of America in Congress assembled, (two-thirds of both houses concurring,) That the following articles be proposed to the legislatures (or conventions) of the several States as amendments to the Constitution of the United States, all or any of which articles when ratified by three-fourths of the said legislatures (or conventions) to be valid as part or parts of the said Constitution, viz:

Article ——.

Every State, wherein slavery now exists, which shall abolish the same therein, at any time, or times, before the first day of January, in the year of our Lord one thousand and nine hundred, shall receive compensation from the United States as follows, to wit:

"The President of the United States shall deliver to every such State, bonds of the United States, bearing interest at the rate of —— per cent, per annum, to an amount equal to the aggregate sum of —— for each slave shown to have been therein, by the eig[h]th census of the United States, said bonds to be delivered to such State by instalments, or in one parcel, at the completion of the abolishment, accordingly as the same shall have been gradual, or at one time, within such State; and interest shall begin to run upon any such bond, only from the proper time of its delivery as aforesaid. Any State having received bonds as aforesaid, and afterwards reintroducing or tolerating slavery therein, shall refund to the United States the bonds so received, or the value thereof, and all interest paid thereon.

Article ——.

All slaves who shall have enjoyed actual freedom by the chances of the war, at any time before the end of the rebellion, shall be forever free; but all owners of such, who shall not have been disloyal, shall be compensated for them, at the same rates as is provided for States adopting abolishment of slavery, but in such way, that no slave shall be twice accounted for.

Article ——.

Congress may appropriate money, and otherwise provide, for colonizing free colored persons, with their own consent, at any place or places without the United States.

I beg indulgence to discuss these proposed articles at some length. Without slavery the rebellion could never have existed; without slavery it could not continue.

Among the friends of the Union there is great diversity, of sentiment, and of policy, in regard to slavery, and the African race amongst us. Some would perpetuate slavery; some would abolish it suddenly, and without compensation; some would abolish it gradually, and with compensation; some would remove the freed people from us, and some would retain them with us; and there are yet other minor diversities. Because of these diversities, we waste much strength in struggles among ourselves. By mutual concession we should harmonize, and act together. This would be compromise; but it would be compromise among the friends, and not with the enemies of the Union. These articles are intended to embody a plan of such mutual concessions. If the plan shall be adopted, it is assumed that emancipation will follow, at least, in several of the States.

As to the first article, the main points are: first, the emancipation; secondly, the length of time for consummating it—thirty-seven years; and thirdly, the compensation.

The emancipation will be unsatisfactory to the advocates of perpetual slavery; but the length of time should greatly mitigate their dissatisfaction. The time spares both races from the evils of sudden derangement—in fact, from the necessity of any derangement—while most of those whose habitual course of thought will be disturbed by the measure will have passed away before its consummation. They will never see it. Another class will hail the prospect of emancipation, but will deprecate the length of time. They will feel that it gives too little to the now living slaves. But it really gives them much. It saves them from the vagrant destitution which must largely attend immediate emancipation in localities where their numbers are very great, and it gives the inspiring assurance that their posterity shall be free forever. The plan leaves to each State, choosing to act under it, to abolish slavery now, or at the end of the century, or at any intermediate time, or by degrees, extending over the whole or any part of the period; and it obliges no two states to proceed alike. It also provides for compensation, and generally the mode of making it. This, it would seem, must further mitigate the dissatisfaction of those who favor perpetual slavery, and especially of those who are to receive the compensation. Doubtless some of those who are to pay, and not to receive will object. Yet the measure is both just and economical. In a certain sense the liberation of slaves is the destruction of property—property acquired by descent, or by purchase, the same as any other property. It is no less true for having been often said, that the people of the south are not more responsible for the original introduction of this property, than are the people of the north; and when it is remembered how unhesitatingly we all use cotton and sugar, and share the profits of dealing in them, it may not be quite safe to say, that the south has been more responsible than the north for its continuance. If then, for a common object, this property is to be sacrificed, is it not just that it be done at a common charge?. . .

As to the second article, I think it would be impracticable to return to bondage the class of persons therein contemplated. Some of them, doubtless, in the property sense, belong to loyal owners; and hence, provision is made in this article for compensating such.

The third article relates to the future of the freed people. It does not oblige, but merely authorizes, Congress to aid in colonizing such as may consent. This ought not to be regarded as objectionable, on the one hand, or on the other, in so much as it comes to nothing, unless by the mutual consent of the people to be deported, and the American voters, through their representatives in Congress.

I cannot make it better known than it already is, that I strongly favor colonization. And yet I wish to say there is an objection urged against free colored people remaining in the country, which is largely imaginary, if not sometimes malicious.

It is insisted that their presence would injure, and displace white labor and white laborers. If there ever could be a proper time for mere catch arguments, that time surely is not now. In times like the present, men should utter nothing for which they would not willingly be responsible through time and eternity. Is it true, then, that colored people can displace any more white labor, by being free, than by remaining slaves? If they stay in their old places, they jostle no white laborers; if they leave their old places, they leave them open to white laborers. Logically, there is neither more nor less of it. Emancipation, even without deportation, would probably enhance the wages of white labor, and, very surely, would not reduce them. Thus, the customary amount of labor would still have to be performed; the freed

people would surely not do more than their old proportion of it, and very probably, for a time, would do less, leaving an increased part to white laborers, bringing their labor into greater demand, and, consequently, enhancing the wages of it. With deportation, even to a limited extent, enhanced wages to white labor is mathematically certain. Labor is like any other commodity in the market—increase the demand for it, and you increase the price of it. Reduce the supply of black labor, by colonizing the black laborer out of the country, and, by precisely so much, you increase the demand for, and wages of, white labor.

But it is dreaded that the freed people will swarm forth, and cover the whole land? Are they not already in the land? Will liberation make them any more numerous? Equally distributed among the whites of the whole country, and there would be but one colored to seven whites. Could the one, in any way, greatly disturb the seven? There are many communities now, having more than one free colored person, to seven whites; and this, without any apparent consciousness of evil from it.... ∾

The Gettysburg Address (1863)

Four score and seven years ago our fathers brought forth on this continent, a new nation, conceived in Liberty, and dedicated to the proposition that all men are created equal.

Now we are engaged in a great civil war; testing whether that nation, or any nation so conceived and so dedicated, can long endure. We are met on a great battle-field of that war. We have come to dedicate a portion of that field, as a final resting place for those who here gave their lives that that nation might live. It is altogether fitting and proper that we should do this.

But, in a larger sense, we can not dedicate—we can not consecrate—we can not hallow—this ground. The brave men, living and dead, who struggled here have consecrated it, far above our poor power to add or detract. The world will little note, nor long remember what we say here, but it can never forget what they did here. It is for us the living, rather, to be dedicated here to the unfinished work which they who fought here have thus far so nobly advanced. It is rather for us to be here dedicated to the great task remaining before us—that from these honored dead we take increased devotion to that cause for which they gave the last full measure of devotion—that we here highly resolve that this nation, under God, shall have a new birth of Freedom—and that government of the people, by the people, for the people, shall not perish from the earth.

~

Second Inaugural Address (1865)

Fellow Countrymen:

At this second appearing to take the oath of the presidential office, there is less occasion for an extended address than there was at the first. Then a statement, somewhat in detail, of a course to be pursued, seemed fitting and proper. Now, at the expiration of four years, during which public declarations have been constantly called forth on every point and phrase of the great contest which still absorbs the attention and engrosses the energies of the nation, little that is new could be presented. The progress of our arms, upon which all else chiefly depends, is as well known to the public as to myself; and it is, I trust, reasonably satisfactory and encouraging to all. With high hope for the future, no prediction in regard to it is ventured.

On the occasion corresponding to this four years ago, all thoughts were anxiously directed to an impending civil war. All dreaded it—all sought to avert it. While the inaugural address was being delivered from this place, devoted altogether to saving the Union without war, insurgent agents were in the city seeking to destroy it without war—seeking to dissolve the Union, and divide effects, by negotiation. Both parties deprecated war; but one of them would make war rather than let the nation survive; and the other would accept war rather than let it perish. And the war came.

One eighth of the whole population were colored slaves, not distributed generally over the Union, but localized in the southern part of it. These slaves constituted a peculiar and powerful interest. All knew that this interest was, somehow, the cause of the war. To strengthen, perpetuate, and extend this interest was the object for which the insurgents would rend the Union, even by war; while the government claimed no right to do more than to restrict the territorial enlargement of it.

Neither party expected for the war the magnitude or the duration which it has already attained. Neither anticipated that the cause of the conflict might cease with, or even before, the conflict itself should cease. Each looked for an easier triumph, and a result less fundamental and astounding. Both read the same Bible, and pray to the same God; and each invokes His aid against the other.

It may seem strange that any men should dare to ask a just God's assistance in wringing their bread from the sweat of other men's faces; but let us judge not, that we be not judged. The prayers of both could not be answered—that of neither has been answered fully.

The Almighty has his own purposes. "Woe unto the world because of offenses! for it must needs be that offenses come; but woe to that man by whom the offense cometh." If we shall suppose that American slavery is one of those offenses which, in the providence of God, must needs come but which, having continued through His appointed time, He now wills to remove, and that He gives to both North and South this terrible war, as the woe due to those by whom the offense came, shall we discern therein any departure from those divine attributes which the believers in a living God always ascribe to him? Fondly do we hope—fervently do we pray—that this mighty scourge of war may speedily pass away. Yet, if God wills that it continue until all the wealth piled up by the bondman's two hundred and fifty years of unrequited toil shall be sunk, and until every drop of blood drawn with the lash shall be paid by another drawn with the sword, as was said three thousand years ago, so still it must be said, "The judgments of the Lord are true and righteous altogether."

With malice toward none; with charity for all; with firmness in the right, as God gives us to see the right, let us strive on to finish the work we are in; to bind up the nation's wounds; to care for him who shall have borne the battle, and for his widow, and his orphan—to do all which may achieve and cherish a just and lasting peace among ourselves, and with all nations.

Primary Sources

Angle, Paul, ed. *Created Equal? The Complete Lincoln-Douglas Debates of 1858.* Chicago: University of Chicago Press, 1958.

Current, Richard N., ed. *The Political Thought of Abraham Lincoln.* Indianapolis: Bobbs-Merrill, 1967.

Elliott, Ian, ed. *Abraham Lincoln, 1809–1865.* Dobbs Ferry, N.Y.: Oceana, 1970.

Fehrenbacher, Don E., ed. *Abraham Lincoln: A Documentary Portrait.* Stanford, Calif.: Stanford University Press, 1964.

Nicolay, John G., and John Hay, eds. *Abraham Lincoln: Complete Works.* 2 vols. New York: Century, 1894.

Secondary Sources

Agar, Herbert. *Abraham Lincoln.* New York: Macmillan, 1952.

Brogan, Denis W. *Abraham Lincoln.* London: Duckworth, 1974.

Current, Richard N. *Lincoln and the First Shot.* Philadelphia: Lippincott, 1963.

———. *The Lincoln Nobody Knows.* New York: Hill and Wang, 1958.

Hesseltine, William B. *Lincoln's Plan of Reconstruction.* Gloucester, Mass.: Peter Smith, 1963.

McPherson, James M. *Abraham Lincoln and the Second American Revolution.* New York: Oxford University Press, 1991.

Oates, Stephen B. *With Malice toward None.* New York: Harper and Row, 1977.

———. *Abraham Lincoln: The Man Behind the Myths.* New York: Harper and Row, 1984.

Part III

Reconstruction and Industrialization: 1865–1900

THIS PERIOD may be divided almost equally between the earlier wartime and Reconstruction years, and the later era of the developing struggle between consolidating capital and the debtor-farmer-labor sectors of the population. The dividing line is 1877, perhaps the most turbulent year in American history, when a presidential election remained undecided for months and railroad service was disrupted by a bloody and destructive national strike. The dominant ethos of the latter period was the Social Darwinist rationale for individual acquisitiveness and laissez-faire: if left free to make the most of available opportunities, the fittest of the species would rise to riches, and the society would be improved by the elimination of the unfit. In reaction to the conditions generated by *hard money* policies (keeping the supply of money low), rapid industrial expansion, and sharp swings in the business cycle, several significant social movements arose. The Greenback and Populist parties, the labor movement, several individual thinkers, and socialists each raised a challenge to the materialist liberal orthodoxy. The climax of this chorus of protest came in the period 1894 to 1896, during which the Supreme Court blocked every major social reform achieved and at the end of which the 1896 election resulted in effective popular acquiescence. After 1896 the new American capitalist system and the positive state associated with it would face no comparable challenge.

Reconstruction

With the war's end at Appomattox in 1865, the questions of how the South was to be restored to the Union and how the rights of former slaves were to be protected became the primary issues. Both presented fundamental constitutional problems, and both led to sharp and continuing controversy.

The eleven Confederate states were not represented in Congress and were essentially governed by Union army commanders on the scene. President Johnson, following Lincoln's moderate intentions, granted widespread amnesty and acted to recognize loyal governments in four states and to establish provisional governments in the other seven. The latter were to hold conventions to amend constitutions to eliminate slavery and repudiate war debts, after which they would be readmitted to the Union. But Congress, dominated by Radical Republicans, repudiated his actions, refused to seat representatives from the Southern states, and declared its intention to conduct its own reconstruction program involving strong national control.

In order to confirm congressional power to so act, the Fourteenth Amendment was drafted and sent to the states in 1866. The potentially sweeping changes in the distribution of power between the states and the national government involved in this amendment (see selection 23) led to its immediate rejection by the Southern states. Such actions, together with race riots in the South and President Johnson's inability to mobilize moderates, led to Radical victories in the congressional elections of 1866 sufficient to give them the two-thirds majorities in each House necessary to override presidential vetoes.

One of the first acts of the new Congress was to establish military districts for the governance of the South and to make ratification of the Fourteenth Amendment one of the conditions of reentry. Only those not excluded as ex-Confederates were eligible to vote. When the Southern states failed to take the required actions, Congress passed new laws requiring military commanders to enroll voters and set up governments. Black voters were in the majority in five states and, along with Republicans, made up governing coalitions in the others. As a result, Radical Republican administrations took office throughout the South and the Fourteenth Amendment was promptly ratified.

The bitter opposition of white Southerners led to the organization of the Ku Klux Klan, which began a campaign of violence against blacks to prevent them from voting and from asserting in other ways the equal rights supposedly guaranteed them. Protection for the black voting rights granted in the new state constitutions was beyond the capacity of Radical administrations. Congress therefore proposed the Fifteenth Amendment early in 1869 as a means of bringing national power to the support of black voters, almost all of whom were Republicans. Giving primacy to blacks over women separated long-term allies in the antislavery and Equal Rights cause, leading first to women's opposing ratification of the Fifteenth Amendment and then to proposals for a sixteenth amendment to provide women's suffrage (see selection 23). Ratification was made a condition of reentry of the four Southern states still not readmitted. The Radical regimes in other states quickly ratified, however, so that the amendment became effective in March 1870, barely a year after it was submitted to the states. To enforce its provisions, Congress promptly passed new laws known as the Ku Klux Klan Acts. The Supreme Court initially took a restrictive view of congressional powers, voiding sections of these as well as the other civil rights acts.

The exigencies of Reconstruction and the goals of Radical Republicans thus led to a surge of national power and, at least potentially, to substantial constitutional change to support that national power at the expense of the states. The Republicans wanted to validate national power, not only to preserve the votes necessary to enable them to stay in office, but also to be of continuing assistance to the industrial and financial interests that they were seeking to win as party allies. The Civil War had led to an economic boom in the North and West; between 1860 and 1865 prices rose 117 percent and wages 43 percent. The Homestead Act of 1862 had spurred agricultural expansion, and growing markets in Europe had absorbed all the United States could produce. Hard-money policies of the Grant Administration were well received by the banking industry if not by the South. Railroad expansion was rapid and profitable, with government land grants and protection aiding railroad financiers. And the Republicans were more than willing to manage tariff policies in behalf of manufacturing interests, as had their Whig predecessors. For all these reasons the Republican party would ride its Union-preserving wave of approval into future permanent existence, the first political party to rise to national power and maintain itself there in nearly a century.

1877

In the latter stages of Reconstruction, Northern concern for the rights of black people was waning. There was decreasing support in Congress for the kind of sustained effort necessary to protect the rights of black citizens against the violent and lawless campaign of the white South to resubjugate them. Moreover, other issues rose to prominence. The Grant administrations were riddled by corruption. Extensive speculation in various securities and too-rapid expansion in several industries had weakened the banking system to such a point that a major bank collapsed. The resulting Panic of 1873 led to several years of falling prices and unemployment. The fact that large numbers of low-wage immigrants had arrived (often as a result of recruiting in Europe by railroad companies) in the postwar years added to tension and resentments in urban areas.

The election of 1876 went to the Democrat Tilden by a popular vote majority of about 250,000. But the Republicans disputed the Tilden electoral college ballots from three Southern states and Oregon, which left him with 184 electoral ballots—one short of the necessary majority. Competing sets of ballots were reported to Congress from each state, and the election was at an impasse. December 1876 and nearly all of January 1877 passed with no resolution; the lame-duck Senate was primarily Republican and anxious to choose the Republican electors, while the lame-duck House was largely Democratic and would select the Democrats. A fifteen-member electoral commission was established, with five senators, five representatives, and five justices of the Supreme Court. As a means of maintaining party balance, the statute specified that of the five justices two would be Democrats, two Republicans, and the fifth chosen by the first four. The justice chosen was a nominal Republican who wrote an opinion favoring Tilden and then, wavering under pressure, voted for Hayes, giving Hayes an eight-to-seven party-line majority. The issue was not decided, however, until 28 February, and Hayes was declared elected only on 2 March, two days before inauguration was to take place.

Southern Democrats accepted the results because, behind the scenes, a momentous compromise had been reached. The Republicans promised to withdraw all remaining federal troops from the South and in effect return the Southern states to white supremacy. For blacks in the South this resulted in a return to economic and social conditions not much better than those during slavery, loss of the right to vote, and continued physical harassment. Blacks were clearly the losers of the election dispute. But the extended uncertainty about when the presidency would be filled gave rise to widespread anxiety that the society would not hold together under the combined weights of economic depression, social unrest, and political turmoil.

The depression following the Panic of 1873 led to particularly hard times for the labor movement. Unions dissolved or lost members due to layoffs, fierce competition for jobs, and low wages. Police and employers made organization difficult at best: the Tompkins Square Riot occurred in New York City in 1874 and the "Molly Maguires" were convicted in Pennsylvania in 1875 with ten hanged for murder.

It was in this context that another wage cut triggered the spontaneous general railroad strike in July 1877. The strike began in West Virginia and quickly spread to nearly all railroad lines east of the Mississippi. Major riots occurred in Baltimore, Pittsburgh, Chicago, and St. Louis. State militia for the most part either refused to fight or joined the strikers in sympathy. When distant militia were brought in, as when the Philadelphia militia were sent to Pittsburgh, the strikers resisted them. In the latter case, twenty-six people were killed, and $10 million worth of damage was done to railroad cars, depots, and trackage. Nine deaths at Martinsburg, West Virginia, led President Hayes, in office less than five months, to send the federal troops just withdrawing from the South to both cities to restore order. In Chicago and St. Louis large numbers of strikers and their sympathizers began to demand political reforms and in St. Louis actually took over some governmental functions for a period.

The great strike ultimately disintegrated, however, with the restoration of some wages and for lack of larger goals. Nevertheless, the shock wave from what had happened—and from what might have happened—was felt throughout the country, effectively changing the frame of reference of politics and political ideas. Abandonment of Reconstruction and the dramatic confrontation of the railroad strike together in the same year served to symbolize the rise of industrial politics with its class lines to challenge (but not yet to replace) sectional politics. The residue of the Civil War and Reconstruction would remain an important political factor for decades to come, but the nation was now in the process of shifting toward a conflict between capital and labor. The political values and ideas of agrarian liberalism would have to be adapted to the new conditions of an urban, industrial society.

These new conditions included the development of a wide variety of machinery for mass production and transportation, burgeoning immigrant populations, vast accumulations of capital in corporations controlling entire industries and markets, and a steadily declining agricultural sector—to name but a few. The industries of mining, steel, and petroleum developed rapidly in the postwar years, giving rise to other new industries and capabilities. The heavy immigration of 1849 to 1854, which was mostly German (and among them some early Marxists), resumed in 1865 to 1873 with Germans, Irish, and Scandinavians, and again in 1880 to 1893 with Eastern and Southern Europeans and some Chinese. In the 1880s, trusts and holding companies became regular means of establishing monopoly control in one or a few hands; efforts to regulate monopolies began with the Sherman Anti-Trust Act of 1890. The period of 1873 to 1896 was one of continuing depression for farmers, many of whom lost farms and went to the cities to become factory hands. Panics followed by recessions occurred in 1873, 1882, 1890, and 1893; recoveries were experienced chiefly in heavy industry and the financial system. Unemployment remained substantial throughout the period. Great riches were achieved by a few, and great hardship suffered by many.

Social Darwinism

A large number of essayists, ministers, politicians, and others kept their eyes firmly fixed on the successes of leading entrepreneurs and financiers, issuing a chorus of praise for their achievements and for the proof they provided of the opportunities that were there for all. Riches were to be gathered, and merit was measured by money. The masses were taught to respect thrift and hard work, which when added to virtue were lauded as the means by which individuals such as Rockefeller, Vanderbilt, Carnegie, and Morgan had amassed their fortunes. Famous in this campaign were the *McGuffey's Readers,* books for elementary schools that systematically taught orthodox patriotic, moral, and social values. An estimated 122 million copies were printed in several editions and used and reused all across the country.

The basic theme of most of these writers

and lecturers was that individuals were located on the social and economic ladder in strict accordance with their talent and effort. Moreover, as the unfit were eliminated, the society as a whole would benefit. Thus any kind of government intrusion into the economy—particularly on behalf of the poorer or disadvantaged sectors—was considered a serious disservice to the social order as a whole. In short, the principle of laissez-faire was rhetorically endorsed by nearly every salient voice, although some were quite ready to employ government assistance when it was in their interest to do so.

Many selections might have been assembled to show the breadth of support enjoyed by the Social Darwinist gospel. Instead, the subtlest and most principled of its advocates, William Graham Sumner, has been presented at greater length (selection 24) to permit a full glimpse of what strict laissez-faire liberalism contains and implies. Sumner rose from humble origins, went to Yale, and then entered the ministry. He soon returned to Yale and established a distinguished academic career as one of the leading American sociologists. His ideas are a consistent expression of orthodox laissez-faire with its emphasis on individualism, property rights, and governmental non-intervention. Sumner deplored all uses of government, not just the ones designed to benefit the poor or the weak; he castigated violations of free-trade principles and the very kinds of special considerations for particular economic interests that Hamilton endorsed.

The rationale for Sumner's utter individualism lay in his classical liberal conviction that progress for all was dependent on the economic successes of those specially talented individuals who might be able to amass fortunes amidst truly competitive conditions. If the natural processes of competition were allowed to run their courses, Sumner believed, all would receive their just rewards and the society would eliminate its weaker members. The problems inherent in analogizing from natural-selection analyses of biological evolution did not much trouble Sumner or other Social Darwinists of the time, perhaps because there already were so many precedents in the liberal tradition for individualism, laissez-faire, and limited government. Sumner saw a person's failure to attain wealth as solely attributable to a lack of capacity to compete, not to disadvantages of education, birth, environment, or fortune.

The success with which this argument was established as a dominant theme in American political thinking has been characterized as the "capture of the American democrat by the Whigs": by use of the Horatio Alger myth and the other accoutrements of the gospel of wealth, the possessors of property captured the thinking of democrats who might otherwise have viewed their success as illegitimate and sought redistribution by means of government.[1] This analysis makes an important point: much of the fear that property holders in the United States have had of the masses has been unfounded because the populace has been as much imbued with respect for, and motivated to possess, property as the most thoroughgoing capitalist. Redistribution has not occurred primarily because there have never been many who thought it justifiable or appropriate. One reason pragmatic politicians were unable to handle the slavery issue in the early nineteenth century was that the property status of slaves could not be eliminated without compensation which would have involved sums too vast to seem possible. The property-oriented American capitalists, the local version of Whiggery, never succeeded in gaining explicit recognition for their status. Indeed, on

---

1. Louis Hartz, *The Liberal Tradition in America* (New York: Harcourt, Brace & World, 1955), chap. 6.

most occasions when they sought to establish themselves or their interests as supreme by right or entitlement, they were rejected by the aroused American individualist democrat. But the substance of their ends, in its economic dimensions and to a considerable extent in the personal supremacy of representative capitalists, was still fully realized—under the banner of individualism, limited government, competitive enterprise, laissez-faire, and "democracy."

Sumner was a contributor to this "capture," although this was not one of his conscious purposes. This contribution is visible in the way Sumner evolved definitions of familiar terms to fit the conditions of the times and the value preferences he held. To Sumner, for example, equality meant equality of opportunity, narrowly construed as the right to compete if a person was otherwise able to. For him the balance was in all other respects on the side of liberty in the sense of strictly prohibiting government interference with a person's enjoyment of the rewards realized from success in the competition. It was both immoral and ultimately dysfunctional to use government for the purpose of taking from those who had succeeded and giving to those who had not. This was more than just a convenient rationale for justifying the possessions of the rich with a moral or social gloss; Sumner followed it consistently to the point of condemning instances where particular interests had enriched themselves through the use of government. He is best understood as marking a high point in the individualist, limited-government, laissez-faire, and exclusively property rights version of the American liberal tradition. The mainstream nature of his position may be estimated from the considerable power that it maintains now, nearly a century later and amidst drastically different circumstances.

Sumner also has another claim to contemporary relevance, one that further documents the principled nature of his positions. In a con-sistent application of a view that sought not just to sustain economic aggrandizement but within the range of its assumptions to improve qualities of life as well, he attacked what he saw as an imperialist foreign policy. His concern was that a nation could not act on one set of principles in regard to other nations and use another set at home. Given his assumption that the territories at stake in the Spanish-American War could not and should not be incorporated into the United States, this concern led him to fear for the domestic effects of an essentially colonialist approach to governing the new territories. If not observed abroad, he asked, could democracy be long sustained at home? A rationalization which permitted the exclusion of some from self-determination and opportunity might eventually undermine commitments to those principles generally or at least sustain exceptions to them. Or, conversely, a government active for foreign-policy purposes might soon become active for domestic purposes as well. To Sumner it appeared that there was a choice to be made, and he opted for avoiding both possibilities by not undertaking the acquisition of territories.

Alternatives

While the Social Darwinist ethos was clearly dominant, at least among the most visible national spokespeople and the major media channels, several social movements arose during this period and presented significant ideological challenges. Some took the form of electoral political action based on their distinctive programs, such as the Greenback and Populist (People's) parties. A major source of social confrontation, perhaps the most fundamental of the era, was the growing labor movement. Although it was weakened by economic conditions and internal divisions, labor was the only major force besides the farmers that was opposed to Social Darwinism. The history of the times might have been very different if workers had been able to come together as a single coherent force *and* if they had been able to develop a coalition with the farmers.

Another kind of challenge was mounted by several salient journalists and reformers, whose critiques drew support chiefly from reform-oriented middle classes and resulted typically in solutions more satisfying in concept than possible of achievement. Behind all of this activity were those who sought to build unity of opposition around a concrete alternative. Some were socialists with Marxist doctrinal guidance of one kind or another, while others simply sought to build the necessary coalitions to serve peoples' needs first and worry about subtleties later. All of these movements were caught up in the great confrontation of 1894–96, and only the socialists gained social momentum afterwards.

The Greenback and Populist (People's) Parties

The farmer-labor protest movements of the period actually began with the Granger movement in 1867. Initially a secret society, the Grangers moved into politics in the 1870s. Independent political parties were formed in several plains states, but their influence was strong throughout the Midwest. Goals included cooperation among farmers to eliminate brokers and processors, and legislative regulation of monopolies, particularly those that controlled railroad and grain storage rates.

But a greater challenge to the system itself was posed first by the Greenback Labor party (1878–84) and then by the People's party (1889–96), as the political arm of the Populists was known. Although these two parties had no lineal connections, they are related in that each was centrally concerned with the character of the monetary system. Generally, neither their contemporary opponents nor historians have been kind to their views in this respect,

usually treating them as at best naive and simplistic, and often as hopelessly utopian or wildly radical. But there are two quite serious issues concealed by such reactions, and they go right to the banking heart of the capitalist political economy. One has to do with the supply of money. When more money is available, prices tend to rise and business activity to pick up; debtors find it easier to repay their creditors with cheaper dollars. Keeping the money supply low (*hard money*) may preserve its value and keep creditors satisfied, but it makes credit for various productive and job-generating activities much less available.

The other issue was who was to decide what the supply of money should be and thus to manage the availability of credit, the level of prices, and the financial core of the economy in general. Both Greenbackers and Populists insisted that such an important power should be kept accountable to the people by being placed in the hands of the national government. They bitterly opposed its possession by a few large banks and its use on behalf of private profit-seeking interests. They saw their jobs, land, and livelihoods being sacrificed to "the money power" and demanded a voice in determining such policies.

These were, and still are, profoundly important issues with the strong potential of forcing a class-based conflict into the political arena. But they contained their own sources of confusion to add to the vigorous and distorting opposition they encountered. Behind them was the concept of money itself: must money have an independent value of its own (gold or silver), or may it be any convenient item (such as paper notes) provided only that the government declare that it is *legal tender* (accepted for payment of debts) and guarantee it in some fashion? Historically the scarcity of gold has maintained its precious nature, thus serving as a standard; many people, then and now, assume there is no other proper method. But there is no logical reason why a publicly accountable government could not be the source of money and hence its value. The issue is really one of what that value and supply are to be, who is to control them, and who wins and loses thereby.

Another source of confusion was the effort of western owners of newly found silver deposits to expand their markets by getting silver into circulation as money. Their appeals drew support from some Greenbackers and Populists because this would expand the supply of money and grant debtors relief from the bankers' hard-money policies. But this reasoning sustains the assumption that money must have an independent value, and it does not reach the concept connecting money management to the democratic character of the system. And it was the latter point that the more thoughtful Greenbackers and Populists were really trying to raise. What was at stake for them was whether the American democracy was to include the people's right to participate in controlling their economic life conditions. Selection 26 poses all these issues as the Populists saw them.

The Labor Movement

Millions of working people were engaged in day-to-day struggles with their employers throughout this period, chiefly over working conditions and wages. The length of the working day (first ten hours and then eight) was a principal issue, as was the often-related one of safety on the job. But depressed wages, kept low by repeated panics and the availability of immigrant and black workers as strikebreakers, presented the most fundamental issue of how the economic pie was to be divided. Only through strong collective effort could workers force their giant corporate employers to grant them larger shares of the profits being generated, so the conflict first centered on the question of organization itself. Employers through

the courts challenged workers' rights to organize; they also used a variety of coercive techniques, including spying on and infiltrating unions, discharging "agitators," hiring private armies and strikebreakers, and using government power as the last resort.

There are two different ways of organizing that present entirely different sorts of challenges to the economic-political system. The question of which was the better way became a major source of conflict within the labor movement and (together with employer-government opposition) helped to reduce the impact of labor in this period. The first approach, and the one that predominated until the Great Depression of the 1930s, is that of *craft* unionization. Here workers who have a particular skill organize to bargain with their employers without regard to what other workers around them are doing. Such workers are usually better educated, and their skills in sufficiently short supply to give them real leverage against the employer. Their closely shared work experience (and often their "American" ethnic backgrounds) make them easier to organize. Because they are both irreplaceable and few in number, employers often grant their demands without serious danger to profits. There is thus generated a relatively satisfied labor elite made up of just the workers whose education might provide leadership and whose skills would give leverage to a broader-based workers' struggle.

The other approach is that of *industrial* unionization, in which all workers in a given industry, from the most skilled draftsperson to the most unskilled laborer, are brought together in a single organization. This is the only way that the great bulk of workers, who are relatively unskilled and eminently replaceable, can bring effective pressure on employers to grant wage or other improvements. It is also much more difficult, not only because there may be many unemployed workers so desperate they will serve as strikebreakers, but also because the diversities among workers in a given industry—ethnic and racial as well as related to the specific work involved—make solidarity problematic. Because the impact of even one union can be so powerful and potentially threatening, employers fight hardest against this form of organization.

The political implications of the different approaches are directly related to the numbers of workers involved. Where organization is by crafts, issues posed are principally seen as economic in character, and, once wage increases or other concessions are granted, no fundamental challenge is posed to the nature of the economic (or political) system itself. In other words, craft unionization is entirely consistent with a capitalist system and can be accepted and absorbed by it without difficulty.

Industrial unionization, however, involves vastly more workers. Employers resist more strongly, and strikes are likely to lead to the involvement of state and national governments through court injunctions, police, or the army. Violence is far more probable under such circumstances. The political potential of industrial unionization is thus much higher, for workers (and most others in the population) are likely to see the issues as placing the government and the employers on one side and the workers on the other. Such class-based polarization contains the possibility of fundamental change in the social and economic order, and industrial unionization is much preferred by those with such goals.

The original form of labor organization in the United States was by crafts, with various national coalitions of unions, culminating in the formation of the American Federation of Labor (AFL) in 1886. Under the leadership of Samuel Gompers, the AFL and its member unions for the next forty years defended the interests of craft unions, kept labor out of direct political activity, and effectively opposed the struggling industrial unions that arose from time to time. Gompers developed cooperative relations with the corporate and banking community to the point where he was accepted into its leading organization, the National Civic Federation, as a responsible labor leader.

The Knights of Labor (1878–93) were the first major effort at industrial unionization. Self-consciously democratic in form, they were organized without regard to sex, race, color, or occupation, and they required that three-quarters of each local assembly be composed of lower-level wage earners. Farmers as well as urban workers were members. The Knights sought to maximize cooperative production, marketing, and purchasing and urged such political goals as the progressive income tax. Membership boomed to nearly a million after two successful strikes in the early 1880s but collapsed after the leadership undercut a general strike for the eight-hour day in Chicago and in the aftermath of the Haymarket Massacre in 1886. The American Railway Union was a much less ambitious industrial union, but it was effectively reduced to craft status when the Pullman Strike of 1894 was broken.

One of the major consequences of efforts at industrial unionization and the other major strikes of the period was to put the question of the equity of income distribution on the political agenda. To what extent this issue was seen as "merely" an economic one and to what extent properly subject to decision through collective popular participation would profoundly affect the nature of democracy in the future.

Other Reform Movements

Several other movements, often involving middle-class people, grew up around prominent thinkers and played significant political roles in this period. Perhaps the most potent of these thinkers was Henry Demarest Lloyd (selection 27). After gaining visibility and respect through trenchant critiques of various aspects of the corporate capitalist economy, Lloyd set about to achieve the needed coalition between labor and the farmers. On the verge of important successes from his Chicago base, Lloyd's efforts were vitiated by the Populists' collapse into the arms of Bryan and by the silver issue in 1896.

A different kind of movement was generated by the publication of a utopian novel by Edward Bellamy in 1888. *Looking Backward* gained immediate popularity by providing a glimpse of a wholly new society in which a democratically controlled national government organized the society and economy to maximize individual well-being and happiness. Nationalism, as the succeeding movement was known, began to make collective ownership and management seem respectable (see selection 26).

Another and more directly electoral political movement was centered around the ideas, and ultimately the New York City mayoralty candidacy, of Henry George. Initially a reforming journalist in San Francisco, George completed his major work, *Progress and Poverty*, in 1879. His basic argument was that land values were created by population expansion, and therefore land should be the sole basis of taxation to reverse the otherwise steady process of impoverishment of those who had to rent land or buy its products. His book soon caught on, spawning the "single tax" movement and leading to his near-election in New York in 1886. Clubs and groups of disciples continued to spread his ideas throughout the 1890s.

Socialism

Scatterings of socialists, both native successors to the early utopians and newly arrived (but divided) Marxists, became active in this period. Their major impact would not be felt un-

til after 1900, but they were putting their analysis and prescription on record through formation of the Socialist Labor party in 1877 and through work in the labor movement. Because so many socialists were German immigrants, however, they tended to be isolated from the native American mainstream. And their arguments were often distorted or discredited by the spectacular acts of the relatively few anarchists who believed in the "propaganda of the deed" and engaged in terrorism. Nevertheless, inherent in many of the protest and reform movements of the times was the germ of democratic collectivism. The field for socialism appeared fertile if European ideas and indigenous American experience could be fused into a broad-based movement.

The Climax: 1894–96

Economic depression and widespread unrest focused protests and calls for reform into the short period between 1894 and 1896. The major events were, first, the dramatic confrontation of the Pullman Strike in 1894; second, the Supreme Court decisions of 1894 and 1895 that blocked existing (and prevented future) legislative reforms, leaving labor subject to court injunctions and the army; third and finally, the election of 1896, which became the referendum on the basic character and direction of the American political economy. The consequence of these events was to establish the frame of reference and boundaries for political thinking that would dominate the century to follow.

In retrospect, the election of 1896 may have been the most significant election in modern (post–Civil War) American history. Up to this point, Grover Cleveland, a conservative, Democratic president, had grudgingly accepted the revival of the income tax as spurred by William Jennings Bryan and the Democratic-controlled House; had pursued a hard-money policy; and had broken the Pullman Strike by sending federal troops to Illinois over the protests of Illinois's leftish, Democratic governor, John Peter Altgeld. The Supreme Court had just declared the income tax unconstitutional; had cut back the ability of Congress to regulate trusts and monopolies through its interstate commerce power; had prevented the states from enacting regulatory legislation; and had endorsed the powers of federal judges to break strikes through injunctions. The People's party appeared to be building from its remarkable achievements of 1892 and joining with urban labor to become a vehicle for radical political change. In short, class lines appeared to be forming and replacing memories of the Civil War as the basis for divisions in American politics. The Panic of 1893 was deepening with high unemployment and frequent strikes. Certainly the election would be an effective national referendum on the questions of labor, monetary policy, means of raising tax revenues, and the status of monopolies. If ever the status quo seemed to be set against social reform, and class set against class, 1896 was the time.

But what actually transpired in the election was another story. The Republicans nominated William McKinley, an Ohio senator known for his conservatism and his effective advocacy of high protective tariffs. The Democratic convention, split between left and right factions, was captured by the "pro-silver" rhetoric (favoring silver-backed currency) of the Nebraskan Bryan. The mostly urban left had no prominent candidate—their leader, Altgeld, was ineligible for the presidency because he had been born in Germany—and reluctantly acquiesced. "Gold" Democrats, a substantial conservative faction, bolted the party, as did a lesser number of "silver" Republicans. The populists, suffering from an influx of "silver" factions and an excess of traditional politics, were unable to prevent the People's Party from nominating Bryan. Their

program was partially absorbed into the Democratic platform and Bryan's rhetoric, and the People's party itself began to disintegrate into socialist and Democratic fragments even before the election.

The campaign was a classic contest between money and managerial organization on the Republican side and a bumbling but a large personal investment by Bryan on the Democratic side. In the first of the "modern" campaigns, the Republican organizer Mark Hanna orchestrated a well-financed media campaign on top of a systematic drive to get out the vote. The "bloody shirt" of the Civil War was revived. Bryan was painted as a raving radical out to destroy the American system, while the Republicans were once again promoted as the saviors of the Constitution and the nation it represented. Bryan made a massive miscalculation in regard to the issues when he made silver coinage the centerpiece of his campaign. This drove away potential support from those who stood to lose from inflation, particularly workers and the urban middle class. He failed to capitalize on the many other real grievances people had. McKinley stayed serenely at home, receiving delegations of supporters. Bryan set records for distance traveled and speeches given. McKinley won the election by half a million votes, receiving 52 percent of the total and taking a comfortable 271 electoral-college votes to Bryan's 176. And the Republicans regained control of both Houses of Congress.

Although the issues at stake in the election were blurred if not concealed by the nomination of Bryan and the nature of the campaign, the election was in practical terms a national referendum on the future directions of the American political system. The Republicans were in power; there would be no income tax or serious attack on corporations; and the Court was safe. Business and employment improved in 1897. The "splendid little war" of

1898 with Spain was a major diversion, awakening latent nationalism. And finally, the Democrats eased another Republican victory by renominating Bryan in 1900.

Summary

Liberalism in the last half of the nineteenth century was decisively individualist, property oriented, and laissez-faire. Its doctrines were synonymous with the needs of capitalist expansion. For increasing numbers of people, the concept of equality was beginning to expand, though the mainstream acceptance of equality of opportunity and before the law, in the narrowest of terms, provided a brake. Blacks were struggling with the conflict between the words of the newly amended Constitution and the reality of their abandonment to systematic subjugation. Women had not achieved even the right to vote, let alone equality in other dimensions. Farmers and workers were pressing for a concept of equality which included minimum economic protection from the worst hardships of the economy. Social conditions themselves seemed to suggest that the combination of all of these pressures would force some future expansion in, or higher priority for, the value of equality in the liberal belief system. For the moment, however, property rights and laissez-faire were at their zenith.

The law was also supreme: the Court, and behind it the Constitution, had never played such a powerful governing role. A kind of civil religion was developing, with the Constitution as its principal liturgy and lawyers as its priests. The organized churches were strongly committed to the social and economic system in which they were embedded. Most ministers were engaged in justifying the laissez-faire status quo and in playing a much lesser role in support of reform and social justice. The impact of religion thus comes primarily from its fusion with the purposes and character of the political economy, lending its legitimacy and moral sanction to the existing order and providing it with nonearthly justifications.

The advances of science and technology that translated into new productive techniques seemed to give industrialization the character of inevitability and progress. Increasing corporate organization appeared to go hand in hand with such advances. Bigness was attributed to the need for efficiency and justified by the managerial skills of the great entrepreneurs —in short, it was for the best, and incidentally consistent with traditional American values.

23. The Civil War Constitutional Amendments and the Failure of the "Sixteenth" Amendment

THE THIRTEENTH AMENDMENT to the Constitution (1865) abolished slavery. The Fourteenth (1868) made all persons born in the United States citizens of the United States and of the state in which they reside, and it prohibited the states from denying them certain rights and privileges. The Fifteenth Amendment (1870) prohibited denial of the right to vote on account of race, color, or previous condition of servitude. In addition, each amendment contained a final section granting Congress the power to enforce its provisions. The Thirteenth Amendment had the one-time significance of completely abolishing slavery in the entire country, not just in the Confederate-held areas as did Lincoln's war-induced Emancipation Proclamation of 1863. The Fourteenth and Fifteenth Amendments, however, together amounted to a constitutional revolution of profound importance; their purposes and impact were vital elements that would shape the American system for the next century.

The Fourteenth and Fifteenth Amendments were initiated by Republicans in Congress, partly in fulfillment of the Civil War's commitment to achieving equality for ex-slaves but more for the practical political purpose of staying in power in the national government. Without Republican black votes in the South, the Democratic party might well have quickly returned to majority status and perhaps might have sent the Republican party the way of the Federalists and Whigs before them.

The revolutionary implications of the amendments lay in the fact that, for the first time, the national Constitution made a large number of rights of individuals enforceable against the states. Before these amendments were passed, the rights enumerated in the Constitution were enforceable only against the national government itself; for infringement of their rights by their states or by other people, people could only look to their state governments for relief. Now they would have the enforcement authority of the United States Supreme Court, and (if the Congress chose to legislate in the area) the support of federal statutes and executive enforcement thereof behind their claims for the rights enumerated. Such rights were broad: the right to have privileges and immunities of citizens of the United States; the right not to be deprived of life, liberty or property by a state without due process of law; and the right not to be denied equal protection of the laws by a state. Moreover, these rights were nonspecific and therefore potentially very broad—depending entirely on how the Supreme Court interpreted them. It was a nationalizing surge nearly equal to the Constitution itself, if and when the Court chose to so view its powers. And every time the Court acted to confirm a new limitation on the states under these amendments, Congress would simultaneously acquire new legislative power under the empowering "enforcement clauses."

The Court's initial reaction was to construe its new powers, and therefore the scope of the change wrought by the amendments, in a very narrow manner. In part this was because the Court wished to minimize the change in existing legal arrangements and to retain the states as viable governments. But in larger part it was quite simply because northern support for black civil rights, never very strong, was waning sharply. White Southerners were being allowed to regain control of their state governments and to reinstitute white supremacy in southern social and economic life, sometimes violently. In the *Civil Rights Cases* (1883), for example, the Court cut back the scope of a congressional postwar statute requiring equal accommodations in public places. It held that the Fourteenth Amendment prohibited only "state action" denying rights. Congressional power, therefore, did not extend to the control of what "private" inns, theaters, and similar establishments did in the way of discrimination against blacks.

The early years of Reconstruction also saw a sometimes bitter argument develop between those who advocated a constitutional amendment to enfranchise black men and those who wanted such an amendment to enfranchise women also. The issue split the Equal Rights Association, the postwar successor to the various antislavery associations, and gave rise to the separate National Woman Suffrage Association, which thereafter opposed the Fifteenth Amendment in Congress. It also temporarily separated former allies Frederick Douglass and the leaders of the women's movement, Elizabeth Cady Stanton and Susan B. Anthony. Douglass argued that endangered black men in the South had greater need of the vote; Stanton, Anthony, and others insisted that the entitlement of women (including black women) was at least as important.

Congress saw the Fifteenth Amendment as less controversial in the form limiting the vote to black males and sent it to the states that way. Ratification was complete by 1870. Defeated in the legislatures of the nation, suffragists responded by having an analogous amendment proposed in the House and Senate. This might-have-been Sixteenth Amendment was then the subject of decades of fruitless petitioning by local and national women's organizations around the country. Ironically, it was not until another practical political necessity converged with women's claims that the suffrage amendment was passed and ratified in 1920 as the Nineteenth Amendment. What finally put it across was concern on the part of middle-class Protestants that the influx of immigrant, largely Catholic and Jewish, lower-class males would result in a voting majority in their favor.

Susan B. Anthony (1820–1906) taught school in upstate New York before becoming involved in the temperance, abolitionist, and women's movements. She was president of the National Woman Suffrage Association during the critical years described above and for many years edited and published *The Revolution,* the semiofficial organ of the women's suffrage movement. She was a courageous and indefatigable leader, who in 1872 created a national sensation by boldly voting and then challenging the government's efforts to prosecute her for doing so. Her name has come to be synonymous with the cause of women's suffrage. Her leadership role was symbolized when she was chosen in 1978 to be the first woman to have her portrait on a United States coin.

The selections excerpted here include the text of the proposed Sixteenth Amendment and related arguments drawn from *The Revo-*

lution; some representative passages from the debates within the Equal Rights Association between Douglass and women leaders, principally Anthony; and documents surrounding Anthony's federal court trial for her indictment for voting in the 1872 election. This last group consists of her memorial to Congress, setting forth the facts surrounding the case and her statement to the court as it was about to pronounce sentence. Anthony's act of voting was part of a coordinated national effort by women to establish that their right to vote had been guaranteed by the Fourteenth Amendment. It should be noted that the statute under which she was tried and convicted was a post–Civil War "Ku Klux Klan" statute, the intent of which was to punish those who falsely cast ballots. ᴄᴡ

The Thirteenth, Fourteenth, and Fifteenth Amendments (1865–1870)

AMENDMENT XIII (1865)

Section 1. Neither slavery nor involuntary servitude, except as a punishment for crime whereof the party shall have been duly convicted, shall exist within the United States, or any place subject to their jurisdiction.

Section 2. Congress shall have power to enforce this article by appropriate legislation.

AMENDMENT XIV (1868)

Section 1. All persons born or naturalized in the United States and subject to the jurisdiction thereof, are citizens of the United States and of the State wherein they reside. No State shall make or enforce any law which shall abridge the privileges or immunities of citizens of the United States; nor shall any State deprive any person of life, liberty, or property, without the due process of law; nor deny to any person within its jurisdiction the equal protection of the laws.

Section 2. Representatives shall be apportioned among the several States according to their respective numbers, counting the whole number of persons in each State, excluding Indians not taxed. But when the right to vote at any election for the choice of electors for President and Vice-President of the United States, Representatives in Congress, the Executive and Judicial Officers of a State, or the members of the Legislature thereof, is denied to any of the male inhabitants of such State, being twenty-one years of age, and citizens of the United States, or in any way abridged, except for participation in rebellion, or other crime, the basis of representation therein shall be reduced in the proportion which the number of such male citizens shall bear to the whole number of male citizens twenty-one years of age in such State.

Section 3. No person shall be a Senator or Representative in Congress, or elector of President and Vice-President, or hold any office, civil or military, under the United States, or under any State, who, having previously taken an oath, as a member of Congress, or as an officer of the United States, or as a member of any State legislature, or as an executive or judicial officer of any State, to support the Constitution of the United States, shall have engaged in insurrection or rebellion against the same, or given aid or comfort to the enemies thereof. But Congress may by a vote of two-thirds of each House, remove such disability.

Section 4. The validity of the public debt of the United States, authorized by law, including debts incurred for payment of pensions and bounties for services in suppressing insurrection or rebellion, shall not be questioned. But neither the United States nor any State shall assume or pay any debt or obligation incurred in aid of insurrection or rebellion against the United States, or any claim for the loss or emancipation of any slave; but all such debts, obligations and claims shall be held illegal and void.

Section 5. The Congress shall have power to enforce, by appropriate legislation, the provisions of this article.

AMENDMENT XV (1870)

Section 1. The right of citizens of the United States to vote shall not be denied or abridged by the United States or by any State on account of race, color, or previous condition of servitude.

Section 2. The Congress shall have power to enforce this article by appropriate legislation. ∾

Excerpts from *The Revolution* (1869)

EDITORIAL

April 29, 1869

The Sixteenth Amendment.—March 15, 1869, will be held memorable in all coming time as the day when the Hon. George W. Julian submitted a "Joint Resolution" to Congress to enfranchise the women of the Republic by proposing a Sixteenth Amendment to the Federal Constitution, which reads as follows:

Art. 16. The Right of Suffrage in the United States shall be based on citizenship, and shall be regulated by Congress; and all citizens of the United States, whether native or naturalized, shall enjoy this right equally without any distinction or discrimination whatever founded on sex.

STATEMENT OF ELIZABETH CADY STANTON

October 21, 1869

All wise women should oppose the Fifteenth Amendment for two reasons: 1st. Because it is invidious to their sex. Look at it from what point you will, and in every aspect, it reflects the old idea of woman's inferiority, her subject

Since our famous Bill of Rights was given to the world declaring all men equal, there has been no other proposition, in its magnitude, beneficence, and far-reaching consequences, so momentous as this. The specific work now before us, is to press the importance of this Amendment on the consideration of the people, and to urge Congress to its speedy adoption. Suffrage associations should be formed at once and newspapers established in every State to press Woman's Enfranchisement, and petitions should be circulated in every school district from Maine to California praying the adoption of the Sixteenth Amendment, that when the Forty-second Congress assembles it may understand the work before it.

condition. And yet the one need to secure an onward step in civilization is a new dignity and self-respect in women themselves. No one can think that the pending proposition of "manhood suffrage" exalts woman, either in her own eyes or those of the man by her side, but it does degrade her practically and theoretically, just as black men were more degraded when all other men were enfranchised.

2d. We should oppose the measure, because men have no right to pass it without our consent. When it is proposed to change the constitution or fundamental law of the State or Nation, all the people have a right to say what that change shall be.

If women understood this pending proposition in all its bearings, theoretically and practically, there would be an overwhelming vote against the admission of another man to the ruling power of this nation, until they themselves were first enfranchised. There is no true patriotism, no true nobility in tamely and silently submitting to this insult. It is mere sycophancy to man; it is licking the hand that forges a new chain for our degradation; it is indorsing the old idea that woman's divinely ordained position is at man's feet, and not on an even platform by his side.

By this edict of the liberal party, the women of this Republic are now to touch the lowest depths of their political degradation. ⌒

Debates at Meetings of the Equal Rights Association (1869)

Mr. Douglass: — I came here more as a listener than to speak, and I have listened with a great deal of pleasure to the eloquent address of the Rev. Mr. Frothingham and the splendid address of the President. There is no name greater than that of Elizabeth Cady Stanton in the matter of woman's rights and equal rights, but my sentiments are tinged a little against *The Revolution.* There was in the address to which I allude the employment of certain names, such as "Sambo," and the gardener, and the bootblack, and the daughters of Jefferson and Washington, and all the rest that I can not coincide with. I have asked what difference there is between the daughters of Jefferson and Washington and other daughters. (Laughter.) I must say that I do not see how any one can pretend that there is the same urgency in giving the ballot to woman as to the negro. With us, the matter is a question of

life and death, at least, in fifteen States of the Union. When women, because they are women, are hunted down through the cities of New York and New Orleans; when they are dragged from their houses and hung upon lamp-posts; when their children are torn from their arms, and their brains dashed out upon the pavement; when they are objects of insult and outrage at every turn; when they are in danger of having their homes burnt down over their heads; when their children are not allowed to enter schools; then they will have an urgency to obtain the ballot equal to our own. (Great applause.)

A Voice: — Is that not all true about black women?

Mr. Douglass: — Yes, yes, yes; it is true of the black woman, but not because she is a woman, but because she is black. (Applause.) Julia Ward Howe at the conclusion of her great speech delivered at the convention in Boston last year, said: "I am willing that the negro shall get the ballot before me." (Applause.) Woman! why, she has 10,000 modes of grappling with her difficulties. I believe that all the virtue of the world can take care of all

SOURCE: E.C. Stanton, Susan B. Anthony, and Matilda Joslyn Gage, *History of Woman Suffrage,* (New York: Fowler & Wells, 1882; reprint ed., New York: Arno Press, 1969), 2: 382–84.

the evil. I believe that all the intelligence can take care of all the ignorance. (Applause.) I am in favor of woman's suffrage in order that we shall have all the virtue and vice confronted. Let me tell you that when there were few houses in which the black man could have put his head, this woolly head of mine found a refuge in the house of Mrs. Elizabeth Cady Stanton, and if I had been blacker than sixteen midnights, without a single star, it would have been the same. (Applause.)

Miss Anthony: — The old anti-slavery school say women must stand back and wait until the negroes shall be recognized. But we say, if you will not give the whole loaf of suffrage to the entire people, give it to the most intelligent first. (Applause.) If intelligence, justice, and morality are to have precedence in the Government, let the question of woman be brought up first and that of the negro last. (Applause.) While I was canvassing the State with petitions and had them filled with names for our cause to the Legislature, a man dared to say to me that the freedom of women was all a theory and not a practical thing. (Applause.) When Mr. Douglass mentioned the black man first and the woman last, if he had noticed he would have seen that it was the men that clapped and not the women. There is not the woman born who desires to eat the bread of dependence, no matter whether it be from the hand of father, husband, or brother; for any one who does so eat her bread places herself in the power of the person from whom she takes it. (Applause.) Mr. Douglass talks about the wrongs of the negro; but with all the outrages that he to-day suffers, he would not exchange his sex and take the place of Elizabeth Cady Stanton. (Laughter and applause.)

Mr. Douglass: — I want to know if granting you the right of suffrage will change the nature of our sexes? (Great laughter.)

Miss Anthony: — It will change the pecuniary position of woman; it will place her

where she can earn her own bread. (Loud applause.) She will not then be driven to such employments only as man chooses for her.

Mrs. Norton said that Mr. Douglass's remarks left her to defend the Government from the inferred inability to grapple with the two questions at once. It legislates upon many questions at one and the same time, and it has the power to decide the woman question and the negro question at one and the same time. (Applause.)

Mrs. Lucy Stone: — Mrs. Stanton will, of course, advocate the precedence for her sex, and Mr. Douglass will strive for the first position for his, and both are perhaps right. If it be true that the government derives its authority from the consent of the governed, we are safe in trusting that principle to the uttermost. If one has a right to say that you can not read and therefore can not vote, then it may be said that you are a woman and therefore can not vote. We are lost if we turn away from the middle principle and argue for one class. I was once a teacher among fugitive slaves. There was one old man, and every tooth was gone, his hair was white, and his face was full of wrinkles, yet, day after day and hour after hour, he came up to the school-house and tried with patience to learn to read, and by-and-by, when he had spelled out the first few verses of the first chapter of the Gospel of St. John, he said to me, "Now, I want to learn to write." I tried to make him satisfied with what he had acquired, but the old man said, "Mrs. Stone, somewhere in the wide world I have a son; I have not heard from him in twenty years; if I should hear from him, I want to write to him, so take hold of my hand and teach me." I did, but before he had proceeded in many lessons, the angels came and gathered him up and bore him to his Father. Let no man speak of an educated suffrage. The gentleman who addressed you claimed that the negroes had the first right to the suffrage, and drew a picture which only his great word-power can do. He again in Massachusetts, when it had cast a majority in favor of Grant and negro suffrage, stood upon the platform and said that woman had better wait for the negro; that is, that both could not be carried, and that the negro had better be the one. But I freely forgave him because he felt as he spoke. But woman suffrage is more imperative than his own; and I want to remind the audience that when he says what the Ku-Kluxes did all over the South, the Ku-Kluxes here in the North in the shape of men, take away the children from the mother, and separate them as completely as if done on the block of the auctioneer. Over in New Jersey they have a law which says that *any* father—he might be the most brutal man that ever existed—*any* father, it says, whether he be under age or not, may by his last will and testament dispose of the custody of his child, born or to be born, and that such disposition shall be good against all persons, and that the mother may not recover her child; and that law modified in form exists over every State in the Union except in Kansas. Woman has an ocean of wrongs too deep for any plummet, and the negro, too, has an ocean of wrongs that can not be fathomed. There are two great oceans; in the one is the black man, and in the other is the woman. But I thank God for that XV. Amendment, and hope that it will be adopted in every State. I will be thankful in my soul if *any* body can get out of the terrible pit. But I believe that the safety of the government would be more promoted by the admission of woman as an element of restoration and harmony than the negro. I believe that the influence of woman will save the country before every other power. (Applause.) I see the signs of the times pointing to this consummation, and I believe that in some parts of the country women will vote for the President of these United States in 1872. (Applause.) ◠

Susan B. Anthony's Statement at the Close of Her Trial (1873)

The Court: The prisoner will stand up. Has the prisoner anything to say why sentence shall not be pronounced?

Miss Anthony: Yes, your honor, I have many things to say; for in your ordered verdict of guilty, you have trampled underfoot every vital principle of our government. My natural rights, my civil rights, my political rights, are all alike ignored. Robbed of the fundamental privilege of citizenship, I am degraded from

SOURCE: E.C. Stanton, Susan B. Anthony, and Matilda Joslyn Gage, *History of Woman Suffrage,* (New York: Fowler & Wells, 1882; reprint ed. New York: Arno Press, 1969), 2: 687–89.

the status of a citizen to that of a subject; and not only myself individually, but all of my sex, are, by your honor's verdict, doomed to political subjection under this so-called Republican government.

Judge Hunt: The Court can not listen to a rehearsal of arguments the prisoner's counsel has already consumed three hours in presenting.

Miss Anthony: May it please your honor, I am not arguing the question, but simply stating the reasons why sentence can not, in justice, be pronounced against me. Your denial of my citizen's right to vote is the denial of my right of consent as one of the governed, the denial of my right of representation as one of the taxed, the denial of my right to a trial by a jury of my peers as an offender against law, therefore, the denial of my sacred rights to life, liberty, property, and—

Judge Hunt: The Court can not allow the prisoner to go on.

Miss Anthony: But your honor will not deny me this one and only poor privilege of protest against this high-handed outrage upon my citizen's rights. May it please the Court to remember that since the day of my arrest last November, this is the first time that either myself or any person of my disfranchised class has been allowed a word of defense before judge or jury—

Judge Hunt: The prisoner must sit down; the Court can not allow it.

Miss Anthony: All my prosecutors, from the 8th Ward corner grocery politician, who entered the complaint, to the United States Marshal, Commissioner, District Attorney, District Judge, your honor on the bench, not one is my peer, but each and all are my political sovereigns; and had your honor submitted my case to the jury, as was clearly your duty, even when I should have had just cause of protest, for not one of those men was my peer; but, native or foreign, white or black, rich or poor, educated or ignorant, awake or asleep, sober or drunk, each and every man of them was my political superior; hence, in no sense, my peer. Even, under such circumstances, a commoner of England, tried before a jury of lords, would have far less cause to complain than should I, a woman, tried before a jury of men. Even my counsel, the Hon. Henry R. Selden, who has argued my cause so ably, so earnestly, so unanswerably before your honor, is my political sovereign. Precisely as no disfranchised person is entitled to sit upon a jury, and no woman is entitled to the franchise, so, none but a regularly admitted lawyer is allowed to practice in the courts, and no woman can gain admission to the bar—hence, jury,

judge, counsel, must all be of the superior class.

Judge Hunt: The Court must insist—the prisoner has been tried according to the established forms of law.

Miss Anthony: Yes, your honor, but by forms of law all made by men, interpreted by men, administered by men, in favor of men, and against women; and hence, your honor's ordered verdict of guilty, against a United States citizen for the exercise of "that citizen's right to vote," simply because that citizen was a woman and not a man. But, yesterday, the same man-made forms of law declared it a crime punishable with $1,000 fine and six months' imprisonment, for you, or me, or any of us, to give a cup of cold water, a crust of bread, or a night's shelter to a panting fugitive as he was tracking his way to Canada. And every man or woman in whose veins coursed a drop of human sympathy violated that wicked law, reckless of consequences, and was justified in so doing. As then the slaves who got their freedom must take it over, or under, or through the unjust forms of law, precisely so now must women, to get their right to a voice in this Government, take it; and I have taken mine, and mean to take it at every possible opportunity.

Judge Hunt: The Court orders the prisoner to sit down. It will not allow another word.

Miss Anthony: When I was brought before your honor for trial, I hoped for a broad and liberal interpretation of the Constitution and its recent amendments, that should declare all United States citizens under its protecting aegis—that should declare equality of rights the national guarantee to all persons born or naturalized in the United States. But failing to get this justice—failing, even, to get a trial by a jury *not* of my peers—I ask not leniency at your hands—but rather the full rigors of the law.

Judge Hunt: The Court must insist—(Here

the prisoner sat down.)

Judge Hunt: The prisoner will stand up. (Here Miss Anthony arose again.) The sentence of the Court is that you pay a fine of one hundred dollars and the costs of the prosecution.

Miss Anthony: May it please your honor, I shall never pay a dollar of your unjust penalty. All the stock in trade I possess is a $10,000 debt, incurred by publishing my paper—*The Revolution*—four years ago, the sole object of which was to educate all women to do precisely as I have done, rebel against your man-made, unjust, unconstitutional forms of law, that tax, fine, imprison, and hang women, while they deny them the right of representation in the Government; and I shall work on with might and main to pay every dollar of that honest debt, but not a penny shall go to this unjust claim. And I shall earnestly and persistently continue to urge all women to the practical recognition of the old revolutionary maxim, that "Resistance to tyranny is obedience to God."

Judge Hunt: Madam, the Court will not order you committed until the fine is paid. ⌒

Susan B. Anthony's Petition to Congress for Remission of Her Fine (1874)

Forty-third Congress, First Session, Senate, Mis. Doc. No. 39. A petition of Susan B. Anthony praying for the remission of a fine imposed upon her by the United States Court for the Northern District of New York, for illegal voting. January 22, 1874. Referred to the Committee on the Judiciary and ordered to be printed.

To the Congress of the United States:

The petition of Susan B. Anthony, of the city of Rochester, in the county of Monroe, and State of New York, respectfully represents: That, prior to the late presidential election, your petitioner applied to the Board of Registry in the Eighth Ward of the city of Rochester, in which city she had resided for more than twenty-five years, to have her name placed upon the register of voters; and the Board of Registry, after consideration of the subject, decided that your petitioner was entitled to have her name placed upon the register, and placed it there accordingly. On the day of election your petitioner, in common with hundreds of other American citizens, her neighbors, whose names had also been registered as voters, offered to the inspectors of election her ballots for electors of President and Vice-President, and for members of Congress, which were received and deposited in the ballot-box by the inspectors. For this act of your petitioner an indictment was found against her by the grand jury, at the sitting of the District Court of the United States for the Northern District of New York, at Albany, charging your petitioner, under the nineteenth section of the act of Congress of May 31, 1870, entitled "An act to enforce the rights of citizens of the United States to vote in the several States of this Union, and for other purposes," with having "knowingly voted without having a lawful right to vote."

SOURCE: E.C. Stanton, Susan B. Anthony, and Matilda Joslyn Gage, *History of Woman Suffrage*, (New York: Fowler & Wells, 1882; reprint ed., New York: Arno Press, 1969), 2: 698–700.

To that indictment your petitioner pleaded not guilty, and the trial of the issue thus joined took place at the Circuit Court in Canandaigua, in the county of Ontario, before the Honorable Ward Hunt, one of the Justices of the Supreme Court of the United States, on the 18th day of June last. Upon that trial the facts of voting by your petitioner, and that she was a woman, were not denied; nor was it claimed on the part of the Government than your petitioner lacked any of the qualifications of a voter, unless disqualified by reason of her sex. It was shown on behalf of your petitioner, on the trial, that before voting she called upon a respectable lawyer and asked his opinion whether she had a right to vote, and he advised her that she had such right, and the lawyer was examined as a witness in her behalf, and testified that he gave her such advice, and that he gave it in good faith, believing that she had such right. It also appeared that when she offered to vote, the question whether, as a woman, she had a right to vote, was raised by the inspectors, and considered by them in her presence, and they decided that she had a right to vote, and received her vote accordingly.

It was shown on the part of the Government that, on the examination of your petitioner before the commissioner on whose warrant she was arrested, your petitioner stated that she should have voted if allowed to vote, without reference to the advice of the attorney whose opinion she asked; that she was not induced to vote by that opinion; that she had before determined to offer her vote, and had no doubt about her right to vote. At the close of the testimony, your petitioner's counsel proceeded to address the jury, and stated that he desired to present for consideration three propositions, two of law, and one of fact: 1. That your petitioner had a lawful right to vote. 2. That whether she had a right to vote or not, if she honestly believed that she had that right, and voted in good faith in that belief, she was guilty of no crime. 3. That when your petitioner gave her vote she gave it in good faith, believing that it was her right to do so.

That the two first propositions presented questions for the court to decide, and the last question for the jury. When your petitioner's counsel had proceeded thus far, the judge suggested that the counsel had better discuss, in the first place, the questions of law, which the counsel proceeded to do; and, having discussed the two legal questions at length, asked then to say a few words to the jury on the question of fact. The judge then said to the counsel that he thought that had better be left until the views of the court upon the legal questions should be made known.

The district attorney thereupon addressed the court at length upon the legal questions; and at the close of his argument the judge delivered an opinion adverse to the positions of your petitioner's counsel upon both of the legal questions presented, holding that your petitioner was not entitled to vote; and that if she voted in good faith in the belief in fact that she had a right to vote, it would constitute no defense; the ground of the decision on the last point being that your petitioner was bound to know that by the law she was not a legal voter, and that even if she voted in good faith in the contrary belief, it constituted no defense to the crime with which she was charged.

The decision of the judge upon those questions was read from a written document, and at the close of the reading the judge said that the decision of those questions disposed of the case and left no question of fact for the jury, and that he should therefore direct the jury to find a verdict of guilty. The judge then said to the jury that the decision of the court had disposed of all there was in the case, and that he directed them to find a verdict of guilty; and he instructed the clerk to enter such a verdict.

At this time, before any entry had been

made by the clerk, your petitioner's counsel asked the judge to submit the case to the jury, and to give to the jury the following several instructions.

The judge declined to submit the case to the jury upon any question whatever, and directed them to render a verdict of guilty against your petitioner. Your petitioner's counsel excepted to the decision of the judge upon the legal questions, and to his direction to the jury to find a verdict of guilty, insisting that it was a direction which no court had a right to give in any criminal case.

The judge then instructed the clerk to take the verdict, and the clerk said, "Gentlemen of the jury, hearken to your verdict as the court hath recorded it. You say you find the defendant guilty of the offense charged; so say you all." No response whatever was made by the jury, either by word or sign. They had not consulted together in their seats or otherwise. Neither of them had spoken a word, nor had they been asked whether they had or had not agreed upon a verdict. Your petitioner's counsel then asked that the clerk be requested to poll the jury. The judge said, "That can not be allowed. Gentlemen of the jury, you are discharged;" and the jurors left the box. No juror spoke a word during the trial, from the time when they were empaneled to the time of their discharge. After denying a motion for a new trial, the judge proceeded upon the conviction thus obtained to pass sentence upon your petitioner, imposing upon her a fine of $100 and the costs of the prosecution.

Your petitioner respectfully submits that, in these proceedings, she has been denied the rights guaranteed by the Constitution to all persons accused of crime, the right of trial by jury, and the right to have the assistance of counsel for their defense. It is a mockery to call her trial a trial by jury; and unless the assistance of counsel may be limited to the argument of legal questions, without the privilege of saying a word to the jury upon the question of the guilt or innocence in fact of the party charged, or the privilege of ascertaining from the jury whether they do or do not agree to the verdict pronounced by the court in their name, she has been denied the assistance of counsel for her defense.

Your petitioner also respectfully insists that the decision of the judge that good faith on the part of your petitioner in offering her vote did not constitute a defense, was not only a violation of the deepest and most sacred principle of the criminal law, that no one can be guilty of crime unless a criminal intent exists; but was also a palpable violation of the statute under which the conviction was had; not on the ground that good faith could, in this, or in any case, justify a criminal act, but on the ground that bad faith in voting was an indispensable ingredient in the offense with which your petitioner was charged. Any other interpretation strikes the word "knowingly" out of the statute, the word which alone describes the essence of the offense. The statute means, as your petitioner is advised, and humbly submits, a knowledge in fact, not a knowledge falsely imputed by law to a party not possessing it in fact, as the judge in this case has held. Crimes can not, either in law or in morals, be established by judicial falsehood. If there be any crime in the case, your petitioner humbly insists it is to be found in such an adjudication.

To the decision of the judge upon the question of the right of your petitioner to vote, she makes no complaint. It was a question properly belonging to the court to decide, was fully and fairly submitted to the judge, and of his decision, whether right or wrong, your petitioner is well aware she can not here complain. But in regard to her conviction of crime, which she insists, for the reasons above given, was in violation of the principles of the common law, of common morality, of the statute under which she was charged, and of the Constitution—a crime of which she was as innocent as the judge by whom she was convicted—she respectfully asks, inasmuch as the law has provided no means of reviewing the decisions of the judge, or of correcting his errors, that the fine imposed upon your petitioner be remitted, as an expression of the sense of this high tribunal that her conviction was unjust.

Dated January 12, 1874.

Susan B. Anthony ∾

Secondary Sources

Anthony, Katherine Susan. *Susan B. Anthony: Her Personal History and Her Era.* New York: Russell and Russell, 1975.

Barry, Kathleen. *Susan B. Anthony: A Biography of a Singular Feminist.* New York: Ballantine Books, 1988.

Harper, Ida (Husted). *The Life and Work of Susan B. Anthony: Including Public Addresses, Her Own Letters and Many from Her Contemporaries during Fifty Years.* Indianapolis and Kansas City: Bowen-Merrill, 1898–1908.

Lutz, Alma. *Susan B. Anthony: Rebel, Crusader, Humanitarian.* Boston: Beacon Press, 1959.

24. William Graham Sumner

WILLIAM GRAHAM SUMNER (1840–1910) was born in Paterson, New Jersey. His father, an uneducated immigrant worker but nevertheless a reader and thinker, exerted a strong influence on him. Educated in the public schools of Hartford, Connecticut, Sumner entered Yale in 1859. At Yale his outstanding academic record won him lasting prominent friends, who helped him go abroad after graduation in 1863 for further study. For the next three years Sumner studied for the ministry at Geneva, Göttingen, and Oxford. Returning to the United States, he was an instructor at Yale from 1866 to 1869. During this same period Sumner was admitted to the diaconate of the Episcopal church; by 1870 he had become rector of a church in Morristown, New Jersey.

As his interest turned increasingly to questions of social and political import, Sumner found that he could not express himself freely in the pulpit. Accordingly, in 1872 he accepted the newly created chair of political and social science at Yale University, where he remained for the rest of his career.

Sumner's activities were not confined to his academic duties. From 1873 to 1876 he was a member of New Haven's board of aldermen; from 1882 to 1910 he was an active member of the Connecticut state board of education and contributed much to the improvement of the public schools. His extensive research into the origins of institutions ranked Sumner among the foremost scholars in this field, and he did much to develop the academic study of sociology in the United States.

He is represented here by two selections. The first is from his major political work, *What Social Classes Owe to Each Other.* Perhaps better than any other, this book expresses the dominant individualist, Social Darwinist, laissez-faire ethos of the late nineteenth century. But it is also a consistent, principled statement of liberalism and far from being a mere self-serving defense of the status quo. The second selection is from *The Conquest of the United States by Spain,* another example of the respectable principles underlying Sumner's positions. Here he is concerned about the domestic consequences of imperialistic adventures. ᕈ

What Social Classes Owe to Each Other (1884)

We are told every day that great social problems stand before us and demand a solution, and we are assailed by oracles, threats, and warnings in reference to those problems. There is a school of writers who are playing quite a role as the heralds of the coming duty and the coming woe. They assume to speak for a large, but vague and undefined, constituency, who set the task, exact a fulfillment, and threaten punishment for default. The task or problem is not specifically defined. Part of the task which devolves on those who are subject to the duty is to define the problem. They are told only that something is the matter; that it behooves them to find out what it is, and how to correct it, and then to work out the cure. All this is more or less truculently set forth. After reading and listening to a great deal of this sort of assertion I find that the question forms itself with more and more distinctness in my mind: Who are those who assume to put hard questions to other people and to demand a solution of them? How did they acquire the right to demand that others should solve their world-problems for them? Who are they who

SOURCE: William Graham Sumner, *What Social Classes Owe to Each Other* (New York: Harper Brothers, 1884).

are held to consider and solve all questions, and how did they fall under this duty?

So far as I can find out what the classes are who are respectively endowed with the rights and duties of posing and solving social problems, they are as follows: Those who are bound to solve the problems are the rich, comfortable, prosperous, virtuous, respectable, educated, and healthy; those whose right it is to set the problems are those who have been less fortunate or less successful in the struggle for existence. The problem itself seems to be, How shall the latter be made as comfortable as the former? To solve this problem, and make us all equally well off, is assumed to be the duty of the former class; the penalty, if they fail of this, is to be bloodshed and destruction. If they cannot make everybody else as well off as themselves, they are to be brought down to the same misery as others.

During the last ten years I have read a great many books and articles, especially by German writers, in which an attempt has been made to set up "the State" as an entity having conscience, power, and will sublimated above human limitations, and as constituting a tutelary genius over us all. I have never been able to find in history or experience anything to fit this concept. I once lived in Germany for two years, but I certainly saw nothing of it there then. Whether the State which Bismarck is moulding will fit the notion is at best a matter of faith and hope. My notion of the State has dwindled with growing experience of life. As an abstraction, the State is to me only All-of-us. In practice—that is, when it exercises will or adopts a line of action—it is only a little group of men chosen in a very haphazard way by the majority of us to perform certain services for all of us. The majority do not go about their selection very rationally, and they are almost always disappointed by the results of their own operation. Hence "the State," instead of offering resources of wisdom, right reason, and pure moral sense beyond what the average of us possess, generally offers much less of all those things. Furthermore, it often turns out in practice that "the State" is not even the known and accredited servants of the State, but, as has been well said, is only some obscure clerk, hidden in the recesses of a Government bureau, into whose power the chance has fallen for the moment to pull one of the stops which control the Government machine. . . .

The little group of public servants who, as I have said, constitute the State, when the State determines on anything, could not do much for themselves or anybody else by their own force. If they do anything, they must dispose of men, as in an army, or of capital, as in a treasury. But the army, or police, or *posse comitatus,* is more or less All-of-us, and the capital in the treasury is the product of the labor and saving of All-of-us. Therefore, when the State means power-to-do it means All-of-us, as brute force or as industrial force.

If anybody is to benefit from the action of the State it must be Some-of-us. If, then, the question is raised, What ought the State to do for labor, for trade, for manufactures, for the poor, for the learned professions? etc., etc. —that is, for a class or an interest—it is really the question, What ought All-of-us to do for

Some-of-us? But Some-of-us are included in All-of-us, and, so far as they get the benefit of their own efforts, it is the same as if they worked for themselves, and they may be cancelled out of All-of-us. Then the question which remains is, What ought Some-of-us to do for Others-of-us? or, What do social classes owe to each other?

I now propose to try to find out whether there is any class in society which lies under the duty and burden of fighting the battles of life for any other class, or of solving social problems for the satisfaction of any other class; also, whether there is any class which has the right to formulate demands on "society"—that is, on other classes; also, whether there is anything but a fallacy and a superstition in the notion that "the State" owes anything to anybody except peace, order, and the guarantees of rights. . . .

I. ON A NEW PHILOSOPHY: THAT POVERTY IS THE BEST POLICY

It is commonly asserted that there are in the United States no classes, and any allusion to classes is resented. On the other hand, we constantly read and hear discussions of social topics in which the existence of social classes is assumed as a simple fact. "The poor," "the weak," "the laborers," are expressions which are used as if they had exact and well-understood definitions. Discussions are made to bear upon the assumed rights, wrongs, and misfortunes of certain social classes; and all public speaking and writing consists, in a large measure, of the discussion of general plans for meeting the wishes of classes of people who have not been able to satisfy their own desires. These classes are sometimes discontented, and sometimes not. Sometimes they are discontented and envious. They do not take their achievements as a fair measure of their rights. They do not blame themselves or their parents for their lot, as compared with that of other people. Sometimes they claim that they have a right to everything of which they feel the need for their happiness on earth. To make such a claim against God and Nature would, of course, be only to say that we claim a right to live on earth if we can. But God and Nature have ordained the chances and conditions of life on earth once for all. The case cannot be reopened. We cannot get a revision of the laws of human life. We are absolutely shut up to the need and duty, if we would learn how to live happily, of investigating the laws of Nature, and deducing the rules of right living in the world as it is. These are very wearisome and commonplace tasks. They consist in labor and self-denial repeated over and over again in learning and doing. When the people whose claims we are considering are told to apply themselves to these tasks they become irritated and feel almost insulted. They formulate their claims as rights against society—that is, against some other men. In their view they have a right, not only to *pursue* happiness, but to *get* it; and if they fail to get, they think they have a claim to the aid of other men—that is, to the labor and self-denial of other men—to get it for them. They find orators and poets who tell them that they have grievances, so long as they have unsatisfied desires. . . .

Certain ills belong to the hardships of human life. They are natural. They are part of the struggle with Nature for existence. We cannot blame our fellowmen for our share of these. My neighbor and I are both struggling to free ourselves from these ills. The fact that my neighbor has succeeded in this struggle better than I constitutes no grievance for me. Certain other ills are due to the malice of men, and to the imperfections or errors of civil institutions. These ills are an object of agitation, and a subject of discussion. The former class of ills is to be met only by manly effort and energy; the latter may be corrected by associated effort. The former class of ills is constantly

grouped and generalized, and made the object of social schemes. We shall see, as we go on, what that means. The second class of ills may fall on certain social classes, and reform will take the form of interference by other classes in favor of that one. The last fact is, no doubt, the reason why people have been led, not noticing distinctions, to believe that the same method was applicable to the other class of ills. The distinction here made between the ills which belong to the struggle and those which are due to the faults of human institutions is of prime importance. . . .

The humanitarians, philanthropists, and reformers, looking at the facts of life as they present themselves, find enough which is sad and unpromising in the condition of many members of society. They see wealth and poverty side by side. They note great inequality of social position and social chances. They eagerly set about the attempt to account for what they see, and to devise schemes for remedying what they do not like. In their eagerness to recommend the less fortunate classes to pity and consideration they forget all about the rights of other classes; they gloss over all the faults of the classes in question, and they exaggerate their misfortunes and their virtues. They invent new theories of property, distorting rights and perpetuating injustice, as anyone is sure to do who sets about the readjustment of social relations with the interests of one group distinctly before his mind, and the interests of all other groups thrown into the background. When I have read certain of these discussions I have thought that it must be quite disreputable to be respectable, quite dishonest to own property, quite unjust to go one's own way and earn one's own living, and that the only really admirable person was the good-for-nothing. The man who by his own effort raises himself above poverty appears, in these discussions, to be of no account. The man who has done nothing to raise himself above poverty finds that the social doctors flock about him, bringing the capital which they have collected from the other class, and promising him the aid of the State to give him what the other had to work for. In all these schemes and projects the organized intervention of society through the State is either planned or hoped for, and the State is thus made to become the protector and guardian of certain classes. The agents who are to direct the State action are, of course, the reformers and philanthropists. Their schemes, therefore, may always be reduced to this type—that A and B decide what C shall do for D. It will be interesting to inquire, at a later period of our discussion, who C is, and what the effect is upon him of all these arrangements. In all the discussions attention is concentrated on A and B, the noble social reformers, and on D, the "poor man." I call C the Forgotten Man, because I have never seen that any notice was taken of him in any of the discussions. When we have disposed of A, B, and D we can better appreciate the case of C, and I think that we shall find that he deserves our attention, for the worth of his character and the magnitude of his unmerited burdens. Here it may suffice to observe that, on the theories of the social philosophers to whom I have referred, we should get a new maxim of judicious living: Poverty is the best policy. If you get wealth, you will have to support other people; if you do not get wealth, it will be the duty of other people to support you.

No doubt one chief reason for the unclear and contradictory theories of class relations lies in the fact that our society, largely controlled in all its organization by one set of doctrines, still contains survivals of old social theories which are totally inconsistent with the former. In the Middle Ages men were united by custom and prescription into associations, ranks, guilds, and communities of various kinds. These ties endured as long as life lasted.

Consequently society was dependent, throughout all its details, on status, and the tie, or bond, was sentimental. In our modern state, and in the United States more than anywhere else, the social structure is based on contract, and status is of the least importance. Contract, however, is rational—even rationalistic. It is also realistic, cold, and matter-of-fact. A contract relation is based on a sufficient reason, not on custom or prescription. It is not permanent. It endures only so long as the reason for it endures. In a state based on contract, sentiment is out of place in any public or common affairs. It is relegated to the sphere of private and personal relations, where it depends not at all on class types, but on personal acquaintance and personal estimates. The sentimentalists among us always seize upon the survivals of the old order. They want to save them and restore them. Much of the loose thinking also which troubles us in our social discussions arises from the fact that men do not distinguish the elements of status and of contract which may be found in our society.

Whether social philosophers think it desirable or not, it is out of the question to go back to status or to the sentimental relations which once united baron and retainer, master and servant, teacher and pupil, comrade and comrade. That we have lost some grace and elegance is undeniable. That life once held more poetry and romance is true enough. But it seems impossible that any one who has studied the matter should doubt that we have gained immeasurably, and that our farther gains lie in going forward, not in going backward. The feudal ties can never be restored. If they could be restored they would bring back personal caprice, favoritism, sycophancy, and intrigue. A society based on contract is a society of free and independent men, who form ties without favor or obligation, and co-operate without cringing or intrigue. A society based on contract, therefore, gives the utmost room and chance for individual development, and for all the self-reliance and dignity of a free man. That a society of free men, cooperating under contract, is by far the strongest society which has ever yet existed; that no such society has ever yet developed the full measure of strength of which it is capable; and that the only social improvements which are now conceivable lie in the direction of more complete realization of a society of free men united by contract, are points which cannot be controverted. It followed, however, that one man, in a free state, cannot claim help from and cannot be charged to give help to, another. To understand the full meaning of this assertion it will be worth while to see what a free democracy is. . . .

History is only a tiresome repetition of one story. Persons and classes have sought to win possession of the power of the State in order to live luxuriously out of the earnings of others. Autocracies, aristocracies, theocracies, and all other organizations for holding political power, have exhibited only the same line of action. It is the extreme of political error to say that if political power is only taken away from generals, nobles, priests, millionaires, and scholars, and given to artisans and peasants, these latter may be trusted to do only right and justice, and never to abuse the power; that they will repress all excess in others, and commit none themselves. They will commit abuse, if they can and dare, just as others have done. The reason for the excesses of the old governing classes lies in the vices and passions of human nature—cupidity, lust, vindictiveness, ambition, and vanity. These vices are confined to no nation, class, or age. They appear in the church, the academy, the workshop, and the hovel, as well as in the army or the palace. They have appeared in autocracies, aristocracies, theocracies, democracies, and ochlocracies, all alike. The only thing which has ever restrained these vices of human nature in those who had political power is law sustained by impersonal institutions. If political power be given to the masses who have not hitherto had it, nothing will stop them from abusing it but laws and institutions. To say that a popular government cannot be paternal is to give it a charter that it can do no wrong. The trouble is that a democratic government is in greater danger than any other of becoming paternal, for it is sure of itself, and ready to undertake anything, and its power is excessive and pitiless against dissentients. . . .

The notion of civil liberty which we have inherited is that of *a status created for the individual by laws and institutions, the effect of which is that each man is guaranteed the use of all his own powers exclusively for his own welfare.* It is not at all a matter of elections, or universal suffrage, or democracy. All institutions are to be tested by the degree to which they guarantee liberty. It is not to be admitted for a moment that liberty is a means to social ends, and that it may be impaired for major considerations. Any one who so argues has lost the bearing and relation of all the facts and factors in a free state. A human being has a life to live, a career to run. He is a centre of powers to work, and of capacities to suffer. What his powers may be—whether they can carry him far or not; what his chances may be, whether wide or restricted; what his fortune may be, whether to suffer much or little—are questions of his personal destiny which he must work out and endure as he can; but for all that concerns the bearing of the society and its institutions upon that man, and upon the sum of happiness to which he can attain during his life on earth, the product of all history and all philosophy up to this time is summed up in the doctrine, that he should be left free to do the most for himself that he can, and should be guaranteed the exclusive enjoyment of all that he does. If the society—that is to say, in plain terms, if his fellow-men, either individually, by groups, or in a mass—impinge upon him otherwise than to surround him with neutral conditions of security, they must do so under the strictest responsibility to justify themselves. Jealousy and prejudice against all such interferences are high political virtues in a free man. It is not at all the function of the State to make men happy. They must make themselves happy in their own way, and at their own risk. The functions of the State lie entirely in the conditions or chances which can be affected by civil organization. Hence, liberty for labor and security for earnings are the ends for which civil institutions exist, not means which may be employed for ulterior ends. The free man who steps forward to claim his inheritance and endowment as a free and equal member of a great civil body must understand that his duties and responsibilities are measured to him by the same scale as his rights and his powers. He wants to be subject to no man. He wants to be equal to his fellows, as all sovereigns are equal. So be it; but he cannot escape the deduction that he can call no man to his aid. The other sovereigns will not respect his independence if he becomes dependent, and they cannot respect his equality if he sues for favors. The free man in a free democracy, [is free only] when he cut off all the ties by which he might have made others pull him up. He must take all the consequences of his new status. He is, in a certain sense, an isolated man. The family tie does not bring to him disgrace for the misdeeds of his relatives, as it once would have done, but neither does it furnish him with the support which it once would have given. The relations of men are open and free, but they are also loose. A free man in a free democracy derogates from his rank if he takes a favor for which he does not render an equivalent.

A free man in a free democracy has no duty whatever toward other men of the same rank and standing, except respect, courtesy, and good-will. We cannot say that there are no classes, when we are speaking politically, and then say that there are classes, when we are telling A what it is his duty to do for B. In a free state every man is held and expected to take care of himself and his family, to make no trouble for his neighbor, and to contribute his full share to public interests and common necessities. If he fails in this he throws burdens on others. He does not thereby acquire rights against the others. On the contrary, he only accumulates obligations toward them; and if he is allowed to make his deficiencies a ground of new claims, he passes over into the position of a privileged or petted person—emancipated from duties, endowed with claims. This is the inevitable result of combining democratic political theories with humanitarian social theories. It would be aside from my present purpose to show, but it is worth noticing in passing, that one result of such inconsistency must surely be to undermine democracy, to increase the power of wealth in the democracy, and to hasten the subjection of democracy to plutocracy; for a man who accepts any share which he has not earned in another man's capital cannot be an independent citizen....

The aggregation of large fortunes is not at all a thing to be regretted. On the contrary, it is a necessary condition of many forms of social advance. If we should set a limit to the accumulation of wealth, we should say to our most valuable producers, "We do not want you to do us the services which you best understand how to perform, beyond a certain point," it would be like killing off our generals in war....

Undoubtedly the man who possesses capital has a great advantage over the man who has no capital, in all the struggle for existence. Think of two men who want to lift a weight, one of whom has a lever, and the other must apply his hands directly; think of two men tilling the soil, one of whom uses his hands or a stick, while the other has a horse and a plough; think of two men in conflict with a wild animal, one of whom has only a stick or a stone, while the other has a repeating rifle; think of two men who are sick, one of whom can travel, command medical skill, get space, light, air and water, while the other lacks all these things. This does not mean that one man has an advantage *against* the other, but that, when they are rivals in the effort to get the means of subsistence from Nature, the one who has capital has immeasurable advantages over the other. If it were not so capital would not be formed. Capital is only formed by self-denial, and if the possession of it did not secure advantages and superiorities of a high order men would never submit to what is necessary to get it. The first accumulation costs by far the most, and the rate of increase by profits at first seems pitiful. Among the metaphors which partially illustrate capital—all of which, however, are imperfect and inadequate—the snow-ball is useful to show some facts about capital. Its first accumulation is slow, but as it proceeds the accumulation becomes rapid in a high ratio, and the element of self-denial declines. This fact, also, is favorable to the accumulation of capital, for if the self-denial continued to be as great per unit when the accumulation had become great, there would speedily come a point at which further accumulation would not pay. The man who has capital has secured his future, won leisure which he can employ in winning secondary objects of necessity and advantage, and emancipated himself from those things in life which are gross and belittling. The possession of capital is, therefore, an indispensable prerequisite of educational, scientific, and moral goods. This is not saying that a man in the narrowest circumstances may not be a good man. It is saying that the extension and elevation of all the moral and metaphysical interests of the race are conditioned on that extension of civilization of which capital is the prerequisite,

and that he who has capital can participate in and move along with the highest developments of his time. Hence it appears that the man who has his self-denial before him, however good may be his intention, cannot be as the man who has his self-denial behind him. Some seem to think that this is very unjust, but they get their notions of justice from some occult source of inspiration, not from observing the facts of this world as it has been made and exists.

The maxim, or injunction, to which a study of capital leads us is, Get capital. In a community where the standard of living is high, and the conditions of production are favorable, there is a wide margin within which an individual may practice self-denial and win capital without suffering, if he has not the charge of a family. That it requires energy, courage, perseverance, and prudence is not to be denied. Any one who believes that any good thing on this earth can be got without those virtues may believe in the philosopher's stone or the fountain of youth. If there were any Utopia its inhabitants would certainly be very insipid and characterless.

Those who have neither capital nor land unquestionably have a closer class interest than landlords or capitalists. If one of those who are in either of the latter classes is a spendthrift he loses his advantage. If the non-capitalists increase their numbers, they surrender themselves into the hands of the landlords and capitalists. They compete with each other for food until they run up the rent of land, and they compete with each other for wages until they give the capitalist a great amount of productive energy for a given amount of capital. If some of them are economical and prudent in the midst of a class which saves nothing and marries early, the few prudent suffer for the folly of the rest, since they can only get current rates of wages; and if these are low the margin out of which to make savings by special personal effort is narrow. No instance has yet been seen of a society composed of a class of great capitalists and class of laborers who had fallen into a caste of permanent drudges. Probably no such thing is possible so long as landlords especially remain as a third class, and so long as society continues to develop strong classes of merchants, financiers, professional men, and other classes. If it were conceivable that non-capitalist laborers should give up struggling to become capitalists, should give way to vulgar enjoyments and passions, should recklessly increase their numbers, and should become a permanent caste, they might with some justice be called proletarians. The name has been adopted by some professed labor leaders, but it really should be considered insulting. If there were such a proletariat it would be hopelessly in the hands of a body of plutocratic capitalists, and a society so organized would, no doubt, be far worse than a society composed only of nobles and serfs, which is the worst society the world has seen in modern times.

At every turn, therefore, it appears that the number of men and the quality of men limit each other, and that the question whether we shall have more men or better men is of most importance to the class which has neither land nor capital....

The history of the human race is one long story of attempts by certain persons and classes to obtain control of the power of the State, so as to win earthly gratifications at the expense of others. People constantly assume that there is something metaphysical and sentimental about government. At bottom there are two chief things with which government has to deal. They are, the property of men and the honor of women. These it has to defend against crime. The capital which, as we have seen, is the condition of all welfare on earth, the fortification of existence, and the means of growth, is an object of cupidity. Some want to

get it without paying the price of industry and economy. In ancient times they made use of force. They organized bands of robbers. They plundered laborers and merchants. Chief of all, however, they found that means of robbery which consisted in gaining control of the civil organization—the State—and using its poetry and romance as a glamour under cover of which they made robbery lawful. They developed high-spun theories of nationality, patriotism, and loyalty. They took all the rank, glory, power, and prestige of the great civil organization, and they took all the rights. They threw on others the burdens and the duties. At one time, no doubt, feudalism was an organization which drew together again the fragments of a dissolved society, but when the lawyers had applied the Roman law to modern kings, and feudal nobles had been converted into an aristocracy of court nobles, the feudal nobility no longer served any purpose.

In modern times the great phenomenon has been the growth of the middle class out of the mediaeval cities, the accumulation of wealth, and the encroachment of wealth, as a social power, on the ground formerly occupied by rank and birth. The middle class has been obliged to fight for its rights against the feudal class, and it has, during three or four centuries, gradually invented and established institutions to guarantee personal and property rights against the arbitrary will of kings and nobles.

In its turn wealth is now becoming a power in three or four countries, gradually invented by the State, and, like every other power, it is liable to abuse unless restrained by checks and guarantees. There is an insolence of wealth, as there is an insolence of rank. A plutocracy might be even far worse than an aristocracy. Aristocrats have always had their class vices and their class virtues. They have always been, as a class, chargeable with licentiousness and gambling. They have, however, as a class, despised lying and stealing. They have always pretended to maintain a standard of honor, although the definition and the code of honor have suffered many changes and shocking deterioration. The middle class has always abhorred gambling and licentiousness, but it has not always been strict about truth and pecuniary fidelity. That there is a code and standard of mercantile honor which is quite as pure and grand as any military code, is beyond question, but it has never yet been established and defined by long usage and the concurrent support of a large and influential society. The feudal code has, through centuries, bred a high type of men, and constituted a caste. The mercantile code has not yet done so, but the wealthy class has attempted to merge itself in or to imitate the feudal class.

The consequence is, that the wealth-power has been developed, while the moral and social sanctions by which that power ought to be controlled have not yet been developed. A plutocracy would be a civil organization in which the power resides in wealth, in which a man might have whatever he could buy, in which the rights, interests, and feelings of those who could not pay would be overridden.

There is a plain tendency of all civilized governments toward plutocracy. The power of wealth in the English House of Commons has steadily increased for fifty years. The history of the present French Republic has shown an extraordinary development of plutocratic spirit and measures. In the United States many plutocratic doctrines have a currency which is not granted them anywhere else; that is, a man's right to have almost anything which he can pay for is more popularly recognized here than elsewhere. So far the most successful limitation on plutocracy has come from aristocracy, for the prestige of rank is still great wherever it exists. The social sanctions of aristocracy fell with great force on the plutocrats, more especially on their wives and daughters. It has al-

ready resulted that a class of wealthy men is growing up in regard to whom the old sarcasms of the novels and the stage about *parvenus* are entirely thrown away. They are men who have no superiors, by whatever standard one chooses to measure them. Such an interplay of social forces would, indeed, be a great and happy solution of a new social problem, if the aristocratic forces were strong enough for the magnitude of the task. If the feudal aristocracy, or its modern representative—which is, in reality, not at all feudal —could carry down into the new era and transmit to the new masters of society the grace, elegance, breeding, and culture of the past, society would certainly gain by that course of things, as compared with any such rupture between past and present as occurred in the French Revolution. The dogmatic radicals who assail "on principle" the inherited social notions and distinctions are not serving civilization. Society can do without patricians, but it cannot do without patrician virtues.

In the United States the opponent of plutocracy is democracy. Nowhere else in the world has the power of wealth come to be discussed in its political aspects as it is here. Nowhere else does the question arise as it does here. I have given some reasons for this in former chapters. Nowhere in the world is the danger of plutocracy as formidable as it is here. To it we appose the power of numbers as it is presented by democracy. Democracy itself, however, is new and experimental. It has not yet existed long enough to find its appropriate forms. It has no prestige from antiquity such as aristocracy possesses. It has, indeed, none of the surroundings which appeal to the imagination. On the other hand, democracy is rooted in the physical, economic, and social circumstances of the United States. This country cannot be other than democratic for an indefinite period in the future. Its political processes will also be republican. The affection of the people for democracy makes them blind and uncritical in regard to it, and they are as fond of the political fallacies to which democracy lends itself as they are of its sound and correct interpretation, or fonder. Can democracy develop itself and at the same time curb plutocracy?...

For now I come to the particular point which I desire to bring forward against all the denunciations and complainings about the power of chartered corporations and aggregated capital. If charters have been given which confer undue powers, who gave them? Our legislators did. Who elected these legislators? We did. If we are a free, self-governing people, we must understand that it costs vigilance and exertion to be self-governing. It costs far more vigilance and exertion to be so under the democratic form, where we have no aids from tradition or prestige, than under other forms. If we are a free, self-governing people, we can blame nobody but ourselves for our misfortunes. No one will come to help us out of them. It will do no good to heap law upon law, or to try by constitutional provisions simply to abstain from the use of powers which we find we always abuse. How can we get bad legislators to pass a law which shall hinder bad legislators from passing a bad law? That is what we are trying to do by many of our proposed remedies. The task before us, however, is one which calls for fresh reserves of moral force and political virtue from the very foundations of the social body. Surely it is not a new thing to us to learn that men are greedy and covetous, and that they will be selfish and tyrannical if they dare. The plutocrats are simply trying to do what the generals, nobles, and priests have done in the past—get the power of the State into their hands, so as to bend the rights of others to their own advantage; and what we need to do is to recognize the fact that we are face to face with the same old foes—the vices and passions of human nature. One of the oldest and most

mischievous fallacies in this country has been the notion that we are better than other nations, and that Government has a smaller and easier task here than elsewhere. This fallacy has hindered us from recognizing our old foes as soon as we should have done. Then, again, these vices and passions take good care here to deck themselves out in the trappings of democratic watchwords and phrases, so that they are more often greeted with cheers than with opposition when they first appear. The plan of electing men to represent us who systematically surrender public to private interests, and then trying to cure the mischief by newspaper and platform declamation against capital and corporations, is an entire failure.

The new foes must be met, as the old ones were met—by institutions and guarantees. The problem of civil liberty is constantly renewed. Solved once, it re-appears in a new form. The old constitutional guarantees were all aimed against king and nobles. New ones must be invented to hold the power of wealth to that responsibility without which no power whatever is consistent with liberty. The judiciary has given the most satisfactory evidence that it is competent to the new duty which devolves upon it. The courts have proved, in every case in which they have been called upon, that there are remedies, that they are adequate, and that they can be brought to bear upon the cases. The chief need seems to be more power of voluntary combination and cooperation among those who are aggrieved. Such cooperation is a constant necessity under free self-government; and when, in any community, men lose the power of voluntary cooperation in furtherance or defense of their own interests, they deserve to suffer, with no other remedy than newspaper denunciations and platform declamations. Of course, in such a state of things, political mountebanks come forward and propose fierce measures which can be paraded for political effect. Such measures would be hostile to all our institutions, would destroy capital, overthrow credit, and impair the most essential interests of society. On the side of political machinery there is no ground for hope, but only for fear. On the side of constitutional guarantees and the independent action of self-governing freemen there is every ground for hope. . . .

Every man and woman in society has one big duty. That is, to take care of his or her own self. This is a social duty. For, fortunately, the matter stands so that the duty of making the best of one's self individually is not a separate thing from the duty of filling one's place in society, but the two are one, and the latter is accomplished when the former is done. The common notion, however, seems to be that one has a duty to society, as a special and separate thing, and that this duty consists in considering and deciding what other people ought to do. Now, the man who can do anything for or about anybody else than himself is fit to be head of a family; and when he becomes head of a family he has duties to his wife and his children, in addition to the former big duty. Then, again, any man who can take care of himself and his family is in a very exceptional position, and his family is in a very exceptional position, if he does not find in his immediate surroundings people who need his care and have some sort of a personal claim upon him. If, now, he is able to fulfill all this, and to take care of anybody outside his family and his dependents, he must have a surplus of energy, wisdom, and moral virtue beyond what he needs for his own business. No man has this; for a family is a charge which is capable of infinite development, and no man could suffice to the full measure of duty for which a family may draw upon him. Neither can a man give to society so advantageous an employment of his services, whatever they are, in any other way as by spending them on his family. Upon this, however, I will not insist. I recur to

the observation that a man who proposes to take care of other people must have himself and his family taken care of, after some sort of a fashion, and must have an as yet unexhausted store of energy.

The danger of minding other people's business is twofold. First, there is the danger that a man may leave his own business unattended to; and, second, there is the danger of an impertinent interference with another's affairs. The "friends of humanity" almost always run into both dangers. I am one of humanity, and I do not want any volunteer friends. I regard friendship as mutual, and I want to have my say about it. I suppose that other components of humanity feel in the same way about it. If so, they must regard any one who assumes the *role* of a friend of humanity as impertinent. The reference to the friend of humanity back to his own business is obviously the next step. . . .

The amateur social doctors are like the amateur physicians—they always begin with the question of *remedies,* and they go at this without any diagnosis or any knowledge of the anatomy or physiology of society. They never have any doubt of the efficacy of their remedies. They never take account of any ulterior effects which may be apprehended from the remedy itself. It generally troubles them not a whit that their remedy implies a complete reconstruction of society or even a reconstitution of human nature. Against all such social quackery the obvious injunction to the quacks is, to mind their own business. . . .

The type and formula of most schemes of philanthropy or humanitarianism is this: A and B put their heads together to decide what C shall be made to do for D. The radical vice of all these schemes, from a sociological point of view, is that C is not allowed a voice in the matter, and his position, character, and interests, as well as the ultimate effects on society through C's interests, are entirely overlooked. I call C the Forgotten Man. For once let us look him up and consider his case, for the characteristic of all social doctors, is, that they fix their minds on some man or group of men whose case appeals to the sympathies and the imagination, and they plan remedies addressed to the particular trouble; they do not understand that all the parts of society hold together, and that forces which are set in action act and react throughout the whole organism, until an equilibrium is produced by a readjustment of all interests and rights. They therefore ignore entirely the source from which they must draw all the energy which they employ in their remedies, and they ignore all the effects on other members of society than the ones they have in view. They are always under the dominion of the superstition of government, and, forgetting that a government produces nothing at all, they leave out of sight the first fact to be remembered in all social discussion—that the State cannot get a cent for any man without taking it from some other man, and this latter must be a man who has produced and saved it. This latter is the Forgotten Man. . . .

There is a beautiful notion afloat in our literature and in the minds of our people that men are born to certain "natural rights." If that were true, there would be something on earth which was got for nothing, and this world would not be the place it is at all. The fact is, that there is no right whatever inherited by man which has not an equivalent and corresponding duty by the side of it, as the price of it. The rights, advantages, capital, knowledge, and all other goods which we inherit from past generations have been won by the struggles and sufferings of past generations; and the fact that the race lives, though men die, and that the race can by heredity accumulate within some cycle its victories over Nature, is one of the facts which make civilization possible. The struggles of the race as a

whole produce the possessions of the race as a whole. Something for nothing is not to be found on earth.

If there were such things as natural rights, the question would arise, Against whom are they good? Who has the corresponding obligation to satisfy these rights? There can be no rights against Nature, except to get out of her what ever we can, which is only the fact of the struggle for existence stated over again. The common assertion is, that the rights are good against society; that is, that society is bound to obtain and secure them for the persons interested. Society, however, is only the persons interested plus some other persons; and as the persons interested have by the hypothesis failed to win the rights, we come to this, that natural rights are the claims which certain persons have by prerogative against some other persons. Such is the actual interpretation in practice of natural rights—claims which some people have by prerogative on other people.

This theory is a very far-reaching one, and of course it is adequate to furnish a foundation for a whole social philosophy. In its widest extension it comes to mean that if any man finds himself uncomfortable in this world, it must be somebody else's fault, and that somebody is bound to come and make him comfortable. Now, the people who are most uncomfortable in this world (for if we should tell all our troubles it would not be found to be a very comfortable world for anybody) are those who have neglected their duties, and consequently have failed to get their rights. The people who can be called upon to serve the uncomfortable must be those who have done their duty, as the world goes, tolerably well. Consequently the doctrine which we are discussing turns out to be in practice only a scheme for making injustice prevail in human society by reversing the distribution of rewards and punishments between those who have done their duty and those who have not. . . .

I have said something disparagingly in a previous chapter about the popular rage against combined capital, corporations, corners, selling futures, etc., etc. The popular rage is not without reason, but it is sadly misdirected and the real things which deserve attack are thriving all the time. The greatest social evil with which we have to contend is jobbery. Whatever there is in legislative charters, watering stocks, etc., etc., which is objectionable, comes under the head of jobbery. Jobbery is any scheme which aims to gain, not by the legitimate fruits of industry and enterprise, but by extorting from somebody a part of his product under guise of some pretended industrial undertaking. Of course it is only a modification when the undertaking in question has some legitimate character, but the occasion is used to graft upon it devices for obtaining what has not been earned. Jobbery is the vice of plutocracy, and it is the especial form under which plutocracy corrupts a democratic and republican form of government. The United States is deeply afflicted with it, and the problem of civil liberty here is to conquer it. It affects everything which we really need to have done to such an extent that we have to do without public objects which we need through fear of jobbery. Our public buildings are jobs —not always, but often. They are not needed, or are costly beyond all necessity or even decent luxury. Internal improvements are jobs. They are not made because they are needed to meet needs which have been experienced. They are made to serve private ends, often incidentally the political interests of the persons who vote the appropriations. Pensions have become jobs. In England pensions used to be given to aristocrats, because aristocrats had political influence, in order to corrupt them. Here pensions are given to the great democratic mass, because they have political power, to corrupt them. Instead of going out where there is plenty of land and making a farm there, some people go down under the Mississippi River to make a farm, and then they want to tax all the people in the United States to make dikes to keep the river off their farms. The California gold-miners have washed out gold, and have washed the dirt down into the rivers and on the farms below. They want the Federal Government to now clean out the rivers and restore the farms. The silver-miners found their product declining in value, and they got the Federal Government to go into the market and buy what the public did not want, in order to sustain (as they hoped) the price of silver. The Federal Government is called upon to buy or hire unsailable ships, to build canals which will not pay, to furnish capital for all sorts of experiments, and to provide capital for enterprises of which private individuals will win the profits. All this is called "developing our resources," but it is, in truth, the great plan of all living on each other.

The greatest job of all is a protective tariff. It includes the biggest log-rolling and the widest corruption of economic and political ideas. It was said that there would be a rebellion if the taxes were not taken off whiskey and tobacco, which taxes were paid into the public Treasury. Just then the importations of Sumatra tobacco became important enough to affect the market. The Connecticut tobacco-growers at once called for an import duty on tobacco which would keep up the price of their product. So it appears that if the tax on tobacco is paid to the Federal Treasury there will be a rebellion, but if it is paid to the Connecticut tobacco-raisers there will be no rebellion at all. The farmers have long paid tribute to the manufacturers; now the manufacturing and other laborers are to pay tribute to the farmers. The system is made more comprehensive and complete, and we all are living on each other more than ever.

Now, the plan of plundering each other produces nothing. It only wastes. All the material over which the protected interests wrangle and grab must be got from somebody outside of their circle. The talk is all about the American laborer and American industry, but in every case in which there is not an actual production of wealth by industry there are two laborers and two industries to be considered —the one who gets and the one who gives. Every protected industry has to plead, as the major premise of its argument, that any industry which does not pay *ought* to be carried on at the expense of the consumers of the product, and, as its minor premise, that the industry in question does not pay; that is, that it cannot reproduce a capital equal in value to that which it consumes plus the current rate of profit. Hence every such industry must be a parasite on some other industry. What is the other industry? Who is the other man? This, the real question, is always overlooked.

In all jobbery the case is the same. There is a victim somewhere who is paying for it all. The doors of waste and extravagance stand open, and there seems to be a general agreement to squander and spend. It all belongs to somebody. There is somebody who had to contribute it, and who will have to find more. Nothing is ever said about him. Attention is all absorbed by the clamorous interests, the importunate petitioners, the plausible schemers, the pitiless bores. Now, who is the victim? He is the Forgotten Man. If we go to find him, we shall find him hard at work tilling the soil to get out of it the fund for all the jobbery, the object of all the plunder, the cost of all the economic quackery, and the pay of all the politicians and statesmen who have sacrificed his interests to his enemies. We shall find him an honest, sober, industrious citizen, unknown outside his little circle, paying his debts and his taxes, supporting the church and the school, reading his party newspaper, and cheering for his pet politician. . . .

It is the Forgotten Man who is threatened by every extension of the paternal theory of government. It is he who must work and pay. When, therefore, the statesmen and social philosophers sit down to think what the State can do or ought to do, they really mean to decide what the Forgotten Man shall do. What the Forgotten Man wants, therefore, is a fuller realization of constitutional liberty. He is suffering from the fact that there are yet mixed in our institutions mediaeval theories of protection, regulation, and authority, and modern theories of independence and individual liberty and responsibility. The consequence of this mixed state of things is, that those who are clever enough to get into control use the paternal theory by which to measure their own rights—that is, they assume privileges; and they use the theory of liberty to measure their own duties—that is, when it comes to the duties, they want to be "let alone." The Forgotten Man never gets into control. He has to pay both ways. His rights are measured to him by the theory of liberty—that is, he has only such as he can conquer; his duties are measured to him on the paternal theory—that is, he must discharge all which are laid upon him, as is the fortune of parents. In a paternal relation there are always two parties, a father and a child; and when we use the paternal relation metaphorically, it is of the first importance to know who is to be father and who is to be child. The *role* of parent falls always to the Forgotten Man. What he wants, therefore, is that ambiguities in our institutions be cleared up, and that liberty be more fully realized. . . .

We each owe to the other mutual redress of grievances. It has been said, in answer to my argument in the last chapter about the Forgotten Women and thread, that the tax on thread is "only a little thing," and that it cannot hurt the women much, and also that, if the women do not want to pay two cents a spool tax, there is thread of an inferior quality, which they can buy cheaper. These answers represent the bitterest and basest social injustice. Every honest citizen of a free state owes it to himself, to the community, and especially to those who are at once weak and wronged, to go to their assistance and to help redress their wrongs. Whenever a law or social arrangement acts so as to injure any one, and that one the humblest, then there is a duty on those who are stronger, or who know better, to demand and fight for redress and correction. When generalized this means that it is the duty of All-of-us (that is, the State) to establish justice for all, from the least to the greatest, and in all matters. This, however, is no new doctrine. It is only the old, true, and indisputable function of the State; and in working for a redress of wrongs and a correction of legislative abuses, we are only struggling to a fuller realization of it—that is, working to improve civil government.

We each owe it to the other to guarantee rights. Rights do not pertain to *results,* but only to *chances.* They pertain to the conditions of the struggle for existence, not to any of the results of it; to the *pursuit* of happiness, not to the possession of happiness. It cannot be said that each one has a right to have some property, because if one man had such a right some other man or men would be under a corresponding obligation to provide him with some property. Each has a right to acquire and possess property if he can. It is plain what falla-cies are developed when we overlook this distinction. Those fallacies run through *all* socialistic schemes and theories. If we take rights to pertain to results, and then say that rights must be equal, we come to say that men have a right to be equally happy, and so on in all the details. Rights should be equal, because they pertain to chances, and all ought to have equal chances so far as chances are provided or limited by the action of society. This, however, will not produce equal results, but it is right just because it will produce unequal results —that is, results which shall be proportioned to the merits of individuals. We each owe it to the other to guarantee mutually the chance to earn, to possess, to learn, to marry, etc., etc., against any interference which would prevent the exercise to those rights by a person who wishes to prosecute and enjoy them in peace for the pursuit of happiness. If we generalize this, it means that All-of-us ought to guarantee rights to each of us. But our modern free, constitutional States are constructed entirely on the notion of rights, and we regard them as performing their functions more and more perfectly according as they guarantee rights in consonance with the constantly corrected and expanded notions of rights from one generation to another. Therefore, when we say that we owe it to each other to guarantee rights we only say that we ought to prosecute and improve our political science.... ∽

"The Conquest of the United States by Spain" (1899)

During the last year the public has been familiarized with descriptions of Spain and of Span-

SOURCE: William Graham Sumner, "The Conquest of the United States by Spain," *Yale Law Journal* 8 (January 1899): 168–93.

ish methods of doing things until the name of Spain has become a symbol for a certain well-defined set of notions and policies. On the other hand, the name of the United States has always been, for all of us, a symbol for a state of things, a set of ideas and traditions, a group of views about social and political affairs. Spain was the first, for a long time the greatest, of the modern imperialistic states. The United States, by its historical origin, its traditions, and its principles, is the chief representative of the revolt and reaction against that kind of a state. I intend to show that, by the line of action now proposed to us, which we call expansion and imperialism, we are throwing away some of the most important elements of the American symbols and are adopting some of the most important elements of the Spanish symbol. We have beaten Spain in a military conflict, but we are submitting to be conquered by her on the field of ideas and policies. Expansionism and imperialism are nothing but the old philosophies of national prosperity which have brought Spain to where she now is. Those philosophies appeal to national vanity and national cupidity. They are seductive, especially upon the first view and the most superficial judgment, and therefore it cannot be denied that they are very strong for popular effect. They are delusions, and they will lead us to ruin unless we are hardheaded enough to resist them. . . .

There is another observation, however, about the war which is of far greater importance: that is, that it was a gross violation of self-government. We boast that we are a self-governing people, and in this respect, particularly, we compare ourselves with pride with older nations. What is the difference after all? The Russians, whom we always think of as standing at the opposite pole of political institutions, have self-government, if you mean by it acquiescence in what a little group of people at the head of the government agree to do. The war with Spain was precipitated upon us headlong, without reflection or deliberation, and without any due formulation of public opinion. Whenever a voice was raised in behalf of deliberation and the recognized maxims of statesmanship, it was howled down in a storm

of vituperation and cant. Everything was done to make us throw away sobriety of thought and calmness of judgment and to inflate all expressions with sensational epithets and turgid phrases. It cannot be denied that everything in regard to the war has been treated in an exalted strain of sentiment and rhetoric very unfavorable to the truth. At present the whole periodical press of the country seems to be occupied in tickling the national vanity to the utmost by representations about the war which are extravagant and fantastic. There will be a penalty to be paid for all this. Nervous and sensational newspapers are just as corrupting, especially to young people, as nervous and sensational novels. The habit of expecting that all mental pabulum shall be highly spiced, and the corresponding loathing for whatever is soberly truthful, undermines character as much as any other vice. Patriotism is being prostituted into a nervous intoxication which is fatal to an apprehension of truth. It builds around us a fool's paradise, and it will lead us into errors about our position and relations just like those which we have been ridiculing in the case of Spain. . . .

Now what will hasten the day when our present advantages will wear out and when we shall come down to the conditions of the older and densely populated nations? The answer is: war, debt, taxation, diplomacy, a grand governmental system, pomp, glory, a big army and navy, lavish expenditures, political jobbery—in a word, imperialism. In the old days the democratic masses of this country, who knew little about our modern doctrines of social philosophy, had a sound instinct on these matters, and it is no small ground of political disquietude to see it decline. They resisted every appeal to their vanity in the way of pomp and glory which they knew must be paid for. They dreaded a public debt and a standing army. They were narrow-minded and went too far with these notions, but they were, at least, right, if they wanted to strengthen democracy.

The great foe of democracy now and in the future is plutocracy. Every year that passes brings out this antagonism more distinctly. It is to be the social war of the twentieth century. In that war militarism, expansion, and imperialism will all favor plutocracy. In the first place, war and expansion will favor jobbery, both in the dependencies and at home. In the second place, they will take away the attention of the people from what the plutocrats are do-ing. In the third place, they will cause large expenditures of the people's money, the return for which will not go into the treasury, but into the hands of a few schemers. In the fourth place, they will call for a large public debt and taxes, and these things especially tend to make men unequal, because any social burdens bear more heavily on the weak than on the strong, and so make the weak weaker and the strong stronger. Therefore expansion and imperialism are a grand onslaught on democracy.... ∾

Primary Sources

The Challenge of Facts and Other Essays by William Graham Sumner. Edited by Albert Galloway Keller. New Haven, Conn.: Yale University Press, 1914.

Earth-Hunger and Other Essays by William Graham Sumner. Edited by Albert Galloway Keller. New Haven, Conn.: Yale University Press, 1913.

The Forgotten Man and Other Essays by William Graham Sumner. Edited by Albert Galloway Keller. New Haven, Conn.: Yale University Press, 1919.

Sumner, William Graham. *Folkways.* Boston: Atheneum Press, 1907.

Sumner, William Graham, and Albert Galloway Keller. *The Science of Society.* 4 vols. New Haven, Conn.: Yale University Press, 1927.

War and Other Essays by William Graham Sumner. Edited by Albert Galloway Keller. New Haven, Conn.: Yale University Press, 1911.

Secondary Sources

Curtis, Bruce. *William Graham Sumner.* Boston: Twayne Publishers, 1981.

McClosky, Robert Green. *American Conservatism.* Cambridge, Mass.: Harvard University Press, 1951.

25. Edward Bellamy

EDWARD BELLAMY (1850–98) was born in western Massachusetts, studied law, and turned to journalism for a career. He published his first novel in 1878, and subsequent work drew favorable literary notice. His major work was *Looking Backward* (1889), a novel which became the largest, fastest selling novel in American history to that time. *Looking Backward* combined contemporary social criticism with a look at what American society could be in the year 2000 if cooperation and true social and economic equality were substituted for competition and what he considered the sham of political equality. The device employed was the awakening of a young Bostonian after more than one hundred years of hypnotic sleep and his subsequent observations and conversations. Less than two years after *Looking Backward* was published, more than 150 "New Nationalist" clubs were hard at work organizing support for Bellamy's program to guarantee material welfare and human dignity for all citizens. Nationalism faded as a movement almost as fast as it developed, although the idea continued to have appeal during the Progressive Era. Bellamy wrote *Equality,* a sequel in form and an extension of his program, in 1897, but he died soon after of tuberculosis.

The selection excerpted here is drawn from the early chapters of *Looking Backward.* The principal characters are Julian West, just awakened in A.D. 2000 from the social strife of 1887; Dr. Leete, his knowledgeable host; and Dr. Leete's gracious and charming daughter Edith, who in proper Victorian style educates Julian about other aspects of the new society. ᵔ

Looking Backward (1889)

... "I must know a little more about the sort of Boston I have come back to. You told me when we were upon the house-top that though a century only had elapsed since I fell asleep, it had been marked by greater changes in the conditions of humanity than many a previous millennium. With the city before me I could well believe that, but I am very curious to know what some of the changes have been. To make a beginning somewhere, for the subject is doubtless a large one, what solution, if any, have you found for the labor question? It was the Sphinx's riddle of the nineteenth century, and when I dropped out the Sphinx was threatening to devour society, because the answer was not forthcoming. It is well worth sleeping a hundred years to learn what the right answer was, if, indeed, you have found it yet."

"As no such thing as the labor question is known nowadays," replied Dr. Leete, "and there is no way in which it could arise, I suppose we may claim to have solved it. Society

would indeed have fully deserved being devoured if it had failed to answer a riddle so entirely simple. In fact, to speak by the book, it was not necessary for society to solve the riddle at all. It may be said to have solved itself. The solution came as the result of a process of industrial evolution which could not have terminated otherwise. All the society had to do was to recognize and cooperate with that evolution, when its tendency had become unmistakable."

"I can only say," I answered, "that at the time I fell asleep no such evolution had been recognized."

"It was in 1887 that you fell into this sleep, I think you said."

"Yes, May 30th, 1887."

My companion regarded me musingly for some moments. Then he observed, "And you tell me that even then there was no general recognition of the nature of the crisis which society was nearing? Of course, I fully credit your statement. The singular blindness of your contemporaries to the signs of the times is a phenomenon commented on by many of our historians, but few facts of history are more difficult for us to realize, so obvious and unmistakable as we look back seem the indica-

SOURCE: Edward Bellamy, *Looking Backward, 2000–1887* (Boston: Houghton Mifflin, 1889), 48–58, 86–98.

tions, which must also have come under your eyes, of the transformation about to come to pass. I should be interested, Mr. West, if you would give me a little more definite idea of the view which you and men of your grade of intellect took of the state and prospects of society in 1887. You must, at least, have realized that the widespread industrial and social troubles, and the underlying dissatisfaction of all classes with the inequalities of society, and the general misery of mankind, were portents of great changes of some sort."

"We did, indeed, fully realize that," I replied. "We felt that society was dragging anchor and in danger of going adrift. Whither it would drift nobody could say, but all feared the rocks."

"Nevertheless," said Dr. Leete, "the set of the current was perfectly perceptible if you had but taken pains to observe it, and it was not toward the rocks, but toward a deeper channel."

"We had a popular proverb," I replied, "that 'hindsight is better than foresight,' the force of which I shall now, no doubt, appreciate more fully than ever. All I can say is, that the prospect was such when I went into that long sleep that I should not have been surprised that I looked down from your housetop to-day on a heap of charred and mossgrown ruins instead of this glorious city."

Dr. Leete had listened to me with close attention and nodded thoughtfully as I finished speaking. "What you have said," he observed, "will be regarded as a most valuable vindication of Storiot, whose account of your era has been generally thought exaggerated in its picture of the gloom and confusion of men's minds. That a period of transition like that should be full of excitement and agitation was indeed to be looked for; but seeing how plain was the tendency of the forces in operation, it was natural to believe that hope rather than fear would have been the prevailing temper of the popular mind."

"You have not yet told me what was the answer to the riddle which you found," I said. "I am impatient to know by what contradiction of natural sequence the peace and prosperity which you now seem to enjoy could have been the outcome of an era like my own."

"Excuse me," replied my host, "but do you smoke?" It was not till our cigars were lighted and drawing well that he resumed. "Since you are in the humor to talk rather than to sleep, as I certainly am, perhaps I cannot do better than to try to give you enough idea of our modern industrial system to dissipate at least the impression that there is any mystery about the process of its evolution. The Bostonians of your day had the reputation of being great askers of questions, and I am going to show my descent by asking you one to begin with. What should you name as the most prominent feature of the labor troubles of your day?"

"Why, the strikes, of course," I replied.

"Exactly; but what made the strikes so formidable?"

"The great labor organizations."

"And what was the motive of these great organizations?"

"The workmen claimed they had to organize to get their rights from the big corporations," I replied.

"That is just it," said Dr. Leete; "the organization of labor and the strikes were an effect, merely, of the concentration of capital in greater masses than had ever been known before. Before this concentration began, while as yet commerce and industry were conducted by innumerable petty concerns with small capital, instead of a small number of great concerns with vast capital, the individual workman was relatively important and independent in his relations to the employer. Moreover, when a little capital or a new idea was enough to start a man in business for himself, workingmen were constantly becoming employers and there was no hard and fast line between the two classes. Labor unions were needless then, and general strikes out of the question. But when the era of small concerns with small capital was succeeded by that of the great aggregations of capital, all this was changed. The individual laborer, who had been relatively important to the small employer, was reduced to insignificance and powerlessness over against the great corporation, while at the same time the way upward to the grade of employer was closed to him. Self-defense drove him to union with his fellows.

"The records of the period show that the outcry against the concentration of capital was furious. Men believed that it threatened society with a form of tyranny more abhorrent than it had ever endured. They believed that the great corporations were preparing for them the yoke of a baser servitude than had ever been imposed on the race, servitude not to men but to soulless machines incapable of any motive but insatiable greed. Looking back, we cannot wonder at their desperation, for certainly humanity was never confronted with a fate more sordid and hideous than would have been the era of corporate tyranny which they anticipated.

"Meanwhile, without being in the smallest degree checked by the clamor against it, the absorption of business by ever larger monopolies continued. In the United States there was not, after the beginning of the last quarter of the century, any opportunity whatever for individual enterprise in any important field of industry, unless backed by a great capital. During the last decade of the century, such small businesses as still remained were fast-failing survivals of a past epoch, or mere parasites on the great corporations, or else existed in fields too small to attract the great capitalists. Small businesses, as far as they still remained, were reduced to the condition of rats and mice, living in holes and corners, and counting on evading notice for the enjoyment of existence. The railroads had gone on combining till a few great syndicates controlled every rail in the land. In manufactories, every important staple was controlled by a syndicate. These syndicates, pools, trusts, or whatever their name, fixed prices and crushed all competition except when combinations as vast as themselves arose. Then a struggle, resulting in a still greater consolidation, ensued. The great city bazaar crushed its country rivals with branch stores, and in the city itself absorbed its smaller rivals till the business of a whole quarter was concentrated under one roof, with a hundred former proprietors of shops serving as clerks. Having no business of his own to put his money in, the small capitalist, at the same time that he took service under the corporation, found no other investment for his money but its stocks and bonds, thus becoming doubly dependent upon it.

"The fact that the desperate popular opposition to the consolidation of business in a few powerful hands had no effect to check it proves that there must have been a strong economical reason for it. The small capitalists, with their innumerable petty concerns, had in fact yielded the field to the great aggregations of capital, because they belonged to a day of small things and were totally incompetent to the demands of an age of steam and telegraphs and the gigantic scale of its enterprises. To restore the former order of things, even if possible, would have involved returning to the day of stagecoaches. Oppressive and intolerable as was the régime of the great consolidations of capital, even its victims, while they cursed it, were forced to admit the prodigious increase of efficiency which had been imparted to the national industries, the vast economies effected by concentration of management and unity of organization, and to confess that since the new system had taken the place of the old the wealth of the world had increased at a rate before undreamed of. To be sure this vast increase had gone chiefly to make the rich richer, increasing the gap between them and the poor; but the fact remained that, as a means merely of producing wealth, capital had been proved efficient in proportion to its consolidation. The restoration of the old system with the subdivision of capital, if it were possible, might indeed bring back a greater equality of conditions, with more individual dignity and freedom, but it would be at the price of general poverty and the arrest of material progress.

"Was there, then, no way of commanding the services of the mighty wealth-producing principle of consolidated capital without bowing down to a plutocracy like that of Carthage? As soon as men began to ask themselves these questions, they found the answer ready for them. The movement toward the conduct of business by larger and larger aggregations of capital, the tendency toward monopolies, which had been so desperately and vainly resisted, was recognized at last, in its true significance, as a process which only needed to complete its logical evolution to open a golden future to humanity.

"Early in the last century the evolution was completed by the final consolidation of the entire capital of the nation. The industry and commerce of the country, ceasing to be conducted by a set of irresponsible corporations and syndicates of private persons at their caprice and for their profit, were intrusted to a single syndicate representing the people, to be conducted in the common interest for the common profit. The nation, that is to say, organized as the one great business corporation in which all other corporations were absorbed; it became the one capitalist in the place of all other capitalists, the sole employer, the final monopoly in which all previous and lesser monopolies were swallowed up, a monopoly in the profits and economies of which all citizens shared. The epoch of trusts had ended in The Great Trust. In a word, the people of the United States concluded to assume the conduct of their own business, just as one hundred odd years before they had assumed the conduct of their own government, organizing now for industrial purposes on precisely the same grounds that they had then organized for political purposes. At last, strangely late in the world's history, the obvious fact was perceived that no business is so essentially the public business as the industry and commerce on which the people's livelihood depends, and that to entrust it to private persons to be managed for private profit is a folly similar in kind, though vastly greater in magnitude, to that of surrendering the functions of political government to kings and nobles to be conducted for their personal glorification."

"Such a stupendous change as you describe," said I, "did not, of course, take place without great bloodshed and terrible convulsions."

"On the contrary," replied Dr. Leete, "there was absolutely no violence. The change had been long foreseen. Public opinion had become fully ripe for it, and the whole mass of the people was behind it. There was no more possibility of opposing it by force than by argument. On the other hand the popular sentiment toward the great corporations and those identified with them had ceased to be one of bitterness, as they came to realize their necessity as a link, a transition phase, in the evolution of the true industrial system. The most violent foes of the great private monopolies were now forced to recognize how invaluable and indispensable had been their office in educating the people up to the point of assuming control of their own business. Fifty years before, the consolidation of the industries of the country under national control would have seemed a very daring experiment to the most sanguine. But by a series of object lessons, seen and studied by all men, the great corporations had taught the people an entirely new set of ideas on this subject. They had seen for many years syndicates handling revenues greater than those of states, and directing the labors of hundreds of thousands of men with an efficiency and economy unattainable in smaller operations. It had come to be recognized as an axiom that the larger the business the simpler the principles that can be applied to it; that, as the machine is truer than the hand, so the system, which in a great concern does the work of the master's eye in a small business, turns out more accurate results. Thus it came about that, thanks to the corporations themselves, when it was proposed that the nation should assume their functions, the suggestion implied nothing which seemed impracticable even to the timid. To be sure it was a step beyond any yet taken, a broader generalization, but the very fact that the nation would be the sole corporation in the field would, it was seen, relieve the undertaking of many difficulties with which the partial monopolies had contended."...

"You were surprised," he said, "at my saying that we got along without money or trade, but a moment's reflection will show that trade existed and money was needed in your day simply because the business of production was left in private hands, and that, consequently, they are superfluous now."

"I do not at once see how that follows," I replied.

"It is very simple," said Dr. Leete. "When innumerable different and independent persons produced the various things needful to life and comfort, endless exchanges between individuals were requisite in order that they might supply themselves with what they desired. These exchanges constituted trade, and money was essential as their medium. But as soon as the nation became the sole producer of all sorts of commodities, there was no need of exchanges between individuals that they might get what they required. Everything was procurable from one source, and nothing could be procured anywhere else. A system of direct distribution from the national storehouses took the place of trade, and for this money was unnecessary."

"How is this distribution managed?" I asked.

"On the simplest possible plan," replied Dr. Leete. "A credit corresponding to his share of the annual product of the nation is given to every citizen on the public books at the beginning of each year, and a credit card issued him with which he procures at the public storehouses, found in every community, whatever he desires whenever he desires it. This arrangement, you will see, totally obviates the necessity for business transactions of any sort between individuals and consumers. Perhaps you would like to see what our credit-cards are like.

"You observe," he pursued as I was curiously examining the piece of pasteboard he gave me, "that this card is issued for a certain number of dollars. We have kept the old word, but not the substance. The term, as we use it, answers to no real thing, but merely serves as an algebraical symbol for comparing the values of products with one another. For this purpose they are all priced in dollars and cents, just as in your day. The value of what I procure on this card is checked off by the clerk, who pricks out of these tiers of squares the price of what I order."

"If you wanted to buy something of your neighbor, could you transfer part of your credit to him as consideration?" I inquired.

"In the first place," replied Dr. Leete "our neighbors have nothing to sell us, but in any event our credit would not be transferable, being strictly personal. Before the nation could even think of honoring any such transfer as you speak of, it would be bound to inquire into all the circumstances of the transaction, so as to be able to guarantee its absolute equity. It would have been reason enough, had there been no other, for abolishing money, that its possession was no indication of rightful title to it. In the hands of the man who had stolen it or murdered for it, it was as good as in those which had earned it by industry. People nowadays interchange gifts and favors out of friendship, but buying and selling is considered absolutely inconsistent with the mutual benevolence and disinterestedness which should prevail between citizens and the sense of community of interest which supports our social system. According to our ideas, buying and selling is essentially anti-social in all its tendencies. It is an education in self-seeking at the expense of others, and no society whose citizens are trained in such a school can possibly rise above a very low grade of civilization."

"What if you have to spend more than your card in any one year?" I asked.

"The provision is so ample that we are more likely not to spend it all," replied Dr. Leete. "But if extraordinary expenses should exhaust it, we can obtain a limited advance on the next year's credit, though this practice is not encouraged, and a heavy discount is charged to check it. Of course if a man showed himself a reckless spendthrift he would receive his allowance monthly or weekly instead of yearly, or if necessary not be permitted to handle it all."

"If you don't spend your allowance, I suppose it accumulates?"

"That is also permitted to a certain extent when a special outlay is anticipated. But unless notice to the contrary is given, it is presumed that the citizen who does not fully expend his credit did not have occasion to do so, and the balance is turned into the general surplus."

"Such a system does not encourage saving habits on the part of citizens," I said.

"It is not intended to," was the reply. "The nation is rich, and does not wish the people to deprive themselves of any good thing. In your day, men were bound to lay up goods and money against coming failure of the means of support and for their children. This necessity made parsimony a virtue. But now it would have no such laudable object, and, having lost its utility, it has ceased to be regarded as a virtue. No man any more has any care for the morrow, either for himself or his children, for the nation guarantees the nurture, education, and comfortable maintenance of every citizen from the cradle to the grave."

"That is a sweeping guarantee!" I said. "What certainty can there be that the value of a man's labor will recompense the nation for its outlay on him? On the whole, society may be able to support all its members, but some must earn less than enough for their support, and others more; and that brings us back once more to the wages question, on which you have hitherto said nothing. It was at just this point, if you remember, that our talk ended last evening; and I say again, as I did then, that here I should suppose a national industrial system like yours would find its main difficulty. How, I ask once more, can you adjust satisfactorily the comparative wages or remuneration of the multitude of avocations, so unlike and so incommensurable, which are necessary for the service of society? In our day the market rate determined the price of labor of all sorts, as well as of goods. The employer paid as little as he could, and the worker got as much. It was not a pretty system ethically, I admit; but it did, at least, furnish us a rough and ready formula for settling a question which must be settled ten thousand times a day if the world was ever going to get forward. There seemed to us no other practicable way of doing it."

"Yes," replied Dr. Leete, "it was the only practicable way under a system which made the interests of every individual antagonistic to those of every other; but it would have been a pity if humanity could never have devised a better plan, for yours was simply the application to the mutual relations of men of the devil's maxim, 'Your necessity is my opportunity.' The reward of any service depended not upon its difficulty, danger, or hardship, for throughout the world it seems that the most perilous, severe, and repulsive labor was done by the worst paid classes; but solely upon the strait of those who needed the service."

"All that is conceded," I said. "But, with all its defects, the plan of settling prices by the market rate was a practical plan; and I cannot conceive what satisfactory substitute you can have devised for it. The government being the only possible employer, there is of course no labor market or market rate. Wages of all sorts must be arbitrarily fixed by the government. I cannot imagine a more complex and delicate function than that must be, or one, however performed, more certain to breed universal dissatisfaction."

"I beg your pardon," replied Dr. Leete, "but I think you exaggerate the difficulty. Suppose a board of fairly sensible men were charged with settling the wages for all sorts of trades under a system which, like ours, guaranteed employment to all, while permitting the choice of avocations. Don't you see that, however unsatisfactory the first adjustment might be, the mistakes would soon correct themselves? The favored trades would have too many volunteers, and those discriminated against would lack them till the errors were set right. But this is aside from the purpose, for, though this plan would, I fancy, be practicable enough, it is no part of our system."

"How, then, do you regulate wages?" I once more asked.

Dr. Leete did not reply till after several moments of meditative silence. "I know, of course," he finally said, "enough of the old or-

der of things to understand just what you mean by that question; and yet the present order is so utterly different at this point that I am a little at loss how to answer you best. You ask me how we regulate wages; I can only reply that there is no idea in the modern social economy which at all corresponds with what was meant by wages in your day."

"I suppose you mean that you have no money to pay wages in," said I. "But the credit given the worker at the government storehouse answers to his wages with us. How is the amount of the credit given respectively to the workers in different lines determined? By what title does the individual claim his particular share? What is the basis of allotment?"

"His title," replied Dr. Leete, "is his humanity. The basis of his claim is the fact that he is a man."

"The fact that he is a man!" I repeated, incredulously. "Do you possibly mean that all have the same share?"

"Most assuredly."

The readers of this book never having practically known any other arrangement, or perhaps very carefully considered the historical accounts of former epochs in which a very different system prevailed, cannot be expected to appreciate the stupor of amazement into which Dr. Leete's simple statement plunged me.

"You see," he said, smiling, "that it is not merely that we have no money to pay wages in, but, as I said, we have nothing at all answering to your idea of wages."

By this time I had pulled myself together sufficiently to voice some of the criticisms which, man of the nineteenth century as I was, came uppermost in my mind, upon this to me astounding arrangement. "Some men do twice the work of others!" I exclaimed. "Are the clever workmen content with a plan that ranks them with the indifferent?"

"We leave no possible ground for any complaint of injustice," replied Dr. Leete, "by requiring precisely the same measure of service from all."

"How can you do that, I should like to know, when no two men's powers are the same?"

"Nothing could be simpler," was Dr. Leete's reply. "We require of each that he shall make the same effort; that is, we demand of him the best service it is in his power to give."

"And supposing all do the best they can," I answered, "the amount of the product resulting is twice greater from one man than from another."

"Very true," replied Dr. Leete; "but the amount of the resulting product has nothing whatever to do with the question, which is one of desert. Desert is a moral question, and the amount of the product a material quantity. It would be an extraordinary sort of logic which should try to determine a moral question by a material standard. The amount of the effort alone is pertinent to the question of desert. All men who do their best, do the same. A man's endowments, however godlike, merely fix the measure of his duty. The man of great endowments who does not do all he might, though he may do more than a man of small endowments who does his best, is deemed a less deserving worker than the latter, and dies a debtor to his fellows. The Creator sets men's tasks for them by the faculties he gives them; we simply exact their fulfillment."

"No doubt that is very fine philosophy," I said; "nevertheless it seems hard that the man who produces twice as much as another, even if both do their best, should have only the same share."

"Does it, indeed, seem so to you?" responded Dr. Leete. "Now, do you know, that seems very curious to me? The way it strikes people nowadays is, that a man who can produce twice as much as another with the same effort, instead of being rewarded for doing so,

ought to be punished if he does not do so. In the nineteenth century, when a horse pulled a heavier load than a goat, I suppose you rewarded him. Now, we should have whipped him soundly if he had not, on the ground that, being much stronger, he ought to. It is singular how ethical standards change." The doctor said this with such a twinkle in his eye that I was obliged to laugh.

"I suppose," I said, "that the real reason that we rewarded men for their endowments, while we considered those of horses and goats merely as fixing the service to be severally required of them, was that the animals, not being reasoning beings, naturally did the best they could, whereas men could only be induced to do so by rewarding them according to the amount of their product. That brings me to ask why, unless human nature has mightily changed in a hundred years, you are not under the same necessity."

"We are," replied Dr. Leete. "I don't think there has been any change in human nature in that respect since your day. It is still so constituted that special incentives in the form of prizes, and advantages to be gained, are requisite to call out the best endeavors of the average man in any direction."

"But what inducement," I asked, "can a man have to put forth his best endeavors when, however much or little he accomplishes, his income remains the same? High characters may be moved by devotion to the common welfare under such a system, but does not the average man tend to rest back on his oar, reasoning that it is of no use to make a special effort, since the effort will not increase his income, nor its withholding diminish it?"

"Does it then really seem to you," answered my companion, "that human nature is insensible to any motives save fear of want and love of luxury, that you should expect security and equality of livelihood to leave them without possible incentives to effort? Your contemporaries did not really think so, though they might fancy they did. When it was a question of the grandest class of efforts, the most absolute self-devotion, they depended on quite other incentives. Not higher wages, but honor and the hope of men's gratitude, patriotism and the inspiration of duty, were the motives which they set before their soldiers when it was a question of dying for the nation, and never was there an age of the world when those motives did not call out what is best and noblest in men. And not only this, but when you come to analyze the love of money which was the general impulse to effort in your day, you find that the dread of want and desire of luxury was but one of several motives which the pursuit of money represented; the others, and with many the more influential, being desire of power, of social position, and reputation for ability and success. So you see that though we have abolished poverty and the fear of it, and inordinate luxury with the hope of it, we have not touched the greater part of the motives which underlay the love of money in former times, or any of those which prompted the supremer sorts of effort. The coarser motives, which no longer move us, have been replaced by higher motives wholly unknown to the mere wage earners of your age. Now that

industry of whatever sort is no longer self-service, but service of the nation, patriotism, passion for humanity, impel the worker as in your day they did the soldier. The army of industry is an army, not alone by virtue of its perfect organization, but by reason also of the ardor of self-devotion which animates its members.

"But as you used to supplement the motives of patriotism with the love of glory, in order to stimulate the valor of your soldiers, so do we. Based as our industrial system is on the principle of requiring the same unit of effort from every man, that is, the best he can do, you will see that the means by which we spur the workers to do their best must be a very essential part of our scheme. With us, diligence in the national service is the sole and certain way to public repute, social distinction, and official power. The value of a man's services to society fixes his rank in it. Compared with the effect of our social arrangements in impelling men to be zealous in business, we deem the object-lessons of biting poverty and wanton luxury on which you depended a device as weak and uncertain as it was barbaric. The lust of honor even in your sordid day notoriously impelled men to more desperate effort than the love of money could." ... ⌒

Primary Sources

Bellamy, Edward. *The Duke of Stockbridge: A Romance of Shays' Rebellion.* New York: Silver, Burdett and Co., 1900.

———. *Edward Bellamy Speaks Again! Articles, Public Addresses, Letters.* Kansas City, Mo.: Peerage Press, 1937.

———. *Equality.* New York: AMS Press, 1970.

———. *Looking Backward, 2000–1887.* Edited by John L. Thomas. Cambridge, Mass.: Harvard University Press, Belknap Press, 1967.

Secondary Sources

Bowman, Sylvia. *Edward Bellamy.* Boston: Twayne Publishers, 1986.

———. *Edward Bellamy Abroad: An American Prophet's Influence.* New York: Twayne Publishers, 1962.

———. *The Year 2000: A Critical Biography of Edward Bellamy.* New York: Bookman Associates, 1958.

Morgan, Arthur Ernest. *The Philosophy of Edward Bellamy.* New York: King's Crown Press, 1945.

25. Populism

POPULISM is the label given to the major protest and reform movement that arose principally from the farms of the South and West in the late 1880s and 1890s. The origins of the movement lay in the grievances farmers had against their creditors, particularly banks and railroads, in the context of steadily falling prices for farm products. The organizational forms taken were at first various Farmers' Alliances, and then, as the movement reluctantly entered politics, the People's Party, which contested national and state elections with considerable though fleeting success in 1892 and 1896. The movement was one of the strongest grassroots democratic uprisings in American history, going so far as to call for democratic control over the availability and value of money and credit—the essence of the capitalist economic system. To be sure, historians have only recently recognized Populism's contribution to democratic thought. For many years, it was dismissed as mere nativist, anti-industrial protest—the "little guy" of nostalgic America against the emerging big corporations and big government of the modern world. The movement contained such elements, but it was fully set in the mainstream of a changing sense of dignity and democracy.

No single figure spoke authoritatively for Populism, and therefore the political ideas of the movement are represented here by two documents. First are the "Ocala Demands" of 1890, the product of several Farmers' Alliance meetings in Ocala, Florida. Here, the financial ideas are laid out most fully. The second is the People's Party platform of 1892, when the third-party's candidate, James Weaver, won twenty-two electoral ballots and the party elected several state and national representatives. In this document, the demand for democratic control of the financial system is set in the context of a more general political reform program. These ideas did not go away with the ultimate defeat of Populism; in one or another form, they served as the base of reform proposals and enactments for the next twenty years. ∾

The Ocala Demands (December 1890)

1. a. We demand the abolition of national banks.

b. We demand that the government shall establish sub-treasuries or depositories in the several states, which shall loan money direct to the people at a low rate of interest, not to exceed two per cent per annum, on nonperishable farm products, and also upon real estate, with proper limitations upon the quantity of land and amount of money.

c. We demand that the amount of the circulating medium be speedily increased to not

SOURCE: Henry Commager, ed., *Documents of American History* (New York: Oxford University Press, 1973), 592–93.

less than $50 per capita.

2. We demand that Congress shall pass such laws as will effectually prevent the dealing in futures of all agricultural and mechanical productions; providing a stringent system of procedure in trials that will secure the prompt conviction, and imposing such penalties as shall secure the most perfect compliance with the law.

3. We condemn the silver bill recently passed by Congress, and demand in lieu thereof the free and unlimited coinage of silver.

4. We demand the passage of laws prohibiting alien ownership of land, and that Congress take prompt action to devise some plan to obtain all lands now owned by aliens and foreign syndicates; and that all lands now held by railroads and other corporations in excess of such as is actually used and needed by them be reclaimed by the government and held for actual settlers only.

5. Believing in the doctrine of equal rights to all and special privileges to none, we demand—

a. That our national legislation shall be so framed in the future as not to build up one industry at the expense of another.

b. We further demand a removal of the existing heavy tariff tax from the necessities of life, that the poor of our land must have.

c. We further demand a just and equitable system of graduated tax on incomes.

d. We believe that the money of the country should be kept as much as possible in the hands of the people, and hence we demand that all national and state revenues shall be limited to the necessary expenses of the government economically and honestly administered.

6. We demand the most rigid, honest, and just state and national government control and supervision of the means of public communication and transportation, and if this control and supervision does not remove the abuse now existing, we demand the government ownership of such means of communication and transportation.

7. We demand that the Congress of the United States submit an amendment to the Constitution providing for the election of United States Senators by direct vote of the people of each state. ∽

The Populist Party Platform (4 July 1892)

Assembled upon the 116th anniversary of the Declaration of Independence, the People's Party of America, in their first national convention, invoking upon their action the blessing of Almighty God, put forth in the name and on behalf of the people of this country, the following preamble and declaration of principles: The conditions which surround us best justify our co-operation; we meet in the midst of a nation brought to the verge of moral, political, and material ruin. Corruption dominates the ballot-box, the Legislatures, the Congress, and touches even the ermine of the bench. The people are demoralized; most of the States have been compelled to isolate the voters at the polling places to prevent universal intimidation and bribery. The newspapers are largely subsidized or muzzled, public opinion silenced, business prostrated, homes covered with mortgages, labor impoverished, and the land concentrating in the hands of capitalists. The urban workmen are denied the right to organize for self-protection, imported pauperized labor beats down their wages, a hireling standing army, unrecognized by our laws, is established to shoot them down, and they are rapidly degenerating into European conditions. The fruits of the toil of millions are boldly stolen to build up colossal fortunes for a few, unprecedented in the history of mankind; and the possessors of these, in turn, despise the Republic and endanger liberty. From the same prolific womb of governmental injustice we breed the two great classes—tramps and millionaires.

The national power to create money is appropriated to enrich bond-holders; a vast public debt payable in legal-tender currency has been funded into gold-bearing bonds, thereby adding millions to the burdens of the people.

Silver, which has been accepted as coin since the dawn of history, has been demonetized to add to the purchasing power of gold by decreasing the value of all forms of property as well as human labor, and the supply of currency is purposely abridged to fatten usurers, bankrupt enterprise, and enslave industry. A vast conspiracy against mankind has been organized on two continents, and it is rapidly taking possession of the world. If not met and overthrown at once it forebodes terrible social convulsions, the destruction of civilization, or the establishment of an absolute despotism.

We have witnessed for more than a quarter of a century the struggles of the two great political parties for power and plunder, while grievous wrongs have been inflicted upon the suffering people. We charge that the controlling influences dominating both these parties have permitted the existing dreadful conditions to develop without serious effort to prevent or restrain them. Neither do they now promise us any substantial reform. They have agreed together to ignore, in the coming campaign, every issue but one. They propose to drown the outcries of a plundered people with the uproar of a sham battle over the tariff, so

that capitalists, corporations, national banks, rings, trusts, watered stock, the demonetization of silver, and the oppressions of the usurers may all be lost sight of. They propose to sacrifice our homes, lives, and children on the altar of mammon; to destroy the multitude in order to secure corruption funds from the millionaires.

Assembled on the anniversary of the birthday of the nation, and filled with the spirit of the grand general and chief who established our independence, we seek to restore the government of the Republic to the hands of the "plain people," with which class it originated. We assert our purposes to be identical with the purposes of the National Constitution; to form a more perfect union and establish justice, insure domestic tranquillity, provide for the common defence, promote the general welfare, and secure the blessings of liberty for ourselves and our posterity.

We declare that this Republic can only endure as a free government while built upon the love of the people for each other and for the nation; that it cannot be pinned together by bayonets; that the Civil War is over, and that every passion and resentment which grew out of it must die with it, and that we must be in fact, as we are in name, one united brotherhood of free men.

Our country finds itself confronted by conditions for which there is no precedent in the history of the world; our annual agricultural productions mount to billions of dollars in value, which must, within a few weeks or months, be exchanged for billions of dollars' worth of commodities consumed in their production; the existing currency supply is wholly inadequate to make this exchange; the results are falling prices, the formation of combines and rings, the impoverishment of the producing class. We pledge ourselves that if given power we will labor to correct these evils by wise and reasonable legislation, in accordance with the terms of our platform.

We believe that the power of government—in other words, of the people—should be expanded (as in the case of the postal service) as rapidly and as far as the good sense of an intelligent people and the teachings of experience shall justify, to the end that oppression, injustice, and poverty shall eventually cease in the land.

While our sympathies as a party of reform are naturally upon the side of every proposition which will tend to make men intelligent, virtuous, and temperate, we nevertheless regard these questions, important as they are, as secondary to the great issues now pressing for solution, and upon which not only our individual prosperity but the very existence of free institutions depend; and we ask all men to first help us to determine whether we are to have a republic to administer before we differ as to the conditions upon which it is to be administered, believing that the forces of reform this day organized will never cease to move forward until every wrong is righted and equal rights and equal privileges securely established for all the men and women of this country.

PLATFORM

We declare, therefore—

First.—The the union of the labor forces of the United States this day consummated shall be permanent and perpetual; may its spirit enter into all hearts for the salvation of the Republic and the uplifting of mankind.

Second.—Wealth belongs to him who creates it, and every dollar taken from industry without an equivalent is robbery. "If any will not work, neither shall he eat." The interests of rural and civil labor are the same; their enemies are identical.

Third.—We believe that the time has come when the railroad corporations will either own the people or the people must own the railroads; and should the government enter upon the work of owning and managing all railroads, we should favor an amendment to the Constitution by which all persons engaged in the government service shall be placed under a civil-service regulation of the most rigid character, so as to prevent the increase of the power of the national administration by the use of such additional government employees.

FINANCE.—We demand a national currency, safe, sound, and flexible issued by the general government only, a full legal tender for all debts, public and private, and that without the use of banking corporations; a just, equitable, and efficient means of distribution direct to the people, at a tax not to exceed 2 per cent, per annum, to be provided as set forth in the sub-treasury plan of the Farmers' Alliance, or a better system; also by payments in discharge of its obligations for public improvements.

1. We demand free and unlimited coinage of silver and gold at the present legal ratio of 16 to 1.
2. We demand that the amount of circulating medium be speedily increased to not less than $50 per capita.
3. We demand a graduated income tax.
4. We believe that the money of the country should be kept as much as possible in the hands of the people, and hence we demand that all State and national revenues shall be limited to the necessary expenses of the government, economically and honestly administered.
5. We demand that postal savings banks be established by the government for the safe deposit of the earnings of the people and to facilitate exchange.

TRANSPORTATION.—Transportation being a means of exchange and a public necessity, the government should own and operate the railroads in the interest of the people. The telegraph and telephone, like the post-office system, being a necessity for the transmission of news, should be owned and operated by the government in the interest of the people.

LAND.—The land, including all the natural sources of wealth, is the heritage of the people, and should not be monopolized for speculative purposes, and alien ownership of land should be prohibited. All land now held by railroads and other corporations in excess of their actual needs, and all lands now owned by aliens, should be reclaimed by the government and held for actual settlers only.

EXPRESSION OF SENTIMENTS

Your Committee on Platform and Resolutions beg leave unanimously to report the following:

Whereas, Other questions have been presented for our consideration, we hereby submit the following, not as a part of the Platform of the People's Party, but as resolutions expressive of the sentiment of this Convention.

1. RESOLVED, That we demand a free ballot and a fair count in all elections, and pledge ourselves to secure it to every legal voter without Federal intervention, through the adoption by the States of the unperverted Australian or secret ballot system.

2. RESOLVED, That the revenue derived from a graduated income tax should be applied to the reduction of the burden of taxation now levied upon the domestic industries of this country.

3. RESOLVED, That we pledge our support to fair and liberal pensions to ex-Union soldiers and sailors.

4. RESOLVED, That we condemn the fallacy of protecting American labor under the present system, which opens our ports to the pauper and criminal classes of the world and crowds out our wage-earners; and we denounce the present ineffective laws against contract labor, and demand the further restriction of undesirable emigration.

5. RESOLVED, That we cordially sympathize with the efforts of organized workingmen to shorten the hours of labor, and demand a rigid enforcement of the existing eight-hour law on Government work, and ask that a penalty clause be added to the said law.

6. RESOLVED, That we regard the maintenance of a large standing army of mercenaries, known as the Pinkerton system, as a menace to our liberties, and we demand its abolition; and we condemn the recent invasions of the Territory of Wyoming by the hired assassins of plutocracy, assisted by Federal officers.

7. RESOLVED, That we commend to the favorable consideration of the people and the reform press the legislative system known as the initiative and referendum.

8. RESOLVED, That we favor a constitutional provision limiting the office of President and Vice-President to one term, and providing for the election of Senators of the United States by a direct vote of the people.

9. RESOLVED, That we oppose any subsidy or national aid to any private corporation for any purpose.

10. RESOLVED, That this convention sympathizes with the Knights of Labor and their righteous contest with the tyrannical combine of clothing manufacturers of Rochester, and declare it to be a duty of all who hate tyranny and oppression to refuse to purchase the goods made by the said manufacturers, or to patronize any merchants who sell such goods. ⌒

Secondary Sources

Goodwyn, Lawrence. *The Populist Moment.* New York: Oxford University Press, 1979.

Hicks, John D. *The Populist Revolt: A History of the Farmer's Alliances and the People's Party.* Lincoln: University of Nebraska Press, 1959.

27. Henry Demarest Lloyd

HENRY DEMAREST LLOYD (1847–1903) studied at Columbia Law School and served as financial editor and chief editorial writer for the Chicago *Tribune*. His columns were scholarly critiques of the Chicago Board of Trade, western mining companies, the railroads, and Standard Oil and other trusts. He also wrote magazine articles focusing on the dangers trusts and monopolies posed for democracy in the United States and calling for strong national regulation. But his major work was *Wealth against Commonwealth* (1894), a powerful and well-documented attack on corporate capitalism and its use of Social Darwinism and laissez-faire economics. Lloyd sought to provide a new social and philosophical base for democracy that would enable it to "harmonize and subordinate large scale economic organization to the ideals of freedom, equality, and humanity in the great society."[1]

Turning to direct social reform activity, Lloyd became probably its leading force by trying to build an alliance between urban labor and the Populist movement. He was deeply involved in Chicago politics and succeeded in 1894 in bringing about mutual agreements between labor unions and the People's party on platform adoptions. Other midwestern cities saw similar linkages developing in that year. If the alliance had been accomplished on anything like a national scale, the election of 1896 might have been very different.

The speech presented here is an 1894 address which serves several purposes: it summarizes some of the analysis presented at greater length in *Wealth against Commonwealth;* it suggests how Lloyd proposed to combine the premises and goals of farmers and labor; and finally, it indicates his sense of the relevance of an American socialism. ⌒

---

1. Charles Destler, *Radicalism in America, 1865–1901* (Storrs: University of Connecticut Press, 1947), 138.

"Revolution: The Evolution of Socialism" (1894)

All our parties are Reform parties. The democracy has been lowering the tariff ever since the government was established. They have done so well that their rates are higher in 1894 than they were in 1842. The republicans have been "saving the union" for thirty years, and the tramp, tramp, tramp, of a million men on the march still sounds through the country—the tramp of the tramp. The appearance at the polls of a new party which was not known in 1888, and in 1892, in its first presidential campaign, cast over 1,000,000 votes, is a hint that

SOURCE: Henry Demarest Lloyd, Address in Chicago, 6 October 1894. *The Commonwealth Library,* No. 2 (October 1894).

a new conception of reform is shaping itself in the minds of our fellow citizens. They want reform that will reform, and they want it now. Reform that is reform, and reform in our time, not in our great-grandchildren's, is what the people need and what they mean to have.

Lafayette said in 1791 that it would take twenty years to bring freedom to France; in two years feudalism was dead. Our great Emerson said in 1859—within four years of the emancipation proclamation—"We shall not live to see slavery abolished." Jefferson, the young delegate in the house of burgesses of Virginia, in one year abolished entail, and primogeniture, and the whole fabric of aristocracy, in that colony. The patricians pleaded for delay, for compromise. "Let our eldest sons inherit by law at least a double portion." "Not unless they can do twice as much work and eat twice as much as their younger brothers," was the reply of this first great social democrat, and he finished his reform at the same session at which he began it.

No great idea is ever lost. The greatest of human ideas is democracy. It has often disappeared, but it has never been lost. We have democratized religion, and the humblest men have equal rights with all others to find the Almighty within themselves, without the intervention of a privileged class. We have nearly finished democratizing kings, and we are now about to democratize the millionaire. Under absolutism the people mend their fortunes by insurrection. Under popular government they start a new party. All over the world, wherever popular government exists with its provisions for peaceful revolution instead of violent revolution, the people are forming new parties—in England, France, Germany, Australia, as well as in this country. This is the great political fact of our times. Some of these, like the distinctively workingmen's parties, are class movements. They are the natural and inevitable reaction from class movements against the workingmen. These parties all have practically the same object—to democratize the millionaire, and, as Jefferson did when he democratized the provincial patricians of Virginia, to do it as nearly as possible at one sitting.

THE EVILS OF CONCENTRATED WEALTH

A broad view of the reforms demanded by the new parties rising in Europe and America and Australia shows the substance of them all to be the same. There is nothing, Lowell says, that men prize so much as some kind of privilege, even though it be only the place of chief mourner at a funeral. In all the great industries a few men are building themselves up into the chief places, not as mourners themselves, but to make their fellow citizens mourners. The millions produce wealth; only the tens have it. There is the root of the whole matter. The first and last political issue of our time is with its concentrated wealth. Not with wealth, but with its concentration. "Far-seeing men," says James Russell Lowell, "count the increasing power of wealth and its combinations as one of the chief dangers with which the institutions of the United States are threatened in the not distant future." This concentration of wealth is but another name for the contraction of currency, the twin miseries of monopoly and pauperism, the tyranny of corporations, the corruption of the government, the depopulation of the country, the congestion of the cities, and the host of ills which now form the staple theme of our novelists and magazinists, and the speeches of the new-party orators.

Those faithful watchers who are sounding these alarms are ridiculed as calamity howlers. When strong, shrewd, grasping, covetous men devote themselves to creating calamities, fortunate are the people who are awakened by faithful calamity howlers. Noah was a calamity howler, and the bones of the men who laughed at him have helped to make the phosphate beds out of which fertilizers are now dug for the market. It was a calamity howler who said, "Sweet are the uses of adversity," and another averred that "Man was born to trouble, as the sparks fly upward." There are thirty-two paragraphs in the Declaration of Independence; twenty-nine of the thirty-two are calamity howls about the wrongs and miseries of America under British rule.

The contraction of the currency is a terrible thing, but there is another as terrible —the contraction of commodities and work by stoppage of production, lockout, the dismantling of competitive works, the suppression of patents, and other games of business. The institutions of America were founded to rest on the love of the people for their country; we have a new cement now to hold society together—injunctions and contempt of court.

And we see materializing out of the shadows of our great counting-rooms a new system of government—government by campaign contribution. The people maintain their national, state, city, and local governments at a cost of $1,000,000,000 a year; but the trusts, and armor-plate contractors, and the whisky ring, and the subsidized steamship companies, and the street and other railways, buy the privilege of running these governments to enrich themselves, to send troublesome leaders of the people to jail, to keep themselves out of jail. By campaign contributions of a few millions is thus bought away from the people the government which cost the people $1,000,000,000 a year. There are many marvels of cheapness in the market, but the greatest counter bargains in modern business are such as the sugar trust got when, by contributing a few hundred thousand dollars to both parties, it bought the right to tax the people untold millions a year.

THE COMING REVOLUTION IS HERE

We talk about the coming revolution and hope it will be peaceful. The revolution has come. This use of the government of all for the enrichment and aggrandizement of a few is a revolution. It is a revolution which has created the railroad millionaires of this country. To maintain the highways is one of the sacredest functions of a government. Railroads are possible only by the exercise of the still more sacred governmental power of eminent domain which when citizens will not sell the right of way takes their property through the forms of law by force—none the less by force because the money value is paid. These sovereign powers of the highway and of eminent domain have been given by you and me, all of us, to our government, to be used only for the common and equal benefit of all. Given by all to be used for all, it is a revolution to have made them the perquisite of a few. Only a revolution could have made possible in the speech of a free people such a phrase as a railroad king.

It is a revolution which has given the best parts of the streets that belong to all the people to street-railway syndicates, and gas companies, and telephone companies, and power companies. It is a revolution which has created national-bank millionaires, and bond millionaires, and tariff millionaires, and land-grant millionaires, out of the powers you and I delegated to the government of the United States for the equal good of every citizen. The inter-state commerce act was passed to put into prison the railroad managers who used their highway power to rob the people, to ruin the merchants and manufacturers whose business they wanted to give to favored shippers. The anti-trust law was passed to put into prison the men who make commerce a conspiracy, to compel the people every day to pay a ransom for their lives. It is a revolution which is using these interstate commerce and anti-trust laws to prosecute the employee of the railways for exercising their inalienable rights as free men to unite for defense against intolerable wrong. It is a revolution which lets the presidents, and managers, and owners of the railroads and trusts, go free of all punishment for the crimes they are committing; which sends out no process against any of the corporations or corporation men in the American Railway Association, while it uses all the powers of the attorney-general of the United States to prosecute, and, if possible, to send to prison, the members of the American Railway Union. It is a revolution which is putting the attorneys of corporations into ermine on the bench to be attorneys still.

It is a revolution by which great combinations, using competition to destroy competition, have monopolized entire markets, and as the sole sellers of goods make the people buy dear, and as the sole purchasers of labor make the people sell themselves cheap. The last and deepest and greatest revolution of all is that by which the mines, machinery, factories, currency, land, entrusted to private hands as private property, only as a stewardship, to warm, feed, clothe, serve mankind, are used to make men cold, hungry, naked, and destitute. Coal mines shut down to make coal scarce, mills shut down to make goods scarce, currency used to deprive people of the means of exchange, and the railways used to hinder transportation.

Counter Revolution of the People

This is the revolution that has come. With local variation it is world-wide, and against it the people are rising world-wide in peaceful counter revolutions, in people's parties. It begins now to be seen generally what a few have been pointing out from the beginning, that the working men in organizing to defend themselves have been only pioneers. The power which denied them a fair share of their production was the same power which is now attacking the consumer, the farmer, and even the fellow capitalist. In organizing against modern capitalism the workingmen set the example which all the people are now driven by self-preservation to follow. The trades union of the workingmen was the precursor of the farmers' alliance, the grange, and the people's party.

Chicago to-day leads the van in this great forward movement. Here the workingmen, capitalists, single-taxers, and socialists have come together to join forces with each other and with the farmers, as has been done in no other city. Its meetings are attended here by thousands, as you see to-night. It is the most wonderful outburst of popular hope and enthusiasm in the recent politics of this country. Chicago thus leads in numbers and in enthusiasm and promises of success, because it has led in boldness and sincerity and thoroughness of reform doctrine. The workingmen of Chicago at the Springfield conference, which was the fountainhead of this tidal wave, stood firm as a rock for the principle without which the industrial liberties of the people can never be established—the principle that they have the right at their option to own and operate collectively any or all of the means of production, distribution, and exchange. They already own some; they have the right to own as many more as they want. This is the mother principle of the government we already have, and it covers the whole brood of government railroads, telegraphs, telephones, banks, lands, street railways, all the municipalizations and nationalizations in which everywhere the people are giving utterance to their belief that they are the only proper and the only competent administrators of the wealth which they create.

The Declaration of Independence of 1776 declared that the people felt themselves able to manage for themselves the government, all of whose powers sprang from them. This declaration of 1894 is the proclamation of the next step in independence. The people have done so well that they will move forward again and manage for themselves some more departments of the commonwealth all of whose powers spring from them. The democratization of government, the democratization of collective industry—they are parts of one great upward emancipation. The American idea, says Emerson, is emancipation. The co-operative commonwealth is the legitimate offspring and lawful successor of the republic. Our liberties and our wealth are from the people and by the people and both must be for the people. Wealth, like government, is the product of the co-operation of all, and, like government, must be the property of all its creators, not of a privileged few alone. The principles of liberty, equality, union, which rule in the industries we call government, must rule in all industries. Government exists only by the consent of the governed. Business, property, capital, are also governments and must also rest on the consent of the governed. This assertion of the inherent and inalienable right, and ability, of the people to own and operate, at their option, any or all of the wealth they create, is the fundamental, irrepressible, and uncompromisable keynote of the crisis, and with this trumpet note you can lead the people through any sacrifice to certain victory.

THINGS THE PEOPLE HAVE LEARNED

Jefferson, one of his biographers tells us, was one of the most successful politicians of his time because he kept his ear close to the bosom of the people. If we will do the same we will hear the great heart of the common people beating the world over with this new hope of coming to own their means of production and the fruit of their labor, and so for the first time in history owning themselves. The people always think quicker and straighter than the philosophers, because while the philosopher simply meditates the people suffer. The people here to-night have learned in their

marketing, in their cut wages, in their lockouts and search for employment, in the prices they pay for sugar, and coal, and matches, and meat, and hundreds of other things, that all the other reforms—of the tariff, the banks, the land system, the railroads, and the currency —would leave them still the slaves of syndicates which hold the necessaries of life and means of production in absolute right as private property, beyond the reach of all these reforms, and with wealth which puts them beyond competition. Herein is the inner citadel of monopoly and "plank 10" is the battering-ram which will bring down its walls.

This cardinal principle, to which every candidate of the people's party of Cook county who seeks the support of the workingmen must subscribe, has been adopted in substance by the party in New York. The party in Connecticut in their last platform show themselves ready for it. It will without doubt be adopted overwhelmingly by the next national convention of the people's party, and under the banner of this principle—which is as big as the crisis—the party will move into the presidency, perhaps as soon as 1896. It is not to the parties that have produced the pandemonium of intermittent panic which is called trade and industry that the people can look for relief. To vote for them is to vote for more panics, more pandemoniums. Both these parties have done good work, but their good work is done. The republican party took the black man off the auction block of the slave power, but it has put the white man on the auction block of the money power, to be sold to the lowest bidder under the iron hammer of monopoly. The democratic party for a hundred years has been the pull-back against the centralization in American politics, standing for the individual against the community, the town against the state, and the state against the nation. But in one hour here last July it sacrificed the honorable devotion of a century to its great principle and surrendered both the rights of states and the rights of man to the centralized corporate despotism to which the presidency of the United States was then abdicated.

There ought to be two first-class political funerals in this country in 1896, and if we do our duty the corpses will be ready on time. "Are you going to the funeral of Benedict Arnold?" one of his neighbors asked another, "No, but I approve of it." We will not go to the republican and democratic funerals, but we approve of them. There is a party that the people can trust because in the face of overwhelming odds, without distinguished leaders, money, office, or prestige, it has raised the standard of a principle to save the people. The continual refrain of Mommsen, the great historian of Rome, is that its liberties and prosperity were lost because its reformers were only half reformers, and none of its statesmen would strike at the root of its evils. By that mistake we must profit.

It is a fact of political history that no new party was ever false to the cause for which it was formed. If the people's party as organized in Cook county is supported by the country, and the people get the control of their industries as of the government, the abolition of monopoly will as surely follow as the abolition of slavery followed the entrance of Abraham Lincoln into the white house in 1861. Then we will have the judges and the injunctions, the president and the house of representatives. There will be no senate; we will have the referendum, and the senate will go out when the people come in. The same constitution that could take the property of unwilling citizens for the railroads for rights of way can take the railroads, willing or unwilling, to be the nation's property when the people come in. Then the national debt, instead of representing the waste of war, will represent the railroads and other productive works owned by the people and worth more, as in Australia, than the bonds issued for them. The same constitution that could demonetize silver can remonetize it, or demonetize gold for a better money than either. The honest dollar will come in when the people come in, for it will not be a dollar that can be made scarce, to produce panics, and throw millions of men out of work, and compel the borrower to pay two where he received only one.

WOMEN MUST VOTE NOW

Women will vote, and some day we will have a woman president when the people come in. The post office will carry your telegrams and your parcels as well as your letters, and will be the people's bank for savings, and their life and accident insurance company, as it is elsewhere already. Every dark place in our cities will be brilliant with electricity, made by the municipalities for themselves. Working men and women will ride for 3 cents and school children for 2½ cents, as in Toronto, on streetcar lines owned by the municipalities, and paying by their profits a large part of the cost of government now falling on the tax-payer. When the people come in, political corruption, boss rule, and boodle will go out, because these spring mainly from the intrigues and briberies of syndicates to get hold of public functions for their private profit. We will have a real civil service, the inevitable and logical result of the demands of the people's party, founded, as true civil-service reform must be, on a system of public education which shall give every child of the republic the opportunity to fit himself for the public service. The same constitution which granted empires of public lands to create the Pacific railroad kings will find land for workingmen's homes and land for cooperative colonies of the unemployed.

There will soon be no unemployed when the people come in. They will have no shoemakers locked out or shoe factories shut down while there is a foot unshod, and all the mills and mines and factories the needs of the people require the people will keep going. Every man who works will get a living and every man who gets a living shall work, when the people come in. These are some of the things the people's party of Cook county means. At the coming election let every man and woman vote—for the women must vote through the men until they vote themselves— let every man and woman vote for those, and only for those, who accept this grand principle of the liberation of the people by themselves. Let this platform get a popular indorsement at the polls next November that will advertise to the world that the people have at last risen in their might, not to rest until another great emancipation has been added to the glorious record of the liberties achieved by mankind. ∾

Primary Sources

Lloyd, Henry Demarest. *Labor Copartnership: Notes of a Visit to Co-operative Workshops, Factories and Farms in Great Britain and Ireland, in Which Employer, Employee, and Consumer Share in Ownership, Management and Results.* New York and London: Harper and Brothers, 1898.

———. *Man, the Social Creator.* New York: Doubleday, Page, 1906.

———. *Men, the Workers.* New York: Arno Press, 1969.

Secondary Sources

Destler, Chester McArthur. *Henry Demarest Lloyd and the Empire of Reform.* Philadelphia: University of Pennsylvania Press, 1963.

Jernigan, E. Jay. *Henry Demarest Lloyd.* New York: Twayne Publishers, 1976.

Part IV

The Rise of the Positive State: 1900–1945

THE CENTURY began with laissez-faire capitalism at the height of its power. The return of prosperity, the diversion of the War of 1898, and McKinley's even greater majority win over Bryan in the election of 1900 than in 1896—all seemed to foreshadow a period of complete corporate dominance. But there continued to be social sources of opposition and a growing clamor from "muckrakers" and other middle-class intellectuals for various kinds of social reform. These were fueled by such economic and social conditions as arrogant profiteering by some trusts and speculators, urban degradation, unemployment and harsh working conditions, and corruption at various levels of government.

The power of the reform movements was significant, and fear of anarchist and socialist opposition was widespread among the upper classes.[1] Moreover, the biggest corporations and banks were beginning to see the need for some kind of national rationale for preventing destructive competition and ensuring stability and predictability in their industries.[2] Each of these factors contributed in some fashion to a basic change in liberalism from strict laissez-faire (with exceptions) to government intervention in the economy and society. Specific reforms and regulations of business became more frequent, and new national systems for overseeing key economic activities were created, such as the Federal Reserve system, the Federal Trade Commission, and the Pure Food and Drug Administration.

Historians now disagree over how much this new national government activity actually represented the resumption of popular control over a potentially runaway private economy. Some see it as part of the Progressive Era's more general efforts to improve the quality of working conditions and restore "good government" at all levels. Others see farsighted business leaders employing the façade of reform to penetrate and use the national executive branch for their own purposes; they also tend to view the Progressive Era as a period in which a middle class threatened by rising numbers of immigrants and lower classes asserted its own values. But the momentous nature of the change in liberalism is not at issue, nor is the significance of this period for establishing the basic structure and practices of the increasingly interdependent economic and political system in America.

---

1. James Weinstein, *The Corporate Ideal in the Liberal State, 1900–1918* (Boston: Beacon Press, 1964).
2. Gabriel Kolko, *The Triumph of Conservatism* (New York: Free Press, 1963).

In this part we shall first survey the ideas put forward by the major sources of opposition, with particular concern for their underlying assumptions and how they contrasted with liberalism. Then we shall examine the ways in which the change in liberalism was accomplished, first in the important intellectual synthesis of Hamilton and Jefferson achieved by Herbert Croly and next in the popularizing speeches and actions of Presidents Woodrow Wilson and Franklin Roosevelt. We shall also see that new applications of science, technology, organization, and bureaucracy made these changes a part of everyday working life—and created new problems for "democracy."

Sources of Opposition and Reform

As the modern industrial system began to take shape, some social groups sought to be included in its opportunities or protected against its most severe inequalities. Others opposed it in fundamental ways, criticizing its basic social and economic structure, its values and practices, and the quality of life within it, and calling for its total reconstruction.

The first demands were reformist in character in that the groups making them accepted the basic structures and values of the existing system, asking that these also be applied to them with perhaps some modifications. Examples in the early years of this period included: organized labor, made up chiefly of craft unions and clearly operating on the defensive; the women's movement, now focused almost entirely on gaining the right to vote; most black organizations, still seeking the most traditional civil rights and acceptance as citizens; and the muckrakers and municipal reformers who sought to end the worst corporate abuses and governmental corruption. All of these movements were seeking goals entirely consistent with the dominant capitalist-liberal system. Thus they could be accommodated without seriously challenging that system. Their

cumulative effect was to force the liberal value of equality to rank almost as high a priority as that of property and to add to the momentum that ultimately converted liberalism from being laissez-faire to being interventionist. But there were no new or fundamentally different ideas put forward by these movements.

The second set of demands, however, would have required reconstruction of the social order in the most basic ways. The assumptions and values of these movements posed perhaps the most vigorous challenge liberalism has ever faced in American history, even though the social force behind them was modest and dispersed within two decades. Examples in these early years included anarchism, radical feminism, militant black nationalism, and socialism. The first and last of these were most important at the time and will receive priority here, although the others will be considered briefly in conclusion.

ANARCHISM

Much confusion has been generated over the years, some of it deliberately by its detractors, about anarchism's beliefs and goals. Anarchism is not a synonym for chaos, nor is it exaggerated individualism combined with strict laissez-faire on the part of government. To be sure, there is an American variant, often called *libertarianism,* which takes liberal individualism to its furthest extreme and exalts individual self-determination and "freedom" over all social obligation or restraints. But, however attractive to some in the American context, this is not the primary thrust of anarchist thought.

Instead, the premise of anarchism is that human nature is cooperative and good rather than acquisitive and self-seeking. People naturally seek to live harmoniously with their fellows, to experience a genuine sense of community in their social and interpersonal relationships. What prevents them from doing this, and thus from realizing their highest human potential as individuals, are the hierarchical structures and demands imposed on them —social, economic, and political. Capitalism is the worst of these hierarchical systems because it is based on the exploitation of human by human; because it emphasizes self-seeking, profit, and consumption as the primary motivators in social life; and because it results in profound alienation for working people. The capitalist state is the organized enforcer of these destructive hierarchical relationships and must be destroyed along with the economic system it serves. But the socialist state is considered almost as bureaucratic and hierarchical as the capitalist state and therefore is no real improvement. In other words, although anarchists make much the same critique of capitalism as socialists do, the two split sharply over the proper remedy. They often quarrel as vigorously with each other as they do with their shared enemy, capitalist-liberal society.

The goal that anarchists seek is not a world without order of any kind, nor are they opposed to organization as such. Anarchism holds that people should act spontaneously but that they will also want to do so in concert with their fellows under conditions of true freedom. What evolves then is an order or an organization based on constant discussion and continuing consent on the part of its members, probably with rotating representative responsibilities amidst the accepted equality of all. It is a social system in which people experience no unnecessary constraints, external or internalized, and thus are free to develop all their innate human potential. They can do so, of course, only in a context with other human beings who are equally free of restraints and able to form a reciprocally developing community together.

Finally, anarchism does not hold that violence is necessary or desirable as a means of bringing about its goals. For a period in the late nineteenth century, some anarchists thought that there was something to be gained from "propaganda of the deed," and they committed such terrorist acts as assassinations and bombings. But most anarchists have always thought terrorism counterproductive and inconsistent with principled commitments to human life and its potential. Violence might be necessary at some point to defend against the systematic violence perpetrated by capitalism on working people or to defend the anarchist society once achieved. It forms no integral part of the anarchist belief system, however, and the widely shared impression that it does is the achievement of antianarchist propaganda over the years.

The anarchist movement in the United States was highly visible from the 1880s to about 1920. The Haymarket Massacre of 1886 in Chicago led to the conviction and execution of several anarchist leaders and to a general wave of revulsion against the "foreign" doctrines and their equally foreign advocates. Doubt remains about who actually committed the acts involved, but it seems clear that the executed anarchists did not. The occasion was used as an opportunity to link anarchism with violence and to discredit it. That this tactic was only partially successful may be seen from the dramatic and successful career of the leading anarchist agitator, Emma Goldman, whose impact was greatest in the early decades of the twentieth century. Through her journal *Mother Earth,* her lecture tours, and her own life (particularly as sensationalized in the press), she managed to bring the anarchist message before millions of Americans. Her essay on anarchism presented in selection 28 is one of the classics of American anarchism, even though it contains a thread of the libertarian individualism that makes anarchism confusing in this country.

SOCIALISM

As noted earlier, an indigenous American socialism arose in reaction to capitalism in the

1830s and 1840s. Capitalism was charged with exploitation, promulgation of values destructive to human community, and general degradation of workers' lives. The conditions of the 1880s and 1890s led to a similar reaction among American thinkers, who called for commonsense collective action to take over the most exploitative industries (railroads and mines) and manage them for public good rather than private profit. Marxian socialism proceeded from a more comprehensive interpretation of the historical development of economic systems and the ideological and cultural characteristics of their related social orders. It arrived with the waves of German immigration in the 1850s, 1870s, and 1880s, but remained isolated among Germans for several years.

With the formation of the Socialist party in 1900, the native and Marxian strands began to come together in uneasy coalition. With Eugene Debs as its most visible spokesperson, socialism soon began to make electoral as well as intellectual progress. In 1912, the high point of socialist achievement, there were hundreds of local and state officeholders, and the readership of socialist papers was well into the hundreds of thousands. As a result of its antiwar position, however, the Socialist party suffered vigorous attacks by national and state governments, the press, and patriotic vigilantes. When these were compounded by internal strife and reactions to the Bolshevik revolution of 1917 (for and against), the party began to disintegrate and socialist ideas lost their mass appeal soon afterwards.

Socialism would replace private ownership of the major means of production (but not including such private property as houses, cars, and personal possessions) with public ownership in the hands of a democratically elected government. It would replace what it sees as the irrationality and gross inequalities of capitalism with a national planning system in which social goals would control the uses of resources and the pattern of capital investment. Instead of producing whatever could be sold at a profit, production would be designed to serve human needs in the society. Instead of the appropriation of the major share of the surplus generated by a few capitalist owners, distribution of such wealth and income would be made far more equal, and conditions of employment more satisfactory for workers.

Socialists believe that the profit imperative of capitalism results in low wages, dangerous working conditions, unemployment, and a generally stunted and desperate quality of life for workers. The capitalist ruling class is seen as using a variety of ideological and coercive organizations and techniques (such as the press, organized religion, the schools, the courts, the police, and the army) to maintain control over the population. People are therefore unable to develop in accordance with all the potential inherent in human nature, or —because of their anxiety for mere survival and the power of the internalized cultural values of capitalism—they are even capable of participating in their own oppression.

The task for socialism is therefore to help the masses of people see the nature of the world they live in and help them see how collective action might reconstruct it into a more satisfyingly human society. The socialist critique of capitalism is total, in that structures, values, and practices are all viewed as having a coherent, systemic relationship to one another. Consequently, they must *all* be changed, though not necessarily at the same time. Unlike some earlier labor radicals and populists, socialists specifically reject raising one or a few issues in isolation, and they insist on a deeper causal analysis of what is wrong as well as on a complete program of reconstruction.

The greatest issue for the Socialist party in

this early period was how to make the necessary connections between its analysis, its leaders, and the mass base of working people needed to gain power. Electoral campaigns by the party were an obvious tactic, but divisions developed over the question of how explicitly and comprehensively to make a distinctly socialist program the basis of such campaigns. Continued debates arose over whether socialists should enter existing unions and try to educate within them to bring the members to socialism, or whether this was so unlikely a result that separate unions of socialist orientation should be formed and members recruited directly into them. This is the so-called dual unionism issue, and disagreements about the better tactic to use in the face of hostility from existing labor leaders have always troubled socialists. Nearly all socialists agreed, however, that industrial unions were preferable whenever possible, leading therefore to substantial initial support for the Industrial Workers of the World (IWW or Wobblies) when it formed in 1905.

Most socialists of this period saw eventual electoral victory as the proper route to power. Only a few believed that a future violent revolution was possible and necessary. However, the views of this latter group, though few in number, were given such prominence that a basic fear of socialism was generated on these grounds. The necessity faced by many socialists of meeting force with force—on the picket lines, in labor organizing, or in defense against vigilantes—gave some credence to this impression. But there was even less connection between socialism and violence than there was between anarchism and violence. Indeed, American constitutional law on civil liberties today owes much of its substance to the claims for free speech and freedom of assembly that were made by socialists who had everything to lose when violence occurred.

RADICAL FEMINISM AND MILITANT BLACK NATIONALISM

Some limited representation of the values and goals of both of these movements occurred during this period. In both cases, however, it was due to the distinctive contributions of one or two unusual individuals, rather than to any underlying social force. The importance of these individuals is thus due more to their unique ideas and the forcefulness with which they articulated them—thereby serving to ignite fuses that would explode far in the future—than to any contemporary impact.

Radical feminism is used here to characterize those who saw in women's status both systematic male dominance and the compelling need to reconstruct the social order (starting with how women thought about themselves) to achieve full equality and real freedom. Entering the present society on terms equal to men would not suffice: its defects were too profound and its values too corrupt. What was needed was a new kind of society in which not only sex distinctions but also class and cultural restraints on human freedom would be eliminated. Obtaining the vote for women was considered a tiny and probably delusive step in this process. All of these ideas find cogent expression in Emma Goldman's "Tragedy of Women's Emancipation," an essay that still seems advanced in many respects today.

Militant black nationalism is used to characterize those who demanded white acceptance of black history and culture and sought human equality and dignity as a matter of right rather than a gift grudgingly granted. Some black spokespeople advocated slow assimilation on white terms, and others even acquiesced to segregation while blacks were acquiring the necessary skills to compete in white society. But those such as W.E.B. Du Bois saw a racism so historically and deeply embedded in institutions, values, and practices that to eradicate it, it had to be confronted and the society reconstructed. His scholarly work documented overt and covert institutional racism, and his popular works expressed black outrage in ways equaled only in the post–World War II period. His dispute with other black thinkers is reflected in the major essay in selection 29.

From Laissez-faire to Interventionism and the Positive State

The many calls for specific reforms made by muckrakers and other Progressive elements combined with fear of the much smaller anarchist and socialist movements to generate significant momentum for the idea that some forms of change were necessary and desirable. But the scope of change and its enduring implications for the rise of an interventionist government (ultimately, the "positive" or purposeful as well as powerful state) would probably not have occurred had it not been for the active cooperation of the largest corporations and banks. In a painstakingly documented study of this period, historian Gabriel Kolko has shown how the needs of corporations and banks for economic stability, an end to destructive competition, and a greater voice in government policy led to support for a number of the regulatory reforms pressed by the Theodore Roosevelt and Woodrow Wilson administrations.[3] Their role was obscured at the time, of course, by the loud opposition mounted by smaller and localized businesses and other defenders of the status quo.

Pressures for some kind of reform that would give the national government power to manage parts of the private economy thus emanated from many sources. But such national public policies would clearly have violated the long-established principle of laissez-faire, re-

affirmed so decisively only as recently as 1896 and 1900. Pragmatic American policymakers would probably have gone ahead in any event, but the "New Nationalism" of Roosevelt and the "New Freedom" of Wilson both received their ideological justification from the publication in 1909 of Herbert Croly's *Promise of American Life*. Roosevelt's debt was explicit and acknowledged. Wilson's was clearer in practice than in rhetoric. What Croly caught and expressed was what was "in the air" at the time. His actual impact is less important than the way in which his work symbolizes the change taking place in liberalism during this era.

Croly's problem was that of early twentieth-century liberalism and in some respects of liberalism today: can a system resting on individualism, contract, and property rights act purposefully and comprehensively enough to control excesses in the use of great accumulations of private economic power or to alleviate other social ills? Those key values tend to hold government action to interstitial, limited policies in cases where it is shown to be absolutely necessary. But would it not then be timely and sufficient to do more than temporarily patch up the most extreme dislocations—to attack the fundamental causes to prevent them from generating greater problems for the future? Yet any attempt to employ government in a manner equal to the problems that existed, Croly argued, would run aground against the residue of Jeffersonian individualism and limited government. Thus liberalism was boxed in between problematic conditions, on the one hand, and a self-limiting set of inhibitions against use of government, on the other.

Croly's solution was an explicit synthesis of the traditional Hamiltonian and Jeffersonian positions. He shared Hamilton's willingness to assume responsibility for achieving specific goals through the use of government, and he converted Hamilton's purposes into the broader one of a prosperous economy man-

---

3. Kolko, *The Triumph of Conservatism*.

aged by an intelligent and public-spirited government. But he also endorsed Jefferson's concern for the individual's attainment and for the general social and economic betterment of all members of the society. Croly proposed to harmonize these two sets of goals through the deliberate employment of government as the agent of the people for the purpose of realizing a "morally and socially desirable distribution of wealth." This meant that long-range goals would be defined and basic policy directions set through popular decision-making processes; then public officials would use the powers of government in whatever ways necessary to accomplish those ends. It also emphatically meant the end of limited government and laissez-faire inhibitions on the part of government. Croly was convinced that conditions in the economy were such as to make concentration of capital and certain monopolies inevitable, desirable, and efficient; for him the problem was not to break them up but to enable them to be managed for maximum public benefit. He believed that continued individual self-serving in the context of the times would create intolerable conditions where disparities in wealth and opportunity would destroy all sense of community and all hope for realization of the American promise. He saw his proposals as uniting the nationalist vision of Hamilton with the democratic commitments of Jefferson to raise the possibility of a new era of social and economic achievement.

Croly's argument gave liberalism a new rationale for the interventionist use of government but preserved liberalism's individualist core, its commitment to property rights, and its other traditional goals of individual freedom and equality. In so doing, he set off a debate that continues to this day between 1890s-style liberals, who insist on laissez-faire and limited government (and are sometimes called conservatives for that reason), and modern, or "welfare," liberals, who, in their desire to use

government to manage the economy and serve other social goals, have supported repeated and sustained governmental interventions. Both sides, of course, retain commitments to individualism, property, freedom, and equality in this context.

What makes Croly so fascinating as a watershed figure in American political thought is the ambiguity in his synthesis. The Jeffersonian side would preserve the democratic emphasis on government's managing the economy in the public interest. It is this side that has given the Progressive Era the image of being a period of democratic reform and that has led to understanding the American system as one of *welfare liberalism,* in which the needs of individuals are served by their democratically controlled government. But the Hamiltonian side would emphasize government serving different ends—those of business and finance, or *corporate liberalism.* From this side, today's corporations and banks would in time have gained dominating influence over the actions of the national government, particularly those of the executive branch, and the idea of democratic control would have been a convenient umbrella under which they could work their private will.

Is Croly a modern liberal or a contemporary Hamiltonian conservative? Probably he is some of each. In his day, and in most subsequent understanding, he was viewed as the father of modern liberalism. But inherent in the structures and priorities that he helped to justify are tendencies toward the few using power at the expense of the many. These tendencies are there in Croly, as they are there in the new liberalism he helped to evolve, and it is the actions-in-context of subsequent thinkers and policymakers that have (or will have) determined the eventual outcome.

Which side of Croly's synthesis would come to dominate in later years? Clearly, there has been another, modern round in the struggle between Jefferson and Hamilton, one profoundly influenced by the increasing scale of organization and by demands that international responsibilities and domestic crises have placed on the political economy. In the crucial implementing years of the new liberalism —during the Wilson and Franklin Roosevelt administrations—war and depression played no small part. In both cases the tradition and rhetoric were Jeffersonian. The practice was reformist but sensitive to the needs of business and open to its participation. A case can certainly be made that the consequences more often than not were Hamiltonian.

The practical implementation of Croly's philosophical synthesis of Hamilton and Jefferson and revision of liberalism occurred in the political programs of the following two decades, which built the positive state and have shaped the remainder of the twentieth century. Woodrow Wilson was as good a Progressive as Theodore Roosevelt, and Franklin Roosevelt was the best of them all. The rhetoric of Jefferson and the practice of Hamilton live on today as a result. Three selections document and illustrate this century-shaping framework. First is Progressivism (selection 32), including the party platform of 1912 and the constitutional reforms associated with it. Wilson's "New Democracy" provides early and effective support (selection 34), and then FDR's "New Deal" (selection 36) completes the justification for the positive state with his "Economic Bill of Rights," which was never implemented.

The Roles of Science, Technology, Organization, and Bureaucracy— and the Problem of Democracy

At the same time Croly was articulating the justification for liberalism's reversal of laissez-faire, several less visible but equally important processes were at work to similarly reorganize economic and political life. Bigness had come to be accepted as necessary and efficient in corporate life, and commensurate increases in scale were set underway for the national government. But now large-scale production, distribution, and consumption were to be systematized and expanded through the introduction of new scientific and managerial techniques. The advertising industry, for example, would soon become a major economic factor as forms of communication multiplied and reached more deeply into the society.

Nothing better expresses the penetration of science and managerialism into everyday life, however, than the idea of scientific management promulgated by Frederick W. Taylor. Taylor's principles were designed to make work in mass-production industries more efficient through a combination of time-and-motion studies and a variety of incentives. These principles also tended to reduce each worker's knowledge to but one minor function, making workers more dispensable and easier to control. New layers of management were created to ensure maximum efficiency and productivity.

At first, even the wide impact that scientific management had in the manufacturing, mining, and transportation industries might not seem to be political or involve political thought. But the popularity of such management in these industries and in the press illustrates not only the extent to which the whole country was in thrall to science and managerialism, but also the profoundly political way its effects shaped work life, social mobility, self-understanding, and ways of thinking in the society. Congress thought Taylor's efforts important enough to appoint a select committee to explore its implications and succeeded at least in getting Taylor to acknowledge that one consequence was higher profits with fewer, less skilled employees (selection 33).

As the scale and assets of corporate organizations increased, so did the number and relative power of the bureaucracies needed to manage them. The actual power to control the corporation seemed to be drained from the founding family, the board of directors, or the increasingly numerous body of stockholders. Instead it was located in the managers, in the subordinate bureaucracy, or perhaps in some impersonal way in the organization itself. The whole idea of property, as well as the responsibility for directing the corporation, was confused under these circumstances. By the 1930s prominent New Dealers were arguing that this meant that the public, in the form of the national government, might legitimately exercise control over those kinds of corporations whose lack of coherent direction resulted in failure to meet social responsibilities. (Of course, the argument that large organizations contained their own logic and defied control efforts could be applied to the expanding New Deal government agencies as well.)

The problem of scale and organization and attendant bureaucracy and control questions thus rose to prominence between the Progressive Era and the New Deal. It was a problem for political thought *and* a problem for the everyday life of the growing millions whose lives and work were enmeshed in organizations and subject to bureaucracy. Not least of the problems exacerbated (if not created) by the new conditions of social and economic organization was that of preserving broad democratic participation and accountability. The twin difficulties ordinary people had of acquiring enough information about an increasingly complex and technological world and of effectively exercising control over public institutions and policies seemed insurmountable. One solution, some thought, might be to develop new understandings of democracy that were consistent with what was thought possible. This might readily lead toward reducing the role of popular majorities within the liberal system. But it might also lead toward new opportunities for democracy, using new scientific knowledge-producing and communication techniques. This was proposed by the leading philosopher of the first half of the twentieth century, John Dewey (see selection 35).

The problems generated in the Progressive Era are still with us today because the basic structures and values of that period have become fixed into an enduring framework. From that time forward, we have embellished rather than reconstructed it, in response to new problems and conditions we have encountered. ✇

28. Emma Goldman

EMMA GOLDMAN (1869–1940) was born in Russia and emigrated to the United States in 1886. The Haymarket Riot and the subsequent execution of several leading anarchists gave focus to her developing political concerns, and she soon became one of the best-known authors and lecturers in American history. She was not only a highly visible and persuasive anarchist but also a very modern-sounding advocate of a comprehensive women's liberation. From the 1890s on, she was the constant object of police and press harassment and was imprisoned twice, interrogated at length several times, and prevented from speaking on many occasions. Nevertheless, for several years she edited and published *Mother Earth,* a leading anarchist journal, and repeatedly made speaking tours in the United States and Europe.

Both of the following excerpts were originally contributions to *Mother Earth* and were later published in a collection of such work. "Anarchism: What It Really Stands For" expands on some earlier American individualist thought and amounts to a fairly comprehen-

sive statement of anarchist principles. Some anarchists did not share Goldman's individualist premise that the masses lacked competence to govern and should defer to the wise and talented few, but all accepted her as a leading spokesperson for their cause. The second excerpt develops a comprehensive argument for the liberation of women, expanding on her previous critique of the illusions contained in the woman suffrage movement. ∾

"Anarchism: What It Really Stands For" (1907)

Ever reviled, accursed, ne'er understood,
  Thou art the grisly terror of our age.
"Wreck of all order," cry the multitude,
  "Art thou, and war and murder's
    endless rage."
O, let them cry. To them that ne'er
    have striven
  The truth that lies behind a word to
    find,
To them the word's right meaning was
    not given.
  They shall continue blind among the
    blind.
But thou, O word, so clear, so strong,
    so pure,
  Thou sayest all which I for goal
    have taken.
I give thee to the future! Thine secure
  When each at least unto himself
    shall waken.
Comes it in sunshine? In the tempest's
    thrill?
  I cannot tell—but it the earth shall see!
I am an Anarchist! Wherefore I will
  Not rule, and also ruled I will not be!
      John Henry Mackay

The history of human growth and development is at the same time the history of the terrible struggle of every new idea heralding the approach of a brighter dawn. In its tenacious hold on tradition, the Old has never hesitated to make use of the foulest and cruelest means to stay the advent of the New, in whatever form or period the latter may have asserted itself. Nor need we retrace our steps into the distant past to realize the enormity of opposition, difficulties, and hardships placed in the path of every progressive idea. The rack, the thumbscrew, and the knout are still with us; so are the convict's garb and the social wrath, all conspiring against the spirit that is serenely marching on.

Anarchism could not hope to escape the fate of all other ideas of innovation. Indeed, as the most revolutionary and uncompromising innovator, Anarchism must needs meet with the combined ignorance and venom of the world it aims to reconstruct.

SOURCE: Both excerpts in this selection are from Emma Goldman, *Anarchism and Other Essays* (New York: Dover, 1969).

To deal even remotely with all that is being said and done against Anarchism would necessitate the writing of a whole volume. I shall therefore meet only two of the principal objections. In so doing, I shall attempt to elucidate what Anarchism really stands for.

The strange phenomenon of the opposition to Anarchism is that it brings to light the relation between so-called intelligence and ignorance. And yet this is not so very strange when we consider the relativity of all things. The ignorant mass has in its favor that it makes no pretense of knowledge or tolerance. Acting, as it always does, by mere impulse, its reasons are like those of a child. "Why?" "Because." Yet the opposition of the uneducated to Anarchism deserves the same consideration as that of the intelligent man.

What, then, are the objections? First, Anarchism is impractical, though a beautiful ideal. Second, Anarchism stands for violence and destruction, hence it must be repudiated as vile and dangerous. Both the intelligent man and the ignorant mass judge not from a thorough knowledge of the subject, but either from hearsay or false interpretation.

A practical scheme, says Oscar Wilde, is either one already in existence, or a scheme that could be carried out under the existing conditions; but it is exactly the existing conditions that one objects to, and any scheme that could accept these conditions is wrong and foolish. The true criterion of the practical, therefore, is not whether the latter can keep intact the wrong or foolish; rather is it whether the scheme has vitality enough to leave the stagnant waters of the old, and build, as well as sustain, new life. In the light of this conception, Anarchism is indeed practical. More than any other idea, it is helping to do away with the wrong and foolish; more than any other idea, it is building and sustaining new life.

The emotions of the ignorant man are continuously kept at a pitch by the most blood-curdling stories about Anarchism. Not a thing too outrageous to be employed against this philosophy and its exponents. Therefore Anarchism represents to the unthinking what the proverbial bad man does to the child,—a black monster bent on swallowing everything; in short, destruction and violence.

Destruction and violence! How is the ordinary man to know that the most violent element in society is ignorance; that its power of destruction is the very thing Anarchism is combating? Nor is he aware that Anarchism, whose roots, as it were, are part of nature's forces, destroys, not healthful tissue, but parasitic growths that feed on the life's essence of society. It is merely clearing the soil from weeds and sagebrush, that it may eventually bear healthy fruit.

Someone has said that it requires less mental effort to condemn than to think. The widespread mental indolence, so prevalent in society, proves this to be only too true. Rather than to go to the bottom of any given idea, to examine into its origin and meaning, most people will either condemn it altogether, or rely on some superficial or prejudicial definition of non-essentials.

Anarchism urges man to think, to investigate, to analyze every proposition; but that the brain capacity of the average reader be not taxed too much, I also shall begin with a definition, and then elaborate on the latter.

ANARCHISM:—The philosophy of a new social order based on liberty unrestricted by man-made law; the theory that all forms of government rest on violence, and are therefore wrong and harmful, as well as unnecessary.

The new social order rests, of course, on the materialistic basis of life; but while all Anarchists agree that the main evil today is an economic one, they maintain that the solution of that evil can be brought about only through the consideration of *every phase* of life,—individual, as well as the collective; the internal, as well as the external phases.

A thorough perusal of the history of human development will disclose two elements in bitter conflict with each other; elements that are only now beginning to be understood, not as foreign to each other, but as closely related and truly harmonious, if only placed in proper environment: the individual and social instincts. The individual and society have waged a relentless and bloody battle for ages, each striving for supremacy, because each was blind to the value and importance of the other. The individual and social instincts,—the one a most potent factor for individual endeavor, for growth, aspiration, self-realization; the other an equally potent factor for mutual helpfulness and social well-being.

The explanation of the storm raging within the individual, and between him and his surroundings, is not far to seek. The primitive man, unable to understand his being, much less the unity of all life, felt himself absolutely dependent on blind, hidden forces ever ready to mock and taunt him. Out of that attitude grew the religious concepts of man as a mere speck of dust dependent on superior powers on high, who can only be appeased by complete surrender. All the early sagas rest on that idea, which continues to be the *Leitmotif* of the biblical tales dealing with the relation of man to God, to the State, to society. Again and again the same motif, *man is nothing, the powers are everything*. Thus Jehovah would only endure man on condition of complete surrender. Man can have all the glories of the earth, but he must not become conscious of himself. The State, society, and moral laws all sing the same refrain: Man can have all the glories of the earth, but he must not become conscious of himself.

Anarchism is the only philosophy which brings to man the consciousness of himself; which maintains that God, the State, and society are non-existent, that their promises are null and void, since they can be fulfilled only through man's subordination. Anarchism is therefore the teacher of the unity of life; not merely in nature, but in man. There is no conflict between the individual and the social instincts, any more than there is between the heart and the lungs: the one the receptacle of a precious life essence, the other the repository of the element that keeps the essence pure and strong. The individual is the heart of society, conserving the essence of social life; society is the lungs which are distributing the element to keep the life essence—that is, the individual —pure and strong.

"The one thing of value in the world," says Emerson, "is the active soul; this every man contains within him. The soul active sees absolute truth and utters truth and creates." In other words, the individual instinct is the thing of value in the world. It is the true soul that sees and creates the truth alive, out of which is to come a still greater truth, the re-born social soul.

Anarchism is the great liberator of man from the phantoms that have held him captive; it is the arbiter and pacifier of the two forces for individual and social harmony. To accomplish that unity, Anarchism has declared war on the pernicious influences which have so far prevented the harmonious blending of individual and social instincts, the individual and society.

Religion, the dominion of the human mind; Property, the dominion of human needs; and Government, the dominion of human conduct, represent the stronghold of man's enslavement and all the horrors it entails. Religion! How it dominates man's mind, how it humiliates and degrades his soul. God is everything, man is nothing, says religion. But out of that nothing God has created a kingdom so despotic, so tyrannical, so cruel, so terribly exacting that naught but gloom and tears and blood have ruled the world since gods began. Anarchism rouses man to rebellion against this black monster. Break your mental fetters, says Anarchism to man, for not until you think and judge for yourself will you get rid of the dominion of darkness, the greatest obstacle to all progress.

Property, the dominion of man's needs, the denial of the right to satisfy his needs. Time was when property claimed a divine right, when it came to man with the same refrain, even as religion, "Sacrifice! Abnegate! Submit!" The spirit of Anarchism has lifted man from his prostrate position. He now stands erect, with his face toward the light. He has learned to see the insatiable, devouring, devastating nature of property, and he is preparing to strike the monster dead.

"Property is robbery," said the great French Anarchist Proudhon. Yes, but without risk and danger to the robber. Monopolizing the accumulated efforts of man, property has robbed him of his birthright, and has turned him loose a pauper and an outcast. Property has not even the time-worn excuse that man does not create enough to satisfy all needs. The ABC student of economics knows that the productivity of labor within the last few decades far exceeds normal demand. But what are normal demands to an abnormal institution? The only demand that property recognizes is its own gluttonous appetite for greater wealth, because wealth means power; the power to subdue, to crush, to exploit, the power to enslave, to outrage, to degrade. America is particularly boastful of her great power, her enormous national wealth. Poor America, of what avail is all her wealth, if the individuals comprising the nation are wretchedly poor? If they live in squalor, in filth, in crime, with hope and joy gone, a homeless, soilless army of human prey.

It is generally conceded that unless the returns of any business venture exceed the cost, bankruptcy is inevitable. But those engaged in the business of producing wealth have not yet learned even this simple lesson. Every year the cost of production in human life is growing larger (50,000 killed, 100,000 wounded in America last year); the returns to the masses, who help to create wealth, are ever getting smaller. Yet America continues to be blind to the inevitable bankruptcy of our business of production. Nor is this the only crime of the latter. Still more fatal is the crime of turning the producer into a mere particle of a machine, with less will and decision than his master of steel and iron. Man is being robbed not merely of the products of his labor, but of the power of free initiative, of originality, and the interest in, or desire for, the things he is making.

Real wealth consists in things of utility and beauty, in things that help to create strong, beautiful bodies and surroundings inspiring to live in. But if man is doomed to wind cotton around a spool, or dig coal, or build roads for thirty years of his life, there can be no talk of wealth. What he gives to the world is only gray and hideous things, reflecting a dull and hideous existence,—too weak to live, too cowardly to die. Strange to say, there are people who extol this deadening method of centralized production as the proudest achievement of our age. They fail utterly to realize that if we are to continue in machine subserviency, our slavery is more complete than was our bondage to the King. They do not want to know that centralization is not only the death-knell of liberty, but also of health and beauty, of art and science, all these being impossible in a clock-like, mechanical atmosphere.

Anarchism cannot but repudiate such a method of production: its goal is the freest possible expression of all the latent powers of the individual. Oscar Wilde defines a perfect personality as "one who develops under perfect conditions, who is not wounded, maimed, or in danger." A perfect personality, then, is only possible in a state of society where man is free to choose the mode of work, the conditions of work, and the freedom to work. One to whom the making of a table, the building of a house, or the tilling of the soil, is what the painting is to the artist and the discovery to the scientist,—the result of inspiration, of intense longing, and deep interest in work as a creative force. That being the ideal of Anarchism, its economic arrangements must consist of voluntary productive and distributive associations, gradually developing into free communism, as the best means of producing with the least waste of human energy. Anarchism, however, also recognizes the right of the individual, or numbers of individuals, to arrange at all times for other forms of work, in harmony with their tastes and desires.

Such free display of human energy being possible only under complete individual and social freedom, Anarchism directs its forces against the third and greatest foe of all social equality; namely, the State, organized authority, or statutory law,—the dominion of human conduct.

Just as religion has fettered the human mind, and as property, or the monopoly of things, has subdued and stifled man's needs, so has the State enslaved his spirit, dictating every phase of conduct. "All government in essence," says Emerson, "is tyranny." It matters not whether it is government by divine right or majority rule. In every instance its aim is the absolute subordination of the individual.

Referring to the American government, the greatest American Anarchist, David Thoreau, said: "Government, what is it but a tradition, though a recent one, endeavoring to transmit itself unimpaired to posterity, but each instance losing its integrity; it has not the vitality and force of a single living man. Law never made man a whit more just; and by means of their respect for it, even the well disposed are

daily made agents of injustice."

Indeed, the keynote of government is injustice. With the arrogance and self-sufficiency of the King who could do no wrong, governments ordain, judge, condemn, and punish the most insignificant offenses, while maintaining themselves by the greatest of all offenses, the annihilation of individual liberty. Thus Ouida is right when she maintains that "the State only aims at instilling those qualities in its public by which its demands are obeyed, and its exchequer is filled. Its highest attainment is the reduction of mankind to clockwork. In its atmosphere all those finer and more delicate liberties, which require treatment and spacious expansion, inevitably dry up and perish. The State requires a taxpaying machine in which there is no hitch, an exchequer in which there is never a deficit, and a public, monotonous, obedient, colorless, spiritless, moving humbly like a flock of sheep along a straight high road between two walls."

Yet even a flock of sheep would resist the chicanery of the State, if it were not for the corruptive, tyrannical, and oppressive methods it employs to serve its purposes. Therefore Bakunin repudiates the State as synonymous with the surrender of the liberty of the individual or small minorities,—the destruction of social relationship, the curtailment, or complete denial even, of life itself, for its own aggrandizement. The State is the altar of political freedom and, like the religious altar, it is maintained for the purpose of human sacrifice.

In fact, there is hardly a modern thinker who does not agree that government, organized authority, or the State, is necessary *only* to maintain or protect property and monopoly. It has proven efficient in that function only.

Even George Bernard Shaw, who hopes for the miraculous from the State under Fabianism, nevertheless admits that "it is at present a huge machine for robbing and slave-driving of the poor by brute force." This being the case, it is hard to see why the clever prefacer wishes to uphold the State after poverty shall have ceased to exist.

Unfortunately there are still a number of people who continue in the fatal belief that government rests on natural laws, that it maintains social order and harmony, that it diminishes crime, and that it prevents the lazy man from fleecing his fellows. I shall therefore examine these contentions.

A natural law is that factor in man which asserts itself freely and spontaneously without any external force, in harmony with the requirements of nature. For instance, the demand for nutrition, for sex gratification, for light, air, and exercise, is a natural law. But its expression needs not the machinery of government, needs not the club, the gun, the handcuff, or the prison. To obey such laws, if we may call it obedience, requires only spontaneity and free opportunity. That governments do not maintain themselves through such harmonious factors is proven by the terrible array of violence, force, and coercion all governments use in order to live. Thus Blackstone is right when he says, "Human laws are invalid, because they are contrary to the laws of nature."

Unless it be the order of Warsaw after the slaughter of thousands of people, it is difficult to ascribe to governments any capacity for order or social harmony. Order derived through submission and maintained by terror is not much of a safe guaranty; yet that is the only "order" that governments have ever maintained. True social harmony grows naturally out of solidarity of interests. In a society where those who always work never have anything, while those who never work enjoy everything, solidarity of interests is nonexistent; hence social harmony is but a myth. The only way organized authority meets this grave situation is by extending still greater privileges to those who have already monopolized the

earth, and by still further enslaving the disinherited masses. Thus the entire arsenal of government—laws, police, soldiers, the courts, legislatures, prisons,—is strenuously engaged in "harmonizing" the most antagonistic elements in society.

The most absurd apology for authority and law is that they serve to diminish crime. Aside from the fact that the State is itself the greatest criminal, breaking every written and natural law, stealing in the form of taxes, killing in the form of war and capital punishment, it has come to an absolute standstill in coping with crime. It has failed utterly to destroy or even minimize the horrible scourge of its own creation.

Crime is naught but misdirected energy. So long as every institution of today, economic, political, social, and moral, conspires to misdirect human energy into wrong channels; so long as most people are out of place doing the things they hate to do, living a life they loathe to live, crime will be inevitable, and all the laws on the statutes can only increase, but never do away with, crime. What does society, as it exists today, know of the process of despair, the poverty, the horrors, the fearful struggle the human soul must pass on its way to crime and degradation. Who that knows this terrible process can fail to see the truth in these words of Peter Kropotkin:

"Those who will hold the balance between the benefits thus attributed to law and punishment and the degrading effect of the latter on humanity; those who will estimate the torrent of depravity poured abroad in human society by the informer, favored by the Judge even, and paid for in clinking cash by governments, under the pretext of aiding to unmask crime, those who will go within prison walls and there see what human beings become when deprived of liberty, when subjected to the care of brutal keepers, to coarse cruel words, to a thousand stinging, piercing humiliations, will agree with us that the entire apparatus of prison and punishment is an abomination which ought to be brought to an end."

The deterrent influence of law on the lazy man is too absurd to merit consideration. If society were only relieved of the waste and expense of keeping a lazy class, and the equally great expense of the paraphernalia of protection this lazy class requires, the social tables would contain an abundance for all, including even the occasional lazy individual. Besides, it is well to consider that laziness results either from special privileges, or physical and mental abnormalities. Our present insane system of production fosters both, and the most astounding phenomenon is that people should want to work at all now. Anarchism aims to strip labor of its deadening, dulling aspect, of its gloom and compulsion. It aims to make work an instrument of joy, of strength, of color, of real harmony, so that the poorest sort of a man should find in work both recreation and hope.

To achieve such an arrangement of life, government, with its unjust, arbitrary, repressive measures, must be done away with. At best it has but imposed one single mode of life upon all, without regard to individual and social variations and needs. In destroying government and statutory laws, Anarchism proposes to rescue the self-respect and independence of the individual from all restraint and invasion by authority. Only in freedom can man grow to his full stature. Only in freedom will he learn to think and move, and give the very best in him. Only in freedom will he realize the true force of the social bonds which knit men together, and which are the true foundation of a normal social life.

But what about human nature? Can it be changed? And if not, will it endure under Anarchism?

Poor human nature, what horrible crimes have been committed in thy name! Every fool, from king to policeman, from the flatheaded parson to the visionless dabbler in science, presumes to speak authoritatively of human nature. The greater the mental charlatan, the more definite his insistence on the wickedness and weaknesses of human nature. Yet, how can any one speak of it today, with every soul in a prison, with every heart fettered, wounded, and maimed?

John Burroughs has stated that experimental study of animals in captivity is absolutely useless. Their character, their habits, their appetites undergo a complete transformation when torn from their soil in field and forest. With human nature caged in a narrow space, whipped daily into submission, how can we speak of its potentialities?

Freedom, expansion, opportunity, and, above all, peace and repose, alone can teach us the real dominant factors of human nature and all its wonderful possibilities.

Anarchism, then, really stands for the liberation of the human mind from the dominion of religion; the liberation of the human body from the dominion of property; liberation from the shackles and restraint of government. Anarchism stands for a social order based on the free grouping of individuals for the purpose of producing real social wealth; an order that will guarantee to every human being free access to the earth and full enjoyment of the necessities of life, according to individual desires, tastes, and inclinations.

This is not a wild fancy or an aberration of the mind. It is the conclusion arrived at by hosts of intellectual men and women the world over; a conclusion resulting from the close and studious observation of the tendencies of modern society: individual liberty and economic equality, the twin forces for the birth of what is fine and true in man.

As to methods. Anarchism is not, as some may suppose, a theory of the future to be realized through divine inspiration. It is a living force in the affairs of our life, constantly creating new conditions. The methods of Anarchism therefore do not comprise an iron-clad program to be carried out under all circumstances. Methods must grow out of the economic needs of each place and clime, and of the intellectual and temperamental requirements of the individual. The serene, calm character of a Tolstoy will wish different methods for social reconstruction than the intense, overflowing personality of a Michael Bakunin or a Peter Kropotkin. Equally so it must be apparent that the economic and political needs of Russia will dictate more drastic measures than would England or America. Anarchism does not stand for military drill and uniformity; it does, however, stand for the spirit of revolt, in whatever form, against everything that hinders human growth. All Anarchists agree in that, as they also agree in their opposition to the political machinery as a means of bringing about the great social change.

"All voting," says Thoreau, "is a sort of gaming, like checkers, or backgammon, a playing with right and wrong; its obligation never exceeds that of expediency. Even voting for the right thing is doing nothing for it. A wise man will not leave the right to the mercy of chance, nor wish it to prevail through the power of the majority." A close examination of the machinery of politics and its achievements will bear out the logic of Thoreau.

What does the history of parliamentarism show? Nothing but failure and defeat, not even a single reform to ameliorate the economic and social stress of the people. Laws have been passed and enactments made for the improvement and protection of labor. Thus it was proven only last year that Illinois, with the most rigid laws for mine protection, had the greatest mine disasters. In States where child labor laws prevail, child exploitation is at its highest, and though with us the workers enjoy full political opportunities, capitalism

has reached the most brazen zenith.

Even were the workers able to have their own representatives, for which our good Socialist politicians are clamoring, what chances are there for their honesty and good faith? One has but to bear in mind the process of politics to realize that its path of good intentions is full of pitfalls: wirepulling, intriguing, flattering, lying, cheating; in fact, chicanery of every description, whereby the political aspirant can achieve success. Added to that is a complete demoralization of character and conviction, until nothing is left that would make one hope for anything from such a human derelict. Time and time again, the people were foolish enough to trust, believe, and support with their last farthing aspiring politicians, only to find themselves betrayed and cheated.

It may be claimed that men of integrity would not become corrupt in the political grinding mill. Perhaps not; but such men would be absolutely helpless to exert the slightest influence in behalf of labor, as indeed has been shown in numerous instances. The State is the economic master of its servants. Good men, if such there be, would either remain true to their political faith and lose their economic support, or they would cling to their economic master and be utterly unable to do the slightest good. The political arena leaves one no alternative, one must either be a dunce or a rogue.

The political superstition is still holding sway over the hearts and minds of the masses, but the true lovers of liberty will have no more to do with it. Instead, they believe with Stirner that man has as much liberty as he is willing to take. Anarchism therefore stands for direct action, the open defiance of, and resistance to, all laws and restrictions, economic, social, and moral. But defiance and resistance are illegal. Therein lies the salvation of man. Everything illegal necessitates integrity, self-reliance, and courage. In short, it calls for free, independent spirits, for "men who are men, and who have a bone in their backs which you cannot pass your hand through."

Universal suffrage itself owes its existence to direct action. If not for the spirit of rebellion, of the defiance on the part of the American revolutionary fathers, their posterity would still wear the King's coat. If not for the direct action of a John Brown and his comrades, America would still trade in the flesh of the black man. True, the trade in white flesh is still going on; but that, too, will have to be abolished by direct action. Trade-unionism, the economic arena of the modern gladiator, owes its existence to direct action. It is but recently that law and government have attempted to crush the trade-union movement, and condemned the exponents of man's right to organize to prison as conspirators. Had they sought to assert their cause through begging, pleading, and compromise, trade unionism would today be a negligible quantity. In France, in Spain, in Italy, in Russia, nay even in England (witness the growing rebellion of English labor unions), direct, revolutionary, economic action has become so strong a force in the battle for industrial liberty as to make the world realize the tremendous importance of labor's power. The General Strike, the supreme expression of the, economic consciousness of the workers, was ridiculed in America but a short time ago. Today every great strike, in order to win, must realize the importance of the solidaric general protest.

Direct action, having proven effective along economic lines, is equally potent in the environment of the individual. There a hundred forces encroach upon his being, and only persistent resistance to them will finally set him free. Direct action against the authority in the shop, direct action against the authority of the law, direct action against the invasive, meddlesome authority of our moral code, is the logical, consistent method of Anarchism.

Will it not lead to a revolution? Indeed, it will. No real social change has ever come about without a revolution. People are either not familiar with their history, or they have not yet learned that revolution is but thought carried into action.

Anarchism, the great leaven of thought, is today permeating every phase of human endeavor. Science, art, literature, the drama, the effort for economic betterment, in fact every individual and social opposition to the existing disorder of things, is illumined by the spiritual light of Anarchism. It is the philosophy of the sovereignty of the individual. It is the theory of social harmony. It is the great, surging, living truth that is reconstructing the world, and that will usher in the Dawn. ∾

"The Tragedy of Woman's Emancipation" (1910)

I begin with an admission: Regardless of all political and economic theories, treating of the fundamental differences between various groups within the human race, regardless of class and race distinctions, regardless of all artificial boundary lines between woman's rights and man's rights, I hold that there is a point where these differentiations may meet and grow into one perfect whole.

With this I do not mean to propose a peace treaty. The general social antagonism which has taken hold of our entire public life today, brought about through the force of opposing and contradictory interests, will crumble to pieces when the reorganization of our social life, based upon the principles of economic justice, shall have become a reality.

Peace or harmony between the sexes and individuals does not necessarily depend on a superficial equalization of human beings; nor does it call for the elimination of individual traits and peculiarities. The problem that confronts us today, and which the nearest future is to solve, is how to be one's self and yet in oneness with others, to feel deeply with all human beings and still retain one's own characteristic qualities. This seems to me to be the basis upon which the mass and the individual, the true democrat and the true individuality, man and woman, can meet without antagonism and opposition. The motto should not be: Forgive one another; rather, Understand one another. The oft-quoted sentence of Madame de Staël: "To understand everything means to forgive everything," has never particularly appealed to me; it has the odor of the confessional; to forgive one's fellow-being conveys the idea of pharisaical superiority. To understand one's fellow-being suffices. The admission partly represents the fundamental aspect of my views on the emancipation of woman and its effect upon the entire sex.

Emancipation should make it possible for woman to be human in the truest sense. Everything within her that craves assertion and activity should reach its fullest expression; all artificial barriers should be broken, and the road towards greater freedom cleared of every trace of centuries of submission and slavery.

This was the original aim of the movement for woman's emancipation. But the results so far achieved have isolated woman and have robbed her of the fountain springs of that happiness which is so essential to her. Merely external emancipation has made of the modern woman an artificial being, who reminds one of the products of French arboriculture with its arabesque trees and shrubs, pyramids, wheels,

and wreaths; anything, except the forms which would be reached by the expression of her own inner qualities. Such artificially grown plants of the female sex are to be found in large numbers, especially in the so-called intellectual sphere of our life.

Liberty and equality for woman! What hopes and aspirations these words awakened when they were first uttered by some of the noblest and bravest souls of those days. The sun in all his light and glory was to rise upon a new world; in this world woman was to be free to direct her own destiny—an aim certainly worthy of the great enthusiasm, courage, perseverance, and ceaseless effort of the tremendous host of pioneer men and women, who staked everything against a world of prejudice and ignorance.

My hopes also move towards that goal, but I hold that the emancipation of woman, as interpreted and practically applied today, has failed to reach that great end. Now, woman is confronted with the necessity of emancipating herself from emancipation, if she really desires to be free. This may sound paradoxical, but is, nevertheless, only too true.

What has she achieved through her emancipation? Equal suffrage in a few States. Has that purified our political life, as many well-meaning advocates predicted? Certainly not. Incidentally, it is really time that persons with plain, sound judgment should cease to talk about corruption in politics in a boarding-school tone. Corruption of politics has nothing to do with the morals, or the laxity of morals, of various political personalities. Its cause is altogether a material one. Politics is the reflex of the business and industrial world, the mottos of which are: "To take is more blessed than to give"; "buy cheap and sell dear"; "one soiled hand washes the other." There is no hope even that woman, with her right to vote, will ever purify politics.

Emancipation has brought woman economic equality with man; that is, she can choose her own profession and trade; but as her past and present physical training has not equipped her with the necessary strength to compete with man, she is often compelled to exhaust all her energy, use up her vitality, and strain every nerve in order to reach the market value. Very few ever succeed, for it is a fact that women teachers, doctors, lawyers, architects, and engineers are neither met with the same confidence as their male colleagues, nor receive equal remuneration. And those that do reach that enticing equality, generally do so at the expense of their physical and psychical well-being. As to the great mass of working girls and women, how much independence is gained if the narrowness and lack of freedom of the home is exchanged for the narrowness and lack of freedom of the factory, sweatshop, department store, or office? In addition is the burden which is laid on many women of looking after a "home, sweet home"—cold, dreary, disorderly, uninviting—after a day's hard work. Glorious independence! No wonder that hundreds of girls are so willing to accept the first offer of marriage, sick and tired of their "independence" behind the counter, at the sewing or typewriting machine. They are just as ready to marry as girls of the middle class, who long to throw off the yoke of parental supremacy. A so-called independence which leads only to earning the merest subsistence is not so enticing, not so ideal, that one could expect woman to sacrifice everything for it. Our highly praised independence is, after all, but a slow process of dulling and stifling woman's nature, her love instinct, and her mother instinct.

Nevertheless, the position of the working girl is far more natural and human than that of her seemingly more fortunate sister in the more cultured professional walks of life—teachers, physicians, lawyers, engineers, etc., who have to make a dignified, proper appearance, while the inner life is growing empty and dead.

The narrowness of the existing conception of woman's independence and emancipation; the dread of love for a man who is not her social equal; the fear that love will rob her of her freedom and independence; the horror that love or the joy of motherhood will only hinder her in the full exercise of her profession—all these together make of the emancipated modern woman a compulsory vestal, before whom life, with its great clarifying sorrows and its deep, entrancing joys, rolls on without touching or gripping her soul.

Emancipation, as understood by the majority of its adherents and exponents, is of too narrow a scope to permit the boundless love and ecstasy contained in the deep emotion of the true woman, sweetheart, mother, in freedom.

The tragedy of the self-supporting or economically free woman does not lie in too many, but in too few experiences. True, she surpasses her sister of past generations in knowledge of the world and human nature; it is just because of this that she feels deeply the lack of life's essence, which alone can enrich the human soul, and without which the majority of women have become mere professional automatons.

That such a state of affairs was bound to come was foreseen by those who realized that, in the domain of ethics, there still remained many decaying ruins of the time of the undisputed superiority of man, ruins that are still considered useful. And, what is more important, a goodly number of the emancipated are unable to get along without them. Every movement that aims at the destruction of existing institutions and the replacement thereof with something more advanced, more perfect, has followers who in theory stand for the most radical ideas, but who, nevertheless, in their every-day practice, are like the average Philistine, feigning respectability and clamoring for the good opinion of their opponents. There are, for example, Socialists, and even Anarchists, who stand for the idea that property is robbery, yet who will grow indignant if anyone owe them the value of a half-dozen pins.

The same Philistine can be found in the movement for woman's emancipation. Yellow journalists and milk-and-water litterateurs have painted pictures of the emancipated woman that make the hair of the good citizen and his dull companion stand up on end. Every member of the woman's rights movement was pictured as a George Sand in her absolute disregard of morality. Nothing was sacred to her. She had no respect for the ideal relation between man and woman. In short, emancipation stood only for a reckless life of lust and sin, regardless of society, religion, and morality. The exponents of woman's rights were highly indignant at such misrepresentation, and, lacking humor, they exerted all their energy to prove that they were not at all as bad as they were painted, but the very reverse. Of course, as long as woman was the slave of man, she could not be good and pure, but now that she was free and independent she would prove how good she could be and that her influence would have a purifying effect on all institutions in society. True, the movement for woman's rights has broken many old fetters, but it has also forged new ones. The great movement of true emancipation has not met with a great race of women who could look liberty in the face. Their narrow, Puritanical vision banished man, as a disturber and doubtful character, out of their emotional life. Man was not to be tolerated at any price, except perhaps as the father of a child, since a child could not very well come to life without a father. Fortunately, the most rigid Puritans never will be strong enough to kill the innate craving for motherhood. But woman's freedom is closely allied with man's freedom and many

of my so-called emancipated sisters seem to overlook the fact that a child born in freedom needs the love and devotion of each human being about him, man as well as woman. Unfortunately, it is this narrow conception of human relations that has brought about a great tragedy in the lives of the modern man and woman.

About fifteen years ago appeared a work from the pen of the brilliant Norwegian Laura Marholm, called *Woman, a Character Study.* She was one of the first to call attention to the emptiness and narrowness of the existing conception of woman's emancipation, and its tragic effect upon the inner life of woman. In her work Laura Marholm speaks of the fate of several gifted women of international fame: the genius Eleonora Duse; the great mathematician and writer Sonya Kovalevskaia; the artist and poet-nature Marie Bashkirtzeff, who died so young. Through each description of the lives of these women of such extraordinary mentality runs a marked trail of unsatisfied craving for a full, rounded, complete, and beautiful life, and the unrest and loneliness resulting from the lack of it. Through these masterly psychological sketches one cannot help but see that the higher the mental development of woman, the less possible it is for her to meet a congenial mate who will see in her, not only sex, but also the human being, the friend, the comrade and strong individuality, who cannot and ought not lose a single trait of her character.

The average man with his self-sufficiency, his ridiculously superior airs of patronage towards the female sex, is an impossibility for woman as depicted in the *Character Study* by Laura Marholm. Equally impossible for her is the man who can see in her nothing more than her mentality and her genius, and who fails to awaken her woman nature.

A rich intellect and a fine soul are usually considered necessary attributes of a deep and beautiful personality. In the case of the modern woman, these attributes serve as a hindrance to the complete assertion of her being. For over a hundred years the old form of marriage, based on the Bible, "till death doth part," has been denounced as an institution that stands for the sovereignty of the man over the woman, of her complete submission to his whims and commands, and absolute dependence on his name and support. Time and again it has been conclusively proved that the old matrimonial relation restricted woman to the function of man's servant and the bearer of his children. And yet we find many emancipated women who prefer marriage, with all its deficiencies, to the narrowness of an unmarried life; narrow and unendurable because of the chains of moral and social prejudice that cramp and bind her nature.

The explanation of such inconsistency on the part of many advanced women is to be found in the fact that they never truly understood the meaning of emancipation. They thought that all that was needed was independence from external tyrannies; the internal tyrants, far more harmful to life and growth —ethical and social conventions—were left to take care of themselves; and they have taken care of themselves. They seem to get along as beautifully in the heads and hearts of the most active exponents of woman's emancipation, as in the heads and hearts of our grandmothers.

These internal tyrants, whether they be in the form of public opinion or what will mother say, or brother, father, aunt, or relative of any sort; what will Mrs. Grundy, Mr. Comstock, the employer, the Board of Education say? All these busybodies, moral detectives, jailers of the human spirit, what a greater amount of naturalness, kind-heartedness, and simplicity, than the majority of our emancipated professional women who fill the colleges, halls of learning, and various offices. This does not mean a wish to return to the past, nor does it condemn woman to her old sphere, the kitchen and the nursery.

Salvation lies in an energetic march onward towards a brighter and clearer future. We are in need of unhampered growth out of old traditions and habits. The movement for woman's emancipation has so far made but the first step in that direction. It is to be hoped that it will gather strength to make another. The right to vote, or equal civil rights, may be good demands, but true emancipation begins neither at the polls nor in courts. It begins in woman's soul. History tells us that every oppressed class gained true liberation from its masters through its own efforts. It is necessary that woman learn that lesson, that she realize that her freedom will reach as far as her power to achieve her freedom reaches. It is, therefore, far more important for her to begin with her inner regeneration, to cut loose from the weight of prejudices, traditions, and customs. The demand for equal rights in every vocation of life is just and fair; but, after all, the most vital right is the right to love and be loved. Indeed, if partial emancipation is to become a complete and true emancipation of woman, it will have to do away with the ridiculous notion that to be loved, to be sweetheart and mother, is synonymous with being slave or subordinate. It will have to do away with the absurd notion of the dualism of the sexes, or that man and woman represent two antagonistic worlds.

Pettiness separates; breadth unites. Let us be broad and big. Let us not overlook vital things because of the bulk of trifles confronting us. A true conception of the relation of the sexes will not admit of conqueror and conquered; it knows of but one great thing: to give of one's self boundlessly, in order to find one's self richer, deeper, better. That alone can fill the emptiness, and transform the tragedy of woman's emancipation into joy, limitless joy.

&

Primary Sources

Drinnon, Richard, and Anna Marie Drinnon, eds. *Nowhere at Home: Letters from Exile of Emma Goldman and Alexander Berkman.* New York: Schocken Books, 1975.

Goldman, Emma. *Anarchism and Other Essays.* New York: Dover, 1969.

———. *Living My Life, 1869–1940.* 2 vols. New York: Dover, 1970.

———. *My Disillusionment in Russia.* New York: T.Y. Crowell, 1970.

———, ed. *Mother Earth Bulletin* (October 1917–April 1918). New York: Greenwood Reprint Corp., 1968.

Shulman, Alix Kates, ed. *Red Emma Speaks: Selected Writings and Speeches.* New York: Random House, 1972.

Secondary Sources

Chalberg, John. *Emma Goldman: American Individualist.* New York: HarperCollins, 1991.

Drinnon, Richard. *Rebel in Paradise.* Chicago: University of Chicago Press, 1961.

Rich, Andrea, and Arthur L. Smith, *Rhetoric of Revolution: Samuel Adams, Emma Goldman, Malcolm X.* Durham, N.C.: Moore Publishing, 1970.

Wexler, Alice. *Emma Goldman: An Intimate Life.* New York: Pantheon Books, 1984.

29. W.E.B. Du Bois

WILLIAM EDWARD BURGHARDT DU BOIS (1868–1963) was one of the most powerful intellects, and probably the leading black thinker, in all of American history. He was born and brought up in a small town in the Berkshire hills of western Massachusetts, earned his first bachelor's degree at Fisk University, and then was admitted to Harvard, where he rapidly obtained bachelor's, master's and doctoral degrees. As a professor at Atlanta University, he set high scholarly standards by writing a series of studies of the social history of black people, a field until then characterized chiefly by ignorance, stereotypes, and outright racism. He vigorously championed the black claim for self-determination and dignity (roughly what would come to be known in the 1960s as *black power*), in opposition to the more conservative acceptance of subordinate roles espoused by Booker T. Washington. He was active in the formation of the Niagara Movement and of the National Association for the Advancement of Colored People (NAACP), and he constantly sought to connect American blacks with their African heritage. Always on the militant side of the black freedom movement, Du Bois eventually grew more convinced that only drastic social reconstruction could end American racism. In his last years he joined the Communist party, renounced his American citizenship, and moved to Ghana, where he died in 1963.

The excerpts presented here are both drawn from *The Souls of Black Folk,* a collection of essays published in 1903. "Of Our Spiritual Strivings" was the opening chapter and gives a sense both of the deep feeling pervading all of Du

Bois's work and of his literary style. "Of Mr. Booker T. Washington and Others," written especially for *The Souls of Black Folk,* is a comprehensive statement of the political perspective that Du Bois saw as necessary for the full freedom of black people. ◞

The Souls of Black Folk (1903)

"OF OUR SPIRITUAL STRIVINGS"

Between me and the other world there is ever an unasked question: unasked by some through feelings of delicacy; by others through the difficulty of rightly framing it. All, nevertheless, flutter round it. They approach me in a half-hesitant sort of way, eye me curiously or compassionately, and then, instead of saying directly, How does it feel to be a problem? they say, I know an excellent colored man in my town; or, I fought at Mechanicsville; or, Do not these Southern outrages make your blood boil? At these I smile, or am interested, or reduce the boiling to a simmer, as the occasion may require. To the real question, How does it feel to be a problem? I answer seldom a word.

And yet, being a problem is a strange experience,—peculiar even for one who has never been anything else, save perhaps in babyhood and in Europe. It is in the early days of rollicking boyhood that the revelation first bursts upon one, all in a day, as it were. I remember well when the shadow swept across me. I was a little thing, away up in the hills of New England, where the dark Housatonic winds between Hoosac and Taghkanic to the sea. In a wee wooden schoolhouse, something put it into the boys' and girls' heads to buy gorgeous visiting-cards—ten cents a package—and exchange. The exchange was merry, till one girl, a tall newcomer, refused my card,—refused it

SOURCE: W.E.B. Du Bois, *The Souls of Black Folk* (Chicago: A.C. McClurg, 1903), chaps. 1 and 3.

peremptorily, with a glance. Then it dawned upon me with a certain suddenness that I was different from the others; or like, mayhap, in heart and life and longing, but shut out from their world by a vast veil. I had thereafter no desire to tear down that veil, to creep through; I held all beyond it in common contempt, and lived above it in a region of blue sky and great wandering shadows. That sky was bluest when I could beat my mates at examination-time, or beat them at a foot-race, or even beat their stringy heads. Alas, with the years all this fine contempt began to fade; for the words I longed for, and all their dazzling opportunities, were theirs, not mine. But they should not keep these prizes, I said; some, all, I would wrest from them. Just how I would do it I could never decide: by reading law, by healing the sick, by telling the wonderful tales that swam in my head,—some way. With other black boys the strife was not so fiercely sunny: their youth shrunk into tasteless sycophancy, or into silent hatred of the pale world about them and mocking distrust of everything white; or wasted itself in a bitter cry, Why did God make me an outcast and a stranger in mine own house? The shades of the prison-house closed round about us all: walls strait and stubborn to the whitest, but relentlessly narrow, tall, and unscalable to sons of night who must plod darkly on in resignation, or beat unavailing palms against the stone, or steadily, half hopelessly, watch the streak of blue above.

After the Egyptian and Indian, the Greek

and Roman, the Teuton and Mongolian, the Negro is a sort of seventh son, born with a veil, and gifted with second sight in this American world,—a world which yields him no true self-consciousness, but only lets him see himself through the revelation of the other world. It is a peculiar sensation, this double-consciousness, this sense of always looking at one's self through the eyes of others, of measuring one's soul by the tape of a world that looks on in amused contempt and pity. One ever feels his twoness,—an American, a Negro; two souls, two thoughts, two unreconciled strivings; two warring ideals in one dark body, whose dogged strength alone keeps it from being torn asunder.

The history of the American Negro is the history of this strife,—this longing to attain self-conscious manhood, to merge his double self into a better and truer self. In this merging he wishes neither of the older selves to be lost. He would not Africanize America, for America has too much to teach the world and Africa. He would not bleach his Negro soul in a flood of white Americanism, for he knows that Negro blood has a message for the world. He simply wishes to make it possible for a man to be both a Negro and an American, without being cursed and spit upon by his fellows, without having the doors of Opportunity closed roughly in his face.

This, then, is the end of his striving: to be a co-worker in the kingdom of culture, to escape both death and isolation, to husband and use his best powers and his latent genius. These powers of body and mind have in the past been strangely wasted, dispersed, or forgotten. The shadow of a mighty Negro past flits through the tale of Ethiopia the Shadowy and of Egypt the Sphinx. Through history, the powers of single black men flash here and there like falling stars, and die sometimes before the world has rightly gauged their brightness. Here in America, in the few days since

Emancipation, the black man's turning hither and thither in hesitant and doubtful striving has often made his very strength to lose effectiveness, to seem like absence of power, like weakness. And yet it is not weakness,—it is the contradiction of double aims. The double-aimed struggle of the black artisan—on the one hand to escape white contempt for a nation of mere hewers of wood and drawers of water, and on the other hand to plough and nail and dig for a poverty-stricken horde —could only result in making him a poor craftsman, for he had but half a heart in either cause. By the poverty and ignorance of his people, the Negro minister or doctor was tempted toward quackery and demagogy; and by the criticism of the other world, toward ideals that made him ashamed of his lowly tasks. The would-be black *savant* was confronted by the paradox that the knowledge his people needed was a twice-told tale to his white neighbors, while the knowledge which would teach the white world was Greek to his own flesh and blood. The innate love of harmony and beauty that set the ruder souls of his people a-dancing and a-singing raised but confusion and doubt in the soul of the black artist; for the beauty revealed to him was the soul-beauty of a race which his larger audience despised, and he could not articulate the message of another people. This waste of double aims, this seeking to satisfy two unreconciled ideals, has wrought sad havoc with the courage and faith and deeds of ten thousand thousand people,—has sent them often wooing false gods and invoking false means of salvation, and at times has even seemed about to make them ashamed of themselves.

Away back in the days of bondage they thought to see in one divine event the end of all doubt and disappointment; few men ever worshipped Freedom with half such unquestioning faith as did the American Negro for two centuries. To him, so far as he thought and dreamed, slavery was indeed the sum of all villainies, the cause of all sorrow, the root of all prejudice; Emancipation was the key to a promised land of sweeter beauty than ever stretched before the eyes of wearied Israelites. In song and exhortation swelled one refrain—Liberty; in his tears and curses the God he implored had Freedom in his right hand. At last it came,—suddenly, fearfully, like a dream. With one wild carnival of blood and passion came the message in his own plaintive cadences:—

> "Shout, O children!
> Shout, you're free!
> For God has bought your liberty!"

Years have passed away since then,—ten, twenty, forty; forty years of national life, forty years of renewal and development, and yet the swarthy spectre sits in its accustomed seat at the Nation's feast. In vain do we cry to this our vastest social problem:—

> "Take any shape but that, and my
>   firm nerves
> Shall never tremble!"

The Nation has not yet found peace from its sins; the freedman has not yet found in freedom his promised land. Whatever of good may have come in these years of change, the shadow of a deep disappointment rests upon the Negro people,—a disappointment all the more bitter because the unattained ideal was unbounded save by the simple ignorance of a lowly people.

The first decade was merely a prolongation of the vain search for freedom, the boon that seemed ever barely to elude their grasp,—like a tantalizing will-o'-the-wisp, maddening and misleading the headless host. The holocaust of war, the terrors of the Ku Klux Klan, the lies of carpet-baggers, the disorganization of industry, and the contradictory advice of friends and foes, left the bewildered serf with no new watchword beyond the old cry for freedom. As the time flew, however, he began to grasp a new idea. The ideal of liberty demanded for its attainment powerful means, and these the Fifteenth Amendment gave him. The ballot, which before he had looked upon as a visible sign of freedom, he now regarded as the chief means of gaining and perfecting the liberty with which war had partially endowed him. And why not? Had not votes made war and emancipated millions? Had not votes enfranchised the freedmen? Was anything impossible to a power that had done all this? A million black men started with renewed zeal to vote themselves into the kingdom. So the decade flew away, the revolution of 1876 came, and left the half-free serf weary, wondering, but still inspired. Slowly but steadily, in the following years, a new vision began gradually to replace the dream of political power,—a powerful movement, the rise of another ideal to guide the unguided, another pillar of fire by night after a clouded day. It was the ideal of "book learning"; the curiosity, born of compulsory ignorance, to know and test the power of the cabalistic letters of the white man, the longing to know. Here at last seemed to have been discovered the mountain path to Canaan; longer than the highway of Emancipation and law, steep and rugged, but straight, leading to heights high enough to overlook life.

Up the new path the advance guard toiled, slowly, heavily, doggedly; only those who have watched and guided the faltering feet, the misty minds, the dull understandings, of the dark pupils of these schools know how faithfully, how piteously, this people strove to learn. It was weary work. The cold statistician wrote down the inches of progress here and there, noted also where here and there a foot had slipped or some one had fallen. To the tired climbers, the horizon was ever dark, the mists were often cold, the Canaan was always dim and far away. If, however, the vistas disclosed as yet no goal, no resting-place, little but flattery and criticism, the journey at least gave leisure for reflection and self-examination; it changed the child of Emancipation to the youth with dawning self-consciousness, self-realization, self-respect. In those sombre forests of his striving his own soul rose before him, and he saw himself,—darkly as through a veil; and yet he saw in himself some faint revelation of his power, of his mission. He began to have a dim feeling that, to attain his place in the world, he must be himself, and not another. For the first time he sought to analyze the burden he bore upon his back, that deadweight of social degradation partially masked behind a half-named Negro problem. He felt his poverty; without a cent, without a home, without land, tools, or savings, he had entered into competition with rich, landed, skilled neighbors. To be a poor man is hard, but to be a poor race in a land of dollars is the very bottom of hardships. He felt the weight of his ignorance,—not simply of letters, but of life, of business, of the humanities; the accumulated sloth and shirking and awkwardness of decades and centuries shackled his hands and feet. Nor was his burden all poverty and ignorance. The red stain of bastardy, which two centuries of systematic legal defilement of Negro women had stamped upon his race, meant not only the loss of ancient African chastity, but also the hereditary weight of a mass of corruption from white adulterers, threatening almost the obliteration of the Negro home.

A people thus handicapped ought not to be asked to race with the world, but rather allowed to give all its time and thought to its own social problems. But alas! while sociologists gleefully count his bastards and his prostitutes, the very soul of the toiling, sweating black man is darkened by the shadow of a vast despair. Men call the shadow prejudice, and learnedly explain it as the natural defence of culture against barbarism, learning against ignorance, purity against crime, the "higher" against the "lower" races. To which the Negro cries Amen! and swears that to so much of this strange prejudice as is founded on just homage to civilization, culture, righteousness, and progress, he humbly bows and meekly does obeisance. But before that nameless prejudice that leaps beyond all this he stands helpless, dismayed, and well-nigh speechless; before that personal disrespect and mockery, the ridicule and systematic humiliation, the distortion of fact and wanton license of fancy, the cynical ignoring of the better and the boisterous welcoming of the worse, the all-pervading desire to inculcate disdain for everything black, from Toussaint to the devil,—before this there rises a sickening despair that would disarm and discourage any nation save that black host to whom "discouragement" is an unwritten word.

But the facing of so vast a prejudice could not but bring the inevitable self-questioning, self-disparagement, and lowering of ideals which ever accompany repression and breed in an atmosphere of contempt and hate. Whisperings and portents came borne upon the four winds: Lo! we are diseased and dying, cried the dark hosts; we cannot write, our voting is vain; what need of education, since we must always cook and serve? And the Nation echoed and enforced this self-criticism, saying: Be content to be servants, and nothing more; what need of higher culture for half-men? Away with the black man's ballot, by force or fraud,—and behold the suicide of a race! Nevertheless, out of the evil came something of good,—the more careful adjustment of education to real life, the clearer perception of the Negroes' social responsibilities, and the sobering realization of the meaning of progress.

So dawned the time of *Sturm und Drang*: storm and stress to-day rocks our little boat on the mad waters of the world-sea; there is within and without the sound of conflict, the burning of body and rending of soul; inspiration strives with doubt, and faith with vain questionings. The bright ideals of the past, —physical freedom, political power, the training of brains and the training of hands,—all these in turn have waxed and waned, until even the last grows dim and overcast. Are they all wrong,—all false? No, not that, but each alone was over-simple and incomplete,—the dreams of a credulous race-childhood, or the fond imaginings of the other world which does not know and does not want to know our power. To be really true, all these ideals must be melted and welded into one. The training of the schools we need to-day more than ever; —the training of deft hands, quick eyes and ears, and above all the broader, deeper, higher culture of gifted minds and pure hearts. The power of the ballot we need in sheer self-defence,—else what shall save us from a second slavery? Freedom, too, the long-sought, we still seek,—the freedom of life and limb, the freedom to work and think, the freedom to love and aspire. Work, culture, liberty,—all these we need, not singly but together, not successively but together, each growing and aiding each, and all striving toward that vaster ideal that swims before the Negro people, the ideal of human brotherhood, gained through the unifying ideal of Race; the ideal of fostering and developing the traits and talents of the Negro, not in opposition to or contempt for other races, but rather in large conformity to the greater ideals of the American Republic, in order that some day on American soil two world-races may give each to each those characteristics both so sadly lack. We the darker ones come even now not altogether empty-handed: there are to-day no truer exponents of the pure human spirit of the Declaration of Independence than the American Negroes; there is no true American music but the wild sweet melodies of the Negro slave; the American fairy tales and folklore are Indian and African;

and, all in all, we black men seem the sole oasis of simple faith and reverence in a dusty desert of dollars and smartness. Will America be poorer if she replace her brutal dyspeptic blundering with light-hearted but determined Negro humility? or her coarse and cruel wit with loving jovial good-humor? or her vulgar music with the soul of the Sorrow Songs?

Merely a concrete test of the underlying principles of the great republic is the Negro Problem, and the spiritual striving of the freedmen's sons is the travail of souls whose burden is almost beyond the measure of their strength, but who bear it in the name of an historic race, in the name of this the land of their fathers' fathers, and in the name of human opportunity.

And now what I have briefly sketched in large outline let me on coming pages tell again in many ways, with loving emphasis and deeper detail, that men may listen to the striving in the souls of black folk.

"OF MR. BOOKER T. WASHINGTON AND OTHERS"

Easily the most striking thing in the history of the American Negro since 1876 is the ascendancy of Mr. Booker T. Washington. It began at the time when war memories and ideals were rapidly passing; a day of astonishing commercial development was dawning; a sense of doubt and hesitation overtook the freedmen's sons,—then it was that his leading began. Mr. Washington came, with a single definite programme, at the psychological moment when the nation was a little ashamed of having bestowed so much sentiment on Negroes, and was concentrating its energies on Dollars. His programme of industrial education, conciliation of the South, and submission and silence as to civil and political rights, was not wholly original; the Free Negroes from 1830 up to war-time had striven to build industrial schools, and the American Missionary Association had from the first taught various trades; and Price and others had sought a way of honorable alliance with the best of the Southerners. But Mr. Washington first indissolubly linked these things; he put enthusiasm, unlimited energy, and perfect faith into his programme, and changed it from a by-path into a veritable Way of Life. And the tale of the methods by which he did this is a fascinating study of human life.

It startled the nation to hear a Negro advocating such a programme after many decades of bitter complaint; it startled and won the applause of the South, it interested and won the admiration of the North; and after a confused murmur of protest, it silenced if it did not convert the Negroes themselves.

To gain the sympathy and cooperation of the various elements comprising the white South was Mr. Washington's first task; and this, at the time Tuskegee was founded, seemed, for a black man, well-nigh impossible. And yet ten years later it was done in the word spoken at Atlanta: "In all things purely social we can be as separate as the five fingers, and yet one as the hand in all things essential to mutual progress." This "Atlanta Compromise" is by all odds the most notable thing in Mr. Washington's career. The South interpreted it in different ways: the radicals received it as a complete surrender of the demand for civil and political equality; the conservatives, as a generously conceived working basis for mutual understanding. So both approved it, and to-day its author is certainly the most distinguished Southerner since Jefferson Davis, and the one with the largest personal following.

Next to this achievement comes Mr. Washington's work in gaining place and consideration in the North. Others less shrewd and tactful had formerly essayed to sit on these two stools and had fallen between them; but as Mr. Washington knew the heart of the South from birth and training, so by singular insight he intuitively grasped the spirit of the age which was dominating the North. And so thoroughly did he learn the speech and thought of triumphant commercialism, and the ideals of material prosperity, that the picture of a lone black boy poring over a French grammar amid the weeds and dirt of a neglected home soon seemed to him the acme of absurdities. One wonders what Socrates and St. Francis of Assisi would say to this.

And yet this very singleness of vision and thorough oneness with his age is a mark of the successful man. It is as though Nature must needs make men narrow in order to give them force. So Mr. Washington's cult has gained unquestioning followers, his work has wonderfully prospered, his friends are legion, and his enemies are confounded. To-day he stands as the one recognized spokesman of his ten million fellows, and one of the most notable figures in a nation of seventy millions. One hesitates, therefore, to criticise a life which, beginning with so little, has done so much. And yet the time is come when one may speak in all sincerity and utter courtesy of the mistakes and shortcomings of Mr. Washington's career, as well as of his triumphs, without being thought captious or envious, and without forgetting that it is easier to do ill than well in the world.

The criticism that has hitherto met Mr. Washington has not always been of this broad character. In the South especially has he had to walk warily to avoid the harshest judgments, —and naturally so, for he is dealing with the one subject of deepest sensitiveness to that section. Twice—once when at the Chicago celebration of the Spanish-American War he alluded to the color-prejudice that is "eating away the vitals of the South," and once when he dined with President Roosevelt—has the resulting Southern criticism been violent enough to threaten seriously his popularity. In the

North the feeling has several times forced itself into words, that Mr. Washington's counsels of submission overlooked certain elements of true manhood, and that his educational programme was unnecessarily narrow. Usually, however, such criticism has not found open expression, although, too, the spiritual sons of the Abolitionists have not been prepared to acknowledge that the schools founded before Tuskegee, by men of broad ideals and self-sacrificing spirit, were wholly failures or worthy of ridicule. While, then, criticism has not failed to follow Mr. Washington, yet the prevailing public opinion of the land has been but too willing to deliver the solution of a wearisome problem into his hands, and say, "If that is all you and your race ask, take it."

Among his own people, however, Mr. Washington has encountered the strongest and most lasting opposition, amounting at times to bitterness, and even to-day continuing strong and insistent even though largely silenced in outward expression by the public opinion of the nation. Some of this opposition is, of course, mere envy; the disappointment of displaced demagogues and the spite of narrow minds. But aside from this, there is among educated and thoughtful colored men in all parts of the land a feeling of deep regret, sorrow, and apprehension at the wide currency and ascendancy which some of Mr. Washington's theories have gained. These same men admire his sincerity of purpose, and are willing to forgive much to honest endeavor which is doing something worth the doing. They cooperate with Mr. Washington as far as they conscientiously can; and, indeed, it is no ordinary tribute to this man's tact and power that, steering as he must between so many diverse interests and opinions, he so largely retains the respect of all.

But the hushing of the criticism of honest opponents is a dangerous thing. It leads some of the best of the critics to unfortunate silence and paralysis of effort, and others to burst into speech so passionately and intemperately as to lose listeners. Honest and earnest criticism from those whose interests are most nearly touched,—criticism of writers by readers, of government by those governed, of leaders by those led,—this is the soul of democracy and the safeguard of modern society. If the best of the American Negroes receive by outer pressure a leader whom they had not recognized before, manifestly there is here a certain palpable gain. Yet there is also irreparable loss,—a loss of that peculiarly valuable education which a group receives when by search and criticism it finds and commissions its own leaders. The way in which this is done is at once the most elementary and the nicest problem of social growth. History is but the record of such group-leadership; and yet how infinitely changeful is its type and character! And of all types and kinds, what can be more instructive than the leadership of a group within a group?—that curious double movement where real progress may be negative and actual advance be relative retrogression. All this is the social student's inspiration and despair.

Now in the past the American Negro has had instructive experience in the choosing of group leaders, founding thus a peculiar dynasty which in the light of present conditions is worthwhile studying. When sticks and stones and beasts form the sole environment of a people, their attitude is largely one of determined opposition to and conquest of natural forces. But when to earth and brute is added an environment of men and ideas, then the attitude of the imprisoned group may take three main forms,—a feeling of revolt and revenge; an attempt to adjust all thought and action to the will of the great group; or, finally, a determined effort at self-realization and self-development despite environing opinion. The influence of all of these attitudes at various times can be traced in the history of the American Negro, and in the evolution of his successive leaders.

Before 1750, while the fire of African freedom still burned in the veins of the slaves, there was in all leadership or attempted leadership but the one motive of revolt and revenge,—typified in the terrible Maroons, the Danish blacks, and Cato of Stono, and veiling all the Americas in fear of insurrection. The liberalizing tendencies of the latter half of the eighteenth century brought, along with kindlier relations between black and white, thoughts of ultimate adjustment and assimilation. Such aspiration was especially voiced in the earnest songs of Phyllis, in the martyrdom of Attucks, the fighting of Salem and Poor, the intellectual accomplishments of Banneker and Derham, and the political demands of the Cuffes.

Stern financial and social stress after the war cooled much of the previous humanitarian ardor. The disappointment and impatience of the Negroes at the persistence of slavery and serfdom voiced itself in two movements. The slaves in the South, aroused undoubtedly by vague rumors of the Haytian revolt, made three fierce attempts at insurrection,—in 1800 under Gabriel in Virginia, in 1822 under Vesey in Carolina, and in 1831 again in Virginia under the terrible Nat Turner. In the Free States, on the other hand, a new and curious attempt at self-development was made. In Philadelphia and New York color-prescription led to a withdrawal of Negro communicants from white churches and the formation of a peculiar socioreligious institution among the Negroes known as the African Church,—an organization still living and controlling in its various branches over a million of men.

Walker's wild appeal against the trend of the times showed how the world was changing after the coming of the cotton gin. By 1830 slavery seemed hopelessly fastened on the South, and the slaves thoroughly cowed into submission. The free Negroes of the North, inspired by the mulatto immigrants from the West Indies, began to change the basis of their demands; they recognized the slavery of slaves, but insisted that they themselves were freemen, and sought assimilation and amalgamation with the nation on the same terms with other men. Thus, Forten and Purvis of Philadelphia, Shad of Wilmington, Du Bois of New Haven, Barbadoes of Boston, and others, strove singly and together as men, they said, not as slaves; as "people of color," not as "Negroes." The trend of the times, however, refused them recognition save in individual and exceptional cases, considered them as one with all the despised blacks, and they soon found themselves striving to keep even the rights they formerly had of voting and working and moving as freemen. Schemes of migration and colonization arose among them; but these they refused to entertain, and they eventually turned to the Abolition movement as a final refuge.

Here, led by Remond, Nell, Wells-Brown, and Douglass, a new period of self-assertion and self-development dawned. To be sure, ultimate freedom and assimilation was the ideal before the leaders, but the assertion of the manhood rights of the Negro by himself was the main reliance, and John Brown's raid was the extreme of its logic. After the war and emancipation, the great form of Frederick Douglass, the greatest of American Negro leaders, still led the host. Self-assertion, especially in political lines, was the main programme, and behind Douglass came Elliot, Bruce, and Langston, and the Reconstruction politicians, and, less conspicuous but of greater social significance, Alexander Crummell and Bishop Daniel Payne.

Then came the Revolution of 1876, the suppression of the Negro votes, the changing and shifting of ideals, and the seeking of new lights in the great night. Douglass, in his old age, still bravely stood for the ideals of his early manhood,—ultimate assimilation *through* self-assertion, and on no other terms. For a time Price arose as a new leader, destined, it seemed, not to give up, but to re-state the old ideals in a form less repugnant to the white South. But he passed away in his prime. Then 'came the new leader. Nearly all the former ones had become leaders by the silent suffrage of their fellows, had sought to lead their own people alone, and were usually, save Douglass, little known outside their race. But Booker T. Washington arose as essentially the leader not of one race but of two,—a compromiser between the South, the North, and the Negro. Naturally the Negroes resented, at first bitterly, signs of compromise which surrendered their civil and political rights, even though this was to be exchanged for larger chances of economic development. The rich and dominating North, however, was not only weary of the race problem, but was investing largely in Southern enterprise, and welcomed any method of peaceful cooperation. Thus, by national opinion, the Negroes began to recognize Mr. Washington's leadership; and the voice of criticism was hushed.

Mr. Washington represents in Negro thought the old attitude of adjustment and submission; but adjustment at such a peculiar time as to make his programme unique. This is an age of unusual economic development, and Mr. Washington's programme naturally takes an economic cast, becoming a gospel of Work and Money to such an extent as apparently almost completely to overshadow the higher aims of life. Moreover, this is an age when the more advanced races are coming in closer contact with the less developed races, and the race-feeling is therefore intensified; and Mr. Washington's programme practically accepts the alleged inferiority of the Negro races. Again, in our own land, the reaction from the sentiment of war time has given impetus to race-prejudice against Negroes, and Mr. Wash-

ington withdraws many of the high demands of Negroes as men and American citizens. In other periods of intensified prejudice all the Negro's tendency to self-assertion has been called forth; at this period a policy of submission is advocated. In the history of nearly all other races and peoples the doctrine preached at such crises has been that manly self-respect is worth more than lands and houses, and that a people who voluntarily surrender such respect, or cease striving for it, are not worth civilizing.

In answer to this, it has been claimed that the Negro can survive only through submission. Mr. Washington distinctly asks that black people give up, at least for the present, three things,—

First, political power,
Second, insistence on civil rights,
Third, higher education of Negro
    youth,—

and concentrate all their energies on industrial education, and accumulation of wealth, and the conciliation of the South. This policy has been courageously and insistently advocated for over fifteen years, and has been triumphant for perhaps ten years. As a result of this tender of the palm-branch, what has been the return? In these years there have occurred:

1. The disfranchisement of the Negro.
2. The legal creation of a distinct status of civil inferiority for the Negro.
3. The steady withdrawal of aid from institutions for the higher training of the Negro.

These movements are not, to be sure, direct results of Mr. Washington's teachings; but his propaganda has, without a shadow of doubt, helped their speedier accomplishment. The question then comes: Is it possible, and probable, that nine millions of men can make effective progress in economic lines if they are deprived of political rights, made a servile caste, and allowed only the most meagre chance for developing their exceptional men? If history and reason give any distinct answer to these questions, it is an emphatic *No*. And Mr. Washington thus faces the triple paradox of his career:

1. He is striving nobly to make Negro artisans business men and property-owners; but it is utterly impossible, under modern competitive methods, for workingmen and property-owners to defend their rights and exist without the right of suffrage.

2. He insists on thrift and self-respect, but at the same time counsels a silent submission to civic inferiority such as is bound to sap the manhood of any race in the long run.

3. He advocates common-school and industrial training, and depreciates institutions of higher learning, but neither the Negro common-schools, nor Tuskegee itself, could remain open a day were it not for teachers trained in Negro colleges, or trained by their graduates.

This triple paradox in Mr. Washington's position is the object of criticism by two classes of colored Americans. One class is spiritually descended from Toussaint the Savior, through Gabriel, Vesey, and Turner, and they represent the attitude of revolt and revenge; they hate the white South blindly and distrust the white race generally, and so far as they agree on definite action, think that the Negro's only hope lies in emigration beyond the borders of the United States. And yet, by the irony of fate, nothing has more effectually made this programme seem hopeless than the recent course of the United States toward weaker and darker peoples in the West Indies, Hawaii, and the Philippines,—for where in the world may we go and be safe from lying and brute force?

The other class of Negroes who cannot agree with Mr. Washington has hitherto said little aloud. They deprecate the sight of scattered counsels, of internal disagreement; and especially they dislike making their just criticism of a useful and earnest man an excuse for a general discharge of venom from small-minded opponents. Nevertheless, the questions involved are so fundamental and serious that it is difficult to see how men like the Grimkes, Kelly Miller, J.W.E. Bowen, and other representatives of this group, can much longer be silent. Such men feel in conscience bound to ask of this nation three things:

1. The right to vote.
2. Civic equality.
3. The education of youth according to ability.

They acknowledge Mr. Washington's invaluable service in counselling patience and courtesy in such demands; they do not ask that ignorant black men vote when ignorant whites are debarred, or that any reasonable restrictions in the suffrage should not be applied; they know that the low social level of the mass of the race is responsible for much discrimination against it, but they also know, and the nation knows, that relentless color-prejudice is more often a cause than a result of the Negro's degradation; they seek the abatement of this relic of barbarism, and not its systematic encouragement and pampering by all agencies of social power from the Associated Press to the Church of Christ. They advocate, with Mr. Washington, a broad system of Negro common schools supplemented by thorough industrial training; but they are surprised that a man of Mr. Washington's insight cannot see that no such educational system ever has rested or can rest on any other basis than that of the well-equipped college and university, and they insist that there is a demand for a few such institutions throughout the South to train the best of the Negro youth as teachers, professional men, and leaders.

This group of men honor Mr. Washington for his attitude of conciliation toward the white South; they accept the "Atlanta Compromise" in its broadest interpretation; they recognize, with him, many signs of promise, many men of high purpose and fair judgment, in this section; they know that no easy task has been laid upon a region already tottering under heavy burdens. But, nevertheless, they insist that the way to truth and right lies in straightforward honesty, not in indiscriminate flattery; in praising those of the South who do well and criticising uncompromisingly those who do ill; in taking advantage of the opportunities at hand and urging their fellows to do the same, but at the same time in remembering that only a firm adherence to their higher ideals and aspirations will ever keep those ideals within the realm of possibility. They do not expect that the free right to vote, to enjoy civic rights, and to be educated, will come in a moment; they do not expect to see the bias and prejudices of years disappear at the blast of a trumpet; but they are absolutely certain that the way for a people to gain their reasonable rights is not by voluntarily throwing them away and insisting that they do not want them; that the way for a people to gain respect is not by continually belittling and ridiculing themselves; that, on the contrary, Negroes must insist continually, in season and out of season, that voting is necessary to modern manhood, that color discrimination is barbarism, and that black boys need education as well as white boys.

In failing thus to state plainly and unequivocally the legitimate demands of their people, even at the cost of opposing an honored leader, the thinking classes of American Negroes would shirk a heavy responsibility,—a responsibility to themselves, a responsibility to the struggling masses, a responsibility to the darker races of men whose future depends so largely on this American experiment, but especially a responsibility to this nation,—this common Fatherland. It is wrong to encourage a man or a people in evil-doing; it is wrong to aid and abet a national crime simply because it is unpopular not to do so. The growing spirit of kindliness and reconciliation between the North and South after the frightful difference of a generation ago ought to be a source of deep congratulation to all, and especially to those whose mistreatment caused the war; but if that reconciliation is to be marked by the industrial slavery and civic death of those same black men, with permanent legislation into a position of inferiority, then those black men, if they are really men, are called upon by every consideration of patriotism and loyalty to oppose such a course by all civilized methods, even though such opposition involves disagreement with Mr. Booker T. Washington. We have no right to sit silently by while the inevitable seeds are sown for a harvest of disaster to our children, black and white.

First, it is the duty of black men to judge the South discriminatingly. The present generation of Southerners are not responsible for the past, and they should not be blindly hated or blamed for it. Furthermore, to no class is the indiscriminate endorsement of the recent course of the South toward Negroes more nauseating than to the best thought of the South. The South is not "solid," it is a land in the ferment of social change, wherein forces of all kinds are fighting for supremacy; and to praise the ill the South is to-day perpetrating is just as wrong as to condemn the good. Discriminating and broad-minded criticism is what the South needs,—needs it for the sake of her own white sons and daughters, and for the insurance of robust, healthy mental and moral development.

To-day even the attitude of the Southern whites toward the blacks is not, as so many assume, in all cases the same; the ignorant Southerner hates the Negro, the workingmen fear his competition, the moneymakers wish to use him as a laborer, some of the educated see a menace in his upward development, while others—usually the sons of the masters—wish to help him to rise. National opinion has enabled this last class to maintain the Negro common schools, and to protect the Negro partially in property, life, and limb. Through the pressure of the money-makers, the Negro is in danger of being reduced to semislavery, especially in the country districts; the workingmen, and those of the educated who fear the Negro, have united to disfranchise him, and some have urged his deportation; while the passions of the ignorant are easily aroused to lynch and abuse any black man. To praise this intricate whirl of thought and prejudice is nonsense; to inveigh indiscriminately against "the South" is unjust; but to use the same breath in praising Governor Aycock, exposing Senator Morgan, arguing with Mr. Thomas Nelson Page, and denouncing Senator Ben Tillman, is not only sane, but the imperative duty of thinking black men.

It would be unjust to Mr. Washington not to acknowledge that in several instances he has opposed movements in the South which were unjust to the Negro; he sent memorials to the Louisiana and Alabama constitutional conventions, he has spoken against lynching, and in other ways has openly or silently set his influence against sinister schemes and unfortunate happenings. Notwithstanding this, it is equally true to assert that on the whole the distinct impression left by Mr. Washington's propaganda is, first, that the South is justified in its present attitude toward the Negro because of the Negro's degradation; secondly, that the prime cause of the Negro's failure to rise more quickly is his wrong education in the past; and, thirdly, that his future rise depends primarily on his own efforts. Each of these propositions is a dangerous half-truth. The supplementary truths must never be lost sight of: first, slavery and race-prejudice are potent if not sufficient causes of the Negro's position; second, industrial and common-school training were necessarily slow in planting because they had to await the black teachers trained by higher institutions,—it being extremely doubtful if any essentially different development was possible, and certainly a Tuskegee was unthinkable before 1880; and, third, while it is a great truth to say that the Negro must strive and strive mightily to help himself, it is equally true that unless his striving be not simply seconded, but rather aroused and encouraged, by the initiative of the richer and wiser environing group, he cannot hope for great success.

In his failure to realize and impress this last point, Mr. Washington is especially to be criticized. His doctrine has tended to make the whites, North and South, shift the burden of the Negro problem to the Negro's shoulders and stand aside as critical and rather pessimistic spectators; when in fact the burden belongs to the nation, and the hands of none of us are clean if we bend not our energies to righting these great wrongs.

The South ought to be led, by candid and honest criticism, to assert her better self and do her full duty to the race she has cruelly wronged and is still wronging. The North —her co-partner in guilt—cannot salve her conscience by plastering it with gold. We cannot settle this problem by diplomacy and suaveness, by "policy" alone. If worse come to worst, can the moral fibre of this country survive the slow throttling and murder of nine millions of men?

The black men of America have a duty to perform, a duty stern and delicate,—a forward movement to oppose a part of the work of their greatest leader. So far as Mr. Washington preaches Thrift, Patience, and Industrial Training for the masses, we must hold up his hands and strive with him, rejoicing in his honors and glorying in the strength of this Joshua called of God and of man to lead the headless host. But so far as Mr. Washington apologizes for injustice, North or South, does not rightly value the privilege and duty of voting, belittles the emasculating effects of caste distinctions, and opposes the higher training and ambition of our brighter minds,—so far as he, the South, or the Nation does this,—we must unceasingly and firmly oppose them. By every civilized and peaceful method we must strive for the rights which the world accords to men, clinging unwaveringly to those great words which the sons of the Fathers would fain forget: "We hold these truths to be self-evident: That all men are created equal; that they are endowed by their Creator with certain unalienable rights; that among these are life, liberty, and the pursuit of happiness." ∽

Primary Sources

Aptheker, Herbert, ed. *The Correspondence of W.E.B. Du Bois*. 3 vols. Amherst: University of Massachusetts Press, 1973–78.

Clarke, John Henrik, et al., eds. *Black Titan: W.E.B. Du Bois, an Anthology by the Editors of Freedomways*. Boston: Beacon Press, 1970.

Du Bois, W.E.B. *An ABC of Color: Selections Chosen by the Author from over Half a Century of His Writings*. New York: International Publishers, 1969.

———. *The Autobiography of W.E.B. Du Bois: A Soliloquy on Viewing My Life from the Last Decade of Its First Century*. New York: International Publishers, 1968.

———. *The Black Flame: A Trilogy*. New York: Mainstream Publishers, 1957–61.

———. *Black Folk, Then and Now*. New introduction by Herbert Aptheker. Millwood, N.Y.: Kraus-Thomson Organization, 1975.

———. *Black Reconstruction*. New introduction and bibliography by Herbert Aptheker. Millwood, N.Y.: Kraus-Thomson Organization, 1975.

———. *Dusk of Dawn*. New introduction by Herbert Aptheker. Millwood, N.Y.: Kraus-Thomson Organization, 1975.

———. *The Souls of Black Folk*. New introduction by Herbert Aptheker. N.Y.: Kraus-Thomson Organization, 1973.

———. *W.E.B. Du Bois on Sociology and the Black Community*. Chicago: University of Chicago Press, 1978.

Lester, Julius, ed. *The Seventh Son: The Thought and Writings of W.E.B. Du Bois*. Introduction by J. Lester. New York: Random House, 1971.

Partington, Paul G., ed. *W.E.B. Du Bois: A Bibliography of His Published Writings*. Whittier, Calif.: Partington, 1977.

Secondary Sources

Broderick, F.L. *W.E.B. Du Bois: A Negro Leader in a Time of Crisis*. Stanford, Calif.: Stanford University Press, 1959.

Logan, Rayford W., ed. *W. E.B. Du Bois: A Profile*. New York: Hill and Wang, 1971.

Marable, Manning. *W.E.B. Du Bois, Black Radical Democrat*. Boston: Twayne Publishers, 1986.

Patterson, Anita H. *From Emerson to King: Democracy, Race, and the Politics of Protest*. New York: Oxford University Press, 1997.

Rudwick, E.M. *W.E.B. Du Bois: A Study in Minority Group Leadership*. Philadelphia: University of Pennsylvania Press, 1961.

30. Eugene V. Debs

EUGENE V. DEBS (1855–1926) was born in Terre Haute, Indiana, where he went to work for the railroad at the age of fifteen. In time he rose through the ranks of the Brotherhood of Locomotive Firemen to become national secretary and editor of the newspaper. He helped to form the (industrial) American Railway Union and became its president in 1893. Although he had thought the Pullman Strike of 1894 unwise, he supported it and so was included in the injunction order issued by the federal district court (see the introduction to part IV). Disobeying it, he was held in contempt of court and sent to prison, where the chance to read and reflect on his experiences led to his becoming a socialist. He was a founding leader first of the Social Democratic party (1897) and then of the Socialist party (1900). Always an advocate of industrial unionism, he supported the formation of the International Workers of the World in 1905, though not all of the tactics subsequently employed in its name. He was the presidential candidate of the Socialist party five times, receiving nearly a million votes in both the 1912 and 1920 elections (during the second of which he was serving a ten-year sentence in prison for seditious speech). Thoroughly American and always militant, Debs stands as one of the foremost spokespersons for socialism and the working class generally.

The materials included here center around the latter trial and conviction, although the first speech is a characteristic call for politically active industrial unionism. Debs made his famous Canton, Ohio, speech in 1918 at a time when prowar forces were actively trying to suppress antiwar sentiments. The Socialist party had taken a principled stand against the war and on behalf of the international working class in 1917. It had run many local candidates on this antiwar platform in the elections of 1917 and several of them won. Such opposition sparked Congress to enact new sedition laws, and the press and the national government collaborated in a campaign against radicals, socialists, and foreigners. Like Goldman, Debs spoke out deliberately and sought to raise the shield of protection of free speech under the First Amendment. The reader may judge whether his Canton speech should have been entitled to such guarantees. Debs's plea to his trial jury argues that it was, while Justice Oliver Wendell Holmes, speaking later for the Supreme Court, concluded that Debs's words were so close to being "action that the government had power to prevent" that they were not protected by the apparently clear language of the amendment. ᘒ

"Revolutionary Unionism" (1905)

The unity of labor, economic and political, upon the basis of the class struggle, is at this time the supreme need of the working class. The prevailing lack of unity implies lack of class consciousness; that is to say, enlightened self-interest; and this can, must and will be overcome by revolutionary education and organization. Experience, long, painful, and dearly bought, has taught some of us that craft division is fatal to class unity. To accomplish its mission the working class must be united. They must act together; they must assert their combined power, and when they do this upon the basis of the class struggle, then and then only will they break the fetters of wage slavery.

We are engaged today in a class war; and why? For the simple reason that in the evolution of the capitalist system in which we live, society has been mainly divided into two economic classes—a small class of capitalists who own the tools with which work is done and wealth is produced, and a great mass of workers who are compelled to use those tools. Between these two classes there is an irrepressible economic conflict. Unfortunately for himself, the workingman does not yet understand the nature of this conflict, and for this reason has hitherto failed to accomplish any effective unity of his class.

It is true that workers in the various departments of industrial activity have organized trade unions. It is also true that in this capacity they have from time to time asserted such power as this form of organization has conferred upon them. It is equally true that mere craft unionism, no matter how well it may be

organized, is in the present highly developed capitalist system utterly unable to successfully cope with the capitalist class. The old craft union has done its work and belongs to the past. Labor unionism, like everything else, must recognize and bow to the inexorable law of evolution.

The craft union says that the worker shall receive a fair day's pay for a fair day's work. What is a fair day's pay for a fair day's work? Ask the capitalist and he will give you his idea about it. Ask the worker and, if he is intelligent, he will tell you that a fair day's pay for a fair day's work is all the workingman produces.

While the craft unionist still talks about a fair day's pay for a fair day's work, implying that the economic interests of the capitalist and the worker can be harmonized upon a basis of equal justice to both, the Industrial Worker says, "I want all I produce by my labor."

If the worker is not entitled to all he produces, then what share is anybody else entitled to?

Does the worker today receive all he produces? Does he receive anything like a fair (?) share of the product of his labor? Will any trade unionist of the old school make any such claim, and if he is bold enough to make it, can he verify it?

The student of this question knows that, as a matter of fact, in the capitalist system in which we live today the worker who produces all wealth receives but enough of his product to keep him in working and producing order. His wage, in the aggregate, is fixed by his living necessities. It suffices, upon the average, to maintain him according to the prevailing standard of living and to enable him to reproduce himself in the form of labor power. He

SOURCE: Eugene Debs, Speech in Chicago, 25 November 1905. In Ronald Radosh, ed., *Debs* (Englewood Cliffs, N.J.: Prentice-Hall, 1971).

receives, as a matter of fact, but about 17 percent of what his labor produces. . . .

The evolution is not yet complete.

By virtue of his private ownership of the social tool—made and used by the cooperative labor of the working class—the employer has the economic power to appropriate to himself, as a capitalist, what is produced by the social labor of the working class. This accounts for the fact that the capitalist becomes fabulously rich, lives in a palace where there is music and singing and dancing, and where there is the luxury of all climes, while the workingmen who do the work and produce the wealth and endure the privations and make the sacrifices of health and limb and life, remain in a wretched state of poverty and dependence.

The exploiting capitalist is the economic master and the political ruler in capitalist society, and as such holds the exploited wage worker in utter contempt.

No master ever had any respect for his slave, and no slave ever had, or ever could have, any real love for his master. . . .

Alert, vigilant, argus-eyed as the capitalist dailies of Chicago are, there is not one of them that knows of this meeting of the Industrial Workers. But if this were a meeting of the American Federation of Labor and an old trade union leader were here, you would read tomorrow morning a full account of it and him in every capitalist paper in the city. There is a reason for this that explains itself.

The capitalist papers know that there is such an organization as the Industrial Workers, because they have lied about it. Just now they are ignoring it. Let me serve notice on them through you and the thousands of others who flock to our meetings everywhere, that they will reckon with the Industrial Workers before six months have rolled around.

There are those wage workers who feel their economic dependence, who know that the capitalist for whom they work is the owner of their job, and therefore the master of their fate, who are still vainly seeking by individual effort and through waning craft unions to harmonize the conflicting interests of the exploiting capitalist and the exploited wage slave. They are engaged in a vain and hopeless task. They are wasting time and energy worthy of a better cause. These interests never can and never will be harmonized permanently, and when they are adjusted even temporarily it is always at the expense of the working class.

It is no part of the mission of this revolutionary working-class union to conciliate the capitalist class. We are organized to fight that class, and we want that class to distinctly understand it. And they do understand it, and in time the working class will also understand it; and then the capitalist class will have reason to understand it better still. Their newspapers understand it so well even now that they have not a single favorable comment to make upon it. . . .

There was a time when the craft union expressed in terms of unionism the prevailing mode of industry. That was long ago when production was still mainly carried on by handicraftmen with hand tools; when one man worked for another to learn his trade that he might become its master. The various trades involved skill and cunning; considerable time was required to master them. This was in the early stages of the capitalist system. Even at that early day the antagonism between employer and employed found expression, although the employer was not at that time the capitalist as he is today. The men who followed these trades found it necessary in order to protect themselves in their trade interests to band together, form a union, so that they might act together in resisting the encroachments of the "boss." So the trade union came into existence. . . .

The pure and simple trade union, in seeking to preserve its autonomy, is forced into conflict with other trade unions by the unceasing operation of the laws of industrial evolution. How many of the skilled trades that were in operation half a century ago are still practiced? ...

We insist that all the workers in the whole of any given plant shall belong to one and the same union.

This is the very thing the workers need and the capitalist who owns the establishment does not want. He believes in labor unionism if it is the "right kind." And if it is the right kind for him it is the wrong kind for you. He is more than willing that his employees shall join the craft union. He has not the slightest objection. On the contrary, it is easily proven that capitalists are among the most active upholders of the old craft unions.

The capitalists are perfectly willing that you shall organize, as long as you don't do a thing against them, as long as you don't do a thing for yourselves. You cannot do a thing for yourselves without antagonizing them; and you don't antagonize them through your craft unions nearly as much as you buttress their interests and prolong their mastery. ...

President Roosevelt would have you believe that there are no classes in the United States. He was made president by the votes of the working class. Did you ever know of his stopping overnight in the home of a workingman? Is it by mere chance that he is always sheltered beneath the hospitable roof of some plutocrat? Not long ago he made a visit here and he gave a committee representing the workers about fifteen minutes of his precious time, just time enough to rebuke them with the intimation that organized labor consisted of a set of lawbreakers, and then he gave fifteen hours to the plutocrats of Chicago, being wined and dined by them to prove that there are no classes in the United States, and that you, horny-handed

veteran, with your wage of $1.50 a day, with six children to support on that, are in the same class with John D. Rockefeller! Your misfortune is that you do not know you are in the same class. But on election day it dawns upon you and you prove it by voting the same ticket.

Since you have looked yourself over thoroughly, you realize by this time that, as a workingman, you have been supporting, through your craft unions and through your ballots, a social system that is the negation of your manhood.

The capitalist for whom you work doesn't have to go out and look for you; you have to look for him, and you belong to him just as completely as if he had a title to your body; as if you were his chattel slave.

He doesn't own you under the law, but he does under the fact.

Why? Because he owns the tool with which you work, and you have got to have access to that tool if you work; and if you want to live you have got to work. If you don't work you don't eat; and so, scourged by hunger pangs, you look about for that tool and you locate it, and you soon discover that between yourself, a workingman, and that tool that is an essential part of yourself in industry, there stands the capitalist who owns it. He is your boss; he owns your job, takes your product, and controls your destiny. Before you can touch that tool to earn a dime you must petition the owner of it to allow you to use it, in consideration of your giving to him all you produce with it, except just enough to keep you alive and in working order.

Observe that you are displaced by the surplus product of your own labor; that what you produce is of more value under capitalism than you who produce it; that the commodity which is the result of your labor is of greater value under capitalism than your own life.

You consist of palpitating flesh; you have wants. You have necessities. You cannot satisfy them, and you suffer. But the product of your labor, the property of the capitalist, that is sacred; that must be protected at all hazards. After you have been displaced by the surplus product of your labor and you have been idle long enough, you become restive and you begin to speak out, and you become a menace. The unrest culminates in trouble. The capitalist presses a button and the police are called into action. Then the capitalist presses button No. 2 and injunctions are issued by the judges, the judicial allies and servants of the capitalist class. Then button No. 3 is pressed and the state troops fall into line; and if this is not sufficient, button No. 4 is pressed and the regular soldiers come marching to the scene. That is what President Roosevelt meant when he said that back of the mayor is the governor, back of the governor, the president; or, to use his own words, back of the city, the state, and back of the state the nation—the capitalist nation.

If you have been working in a steel mill and you have made more steel than your master can sell, and you are locked out and get hungry, and the soldiers are called out, it is to protect the steel and shoot you who made the steel—to guard the men who steal the steel and kill the men who made it.

I am not asking you to withdraw from the craft unions simply because the Industrial Workers has been formed. I am asking you to think about these matters for yourselves....

I have said and say again that no strike was ever lost; that it has always been worth all it cost. An essential part of a workingman's education is the defeats he encounters. The strikes he loses are after all the only ones he wins. I am heartily glad for myself that I lost the strike. It is the best thing that ever happened to me. I lost the strike of the past that I may win the strike of the future.

I am a discredited labor leader, but I have good staying qualities. The very moment the capitalist press credits me with being a wise labor leader, I will invite you to investigate me upon the charge of treason. I am discredited by the capitalist simply because I am true to his victim. I don't want his favors. I do not court his approbation. I would not have it. I can't afford it. If I had his respect it would be at the price of my own.

I don't care anything about what is called public opinion. I know precisely what that means. It is but the reflection of the interests of the capitalist class. As between the respect of the public and my own, I prefer my own; and I am going to keep it until I can have both.

When I pick up a capitalist newspaper and read a eulogy of some labor leader, I know that that leader has at least two afflictions; the one is mental weakness and the other is moral cowardice—and they go together. Put it down that when the capitalist who is exploiting you credits your leader with being safe and conservative and wise, that leader is not serving you. And if you take exception to that statement, just ask me to prove it.

The rank and file of all unions, barring their ignorance, are all right. The working class as a whole is all right. Many of them are misguided, and stand in the light of their own interest.

It is sometimes necessary that we offend you and even shock you, that you may understand that we are your friends and not your enemies. And if we are against your unions it is because we are for you. We know that you have paid your dues into them for years and that you are animated by a spirit of misdirected loyalty to those unions.

I can remember that it was not a very easy matter for me to give up the union in which I had spent my boyhood and all the years of my young manhood. I remember that I felt there was something in it in the nature of a sacrifice, and yet I had to make it in the interest of the larger duty that I owed myself and the working class.

Let me say to you, if you are a craft unionist, that infinitely greater than your loyalty to your craft is your loyalty to the working class as a whole. No craft union can fight this great battle successfully alone. The craft is a part, a part only, of the great body of the working class. And the time has come for this class, numerically overwhelmingly in the majority, to follow in one respect at least the example of its capitalist masters and unite as a whole.

In this barbarous competitive struggle in which we are engaged, the workers, the millions, are fighting each other to sell themselves into slavery; the middle class are fighting each other to get enough trade to keep soul and body together, and the professional class are fighting each other like savages for practice. And this is called civilization! What a mockery! What a sham! There is no real civilization in the capitalist system.

Today there is nothing so easily produced as wealth. The whole earth consists of raw materials; and in every breath of nature, in sunshine, and in shower, hidden everywhere, are the subtle forces that may, by the touch of the hand of labor, be set into operation to transmute these raw materials into wealth, the finished products, in all their multiplied forms and in opulent abundance for all. The merest child can press a button that will set in operation a forest of machinery and produce wealth enough for a community.

Whatever may be said of the ignorant, barbarous past, there is no excuse for poverty today. And yet it is the scourge of the race. It is the Nemesis of capitalist civilization. Ten millions, one-eighth of our whole population, are in a state of chronic poverty. Three millions of these have been sunk to unresisting pauperism.

The whole working class is in a sadly dependent state, and even the most favored wage worker is left suspended by a single thread. He does not know what hour a machine may be invented to make his trade useless, displace him and throw him into the increasing army of the unemployed....

You can change this condition—not tomorrow, not next week, nor next year; but in the meantime the next thing to changing it is making up your mind that it shall be changed. That is what we Industrial Unionists have done. And so there has come to us a new state of mind, and in our hearts there is the joy of service and the serenity of triumph.

We are united and we cannot be disunited. We cannot be stampeded. We know that we are confronted by ten thousand difficulties. We know that all the powers of capitalism are to be arrayed against us. But were these obstacles multiplied by a million, it would simply have the effect of multiplying our determination by a million, to overcome them all. And so we are organizing and appealing to you.

The workingman today does not understand his industrial relation to his fellow workers. He has never been correlated with others in the same industry. He has mechanically done his part. He has simply been a cog, with little reference to, or knowledge of, the rest of the cogs. Now, we teach him to hold up his head and look over the whole mechanism. If he is employed in a certain plant, as an Industrial Unionist, his eyes are opened. He takes a survey of the entire productive mechanism, and he understands his part in it, and his relation to every other worker in that industry. The very instant he does that he is buoyed by a fresh hope and thrilled with a new aspiration. He becomes a larger man. He begins to feel like a collective son of toil.

Then he and his fellows study to fit themselves to take control of this productive mechanism when it shall be transferred from the idle capitalist to the workers to whom it rightfully belongs.

In every mill and every factory, every mine and every quarry, every railroad and every shop, everywhere, the workers, enlightened, understanding their self-interest, are correlating themselves in the industrial and economic mechanism. They are developing their industrial consciousness, their economic and political power; and when the revolution comes, they will be prepared to take possession and assume control of every industry. With the education they will have received in the Industrial Workers they will be drilled and disciplined, trained and fitted for Industrial Mastery and Social Freedom. ∾

Speech to the Jury (1918)

"May it please the Court, and Gentlemen of the Jury:

"For the first time in my life I appear before a jury in a court of law to answer to an indictment for crime. I am not a lawyer. I know little about court procedure, about the rules of evidence or legal practice. I know only that you gentlemen are to hear the evidence brought against me, that the Court is to instruct you in the law, and that you are then to determine by your verdict whether I shall be branded with criminal guilt and be consigned, perhaps to the end of my life, in a felon's cell.

"Gentlemen, I do not fear to face you in this hour of accusation, nor do I shrink from the consequences of my utterances or my acts. Standing before you, charged as I am with crime, I can yet look the Court in the face, I can look you in the face, I can look the world in the face, for in my conscience, in my soul, there is festering no accusation of guilt.

"Permit me to say in the first place that I am entirely satisfied with the Court's ruling. I have no fault to find with the district attorney or with the counsel for the prosecution.

"I wish to admit the truth of all that has been testified to in this proceeding. I have no disposition to deny anything that is true. I would not, if I could, escape the results of an adverse verdict. I would not retract a word that I have uttered that I believe to be true to save myself from going to the penitentiary for the rest of my days.

"I am charged in the indictment, first, that I did willfully cause and attempt to cause or incite, insubordination, mutiny, disloyalty and refusal of duty within the military forces of the United States; that I did obstruct and attempt to obstruct the recruiting and enlistment service of the United States. I am charged also with uttering words intended to bring into contempt and disrepute the form of government of the United States, the Constitution of the United States, the military forces of the United States, the flag of the United States, and the uniform of the army and navy."

The Court: "Mr. Debs, permit me to say that the last charge which you have read to the jury has been withdrawn from their consideration by the Court."

Debs: "Pardon me. I was not aware of that."

The Court: "I have directed a verdict of 'not guilty' as to that charge."

SOURCE: David Karsner, *Debs: His Authorized Life and Letters* (New York: Boni and Liveright, 1919).

Debs: "I am accused further of uttering words intended to procure and incite resistance to the United States and to promote the cause of the Imperial German Government.

"Gentlemen, you have heard the report of my speech at Canton on June 16, and I submit that there is not a word in that speech to warrant these charges. I admit having delivered the speech. I admit the accuracy of the speech in all of its main features as reported in this proceeding. There were two distinct reports. They vary somewhat, but they are agreed upon all the material statements embodied in that speech.

"In what I had to say there my purpose was to educate the people to understand something about the social system in which we live and to prepare them to change this system by perfectly peaceable and orderly means into what I, as a Socialist, conceive to be a real democracy.

"From what you heard in the address of counsel for the prosecution, you might naturally infer that I am an advocate of force and violence. It is not true. I have never advocated violence in any form. I always believed in education, in intelligence, in enlightenment, and I have always made my appeal to the reason and to the conscience of the people.

"I admit being opposed to the present form of government. I admit being opposed to the present social system. I am doing what little I can, and have been for many years, to bring about a change that shall do away with the rule of the great body of the people by a relatively small class and establish in this country an industrial and social democracy.

"In the course of the speech that resulted in this indictment, I am charged with having expressed sympathy for Kate Richards O'Hare, for Rose Pastor Stokes, for Ruthenberg, Wagenknecht and Baker. I did express my perfect sympathy with these comrades of mine. I have known them for many years. I have every rea-

son to believe in their integrity, every reason to look upon them with respect, with confidence and with approval.

"Kate Richards O'Hare never uttered the words imputed to her in the report. The words are perfectly brutal. She is not capable of using such language. I know that through all of the years of her life she has been working in the interests of the suffering, struggling poor, that she has consecrated all of her energies, all of her abilities, to their betterment. The same is true of Rose Pastor Stokes. Through all her life she has been on the side of the oppressed and downtrodden. If she were so inclined she might occupy a place of ease. She might enjoy all of the comforts and leisures of life. Instead of this, she has renounced them all. She has taken her place among the poor, and there she has worked with all of her ability, all of her energy, to make it possible for them to enjoy a little more of the comforts of life.

"I said that if these women whom I have known all of these years—that if they were criminals, if they ought to go to the penitentiary, then I, too, am a criminal, and I ought to be sent to prison. I have not a word to retract—not one. I uttered the truth. I made no statement in that speech that I am not prepared to prove. If there is a single falsehood in it, it has not been exposed. If there is a single statement in it that will not bear the light of truth, I will retract it. I will make all of the reparation in my power. But if what I said is true, and I believe it is, then whatever fate or fortune may have in store for me I shall preserve inviolate the integrity of my soul and stand by it to the end.

"When I said what I did about the three comrades of mine who are in the workhouse at Canton, I had in mind what they had been ever since I have known them in the service of the working class. I had in mind the fact that these three working men had just a little while before had their hands cuffed and were strung up in that prison house for eight hours at a time until they fell to the floor fainting from exhaustion. And this because they had refused to do some menial, filthy services that were an insult to their dignity and their manhood.

"I have been accused of expressing sympathy for the Bolsheviki of Russia. I plead guilty to the charge. I have read a great deal about the Bolsheviki of Russia that is not true. I happen to know of my knowledge that they have been grossly misrepresented by the press of this country. Who are these much-maligned revolutionists of Russia? For years they had been the victims of a brutal Czar. They and their antecedents were sent to Siberia, lashed with a knout, if they even dreamed of freedom. At last the hour struck for a great change. The revolution came. The Czar was overthrown and his infamous regime ended. What followed? The common people of Russia came into power—the peasants, the toilers, the soldiers—and they proceeded as best they could to establish a government of the people."

District Attorney Wertz: "If the Court please, I would like to ask the Court to instruct the defendant that his arguments are to be confined to the evidence in the case. There isn't any evidence in this case about the Bolsheviki at all or the Russian revolution."

The Court: "I think I will permit the defendant to proceed in his own way. Of course, you are not a lawyer, Mr. Debs. The usual rule is that the remarks of counsel should be confined to the testimony in the case, but it does not forbid counsel from making references to facts or matters of general public history or notoriety by way of illustrating your arguments and comments upon the testimony in the case. So I will permit you to proceed in your own way."

Debs: "Thank you. It may be that the much-despised Bolsheviki may fail at last, but let me say to you that they have written a chapter of glorious history. It will stand to their eternal credit. The leaders are now denounced as criminals and outlaws. Let me remind you that there was a time when George Washington, who is now revered as the father of his country, was denounced as a disloyalist; when Sam Adams, who is known to us as the father of the American Revolution, was condemned as an incendiary, and Patrick Henry, who delivered that inspired and inspiring oration, that aroused the Colonists, was condemned as a traitor. They were misunderstood at the time. They stood true to themselves, and they won an immortality of gratitude and glory.

"When great changes occur in history, when great principles are involved, as a rule the majority are wrong. The minority are right. In every age there have been a few heroic souls who have been in advance of their time who have been misunderstood, maligned, persecuted, sometimes put to death. Long after their martyrdom monuments were erected to them and garlands were woven for their graves.

"I have been accused of having obstructed the war. I admit it. Gentlemen, I abhor war. I would oppose the war if I stood alone. When I think of a cold, glittering steel bayonet being plunged in the white, quivering flesh of a human being, I recoil with horror. I have often wondered if I could take the life of my fellow man, even to save my own.

"Men talk about holy wars. There are none. Let me remind you that it was Benjamin Franklin who said, 'There never was a good war or a bad peace.'

"Napoleon Bonaparte was a high authority upon the subject of war. And when in his last days he was chained to the rock at St. Helena, when he felt the skeleton hand of death reaching for him, he cried out in horror, 'War is the trade of savages and barbarians.'

"I have read some history. I know that it is

ruling classes that make war upon one another, and not the people. In all the history of this world the people have never yet declared a war. Not one. I do not believe that really civilized nations would murder one another. I would refuse to kill a human being on my own account. Why should I at the command of any one else, or at the command of any power on earth?

"Twenty centuries ago there was one appeared upon earth we know as the Prince of Peace. He issued a command in which I believe. He said, 'Love one another.' He did not say, 'Kill one another,' but 'love one another.' He espoused the cause of the suffering poor —just as Rose Pastor Stokes did, just as Kate Richards O'Hare did—and the poor heard him gladly. It was not long before he aroused the ill will and hatred of the usurers, the money changers, the profiteers, the high priests, the lawyers, the judges, the merchants, the bankers—in a word, the ruling class. They said of him just what the ruling class says of the Socialist to-day, 'He is preaching dangerous doctrine. He is inciting the common rabble. He is a menace to peace and order.' And they had him arraigned, tried, convicted, condemned, and they had his quivering body spiked to the gates of Jerusalem.

"This has been the tragic history of the race. In the ancient world Socrates sought to teach some new truths to the people, and they made him drink the fatal hemlock. It has been true all along the track of the ages. The men and women who have been in advance, who have had new ideas, new ideals, who have had the courage to attack the established order of things, have all had to pay the same penalty.

"A century and a half ago, when the American colonists were still foreign subjects, and when there were a few men who had faith in the common people and believed that they could rule themselves without a king, in that day to speak against the king was treason. If

you read Bancroft or any other standard historian, you will find that a great majority of the colonists believed in the king and actually believed that he had a divine right to rule over them. They had been taught to believe that to say a word against the king, to question his socalled divine right, was sinful. There were ministers who opened their Bibles to prove that it was the patriotic duty of the people to loyally serve and support the king. But there were a few men in that day who said, 'We don't need a king. We can govern ourselves.' And they began an agitation that has been immortalized in history.

"Washington, Adams, Paine—these were the rebels of their day. At first they were opposed by the people and denounced by the press. You can remember that it was Franklin who said to his compeers, 'We have now to hang together or we'll hang separately by and by.' And if the Revolution had failed, the revolutionary fathers would have been executed as felons. But it did not fail. Revolutions have a habit of succeeding when the time comes for them. The revolutionary forefathers were opposed to the form of government in their day. They were opposed to the social system of their time. They were denounced, they were condemned. But they had the moral courage to stand erect and defy all the storms of detraction; and that is why they are in history, and that is why the great respectable majority of their day sleep in forgotten graves. The world does not know they ever lived.

"At a later time there began another mighty agitation in this country. It was against an institution that was deemed a very respectable one in its time, the institution of chattel slavery, that became all-powerful, that controlled the President, both branches of Congress, the Supreme Court, the press, to a very large extent the pulpit. All of the organized forces of society, all the powers of government, upheld chattel slavery in that day. And again there were a few lovers of liberty who appeared. One of them was Elijah Lovejoy. Elijah Lovejoy was as much despised in his day as are the leaders of the I.W.W. in our day. Elijah Lovejoy was murdered in cold blood in Alton, Illinois, in 1837 simply because he was opposed to chattel slavery—just as I am opposed to wage slavery. When you go down the Mississippi River and look up at Alton, you see a magnificent white shaft erected there in memory of a man who was true to himself and his convictions of right and duty unto death.

"It was my good fortune to personally know Wendell Phillips. I heard the story of his persecution in part, at least, from his own eloquent lips just a little while before they were silenced in death.

"William Lloyd Garrison, Garret Smith, Thaddeus Stevens—these leaders of the abolition movement, who were regarded as monsters of depravity, were true to the faith and stood their ground. They are all in history. You are teaching your children to revere their memories, while all of their detractors are in oblivion.

"Chattel slavery disappeared. We are not yet free. We are engaged in another mighty agitation to-day. It is as wide as the world. It is the rise of the toiling and producing masses who are gradually becoming conscious of their interest, their power, as a class, who are organizing industrially and politically, who are slowly but surely developing the economic and political power that is to set them free. They are still in the minority, but they have learned how to wait, and to bide their time.

"It is because I happen to be in this minority that I stand in your presence today, charged with crime. It is because I believe, as the revolutionary fathers believed in their day, that a change was due in the interests of the people, that the time had come for a better form of government, an improved system, a higher social order, a nobler humanity and a grander

civilization. This minority that is so much misunderstood and so bitterly maligned is in alliance with the forces of evolution, and as certain as I stand before you this afternoon, it is but a question of time until this minority will become the conquering majority and inaugurate the greatest change in all of the history of the world. You may hasten the change; you may retard it; you can no more prevent it than you can prevent the coming of the sunrise on the morrow.

"My friend, the assistant prosecutor, doesn't like what I had to say in my speech about internationalism. What is there objectionable to internationalism? If we had internationalism there would be no war. I believe in patriotism. I have never uttered a word against the flag. I love the flag as a symbol of freedom. I object only when that flag is prostituted to base purposes, to sordid ends, by those who, in the name of patriotism, would keep the people in subjection.

"I believe, however, in a wider patriotism. Thomas Paine said, 'My country is the world. To do good is my religion.' Garrison said, 'My country is the world and all mankind are my countrymen.' That is the essence of internationalism. I believe in it with all of my heart. I believe that nations have been pitted against nations long enough in hatred, in strife, in warfare. I believe there ought to be a bond of unity between all of these nations. I believe that the human race consists of one great family. I love the people of this country, but I don't hate the people of any country on earth —not even the Germans. I refuse to hate a human being because he happens to be born in some other country. Why should I? To me it does not make any difference where he was born or what the color of his skin may be. Like myself, he is the image of his creator. He is a human being endowed with the same faculties, he has the same aspirations, he is entitled to the same rights, and I would infinitely rather serve him and love him than to hate him and kill him.

"We hear a great deal about human brotherhood—a beautiful and inspiring theme. It is preached from a countless number of pulpits. It is vain for us to preach of human brotherhood while we tolerate this social system in which we are a mass of warring units, in which millions of workers have to fight one another for jobs, and millions of business men and professional men have to fight one another for trade, for practice—in which we have individual interests and each is striving to care for himself alone without reference to his fellow men. Human brotherhood is yet to be realized in this world. It can never be under the capitalist-competitive system in which we live.

"Yes, I was opposed to the war. I am perfectly willing, on that count, to be branded as a disloyalist, and if it is a crime under the American law, punishable by imprisonment, for being opposed to human bloodshed, I am perfectly willing to be clothed in the stripes of a convict and to end my days in a prison cell.

"If my friends, the attorneys, had known me a little better they might have saved themselves some trouble in procuring evidence to prove certain things against me which I have not the slightest inclination to deny, but rather, upon the other hand, I have a very considerable pride in.

"You have heard a great deal about the St. Louis platform. I wasn't at the convention when that platform was adopted, but I don't ask to be excused from my responsibility on that account. I voted for its adoption. I believe in its essential principles. There was some of its phrasing that I would have otherwise. I afterwards advocated a restatement. The testimony to the effect that I had refused to repudiate it was true.

"At the time that platform was adopted the nation had just entered upon the war and there were millions of people who were not Socialists who were opposed to the United States being precipitated into that war. Time passed; conditions changed. There were certain new developments and I believed there should be a restatement. I have been asked why I did not favor a repudiation of what was said a year before. For the reason that I believed then, as I believe now, that the statement correctly defined the attitude of the Socialist Party toward war. That statement, bear in mind, did not apply to the people of this country alone, but to the people of the world. It said, in effect, to the people, especially to the workers, of all countries, 'Quit going to war. Stop murdering one another for the profit and glory of the ruling classes. Cultivate the arts of peace. Humanize humanity. Civilize civilization.' That is the essential spirit and the appeal of the much-hated, condemned St. Louis platform.

"Now, the Republican and Democratic parties hold their conventions from time to time. They revise their platforms and their declarations. They do not repudiate previous platforms. Nor is it necessary. With the change of conditions these platforms are outgrown and others take their places. I was not in the convention, but I believed in that platform. I do today. But from the beginning of the war to this day, I have never, by word or act, been guilty of the charges that are embraced in this indictment. If I have criticized, if I ever condemned, it is because I have believed myself justified in doing so under the laws of the land. I have had precedents for my attitude. This country has been engaged in a number of wars, and every one of them has been opposed, every one of them has been condemned by some of the most eminent men in the country. The war of the Revolution was opposed. The Tory press denounced its leaders as criminals and outlaws. And that was when they were under the 'divine right' of a king to rule men.

"The War of 1812 was opposed and condemned; the Mexican war was bitterly condemned by Abraham Lincoln, by Charles Sumner, by Daniel Webster and by Henry Clay. That war took place under the Polk administration. These men denounced the President; they condemned his administration; and they said that the war was a crime against humanity. They were not indicted; they were not tried for crime. They are honored to-day by all of their countrymen. The War of the Rebellion was opposed and condemned. In 1864 the Democratic Party met in convention at Chicago and passed a resolution condemning the war as a failure. What would you say if the Socialist Party were to meet in convention to-day and condemn the present war as a failure? You charge us with being disloyalists and traitors. Were the Democrats of 1864 disloyalists and traitors because they condemned the war as a failure?

"I believe in the Constitution of the United States. Isn't it strange that we Socialists stand almost alone to-day in defending the Constitution of the United States? The revolutionary fathers who had been oppressed under king rule understood that free speech and free press and the right of free assemblage by the people were the fundamental principles of democratic government. The very first amendment to the Constitution reads: 'Congress shall make no law respecting an establishment of religion, or prohibiting the free exercise thereof; or abridging the freedom of speech, or of the press; or the right of the people peaceably to assemble, and to petition the government for a redress of grievances.' That is perfectly plain English. It can be understood by a child. I believe that the revolutionary fathers meant just what is here stated—that Congress shall make no law abridging the freedom of speech or of the press, or of the right of the people to peaceably assemble, and to petition the government for a redress of grievances.

"That is the right that I exercised at Can-

ton on the 16th day of last June; and for the exercise of that right I now have to answer to this indictment. I believe in the right of free speech in war as well as in peace. I would not, under any circumstances, gag the lips of my biggest enemy. I would under no circumstances suppress free speech. It is far more dangerous to attempt to gag the people than to allow them to speak freely of what is in their hearts. I do not go as far as Wendell Phillips did. Wendell Phillips said that the glory of free men is that they trample unjust laws under their feet. That is how they repealed them. If a human being submits to having his lips sealed, to be in silence reduced to vassalage, he may have all else, but he is still lacking in all that dignifies and glorifies real manhood.

"Now, notwithstanding this fundamental provision in the national law, Socialists' meetings have been broken up all over this country. Socialist speakers have been arrested by hundreds and flung into jail, where many of them are lying now. In some cases not even a charge was lodged against them, guilty of absolutely no crime except the crime of attempting to exercise the right guaranteed to them by the Constitution of the United States.

"I have told you that I am no lawyer, but it seems to me that I know enough to know that if Congress enacts any law that conflicts with this provision in the Constitution, that law is void. If the Espionage Law finally stands, then the Constitution of the United States is dead. If that law is not the negation of every fundamental principle established by the Constitution, then certainly I am unable to read or to understand the English language.

To the Court: "Your Honor, I don't know whether I would be in order to quote from a book I hold in my hand, called 'The New Freedom,' by Woodrow Wilson, President of the United States."

The Court: "I will grant you that permission."

Debs: "I want to show the gentlemen of the jury, if I can, that every statement I made in my Canton speech is borne out in this book by Woodrow Wilson, called 'The New Freedom.' It consists of his campaign speeches while a candidate for the presidency. Of course, he uses different language than I did, for he is a college professor. He is an educated gentleman. I never had a chance to get an education. I had to go to work in my childhood. I want to show you that the statement made by Rose Pastor Stokes, for which she has been convicted, and the approval of which has brought condemnation upon me, is substantially the same statement made by Mr. Wilson when he was a candidate for the presidency of the United States:

" 'To-day, when our government has so far passed into the hands of special interests; to-day, when the doctrine is implicitly avowed that only select classes have the equipment necessary for carrying on government; to-day, when so many conscientious citizens, smitten with the scene of social wrong and suffering, have fallen victims to the fallacy that benevolent government can be meted out to the people by kind-hearted trustees of prosperity and guardians of the welfare of dutiful employees—to-day, supremely does it behoove this nation to remember that a people shall be saved by the power that sleeps in its own deep bosom, or by none; shall be renewed in hope, in conscience, in strength, by waters welling up from its own sweet, perennial springs.'

"So this government has passed into the hands of special interests. Rose Pastor Stokes' language is somewhat different. Instead of 'special interests' she said 'profiteers.' She said that a government that was for the profiteers could not be for the people, and that as long as the government was for the profiteers, she was for the people. That is the statement that I indorsed, approved and believed in with all my heart. The President of the United States tells us that our government has passed into the control of special interests. When we Socialists make the same contention, we are branded as disloyalists, and we are indicted as criminals. But that is not all, nor nearly all:

" 'There are, of course, Americans who have not yet heard that anything is going on. The circus might come to town, have the big parade and go, without their catching a sight of the camels or a note of the calliope. There are people, even Americans, who never move themselves or know that anything else is moving.'

"Just one other quotation: 'For a long time this country of ours has lacked one of the institutions which free men have always and everywhere held fundamental. For a long time there has been no sufficient opportunity of counsel among the people; no place and method of talk, of exchange of opinion, of parley. Communities have outgrown the folk-moot and the town meeting. Congress, in accordance with the genius of the land, which asks for action and is impatient of words —Congress has become an institution which does its work in the privacy of committee rooms and not on the floor of the Chamber; a body that makes laws, a legislature; not a body that debates, not a parliament. Party conventions afford little or no opportunity for discussion; platforms are privately manufactured and adopted with a whoop. It is partly because citizens have foregone the taking of counsel together that the unholy alliances of bosses and Big Business have been able to assume to govern for us.

" 'I conceive it to be one of the needs of the hour to restore the processes of common counsel, and to substitute them for the processes of private arrangement which now determine the policies of cities, states and nation. We must learn, we freemen, to meet, as our fathers did, somehow, somewhere, for consultation. There must be discussion and debate, in which all freely participate.' "

"Well, there has been something said in connection with this about profiteering—in connection with this indictment.

To the Court: "Would it be in order for me to read a brief statement, showing to what extent profiteering has been carried on during the last three years?"

The Court: "No. There would be no consensus of opinion or agreement upon that statement. It is a matter that is not really in the case, and when you go to compile a statement, you are then undertaking to assume something without producing evidence to substantiate it."

Debs: "Now, in the course of this proceeding you, gentlemen, have perhaps drawn the inference that I am pro-German, in the sense that I have any sympathy with the Imperial Government of Germany. My father and mother were born in Alsace. They loved France with a passion that is holy. They understood the meaning of Prussianism, and they hated it with all their hearts. I did not need to be taught to hate Prussian militarism. I knew from them what a hateful, what an oppressive, what a brutalizing thing it was and is. I cannot imagine how any one could suspect that for one moment I could have the slightest sympathy with such a monstrous thing. I have been speaking and writing against it practically all of my life. I know that the Kaiser incarnates all there is of brute force and of murder. And yet I would not, if I had the power, kill the Kaiser. I would do to him what Thomas Paine wanted to do to the king of England. He said, 'I destroy the king, but save the man.'

"The thing that the Kaiser incarnates and embodies, called militarism, I would, if I could, wipe from the face of the earth,—not only the militarism of Germany, but the militarism of the whole world. I am quite well aware of the fact that the war now deluging the world with blood was precipitated there. Not by the German people, but by the class that rules, oppresses, robs and degrades the German people. President Wilson has repeatedly said that we were not making war on the German people, and yet in war it is the people who are slain, and not the rulers who are responsible for the war.

"With every drop in my veins I despise kaiserism, and all that kaiserism expresses and implies. I have sympathy with the suffering, struggling people everywhere. It does not make any difference under what flag they were born, or where they live, I have sympathy with them all. I would, if I could, establish a social system that would embrace them all. It is precisely at this point that we come to realize that there is a reason why the peoples of the various nations are pitted against each other in brutal warfare instead of being united in one all-embracing brotherhood.

"War does not come by chance. War is not the result of accident. There is a definite cause for war, especially a modern war. The war that began in Europe can readily be accounted for. For the last forty years, under this international capitalist system, this exploiting system, these various nations of Europe have been preparing for the inevitable. And why? In all these nations the great industries are owned by a relatively small class. They are operated for the profit of that class. And great abundance is produced by the workers; but their wages will only buy back a small part of their product. What is the result? They have a vast surplus on hand; they have got to export it; they have got to find a foreign market for it. As a result of this these nations are pitted against each other. They are industrial rivals—competitors. They begin to arm themselves to open, to maintain the market and quickly dispose of their surplus. There is but the one market. All these nations are competitors for it, and sooner or later every war of trade becomes a war of blood.

"Now, where there is exploitation there

must be some form of militarism to support it. Wherever you find exploitation you find some form of military force. In a smaller way you find it in this country. It was there long before war was declared. For instance, when the miners out in Colorado entered upon a strike about four years ago, the state militia, that is under the control of the Standard Oil Company, marched upon a camp, where the miners and their wives and children were in tents,—and, by the way, a report of this strike was issued by the United States Commission on Industrial Relations. When the soldiers approached the camp at Ludlow, where these miners, with their wives and children, were, the miners, to prove that they were patriotic, placed flags above their tents, and when the state militia, that is paid by Rockefeller and controlled by Rockefeller, swooped down upon that camp, the first thing they did was to shoot these United States flags into tatters. Not one of them was indicted or tried because he was a traitor to his country. Pregnant women were killed, and a number of innocent children slain. This in the United States of America, —the fruit of exploitation. The miners wanted a little more of what they had been producing. But the Standard Oil Company wasn't rich enough. It insisted that all they were entitled to was just enough to keep them in working order. There is slavery for you. And when at last they protested, when they were tormented by hunger, when they saw their children in tatters, they were shot down as if they had been so many vagabond dogs.

"And while I am upon this point let me say just another word. Workingmen who organize, and who sometimes commit overt acts, are very often times condemned by those who have no conception of the conditions under which they live. How many men are there, for instance, who know anything of their own knowledge about how men work in a lumber camp—a logging camp, a turpentine camp? In

this report of the United States Commission on Industrial Relations you will find the statement proved that peonage existed in the state of Texas. Out of these conditions springs such a thing as the I.W.W.—When men receive a pittance for their pay, when they work like galley slaves for a wage that barely suffices to keep their protesting souls within their tattered bodies. When they can endure the conditions no longer, and they make some sort of a demonstration, or perhaps commit acts of violence, how quickly are they condemned by those who do not know anything about the conditions under which they work!

"Five gentlemen of distinction, among them Professor John Graham Brooks, of Harvard University, said that a word that so fills the world as the I.W.W. must have something in it. It must be investigated. And they did investigate it, each along his own lines, and I wish it were possible for every man and woman in this country to read the result of their investigation. They tell you why and how the I.W.W. was instituted. They tell you, moreover, that the great corporations, such as the Standard Oil Company, such as the Coal Trust, and the Lumber Trust, have, through their agents, committed more crimes against the I.W.W. than the I.W.W. have ever committed against them.

"I was asked not long ago if I was in favor of shooting our soldiers in the back. I said, 'No, I would not shoot them in the back. I wouldn't shoot them at all. I would not have them shot.' Much has been made of a statement that I declared that men were fit for something better than slavery and cannon fodder. I made the statement. I make no attempt to deny it. I meant exactly what I said. Men are fit for something better than slavery and cannon fodder; and the time will come, though I shall not live to see it, when slavery will be wiped from the earth, and when men will marvel that there ever was a time when men who called themselves civilized rushed upon each other like wild beasts and murdered one another, by methods so cruel and barbarous that they defy the power of man to describe. I can hear the shrieks of the soldiers of Europe in my dreams. I have imagination enough to see a battlefield. I can see it strewn with the legs of human beings, who but yesterday were in the flush and glory of their young manhood. I can see them at eventide, scattered about in remnants, their limbs torn from their bodies, their eyes gouged out. Yes, I can see them, and I can hear them. I have looked above and beyond this frightful scene. I think of the mothers who are bowed in the shadow of their last great grief—whose hearts are breaking. And I say to myself, 'I am going to do the little that lies in my power to wipe from this earth that terrible scourge of war.'

"If I believed in war I could not be kept out of the first line trenches. I would not be patriotic at long range. I would be honest enough, if I believed in bloodshed, to shed my own. But I do not believe that the shedding of blood bears any actual testimony to patriotism, to lead a country to civilization. On the contrary, I believe that warfare, in all of its forms, is an impeachment of our social order, and a rebuke to our much vaunted Christian civilization.

"And now, Gentlemen of the Jury, I am not going to detain you too long. I wish to admit everything that has been said respecting me from this witness chair. I wish to admit everything that has been charged against me except what is embraced in the indictment which I have read to you. I cannot take back a word. I can't repudiate a sentence. I stand before you guilty of having made this speech. I stand before you prepared to accept the consequences of what there is embraced in that speech. I do not know, I cannot tell, what your verdict may be; nor does it matter much, so far as I am concerned.

"Gentlemen, I am the smallest part of this trial. I have lived long enough to appreciate my own personal insignificance in relation to a great issue that involves the welfare of the whole people. What you may choose to do to me will be of small consequence after all. I am not on trial here. There is an infinitely greater issue that is being tried in this court, though you may not be conscious of it. American institutions are on trial here before a court of American citizens. The future will tell.

"And now, Your Honor, permit me to return my hearty thanks for your patient consideration. And to you, Gentlemen of the Jury, for the kindness with which you have listened to me.

"My fate is in your hands. I am prepared for the verdict."

Primary Sources

Bernstein, Joseph M., ed. *Writing and Speeches of Eugene V. Debs.* New York: Hermitage Press, 1948.

Debs, Eugene. *Walls and Bars.* Chicago: Socialist Party, 1927.

Tussey, Jean Y., ed. *Eugene V. Debs Speaks.* New York: Path Press, 1970.

Secondary Sources

Ginger, Ray. *Eugene V. Debs: A Biography.* Reprint ed., New York: Macmillan, 1962.

Herreshoff, David. *The Origins of American Marxism: From Transcendentalist to De Leon.* Reprint ed., New York: Monad Press, 1973.

Radosh, Ronald. *Debs.* Englewood Cliffs, New Jersey: Prentice-Hall, 1971.

White, Terry Anne. *Eugene Debs: American Socialist.* New York: L. Hill, 1974.

31. Herbert Croly

HERBERT CROLY (1869–1930) was born in New York City and from 1893 to 1899 attended first The City College of New York and then Harvard University. He served as editor of the *Architectural Record* from 1900 to 1906, and he wrote the major work of the Progressive Era, *The Promise of American Life,* for publication in 1909. The latter work justified a powerful Hamiltonian government as a means of realizing Jeffersonian goals of democracy and individual happiness and served as the intellectual rationale for both Roosevelt's New Nationalism and Wilson's New Freedom. Croly was later editor of *The New Republic* from its founding in 1914 to his death in 1930. From this progressive-liberal platform Croly helped to bring about the entry of the United States into World War I and provided a continuing forum for those who advocated national governmental responsibility for national well-being.

This selection is from the key chapter of *The Promise of American Life,* in which Croly synthesizes Hamiltonian and Jeffersonian viewpoints to produce the basic rationale of the new positive state: big government will control big corporations in the name of the people, thus serving the causes of democracy, equal rights, and ultimate social harmony. Croly's work should be analyzed carefully. Not only does it mark the shift in liberalism from an emphasis on laissez-faire to one on interventionist government, but it also contains significant elements of conservatism. Perhaps the ultimate significance of this work, in light of its effects on the New Deal through the post–World War II era, is rather that it has become a rationale for corporate dominance over the society and the state. The national government then becomes the purposeful molder of the society, the agency by which goals are to be achieved—but whose goals, and what interests should receive highest priority? ∽

The Promise of American Life (1909)

RECONSTRUCTION: ITS CONDITIONS AND PURPOSES

The best method of approaching a critical reconstruction of American political ideas will be by means of an analysis of the meaning of democracy. A clear popular understanding of

SOURCE: Herbert Croly, *The Promise of American Life* (New York: Macmillan, 1909), chap. 7.

the contents of the democratic principle is obviously of the utmost practical political importance to the American people. Their loyalty to the idea of democracy, as they understand it, cannot be questioned. Nothing of any considerable political importance is done or left undone in the United States, unless such action or inaction can be plausibly defended on democratic grounds; and the only way to secure for the American people the benefit of a comprehensive and consistent political policy will be to derive it from a comprehensive and consistent conception of democracy.

Democracy as most frequently understood is essentially and exhaustively defined as a matter of popular government; and such a definition raises at once a multitude of time-honored, but by no means superannuated, controversies. The constitutional liberals in England, in France, and in this country have always objected to democracy as so understood, because of the possible sanction it affords for the substitution of a popular despotism in the place of the former royal or oligarchic despotisms. From their point of view individual liberty is the greatest blessing which can be secured to a people by a government; and individual liberty can be permanently guaranteed only in case political liberties are in theory and practice subordinated to civil liberties. Popular political institutions constitute a good servant, but a bad master. When introduced in moderation they keep the government of a country in close relation with well-informed public opinion, which is a necessary condition of political sanitation; but if carried too far, such institutions compromise the security of the individual and the integrity of the state. They erect a power in the state, which in theory is unlimited and which constantly tends in practice to dispense with restrictions. A power which is theoretically absolute is under no obligation to respect the rights either of individuals or minorities; and sooner or later such power will be used for the purpose of oppressing the individual. The only way to secure individual liberty is, consequently, to organize a state in which the Sovereign power is deprived of any rational excuse or legal opportunity of violating certain essential individual rights.

The foregoing criticism of democracy, defined as popular government, may have much practical importance; but there are objections to it on the score of logic. It is not a criticism of a certain conception of democracy, so much as of democracy itself. Ultimate responsibility for the government of a community must reside somewhere. If the single monarch is practically dethroned, as he is by these liberal critics of democracy, some Sovereign power must be provided to take his place. In England Parliament, by means of a steady encroachment on the royal prerogatives, has gradually become Sovereign; but other countries, such as France and the United States, which have wholly dispensed with royalty, cannot, even if they would, make a legislative body Sovereign by the simple process of allowing it to usurp power once enjoyed by the Crown....

To be sure, a democracy may impose rules of action upon itself—as the American democracy did in accepting the Federal Constitution. But in adopting the Federal Constitution the American people did not abandon either its responsibilities or rights as Sovereign. Difficult as it may be to escape from the legal framework defined in the Constitution, that body of law in theory remains merely an instrument which was made for the people and which if necessary can and will be modified. A people, to whom was denied the ultimate responsibility for its welfare, would not have obtained the prime condition of genuine liberty. Individual freedom is important, but more important still is the freedom of a whole people to dispose of its own destiny; and I do not see how the existence of such an ultimate popular political freedom and responsibility can be denied by any one who has rejected the theory of a divinely appointed political order. The fallibility of human nature being what it is, the practical application of this theory will have its grave dangers; but these dangers are only evaded and postponed by a failure to place ultimate political responsibility where it belongs. While a country in the position of Germany or Great Britain may be fully justified from the point of view of its national tradition in merely compromising with democracy, other countries, such as the United States and France, which have earned the right to dispense with these compromises; are at least building their political structure on the real and righteous source of political authority. Democracy may mean something more than a theoretically absolute popular government, but it assuredly cannot mean anything less.

If, however, democracy does not mean anything less than popular Sovereignty, it assuredly does mean something more. It must at least mean an expression of the Sovereign will, which will not contradict and destroy the continuous existence of its own Sovereign power. Several times during the political history of France in the nineteenth century, the popular will has expressed itself in a manner adverse to popular political institutions. Assemblies have been elected by universal suffrage, whose tendencies have been reactionary and undemocratic, and who have been supported in this reactionary policy by an effective public opinion. Or the French people have by means of a plebiscite delegated their Sovereign power to an Imperial dictator, whose whole political system was based on a deep suspicion of the source of his own authority. A particular group of political institutions or course of political action may, then, be representative of the popular will, and yet may be undemocratic. Popular Sovereignty is self-contradictory, unless it is expressed in a manner favorable to its own perpetuity and integrity.

The assertion of the doctrine of popular Sovereignty is, consequently, rather the beginning than the end of democracy. There can be no democracy where the people do not rule; but government by the people is not necessarily democratic. The popular will must in a democratic state be expressed somehow in the interest of democracy itself; and we have not traveled very far towards a satisfactory conception of democracy until this democratic purpose has received some definition. In what way must a democratic state behave in order to contribute to its own integrity?

The ordinary American answer to this question is contained in the assertion of Lincoln, that our government is "dedicated to the proposition that all men are created equal." Lincoln's phrasing of the principle was due to the fact that the obnoxious and undemocratic system of Negro slavery was uppermost in his mind when he made his Gettysburg address; but he meant by his assertion of the principle of equality substantially what is meant today by the principle of "equal rights for all and special privileges for none." Government by the people has its natural and logical complement in government for the people. Every state with a legal framework must grant certain rights to individuals; and every state, in so far as it is efficient, must guarantee to the individual that his rights, as legally defined, are secure. But an essentially democratic state consists in the circumstance that all citizens enjoy these rights equally. If any citizen or any group of citizens enjoys by virtue of the law any advantage over their fellow-citizens, then the most sacred principle of democracy is violated. On the other hand, a community in which no man or no group of men are granted by law any advantage over their fellow-citizens is the type of the perfect and fruitful democratic state. Society is organized politically for the benefit of all the people. Such an organization may permit radical differences among individuals in the opportunities and possessions they actually enjoy; but no man would be able to impute his own success or failure to the legal framework of society. Every citizen would be getting a "Square Deal."

Such is the idea of the democratic state, which the majority of good Americans believe to be entirely satisfactory. It should endure indefinitely, because it seeks to satisfy every interest essential to associated life. The interest of the individual is protected, because of the liberties he securely enjoys. The general social interest is equally well protected, because the liberties enjoyed by one or by a few are enjoyed by all. Thus the individual and the social interests are automatically harmonized. The virile democrat in pursuing his own interest "under the law" is contributing effectively to the interest of society, while the social interest consists precisely in the promotion of these individual interests, in so far as they can be equally exercised. The divergent demands of the individual and the social interest can be reconciled by grafting the principle of equality on the thrifty tree of individual rights, and the ripe fruit thereof can be gathered merely by shaking the tree.

It must be immediately admitted, also, that the principle of equal rights, like the principle of ultimate popular political responsibility, is the expression of an essential aspect of democracy. There is no room for permanent legal privileges in a democratic state. Such privileges may be and frequently are defended on many excellent grounds. They may unquestionably contribute for a time to social and economic efficiency and to individual independence. But whatever advantage may be derived from such permanent discriminations must be abandoned by a democracy. It cannot afford to give any one class of its citizens a permanent advantage or to others a permanent grievance. It ceases to be a democracy, just as soon as any permanent privileges are conferred by its institutions or its laws; and this equality of right and absence of permanent privilege is the expression of a fundamental social interest.

But the principle of equal rights, like the principle of ultimate popular political responsibility, is not sufficient; and because of its insufficiency results in certain dangerous ambiguities and self-contradictions. American political thinkers have always repudiated the idea

that by equality of rights they meant anything like equality of performance or power. The utmost varieties of individual power and ability are bound to exist and are bound to bring about many different levels of individual achievement. Democracy both recognizes the right of the individual to use his powers to the utmost, and encourages him to do so by offering a fair field and, in case of success, an abundant reward. The democratic principle requires an equal start in the race, while expecting at the same time an unequal finish. But Americans who talk in this way seem wholly blind to the fact that under a legal system which holds private property sacred there may be equal rights, but there cannot possibly be any equal opportunities for exercising such rights. The chance which the individual has to compete with his fellows and take a prize in the race is vitally affected by material conditions over which he has no control. It is as if the competitor in a Marathon cross country run were denied proper nourishment or proper training, and was obliged to toe the mark against rivals who had every benefit of food and discipline. Under such conditions he is not as badly off as if he were entirely excluded from the race. With the aid of exceptional strength and intelligence he may overcome the odds against him and win out. But it would be absurd to claim that, because all the rivals toed the same mark, a man's victory or defeat depended exclusively on his own efforts. Those who have enjoyed the benefits of wealth and thorough education start with an advantage which can be overcome only by very exceptional men,—men so exceptional, in fact, that the average competitor without such benefits feels himself disqualified for the contest.

Because of the ambiguity indicated above, different people with different interests, all of them good patriotic Americans, draw very different inferences from the doctrine of equal rights. The man of conservative ideas and interests means by the rights, which are to be equally exercised, only those rights which are defined and protected by the law—the more fundamental of which are the rights to personal freedom and to private property. The man of radical ideas, on the other hand, observing, as he may very clearly, that these equal rights cannot possibly be made really equivalent to equal opportunities, bases upon the same doctrine a more or less drastic criticism of the existing economic and social order and sometimes of the motives of its beneficiaries and conservators. The same principle, differently interpreted, is the foundation of American political orthodoxy and American political heterodoxy. The same measure of reforming legislation, such as the new Interstate Commerce Law, seems to one party a wholly inadequate attempt to make the exercise of individual rights a little more equal, while it seems to others an egregious violation of the principle itself. What with reforming legislation on the one hand and the lack of it on the other, the once sweet air of the American political mansion is soured by complaints. Privileges and discriminations seem to lurk in every political and economic corner. The "people" are appealing to the state to protect them against the usurpations of the corporations and the Bosses. The government is appealing to the courts to protect the shippers against the railroads. The corporations are appealing to the Federal courts to protect them from the unfair treatment of state legislatures. Employers are fighting trades-unionism, because it denies equal rights to their employee. The unionists are entreating public opinion to protect them against the unfairness of "government by injunction." To the free trader the whole protectionist system seems a flagrant discrimination on behalf of a certain portion of the community. Everybody seems to be clamoring for a "Square Deal" but nobody seems to be getting it.

The ambiguity of the principle of equal rights and the resulting confusion of counsel are so obvious that there must be some good reason for their apparently unsuspected existence. The truth is that Americans have not readjusted their political ideas to the teaching of their political and economic experience. For a couple of generations after Jefferson had established the doctrine of equal rights as the fundamental principle of the American democracy, the ambiguity resident in the application of the doctrine was concealed. The Jacksonian Democrats, for instance, who were constantly nosing the ground for a scent of unfair treatment, could discover no example of political privileges, except the continued retention of their offices by experienced public servants; and the only case of economic privilege of which they were certain was that of the National Bank. The fact is, of course, that the great majority of Americans were getting a "Square Deal" as long as the economic opportunities of a new country had not been developed and appropriated. Individual and social interest did substantially coincide as long as so many opportunities were open to the poor and untrained man, and as long as the public interest demanded first of all the utmost celerity of economic development. But, as we have seen in a preceding chapter, the economic development of the country resulted inevitably in a condition which demanded on the part of the successful competitor either increasing capital, improved training, or a larger amount of ability and energy. With the advent of comparative economic and social maturity, the exercise of certain legal rights became substantially equivalent to the exercise of a privilege; and if equality of opportunity was to be maintained, it could not be done by virtue of non-interference. The demands of the "Higher Law" began to diverge from the results of the actual legal system.

Public opinion is, of course, extremely

loath to admit that there exists any such divergence of individual and social interest, or any such contradiction in the fundamental American principle. Reformers no less than conservatives have been doggedly determined to place some other interpretation upon the generally recognized abuses; and the interpretation on which they have fastened is that some of the victors have captured too many prizes, because they did not play fair. There is just enough truth in this interpretation to make it plausible, although, as we have seen, the most flagrant examples of apparent cheating were due as much to equivocal rules as to any fraudulent intention. But orthodox public opinion is obliged by the necessities of its own situation to exaggerate the truth of its favorite interpretation; and any such exaggeration is attended with grave dangers, precisely because the ambiguous nature of the principle itself gives a similar ambiguity to its violations. The cheating is understood as disobedience to the actual law, or as violation of a Higher Law, according to the interests and preconceptions of the different reformers; but however it is understood, they believe themselves to be upholding some kind of a Law, and hence endowed with some kind of sacred mission. . . .

DEMOCRACY AND DISCRIMINATION

The principle of equal rights has always appealed to its more patriotic and sensible adherents as essentially an impartial rule of political action—one that held a perfectly fair balance between the individual and society, and between different and hostile individual and class interests. But as a fundamental principle of democratic policy it is as ambiguous in this respect as it is in other respects. In its traditional form and expression it has concealed an extremely partial interest under a formal proclamation of impartiality. The political thinker who popularized it in this country was not concerned fundamentally with harmonizing the essential interest of the individual with the essential popular or social interest. Jefferson's political system was intended for the benefit only of a special class of individuals, viz., those average people who would not be helped by any really formative rule or method of discrimination. In practice it has proved to be inimical to individual liberty, efficiency, and distinction. An insistent demand for equality, even in the form of a demand for equal rights, inevitably has a negative and limiting effect upon the free and able exercise of individual opportunities. From the Jeffersonian point of view democracy would incur a graver danger from a violation of equality than it would profit from a triumphant assertion of individual liberty. Every opportunity for the edifying exercise of power, on the part either of an individual, a group of individuals, or the state is by its very nature also an opportunity for its evil exercise. The political leader whose official power depends upon popular confidence may betray the trust. The corporation employing thousands of men and supplying millions of people with some necessary service or commodity may reduce the cost of production only for its own profit. The state may use its great authority chiefly for the benefit of special interests. The advocate of equal rights is preoccupied by these opportunities for the abusive exercise of power, because from his point of view rights exercised in the interest of inequality have ceased to be righteous. He distrusts those forms of individual and associated activity which give any individual or association substantial advantages over their associates. He becomes suspicious of any kind of individual and social distinction with the nature and effects of which he is not completely familiar. . . .

Thus the Jeffersonian principle of national irresponsibility can no longer be maintained by those Democrats who sincerely believe that the inequalities of power generated in the

American economic and political system are dangerous to the integrity of the democratic state. To this extent really sincere followers of Jefferson are obliged to admit the superior political wisdom of Hamilton's principle of national responsibility, and once they have made this admission, they have implicitly abandoned their contention that the doctrine of equal rights is a sufficient principle of democratic political action. They have implicitly accepted the idea that the public interest is to be asserted, not merely by equalizing individual rights, but by controlling individuals in the exercise of those rights. The national public interest has to be affirmed by positive and aggressive action. The nation has to have a will and a policy as well as the individual; and this policy can no longer be confined to the merely negative task of keeping individual rights from becoming in any way privileged.

The arduous and responsible political task which a nation in its collective capacity must seek to perform is that of selecting among the various prevailing ways of exercising individual rights those which contribute to national perpetuity and integrity. Such selection implies some interference with the natural course of popular action; and that interference is always costly and may be harmful either to the individual or the social interest must be frankly admitted. He would be a foolish Hamiltonian who would claim that a state, no matter how efficiently organized and ably managed, will not make serious and perhaps enduring mistakes; but he can answer that inaction and irresponsibility are more costly and dangerous than intelligent and responsible interference. The practice of non-interference is just as selective in its effects as the practice of state interference. It means merely that the nation is willing to accept the results of natural selection instead of preferring to substitute the results of artificial selection. In one way or another a nation is bound to recognize the re-

sults of selection. The Hamiltonian principle of national responsibility recognizes the inevitability of selection; and since it is inevitable, is not afraid to interfere on behalf of the selection of the really fittest. If a selective policy is pursued in good faith and with sufficient intelligence, the nation will at least be learning from its mistakes. It should find out gradually the kind and method of selection, which is most desirable, and how far selection by non-interference is to be preferred to active selection....

As a matter of fact the American democracy both in its central and in its local governments has always practiced both methods of selection. The state governments have sedulously indulged in a kind of interference conspicuous both for its activity and its inefficiency. The Federal government, on the other hand, has been permitted to interfere very much less; but even during the palmiest days of national irresponsibility it did not altogether escape active intervention. A protective tariff is of course, a plain case of preferential class legislation, and so was the original Interstate Commerce Act. They were designed to substitute artificial preferences for those effected by unregulated individual action, on the ground that the proposed modification of the natural course of trade would contribute to the general economic prosperity. No less preferential in purpose are the measures of reform recently enacted by the central government. The amended Interstate Commerce Law largely increases the power of possible discrimination possessed by the Federal Commission. The Pure Food Bill forbids many practices, which have arisen in connection with the manufacture of food products, and discriminates against the perpetrators of such practices. Factory legislation or laws regulating the hours of labor have a similar meaning and justification. It is not too much to say that substantially all the industrial legislation, demanded by the "people" both here and abroad and passed in the popular interest, has been based essentially on class discrimination.

The situation which these laws are supposed to meet is always the same. A certain number of individuals enjoy, in the beginning, equal opportunities to perform certain acts; and in the competition resulting therefrom some of these individuals or associations obtain advantages over their competitors, or over their fellow-citizens whom they employ or serve. Sometimes these advantages and the practices whereby they are obtained are profitable to a larger number of people than they injure. Sometimes the reverse is true. In either event the state is usually asked to interfere by the class whose economic position has been compromised. It by no means follows that the state should acquiesce in this demand. In many cases interference may be more costly than beneficial. Each case must be considered on its merits. But whether in any particular case the state takes sides or remains impartial, it most assuredly has a positive function to perform on the premises. If it remains impartial, it simply agrees to abide by the results of natural selection. If it interferes, it seeks to replace natural with artificial discrimination. In both cases it authorizes discriminations which in their effect violate the doctrines of "equal rights." Of course, a reformer can always claim that any particular measure of reform proposes merely to restore to the people a "Square Deal"; but that is simply an easy and thoughtless way of concealing novel purposes under familiar formulas. Any genuine measure of economic or political reform will, of course, give certain individuals better opportunities than those they have been recently enjoying, but it will reach this result only by depriving other individuals of advantages which they have earned.

Impartiality is the duty of the judge rather than the statesman, of the courts rather than the government. The state which proposes to draw a ring around the conflicting interests of its citizens and interfere only on behalf of a fair fight will be obliged to interfere constantly and will never accomplish its purpose. In economic warfare, the fighting can never be fair for long, and it is the business of the state to see that its own friends are victorious. It holds, if you please, itself a hand in the game. The several players are playing, not merely with one another, but with the political and social bank. The security and perpetuity of the state, and of the individual in so far as he is a social animal, depend upon the victory of the national interest—as represented both in the assurance of the national profit and in the domination of the nation's friends. It is in the position of the bank at Monte Carlo, which does pretend to play fair, but which frankly promulgates rules advantageous to itself. Considering the percentage in its favor and the length of its purse, it cannot possibly lose. It is not really gambling; and it does not propose to take any unnecessary risks. Neither can a state, democratic or otherwise, which believes in its own purpose. While preserving at times an appearance of impartiality so that its citizens may enjoy for a while a sense of the reality of their private game, it must on the whole make the rules in its own interest. It must help those men to win who are most capable of using their winnings for the benefit of society.

CONSTRUCTIVE DISCRIMINATION

Assuming, then, that a democracy cannot avoid the constant assertion of national responsibility for the national welfare, an all-important question remains as to the way in which and the purpose for which this interference should be exercised. Should it be exercised on behalf of individual liberty? Should it be exercised on behalf of social equality? Is there any way in which it can be exercised on behalf of both liberty and equality?

Hamilton and the constitutional liberals

asserted that the state should interfere exclusively on behalf of individual liberty; but Hamilton was no democrat and was not outlining the policy of a democratic state. In point of fact democracies have never been satisfied with a definition of democratic policy in terms of liberty. Not only have the particular friends of liberty usually been hostile to democracy, but democracies both in idea and behavior have frequently been hostile to liberty; and they have been justified in distrusting a political regime organized wholly or even chiefly for its benefit. "La Liberté," says Mr. Emile Faguet, in the preface to his "Politiques et Moralistes du Dix-Neuvième Siècle"—"La Liberté s'oppose à l'Egalité, car La Liberté est aristocratique par essence. La Liberté ne se donne jamais, ne s'octroie jamais; elle se conquiert. Or ne peuvent la conquérir que des groupes sociaux qui ont su se donne la cohérence, l'organisation et la discipline et qui par conséquent, vent des groupes aristocratiques." The fact that states organized exclusively or largely for the benefit of liberty are essentially aristocratic explains the hostile and suspicious attitude of democracies towards such a principle of political action.

Only a comparatively small minority are capable at any one time of exercising political, economic, and civil liberties in an able, efficient, or thoroughly worthy manner; and a regime wrought for the benefit of such a minority would become at best a state, in which economic, political, and social power would be very unevenly distributed—a state like the Orleans Monarchy in France of the "Bourgeoisie" and the "Intellectuals." Such a state might well give its citizens fairly good government, as did the Orleans Monarchy; but just in so far as the mass of the people had any will of its own, it could not arouse vital popular interest and support; and it could not contribute, except negatively, to the fund of popular good sense and experience. The lack of such popular support caused the death of the French liberal monarchy; and no such regime can endure, save, as in England, by virtue of a somewhat abject popular acquiescence. As long as it does endure, moreover, it tends to undermine the virtue of its own beneficiaries. The favored minority, feeling as they do tolerably sure of their position, can scarcely avoid a habit of making it somewhat too easy for one another. The political, economic, and intellectual leaders begin to be selected without any sufficient test of their efficiency. Some sort of a test continues to be required; but the standards which determine it drift into a condition of being narrow, artificial, and lax. Political, intellectual, and social leadership, in order to preserve its vitality needs a feeling of effective responsibility to a body of public opinion as wide, as varied, and as exacting as that of the whole community.

The desirable democratic object, implied in the traditional democratic demand for equality, consists precisely in that of bestowing a share of the responsibility and the benefits, derived from political and economic association, upon the whole community. Democracies have assumed and have been right in assuming that a proper diffusion of effective responsibility and substantial benefits is the one means whereby a community can be supplied with an ultimate and sufficient bond of union. The American democracy has attempted to manufacture a sufficient bond out of the equalization of rights: but such a bond is, as we have seen, either a rope of sand or a link of chains. A similar object must be achieved in some other way; and the ultimate success of democracy depends upon its achievement.

The fundamental political and social problem of a democracy may be summarized in the following terms. A democracy, like every political and social group, is composed of individuals, and must be organized for the benefit of its constituent members. But the individual has no chance of effective personal power except by means of the secure exercise of certain personal rights. Such rights, then, must be secured and exercised; yet when they are exercised, their tendency is to divide the community into divergent classes. Even if enjoyed with some equality in the beginning, they do not continue to be equally enjoyed, but make towards discriminations advantageous to a minority. The state, as representing the common interest, is obliged to admit the inevitability of such classifications and divisions, and has itself no alternative but to exercise a decisive preference on behalf of one side or the other. A well-governed state will use its power to promote edifying and desirable discriminations. But if discriminations tend to divide the community, and the state itself cannot do more than select among the various possible cases of discrimination those which it has some reason to prefer, how is the solidarity of the community to be preserved? And above all, how is a democratic community, which necessarily includes everybody in its benefits and responsibilities, to be kept well united? Such a community must retain an ultimate bond of union which counteracts the divergent effect of the discriminations, yet which at the same time is not fundamentally hostile to individual liberties.

The clew to the best available solution of the problem is supplied by a consideration of the precise manner, in which the advantages derived from the efficient exercise of liberties become inimical to a wholesome social condition. The hostility depends, not upon the existence of such advantageous discriminations for a time, but upon their persistence for too long a time. When, either from natural or artificial causes, they are properly selected, they contribute at the time of their selection both to individual and to social efficiency. They have been earned, and it is both just and edifying that, in so far as they have been earned, they should be freely enjoyed. On the other hand,

they should not, so far as possible, be allowed to outlast their own utility. They must continue to be earned. It is power and opportunity enjoyed without being earned which help to damage the individual—both the individuals who benefit and the individuals who consent—and which tend to loosen the ultimate social bond. A democracy, no less than a monarchy or an aristocracy, must recognize political, economic, and social discriminations, but it must also manage to withdraw its consent whenever these discriminations show any tendency to excessive endurance. The essential wholeness of the community depends absolutely on the ceaseless creation of a political, economic, and social aristocracy and their equally incessant replacement.

Both in its organization and in its policy a democratic state has consequently to seek two different but supplementary objects. It is the function of such a state to represent the whole community; and the whole community includes the individual as well as the mass, the many as well as the few. The individual is merged in the mass, unless he is enabled to exercise efficiently and independently his own private and special purposes. He must not only be permitted, he must be encouraged to earn distinction; and the best way in which he can be encouraged to earn distinction is to reward distinction both by abundant opportunity and cordial appreciation. Individual distinction, resulting from the efficient performance of special work, is not only the foundation of all genuine individuality, but is usually of the utmost social value. In so far as it is efficient, it has a tendency to be constructive. It both inserts some member into the social edifice which forms for the time being a desirable part of the whole structure, but it tends to establish a standard of achievement which may well form a permanent contribution to social amelioration. It is useful to the whole community, not because it is derived from popular sources or conforms to popular standards, but because it is formative and so helps to convert the community into a well-formed whole. . . .

THE BRIDGE BETWEEN DEMOCRACY AND NATIONALITY

We are now prepared, I hope, to venture upon a more fruitful definition of democracy. The popular definitions err in describing it in terms of its machinery or of some partial political or economic object. Democracy does not mean merely government by the people, or majority rule, or universal suffrage. All of these political forms or devices are a part of its necessary organization; but the chief advantage such methods of organization have is their tendency to promote some salutary and formative purpose. The really formative purpose is not exclusively a matter of individual liberty, although it must give individual liberty abundant scope. Neither is it a matter of equal rights alone, although it must always cherish the social bond which the principle represents. The salutary and formative democratic purpose consists in using the democratic organization for the joint benefit of individual distinction and social improvement.

To define the really democratic organization as one which makes expressly and intentionally for individual distinction and social improvement is nothing more than a translation of the statement that such an organization should make expressly and intentionally for the welfare of the whole people. The whole people will always consist of individuals, constituting small classes, who demand special opportunities, and the mass of the population who demand for their improvement more generalized opportunities. At any particular time or in any particular case, the improvement of the smaller classes may conflict with that of the larger class, but the conflict becomes permanent and irreconcilable only when it is intensified by the lack of a really binding and edifying public policy, and by the consequent

stimulation of class and factional prejudices and purposes. A policy, intelligently informed by the desire to maintain a joint process of individual and social amelioration, should be able to keep a democracy sound and whole both in sentiment and in idea. Such a democracy would not be dedicated either to liberty or to equality in their abstract expressions, but to liberty and equality, in so far as they made for human brotherhood. As M. Faguet says in the introduction to his "Politiques et Moralistes du Dix-Neuvième Siècle," from which I have already quoted: "Liberté et Egalité sont donc contradictoires et exclusives l'une et l'autre; mais la Fraternité les concilierait. La Fraternité non seulement concilierait la Liberté et l'Egalité, mais elle les ferait génératrices l'une et l'autre." The two subordinate principles, that is, one representing the individual and the other the social interest, can by their subordination to the principle of human brotherhood, be made in the long run mutually helpful.

The foregoing definition of the democratic purpose is the only one which can entitle democracy to an essential superiority to other forms of political organization. Democrats have always tended to claim some such superiority for their methods and purposes, but in case democracy is to be considered merely as political machinery, or a partial political idea, the claim has no validity. Its superiority must be based upon the fact that democracy is the best possible translation into political and social terms of an authoritative and comprehensive moral idea; and, provided a democratic state honestly seeks to make its organization and policy contribute to a better quality of individuality and a higher level of associated life, it can within certain limits claim the allegiance of mankind on rational moral grounds.

The proposed definition may seem to be both vague and commonplace; but it none the less brings with it practical consequences of paramount importance. The subordination of the machinery of democracy to its purpose, and the comprehension within that purpose of the higher interests both of the individual and society, is not only exclusive of many partial and erroneous ideas, but demands both a reconstructive programme and an efficient organization. A government by the people, which seeks an organization and a policy beneficial to the individual and to society, is confronted by a task as responsible and difficult as you please; but it is a specific task which demands the adoption of certain specific and positive means. Moreover it is a task which the American democracy has never sought consciously to achieve. American democrats have always hoped for individual and social amelioration as the result of the operation of their democratic system; but if any such result was to follow, its achievement was to be a happy accident. The organization and policy of a democracy should leave the individual and society to seek their own amelioration. The democratic state should never discriminate in favor of anything or anybody. It should only discriminate against all sorts of privilege. Under the proposed definition, on the other hand, popular government is to make itself expressly and permanently responsible for the amelioration of the individual and society; and a necessary consequence of this responsibility is an adequate organization and a reconstructive policy.

The majority of good Americans will doubtless consider that the reconstructive policy, already indicated, is flagrantly socialistic both in its methods and its objects; and if any critic likes to fasten the stigma of socialism upon the foregoing conception of democracy, I am not concerned with dodging the odium of the word. The proposed definition of democracy is socialistic, if it is socialistic to consider democracy inseparable from a candid, patient, and courageous attempt to advance the social problem towards a satisfactory solution. It is

also socialistic in case socialism cannot be divorced from the use, wherever necessary, of the political organization in all its forms to realize the proposed democratic purpose. On the other hand, there are some doctrines frequently associated with socialism, to which the proposed conception of democracy is wholly inimical; and it should be characterized not so much socialistic, as unscrupulously and loyally nationalistic.

A democracy dedicated to individual and social betterment is necessarily individualistic as well as socialist. It has little interest in the mere multiplication of average individuals, except in so far as such multiplication is necessary to economic and political efficiency; but it has the deepest interest in the development of a higher quality of individual self-expression. There are two indispensable economic conditions of qualitative individual self-expression. One is the preservation of the institution of private property in some form, and the other is the radical transformation of its existing nature and influence. A democracy certainly cannot fulfill its mission without the eventual assumption by the state of many functions now performed by individuals, and without becoming expressly responsible for an improved distribution of wealth; but if any attempt is made to accomplish these results by violent means, it will most assuredly prove to be a failure. An improvement in the distribution of wealth or in economic efficiency which cannot be accomplished by purchase on the part of the state or by a legitimate use of the power of taxation, must be left to the action of time, assisted, of course, by such arrangements as are immediately practical. But the amount of actual good to the individual and society which can be effected *at any one time* by an alteration in the distribution of wealth is extremely small; and the same statement is true of any proposed state action in the interest of the democratic purpose. Consequently, while responsible state action is an essential condition of any steady approach to the democratic consummation, such action will be wholly vain unless accompanied by a larger measure of spontaneous individual amelioration. In fact one of the strongest arguments on behalf of a higher and larger conception of state responsibilities in a democracy is that the candid, courageous, patient, and intelligent attempt to redeem those responsibilities provides one of the highest types of individuality—viz., the public-spirited man with a personal opportunity and a task which should be enormously stimulating and edifying.

The great weakness of the most popular form of socialism consists, however, in its mixture of a revolutionary purpose with an international scope. It seeks the abolition of national distinctions by revolutionary revolts of the wage-earner against the capitalist; and in so far as it proposes to undermine the principle of national cohesion and to substitute for it an international organization of a single class, it is headed absolutely in the wrong direction. Revolutions may at times be necessary and on the whole helpful, but not in case there is any other practicable method of removing grave obstacles to human amelioration; and in any event their tendency is socially disintegrating. The destruction or the weakening of nationalities for the ostensible benefit of an international socialism would in truth gravely imperil the bond upon which actual human association is based. The peoples who have inherited any share in Christian civilization are effectively united chiefly by national habits, traditions, and purposes; and perhaps the most effective way of bringing about an irretrievable division of purpose among them would be the adoption by the class of wage-earners of the programme of international socialism. It is not too much to say that no permanent good can, under existing conditions, come to the individual and society except through the preservation and the development of the existing system of nationalized states.

Radical and enthusiastic democrats have usually failed to attach sufficient importance to the ties whereby civilized men are at the present time actually united. Inasmuch as national traditions are usually associated with all sorts of political, economic, and social privileges and abuses, they have sought to identify the higher social relation with the destruction of the national tradition and the substitution of an ideal bond. In so doing they are committing a disastrous error; and democracy will never become really constructive until this error is recognized and democracy abandons its former alliance with revolution. The higher human relation must be brought about chiefly by the improvement and the intensification of existing human relations. The only possible foundation for a better social structure is the existing social order, of which the contemporary system of nationalized states forms the foundation.

Loyalty to the existing system of nationalized states does not necessarily mean loyalty to an existing government merely because it exists. There have been, and still are, governments whose ruin is a necessary condition of popular liberation; and revolution doubtless still has a subordinate part to play in the process of human amelioration. The loyalty which a citizen owes to a government is dependent upon the extent to which the government is representative of national traditions and is organized in the interest of valid national purposes. National traditions and purposes always contain a large infusion of dubious ingredients; but loyalty to them does not necessarily mean the uncritical and unprotesting acceptance of the national limitations and abuses. Nationality is a political and social idea as well as the great contemporary political fact. Loyalty to the national interest implies devotion to a progressive principle. It demands, to be sure, that the progressive principle be realized without any violation of fundamental national ties. It demands that any national action taken for the benefit of the progressive principle be approved by the official national organization. But it also serves as a ferment quite as much as a bond. It bids the loyal national servants to fashion their fellow-countrymen into more of a nation; and the attempt to perform this bidding constitutes a very powerful and wholesome source of political development. It constitutes, indeed, a source of political development which is of decisive importance for a satisfactory theory of political and social progress, because a people which becomes more of a nation has a tendency to become for that very reason more of a democracy.

The assertion that a people which becomes more of a nation becomes for that very reason more of a democracy, is, I am aware, a hazardous assertion, which can be justified, if at all, only at a considerable expense. As a matter of fact, the two following chapters will be devoted chiefly to this labor of justification. In the first of these chapters I shall give a partly historical and partly critical account of the national principle in its relation to democracy; and in the second I shall apply the results, so achieved, to the American national principle in its relation to the American democratic idea. But before starting this complicated task, a few words must be premised as to the reasons which make the attempt well worth the trouble.

If a people, in becoming more of a nation, become for that very reason more of a democracy, the realization of the democratic purpose is not rendered any easier, but democracy is provided with a simplified, a consistent, and a practicable programme. An alliance is established thereby between the two dominant political and social forces in modern life. The suspicion with which aggressive advocates of the national principle have sometimes regarded democracy would be shown to have only a conditional justification, and the suspicion with which many ardent democrats have regarded aggressive nationalism would be similarly disarmed. A democrat, so far as the statement is true, could trust the fate of his cause in each particular state to the friends of national progress. Democracy would not need for its consummation the ruin of the traditional political fabrics; but so far as those political bodies were informed by genuinely national ideas and aspirations, it could await confidently the process of national development. In fact, the first duty of a good democrat would be that of rendering to his country loyal patriotic service. Democrats would abandon the task of making over the world to suit their own purposes, until they had come to a better understanding with their own countrymen. One's democracy, that is, would begin at home and it would for the most part stay at home, and the cause of national well-being would derive invaluable assistance from the loyal cooperation of good democrats.

A great many obvious objections will, of course, be immediately raised against any such explanation of the relation between democracy and nationality; and I am well aware that those objections demand the most serious consideration. A generation or two ago the European democrat was often by way of being an ardent nationalist; and a constructive relation between the two principles was accepted by many European political reformers. The events of the last fifty years have, however, done much to sever the alliance, and to make European patriots suspicious of democracy, and European democrats suspicious of patriotism. To what extent these suspicions are justified, I shall discuss in the next chapter; but that discussion will be undertaken almost exclusively for obtaining, if possible, some light upon our domestic situation. The formula of a constructive relation between the national and democratic principles has certain importance for European peoples, and particularly for Frenchmen: but, if true, it is of a far superior importance to Americans. It supplies a constructive form for the progressive solution of their political and social problems; and while it imposes on them responsibilities which they have sought to evade, it also offers compensations, the advantage of which they have scarcely expected.

Americans have always been both patriotic and democratic, just as they have always been friendly both to liberty and equality, but in neither case have they brought the two ideas or aspirations into mutually helpful relations. As democrats they have often regarded nationalism with distrust, and have consequently deprived their patriotism of any sufficient substance and organization. As nationalists they have frequently regarded essential aspects of democracy with a wholly unnecessary and embarrassing suspicion. They have been after a fashion Hamiltonian, and Jeffersonian after more of a fashion; but they have never recovered from the initial disagreement between Hamilton and Jefferson. If there is any truth in the idea of a constructive relation between democracy and nationality this disagreement must be healed. They must accept both principles loyally and unreservedly; and by such acceptance their "noble national theory" will obtain a wholly unaccustomed energy and integrity. The alliance between the two principles will not leave either of them intact; but it will necessarily do more harm to the Jeffersonian group of political ideas than it will to the Hamiltonian. The latter's nationalism can be adapted to democracy without an essential injury to itself, but the former's democracy cannot be nationalized without being transformed. The manner of its transformation has already been discussed in detail. It must cease to be a democracy of indiscriminate individualism, and become one of selected individuals who are obliged constantly to justify their selection; and its members must be united not by a sense of joint irresponsibility, but by a sense of joint responsibility for the success of their political and social ideal. They must become, that is, a democracy devoted to the welfare of the whole people by means of a conscious labor of individual and social improvement; and that is precisely the sort of democracy which demands for its realization the aid of the Hamiltonian nationalistic organization and principle. ∼

Primary Sources

Croly, Herbert. *Marcus Alonzo Hanna.* New York: Macmillan, 1923.
———. *Progressive Democracy.* New York: Macmillan, 1914.
———. *The Promise of American Life.* New York: Macmillan, 1909.

Secondary Sources

Forcey, Charles B. "Croly and Nationalism," *New Republic,* 22 November 1954, 17–23.
———. *The Crossroads of Liberalism: Croly, Weyl, Lippmann, and the Progressive Era.* New York: Oxford University Press, 1961.
Frankfurter, Felix. "Croly and Opinion," *New Republic,* 22 November 1954, 112–14.
Smith, Henry Ladel. "Editing for the Superior Few," *New Republic,* 22 November 1954, 23–26.
Straight, Michael. "The Ghost at the Banquet," *New Republic,* 22 November 1954, 11–16.

32. Progressivism

PROGRESSIVISM is the name given to the reform movement of the early twentieth century, chiefly from 1908 to 1916, which resulted in several significant changes in politics and public policy, some of which were versions of the Populists' earlier demands. Like the Populists, the Progressives included several different groups of people and ideas who were united around the restoration of popular control over government and the big corporations. Unlike the Populists, Progressives tended to be middle-class people with stronger ties to established politics and the major parties, particularly the Republican party. Progressivism was a broad-based spirit of mostly democratic reform, but one in which the working classes and immigrants (and the political "machines" that catered to them) were part of the problem requiring Americanization.

The various strands of Progressivism are represented here by three documents. First is the Progressive party platform of 1912. In this year the party, originally started and later carried on by Robert La Follette of Wisconsin, was almost entirely the personal vehicle of Theodore Roosevelt's effort to supplant his successor, Republican William Howard Taft. But the platform was characteristic of the party's moderate reform principles. Second is an example of one of the movement's enduring causes, the institution of the initiative and referendum at the state level—in this case, Colorado in 1910. These provisions, allowing voters to introduce and vote on legislation and to force a legislative enactment to the ballot for a popular vote, were achieved in twenty states during this period. Colorado's is included here because the powers involved apply to amending the state constitution as well as to ordinary legislation. The final selection is the set of Progressive era constitutional amendments added to the U.S. Constitution as part of the democratizing effort. Prohibition was closely associated with the purification of politics and the role of women in political life. ∾

The Progressive Party Platform (5 August 1912)

The conscience of the people, in a time of grave national problems, has called into being a new party, born of the nation's sense of justice. We of the Progressive party here dedicate ourselves to the fulfillment of the duty laid upon us by our fathers to maintain the government of the people, by the people and for the people whose foundations they laid....

THE OLD PARTIES

Political parties exist to secure responsible government and to execute the will of the people.

From these great tasks both of the old parties have turned aside. Instead of instruments

SOURCE: Henry Commager, ed., *Documents of American History* (New York: Oxford University Press, 1973), 2:73–75.

to promote the general welfare, they have become the tools of corrupt interests which use them impartially to serve their selfish purposes. Behind the ostensible government sits enthroned an invisible government owing no allegiance and acknowledging no responsibility to the people.

To destroy this invisible government, to dissolve the unholy alliance between corrupt business and corrupt politics is the first task of the statesmanship of the day.

The deliberate betrayal of its trust by the Republican party, the fatal incapacity of the Democratic party to deal with the new issues of the new time, have compelled the people to forge a new instrument of government through which to give effect to their will in laws and institutions.

Unhampered by tradition, uncorrupted by power, undismayed by the magnitude of the task, the new party offers itself as the instrument of the people to sweep away old abuses, to build a new and nobler commonwealth....

THE RULE OF THE PEOPLE

... In particular, the party declares for direct primaries for the nomination of State and National officers, for nation-wide preferential primaries for candidates for the presidency; for the direct election of United States Senators by the people; and we urge on the States the policy of the short ballot, with responsibility to the people secured by the initiative, referendum and recall....

EQUAL SUFFRAGE

The Progressive party, believing that no people can justly claim to be a true democracy which denies political rights on account of sex, pledges itself to the task of securing equal suffrage to men and women alike.

CORRUPT PRACTICES

We pledge our party to legislation that will compel strict limitation of all campaign contributions and expenditures, and detailed publicity of both before as well as after primaries and elections.

PUBLICITY AND PUBLIC SERVICE

We pledge our party to legislation compelling the registration of lobbyists; publicity of committee hearings except on foreign affairs, and recording of all votes in committee; and forbidding federal appointees from holding office in State or National political organizations, or taking part as officers or delegates in political conventions for the nomination of elective State or National officials.

THE COURTS

The Progressive party demands such restriction of the power of the courts as shall leave to the people the ultimate authority to determine fundamental questions of social welfare and public policy. To secure this end, it pledges itself to provide:

1. That when an Act, passed under the police power of the State, is held unconstitutional under the State Constitution, by the courts, the people, after an ample interval for deliberation, shall have an opportunity to vote on the question whether they desire the Act to become law, notwithstanding such decision.

2. That every decision of the highest appellate court of a State declaring an Act of the Legislature unconstitutional on the ground of its violation of the Federal Constitution shall be subject to the same review by the Supreme Court of the United States as is now accorded to decisions sustaining such legislation.

ADMINISTRATION OF JUSTICE

... We believe that the issuance of injunctions in cases arising out of labor disputes should be prohibited when such injunctions would not apply when no labor disputes existed.

We believe also that a person cited for contempt in labor disputes, except when such contempt was committed in the actual presence of the court or so near thereto as to interfere with the proper administration of justice, should have a right to trial by jury.

SOCIAL AND INDUSTRIAL JUSTICE

The supreme duty of the Nation is the conservation of human resources through an enlightened measure of social and industrial justice. We pledge ourselves to work unceasingly in State and Nation for:

Effective legislation looking to the prevention of industrial accidents, occupational diseases, overwork, involuntary unemployment, and other injurious effects incident to modern industry;

The fixing of minimum safety and health standards for the various occupations, and the exercise of the public authority of State and Nation, including the Federal Control over interstate commerce, and the taxing power, to maintain such standards;

The prohibition of child labor;

Minimum wage standards for working women, to provide a "living wage" in all industrial occupations;

The general prohibition of night work for women and the establishment of an eight hour day for women and young persons;

One day's rest in seven for all wage workers;

The eight hour day in continuous twenty-four-hour industries;

The abolition of the convict contract labor system; substituting a system of prison production for governmental consumption only; and the application of prisoners' earnings to the support of their dependent families;

Publicity as to wages, hours and conditions of labor; full reports upon industrial accidents and diseases, and the opening to public inspection of all tallies, weights, measures and check systems on labor products;

Standards of compensation for death by industrial accident and injury and trade disease which will transfer the burden of lost earnings from the families of working people to the industry, and thus to the community;

The protection of home life against the hazards of sickness, irregular employment and old age through the adoption of a system of social insurance adapted to American use;

The development of the creative labor power of America by lifting the last load of illiteracy from American youth and establishing continuation schools for industrial education under public control and encouraging agricultural education and demonstration in rural schools;

The establishment of industrial research laboratories to put the methods and discoveries of science at the service of American producers;

We favor the organization of the workers, men and women, as a means of protecting their interests and of promoting their progress. . . .

CURRENCY

. . . The issue of currency is fundamentally a Government function and the system should have as basic principles soundness and elasticity. The control should be lodged with the Government and should be protected from domination or manipulation by Wall Street or any special interests.

We are opposed to the so-called Aldrich currency bill, because its provisions would place our currency and credit system in private hands, not subject to effective public control. . . .

CONSERVATION

. . . We believe that the remaining forests, coal and oil lands, water powers and other natural resources still in State or National control (except agricultural lands) are more likely to be wisely conserved and utilized for the general welfare if held in the public hands.

In order that consumers and producers, managers and workmen, now and hereafter, need not pay toll to private monopolies of power and raw material, we demand that such resources shall be retained by the State or Nation, and opened to immediate use under laws which will encourage development and make to the people a moderate return for benefits conferred. . . . ∽

The Progressive Era Constitutional Amendments, Sixteen through Twenty-One (1913–1933)

AMENDMENT XVI
(25 FEBRUARY 1913)

The Congress shall have power to lay and collect taxes on incomes, from whatever source derived, without apportionment among the several States and without regard to any census or enumeration.

AMENDMENT XVII
(31 MAY 1913)

The Senate of the United States shall be composed of two senators from each State, elected by the people thereof, for six years; and each Senator shall have one vote. The electors in each State shall have the qualifications requisite for electors of the most numerous branch of the State legislature.

When vacancies happen in the representation of any State in the Senate, the executive authority of such State shall issue writs of election to fill such vacancies: *Provided,* That the legislature of any State may empower the executive thereof to make temporary appointments until the people fill the vacancies by election as the legislature may direct.

This amendment shall not be so construed as to affect the election or term of any senator chosen before it becomes valid as part of the Constitution.

AMENDMENT XVIII
(29 JANUARY 1919)

After one year from the ratification of this article, the manufacture, sale, or transportation of intoxicating liquors within, the importation thereof into, or the exportation thereof from the United States and all territory subject to the jurisdiction thereof for beverage purposes is hereby prohibited.

The Congress and the several States shall have concurrent power to enforce this article by appropriate legislation.

This article shall be inoperative unless it shall have been ratified as an amendment to the Constitution by the legislatures of the several States, as provided in the Constitution, within seven years from the date of the submission hereof to the States by Congress.

[Repealed by Amendment XXI, 19 December 1933]

AMENDMENT XIX
(26 AUGUST 1920)

The right of citizens of the United States to vote shall not be denied or abridged by the United States or by any States on account of sex.

The Congress shall have power by appropriate legislation to enforce the provisions of this article.

AMENDMENT XX
(6 FEBRUARY 1933)

Sec. 1. The terms of the President and Vice-President shall end at noon on the twentieth day of January, and the terms of Senators and Representatives at noon on the third day of January, of the years in which such terms would have ended if this article had not been ratified; and the terms of their successors shall then begin.

Sec. 2. The Congress shall assemble at least once in every year, and such meeting shall begin at noon on the third day of January, unless they shall by law appoint a different day.

Sec. 3. If, at the time fixed for the beginning of the term of the President, the President-elect shall have died, the Vice-President-elect shall become President. If a President shall not have been chosen before the time fixed for the beginning of his term, or if the President-elect shall have failed to qualify, then the Vice-President-elect shall act as President until a President shall have qualified; and the Congress may by law provide for the case wherein neither a President-elect nor a Vice-President-elect shall have qualified, declaring who shall then act as President, or the manner in which one who is to act shall be selected, and such person shall act accordingly until a President or Vice-President shall have qualified.

Sec. 4. The Congress may by law provide for the case of the death of any of the persons from whom the House of Representatives may choose a President whenever the right of choice shall have devolved upon them, and for the case of the death of any of the persons from whom the Senate may choose a Vice-President whenever the right of choice shall have devolved upon them.

Sec. 5. Sections 1 and 2 shall take effect on the 15th day of October following the ratification of this article.

Sec. 6. This article shall be inoperative unless it shall have been ratified as an amendment to the Constitution by the legislatures of three-fourths of the several States within seven years from the date of its submission.

AMENDMENT XXI
(15 DECEMBER 1933)

Sec. 1. The Eighteenth Article of amendment to the Constitution of the United States is hereby repealed.

Sec. 2. The transportation or importation into any State, Territory, or possession of the United States for delivery or use therein of intoxicating liquors in violation of the laws thereof, is hereby prohibited.

Sec. 3. This article shall be inoperative unless it shall have been ratified as an amendment to the Constitution by conventions in the several States, as provided in the Constitution, within seven years from the date of the submission thereof to the States by the Congress. ∾

Article V of the Colorado State Constitution, as Amended 8 November 1910

LEGISLATIVE DEPARTMENT

Section 1. General assembly—initiative and referendum. The legislative power of the state shall be vested in the general assembly consisting of a senate and house of representatives, both to be elected by the people, but the people reserve to themselves the power to propose laws and amendments to the constitution

and to enact or reject the same at the polls independent of the general assembly, and also reserve power at their own option to approve or
reject at the polls any act, item, section or part
of any act of the general assembly.

The first power hereby reserved by the
people is the initiative, and at least eight percent of the legal voters shall be required to
propose any measure by petition, and every
such petition shall include the full text of the
measure so proposed. Initiative petitions for
state legislation and amendments to the constitution, shall be addressed to and filed with the
secretary of state at least four months before
the election at which they are to be voted
upon.

The second power hereby reserved is the
referendum, and it may be ordered, except as
to laws necessary for the immediate preservation of the public peace, health or safety, and
appropriations for the support and maintenance of the department of state and state institutions, against any act, section or part of
any act or the general assembly, either by a petition signed by five percent of the legal voters
or by the general assembly. Referendum petitions shall be addressed to and filed with the
secretary of state not more than ninety days
after the final adjournment of the session of
the general assembly, that passed the bill on
which the referendum is demanded. The filing
of a referendum petition against any item, section or part of any act, shall not delay the remainder of the act from becoming operative.
The veto power of the governor shall not extend to measures initiated by, or referred to
the people. All elections on measures referred
to the people of the state shall be held at the
biennial regular general election, and all such
measures shall become the law or a part of the
constitution, when approved by a majority of
the votes cast thereon, and not otherwise, and
shall take effect from and after the date of the
official declaration of the vote thereon by

proclamation of the governor, but not later
than thirty days after the vote has been canvassed. This section shall not be construed to
deprive the general assembly of the right to enact any measure. The whole number of votes
cast for secretary of state at the regular general
election last preceding the filing of any petition
for the initiative or referendum shall be the basis on which the number of legal voters necessary to sign such petition shall be counted.

The secretary of state shall submit all
measures initiated by or referred to the people
for adoption or rejection at the polls, in compliance herewith. The petition shall consist of
sheets having such general form printed or
written at the top thereof as shall be designated or prescribed by the secretary of state;
such petition shall be signed by qualified electors in their own proper persons only, to
which shall be attached the residence address
of such person and the date of signing the
same. To each of such petitions which may
consist of one or more sheets, shall be attached an affidavit of some qualified elector,
that each signature of the person whose name
it purports to be, and that to the best of the
knowledge and belief of the affiant, each of the
persons signing said petition was at the time of
signing, a qualified elector. Such petition so
verified shall be prima facie evidence that the
signatures thereon are genuine and true and
that the persons signing the same are qualified
electors. The text of all measures to be submitted shall be published as constitutional
amendments are published, and in submitting
the same and in all matters pertaining to the
form of all petitions the secretary of state and
all other officers shall be guided by the general
laws, and the act submitting this amendment,
until legislation shall be especially provided
therefor.

The style of all laws adopted by the people
through the initiative shall be, "Be It Enacted
by the People of the State of Colorado."

The initiative and referendum powers reserved to the people by this section are hereby further reserved to the legal voters of every city, town and municipality as to all local, special and municipal legislation of every character in or for their respective municipalities. The manner of exercising said powers shall be prescribed by general laws, except that cities, towns and municipalities may provide for the manner of exercising the initiative and referendum powers as to their municipal legislation. Not more than ten percent of the legal voters may be required to order the referendum, nor more than fifteen percent to propose any measure by the initiative in any city, town or municipality.

This section of the constitution shall be in all respects self-executing. ~

Secondary Sources

Chambers, John W. *The Tyranny of Change: America in the Progressive Era, 1900–1917.* New York: St. Martin's Press, 1980.

Colburn, David R., and George E. Pozzetta, eds. *Reform and Reformers in the Progressive Era.* Westport, Conn.: Greenwood Press, 1983.

Haber, Samuel. *Efficiency and Uplife: Scientific Management in the Progressive Era, 1890–1920.* Chicago: University of Chicago Press, 1964.

Sarasohn, David. *The Party of Reform: Democrats in the Progressive Era.* Jackson: University of Mississippi Press, 1989.

Weinstein, James. *The Corporate Ideal in the Liberal State, 1900–1918.* Boston: Beacon Press, 1968.

33. Frederick W. Taylor

FREDERICK W. TAYLOR (1856–1915) graduated from a New England private school and went to work as a machinist for several years. He rose to the position of chief engineer at a steel company, acquired an engineering degree, and developed the concept of scientific management. By the turn of the century his technical papers and consulting had led to wide interest in time and motion studies, work reorganization, and efficiency-maximizing—all of which were part of scientific management. His two major works were the paper "Shop Management" (1903) and the book *Principles of Scientific Management* (1911).

By the latter date, scientific management had become controversial in the popular press. Organized labor viewed it as a rationale for reducing the number of employees, for lowering the skill level required in each job, and for speeding up the remaining workers. Early in 1912 a special committee of the House of Representatives, chaired by labor-sympathizing Representative William B. Wilson (D-Penn.), explored the nature of scientific management with Taylor as its major witness. The selection excerpted here is drawn from that testimony, in which Taylor's succinct description is followed by Wilson's blunt challenges and Taylor's responses. ~

The Nature of Scientific Management (1912)

Scientific management is not any efficiency device, not a device of any kind for securing efficiency; nor is it any bunch or group of efficiency devices. It is not a new system of figuring costs; it is not a new scheme of paying men; it is not a piecework system; it is not a bonus system; it is not a premium system; it is no scheme for paying men; it is not holding a stop watch on a man and writing things down about him; it is not time study; it is not motion study nor an analysis of the movements of men; it is not the printing and ruling and unloading of a ton or two of blanks on a set of men and saying, "Here's your system; go use it." It is not divided foremanship or functional foremanship; it is not any of the devices which the average man calls to mind when scientific management is spoken of. The average man thinks of one or more of these things when he hears the words "scientific management" mentioned, but scientific management is not any of these devices. I am not sneering at cost-keeping systems, at time study, at functional foremanship, nor at any new and improved scheme of paying men, nor at any efficiency devices, if they are really devices that make for efficiency. I believe in them; but what I am emphasizing is that these devices in whole or in part are not scientific management; they are useful adjuncts to scientific management, so are they also useful adjuncts of other systems of management. Now, in its essence, scientific management involves a complete mental revolution on the part of the workingman engaged in any particular establishment or industry—a complete mental revolution on the part of

these men as to their duties toward their work, toward their fellow men, and toward their employers. And it involves the equally complete mental revolution on the part of those on the management's side—the foreman, the super intendent, the owner of the business, the board of directors—a complete mental revolution on their part as to their duties toward their fellow workers in the management, toward their workmen, and toward all of their daily problems. And without this complete mental revolution on both sides scientific management does not exist.

That is the essence of scientific management, this great mental revolution. Now, later on, I want to show you more clearly what I mean by this great mental revolution. I know that perhaps it sounds to you like nothing but bluff—like buncombe—but I am going to try and make clear to you just what this great mental revolution involves, for it does involve an immense change in the minds and attitude of both sides, and the greater part of what I shall say today has relation to the bringing about of this great mental revolution. So that whether the details may be interesting or uninteresting, what I hope you will see is that this great change in attitude and viewpoint must produce results which are magnificent for both sides, just as fine for one as for the other. Now, perhaps I can make clear to you at once one of the very great changes in outlook which come to the workmen, on the one hand, and to those in the management on the other hand.

I think it is safe to say that in the past a great part of the thought and interest both of the men, on the side of the management, and of those on the side of the workmen in manufacturing establishments has been centered upon what may be called the proper division of the surplus resulting from their joint efforts,

SOURCE: Testimony by Frederick W. Taylor before the House Committee, January 1912. In *Scientific Management* (New York: Harper and Row, 1947).

between the management on the one hand, and the workmen on the other hand. The management have been looking for as large a profit as possible for themselves, and the workmen have been looking for as large wages as possible for themselves, and that is what I mean by the division of the surplus. Now this question of the division of the surplus is a very plain and simple one (for I am announcing no great fact in political economy or anything of that sort). Each article produced in the establishment has its definite selling price. Into the manufacture of this article have gone certain expenses, namely, the cost of materials, the expenses connected with selling it, and certain indirect expenses, such as the rent of the building, taxes, insurance, light and power, maintenance of machinery, interest on the plant, etc. Now, if we deduct these several expenses from the selling price, what is left over may be called the surplus. And out of this surplus comes the profit to the manufacturer on the one hand, and the wages of the workmen on the other hand. And it is largely upon the division of this surplus that the attention of the workman and of the management has been centered in the past. Each side has had its eye upon this surplus, the working man wanting as large a share in the form of wages as he could get, and the management wanting as large a share in the form of profits as it could get; I think I am safe in saying that in the past it has been in the division of this surplus that the great labor troubles have come between employers and employees.

Frequently, when the management have found the selling price going down they have turned toward a cut in the wages—toward reducing the workman's share of the surplus—as their way of getting out whole, of preserving their profits intact. While the workman (and you can hardly blame him) rarely feels willing to relinquish a dollar of his wages, even in dull times, he wants to keep all that he has had in the past, and when busy times come again very naturally he wants to get more. Thus it is over this division of the surplus that most of the troubles have arisen; in the extreme cases this has been the cause of serious disagreements and strikes. Gradually the two sides have come to look upon one another as antagonists, and at times even as enemies—pulling apart and matching the strength of the one against the strength of the other.

The great revolution that takes place in the mental attitude of the two parties under scientific management is that both sides take their eyes off of the division of the surplus as the all-important matter, and together turn their attention toward increasing the size of the surplus until this surplus becomes so large that it is unnecessary to quarrel over how it shall be divided. They come to see that when they stop pulling against one another, and instead both turn and push shoulder to shoulder in the same direction, the size of the surplus created by their joint efforts is truly astounding. They both realize that when they substitute friendly cooperation and mutual helpfulness for antagonism and strife they are together able to make this surplus so enormously greater than it was in the past that there is ample room for a large increase in wages for the workmen and an equally great increase in profits for the manufacturer. This, gentlemen, is the beginning of the great mental revolution which constitutes the first step toward scientific management. It is along this line of complete change in the mental attitude of both sides; of the substitution of peace for war; the substitution of hearty brotherly cooperation for contention and strife; of both pulling hard in the same direction instead of pulling apart; of replacing suspicious watchfulness with mutual confidence; of becoming friends instead of enemies; it is along this line, I say, that scientific management must be developed.

The substitution of this new outlook—this

new viewpoint—is of the very essence of scientific management, and scientific management exists nowhere until after this has become the central idea of both sides; until this new idea of cooperation and peace ...

The Chairman. Mr. Taylor, what percentage of the increased efficiency under scientific management is due to the systematizing of the work and what percent to the speeding up of the workman?

Mr. Taylor. In the ordinary sense of "speeding up," there is no increase in efficiency due to that. Using the term "speeding up" in its technical meaning, it means getting the workmen to go faster than they properly ought to go. There is no speeding up that occurs under scientific management in this sense.

The Chairman. How much in the sense in which it has been used—that the workman is required to go faster than he normally did go prior to the introduction of the system? Using it in that sense, what percentage of the increased efficiency is due to the systematizing of work and what percentage to the speeding up of the workmen under the definition which I have given?

Mr. Taylor. That depends, Mr. Chairman, upon the workman and the extent to which the workman was soldiering beforehand—that is, upon whether he was purposely going slow or not. As I have indicated, the amount of soldiering that takes place varies with the varying conditions, and there is no standard or uniform condition with relation to soldiering.

In some trades there is a very great deal of soldiering, in other trades there is less soldiering, so that the question can only be answered in its relation to some specific case. There is no general rule that I know of.

The Chairman. What social or economic necessity is there for speeding up the workman beyond the normal conditions under which he worked before the introduction of these scientific systems?

Mr. Taylor. Again, in its technical sense, there is no "speeding up" that occurs under scientific management. There is merely the elimination of waste movements—the elimination of soldiering, and the substitution of the very quickest, best, and easiest way of doing each thing for the older, inefficient way of doing the same thing; and this does not involve what is known as "speeding up."

The Chairman. If I recall your direct testimony, Mr. Taylor, you have stated that you found a condition of soldiering existing in the plants that you had to do with?

Mr. Taylor. Yes.

The Chairman. Does not your system propose to eliminate that soldiering?

Mr. Taylor. It certainly does.

The Chairman. Who is to determine what constitutes soldiering and what constitutes a proper amount of physical energy to be expended?

Mr. Taylor. The determination of what it is right for the man to do, of what constitutes a proper day's work, in all trades, is a matter for accurate, careful scientific investigation. It must be done by men who are earnest, honest, and impartial, and the standards which are gradually adopted by men who are undertaking this scientific investigation of every movement of every man connected with every trade establishes in time standards which are accepted both by the workmen and the management as correct.

The Chairman. Would not an employer be an interested party because he might profit or lose, as the circumstances might be?

Mr. Taylor. I can conceive that a dishonest employer or a heartless employer might very likely desire, in his ignorance of facts, to set a task which was too severe for the workman; but that man would be brought up with a round turn, because he would find that his workmen would not carry out unjust and unfair tasks; and an attempt at injustice on the part of such a man would wind up by his being a complete loser in the transaction. Therefore, the man who attempts any overdriving of that sort would simply fail.

The Chairman. The employer being a profiter by the expenditure of additional energy on the part of the workmen and not having the additional physical discomfort of the workmen to guide him in determining what constitutes a proper day's work, and what is soldiering—in what manner could the workman protect himself against an improper day's work being imposed upon him?

Mr. Taylor. By simply refusing to work at the pace set. He always has that remedy under scientific management; and as you know under scientific management he gets his regular day's pay, whether he works at the pace set or not. When he falls short of the day's work asked of him he merely fails to earn the extra premium of 30 to 100 percent which is paid for doing the piece of work in the time set.

The Chairman. Assuming an employer having a thousand employees, and conditions being imposed upon a workman requiring him to do more work than he believes he ought to do, and his refusal to do the work because he believed it to be too much, and the other 999 men continue on at work: upon what basis of equality would the employer and employee be under a condition of that kind?

Mr. Taylor. There is no earthly reason, if it is desired by the workmen, why there should not be a joint commission of workmen and employers to set these tasks, not the slightest earthly reason. And, as I think I have told you before, Mr. Chairman, the tasks which are set in our establishment are universally set or almost universally set by men who have themselves been workmen, and in most cases those who set the daily tasks have come quite recently from doing work at their trades. They have within the last six months or a year or two years perhaps worked right at those

trades. They are chosen because they are fairminded men, competent men, and because they have the confidence both of the management and the workmen. You must remember, Mr. Chairman, in the first place, that under scientific management the workmen and the management are the best of friends, and, in the second place, that one of the greatest characteristics of scientific management—the one element that distinguishes it from the older type of management—is that all any employee working under scientific management has to do is to bring to the attention of the management the fact that he thinks that he is receiving an injustice, and an impartial and careful investigation will be made. And unless this condition of seeking to do absolute justice to the workman exists, scientific management does not exist. It is the very essence of scientific management.

The Chairman. As I understand, then, very frequently those tasks are set by men who have come fresh from the ranks?

Mr. Taylor. Yes, sir.

The Chairman. Over on the side of management?

Mr. Taylor. Yes, sir.

The Chairman. Now, is it not true that when a man is selected by the management, as a rule, he is selected because they believe in his ability to take care of the interests of the management?

Mr. Taylor. Under scientific management because they believe in his impartiality, his straightforwardness, his truthfulness, and they believe he will have both the confidence of the management and the men, and equally forward the best interests of both sides which are mutual....

The Chairman. In what percentage, if any, of those establishments that have come under your observation where scientific management has been introduced has collective bargaining been introduced, by which the workmen collectively become a party in determining the wages, the task, and the conditions under which they shall work?

Mr. Taylor. Under the old sense of collective bargaining, I know of no single instance in which that has been used under scientific management. That is in the old sense of collective bargaining.

In the new sense of collective bargaining it is done in every establishment in which scientific management exists. During my first day's testimony I tried to make it clear that under the old system of management a very large part of the time and thought of both those on the management side and of the workmen was devoted to securing each for its own side what it looked upon as its proper share of the surplus. I use this word "surplus" as defined by me in my first day's testimony.

Now, a manufacturer who is an unjust man (and that frequently is the case—no more frequently is the manufacturer unjust, however, than is the workman unjust) when the manufacturer is unjust toward his men, without collective bargaining under the old system of management he has the power to secure more than his fair share of this surplus. Therefore, in many establishments under the ordinary system collective bargaining has become and is in my judgment an absolute necessity.

Under the old system of management (not scientific management) the attitude assumed in nine cases out of ten by the leaders of the workmen on the one hand and by the management on the other, is that of semihostility. It is an attitude the existence of which prevents the full measure of cooperation which should exist between both sides in order to produce the largest and best results, and whenever this attitude exists collective bargaining is a necessity.

Now, the moment this attitude of hostility or semihostility between the two sides is abandoned, and the moment it becomes the object of both sides jointly to arrive at what is an eq-

uitable and just series of standards by which they will both be governed; the moment they realize that under this new type of cooperation—by joining together and pushing in the same direction instead of pulling apart—they can so enormously increase this surplus that there will be ample for both sides to divide; then collective bargaining instead of becoming a necessity becomes of trifling importance. In all establishments working under scientific management it is always understood that any single workman or any four or five or six workmen can at any time call to the attention of the management the fact that any element in the management is wrong and should be corrected, and this protest will receive immediate and proper attention. And what I want to emphasize is that the kind of attention which any protest from the men receives under scientific management is not that which is subject to the personal prejudice or to the personal judgment of the employer, but it is the type of attention which immediately starts a careful scientific investigation as to all of the facts in the case, and this investigation is pursued until results have been obtained which satisfy both sides of the justice of the conclusion. Under these circumstances, then, collective bargaining becomes a matter of trifling importance. But there is no reason on earth why there should not be a collective bargaining under scientific management just as under the older type, if the men want it.

The Chairman. If collective bargaining is satisfactory under the conditions first described by you in order to get a proper division of the surplus, because the division of that surplus affects both the employer and the employees, would it not also be just as essential that there should be collective bargaining relative to conditions under which the workmen should work, because those conditions affect both the employer and the employee.

Mr. Taylor. I should make the same answer

to this question as I did to the last: that all that is necessary under true scientific management is for the attention of the management to be called to the fact that a bad condition exists to have a scientific investigation started, the results of which should be satisfactory to both sides.

The Chairman. If the satisfactory handling of scientific management depends on the ideal condition of mind whereby the employer is willing to concede to the workmen that which each workman is entitled to, how, under the other phases of scientific management, is the workman going to be able to protect himself against imposition by any other process than that of collective bargaining?

Mr. Taylor. I think I have already stated, Mr. Chairman, that the workman has it in his power at any minute, under scientific management, to correct any injustice that may be done him in relation to his ordinary every day work by simply choosing his own pace and doing the work as he sees fit. That remedy lies open to him at any minute, and the workman will do it every time he is treated unjustly under scientific management, just as he would under any other management. In other words, injustice on the part of the employer would kill the goose that lays the golden egg.

The Chairman. Would not your suggestion of cooperation on the part of the workman with the management (the management being the sole and arbitrary judge of the issue) be very much like the lion and the lamb lying down together with the lamb inside?

Mr. Taylor. Just the opposite. The lion is proverbial of everything that is bad. The lion is proverbial of strife, arrogance—of everything that is vicious. Scientific management cannot exist in establishments with lions at the head of them. It ceases to exist when injustice knowingly exists. Injustice is typical of some other management, not of scientific management.

The Chairman. Mr. Taylor, do you believe that any system of scientific management induced by a desire for greater profit would revolutionize the minds of the employers to such an extent that they would immediately, voluntarily, and generally enforce the golden rule?

Mr. Taylor. If they had sense they would. And let me tell you, Mr. Chairman, that that is the best answer. Not immediately. I have never said that. You cannot persuade any set of men, employers or employees, to adopt the principles of scientific management immediately. I have always said that it takes a period of from two to five years to get both sides completely imbued with the principles of scientific management. And I have further said, which I wish to repeat and emphasize, that nine-tenths of the trouble comes from those on the management side in taking up and operating a new device, and only one-tenth on the workmen's side. Our difficulties are almost entirely with the management.

The Chairman. Is it not true that scientific management has been developed with a desire to cheapen the production in order that there might be greater profits?

Mr. Taylor. Mr. Chairman, in one of the books which I have written on scientific management, in paragraph 21, page 1343, in the paper-covered pamphlet entitled "Shop Management," and which is in the possession of the Chair, in large print—and I believe this is perhaps the only paragraph in that whole book written in this very large print—is emphasized this fact:

This paper is written mainly with the object of advocating high wages and a low labor cost as a foundation of the best management and of pointing out the general principles which render it possible to maintain these conditions, even under the most trying circumstances, and of indicating the various steps which the writer thinks should be taken in making a change from a poor system to the better types of management.

The Chairman. In the same book, Mr. Taylor, do you not undertake to show that high wages are brought about by taking a workman who has been employed at a lower-priced class of work and putting him at work on a portion of the work formerly performed by the high-class workman and then giving him a higher rate of wage than he had before in the lower class of work, and yet a lower rate than was actually paid to the skilled workman who performed that work prior to that time?

Mr. Taylor. I have pointed out that under the principles of scientific management, with the teaching and kindly guidance which the workmen receive from the teachers who are over them in the management—I won't say over them; who are helping them in the management—with the high standards which are placed before them and taught to them; with the better methods of doing work (which are gradually developed through the joint efforts of hundreds of men) I have pointed out that when any workman of any caliber receives this unusual training and is given these unusual opportunities, that he is thereby enabled to do a higher and a better and a more interesting job.... ∽

Primary Source

Taylor, Frederick Winslow. *Scientific Management, Comprising Shop Management, the Principles of Scientific Management and Testimony before the Special House Committee.* New York: Harper and Row, 1947.

Secondary Sources

Braverman, Harry. *Labor and Monopoly Capital: The Degradation of Work in the Twentieth Century.* New York: Monthly Review Press, 1974.

Edwards, Richard. *Contested Terrain: The Transformation of the Workplace in the Twentieth Century.* New York: Basic Books, 1979.
Kakar, Sudhir. *Frederick Taylor: A Study in Personality and Innovation.* Cambridge, Mass.: MIT Press, 1970.
Wrege, Charles D. *Frederick W. Taylor, the Father of Scientific Management: Myth and Reality.* Homewood, Ill.: Business One Irwin, 1991.

34. Woodrow Wilson

WOODROW WILSON (1856–1924) was born in Virginia and graduated from Princeton in 1879. He studied law and was admitted to the Virginia bar, but after briefly practicing privately he entered graduate school at Johns Hopkins University. His doctoral thesis, *Congressional Government* (1885), remains a classic of political science today. During the years 1902 to 1910 Wilson was professor of jurisprudence and political economy at Princeton and later its president. An articulate, visible advocate of educational and other social reforms but with an underlying conservative perspective, he was elected governor of New Jersey as a Democrat in 1910. In 1912 he won the Democratic nomination for president as the conservative alternative to Bryan and was elected after the majority Republican party split and Roosevelt ran against Taft.

The selection given here is drawn from Wilson's campaign speeches of 1912, which together make up the substance of his New Free-dom. The Jeffersonian heritage should be clear, as well as its coming merger with the Hamiltonian concept of an interventionist national government. Croly's argument for combining nationalism and democracy finds fulfillment in Wilson's critique of big corporations and in his advocacy of restoring popular control of national government. ᐯᐯ

"The Meaning of Democracy" (1912)

I know that the government of the United States is not a free instrument, and that it is our duty to set it free. Very well, set it free from whom? And how set it free? ... I have always been impatient of the talk of abstract propositions. That may seem a strange statement to be made by a man whose opponents whenever they can't answer his arguments call him "academic," but I have always been opposed to the mere presentation to audiences of the abstract conceptions of government.

Of course, this was intended to be a government of free citizens and of equal opportunity, but how are we going to make it such? That is the question. Because I realize that while we are followers of Jefferson, there is one principle of Jefferson's which no longer can obtain in the practical politics of America. You know that it was Jefferson who said that the best government is that which does as little governing as possible, which exercises its power as little as possible. That was said in a day when the opportunities of America were so obvious to every man, when every individual was so free to use his powers without let or hindrance, that all that was necessary was that the government should withhold its hand and see to it that every man got an opportunity to act if he would. But that time is past. America is not now, and cannot in the future be, a place for unrestricted individual enterprise. It is true that we have come upon an age of great cooperative industry. It is true that we must act absolutely upon that principle.

Let me illustrate what I mean. You know that it used to be true in our cities that every family occupied a separate house of its own, that every family had its own little premises, that every family was separated in its life from every other family. But you know that that is no longer the case, and that it cannot be the case, in our great cities. Families live in layers, they live in tenements, they live in flats, they live on floors; they are piled layer upon layer in the great tenement houses of our crowded districts, and not only are they piled layer upon layer, but they are associated room by room, so that there is in each room, sometimes, in our congested districts, a separate family.

Now, what has happened in foreign countries, in some of which they have made much more progress than we in handling these things, is this: In the city of Glasgow, for example, which is one of the model cities of the world, they have made up their minds that the

SOURCE: A Campaign Speech, 23 September 1912, Scranton, Pennsylvania. In John W. Davidson, ed., *A Crossroads of Freedom: The 1912 Campaign Speeches* (New Haven, Conn.: Yale University Press, 1956).

entries and the hallways of great tenements are public streets. Therefore, the policeman goes up the stairway, and patrols the corridors; the lighting department of the city sees to it that the corridors are abundantly lighted and the staircases. The city does not deceive itself into supposing that that great building is a unit from which the police are to keep out and the city authority to be excluded, but it says: "These are the highways of human movement; and wherever light is needed, wherever order is needed, there we will carry the authority of the city."

I have likened that to our modern industrial enterprises. You know that a great many corporations, like the Steel Corporation, for example, [are] very like a great tenement house; it isn't the premises of a single commercial family; it is just as much a public business as a great tenement house is a public highway.

When you offer the securities of a great corporation to anybody who wishes to purchase them, you must open that corporation to the inspection of everybody who wants to purchase. There must, to follow out the figure of the tenement house, be lights along the corridor, there must be police patrolling the openings, there must be inspection wherever it is known that men may be deceived with regard to the contents of the premises. If we believe that fraud lies in wait for us, we must have the means of determining whether fraud lies there or not. Similarly, treatment of labor by the great corporations is not now what it was in Jefferson's time. Who in this great audience knows his employer? I mean among those who go down into the mines or go into the mills and factories. You never see, you practically never deal with, the president of the corporation. You probably don't know the directors of the corporation by sight. The only thing you know is that by the score, by the hundred, by the thousand, you are employed with your fellow workmen by some agent of an invisible employer. Therefore, whenever bodies of men employ bodies of men, it ceases to be a private relationship. So that when a court, when a court in my own state, held that workingmen could not peaceably dissuade other workingmen from taking employment and based the decision upon the analogy of domestic servants, they simply showed that their minds and understandings were lingering in an age which had passed away two or three generations ago. This dealing of great bodies of men with other bodies of men is a matter of public scrutiny, and should be a matter of public regulation.

Similarly, it was no business of the law in the time of Jefferson to come into my house and see how I kept house. But when my house, when my property, when my so-called private property, became a great mine, and men went along dark corridors amidst every kind of danger to dig out of the bowels of the earth things necessary for the industries of a whole nation and when it was known that no individual owned these mines, that they were owned by great stock companies, that their partnership was as wide as great communities, then all the old analogies absolutely collapsed and it became the right of the government to go down into those mines and see whether human beings were properly treated in them or not; to see whether accidents were properly safeguarded against; to see whether the modern methods of using these inestimable riches of the world were followed or were not followed. And so you know that by the action of a Democratic House only two years ago the Bureau of Mines and Mining was first equipped to act as foster father of the miners of the United States, and to go into these so-called private properties and see that the life of human beings was just as much safeguarded there as it could be in the circumstances, just as much safeguarded as it would be upon the streets of Scranton, because there are dangers on the streets of Scranton. If somebody puts a derrick improperly erected and secured on top of a building or overtopping the street upon any kind of structure, then the government of the city has the right to see that that derrick is so secured that you and I can walk under it and not be afraid that the heavens are going to fall on us. Similarly, in these great beehives where in every corridor swarm men of flesh and blood it is similarly the privilege of the government, whether of the state or of the United States, as the case may be, to see that human life is properly cared for and that the human lungs have something to breathe.

What I am illustrating for you is this: it is something that our Republican opponents don't seem to credit us with intelligence enough to comprehend. Because we won't take the dictum of a leader who thinks he knows exactly what should be done for everybody, we are accused of wishing to minimize the powers of the government of the United States. I am not afraid of the utmost exercise of the powers of the government of Pennsylvania, or of the Union, provided they are exercised with patriotism and intelligence and really in the interest of the people who are living under them. But when it is proposed to set up guardians over those people to take care of them by a process of tutelage and supervision in which they play no active part, I utter my absolute objection. Because the proposal of the third party, for example, is not to take you out of the hands of the men who have corrupted the government of the United States but to see to it that you remain in their hands and that that government guarantees to you that it will be humane to you.

The most corrupting thing in this country has been this self-same tariff.... The workingmen of America are not going to allow themselves to be deceived by a colossal bluff any longer. One of the corporations in the United States which has succeeded in mastering the laborer and saying to him, "You shall not organize; you shall not exercise your liberty of cooperating though we who employ you are using the power of organization to the outmost point of absolute control"—namely, the United States Steel Corporation—paid enormous dividends and still more enormous bonuses to those who promoted its organization at the same time that it was making men work twelve hours, seven days in the week, at wages which in the three hundred and sixty-five days of the year did not allow enough to support a family. If they have millions to divide among themselves and get those millions as they profess to get them from the opportunities created by the tariff, where does the workingman come in?

Mr. Roosevelt himself has spoken of the profits which they get as "prize money." And his objection is just the objection that I am raising. He says that not enough of the prize money gets into the pay envelope. And I quite agree with him. But I want to know how he proposes to get it there. I search his program from top to bottom, and the only proposal I can find is this: that there shall be an industrial commission charged with the supervision of the great monopolistic combinations which have been formed under the protection of the tariff, and that the government of the United States shall see to it that these gentlemen who have conquered labor shall be kind to labor.

I say, then, the proposition is this: that there shall be two masters, the great corporation and over it the government of the United States; and I ask: Who is going to be the master of the government of the United States? It has a master now—those who in combination control these monopolies. And if the government controlled by the monopolies in its turn controls the monopolies, the partnership is finally consummated.

I don't care how benevolent the master is going to be. I will not live under a master. That is not what America was created for.

America was created in order that every man should have the same chance with every other man to exercise mastery over his own fortunes. Now, what I want to do is to follow the example of the authorities of the city of Glasgow. I want to light and patrol the corridors of these great organizations in order to see that nobody who tries to traverse them is waylaid and maltreated. If you will but hold them off, if you will but see to it that the weak are protected, I will venture a wager with you that there are some men in the United States, now weak, economically weak, who have brains enough to compete with these gentlemen. If you will but protect them, they will presently come into the market and put these gentlemen on their mettle. And the minute they come into the market there will be a bigger market for labor and a different wage scale for labor, because it is susceptible of absolute proof that the high-paid labor of America—where it is high paid—is cheaper than the low-paid labor of the continent of Europe.

Do you know that about ninety per cent (I am told) of those who are employed in labor in this country are not employed in the "protected" industries, and that their wages are almost without exception higher than the wages of those who are employed in the "protected" industries? There is no corner on carpenters, there is no corner on bricklayers, there is no corner on scores of individual instances of classes of skilled laborers but there is a corner on the poolers in the furnaces, there is a corner on the men who dive down into the mines; they are in the grip of a controlling power which determines the market rates of wages in the United States. Only where labor is free is labor highly paid in America. So that when I am fighting against monopolistic control, I am fighting for the liberty of every man in America, and I am fighting for the liberty of American industry.

These gentlemen say that this commission

which they wish to set up should not be bound too much by laws but that they should be allowed to indulge in what they call "constructive regulation," which amounts to administration. And they intimate, though they do not say, that it will be perfectly feasible for this commission to regulate prices; and also to regulate, I dare say, in the long run though they do not now propose it, the rates of wages. How are they going to regulate them? Suppose that they take the net profits of a great concern ... and suppose they say these net profits are too large. How are they going to tell how much of those profits came from efficiency of administration and how much from excessive prices? Now, if you tax efficiency, you discourage industry. If you tax excessive profits, you destroy your monopoly; that is to say, you discourage your monopoly without increasing its efficiency, because without competition there isn't going to be efficiency.

Do you know that railway rates in the United States came down and came steadily down during the period which preceded the regulation of the Interstate Commerce Commission; and that since the regulation of the Interstate Commerce Commission the rates have steadily, though not rapidly, gone up? That means that the cost of operation in the railways in the competitive period under the stimulation of competition went down and that the cost of operation since the period of competition was closed has not gone down. I am not going to explain it but I suspect that nobody brings his operating costs down unless he has to, and that he would not have to unless somebody more intelligent and more efficient than himself gets in the field against him.

We believe that the power of America resides not in the men who have made good and gained a great supremacy in the field of business but in the men who are to make good. Where is the power, where is the distinction, of the great office of President of the United

States? Is America going to be saved because George Washington was great, because Lincoln was great, because men of devoted characters have served in that great office? Don't you know that America is safe only because we do not know who the future presidents of the United States are going to be? If we had depended upon the lineage of these gentlemen they might have failed to have sons like themselves. But we are not depending on anybody except the great American people, and we know that when the time comes some figure, it may be hitherto unknown and from some family whose name and fame the country has never heard, will come—a man fated for the great task by the gift of God and by virtue of his own indomitable character. I say this with a certain degree of embarrassment because I am a candidate for that great office, and I am not going to pretend to any body of my fellow citizens that I have any sort of confidence that I am a big enough man for the place. But I do feel proud of this: that no law, no rule of blood, no privilege of money, picked me out to be a candidate even. It may be a mistake but you can't blame your system for it; because it is a fine system where some remote, severe, academic schoolmaster may become President of the United States. He is not connected at least with the powers that have been, and has even upon occasion set himself against the powers that are.

Men speculate as to what he might be ignorant or audacious enough to do, but all of that is the excitement of the democratic game. We are sports. We aren't going to tie up to a particular family. We aren't going to tie up to a particular class. We are going to say: "We have played this game long enough now to be perfectly serene about it, and we are going to take the chances of the game." That is the beauty of democracy. Democracy means that, instead of depending for the fertility of your chances upon a little acre long tilled, you are going to depend upon all the wide prairies and the hillsides and the forested mountains; and that you don't care whether a man comes from Maine or from Texas, from Washington or from Florida—or anywhere in between—provided when he comes and you look at him you like him. Your confidence of the future is in this: that some man of some kind, probably from an uncalculated quarter, is going to come. You see, therefore, that I am simply going about to illustrate a single thing. I am simply trying to hold your attention to one theme, namely this, that America must be fertile or she cannot be great; that if you confine the processes of your industry or the processes of your politics to those lines where there may be, or has been, monopoly, you impoverish the great country which we would enrich. That to my mind is the whole lesson of history.

Men have always, sooner or later, kicked over the traces after they had for a little while lived upon the theory that some of them ought to take care of the rest of them. There is no man, there is no group of men, there is no class of men, big enough or wise enough to take care of a free people. If the free people can't take care of itself, then it isn't free. It hasn't grown up. That is the very definition of freedom. If you are afraid to trust any and every man to put forth his powers as he pleases, then you are afraid of liberty itself. I am willing to risk liberty to the utmost, and I am not willing to risk anything else. So that for my part, having once got blood in my eye and felt the zest of the active quest for the scalps of the men who don't know any better than to resist the liberties of a great people, it doesn't make any difference to me whether I am elected President or not. I'll find some means, somewhere, of making it infinitely uncomfortable for them.

The vision of America will never change. America once, when she was a little people, sat upon a hill of privilege and had a vision of the future. She saw men happy because they were free. She saw them free because they were equal. She saw them banded together because they had the spirit of brothers. She saw them safe because they did not wish to impose upon one another. And the vision is not changed. The multitude has grown, that welcome multitude that comes from all parts of the world to seek a safe place of life and of hope in America. And so America will move forward, if she moves forward at all, only with her face to that same sun of promise. Just so soon as she forgets the sun in the heavens, just so soon as she looks so intently upon the road before her and around her that she does not know where it leads, then will she forget what America was created for; her light will go out; the nations will grope again in darkness and they will say: "Where are those who prophesied a day of freedom for us? Where are the lights that we followed? Where is the torch that the runners bore? Where are those who bade us hope? Where came in these whispers of dull despair? Has America turned back? Has America forgotten her mission? Has America forgotten that her politics are part of her life, and that only as the red blood of her people flows in the veins of her polity shall she occupy that point of vantage which has made her the beacon and the leader of mankind?" 〜

Primary Sources

Davidson, John Wells, ed. *A Crossroads of Freedom: The 1912 Campaign Speeches*. New Haven, Conn.: Yale University Press for the Woodrow Wilson Foundation, 1956.

Fried, Albert, ed. *A Day of Dedication: The Essential Writings and Speeches of Woodrow Wilson*. New York: Macmillan, 1965.

Wilson, Woodrow. *Congressional Government: A Study in American Politics*. New York: Meridian Books, 1965.

———. *The Road Away from Revolution*. Boston: Atlantic Monthly Press, 1923.

———. *The State: Elements of Historical and Practical Politics*. Boston: Heath, 1918.

———. *Woodrow Wilson: A Selected Bibliography of His Published Writings, Addresses, and Public Papers*. Princeton, N.J.: Princeton University Press, 1948.

Secondary Sources

Braeman, John. *Woodrow Wilson*. Englewood Cliffs, N.J.: Prentice-Hall, 1972.

Buckingham, Peter H. *Woodrow Wilson: A Bibliography of his Times and Presidency*. Wilmington, Del.: Scholarly Resource, 1990.

Freud, Sigmund, and William C. Bullitt, *Thomas Woodrow Wilson, Twenty-eighth President of the U.S.: A Psychological Study*. Boston: Houghton Mifflin, 1966.

Hugh-Jones, Edward Maurice. *Woodrow Wilson and American Liberalism*. New York: Macmillan, 1948.

Link, Stanley Arthur. *Woodrow Wilson and the Progressive Era, 1910–1917*. New York: Harper and Row, 1954.

Urofsky, Melvin I. *Big Steel and the Wilson Administration*. Columbus: Ohio State University Press, 1969.

35. John Dewey

JOHN DEWEY (1859–1952) was born and raised in a small town in Vermont, graduated from the University of Vermont in 1879, and received his doctorate from Johns Hopkins University in 1884. Dewey taught philosophy at the Universities of Michigan, Minnesota, and Chicago until 1904, when he accepted a chair as professor of philosophy at Columbia University, a position he held until his retirement from full-time teaching in 1931.

For several decades, Dewey had wide influence, some of which still continues, on social thought in the United States. He was the leading advocate of the reforms embodied in "progressive education," the learning-by-doing methods particularly popular in the 1930s and 1940s. He endorsed the pragmatism of William James and sought to make the fields of education, social organization, and politics more sensitive to the way people think and how they acquire knowledge.

In this excerpt from *The Public and Its Problems* (1927), Dewey is searching for ways to accommodate democracy and the human need for community, on the one hand, with the growing scale of organization and impersonality of the American social-economic order, on the other. What does democracy require? How can the general public obtain such requirements in the complex modern world? Dewey argues that changes in both the nature of the society and the way we think are necessary to realize democracy under current conditions. ∾

The Public and Its Problems (1927)

We have had occasion to refer in passing to the distinction between democracy as a social idea and political democracy as a system of government. The two are, of course, connected. The idea remains barren and empty save as it is incarnated in human relationships. Yet in discussion they must be distinguished. The idea of democracy is a wider and fuller idea than can be exemplified in the state even at its best. To be realized it must affect all modes of human association, the family, the school, industry, religion. And even as far as

political arrangements are concerned, governmental institutions are but a mechanism for securing to an idea channels of effective operation. It will hardly do to say that criticisms of the political machinery leave the believer in the idea untouched. For, as far as they are justified—and no candid believer can deny that many of them are only too well grounded—they arouse him to bestir himself in order that the idea may find a more adequate machinery through which to work. What the faithful insist upon, however, is that the idea and its external organs and structures are not to be identified. We object to the common supposition of the foes of existing democratic government that the accusations against it touch

SOURCE: Reprinted from *The Public and Its Problems* (1927), by permission of Ohio University Press. The footnotes are Dewey's.

the social and moral aspirations and ideas which underlie the political forms. The old saying that the cure for the ills of democracy is more democracy is not apt if it means that the evils may be remedied by introducing more machinery of the same kind as that which already exists, or by refining and perfecting that machinery. But the phrase may also indicate the need of returning to the idea itself, of clarifying and deepening our apprehension of it, and of employing our sense of its meaning to criticize and remake its political manifestations.

Confining ourselves, for the moment, to political democracy, we must, in any case, renew our protest against the assumption that the idea has itself produced the governmental practices which obtain in democratic states; General suffrage, elected representatives, majority rule, and so on. The idea has influenced the concrete political movement, but it has not caused it. The transition from family and dynastic government supported by the loyalties of tradition to popular government was the outcome primarily of technological discoveries and inventions working a change in the customs by which men had been bound together. It was not due to the doctrines of doctrinaires. The forms to which we are accustomed in democratic governments represent the cumulative effect of a multitude of events, unpremeditated as far as political effects were concerned and having unpredictable consequences. There is no sanctity in universal suffrage, frequent elections, majority rule, congressional and cabinet government. These things are devices evolved in the direction in which the current was moving, each wave of which involved at the time of its impulsion a minimum of departure from antecedent custom and law. The devices served a purpose; but the purpose was rather that of meeting existing needs which had become too intense to be ignored, than that of forwarding the democratic idea. In

spite of all defects, they served their own purpose well.

Looking back, with the aid which *ex post facto* experience can give, it would be hard for the wisest to devise schemes which, under the circumstances, would have met the needs better. In this retrospective glance, it is possible, however, to see how the doctrinal formulations which accompanied them were inadequate, one-sided and positively erroneous. In fact they were hardly more than political warcries adopted to help in carrying on some immediate agitation or in justifying some particular practical polity struggling for recognition, even though they were asserted to be absolute truths of human nature or of morals. The doctrines served a particular local pragmatic need. But often their very adaptation to immediate circumstances unfitted them, pragmatically, to meet more enduring and more extensive needs. They lived to cumber the political ground, obstructing progress, all the more so because they were uttered and held not as hypotheses with which to direct social experimentation but as final truths, dogmas. No wonder they call urgently for revision and displacement.

Nevertheless the current has set steadily in one direction: toward democratic forms. That government exists to serve its community, and that this purpose cannot be achieved unless the community itself shares in selecting its governors and determining their policies, are a deposit of fact left, as far as we can see, permanently in the wake of doctrines and forms, however transitory the latter. They are not the whole of the democratic idea, but they express it in its political phase. Belief in this political aspect is not a mystic faith as if in some overruling providence that cares for children, drunkards and others unable to help themselves. It marks a well-attested conclusion from historic facts. We have every reason to think that whatever changes may take place in existing democratic machinery, they will be of a sort to make the interest of the public a more supreme guide and criterion of governmental activity, and to enable the public to form and manifest its purposes still more authoritatively. In this sense the cure for the ailments of democracy is more democracy. The prime difficulty, as we have seen, is that of discovering the means by which a scattered, mobile and manifold public may so recognize itself as to define and express its interests. This discovery is necessarily precedent to any fundamental change in the machinery. We are not concerned therefore to set forth counsels as to advisable improvements in the political forms of democracy. Many have been suggested. It is no derogation of their relative worth to say that consideration of these changes is not at present an affair of primary importance. The problem lies deeper; it is in the first instance an intellectual problem: the search for conditions under which the Great Society may become the Great Community. When these conditions are brought into being they will make their own forms. Until they have come about, it is somewhat futile to consider what political machinery will suit them. . . .

We have returned, through this apparent excursion, to the question in which our earlier discussion culminated: What are the conditions under which it is possible for the Great Society to approach more closely and vitally the status of a Great Community, and thus take form in genuinely democratic societies and state? What are the conditions under which we may reasonably picture the Public emerging from its eclipse?

The study will be an intellectual or hypothetical one. There will be no attempt to state how the required conditions might come into existence, nor to prophesy that they will occur. The object of the analysis will be to show that *unless* ascertained specifications are realized, the Community cannot be organized as a democratically effective Public. It is not claimed

that the conditions which will be noted will suffice, but only that at least they are indispensable. In other words, we shall endeavor to frame a hypothesis regarding the democratic state to stand in contrast with the earlier doctrine which has been nullified by the course of events.

Two essential constituents in that older theory, as will be recalled, were the notions that each individual is of himself equipped with the intelligence needed, under the operation of self-interest, to engage in political affairs; and that general suffrage, frequent elections of officials and majority rule are sufficient to ensure the responsibility of elected rulers to the desires and interests of the public. As we shall see, the second conception is logically bound up with the first and stands or falls with it. At the basis of the scheme lies what Lippmann has well called the idea of the "omnicompetent" individual: competent to frame policies, to judge their results; competent to know in all situations demanding political action what is for his own good, and competent to enforce his idea of good and the will to effect it against contrary forces. Subsequent history has proved that the assumption involved illusion. Had it not been for the misleading influence of a false psychology, the illusion might have been detected in advance. But current philosophy held that ideas and knowledge were functions of a mind or consciousness which originated in individuals by means of isolated contact with objects. But in fact, knowledge is a function of association and communication; it depends upon tradition, upon tools and methods socially transmitted, developed and sanctioned. Faculties of effectual observation, reflection and desire are habits acquired under the influence of the culture and institutions of society, not ready-made inherent powers. The fact that man acts from crudely intelligized emotion and from habit rather than from rational consideration, is now so familiar that it is not easy to appreciate that the other idea was taken seriously as the basis of economic and political philosophy. The measure of truth which it contains was derived from observation of a relatively small group of shrewd business men who regulated their enterprises by calculation and accounting, and of citizens of small and stable local communities who were so intimately acquainted with the persons and affairs of their locality that they could pass competent judgment upon the bearing of proposed measures upon their own concerns.

Habit is the mainspring of human action, and habits are formed for the most part under the influence of the customs of a group. The organic structure of man entails the formation of habit, for, whether we wish it or not, whether we are aware of it or not, every act effects a modification of attitude and set which directs future behavior. The dependence of habit-forming upon those habits of a group which constitute customs and institutions is a natural consequence of the helplessness of infancy. The social consequences of habit have been stated once for all by James:

Habit is the enormous fly-wheel of society, its most precious conservative influence. It alone is what keeps up within the bounds of ordinance, and saves the children of fortune from the uprisings of the poor. It alone prevents the hardest and most repulsive walks of life from being deserted by those brought up to tread therein. It keeps the fisherman and the deck-hand at sea through the winter; it holds the miner in his darkness, and nails the country-man to his log cabin and his lonely farm through all the months of snow; it protects us from invasion by the natives of the desert and the frozen zone. It dooms us all to fight out the battle of life upon the lines of our nurture or our early choice, and to make the best of a pursuit that disagrees, because there is no other for which we are fitted and it is too late to begin again. It keeps different social strata from mixing.

The influence of habit is decisive because all distinctively human action has to be learned, and the very heart, blood and sinews of learning is creation of habitudes. Habits bind us to orderly and established ways of action because they generate ease, skill and interest in things to which we have grown used and because they instigate fear to walk in different ways, and because they leave us incapacitated for the trial of them. Habit does not preclude the use of thought, but it determines the channels within which it operates. Thinking is secreted in the interstices of habits. The sailor, miner, fisherman and farmer think, but their thoughts fall within the framework of accustomed occupations and relationships. We dream beyond the limits of use and wont, but only rarely does revery become a source of acts which break bounds; so rarely that we name those in whom it happens demonic geniuses and marvel at the spectacle. Thinking itself becomes habitual along certain lines; a specialized occupation. Scientific men, philosophers, literary persons, are not men and women who have so broken the bonds of habits that pure reason and emotion undefiled by use and wont speak through them. They are persons of a specialized infrequent habit. Hence the idea that men are moved by an intelligent and calculated regard for their own good is pure mythology. Even if the principle of self-love actuated behavior, it would still be true that the *objects* in which men find their love manifested, the objects which they take as constituting their peculiar interests, are set by habits reflecting social customs.

These facts explain why the social doctrinaires of the new industrial movement had so little prescience of what was to follow in consequence of it. These facts explain why the more things changed, the more they were the same; they account, that is, for the fact that instead of the sweeping revolution which was expected to result from democratic political machinery, there was in the main but a transfer of vested power from one class to another. A few men, whether or not they were good judges of their own true interest and good, were competent judges of the conduct of business for pecuniary profit, and of how the new governmental machinery could be made to serve their ends. It would have taken a new race of human beings to escape, in the use made of political forms, from the influence of deeply engrained habits, of old institutions and customary social status, with their inwrought limitations of expectation, desire and demand. And such a race, unless of disembodied angelic constitution, would simply have taken up the task where human beings assumed it upon emergency from the condition of anthropoid apes. In spite of sudden and catastrophic revolutions, the essential continuity of history is doubly guaranteed. Not only are personal desire and belief functions of habit and custom, but the objective conditions which provide the resources and tools of action, together with its limitations, obstructions and traps, are precipitates of the past, perpetuating, willy-nilly, its hold and power. The creation of a *tabula rasa* in order to permit the creation of a new order is so impossible as to set at naught both the hope of buoyant revolutionaries and the timidity of scared conservatives.

Nevertheless, changes take place and are cumulative in character. Observation of them in the light of their recognized consequences arouses reflection, discovery, invention, experimentation. When a certain state of accumulated knowledge, of techniques and instrumentalities is attained, the process of change is so accelerated, that, as to-day, it appears exter-

nally to be the dominant trait. But there is a marked lag in any corresponding change of ideas and desires. Habits of opinion are the toughest of all habits; when they have become second nature, and are supposedly thrown out of the door, they creep in again as stealthily and surely as does first nature. And as they are modified, the alteration first shows itself negatively, in the disintegration of old beliefs, to be replaced by floating, volatile and accidentally snatched up opinions. Of course there has been an enormous increase in the amount of knowledge possessed by mankind, but it does not equal, probably, the increase in the amount of errors and half-truths which have got into circulation. In social and human matters, especially, the development of a critical sense and methods of discriminating judgment has not kept pace with the growth of careless reports and of motives for positive misrepresentation. . . .

There can be no public without full publicity in respect to all consequences which concern it. Whatever obstructs and restricts publicity, limits and distorts public opinion and checks and distorts thinking on social affairs. Without freedom of expression, not even methods of social inquiry can be developed. For tools can be evolved and perfected only in operation; in application to observing, reporting and organizing actual subject matter; and this application cannot occur save through free and systematic communication. The early history of physical knowledge, of Greek conceptions of natural phenomena, proves how inept become the conceptions of the best endowed minds when those ideas are elaborated apart from the closest contact with the events which they purport to state and explain. The ruling ideas and methods of the human sciences are in much the same condition today. They are also evolved on the basis of past gross observations, remote from constant use in regulation of the material of new observations.

The belief that thought and its communication are now free simply because legal restrictions which once obtained have been done away with is absurd. Its currency perpetuates the infantile state of social knowledge. For it blurs recognition of our central need to possess conceptions which are used as tools of directed inquiry and which are tested, rectified and caused to grow in actual use. No man and no mind was ever emancipated merely by being left alone. Removal of formal limitations is but a negative condition, positive freedom is not a state but an act which involves methods and instrumentalities for control of conditions. Experience shows that sometimes the sense of external oppression, as by censorship, acts as a challenge and arouses intellectual energy and excites courage. But a belief in intellectual freedom where it does not exist contributes only to complacency in virtual enslavement, to sloppiness, superficiality and recourse to sensations as a substitute for ideas: marked traits of our present estate with respect to social knowledge. On one hand, thinking deprived of its normal course takes refuge in academic specialism, comparable in its way to what is called scholasticism. On the other hand, the physical agencies of publicity which exist in such abundance are utilized in ways which constitute a large part of the present meaning of publicity: advertising, propaganda, invasion of private life, the "featuring" of passing incidents in a way which violates all the moving logic of continuity, and which leaves us with those isolated intrusions and shocks which are the essence of "sensations." ...

Opinions and beliefs concerning the public presuppose effective and organized inquiry. Unless there are methods for detecting the energies which are at work and tracing them through an intricate network of interactions to their consequences, what passes as public opinion will be "opinion" in its derogatory sense rather than truly public, no matter how widespread the opinion is. The number who share error as to fact and who partake of a false belief measures power for harm. Opinion casually formed and formed under the direction of those who have something at stake in having a lie believed can be *public* opinion only in name. Calling it by this name, acceptance of the name as a kind of warrant, magnifies its capacity to lead action astray. The more who share it, the more injurious its influence. Public opinion, even if it happens to be correct, is intermittent when it is not the product of methods of investigation and reporting constantly at work. It appears only in crises. Hence its "rightness" concerns only an immediate emergency. Its lack of continuity makes it wrong from the standpoint of the course of events. It is as if a physician were able to deal for the moment with an emergency in disease but could not adapt his treatment of it to the underlying conditions which brought it about. He may then "cure" the disease—that is, cause its present alarming symptoms to subside— but he does not modify its causes; his treatment may even affect them for the worse. Only continuous inquiry, continuous in the sense of being connected as well as persistent, can provide the material of enduring opinion about public matters.

There is a sense in which "opinion" rather than knowledge, even under the most favorable circumstances, is the proper term to use —namely, in the sense of judgment, estimate. For in its strict sense, knowledge can refer only to what *has* happened and been done. What is still *to be* done involves a forecast of a future still contingent, and cannot escape the liability to error in judgment involved in all anticipation of probabilities. There may well be honest divergence as to policies to be pursued, even when plans spring from knowledge of the same facts. But genuinely public policy cannot be generated unless it be informed by knowledge, and this knowledge does not exist except when there is systematic, thorough, and well-equipped search and record.

Moreover, inquiry must be as nearly contemporaneous as possible; otherwise it is only of antiquarian interest. Knowledge of history is evidently necessary for connectedness of knowledge. But history which is not brought down close to the actual scene of events leaves a gap and exercises influence upon the formation of judgments about the public interest only by guess-work about intervening events. Here, only too conspicuously, is a limitation of the existing social sciences. Their material comes too late, too far after the event, to enter effectively into the formation of public opinion about the immediate public concern and what is to be done about it.

A glance at the situation shows that the physical and external means of collecting information in regard to what is happening in the world have far outrun the intellectual phase of inquiry and organization of its results. Telegraph, telephone, and now the radio, cheap and quick mails, the printing press, capable of swift reduplication of materials at low cost, have attained a remarkable development. But when we ask what sort of material is recorded and how it is organized, when we ask about the intellectual form in which the material is presented, the tale to be told is very different. "News" signifies something which has just happened, and which is new just because it deviates from the old and regular. But its *meaning* depends upon relation to what it imports, to what its social consequences are. This import cannot be determined unless the new is placed in relation to the old, to what has happened and been integrated into the course of events. Without coordination and consecutiveness, events are not events, but mere occurrences, intrusions; an event implies that out of which a happening proceeds. Hence even if we discount the influence of private interests in procuring suppression, secrecy

and misrepresentation, we have here an explanation of the triviality and "sensational" quality of so much of what passes as news. The catastrophic, namely, crime, accident, family rows, personal clashes and conflicts, are the most obvious forms of breaches of continuity; they supply the element of shock which is the strictest meaning of sensation; they are the *new* par excellence, even though only the date of the newspaper could inform us whether they happened last year or this, so completely are they isolated from their connections.

So accustomed are we to this method of collecting, recording and presenting social changes, that it may well sound ridiculous to say that a genuine social science would manifest its reality in the daily press, while learned books and articles supply and polish tools of inquiry. But the inquiry which alone can furnish knowledge as a precondition of public judgments must be contemporary and quotidian. Even if social sciences as a specialized apparatus of inquiry were more advanced than they are, they would be comparatively impotent in the office of directing opinion on matters of concern to the public as long as they are remote from application in the daily and unremitting assembly and interpretation of "news." On the other hand, the tools of social inquiry will be clumsy as long as they are forged in places and under conditions remote from contemporary events.

What has been said about the formation of ideas and judgments concerning the public apply as well to the distribution of the knowledge which makes it an effective possession of the members of the public. Any separation between the two sides of the problem is artificial. The discussion of propaganda and propagandism would alone, however, demand a volume, and could be written only by one much more experienced than the present writer. Propaganda can accordingly only be mentioned, with the remark that the present situation is one unprecedented in history. The political forms of democracy and quasi-democratic habits of thought on social matters have compelled a certain amount of public discussion and at least the simulation of general consultation in arriving at political decisions. Representative government must at least seem to be founded on public interests as they are revealed to public belief. The days are past when government can be carried on without any pretense of ascertaining the wishes of the governed. In theory, their assent must be secured. Under the older forms, there was no need to muddy the sources of opinion on political matters. No current of energy flowed from them. Today the judgments popularly formed on political matters are so important, in spite of all factors to the contrary, that there is an enormous premium upon all methods which affect their formation.

The smoothest road to control of political conduct is by control of opinion. As long as interests of pecuniary profit are powerful, and a public has not located and identified itself, those who have this interest will have an unresisted motive for tampering with the springs of political action in all that affects them. Just as in the conduct of industry and exchange generally the technological factor is obscured, deflected and defeated by "business," so specifically in the management of publicity. The gathering and sale of subject-matter having a public import is part of the existing pecuniary system. Just as industry conducted by engineers on a factual technological basis would be a very different thing from what it actually is, so the assembling and reporting of news would be a very different thing if the genuine interests of reporters were permitted to work freely.

One aspect of the matter concerns particularly the side of dissemination. It is often said, and with a great appearance of truth, that the freeing and perfecting of inquiry would not have any especial effect. For, it is argued, the mass of the reading public is not interested in learning and assimilating the results of accurate investigation. Unless these are read, they cannot seriously affect the thought and action of members of the public; they remain in secluded library alcoves, and are studied and understood only by a few intellectuals. The objection is well taken save as the potency of art is taken into account. A technical high-brow presentation would appeal only to those technically highbrow; it would not be news to the masses. Presentation is fundamentally important, and presentation is a question of art. A newspaper which was only a daily edition of a quarterly journal of sociology or political science would undoubtedly possess a limited circulation and a narrow influence. Even at that, however, the mere existence and accessibility of such material would have some regulative effect. But we can look much further than that. The material would have such an enormous and widespread human bearing that its bare existence would be an irresistible invitation to a presentation of it which would have a direct popular appeal. The freeing of the artist in literary presentation, in other words, is as much a precondition of the desirable creation of adequate opinion on public matters as is the freeing of social inquiry. Men's conscious life of opinion and judgment often proceeds on a superficial and trivial plane. But their lives reach a deeper level. The function of art has always been to break through the crust of conventionalized and routine consciousness. Common things, a flower, a gleam of moonlight, the song of a bird, not things rare and remote, are means with which the deeper levels of life are touched so that they spring up as desire and thought. This process is art. Poetry, the drama, the novel, are proofs that the problem of presentation is not insoluble. Artists have always been the real purveyors of news, for it is not the outward happening in itself which is new, but the kindling by it of emotion, perception and appreciation.

We have but touched lightly and in passing upon the conditions which must be fulfilled if the Great Society is to become a Great Community; a society in which the ever-expanding and intricately ramifying consequences of associated activities shall be known in the full sense of that word, so that an organized, articulate Public comes into being. The highest and most difficult kind of inquiry and a subtle, delicate, vivid and responsive art of communication must take possession of the physical machinery of transmission and circulation and breathe life into it. When the machine age has thus perfected its machinery it will be a means of life and not its despotic master. Democracy will come into its own, for democracy is a name for a life of free and enriching communion. It had its seer in Walt Whitman. It will have its consummation when free social inquiry is indissolubly wedded to the art of full and moving communication. ❧

Primary Sources

Dewey, John. *Experience and Education.* New York: Macmillan, 1938.

———. *Individualism Old and New.* New York: Milton, Balch, 1930.

———. *Liberalism and Social Action.* New York: Putnam's, 1935.

———. *The Quest for Certainty: A Study of the Relation of Knowledge and Action.* New York: Milton, Balch, 1929.

———. *The School and Society.* Chicago: University of Chicago Press, 1899.

Dewey, John, and James H. Tufts. *Ethics.* New York: Henry Holt, 1908.

Secondary Sources

Blewett, John, ed. *John Dewey.* New York: Fordham University Press, 1960.

Hook, Sidney, ed. *John Dewey.* New York: Dial Press, 1950.

Laidler, Harry W. *John Dewey at Ninety.* New York: League for Industrial Democracy, 1950.

Lamont, Corliss, ed. *Dialogue on John Dewey.* New York: Horizon Press, 1959.

Moore, Edward C. *American Pragmatism: Pierce, James and Dewey.* New York: Columbia University Press, 1961.

Ryan, Alan. *John Dewey and the High Tide of American Liberalism.* New York: Norton, 1995.

36. Franklin D. Roosevelt

FRANKLIN D. ROOSEVELT (1882–1945) graduated from Harvard in 1904, practiced law in New York briefly, and then entered politics. He was a New York state senator, an assistant secretary of the navy during World War I, and in 1920 the Democratic vice-presidential candidate. In 1921 he was stricken with infantile paralysis but recovered partially and resumed his political career in New York. Elected governor in 1928 and 1930, he won the nomination to oppose President Hoover in the Depression-year election of 1932. His New Deal was slow to take form: first it was just a campaign slogan; later it seemed to be as much a series of responses to various crises as it was a coherent program. Initially, FDR articulated traditional Democratic economic principles, drawing perhaps most from Wilson's New Freedom. But his determination to preserve both popular support and the essence of the existing economic system led him to adopt more of Croly's nationalism, and the advent of World War II cemented the business-government relationship set in place over the preceding three decades.

Roosevelt was not a deep thinker and never wrote a major book. From his various speeches and major policy departures, however, it is possible to piece together the philosophy of government that would dominate in the United States for decades. Some of his speeches consist of mere rhetoric for purposes of holding popular support, but many provide rich substance and the rationale for a government-business partnership in which the executive branch and the corporate community would be the key elements. The proposal of an Economic Bill of Rights in 1944 represented the furthest extension of New Deal aspirations—a set of ideas no longer endorsed by any major political party. ∿

The Commonwealth Club Address (1932)

I want to speak not of politics but of Government. I want to speak not of parties, but of universal principles. They are not political, except in that larger sense in which a great American once expressed a definition of politics, that nothing in all of human life is foreign to the science of politics. . . .

The issue of Government has always been whether individual men and women will have to serve some system of Government or economics, or whether a system of Government and economics exists to serve individual men and women. This question has persistently dominated the discussion of Government for many generations. On questions relating to these things men have differed, and for time immemorial it is probable that honest men will continue to differ.

The final word belongs to no man; yet we can still believe in change and in progress. Democracy, as a dear old friend of mine in Indiana, Meredith Nicholson, has called it, is a quest, a never-ending seeking for better things, and in the seeking for these things and the striving for them, there are many roads to follow. But, if we map the course of these roads, we find that there are only two general directions.

When we look about us, we are likely to forget how hard people have worked to win the privilege of Government. The growth of the national Governments of Europe was a struggle for the development of a centralized force in the Nation, strong enough to impose peace upon ruling barons. In many instances the victory of the central Government, the creation of a strong central Government, was a haven of refuge to the individual. The people preferred the master far away to the exploitation and cruelty of the smaller master near at hand.

But the creators of national Government were perforce ruthless men. They were often cruel in their methods, but they did strive steadily toward something that society needed and very much wanted, a strong central State able to keep the peace, to stamp out civil war, to put the unruly nobleman in his place, and to permit the bulk of individuals to live safely.

SOURCE: Campaign Speech, San Francisco, 23 September 1932. This and the two following passages are in Samuel Rosenman, ed., *The Public Papers and Addresses of Franklin D. Roosevelt* (New York: Russell & Russell, 1969).

The man of ruthless force had his place in developing a pioneer country, just as he did in fixing the power of the central Government in the development of Nations. Society paid him well for his services and its development. When the development among the Nations of Europe, however, had been completed, ambition and ruthlessness, having served their term, tended to overstep their mark.

There came a growing feeling that Government was conducted for the benefit of a few who thrived unduly at the expense of all. The people sought a balancing—a limiting force. There came gradually, through town councils, trade guilds, national parliaments, by constitution and by popular participation and control, limitations on arbitrary power.

Another factor that tended to limit the power of those who ruled, was the rise of the ethical conception that a ruler bore a responsibility for the welfare of his subjects.

The American colonies were born in this struggle. The American Revolution was a turning point in it. After the Revolution the struggle continued and shaped itself in the public life of the country. There were those who because they had seen the confusion which attended the years of war for American independence surrendered to the belief that popular Government was essentially dangerous and essentially unworkable. They were honest people, my friends, and we cannot deny that their experience had warranted some measure of fear. The most brilliant, honest and able exponent of this point of view was Hamilton. He was too impatient of slow-moving methods. Fundamentally he believed that the safety of the republic lay in the autocratic strength of its Government, that the destiny of individuals was to serve that Government, and that fundamentally a great and strong group of central institutions, guided by a small group of able and public-spirited citizens, could best direct all Government.

But Mr. Jefferson, in the summer of 1776, after drafting the Declaration of Independence turned his mind to the same problem and took a different view. He did not deceive himself with outward forms. Government to him was a means to an end, not an end in itself; it might be either a refuge and a help or a threat and a danger, depending on the circumstances. We find him carefully analyzing the society for which he was to organize a Government. "We have no paupers. The great mass of our population is of laborers, our rich who cannot live without labor, either manual or professional, being few and of moderate wealth. Most of the laboring class possess property, cultivate their own lands, have families and from the demand for their labor, are enabled to exact from the rich and the competent such prices as enable them to feed abundantly, clothe above mere decency, to labor moderately and raise their families."

These people, he considered, had two sets of rights, those of "personal competency" and those involved in acquiring and possessing property. By "personal competency" he meant the right of free thinking, freedom of forming and expressing opinions, and freedom of personal living, each man according to his own lights. To insure the first set of rights, a Government must so order its functions as not to interfere with the individual. But even Jefferson realized that the exercise of the property rights might so interfere with the rights of the individual that the Government, without whose assistance the property rights could not exist, must intervene, not to destroy individualism, but to protect it.

You are familiar with the great political duel which followed; and how Hamilton, and his friends, building toward a dominant centralized power were at length defeated in the great election of 1800, by Mr. Jefferson's party. Out of that duel came the two parties, Republican and Democratic, as we know them today.

THE DAY OF THE INDIVIDUAL
AGAINST THE SYSTEM

So began, in American political life, the new day, the day of the individual against the system, the day in which individualism was made the great watchword of American life. The happiest of economic conditions made that day long and splendid. On the Western frontier, land was substantially free. No one, who did not shirk the task of earning a living, was entirely without opportunity to do so. Depressions could, and did, come and go; but they could not alter the fundamental fact that most of the people lived partly by selling their labor and partly by extracting their livelihood from the soil, so that starvation and dislocation were practically impossible. At the very worst there was always the possibility of climbing into a covered wagon and moving west where the untilled prairies afforded a haven for men to whom the East did not provide a place. So great were our natural resources that we could offer this relief not only to our own people, but to the distressed of all the world; we could invite immigration from Europe, and welcome it with open arms. Traditionally, when a depression came a new section of land was opened in the West; and even our temporary misfortune served our manifest destiny.

It was in the middle of the nineteenth century that a new force was released and a new dream created. The force was what is called the industrial revolution, the advance of steam and machinery and the rise of the forerunners of the modern industrial plant. The dream was the dream of an economic machine, able to raise the standard of living for everyone; to bring luxury within the reach of the humblest; to annihilate distance by steam power and later by electricity, and to release everyone from the drudgery of the heaviest manual toil. It was to be expected that this would necessarily affect Government. Heretofore, Government had merely been called upon to produce

conditions within which people could live happily, labor peacefully, and rest secure. Now it was called upon to aid in the consummation of this new dream. There was, however, a shadow over the dream. To be made real, it required use of the talents of men of tremendous will and tremendous ambition, since by no other force could the problems of financing and engineering and new developments be brought to a consummation.

So manifest were the advantages of the machine age, however, that the United States fearlessly, cheerfully, and, I think, rightly, accepted the bitter with the sweet. It was thought that no price was too high to pay for the advantages which we could draw from a finished industrial system. The history of the last half century is accordingly in large measure a history of a group of financial Titans, whose methods were not scrutinized with too much care, and who were honored in proportion as they produced the results, irrespective of the means they used. The financiers who pushed the railroads to the Pacific were always ruthless, often wasteful, and frequently corrupt; but they did build railroads, and we have them today. It has been estimated that the American investor paid for the American railway system more than three times over in the process; but despite this fact the net advantage was to the United States. As long as we had free land; as long as population was growing by leaps and bounds; as long as our industrial plants were insufficient to supply our own needs, society chose to give the ambitious man free play and unlimited reward provided only that he produced the economic plant so much desired.

During this period of expansion, there was equal opportunity for all and the business of Government was not to interfere but to assist in the development of industry. This was done at the request of business men themselves. The tariff was originally imposed for the purpose of "fostering our infant industry," a phrase I think the older among you will remember as a political issue not so long ago. The railroads were subsidized, sometimes by grants of money, oftener by grants of land; some of the most valuable oil lands in the United States were granted to assist the financing of the railroad which pushed through the Southwest. A nascent merchant marine was assisted by grants of money, or by mail subsidies, so that our steam shipping might ply the seven seas. Some of my friends tell me that they do not want the Government in business. With this I agree; but I wonder whether they realize the implications of the past. For while it has been American doctrine that the Government must not go into business in competition with private enterprise, still it has been traditional, particularly in Republican administrations, for business urgently to ask the Government to put at private disposal all kinds of Government assistance. The same man who tells you that he does not want to see the Government interfere in business—and he means it, and has plenty of good reasons for saying so—is the first to go to Washington and ask the Government for a prohibitory tariff on his product. When things get just bad enough, as they did two years ago, he will go with equal speed to the United States Government and ask for a loan; and the Reconstruction Finance Corporation is the outcome of it. Each group has sought protection from the Government for its own special interests, without realizing that the function of Government must be to favor no small group at the expense of its duty to protect the rights of personal freedom and of private property of all its citizens.

In retrospect we can now see that the turn of the tide came with the turn of the century. We were reaching our last frontier; there was no more free land and our industrial combinations had become great uncontrolled and irresponsible units of power within the State. Clear-sighted men saw with fear the danger that opportunity would no longer be equal; that the growing corporation, like the feudal baron of old, might threaten the economic freedom of individuals to earn a living. In that hour, our antitrust laws were born. The cry was raised against the great corporations. Theodore Roosevelt, the first great Republican Progressive, fought a Presidential campaign on the issue of "trust busting," and talked freely about malefactors of great wealth. If the Government had a policy it was rather to turn the clock back, to destroy the large combinations and to return to the time when every man owned his individual small business.

This was impossible; Theodore Roosevelt, abandoning the idea of "trust busting," was forced to work out a difference between "good" trusts and "bad" trusts. The Supreme Court set forth the famous "rule of reason" by which it seems to have meant that a concentration of industrial power was permissible if the method by which it got its power, and the use it made of that power, were reasonable.

THE NEW FINANCIAL POWER

Woodrow Wilson, elected in 1912, saw the situation more clearly. Where Jefferson had feared the encroachment of political power on the lives of individuals, Wilson knew that the new power was financial. He saw, in the highly centralized economic system, the despot of the twentieth century, on whom great masses of individuals relied for their safety and their livelihood, and whose irresponsibility and greed (if they were not controlled) would reduce them to starvation and penury. The concentration of financial power had not proceeded so far in 1912 as it has today, but it had grown far enough for Mr. Wilson to realize fully its implications. It is interesting, now, to read his speeches. What is called "radical" today (and I have reason to know whereof I speak) is mild compared to the campaign of Mr. Wilson. "No man can deny," he said, "that the lines of endeavor have more and more narrowed and stiffened; no man who knows anything about the development of industry in this country can have failed to observe that the larger kinds of credit are more and more difficult to obtain unless you obtain them upon terms of uniting your efforts with those who already control the industry of the country, and nobody can fail to observe that every man who tries to set himself up in competition with any process of manufacture which has taken place under the control of large combinations of capital will presently find himself either squeezed out or obliged to sell and allow himself to be absorbed." Had there been no World War—had Mr. Wilson been able to devote eight years to domestic instead of to international affairs —we might have had a wholly different situation at the present time. However, the then distant roar of European cannon, growing ever louder, forced him to abandon the study of this issue. The problem he saw so clearly is left with us as a legacy; and no one of us on either side of the political controversy can deny that it is a matter of grave concern to the Government.

A glance at the situation today only too clearly indicates that equality of opportunity as we have known it no longer exists. Our industrial plant is built, the problem just now is whether under existing conditions it is not overbuilt. Our last frontier has long since been reached, and there is practically no more free land. More than half of our people do not live on the farms or on lands and cannot derive a living by cultivating their own property. There is no safety valve in the form of a Western prairie to which those thrown out of work by the Eastern economic machines can go for a new start. We are not able to invite the immigration from Europe to share our endless plenty. We are now providing a drab living for our own people.

Our system of constantly rising tariffs has

at last reacted against us to the point of closing our Canadian frontier on the north, our European markets on the east, many of our Latin-American markets to the south, and a goodly proportion of our Pacific markets on the west, through the retaliatory tariffs of those countries. It has forced many of our great industrial institutions which exported their surplus production to such countries, to establish plants in such countries, within the tariff walls. This has resulted in the reduction of the operation of their American plants, and opportunity for employment.

Just as freedom to farm has ceased, so also the opportunity in business has narrowed. It still is true that men can start small enterprises, trusting to native shrewdness and ability to keep abreast of competitors; but area after area has been preempted altogether by the great corporations, and even in the fields which still have no great concerns, the small man starts under a handicap. The unfeeling statistics of the past three decades show that the independent business man is running a losing race. Perhaps he is forced to the wall; perhaps he cannot command credit; perhaps he is "squeezed out," in Mr. Wilson's words, by highly organized corporate competitors, as your corner grocery man can tell you. Recently a careful study was made of the concentration of business in the United States. It showed that our economic life was dominated by some six hundred odd corporations who controlled two-thirds of American industry. Ten million small business men divided the other third. More striking still, it appeared that if the process of concentration goes on at the same rate, at the end of another century we shall have all American industry controlled by a dozen corporations, and run by perhaps a hundred men. Put plainly, we are steering a steady course toward economic oligarchy, if we are not there already.

Clearly, all this calls for a re-appraisal of

values. A mere builder of more industrial plants, a creator of more railroad systems, an organizer of more corporations, is as likely to be a danger as a help. The day of the great promoter or the financial Titan, to whom we granted anything if only he would build, or develop, is over. Our task now is not discovery or exploitation of natural resources, or necessarily producing more goods. It is the soberer, less dramatic business of administering resources and plants already in hand, of seeking to reestablish foreign markets for our surplus production, of meeting the problem of underconsumption, of adjusting production to consumption, of distributing wealth and products more equitably, of adapting existing economic organizations to the service of the people. The day of enlightened administration has come.

Just as in older times the central Government was first a haven of refuge, and then a threat, so now in a closer economic system the central and ambitious financial unit is no longer a servant of national desire, but a danger. I would draw the parallel one step farther. We did not think because national Government had become a threat in the 18th century that therefore we should abandon the principle of national Government. Nor today should we abandon the principle of strong economic units called corporations, merely because their power is susceptible of easy abuse. In other times we dealt with the problem of an unduly ambitious central Government by modifying it gradually into a constitutional democratic Government. So today we are modifying and controlling our economic units.

THE TASK OF GOVERNMENT IN THE ECONOMIC ORDER

As I see it, the task of Government in its relation to business is to assist the development of an economic declaration of rights, an economic constitutional order. This is the common task of statesman and business man. It is

the minimum requirement of a more permanently safe order of things.

Happily, the times indicate that to create such an order not only is the proper policy of Government, but it is the only line of safety for our economic structures as well. We know, now, that these economic units cannot exist unless prosperity is uniform, that is, unless purchasing power is well distributed throughout every group in the Nation. That is why even the most selfish of corporations for its own interest would be glad to see wages restored and unemployment ended and to bring the Western farmer back to his accustomed level of prosperity and to assure a permanent safety to both groups. That is why some enlightened industries themselves group within the industry in the common interest of all; why business men everywhere are asking a form of organization which will bring the scheme of things into balance, even though it may in some measure qualify the freedom of action of individual units within the business.

The exposition need not further be elaborated. It is brief and incomplete, but you will be able to expand it in terms of your own business or occupation without difficulty. I think everyone who has actually entered the economic struggle—which means everyone who was not born to safe wealth—knows in his own experience and his own life that we have now to apply the earlier concepts of American Government to the conditions of today.

The Declaration of Independence discusses the problems of Government in terms of a contract. Government is a relation of give and take, a contract, perforce, if we would follow the thinking out of which it grew. Under such a contract rulers were accorded power, and the people consented to that power on consideration that they be accorded certain rights. The task of statesmanship has always been the redefinition of these rights in terms of a changing and growing social order. New conditions impose new requirements upon Government and those who conduct Government.

I held, for example, in proceedings before me as Governor, the purpose of which was the removal of the Sheriff of New York, that under modern conditions it was not enough for a public official merely to evade the legal terms of official wrongdoing. He owed a positive duty as well. I said in substance that if he had acquired large sums of money, he was when accused required to explain the sources of such wealth. To that extent this wealth was colored with a public interest. I said that in financial matters, public servants should, even beyond private citizens, be held to a stern and uncompromising rectitude.

I feel that we are coming to a view through the drift of our legislation and our public thinking in the past quarter century that private economic power is, to enlarge an old phrase, a public trust as well. I hold that continued enjoyment of that power by any individual or group must depend upon the fulfillment of that trust. The men who have reached the summit of American business life know this best; happily, many of these urge the binding quality of this greater social contract.

The terms of that contract are as old as the Republic, and as new as the new economic order.

Every man has a right to life, and this means that he has also a right to make a comfortable living. He may by sloth or crime decline to exercise that right; but it may not be denied him. We have no actual famine or dearth; our industrial and agricultural mechanism can produce enough and to spare. Our Government formal and informal, political and economic, owes to everyone an avenue to possess himself of a portion of that plenty sufficient for his needs, through his own work.

Every man has a right to his own property; which means a right to be assured, to the full-

est extent attainable, in the safety of his savings. By no other means can men carry the burdens of those parts of life which, in the nature of things, afford no chance of labor; childhood, sickness, old age. In all thought of property, this right is paramount; all other property rights must yield to it. If, in accord with this principle, we must restrict the operations of the speculator, the manipulator, even the financier, I believe we must accept the restriction as needful, not to hamper individualism but to protect it.

These two requirements must be satisfied, in the main, by the individuals who claim and hold control of the great industrial and financial combinations which dominate so large a part of our industrial life. They have undertaken to be, not business men, but princes of property. I am not prepared to say that the system which produces them is wrong. I am very clear that they must fearlessly and competently assume the responsibility which goes with the power. So many enlightened business men know this that the statement would be little more than a platitude, were it not for an added implication.

GOVERNMENT AS A RESTRAINING INFLUENCE

This implication is, briefly, that the responsible heads of finance and industry instead of acting each for himself, must work together to achieve the common end. They must, where necessary, sacrifice this or that private advantage; and in reciprocal self-denial must seek a general advantage. It is here that formal Government—political Government, if you choose—comes in. Whenever in the pursuit of this objective the lone wolf, the unethical competitor, the reckless promoter, the Ishmael or Insull whose hand is against every man's, declines to join in achieving an end recognized as being for the public welfare, and threatens to drag the industry back to a state of anarchy, the Government may properly be asked to apply restraint. Likewise, should the group ever use its collective power contrary to the public welfare, the Government must be swift to enter and protect the public interest.

The Government should assume the function of economic regulation only as a last resort, to be tried only when private initiative, inspired by high responsibility, with such assistance and balance as Government can give, has finally failed. As yet there has been no final failure, because there has been no attempt; and I decline to assume that this Nation is unable to meet the situation.

The final term of the high contract was for liberty and the pursuit of happiness. We have learned a great deal of both in the past century. We know that individual liberty and individual happiness mean nothing unless both are ordered in the sense that one man's meat is not another man's poison. We know that the old "rights of personal competency," the right to read, to think, to speak, to choose and live a mode of life, must be respected at all hazards. We know that liberty to do anything which deprives others of those elemental rights is outside the protection of any compact; and that Government in this regard is the maintenance of a balance, within which every individual may have a place if he will take it; in which every individual may find safety if he wishes it; in which every individual may attain such power as his ability permits, consistent with his assuming the accompanying responsibility.

THE DUTY OF A STATESMAN IS TO EDUCATE

All this is a long, slow talk. Nothing is more striking than the simple innocence of the men who insist, whenever an objective is present, on the prompt production of a patent scheme guaranteed to produce a result. Human endeavor is not so simple as that. Government includes the art of formulating a policy, and using the political technique to attain so much of that policy as will receive general support; persuading, leading, sacrificing, teaching always, because the greatest duty of a statesman is to educate. But in the matters of which I have spoken, we are learning rapidly, in a severe school. The lessons so learned must not be forgotten, even in the mental lethargy of a speculative upturn. We must build toward the time when a major depression cannot occur again; and if this means sacrificing the easy profits of inflationist booms, then let them go; and good riddance.

Faith in America, faith in our tradition of personal responsibility, faith in our institutions, faith in ourselves demands that we recognize the new terms of the old social contract. We shall fulfill them, as we fulfilled the obligation of the apparent Utopia which Jefferson imagined for us in 1776, and which Jefferson, Roosevelt and Wilson sought to bring to realization. We must do so, lest a rising tide of misery, engendered by our common failure, engulf us all. But failure is not an American habit; and in the strength of great hope we must all shoulder our common load. ◃

Campaign Address (1936)

I seem to have been here before. Four years ago I dropped into this city from the airways—an old friend come in a new way—to accept in this hall the nomination for the Presidency of the United States. I came to a Chicago fighting with its back to the wall—factories closed, markets silent, banks shaky, ships and trains empty. Today those factories sing the song of industry; markets hum with bustling movement; banks are secure; ships and trains are running full. Once again it is Chicago as Carl Sandburg saw it—"The City of the Big Shoulders"—the city that smiles. And with Chicago a whole Nation that had not been cheerful for years is full of cheer once more.

On this trip through the Nation I have talked to farmers, I have talked to miners, I have talked to industrial workers; and in all that I have seen and heard one fact has been clear as crystal—that they are part and parcel of a rounded whole, and that none of them can succeed in his chosen occupation if those in the other occupations fail in their prosperity. I have driven home that point.

Tonight, in this center of business, I give the same message to the business men of America—to those who make and sell the processed goods the Nation uses and to the men and women who work for them.

To them I say:

Do you have a deposit in the bank? It is safer today than it has ever been in our history. It is guaranteed. Last October first marked the end of the first full year in fifty-five years without a single failure of a national bank in the United States. Is that not on the credit side of the Government's account with you?

Are you an investor? Your stocks and bonds are up to five- and six-year high levels.

Are you a merchant? Your markets have the precious life-blood of purchasing power. Your customers on the farms have better incomes and smaller debts. Your customers in the cities have more jobs, surer jobs, better jobs. Did not your Government have something to do with that?

Are you in industry? Industrial earnings, industrial profits are the highest in four, six, or even seven years! Bankruptcies are at a new low. Your Government takes some credit for that.

Are you in railroads? Freight loadings are steadily going up. Passenger receipts are steadily going up—have in some cases doubled—because your Government made the railroads cut rates and make money.

Are you a middleman in the great stream of farm products? The meat and grain that move through your yards and elevators have a steadier supply, a steadier demand and steadier prices than you have known for years. And your Government is trying to keep it that way.

Some people say that all this recovery has just happened. But in a complicated modern world recoveries from depressions do not just happen. The years from 1929 to 1933, when we waited for recovery just to happen, prove the point.

But in 1933 we did not wait. We acted. Behind the growing recovery of today is a story of deliberate Government acceptance of responsibility to save business, to save the American system of private enterprise and economic democracy—a record unequaled by any modern Government in history.

What had the previous Administration in Washington done for four years? Nothing. Why? For a very fundamental reason. That Administration was not industrially-minded or agriculturally-minded or business-minded. It was high-finance-minded—manned and controlled by a handful of men who in turn controlled and by one financial device or another took their toll from the greater part of all other business and industry.

Let me make one simple statement. When I refer to high finance I am not talking about all great bankers, or all great corporation executives, or all multimillionaires—any more than Theodore Roosevelt, in using the term "malefactors of great wealth," implied that all men of great wealth were "malefactors." I do not even imply that the majority of them are bad citizens. The opposite is true.

Just in the same way, the overwhelming

majority of business men in this country are good citizens and the proportion of those who are not is probably about the same proportion as in the other occupations and professions of life.

When I speak of high finance as a harmful factor in recent years, I am speaking about a minority which includes the type of individual who speculates with other people's money— and you in Chicago know the kind I refer to —and also the type of individual who says that popular government cannot be trusted and, therefore, that the control of business of all kinds and, indeed, of Government itself should be vested in the hands of one hundred or two hundred all-wise individuals controlling the purse-strings of the Nation.

High finance of this type refused to permit Government credit to go directly to the industrialist, to the business man, to the homeowner, to the farmer. They wanted it to trickle down from the top, through the intricate arrangements which they controlled and by which they were able to levy tribute on every business in the land.

They did not want interest rates to be reduced by the use of Government funds, for that would affect the rate of interest which they themselves wanted to charge. They did not want Government supervision over financial markets through which they manipulated their monopolies with other people's money.

And in the face of their demands that Government do nothing that they called "unsound," the Government, hypnotized by its indebtedness to them, stood by and let the depression drive industry and business toward bankruptcy.

America is an economic unit. New means and methods of transportation and communications have made us economically as well as politically a single Nation.

Because kidnappers and bank robbers could in high-powered cars speed across state lines it became necessary, in order to protect our people, to invoke the power of the Federal Government. In the same way speculators and manipulators from across State lines, and regardless of State laws, have lured the unsuspecting and the unwary to financial destruction. In the same way across State lines, there have been built up intricate corporate structures, piling bond upon stock and stock upon bond—huge monopolies which were stifling independent business and private enterprise.

There was no power under Heaven that could protect the people against that sort of thing except a people's Government at Washington. All that this Administration has done, all that it proposes to do—and this it does propose to do—is to use every power and authority of the Federal Government to protect the commerce of America from the selfish forces which ruined it.

Always, month in and month out, during these three and a half years, your Government has had but one sign on its desk—"Seek only the greater good of the greater number of Americans." And in appraising the record, remember two things. First, this Administration was called upon to act after a previous Administration and all the combined forces of private enterprise had failed. Secondly, in spite of all the demand for speed, the complexity of the problem and all the vast sums of money involved, we have had no Teapot Dome.

We found when we came to Washington in 1933, that the business and industry of the Nation were like a train which had gone off the rails into a ditch. Our first job was to get it out of the ditch and start it up the track again as far as the repair shops. Our next job was to make repairs—on the broken axles which had gotten it off the road, on the engine which had been worn down by gross misuse.

What was it that the average businessman wanted Government to do for him—to do immediately in 1933?

1. Stop deflation and falling prices—and we did it.
2. Increase the purchasing power of his customers who were industrial workers in the cities—and we did it.
3. Increase the purchasing power of his customers on the farms—and we did it.
4. Decrease interest rates, power rates and transportation rates—and we did it.
5. Protect him from the losses due to crime, bank robbers, kidnappers, blackmailers—and we did it.

How did we do it? By a sound monetary policy which raised prices. By reorganizing the banks of the Nation and insuring their deposits. By bringing the business men of the Nation together and encouraging them to pay higher wages, to shorten working hours, and to discourage that minority among their own members who were engaging in unfair competition and unethical business practices.

Through the AAA, through our cattle-buying program, through our program of drought relief and flood relief, through the Farm Credit Administration, we raised the income of the customers of business who lived on the farms. By our program to provide work for the unemployed, by our CCC camps, and other measures, greater purchasing power was given to those who lived in our cities.

Money began going round again. The dollars paid out by Government were spent in the stores and shops of the Nation; and spent again to the wholesaler; and spent again to the factory; and spent again to the wage earner; and then spent again in another store and shop. The wheels of business began to turn again; the train was back on the rails.

Mind you, it did not get out of the ditch itself, it was hauled out by your Government.

And we hauled it along the road. PWA, WPA, both provided normal and useful employment for hundreds of thousands of work-ers. Hundreds of millions of dollars got into circulation when we liquidated the assets of closed banks through the Reconstruction Finance Corporation; millions more when we loaned money for home building and home financing through the Federal Housing program; hundreds of millions more in loans and grants to enable municipalities to build needed improvements; hundreds of millions more through the CCC camps.

I am not going to talk tonight about how much our program to provide work for the unemployed meant to the Nation as a whole. That cannot be measured in dollars and cents. It can be measured only in terms of the preservation of the families of America.

But so far as business goes, it can be measured in terms of sales made and goods moving.

The train of American business is moving ahead.

But you people know what I mean when I say it is clear that if the train is to run smoothly again the cars will have to be loaded more evenly. We have made a definite start in getting the train loaded more evenly, in order that axles may not break again.

For example, we have provided a sounder and cheaper money market and a sound banking and securities system. You business men know how much legitimate business you lost in the old days because your customers were robbed by fake securities or impoverished by shaky banks.

By our monetary policy we have kept prices up and lightened the burden of debt. It is easier to get credit. It is easier to repay.

We have encouraged cheaper power for the small factory owner to lower his cost of production.

We have given the business man cheaper transportation rates.

But above all, we have fought to break the deadly grip which monopoly has in the past been able to fasten on the business of the Nation.

Because we cherished our system of private property and free enterprise and were determined to preserve it as the foundation of our traditional American system, we recalled the warning of Thomas Jefferson that "widespread poverty and concentrated wealth cannot long endure side by side in a democracy."

Our job was to preserve the American ideal of economic as well as political democracy, against the abuse of concentration of economic power that had been insidiously growing up among us in the past fifty years, particularly during the twelve years of preceding Administrations. Free economic enterprise was being weeded out at an alarming pace.

During those years of false prosperity and during the more recent years of exhausting depression, one business after another, one small corporation after another, their resources depleted, had failed or had fallen into the lap of a bigger competitor.

A dangerous thing was happening. Half of the industrial corporate wealth of the country had come under the control of less than two hundred huge corporations. That is not all. These huge corporations in some cases did not even try to compete with each other. They themselves were tied together by interlocking directors, interlocking bankers, interlocking lawyers.

This concentration of wealth and power has been built upon other people's money, other people's business, other people's labor. Under this concentration independent business was allowed to exist only by sufferance. It has been a menace to the social system as well as to the economic system which we call American democracy.

There is no excuse for it in the cold terms of industrial efficiency.

There is no excuse for it from the point of view of the average investor.

There is no excuse for it from the point of view of the independent business man.

I believe, I have always believed, and I will always believe in private enterprise as the backbone of economic well-being in the United States.

But I know, and you know, and every independent business man who has had to struggle against the competition of monopolies knows, that this concentration of economic power in all-embracing corporations does not represent private enterprise as we Americans cherish it and propose to foster it. On the contrary, it represents private enterprise which has become a kind of private government, a power unto itself—a regimentation of other people's money and other people's lives.

Back in Kansas I spoke about bogey-men and fairy tales which the real Republican leaders, many of whom are part of this concentrated power, are using to spread fear among the American people.

You good people have heard about these fairy tales and bogey-men too. You have heard about how antagonistic to business this Administration is supposed to be. You have heard all about the dangers which the business of America is supposed to be facing if this Administration continues.

The answer to that is the record of what we have done. It was this Administration which saved the system of private profit and free enterprise after it had been dragged to the brink of ruin by these same leaders who now try to scare you.

Look at the advance in private business in the last three and a half years; and read there what we think about private business.

Today for the first time in seven years the banker, the storekeeper, the small factory owner, the industrialist, can all sit back and enjoy the company of their own ledgers. They are in the black. That is where we want them to be; that is where our policies aim them to be; that is where we intend them to be in the future.

Some of these people really forget how sick

they were. But I know how sick they were. I have their fever charts. I know how the knees of all of our rugged individualists were trembling four years ago and how their hearts fluttered. They came to Washington in great numbers. Washington did not look like a dangerous bureaucracy to them then. Oh, no! It looked like an emergency hospital. All of the distinguished patients wanted two things—a quick hypodermic to end the pain and a course of treatment to cure the disease. They wanted them in a hurry; we gave them both. And now most of the patients seem to be doing very nicely. Some of them are even well enough to throw their crutches at the doctor.

The struggle against private monopoly is a struggle for, and not against, American business. It is a struggle to preserve individual enterprise and economic freedom.

I believe in individualism. I believe in it in the arts, the sciences and professions. I believe in it in business. I believe in individualism in all of these things—up to the point where the individualist starts to operate at the expense of society. The overwhelming majority of American business men do not believe in it beyond that point. We have all suffered in the past from individualism run wild. Society has suffered and business has suffered.

Believing in the solvency of business, the solvency of farmers and the solvency of workers, I believe also in the solvency of Government. Your Government is solvent.

The net Federal debt today is lower in proportion to the income of the Nation and in proportion to the wealth of the Nation than it was on March fourth, 1933.

In the future it will become lower still because with the rising tide of national income and national wealth, the very causes of our emergency spending are starting to disappear. Government expenditures are coming down and Government income is going up. The opportunities for private enterprise will continue to expand.

The people of America have no quarrel with business. They insist only that the power of concentrated wealth shall not be abused.

We have come through a hard struggle to preserve democracy in America. Where other Nations in other parts of the world have lost that fight, we have won.

The business men of America and all other citizens have joined in a firm resolve to hold the fruits of that victory, to cling to the old ideals and old fundamentals upon which America has grown great. ∾

An Economic Bill of Rights (11 January 1944)

If ever there was a time to subordinate individual or group selfishness to the national good, that time is now. Disunity at home—bickerings, self-seeking partisanship, stoppages of work, inflation, business as usual, luxury as usual—these are the influences which can undermine the morale of the brave men ready to die at the front for us here.

Those who are doing most of the complaining are not deliberately striving to sabotage the national war effort. They are laboring under the delusion that the time is past when we must make prodigious sacrifices—that the war is already won and we can begin to slacken off. But the dangerous folly of that point of view can be measured by the distance that separates our troops from their ultimate objectives in Berlin and Tokyo—and by the sum of all the perils that lie along the way.

Let us remember the lessons of 1918. In the summer of that year the tide turned in favor of the Allies. But this Government did not relax. In fact, our national effort was stepped up. In August, 1918, the draft age limits were broadened from 21–31 to 18–45. the President called for "Force to the utmost," and his call was heeded. And in November, only three months later, Germany surrendered.

That is the way to fight and win a war—all out—and not with half-an-eye on the battle-fronts abroad and the other eye-and-a-half on personal, selfish, or political interests here at home.

Therefore, in order to concentrate all our energies and resources on winning the war, and to maintain a fair and stable economy at home, I recommend that the Congress adopt:

1. A realistic tax law—which will tax all unreasonable profits, both individual and corporate, and reduce the ultimate cost of the war to our sons and daughters. The tax bill now under consideration by the Congress does not begin to meet this test.

2. A continuation of the law for the renegotiation of war contracts—which will prevent exorbitant profits and assure fair prices to the Government. For two long years I have pleaded with the Congress to take undue profits out of the war.

3. A cost of food law—which will enable the Government (a) to place a reasonable floor under the prices the farmer may expect for his production, and (b) to place a ceiling on the prices a consumer will have to pay for the food he buys. This should apply to necessities only; and will require public funds to carry out. It will cost in appropriations about 1 per cent of the present annual cost of the war.

4. Early enactment of the stabilization statute of October, 1942. This expires June 30, 1944, and if it is not extended well in advance the country might just as well expect price chaos by summer. We cannot have stabilization by wishful thinking. We must take positive action to maintain the integrity of the American dollar.

5. A national service law—which, for the duration of the war, will prevent strikes, and with certain appropriate exceptions, will make available for war production or for any other essential services every able-bodied adult in the nation.

These five measures together form a just and equitable whole. I would not recommend a national service law unless the other laws were passed to keep down the cost of living, to share equitably the burdens of taxation, to hold the stabilization line, and to prevent undue profits.

The Federal Government already has the basic power to draft capital and property of all kinds for war purposes on a basis of just compensation.

As you know, I have for three years hesitated to recommend a national service act. Today, however, I am convinced of its necessity. Although I believe that we and our Allies can win the war without such a measure, I am certain that nothing less than total mobilization of all our resources of manpower and capital will guarantee an earlier victory, and reduce the toll of suffering and sorrow and blood.

I have received a joint recommendation for this law from the heads of the War Department, the Navy Department, and the Maritime Commission. These are the men who bear responsibility for the procurement of the necessary arms and equipment, and for the successful prosecution of the war in the field. They say:

When the very life of the nation is in peril the responsibility for service is common to all men and women. In such a time there can be no discrimination between the men and women who are assigned by the Government to its defense at the battle front and the men and women assigned to produce the vital materials essential to successful military operations. A prompt enactment of a national service law would be merely an expression of the universality of this responsibility.

It is our duty now to begin to lay plans and determine the strategy for the winning of a lasting peace and the establishment of an American standard of living higher than ever before known. We cannot be content, no matter how high the general standard of living may be, if some fraction of our people—whether it be one-third or one-fifth or one-tenth—is ill-fed, ill-clothed, ill-housed, and insecure.

This Republic had its beginning, and grew to its present strength, under the protection of certain inalienable political rights—among them the right of free speech, free press, free worship, trial by jury, freedom from unreasonable searches and seizures. They were our rights to life and liberty.

As our nation has growing size and stature, however—as our industrial economy expanded—these political rights proved inadequate to assure us equality in the pursuit of happiness.

We have come to a clear realization of the fact that true individual freedom cannot exist without economic security and independence. "Necessitous men are not free men." People who are hungry and out of a job are the stuff of which dictatorships are made.

In our day these economic truths have become accepted as self-evident. We have accepted, so to speak, a second Bill of Rights under which a new basis of security and prosperity can be established for all, regardless of station, race or creed.

Among these are:

The right to a useful and remunerative job in the industries or shops or farms or mines of the nation;

The right to earn enough to provide adequate food and clothing and recreation;

The right of every farmer to raise and sell his products at a return which will give him and his family a decent living;

The right of every business man, large and small, to trade in an atmosphere of freedom from unfair competition and domination by monopolies at home or abroad;

The right of every family to a decent home;

The right to adequate medical care and the opportunity to achieve and enjoy good health;

The right to adequate protection from the economic fears of old age, sickness, accident and unemployment;

The right to a good education.

All of these rights spell security. And after this war is won we must be prepared to move forward, in the implementation of these rights, to new goals of human happiness and well-being.

America's own rightful place in the world depends in large part upon how fully these and similar rights have been carried into practice for our citizens. For unless there is security here at home there cannot be lasting peace in the world. ⌒

Primary Sources

Roosevelt, Franklin D. *On Our Way*. New York: Da Capo Press, 1973.

———. *Rendezvous with Destiny*. New York: Dryden Press, 1944.

Rosenman, Samuel I. *The Public Papers and Addresses of Franklin D. Roosevelt*. Introduction and explanatory notes by Roosevelt. New York: Russell and Russell, 1969.

Secondary Sources

Fusfeld, Daniel Roland. *The Economic Thought of F.D.R. and the Origins of the New Deal*. New York: Columbia University Press, 1956.

Rosen, Elliot. *Hoover, Roosevelt and the Brains Trust: From Depression to New Deal*. New York: Columbia University Press, 1977.

Tugwell, Guy Rexford. *The Democratic Roosevelt: A Biography of Franklin D. Roosevelt*. Garden City, N.Y.: Doubleday, 1957.

———. *Franklin D. Roosevelt, Architect of an Era*. New York: Macmillan, 1967.

———. *Roosevelt's Revolution, The First Year: A Personal Perspective*. New York: Macmillan, 1977.

Part V

The Postwar Period: Change versus Continuity, 1945–2000

T HIS PERIOD began with the United States at the height of its power and influence in the world. No economy approached the United States in wealth or productivity at the end of World War II, and only the Soviet Union could claim military power in any way close to that of the United States. Such a level of dominance could not be sustained, however, in part because the United States set out to help reconstruct war-ravaged economies in Europe and Japan.

By the end of the 1960s, the United States was being overtaken by these newly modernized economies and was struggling with the burden of fighting an unpopular war in Southeast Asia. As first the war and then social and economic conditions revived domestic political debate, questions arose about the extent to which the United States was actually in "decline" as a great power, and if so, where responsibility should be placed and what the remedy might be. "Liberalism" got the bulk of the blame. By the 1990s, a whole new range of political issues and ideas seemed to be taking shape as alternatives. But some of these had much in common with unexpectedly tenacious elements of that durable and characteristically American way of thinking, liberalism.

As we reach this current period in the evolution of American political thought and begin to think about the future, it helps to gain perspective by first looking back at the enduring themes and conflicts of the past. What is immediately striking is how many of them continue into the present and seem very likely to shape the future. Today's issues and problems raise questions that have been raised before, and thinkers who address them draw heavily, not just rhetorically, from the ideas of their predecessors.

Continuities in American Political Thought

Three sets of questions run through all of American political thought. They are answered from distinctive but continuing perspectives in different eras. Thus they provide a way of organizing our approach to this very complex and lively period that is superior to a chronology of decades.

1. The first set of questions has to do with the character of economic development and the basic pattern of distribution of the rewards of the economy. How should the American economy be structured, and how should the burdens and

benefits of this economy be distributed among owners, investors, workers, and others? What, if anything, does the concept of equality or economic justice require in the way of distribution of wealth and income? This central set of questions is sometimes obscured by highly visible diversions, such as wars or racial or cultural tensions, but it ultimately returns to the forefront. Buried within it, but never to be ignored, is the strong possibility of class-based conflict. The "haves" tend to dismiss this aspect of the question, deny its existence, and/or chastise those who think in class terms as promoting "class warfare." The "have-nots" are far more aware of its implications, but even they may not identify with class as their principal focus.

2. The second set of questions has to do with the relationship between individuality and individual rights on the one hand and the community as a whole on the other. Are the individual's rights paramount and the rights of the community always secondary? Or does individual self-realization imply interdependence and belonging, such that the community has legitimate claims for loyalty and adherence to certain values and behavioral standards? Involved here are the nature and definition of both the "democracy" that can develop within such a society and the basic cultural values that will be central to social life.

Two connected subissues give this set of questions special conflict potential. One is race and gender relations. Race, particularly the conflict first generated by slavery, is the basic fault line of American politics, and gender issues are only somewhat more muted. Race and gender issues tend to blur class-based conflicts, although ethnicity and cultural values sometimes serve as surrogates for class.

The second subissue is the enduring tension between the central values of freedom and equality. Here, class conflict readily appears as one of the flash points, particularly when the

distribution of wealth and income is at stake. For the "have-nots" to gain greater equality, the "haves" must accept what they view as a loss of freedom. Not all freedom versus equality issues involve economic distributions, of course. Questions of race and gender, and cultural and other diversity, pose similar conflicts.

3. The third set of questions focuses on the proper role of government in addressing these basic issues and conflicts. What kind of responsibility should government have with respect to the economy? How far should government go in promoting racial or gender equality? Included are issues about the scale and responsiveness of the bureaucracy that develops as government functions are multiplied. The United States is a country born of early tax revolt, and Americans have always had profound skepticism about the capabilities and efficiency of governments.

Addressing the Key Questions: The Heritage of the Past

These questions are often addressed as if they were separate and soluble one at a time by concerned people; Americans are distinctively "single issue" oriented. But the more deeply one analyzes the sources and character of the problems raised by these questions, the more connected and interdependent they appear to be—and the more grounded they are in underlying cultural assumptions about human nature and the good society. This way of addressing the key questions amounts to a comprehensive worldview or ideology.

The basic American worldview or ideology is, of course, liberalism. With the individual and the notion of individual rights, particularly property rights, as the cornerstone, the thinkers of earlier periods built and justified a liberal state. The Constitution and Bill of Rights embody these assumptions and values and add the principles of contract, freedom over equality, limited government, and the rule of law. Striving by the rational, self-interested individual in the private sector, with all the opportunities of the free economic market, was relied on to fulfill all individual and social goals.

The views of some in this early period —notably John Adams and Alexander Hamilton—were substantially conservative. They were unwilling to trust the mass of individuals even to serve their own self-interest and insisted on a strong government that could assert the primacy of the organic community and direct individual behavior into appropriate channels. At the time, they represented the principal challenge to early liberalism and helped shape its basic orientation. Challenges from the left were raised among the masses of people, but were far less visible or audible at the elite level.

With the rise of abolitionism and feminism in the nineteenth century, claims for greater equality and democracy were more often heard, but only occasionally in unison. After the Civil War and the transformation to industrialism, farmers and workers were added to the ranks of dissenting or protesting groups —but also as "single issue" advocates, rather than in an integrated movement. Liberals and conservatives tended to close ranks as a coherent establishment that, despite some internal difference, could stand firm against the excesses of popular aspirations.

The characteristic American opposition to the status quo therefore became *populism* —protest by ordinary citizens against the actions of big business or big government that are seen as denying equality, traditional individual rights and opportunities, or both. Such movements are fragile, usually held together only by opposition to what is happening and not by a shared vision or program for the future. Their component elements are more aware of their differences than of their commonalities and readily disrupt coalitions, ac-

cept partial successes, or both. Populism can tend *either* to the left, toward greater equality and democracy, or to the right, toward authoritarian assertion of past standards, beliefs, and practices.

In the first decades of the twentieth century, the liberal-conservative establishment took a turn that has confused people who seek consistent labels for ideas ever since. Abandoning its classical posture of primacy for the free market and limited or laissez-faire government, the new corporate liberalism of Theodore Roosevelt and Woodrow Wilson embraced the Hamiltonian use of the central government as a modern necessity. Those who held to the classical liberal laissez-faire position now became known as *conservatives*. True or organic conservatives fought continuously for their traditional label, with little visibility or success.

The new growth-promoting, economy-managing, and social-welfare-oriented establishment became *liberals*. There were differences in priority among them, roughly but not completely following Republican-Democratic party lines: those who emphasized growth first were *corporate liberals;* those who put social welfare claims first were *welfare liberals*. But the real differences were between the classical liberals (the newly named *conservatives*), who retained a strong minority position in the Republican party, and the new corporate-welfare *liberals,* the liberal-conservative establishment, which dominated both major parties.

Avoiding the Key Questions in the Post–World War II Era

The period began with a heavy emphasis on the values and beliefs that all Americans were assumed to share and a determined refusal to acknowledge that there were *any* questions that remained to be dealt with in the United States. The triumph of American values and practices was demonstrated by the great victory of World War II and the dominant status of the United States after the war. Americans turned inward, toward individualism and material achievements, in order to make up for time lost during the war.

There was one major obstacle to realization of the American dream at home and peaceful prosperity abroad. Communism and the Soviet Union appeared to threaten the United States and "the free world" both militarily and as an ideology attractive to Third World countries and industrial workers generally. This led to increased emphasis in the United States on shared values and beliefs, and even stronger denial that there were really grounds for class conflict or complaints about things American. Whatever existed in the United States was taken as the universal standard, for example as the proper definition of democracy or the model of a benevolent economy. Officially, the United States saw itself in a "battle for men's minds" throughout the world.

Characteristic of the first fifteen years of the postwar period was the emergence of a "consensus interpretation" about wisdom of scholars and citizens alike. This thesis held that all Americans subscribed so strongly and often unconsciously to the core values of liberalism that there was no real disagreement within the United States. In his widely accepted *The Liberal Tradition in America* (1955), for example, Louis Hartz argued that liberalism reigned unchallenged from either left or right because the lack of a feudal past precluded a social base for either socialism or conservatism. In Europe, classes founded on the remains of feudalism (the aristocracy, the middle-class bourgeoisie, and the peasant-proletariat working class) gave rise to conservatism, liberalism, and socialism. Lacking feudalism and such contrasts, the United States had only the liberal middle, which, allowed to remain unchallenged, therefore lost its self-con-

sciousness, clear justifications, and principled edge.

Hartz foresaw and was concerned about two possibilities. One was that liberalism at home might devolve into irrational and compulsive insistence on acceptance of whatever existed in the American past. The other was that liberalism's principles might be so poorly understood by Americans that they would not be effective advocates for liberal democracy in the worldwide "battle for men's minds." His image of a vast and unchallenged consensus among all Americans may seem naïve, elite oriented, or even deliberately manipulative from today's perspective, but it was broadly accepted in its time.

The consensus thesis was articulated in different but supportive ways by two other major scholars in this era. Daniel Boorstin asserted in *The Genius of American Politics* (1953) that Americans, feeling themselves to have been "born free," had never felt the need for an articulated political theory that would contrast American beliefs and practices with those of other systems. In other words, because all Americans agreed on what to do and how to do it, why bother with developing a rationale for it?

Daniel Bell joined the chorus with a major book entitled *The End of Ideology* (1953), in which he argued that the material benefits of modern capitalism had been so widely shared that there were no longer any major economic issues between classes or groups of people. Therefore there was no more need for ideologies that would serve to organize and express the claims of "have-not" movements.

There cannot be many times in American history when such an authoritative and widely accepted interpretation has been so completely wrong. Today, the question might better be: How could that impression have gained such widespread credibility in the first place? The inescapable fact is that the civil rights movement—heir to black abolitionism—had been at work in the courts and in the lunchrooms, bus terminals, schools, and other public places of the nation throughout this period. African-American leaders and major white thinkers as well were articulating the ideas and writing the documents that would shape the American future for the next three decades. The key questions of American political thought were about to reassert themselves in a compelling manner.

Addressing the Key Questions in the Current Period

RACE AND GENDER EQUALITY — AND THE VIETNAM WAR

This continuing question was restored to the national agenda by the civil rights movement in the 1950s. Initially, the cause was led by the litigation strategy of the National Association for the Advancement of Colored People (NAACP), originally founded by W.E.B. Du Bois. More militant and direct action efforts were mounted by southern blacks, working through the Southern Christian Leadership Council (SCLC), the Congress of Racial Equality (CORE), and the Student Non-Violent Coordinating Committee (SNCC).

A leading spokesperson for desegregation, voting rights, and civil rights generally was the Reverend Martin Luther King Jr. Continuing the tradition of Frederick Douglass and W.E.B. Du Bois, King mobilized blacks and whites in behalf of equality of opportunity and full citizenship for black people. His famous "I Have a Dream" speech at a rally of more than a quarter million people in Washington, D.C., in 1963 offered a stirring vision of an American society where people were judged by the content of their character rather than the color of their skin.

In a more militant and equally famous letter, recalling Thoreau's "On Civil Disobedi-

ence" and written from jail where he was awaiting trial for leading a demonstration, King defended the moral right of blacks to defy unjust laws. In the context of the times, however, King was a relative moderate. Malcolm X of the Nation of Islam and the Black Power movement of the late 1960s recalled the black nationalists of earlier decades, regularly threatening violence in self-defense rather than the passive nonviolent strategy of King's model.

As the civil right movement took shape and gained momentum, white college students in the North at first joined in support and then sought to develop their own organizations and programs. The leading organization was Students for a Democratic Society (SDS), which issued perhaps the most widely known manifesto of the decade, the "Port Huron Statement," at its founding convention in 1962. SDS made a broad critique of American society, indicting it for promoting militarism and the Cold War, denying democracy and civil rights, failing to cope with poverty amid affluence, and particularly for excessive bureaucracy. At the outset, however, the SDS critique was strictly a liberal one: The country was acting on the wrong priorities and policies, and the character of the economy and basic values were not mentioned.

The universities were a principal target for SDS-sponsored reforms; they were seen as captives of national military and bureaucratic purposes and as unresponsive to both moral standards and students' needs. By 1965, SDS had taken on a major new responsibility, that of organizing the student movement against the Vietnam war. Again, colleges and universities were implicated, in part because they cooperated with the war effort by conducting military research, and in part because most of them refused to take public stands to the effect that the war was immoral.

Soon, SDS was a frantically active national organization of hundreds of thousands of student members, with several hundred chapters on campuses across the country. Its programs included civil rights efforts, antipoverty neighborhood organizing in urban areas, university reforms—and most of all, the antiwar movement. A major portion of the civil rights movement, led by Reverend King, also called for a broad antipoverty program and began actively to oppose the war. As more and more people came to see poverty, war, and racial discrimination as connected issues—products of imperatives flowing from the U.S. economy and basic values—their critique deepened and became more radical. The label *socialism* was heard in public for the first time in thirty years, and often favorably.

In an interesting parallel to nineteenth-century experience, a third major movement was reborn in the early 1960s: feminism. Initially, Betty Friedan's *The Feminine Mystique* (1962) reflected the frustration and isolation of the middle-class housewife, and like Susan B. Anthony decades earlier, demanded full participation for women in all aspects of American economic and social life. The rebirth of feminism got a major boost from women SDS activists, who saw their male colleagues failing to practice the gender equality that should be a cornerstone of a democratic society. Sounding more like Emma Goldman than the suffragists, these militant feminists developed their own radical analyses including first a new socialist feminism and ultimately an ecological feminism—ecofeminism.

THE CULTURAL-POLITICAL BACKLASH

Too much attention can be paid to those on the change-seeking side of the great question of equality. The various militant movements and many demonstrations for racial and gender equality, particularly the antiwar movement, certainly captured the media headlines for a period of years. Meanwhile, even deeper currents of change in lifestyles, music, and sexual relations were running strongly. The fundamental values and practices of American life seemed to be in upheaval, with change the dominant theme everywhere.

But the fact is that a substantial majority of Americans was opposed, often deeply and bitterly, not only to the tactics but also to the goals of these movements. They were appalled at the televised scenes of demonstrators clashing violently with police and acting in disregard for established authority. Disrespect for the military and the American flag, and violation of traditional values and lifestyle standards, helped set in motion a cultural-political backlash that began to wane only in the 1990s.

As early as 1966, Ronald Reagan won the governorship in California on a platform of controlling dissent and restoring traditional values. In 1968 George Wallace (the American party candidate) and Richard Nixon widely outpolled the Democratic candidate by calling for law and order and the values and standards of the past. Thinly veiled racist appeals, direct opposition to feminism, and patriotic symbols began to be used effectively to blunt the momentum of those seeking to expand equality and stop the war. Greater willingness on the part of the police and National Guard to use force against black and antiwar militants was applauded—and it helped reduce the numbers and self-confidence of the change seekers.

By the mid-1970s, the backlash had succeeded in stalling all the movements that had been so strong a decade earlier. Only feminism had significant energy left, but not enough to carry the Equal Rights Amendment to the Constitution to ratification in the requisite number of states. The much less radical environmentalist movement (see below) became the principal source of change in public policy. With the election of Ronald Reagan as president in 1980, the backlash was validated at the highest possible level, and the process of "Undoing the Sixties" was initiated.

Reagan himself was the principal spokesperson for the revival of classical laissez-faire liberalism, expansion of the military, and restoration of traditional American values. Rarely has a president so effectively dominated the media and so well employed the basic cultural symbols to promote public support. But Reagan was not alone in this effort. Many former liberals rallied to the cultural backlash cause, documenting the failures of liberalism and arguing the merits of free-market solutions and individual responsibility. In particular, African-American conservatives such as Clarence Thomas, Shelby Steele, Stephen Carter, and Glenn Loury gained special visibility for arguing against compensatory policies such as affirmative action on the grounds that they preserved a "victim mentality" and undermined individual responsibility.

THE ECONOMIC QUESTION — AND POPULISM

The question of equity in the distribution of wealth, income, and economic opportunities generally has been fundamental to American political thought. Madison provided a definitive and widely accepted argument in *Federalist No. 10,* in which he made clear that the intent of the Framers of the Constitution was to protect the "haves" from the redistributive intentions of the "have-nots." Hamilton's program as secretary of the treasury made clear that the new government would be a willing ally of the financial and merchant establishment.

For several decades, the issue seemed to be whether the "have-nots" had a moral claim to a larger share of the nation's wealth. The Unitarian minister Orestes Brownson challenged the emerging industrial capitalism in 1840 on behalf of workers, demanding to know how they could be denied their fair share of what they produced. The Gilded Age answer came in 1884 from William Graham Sumner, who refused to accept the idea that any social class owed anything to another.

By this time, the question was starting to become an openly political one in which class interests were well recognized. Unions struggled to organize workers despite determined resistance from employers, and small farmers were building a new political party to seek freer credit and better prices. Perhaps the strongest call for class mobilization came ultimately from the socialist trade union leader Eugene Debs in 1905.

The strength of the socialist movement in the early years of the century actually helped enable the liberal-conservative establishment to achieve its shift from strict laissez faire to the corporate-welfare brand of liberalism. Accommodation and harmony of interests were stressed, until the patriotic fervor of World War I muted dissent. Later, the dominant explanation, dramatically confirmed in the New Deal and World War II, was that an active national government could promote growth and manage the economy for the greater benefit of all. The American economy seemed so productive that the United States could fight a war in Vietnam and a War on Poverty at home at the same time.

By the 1970s, however, images of harmony and affluence were giving way to inflation, unemployment, and sustained hardship for many people. The global economy was changing in fundamental ways as corporations moved to low-wage areas, adopted new technologies, and downsized to cut costs. The economic question—initially restoring growth and then equity of distribution—has dominated politics since the late 1970s. The Catholic bishops' pastoral letter "Economic Justice for All" (1986) is a very good example of the revival of moral thinking about the distribution of wealth and income in this period.

This issue got a major boost in the late 1980s from the repeated release of new data on which classes had benefited from the apparently sustained recovery of the 1980s. It was noted first that the national debt had been quadrupled by the most conservative presidents of the century, with resulting limits on future social services for the needy. Next, the data showed clearly that the wealthiest strata of the population had benefited greatly, and the lower strata had actually lost income, during the 1980s. National government policy had contributed to one of the greatest surges of upward redistribution in American history—one that rivaled anything known in the age of the "Robber Barons" of the 1890s.

This news set off another of the characteristic waves of populist protest that mark American political thought. From the 1890s on, farmers and workers have sought to organize against the power of big business and big government and to demand their individual rights and equal economic opportunities. For almost a century, this popular base supported social welfare legislation, political reforms, and downward economic redistribution.

In the 1990s, however, the ranks of populists were split by the cultural backlash. Those most concerned with the restoration of traditional values, particularly the Christian Right, tended to continue in support of conservative leaders. Others who might have joined a popular protest movement had such low confidence in government as a vehicle for serving their interests that they essentially gave up. A relatively small proportion (even smaller when low voting turnout is considered) ended up in support of the more redistributive candidates and arguments. The principal source of "progressive" political argument and public policy was thus diffused and ineffective at a key moment.

THE GOVERNMENT-BUREAUCRACY QUESTION

The major questions and the issues involved in them all sooner or later revolve around the question of how government is to be empowered to serve which goals. The issue goes beyond the abstract one of whether in a good society government should be *active* or *passive*. If active, in whose interests? On behalf of elites and/or the wealthy? Or on behalf of the poor and needy, who have no other means of achieving their goals? If passive, with what assumptions about how the private sector will work and for whom? Will the free market reward all equally according to their efforts, or will it advantage primarily those who already have the most?

The centrality of government as a potential vehicle for achieving or blocking social goals has always made its actions controversial and its management a matter of conflict. Control of the government becomes an end in itself because it is the key to so many other goals. Because government absorbs so much in taxes, seems so threatening, and appears so readily subject to control by one's opponents, there is a continuing tendency to believe the worst about its leaders and institutions, or their efficiency.

During the New Deal and World War II, most Americans thought highly of their government; it was, after all, the engine of economic recovery and the means of fighting the good war against German fascism and Japanese imperialism. For many people, however, confidence in government began to drop sharply in the 1960s and 1970s. Ultimately, an ever-expanding government bureaucracy began to seem like the necessary expression of liberalism, and to share the blame for those changes that people disliked. Government stubbornly and undemocratically prolonged an unjust war, or government failed to firmly prosecute the war and control dissent at home, depending on one's perspective. The Watergate scandal and official cover-up—and a number of apparent subsequent violations of law and associated cover-ups—gave rise to widespread cynicism about government and politicians and public employees generally. Government itself seemed to be the problem, or at least one of the major obstacles to realizing a better world.

The call to "reinvent" government, consistent with the "flattening" of hierarchies in corporations, thus fell on highly fertile ground. Political candidates actually ran campaigns *against* the government in which they sought office. Others sought to provide quick government-change answers for complex problems that had defied solution for generations. Emphasizing means over ends—methods and practices of governments over goals and purposes—the reinventing movement explicitly disclaimed concern for *what* government did in favor of *how* it did it. In these respects, it was reminiscent of the "scientific management" movement of the early twentieth century and many others in our long history of government reorganization efforts. But it was also more fundamental, indicative of a deep feeling that the times required basic changes in values, ideas, and institutions.

BEYOND LEFT AND RIGHT — AND ENVIRONMENTALISM

By the 1990s, the mix of issues and problems facing Americans seemed to be posing new questions and demanding new answers. The old ideologies—conservatism, liberalism, and socialism—seemed to be inapplicable as sources of solutions; they addressed a century-old industrial society. The external focus and internal unity compelled by the Cold War were no longer available to deflect attention from domestic problems. Race and gender issues were part of the reason, but so were new economic and social realities, new cultural differences, and the new set of environmental issues.

The environmental movement had its recent origins in the publication of Rachel Carson's *Silent Spring* in 1962. It had deep roots

in the American experience, however, reaching back to the early deists, naturalists such as Thoreau, and the conservationists of the Progressive era. Originally, revived environmentalism was a broad middle-class movement that sought to conserve scarce natural resources and prevent further damage to the earth's vital ecosystems. Despite these modest goals, environmentalism was controversial. Advocates of economic growth argued that regulatory and other requirements were making economic development costly and slow. Environmentalists countered that sustainable economic development required a balance between industrial expansion and protection for the planet's life-support systems.

The great importance of environmentalism today lies in the two ways that its version of science (*ecology*) serves to catalyze distinctly different kinds of economic and political thought. First, the new notion that humans must live with and subject to nature, rather than attempt to dominate nature, carries profound implications. It challenges the very idea of nature as a set of objects to be manipulated for the benefit of (some) humans and (indirectly) the idea of dominance by some people over others. Racial, cultural, and gender discrimination, and capitalism itself, are ultimately called into question.

Second, inherent in this manner of thinking about nature is a fundamental change in epistemology—the means by which people recognize knowledge and truth. The way of knowing that developed during the British Enlightenment (*positivism*) asserted a fact-value distinction. Facts have testable, demonstrable reality enabling subjects to know objects by their positive features, the empirical sense data flowing from the object to the subject. Values are intangible subjective preferences, lacking real-world references or provability and therefore are relegated to a lesser status.

The purpose of this way of knowing was

to grasp the laws of nature in order to predict and control the natural world for human benefit. It was only a small step from that point to using this way of knowing to organize and control economies, societies, and human relations generally. Modern Western civilization, and particularly liberalism and capitalism (and socialism), rests almost entirely on this nearly 500-year-old epistemology.

The holistic perspective of the new ecology sees the human and natural worlds together and denies the fact-value and subject-object distinctions. Nature is alive, humans are integrated with nature, and reality is known through seeing facts and values, feelings and things, as extensions of one another. There is a far greater and wholly legitimate role for ways of thinking formerly dismissed as mystical, merely spiritual, or the quaint folklore of lesser cultures.

This new openness translates into different standards of "science," different human relationships, and potentially the epistemological basis for what advocates have come to call a *paradigm shift* or fundamental change in worldview. The call for a social-ecological revolution by the ecofeminist Carolyn Merchant in this collection is a good example of this approach. Whether in time it will actually catalyze such profound change depends as much on economic and social conditions as on the efforts of political thinkers. But it appears that the potential is there, for the first time, to go beyond liberalism, capitalism, and industrial society—and thus truly "beyond left and right." ℰ

37. Martin Luther King Jr.

THE INSPIRATION that led eventually to the Black Power movement and to a growing student movement, the New Left, was the civil rights movement of the late 1950s and early 1960s. The leading figure of that movement, and perhaps of the entire change in national mood symbolized by the phrase "the Sixties," was the Reverend Martin Luther King Jr. (1919–68). As a minister in Montgomery, Alabama, King helped to organize the first black bus boycott (1955 to 1956) and was founder and president of the Southern Christian Leadership Conference (SCLC). The SCLC sponsored various civil rights demonstrations and activities, mobilizing blacks throughout the South and adhering to King's philosophy of nonviolent direct action. Through a combination of personal courage, moral eloquence, and religious appeal, King became the leading symbol of the early civil rights movement. He was assassinated in 1968 as he was about to begin building a coalition of all poor people, black and white, to seek economic justice and an end to the Vietnam war.

The selection presented here is King's "Letter from the Birmingham City Jail." This was written in April 1963, while King was under arrest in Birmingham, Alabama, for leading an unauthorized demonstration. ∿

Letter from the Birmingham City Jail (16 April 1963)

My dear Fellow Clergymen,

While confined here in the Birmingham City Jail, I came across your recent statement calling our present activities "unwise and untimely." Seldom, if ever, do I pause to answer criticism of my work and ideas. If I sought to answer all of the criticisms that cross my desk, my secretaries would be engaged in little else in the course of the day and I would have no time for constructive work. But since I feel that you are men of genuine goodwill and your criticisms are sincerely set forth, I would like to answer your statement in what I hope will be patient and reasonable terms. I think I should give the reason for my being in Birm-

SOURCE: Philadelphia: American Friends Service Committee, 1963. Editor's abridgement.

ingham, since you have been influenced by the argument of "outsiders coming in." I have the honor of serving as president of the Southern Christian Leadership Conference, an organization operating in every Southern state with headquarters in Atlanta, Georgia. We have some eighty-five affiliate organizations all across the South—one being the Alabama Christian Movement for Human Rights. Whenever necessary and possible we share staff, educational, and financial resources with our affiliates. Several months ago our local affiliate here in Birmingham invited us to be on call to engage in a nonviolent direct action program if such were deemed necessary. We readily consented and when the hour came we lived up to our promises. So I am here, along with several members of my staff, because we were invited here. I am here because I have basic organizational ties here. Beyond this, I am in Birmingham because injustice is here. Just as the eighth century prophets left their little villages and carried their "thus saith the Lord" far beyond the boundaries of their home town, and just as the Apostle Paul left his little village of Tarsus and carried the gospel of Jesus Christ to practically every hamlet and city of the Graeco-Roman world, I too am compelled to carry the gospel of freedom beyond my particular home town. Like Paul, I must constantly respond to the Macedonian call for aid.

Moreover, I am cognizant of the interrelatedness of all communities and states. I cannot sit idly by in Atlanta and not be concerned about what happens in Birmingham. Injustice anywhere is a threat to justice everywhere. We are caught in an inescapable network of mutuality tied in a single garment of destiny. Whatever affects one directly affects all indirectly. Never again can we afford to live with the narrow, provincial "outside agitator" idea. Anyone who lives inside the United States can never be considered an outsider anywhere in this country.

You deplore the demonstrations that are presently taking place in Birmingham. But I am sorry that your statement did not express a similar concern for the conditions that brought the demonstrations into being. I am sure that each of you would want to go beyond the superficial social analyst who looks merely at effects, and does not grapple with underlying causes. I would not hesitate to say that it is unfortunate that so-called demonstrations are taking place in Birmingham at this time, but I would say in more emphatic terms that it is even more unfortunate that the white power structure of this city left the Negro community with no other alternative.

In any nonviolent campaign there are four basic steps: (1) collection of the facts to determine whether injustices are alive; (2) negotia-

tion; (3) self-purification; and (4) direct action. We have gone through all of these steps in Birmingham. There can be no gainsaying of the fact that racial injustice engulfs this community; Birmingham is probably the most thoroughly segregated city in the United States. Its ugly record of police brutality is known in every section of this country. Its unjust treatment of Negroes in the courts is a notorious reality. There have been more unsolved bombings of Negro homes and churches in Birmingham than any city in this nation. These are the hard, brutal, and unbelievable facts. On the basis of these conditions Negro leaders sought to negotiate with the city fathers. But the political leaders consistently refused to engage in good faith negotiations. . . .

You may well ask, "Why direct action? Why sit-ins, marches, etc.? Isn't negotiation a better path?" You are exactly right in your call for negotiation. Indeed, this is the purpose of direct action. Nonviolent direct action seeks to create such a crisis and establish such creative tension that a community that has constantly refused to negotiate is forced to confront the issue. It seeks so to dramatize the issue that it can no longer be ignored. I just referred to the creation of tension as a part of the work of the nonviolent resister.

This may sound rather shocking. But I must confess that I am not afraid of the word tension. I have earnestly worked and preached against violent tension, but there is a type of constructive nonviolent tension that is necessary for growth. Just as Socrates felt that it was necessary to create a tension in the mind so that individuals could rise from the bondage of myths and half-truths to the unfettered realm of creative analysis and objective appraisal, we must see the need of having nonviolent gadflies to create the kind of tension in society that will help men rise from the dark depths of prejudice and racism to the majestic heights of understanding and brotherhood. So the purpose of the direct action is to create a situation so crisis-packed that it will inevitably open the door to negotiation. We, therefore, concur with you in your call for negotiation. Too long has our beloved Southland been bogged down in the tragic attempt to live in monologue rather than dialogue.

... My friends, I must say to you that we have not made a single gain in civil rights without determined legal and nonviolent pressure. History is the long and tragic story of the fact that privileged groups seldom give up their privileges voluntarily. Individuals may see the moral light and voluntarily give up their unjust posture; but as Reinhold Niebuhr has reminded us, groups are more immoral than individuals.

We know through painful experience that freedom is never voluntarily given by the oppressor; it must be demanded by the oppressed. Frankly I have never yet engaged in a direct action movement that was "well timed," according to the timetable of those who have not suffered unduly from the disease of segregation. For years now I have heard the word "Wait!" It rings in the ear of every Negro with a piercing familiarity. This "wait" has almost always meant "never." It has been a tranquilizing thalidomide, relieving the emotional stress for a moment, only to give birth to an ill-formed infant of frustration. We must come to see with the distinguished jurist of yesterday that "justice too long delayed is justice denied." We have waited for more than three hundred and forty years for our constitutional and God-given rights. The nations of Asia and Africa are moving with jet-like speed toward the goal of political independence, and we still creep at horse and buggy pace toward the gaining of a cup of coffee at a lunch counter.

I guess it is easy for those who have never felt the stinging darts of segregation to say wait. But when you have seen vicious mobs lynch your mothers and fathers at will and drown your sisters and brothers at whim; when you have seen hate-filled policemen curse, kick, brutalize, and even kill your black brothers and sisters with impunity; when you see the vast majority of your twenty million Negro brothers smothering in an air-tight cage of poverty in the midst of an affluent society; when you suddenly find your tongue twisted and your speech stammering as you seek to explain to your six-year-old daughter why she can't go to the public amusement park that has just been advertised on television, and see tears welling up in her little eyes when she is told that Funtown is closed to colored children, and see the depressing clouds of inferiority begin to form in her little mental sky, and see her begin to distort her little personality by unconsciously developing a bitterness toward white people; when you have to concoct an answer for a five-year-old son asking in agonizing pathos: "Daddy, why do white people treat colored people so mean?"; when you take a cross country drive and find it necessary to sleep night after night in the uncomfortable corners of your automobile because no motel will accept you; when you are humiliated day in and day out by nagging signs reading "white" men and "colored"; when your first name becomes "nigger" and your middle name becomes "boy" (however old you are) and your last name becomes "John," and when your wife and mother are never given the respected title "Mrs."; when you are harried by day and haunted by night by the fact that you are a Negro, living constantly at tip-toe stance never quite knowing what to expect next, and plagued with inner fears and outer resentments; when you are forever fighting a degenerating sense of "nobodiness";—then you will understand why we find it difficult to wait. There comes a time when the cup of endurance runs over, and men are no longer willing to be plunged into an abyss of injustice where they experience the bleakness of corroding despair. I hope, sirs, you can understand our legitimate and unavoidable impatience.

You express a great deal of anxiety over our willingness to break laws. This is certainly a legitimate concern. Since we so diligently urge people to obey the Supreme Court's decision of 1954 outlawing segregation in the public schools, it is rather strange and paradoxical to find us consciously breaking laws. One may well ask, "How can you advocate breaking some laws and obeying others?" The answer is found in the fact that there are two types of laws: There are just laws and there are unjust laws. I would be the first to advocate obeying just laws. One has not only a legal but moral responsibility to obey just laws. Conversely, one has a moral responsibility to disobey unjust laws. I would agree with Saint Augustine that "An unjust law is no law at all."

Now what is the difference between the two? How does one determine when a law is just or unjust? A just law is a man-made code that squares with the moral law or the law of God. An unjust law is a code that is out of harmony with the moral law. To put it in the terms of Saint Thomas Aquinas, an unjust law is a human law that is not rooted in eternal and natural law. Any law that uplifts human personality is just. Any law that degrades human personality is unjust. All segregation statutes are unjust because segregation distorts the soul and damages the personality. It gives the segregator a false sense of superiority and the segregated a false sense of inferiority. To use the words of Martin Buber, the great Jewish philosopher, segregation substitutes an "I-it" relationship for the "I-thou" relationship, and ends up relegating persons to the status of things. So segregation is not only politically, economically, and sociologically unsound, but it is morally wrong and sinful. Paul Tillich has said that sin is separation. Isn't segregation an existential expression of man's tragic separation, an expression of his awful estrangement,

his terrible sinfulness? So I can urge men to obey the 1954 decision of the Supreme Court because it is morally right, and I can urge them to disobey segregation ordinances because they are morally wrong.

Let us turn to a more concrete example of just and unjust laws. An unjust law is a code that a majority inflicts on a minority that is not binding on itself. This is difference made legal. On the other hand, a just law is a code that a majority compels a minority to follow that it is willing to follow itself. This is sameness made legal.

Let me give another explanation. An unjust law is a code inflicted upon a minority which that minority had no part in enacting or creating because they did not have the unhampered right to vote. Who can say the legislature of Alabama which set up the segregation laws was democratically elected? Throughout the state of Alabama all types of conniving methods are used to prevent Negroes from becoming registered voters and there are some counties without a single Negro registered to vote despite the fact that the Negro constitutes a majority of the population. Can any law set up in such a state be considered democratically structured?

These are just a few examples of unjust and just laws. There are some instances when a law is just on its face but unjust in its application. For instance, I was arrested Friday on a charge of parading without a permit. Now there is nothing wrong with an ordinance which requires a permit for a parade, but when the ordinance is used to preserve segregation and to deny citizens the First Amendment privilege of peaceful assembly and peaceful protest, then it becomes unjust.

I hope you can see the distinction I am trying to point out. In no sense do I advocate evading or defying the law as the rabid segregationist would do. This would lead to anarchy. One who breaks an unjust law must do it openly, lovingly (not hatefully as the white mothers did in New Orleans when they were seen on television screaming "nigger, nigger, nigger") and with a willingness to accept the penalty. I submit that an individual who breaks a law that conscience tells him is unjust, and willingly accepts the penalty by staying in jail to arouse the conscience of the community over its injustice, is in reality expressing the very highest respect for law.

Of course there is nothing new about this kind of civil disobedience. It was seen sublimely in the refusal of Shadrach, Meshach, and Abednego to obey the laws of Nebuchadnezzar because a higher moral law was involved. It was practiced superbly by the early Christians who were willing to face hungry lions and the excruciating pain of chopping blocks, before submitting to certain unjust laws of the Roman Empire. To a degree academic freedom is a reality today because Socrates practiced civil disobedience.

We can never forget that everything Hitler did in Germany was "legal" and everything thing the Hungarian freedom fighters did in Hungary was "illegal." It was "illegal" to aid and comfort a Jew in Hitler's Germany. But I am sure that, if I had lived in Germany during that time, I would have aided and comforted my Jewish brothers even though it was illegal. If I lived in a communist country today where certain principles dear to the Christian faith are suppressed, I believe I would openly advocate disobeying these antireligious laws.

I must make two honest confessions to you, my Christian and Jewish brothers. First I must confess that over the last few years I have been gravely disappointed with the white moderate. I have almost reached the regrettable conclusion that the Negroes' great stumbling block in the stride toward freedom is not the White Citizens' "Counciler" or the Ku Klux Klanner, but the white moderate who is more devoted to "order" than to justice; who pre-

fers a negative peace which is the absence of tension to a positive peace which is the presence of justice; who constantly says "I agree with you in the goal you seek, but I can't agree with your methods of direct action"; who paternalistically feels that he can set the timetable for another man's freedom; who lives by the myth of time and who constantly advises the Negro to wait until a "more convenient season." Shallow understanding from people of goodwill is more frustrating than absolute misunderstanding from people of ill will. Lukewarm acceptance is much more bewildering than outright rejection.

I had hoped that the white moderate would understand that law and order exist for the purpose of establishing justice, and that when they fail to do this they become the dangerously structured dams that block the flow of social progress. I had hoped that the white moderate would understand that the present tension in the South is merely a necessary phase of the transition from an obnoxious negative peace, where the Negro passively accepted his unjust plight, to a substance-filled positive peace, where all men will respect the dignity and worth of human personality. Actually, we who engage in nonviolent direct action are not the creators of tension. We merely bring to the surface the hidden tension that is already alive. We bring it out in the open where it can be seen and dealt with. Like a boil that can never be cured as long as it is covered up but must be opened with all its pus-flowing ugliness to the natural medicines of air and light, injustice must likewise be exposed, with all of the tension its exposing creates, to the light of human conscience and the air of national opinion before it can be cured.

In your statement you asserted that our actions, even though peaceful, must be condemned because they precipitate violence. But can this assertion be logically made? Isn't this like condemning the robbed man because his possession of money precipitated the evil act of robbery? Isn't this like condemning Socrates because his unswerving commitment to truth and his philosophical delvings precipitated the misguided popular mind to make him drink the hemlock? Isn't this like condemning Jesus because His unique God consciousness and never-ceasing devotion to His will precipitated the evil act of crucifixion? We must come to see, as federal courts have consistently affirmed, that it is immoral to urge an individual to withdraw his efforts to gain his basic constitutional rights, because the quest precipitates violence. Society must protect the robbed and punish the robber.

I had also hoped that the white moderate would reject the myth of time. I received a letter this morning from a white brother in Texas which said: "All Christians know that the colored people will receive equal rights eventually, but is it possible that you are in too great of a religious hurry? It has taken Christianity almost 2000 years to accomplish what it has. The teachings of Christ take time to come to earth." All that is said here grows out of a tragic misconception of time. It is the strangely irrational notion that there is something in the very flow of time that will inevitably cure all ills. Actually time is neutral. It can be used either destructively or constructively. I am coming to feel that the people of ill will have used time much more effectively than the people of goodwill. We will have to repent in this generation not merely for the vitriolic words and actions of the bad people, but for the appalling silence of the good people. We must come to see that human progress never rolls in on wheels of inevitability. It comes through the tireless efforts and persistent work of men willing to be co-workers with God, and without this hard work time itself becomes an ally of the forces of social stagnation.

We must use time creatively, and forever realize that the time is always ripe to do right.

Now is the time to make real the promise of democracy, and transform our pending national elegy into a creative psalm of brotherhood. Now is the time to lift our national policy from the quicksand of racial injustice to the solid rock of human dignity.

You spoke of our activity in Birmingham as extreme. At first I was rather disappointed that fellow clergymen would see my nonviolent efforts as those of the extremist. I started thinking about the fact that I stand in the middle of two opposing forces in the Negro community. One is a force of complacency made up of Negroes who, as a result of long years of oppression, have been so completely drained of self-respect and a sense of "somebodiness" that they have adjusted to segregation, and of a few Negroes in the middle class who, because of a degree of academic and economic security, and because at points they profit by segregation, have unconsciously become insensitive to the problems of the masses. The other force is one of bitterness and hatred and comes perilously close to advocating violence. It is expressed in the various black nationalist groups that are springing up over the nation, the largest and best known being Elijah Muhammad's Muslim movement. This movement is nourished by the contemporary frustration over the continued existence of racial discrimination. It is made up of people who have lost faith in America, who have absolutely repudiated Christianity, and who have concluded that the white man is an incurable "devil." I have tried to stand between these two forces saying that we need not follow the "do-nothingism" of the complacent or the hatred and despair of the black nationalist. There is the more excellent way of love and nonviolent protest. I'm grateful to God that, through the Negro church, the dimension of nonviolence entered our struggle. If this philosophy had not emerged I am convinced that by now many streets of the South would be flowing with floods of blood. And I am further convinced that if our white brothers dismiss us as "rabble rousers" and "outside agitators"— those of us who are working through the channels of nonviolent direct action—and refuse to support our nonviolent efforts, millions of Negroes, out of frustration and despair, will seek solace and security in black nationalist ideologies, a development that will lead inevitably to a frightening racial nightmare.

Oppressed people cannot remain oppressed forever. The urge for freedom will eventually come. This is what has happened to the American Negro. Something within has reminded him of his birthright of freedom; something without has reminded him that he can gain it. Consciously and unconsciously, he has been swept in by what the Germans call the Zeitgeist, and with his black brothers of Africa, and his brown and yellow brothers of Asia, South America, and the Caribbean, he is moving with a sense of cosmic urgency toward the promised land of racial justice. Recognizing this vital urge that has engulfed the Negro community, one should readily understand public demonstrations. The Negro has many pent-up resentments and latent frustrations. He has to get them out. So let him march sometime; let him have his prayer pilgrimages to the city hall; understand why he must have sit-ins and freedom rides. If his repressed emotions do not come out in these nonviolent ways, they will come out in ominous expressions of violence. This is not a threat; it is a fact of history. So I have not said to my people, "Get rid of your discontent." But I have tried to say that this normal and healthy discontent can be channeled through the creative outlet of nonviolent direct action. Now this approach is being dismissed as extremist. I must admit that I was initially disappointed in being so categorized.

But as I continued to think about the matter I gradually gained a bit of satisfaction from being considered an extremist. Was not Jesus an extremist in love? "Love your enemies, bless them that curse you, pray for them that despitefully use you." Was not Amos an extremist for justice—"Let justice roll down like waters and righteousness like a mighty stream." Was not Paul an extremist for the gospel of Jesus Christ—"I bear in my body the marks of the Lord Jesus." Was not Martin Luther an extremist—"Here I stand; I can do none other so help me God." Was not John Bunyan an extremist—"I will stay in jail to the end of my days before I make a butchery of my conscience." Was not Abraham Lincoln an extremist—"This nation cannot survive half slave and half free." Was not Thomas Jefferson an extremist—"We hold these truths to be self-evident; that all men are created equal." So the question is not whether we will be extremist but what kind of extremist will we be. Will we be extremists for hate or will we be extremists for love? Will we be extremists for the preservation of injustice—or will we be extremists for the cause of justice? In that dramatic scene on Calvary's hill three men were crucified. We must never forget that all three were crucified for the same crime—the crime of extremism. Two were extremists for immorality, and thus fell below their environment. The other, Jesus Christ, was an extremist for love, truth, and goodness, and thereby rose above His environment. So, after all, maybe the South, the nation, and the world are in dire need of creative extremists.

I had hoped that the white moderate would see this. . . .

I wish you had commended the Negro sit-inners and demonstrators of Birmingham for their sublime courage, their willingness to suffer, and their amazing discipline in the midst of the most inhuman provocation. One day the South will recognize its real heroes. They will be the James Merediths, courageously and with a majestic sense of purpose, facing jeering and hostile mobs and the agonizing loneliness that characterizes the life of the pioneer. They will be old, oppressed, battered Negro women, symbolized in a seventy-two-year-old woman of Montgomery, Alabama, who rose up with a sense of dignity and with her people decided not to ride the segregated buses, and responded to one who inquired about her tiredness with ungrammatical profundity: "My feets is tired, but my soul is rested." They will be young high school and college students, young ministers of the gospel and a host of the elders, courageously and nonviolently sitting in at lunch counters and willingly going to jail for conscience sake. One day the South will know that when these disinherited children of God sat down at lunch counters they were in reality standing up for the best in the American dream and the most sacred values in our Judeo-Christian heritage, and thus carrying our whole nation back to great wells of democracy which were dug deep by the founding fathers in the formulation of the Constitution and the Declaration of Independence. . . .

> Yours for the cause of
> Peace and Brotherhood
>
> Martin Luther King Jr. ⟳

38. Students for a Democratic Society

SDS WAS THE leading organization of the New Left until it split into competing factions in 1969. It was composed chiefly of white male college students, yet it sought to reach out to blacks through the civil rights movement and to labor and the poor through local organizing projects. SDS was actually founded in 1960 as an offshoot of the League for Industrial Democracy but asserted its independent ideology and program at its 1962 convention in Port Huron, Michigan. The "Port Huron Statement" was authored almost entirely by Tom Hayden, then a leading figure in SDS and a prominent anti-Vietnam war activist throughout the 1960s.

This statement shows the early stages of the New Left critique of American society, calling for reform through existing institutions to implement the basic promises and ideals of the United States for all. For many, the critique deepened in later years and the remedies became far more drastic. But the "Port Huron Statement" remains one of the few comprehensive statements generated during the 1960s and provided the basis on which many people began to engage in political activity for the first time. ⟳

The Port Huron Statement (1962)

INTRODUCTION: AGENDA
FOR A GENERATION

We are people of this generation, bred in at least modest comfort, housed now in universities, looking uncomfortably to the world we inherit.

When we were kids the United States was the wealthiest and strongest country in the world; the only one with the atom bomb, the least scarred by modern war, an initiator of the United Nations that we thought would distribute Western influence throughout the world. Freedom and equality for each individual, government of, by, and for the people —these American values we found good, principles by which we could live as men. Many of us began maturing in complacency.

As we grew, however, our comfort was penetrated by events too troubling to dismiss. First, the permeating and victimizing fact of human degradation, symbolized by the Southern struggle against racial bigotry, compelled most of us from silence to activism. Second, the enclosing fact of the Cold War, symbolized by the presence of the Bomb, brought awareness that we ourselves, and our friends, and millions of abstract "others" we knew more directly because of our common peril, might die at any time. We might deliberately ignore, or avoid, or fail to feel all other human problems, but not these two, for these were too immediate and crushing in their impact, too challenging in the demand that we as individuals take the responsibility for encounter and resolution.

While these and other problems either directly oppressed us or rankled our consciences and became our own subjective concerns, we

begin to see complicated and disturbing paradoxes in our surrounding America. The declaration "all men are created equal" rang hollow before the facts of Negro life in the South and the big cities of the North. The proclaimed peaceful intentions of the United States contradicted its economic and military investments in the Cold War status quo.

We witnessed, and continue to witness, other paradoxes. With nuclear energy whole cities can easily be powered, yet the dominant nation-states seem more likely to unleash destruction greater than that incurred in all wars of human history. Although our own technology is destroying old and creating new forms of social organization, men still tolerate meaningless work and idleness. While two-thirds of mankind suffers undernourishment, our own upper classes revel amidst superfluous abundance. Although world population is expected to double in forty years, the nations still tolerate anarchy as a major principle of international conduct and uncontrolled exploitation governs the sapping of the earth's physical resources. Although mankind desperately needs revolutionary leadership, America rests in national stalemate, its goals ambiguous and tradition-bound instead of informed and clear, its democratic system apathetic and manipulated rather than "of, by, and for the people."

Not only did tarnish appear on our image of American virtue, not only did disillusion occur when the hypocrisy of American ideals was discovered, but we began to sense that what we had originally seen as the American Golden Age was actually the decline of an era. The worldwide outbreak of revolution against colonialism and imperialism, the entrenchment of totalitarian states, the menace of war, overpopulation, international disorder, supertechnology—these trends were testing the tenacity

---

SOURCE: Students for a Democratic Society, 1962. Editor's abridgement.

of our own commitment to democracy and freedom and our abilities to visualize their application to a world in upheaval.

Our work is guided by the sense that we may be the last generation in the experiment with living. But we are a minority—the vast majority of our people regard the temporary equilibriums of our society and world as eternally functional parts. In this is perhaps the outstanding paradox: we ourselves are imbued with urgency, yet the message of our society is that there is no viable alternative to the present. Beneath the reassuring tones of the politicians, beneath the common opinion that America will "muddle through," beneath the stagnation of those who have closed their minds to the future, is the pervading feeling that there simply are no alternatives, that our times have witnessed the exhaustion not only of Utopias, but of any new departures as well. Feeling the press of complexity upon the emptiness of life, people are fearful of the thought that at any moment things might be thrust out of control. They fear change itself, since change might smash whatever invisible framework seems to hold back chaos for them now. For most Americans, all crusades are suspect, threatening. The fact that each individual sees apathy in his fellows perpetuates the common reluctance to organize for change. The dominant institutions are complex enough to blunt the minds of their potential critics, and entrenched enough to swiftly dissipate or entirely repel the energies of protest and reform, thus limiting human expectancies. Then, too, we are a materially improved society, and by our own improvements we seem to have weakened the case for further change.

Some would have us believe that Americans feel contentment amidst prosperity—but might it not be better called a glaze above deeply felt anxieties about their role in the new world? And if these anxieties produce a developed indifference to human affairs, do they not as well produce a yearning to believe there is an alternative to the present, that something *can* be done to change circumstances in the school, the workplaces, the bureaucracies, the government? It is to this latter yearning, at once the spark and engine of change, that we direct our present appeal. The search for truly democratic alternatives to the present, and a commitment to social experimentation with them, is a worthy and fulfilling human enterprise, one which moves us and, we hope, others today. On such a basis do we offer this document of our convictions and analysis: as an effort in understanding and changing the conditions of humanity in the late twentieth century, an effort rooted in the ancient, still unfulfilled conception of man attaining determining influence over his circumstances of life.

Values

Making values explicit—an initial task in establishing alternatives—is an activity that has been devalued and corrupted. The conventional moral terms of the age, the political moralities—"free world," "people's democracies" —reflect realities poorly, if at all, and seem to function more as ruling myths than as descriptive principles. But neither has our experience in the universities brought us moral enlightenment. Our professors and administrators sacrifice controversy to public relations; their curriculums change more slowly than the living events of the world; their skills and silence are purchased by investors in the arms race; passion is called unscholastic. The questions we might want raised—what is really important? can we live in a different and better way? if we wanted to change society, how would we do it?—are not thought to be questions of a "fruitful, empirical nature," and thus are brushed aside.

Unlike youth in other countries, we are used to moral leadership being exercised and moral dimensions being clarified by our elders.

But today, for us, not even the liberal and socialist preachments of the past seem adequate to the forms of the present. Consider the old slogans: Capitalism Cannot Reform Itself, United Front Against Fascism, General Strike, All Out on May Day. Or, more recently, No Cooperation with Commies and Fellow Travellers, Ideologies are Exhausted, Bipartisanship, No Utopias. These are incomplete, and there are few new prophets. It has been said that our liberal and socialist predecessors were plagued by vision without program, while our own generation is plagued by program without vision. All around us there is astute grasp of method, technique—the committee, the ad hoc group, the lobbyist, the hard and soft sell, the make, the projected image—but, if pressed critically, such expertise is incompetent to explain its implicit ideals. It is highly fashionable to identify oneself by old categories, or by naming a respected political figure, or by explaining "how we would vote" on various issues.

Theoretic chaos has replaced the idealistic thinking of old—and, unable to reconstitute theoretic order, men have condemned idealism itself. Doubt has replaced hopefulness—and men act out a defeatism that is labelled realistic. The decline of utopia and hope is in fact one of the defining features of social life today. The reasons are various: the dreams of the older left were perverted by Stalinism and never re-created; the congressional stalemate makes men narrow their view of the possible; the specialization of human activity leaves little room for sweeping thought; the horrors of the twentieth century, symbolized in the gas-ovens and concentration camps and atom bombs, have blasted hopefulness. To be idealistic is to be considered apocalyptic, deluded. To have no serious aspirations, on the contrary, is to be "toughminded."

In suggesting social goals and values, therefore, we are aware of entering a sphere of some disrepute. Perhaps matured by the past, we have no sure formulas, no closed theories—but that does not mean values are beyond discussion and tentative determination. A first task of any social movement is to convince people that the search for orienting theories and the creation of human values is complex but worthwhile. We are aware that to avoid platitudes we must analyze the concrete conditions of social order. But to direct such an analysis we must use the guideposts of basic principles. Our own social values involve conceptions of human beings, human relationships, and social systems.

We are *men* as infinitely precious and possessed of unfulfilled capacities for reason, freedom, and love. In affirming these principles we are aware of countering perhaps the dominant conceptions of man in the twentieth century: that he is a thing to be manipulated, and that he is inherently incapable of directing his own affairs. We oppose the depersonalization that reduces human beings to the status of things —if anything, the brutalities of the twentieth century teach that means and ends are intimately related, that vague appeals to "posterity" cannot justify the mutilations of the present. We oppose, too, the doctrine of human incompetence because it rests essentially on the modern fact that men have been "competently" manipulated into incompetence—we see little reason why men cannot meet with increasing skill the complexities and responsibilities of their situation, if society is organized not for minority, but for majority, participation in decision-making.

Men have unrealized potential for self-cultivation, self-direction, self-understanding, and creativity. It is this potential that we regard as crucial and to which we appeal, not to the human potentiality for violence, unreason, and submission to authority. The goal of man and society should be human independence: a concern not with image or popularity but with finding a meaning in life that is personally authentic; a quality of mind not compulsively driven by a sense of powerlessness, nor one which unthinkingly adopts status values, nor one which represses all threats to its habits, but one which has full spontaneous access to present and past experiences, one which easily unites the fragmented parts of personal history, one which openly faces problems which are troubling and unresolved; one with an intuitive awareness of possibilities, an active sense of curiosity, an ability and willingness to learn.

This kind of independence does not mean egotistic individualism—the object is not to have one's way so much as it is to have a way that is one's own. Nor do we deify man—we merely have faith in his potential.

Human relationships should involve fraternity and honesty. Human interdependence is contemporary fact; human brotherhood must be willed, however, as a condition of future survival and as the most appropriate form of social relations. Personal links between man and man are needed, especially to go beyond the partial and fragmentary bonds of function that bind men only as worker to worker, employer to employee, teacher to student, American to Russian.

Loneliness, estrangement, isolation describe the vast distance between man and man today. These dominant tendencies cannot be overcome by better personnel management, nor by improved gadgets, but only when a love of man overcomes the idolatrous worship of things by man. As the individualism we affirm is not egoism, the selflessness we affirm is not self-elimination. On the contrary, we believe in generosity of a kind that imprints one's unique individual qualities in the relation to other men, and to all human activity. Further, to dislike isolation is not to favor the abolition of privacy; the latter differs from isolation in that it occurs or is abolished according to individual will.

We would replace power rooted in possession, privilege, or circumstance by power and uniqueness rooted in love, reflectiveness, reason, and creativity. As a *social system* we seek the establishment of a democracy of individual participation, governed by two central aims: that the individual share in those social decisions determining the quality and direction of his life; that society be organized to encourage independence in men and provide the media for their common participation.

In a participatory democracy, the political life would be based in several root principles:

that decision-making of basic social consequence be carried on by public groupings;

that politics be seen positively, as the art of collectively creating an acceptable pattern of social relations;

that politics has the function of bringing people out of isolation and into community, thus being a necessary, though not sufficient, means of finding meaning in personal life;

that the political order should serve to clarify problems in a way instrumental to their solution; it should provide outlets for the expression of personal grievance and aspiration; opposing views should be organized so as to illuminate choices and facilitate the attainment of goals; channels should be commonly available to relate men to knowledge and to power so that private problems—from bad recreation facilities to personal alienation—are formulated as general issues.

The economic sphere would have as its basis the principles:

that work should involve incentives worthier than money or survival. It should be educative, not stultifying; creative, not mechanical; self-directed, not manipulated, encouraging independence, a respect for others, a sense of dignity and a willingness to accept social responsibility, since it is this experience that has crucial influence on habits, perceptions and individual ethics;

that the economic experience is so personally decisive that the individual must share in its full determination;

that the economy itself is of such social importance that its major resources and means of production should be open to democratic participation and subject to democratic social regulation.

Like the political and economic ones, major social institutions—cultural, educational, rehabilitative, and others—should be generally organized with the well-being and dignity of man as the essential measure of success.

In social change or interchange, we find violence to be abhorrent because it requires generally the transformation of the target be it a human being or a community of people, into a depersonalized object of hate. It is imperative that the means of violence be abolished and the institutions—local, national, international—that encourage non-violence as a condition of conflict be developed.

These are our central values, in skeletal form. It remains vital to understand their denial or attainment in the context of the modern world. . . .

POLITICS WITHOUT PUBLICS

The American political system is not the democratic model of which its glorifiers speak. In actuality it frustrates democracy by confusing the individual citizen, paralyzing policy discussion, and consolidating the irresponsible power of military and business interests. . . .

What emerges from the party contradiction and insulation of privately held power is the organized political stalemate: calcification dominates flexibility as the principle of parliamentary organization, frustration is the expectancy of legislators intending liberal re-

form, and Congress becomes less and less central to national decision-making, especially in the area of foreign policy. In this context, confusion and blurring is built into the formulation of issues, long-range priorities are not discussed in the rational manner needed for policy-making, the politics of personality and "image" become a more important mechanism than the construction of issues in a way that affords each voter a challenging and real option. The American voter is buffeted from all directions by pseudo-problems, by the structurally initiated sense that nothing political is subject to human mastery. Worried by his mundane problems which never get solved, but constrained by the common belief that politics is an agonizingly slow accommodation of views, he quits all pretense of bothering.

A most alarming fact is that few, if any, politicians are calling for changes in these conditions. Only a handful even are calling on the president to "live up to" platform pledges; no one is demanding structural changes, such as the shuttling of Southern Democrats out of the Democratic Party. Rather than protesting the state of politics, most politicians are reinforcing and aggravating that state. While in practice they rig public opinion to suit their own interests, in word and ritual they enshrine "the sovereign public" and call for more and more letters. Their speeches and campaign actions are banal, based on a degrading conception of what people want to hear. They respond not to dialogue, but to pressure, and knowing this, the ordinary citizen sees even greater inclination to shun the political sphere. The politician is usually a trumpeter to "citizenship" and "service to the nation," but since he is unwilling to seriously rearrange power relationships, his trumpetings only increase apathy by creating no outlets. Much of the time the call to "service" is justified not in idealistic terms, but in the crasser terms of "defending the free world from communism"—thus making future idealistic impulses harder to justify in anything but Cold War terms....

WHAT IS NEEDED?

How to end the Cold War? How to increase democracy in America? These are the decisive issues confronting liberal and socialist forces today. To us, the issues are intimately related, the struggle for one invariably being a struggle for the other. What policy and structural alternatives are needed to obtain these ends?

1. Universal controlled disarmament must replace deterrence and arms control as the national defense goal....
2. Disarmament should be seen as a political issue, not a technical problem....
3. A crucial feature of this political understanding must be the acceptance of status quo possessions....
4. Experiments in disengagement and demilitarization must be conducted as part of the total disarming process....

THE INDUSTRIALIZATION OF THE WORLD

Many Americans are prone to think of the industrialization of the newly developed countries as a modern form of American *noblesse,* undertaken sacrificially for the benefit of others. On the contrary, the task of world industrialization, of eliminating the disparity between have and have-not nations, is as important as any issue facing America. The colonial revolution signals the end of an era for the old Western powers and a time of new beginnings for most of the people of the earth. In the course of these upheavals, many problems will emerge: American policies must be revised or accelerated in several ways.

1. The United States' principal goal should be creating a world where hunger, poverty, disease, ignorance, violence, and exploitation

are replaced as central features by abundance, reason, love, and international cooperation....
2. We should undertake here and now a fifty-year effort to prepare for all nations the conditions of industrialization....
3. We should not depend significantly on private enterprise to do the job....
4. We should not lock the development process into the Cold War: we should view it as a way of ending that conflict....
5. America should show its commitment to democratic institutions not by withdrawing support from undemocratic regimes, but by making domestic democracy exemplary....
6. America should agree that public utilities, railroads, mines, and plantations, and other basic economic institutions should be in the control of national, not foreign, agencies....
7. Foreign aid should be given through international agencies, primarily the United Nations....
8. Democratic theory must confront the problems inherent in social revolutions....

TOWARDS AMERICAN DEMOCRACY

Every effort to end the Cold War and expand the process of world industrialization is an effort hostile to people and institutions whose interests lie in perpetuation of the East-West military threat and the postponement of change in the "have-not" nations of the world. Every such effort, too, is bound to establish greater democracy in America. The major goals of a domestic effort would be:

1. America must abolish its political party stalemate....
2. Mechanisms of voluntary association must be created through which political information can be imparted and political participation encouraged....
3. Institutions and practices which stifle dis-

sent should be abolished, and the promotion of peaceful dissent should be actively promoted. . . .

4. Corporations must be made publicly responsible. . . .

5. The allocation of resources must be based on social needs. A truly "public sector" must be established, and its nature debated and planned. . . .

6. America should concentrate on its genuine social priorities: abolish squalor, terminate neglect, and establish an environment for people to live in with dignity and creativeness. . . .

Alternatives to Helplessness

The goals we have set are not realizable next month, or even next election—but that fact justifies neither giving up altogether nor a determination to work only on immediate, direct, tangible problems. Both responses are a sign of helplessness, fearfulness of visions, refusal to hope, and tend to bring on the very conditions to be avoided. Fearing vision, we justify rhetoric or myopia. Fearing hope, we reinforce despair.

1. The first effort, then, should be to state a vision: what is the perimeter of human possibility in this epoch? This we have tried to do. The second effort, if we are to be politically responsible, is to evaluate the prospects for obtaining at least a substantial part of that vision in our epoch: what are the social forces that exist, or that must exist, if we are to be at all successful? And what role have we ourselves to play as a social force?. . .

2. The broadest movement for *peace* in several years emerged in 1961–62. In its political orientation and goals it is much less identifiable than the movement for civil rights: it includes socialists, pacifists, liberals, scholars, militant activists, middle-class women,

some professionals, many students, a few unionists. Some have been emotionally single-issue: Ban the Bomb. Some have been academically obscurantist. Some have rejected the System (sometimes both systems). Some have attempted, also, to "work within" the system. Amidst these conflicting streams of emphasis, however, certain basic qualities appear. The most important is that the "peace movement" has operated almost exclusively through peripheral institutions —almost never through mainstream institutions. Similarly, individuals interested in peace have nonpolitical social roles that cannot be turned to the support of peace activity. Concretely, liberal religious societies, anti-war groups, voluntary associations and ad hoc committees have been the political unit of the peace movement; and its human movers have been students, teachers, housewives, secretaries, lawyers, doctors, clergy. The units have not been located in spots of major social influence; the people have not been able to turn their resources fully to the issues that concern them. The results are political ineffectiveness and personal alienation. . . .

3. Central to any analysis of the potential for change must be an appraisal of *organized labor*. It would be ahistorical to disregard the immense influence of labor in making modern America a decent place in which to live. It would be confused to fail to note labor's presence today as the most liberal of mainstream institutions. But it would be irresponsible not to criticize labor for losing much of the idealism that once made it a driving movement. Those who expected a labor upsurge after the 1955 AFL-CIO merger can only be dismayed that one year later, in the Stevenson-Eisenhower campaign, the AFL-CIO Committee on Political Education was able to obtain solicited $1.00 contributions from only one of every 24 un-

ionists, and prompt only 40 percent of the rank and file to vote....

A new politics must include a revitalized labor movement: a movement which sees itself, and is regarded by others, as a major leader of the breakthrough to a politics of hope and vision. Labor's role is no less unique or important in the needs of the future than it was in the past; its numbers and potential political strength, its natural interest in the abolition of exploitation, its reach to the grass roots of American society, combine to make it the best candidate for the synthesis of the civil rights, peace, and economic reform movements....

The University and Social Change

... The civil rights, peace, and student movements are too poor and socially slighted, and the labor movement too quiescent, to be counted with enthusiasm. From where else can power and vision be summoned? We believe that the universities are an overlooked seat of influence.

First, the university is located in a permanent position of social influence. Its educational function makes it indispensable and automatically makes it a crucial institution in the formation of social attitudes. Second, in an unbelievably complicated world, it is the central institution for organizing, evaluating, and transmitting knowledge. Third, the extent to which academic resources presently are used to buttress immoral social practice is revealed first, by the extent to which defense contracts make the universities engineers of the arms race. Too, the use of modern social science as a manipulative tool reveals itself in the "human relations" consultants to the modern corporations, who introduce trivial sops to give laborers feelings of "participation" or "belonging," while actually deluding them in or-

der to further exploit their labor. And, of course, the use of motivational research is already infamous as a manipulative aspect of American politics. But these social uses of the universities' resources also demonstrate the unchangeable reliance by men of power on the men and storehouses of knowledge: this makes the university functionally tied to society in new ways, revealing new potentialities, new levers for change. Fourth, the university is the only mainstream institution that is open to participation by individuals of nearly any viewpoint.

These, at least, are facts, no matter how dull the teaching, how paternalistic the rules, how irrelevant the research that goes on. Social relevance, the accessibility to knowledge, and internal openness—these together make the university a potential base and agency in a movement of social change.

1. Any new left in America must be, in large measure, a left with real intellectual skills, committed to deliberativeness, honesty, reflection as working tools. The university permits the political life to be an adjunct to the academic one, and action to be informed by reason.

2. A new left must be distributed in significant social roles throughout the country. The universities are distributed in such a manner.

3. A new left must consist of younger people who matured in the post-war world, and partially be directed to the recruitment of younger people. The university is an obvious beginning point.

4. A new left must include liberals and socialists, the former for their relevance, the latter for their sense of thoroughgoing reforms in the system. The university is a more sensible place than a political party for these two traditions to begin to discuss their differences and look for political synthesis.

5. A new left must start controversy across the land, if national policies and national apathy are to be reversed. The ideal university is a community of controversy, within itself and its effects on communities beyond.

6. A new left must transform modern complexity into issues that can be understood and felt close-up by every human being. It must give form to the feelings of helplessness and indifference, so that people may see the political, social, and economic sources of their private troubles and organize to change society. In a time of supposed prosperity, moral complacency, and political manipulation, a new left cannot rely on only aching stomachs to be the engine force of social reform. The case for change, for alternatives that will involve uncomfortable personal efforts, must be argued as never before. The university is a relevant place for all of these activities.

But we need not indulge in illusions: the university system cannot complete a movement of ordinary people making demands for a better life. From its schools and colleges across the nation, a militant left might awaken its allies, and by beginning the process towards peace, civil rights, and labor struggles, reinsert theory and idealism where too often reign confusion and political barter. The power of students and faculty united is not only potential; it has shown its actuality in the South, and in the reform movements of the North.

The bridge to political power, though, will be built through genuine cooperation, locally, nationally, and internationally, between a new left of young people, and an awakening community of allies. In each community we must look within the university and act with confidence that we can be powerful, but we must look outwards to the less exotic but more lasting struggles for justice.

To turn these possibilities into realities will involve national efforts at university reform by an alliance of students and faculty. They must wrest control of the educational process from the administrative bureaucracy. They must make fraternal and functional contact with allies in labor, *civil* rights, and other liberal forces outside the campus. They must import major public issues into the curriculum—research and teaching on problems of war and peace is an outstanding example. They must make debate and controversy, not dull pedantic cant, the common style for educational life. They must consciously build a base for their assault upon the loci of power.

As students for a democratic society, we are committed to stimulating this kind of social movement, this kind of vision and program in campus and community across the country. If we appear to seek the unattainable, as it has been said, then let it be known that we do so to avoid the unimaginable. ∾

39. Betty Friedan

BETTY FRIEDAN (b. 1921) brought to light "the problem with no name" and revived feminism in the early 1960s. Her first book, *The Feminine Mystique,* inspired the revival of feminism by focusing on the frustration of the middle-class housewife with no clear vocation and then moving on to the lower-paid and denigrated status of women even when employed. Friedan helped to form the National Organization for Women (NOW). The selection excerpted here is from a report to the NOW convention during her presidency in 1968. ⌒

Our Revolution Is Unique (1968)

We new feminists have begun to define ourselves—existentially—through action. We have learned that while we had much to learn from the black civil rights movement and their revolution against economic and racial oppression, our own revolution is unique: it must define its own ideology.

We can cut no corners; we are, in effect, where the black revolution was perhaps fifty years ago; but the speed with which our revolution is moving now is our unearned historical benefit from what has happened in that revolution. Yet there can be no illusion on our part that a separatist ideology copied from black power will work for us. Our tactics and strategy and, above all, our ideology must be firmly based in the historical, biological, economic, and psychological reality of our two-sexed world, which is not the same as the black reality and different also from the reality of the first feminist wave.

Thanks to the early feminists, we who have mounted this second stage of the feminist revolution have grown up with the right to vote, little as we may have used it for our own purposes. We have grown up with the right to higher education and to employment, and with some, not all, of the legal rights of equality. Insofar as we have moved on the periphery of the mainstream of society, with the skills and the knowledge to command its paychecks, even if insufficient, and to make decisions, even if not consulted beyond housework; we begin to have a self-respecting image of ourselves, as women, not just in sexual relation to men, but as full human beings in society. We are able, at least some of us, to see men, in general or in particular, without blind rancor or hostility, and to face oppression as it reveals itself in our concrete experience with politicians, bosses, priests, or husbands. We do not need to suppress our just grievances. We now have enough courage to express them. And yet we are able to conceive the possibility of full affirmation for man. Man is not the enemy, but the fellow victim of the present half-equality. As we speak, act, demonstrate, testify, and appear on television on matters such as sex discrimination in employment, public accommodations, education, divorce-marriage reform, or abortion repeal, we hear from men who feel they can be freed to greater self-fulfillment to the degree that women are released from the binds that now constrain them.

This sense of freeing men as the other half of freeing women has always been there, even in the early writings of Mary Wollstonecraft, Elizabeth Stanton, and the rest; our action-created new awareness has confirmed this.

Another point we are conscious of in the new feminism is that we are a revolution for all, not for an exceptional few. This, above all, distinguishes us from those token spokeswomen of the period since women won the vote, the Aunt Toms who managed to get a place for themselves in society, and who were, I think, inevitably seduced into an accommodating stance, helping to keep the others quiet. We are beginning to know that no woman can achieve a real breakthrough alone, as long as sex discrimination exists in employment, under the law, in education, in mores, and in denigration of the image of women.

... We cannot say that all American women want equality, because we know that women, like all oppressed people, have accepted the traditional denigration by society. Some women have been too much hurt by denigration from others, by self-denigration, by lack of the experiences, education, and training needed to move in society as equal human beings, to have the confidence that they can so move in a competitive society. They say they don't want equality—they have to be happy, adjust to things as they are. Such women find us threatening. They find equality so frightening that they must wish the new feminists did not exist. And yet we see so clearly from younger women and students that to the degree that we push ahead and create opportunities for movement in society, in the process creating the "new women" who are *people* first, to that degree the threat will disappear.

We do not speak for every woman in America, but we speak for the *right* of every woman in America to become all she is capable of becoming—on her own and/or in partnership with a man. And we already know that we speak not for a few, not for hundreds, not for thousands, but for millions—especially for millions in the younger generation who have tasted more equality than their elders. We

know this simply from the resonance, if you will, that our actions have aroused in society....

WOMEN AND SEX

As an example of the new feminism in action, consider the matter of abortion law repeal. NOW was the first organization to speak on the basic rights of women on the question of abortion. We said that it is the inalienable human right of every woman to control her own reproductive process. To establish that right would require that all laws penalizing abortion be repealed, removed from the penal code; the state would not be empowered either to force or prevent a woman from having an abortion. Now many groups are working on abortion law repeal, while at the same time California and Washington, D.C., court decisions have spelled out the right of a woman to control her own reproduction.

What right has any man to say to any woman, "You must bear this child"? What right has any state to say it? The child-bearing decision is a woman's right and not a technical question needing the sanction of the state, nor should the state control access to birth control devices.

This question can only really be confronted in terms of the basic personhood and dignity of woman, which is violated forever if she does not have the right to control her own reproductive process. And the heart of this idea goes far beyond abortion and birth control.

Women, almost too visible as sex objects in this country today, are at the same time invisible people. As the Negro was the invisible man, so women are the invisible people in America today. To be taken seriously as people, women have to share in the decisions of government, of politics, of the church—not just to cook the church supper, but to preach the sermon; not just to look up the zip codes and address the envelopes, but to make the political decisions; not just to do the housework of industry, but to make some of the executive decisions. Women, above all, want to say what their own lives are going to be, what their own personalities are going to be, not permitting male experts to define what is "feminine" or isn't or should be.

The essence of the denigration of women is their definition as sex objects. And to confront our inequality, we must confront our own self-denigration and our denigration by society in these terms.

Am I saying, therefore, that women must be liberated from sex? No. I am saying that sex will only be liberated, will only cease to be a sniggering dirty joke and an obsession in this society, when women are liberated, self-determining people, liberated to a creativity beyond motherhood, to a full human creativity.

Nor am I saying that women must be liberated from motherhood. I am saying that motherhood will only be liberated to be a joyous and responsible human act, when women are free to make, with full conscious choice and full human responsibility, the decision to be mothers. Then, and only then, will they be able to embrace motherhood without conflict. When they are able to define themselves as people, not just as somebody's mother, not just as servants of children, not just as breeding receptacles, but as people for whom motherhood is a freely chosen part of life, and for whom creativity has many dimensions, as it has for men.

... Women today are forced to live too much through their children and husband —too dependent on them, and, therefore, forced to take too much varied resentment, vindictiveness, inexpressible resentment, and rage out on their husbands and their children.

Perhaps the least understood fact of American political life is the enormous buried violence of women in this country today. Like all oppressed people, women have been taking

their violence out on their own bodies, in all the maladies with which they plague the doctors' offices and the psychoanalysts. They have been taking out their violence inadvertently and in subtle and in insidious ways on their children and on their husbands. And sometimes, they are not so subtle, for the battered child syndrome that we are hearing more and more about in our hospitals is almost always to be found in the instance of unwanted children, and women are doing the battering, as much or more than men.

Man, we have said, is not the enemy. Men will only be truly liberated, to love women and to be fully themselves, when women are liberated to be full people. Until that happens, men are going to bear the burden and the guilt of the destiny they have forced upon women, the suppressed resentment of that passive stage —the sterility of love, when love is not between two fully active, fully participant, fully joyous people, but has in it the element of exploitation. And men will also not be fully free to be all they can be as long as they must live up to an image of masculinity that denies to a man all the tenderness and sensitivity that might be considered feminine. Men have in them enormous capacities that they have to repress and fear in themselves, in living up to this obsolete and brutal man-eating, lion-killing, Ernest Hemingway image of masculinity—the image of all-powerful masculine superiority. All the burdens and responsibilities that men are supposed to shoulder alone, make them, I think, resent women's pedestal, while the burden to women is enforced passivity.

So the real sexual revolution is not the cheap headlines in the papers—at what age boys and girls go to bed with each other and whether they do it with or without the benefit of marriage. That's the least of it. The real sexual revolution is the emergence of women from passivity, from thingness, to full self-determination, to full dignity. And insofar as they can do this, men are also emerging from the stage of identification with brutality and masters to full and sensitive complete humanity.

A revolutionary theory that's adequate to the current demand of the sexual revolution must also address itself to the concrete realities of our society. We can only transcend the reality of the institutions that oppress us by confronting them in our actions now; confronting reality, we change it; we begin to create alternatives, not in abstract discussion, but here and now.

Some women who call themselves revolutionaries get into abstractions. They say, "What's really wrong is marriage altogether. What's wrong is having babies altogether; let's have them in test tubes. Man is the oppressor, and women are enslaved. We don't want jobs because who wants to be equal to men who aren't free. All jobs today are just a rat race anyway."

Now we are rationalizing in radical terms of the extremists of the women's liberation ideology. This is a rationalization for inaction, because in the end we're going to weep and go home and yell at our husbands and make life miserable for a while, but we'll eventually conclude that it's hopeless, that nothing can be done.

If we are going to address ourselves to the need for changing the social institutions that will permit women to be free and equal individuals, participating actively in their society and changing that society—with men—then we must talk in terms of what is possible, and not accept what is as what must be. In other words, don't talk to me about test tubes, because I am interested in leading a revolution for the foreseeable future of my society. And I have a certain sense of optimism that things can be changed.

Twenty-five years from now test-tube babies may be a reality. But it is my educated guess as an observer of the scene—both from what I know of psychology and what I've observed of actual women and men, old and young, conservative and radical, in this country and other countries—that for the foreseeable future people are going to want to enjoy sexual relationships and control the procreative act and make more responsible, human decisions whether and when to have babies.

We need not accept marriage as it's currently structured with the implicit idea of man, the breadwinner, and woman, the housewife. There are many different ways we could posit marriage. But there seems to be a reasonable guess that men and women are going to want relationships of long-term intimacy tied in with a sexual relationship, although we can certainly posit a larger variety of sex relationships than now seen conventional. And it's not possible, much less conducive to health, happiness, or self-fulfillment, for women or men to completely suppress their sexual needs.

We can change institutions, but it is a fantasy deviation from a really revolutionary approach to say that we want a world in which there will be no sex, no marriage, that in order for women to be free they must have a manless revolution. We have to deal with the world of reality if we are going to have a real revolution.

I don't happen to think that women and men are so completely different that it is impossible for us to see each other as human beings. I think that it is as possible for men to put themselves finally in woman's place by an act of empathy or by guilt or by awareness of human rights as it has been possible for some whites to do for blacks. But it's perhaps not much more possible than that, although there are more bonds between men and women, and really men's stake in this revolution is greater, because a woman can make a man's life hell if it isn't solved. But I think it would be as much of a mistake to expect men to hand this to women as to consider all men as the enemy, all men as oppressors. This revolution can have the support of men, but women must take the lead in fighting it as any other oppressed group has had to.

I think that it is possible in education to create and disseminate the radical ideology that is needed to influence the great change in expectations and institutions for the revolution of women. In the education of women, I think it is nonsense to keep talking about optional life styles and the freedom of choice that American women have. They do not have them, and we should face this right away. You cannot tell a woman aged eighteen to twenty that she can make a choice to just stay home all her life with her children, her friends, and her husband. This girl is going to live close to a hundred years. There won't be children home to occupy her all her life. If she has intelligence and the opportunity for education it is telling her simply, "Put yourself in a garbage can, except for the years when you have a few little children at home.". . .

It is a perversion of the new feminism for some to exhort those who would join this revolution to cleanse themselves of sex and the need for love or to refuse to have children. This not only means a revolution with very few followers—but is a cop-out from the problem of moving in society for the *majority* of women, who do want love and children. To enable *all* women, not just the exceptional few, to participate in society we must confront the fact of life—as a temporary fact of most women's lives today—that women do give birth to children. But we must challenge the idea that a woman is primarily responsible for raising children. Man and society have to be educated to accept their responsibility for that role as well. And this is first of all a challenge to education.

In Sweden I was impressed that these expectations are considered absolutely normal. The need for child-care centers is accepted as so important by all the fathers as well as the mothers of the younger generation that every major young politician has it high on his agenda. The equivalent of the Sunday editor of *New York Times* in Sweden, or a rising state senator, would each tell me how both he and his wife have part-time schedules so that they can both go on with their professions, and how this is fine but they realize it's only makeshift because what's really needed is more child-care centers. And the editor would pick up the baby and say proudly that she relates to him more than to his wife. And in the Volvo factory, even the public relations man with a crewcut says the same thing.

I couldn't believe it! I asked, "How do you explain this? Why do so many have these attitudes?" And they said, "Education." Eight years ago they decided that they were going to have absolute equality, and the only way to achieve this was to challenge the sex-role idea. The sex-role debate is not considered a woman question, not even an individual woman question or a societal woman question, but a question for men and women alike. In the elementary schools boys and girls take cooking and child care, and boys and girls take shop. Boys and girls take higher mathematics. In the universities the dormitories are sexually integrated. They all have kitchens and boys and girls learn to live together, to cook and study as equals. The kitchens are very important—a boy will boast how good a cook he is, and the idea that this is woman's work is gone. This has been done in the course of one generation, and if Sweden can do it, the United States can do it. . . .

WOMEN AS A POLITICAL POWER

On the question of self-determination, we became painfully aware, in our attempts to get a bill of rights for women into the platforms of both political parties at the last presidential election and as a major issue in the election for all candidates for national office, that we need *political power*. Our only success then was getting the word "sex" added to a rather vague antidiscrimination sentence in the Republican platform.

We must overcome our diversity of varied political beliefs. Our common commitment is to equality for women. And we are not single-issue people; we want a voice for all women, to raise our voices in decision making on all matters from war and peace to the kinds of cities we're going to inhabit. Many large issues concern all of us; on these things we may differ. We will surmount this. Political power is necessary to change the situation of the op-

pressed 51 percent, to realize the power potential in the fact that women *are* 51 percent.

We will do it by getting into city hall ourselves, or by getting into Congress ourselves, regardless of whether our political party is Republican or Democratic or Peace and Freedom. We're only going to do it by getting there ourselves; that's the nitty-gritty of self-determination for us—not to rely on Richard Nixon or a Senate with only one female or a House with only a few women to do it for us.

... We must begin to use the power of our actions: to make women finally *visible* as people in America, as conscious political and social power; to change our society *now*, so all women can move freely, as people, in it. ∾

40. Ronald Reagan

RONALD REAGAN (b. 1910) was a screen actor and radio personality before he became a full-time politician. An early leader of the conservative wing of the Republican party, he was elected governor of California in 1966 and again in 1970. He challenged the incumbent President Gerald Ford for the Republican nomination in 1976 and won the nomination in 1980. In that election, conducted under conditions of high inflation and with scores of Americans held hostage in the U.S. Embassy in Iran, Reagan won a relatively narrow victory over incumbent Democrat Jimmy Carter. The major accomplishments of Reagan's first term in office were release of the hostages, a sharp reduction in inflation, a major tax cut, and substantial military buildup. In 1984 he defeated former Vice President Walter Mondale, winning reelection in a landslide.

Reagan wrote no major book, although he was an accomplished orator able to awaken strong support from his audiences. In the speeches excerpted here, he touches on many traditional American values and beliefs and stresses patriotism and confidence in the future. This combination of tradition and optimism toward the future is often viewed as a key to Reagan's success in drawing support from mass publics, much as did Franklin Roosevelt, one of his frequently acknowledged models. Part of his characteristic style was to include human-interest anecdotes involving real people that were intended to provide moral lessons regarding issues of the day; these have been edited out to avoid excessive topicality and maintain the focus on enduring principles that Reagan espoused. ᴄ᷿

First Inaugural Address (1981)

To a few of us here today this is a solemn and most momentous occasion, and yet in the history of our nation it is a common-place occurrence. The orderly transfer of authority as called for in the Constitution routinely takes place, as it has for almost two centuries, and few of us stop to think how unique we really are. In the eyes of many in the world, this every-four-year ceremony we accept as normal is nothing less than a miracle.

Mr. President, I want our fellow citizens to know how much you did to carry on this tradition. By your gracious cooperation in the transition process, you have shown a watching world that we are a united people pledged to maintaining a political system which guarantees individual liberty to a greater degree than any other, and I thank you and your people for all your help in maintaining the continuity which is the bulwark of our Republic.

The business of our nation goes forward. These United States are confronted with an economic affliction of great proportions. We suffer from the longest and one of the worst sustained inflations in our national history. It distorts our economic decisions, penalizes thrift, and crushes the struggling young and the fixed-income elderly alike. It threatens to shatter the lives of millions of our people.

Idle industries have cast workers into unemployment, human misery, and personal indignity. Those who do work are denied a fair return for their labor by a tax system which penalizes successful achievement and keeps us from maintaining full productivity.

But great as our tax burden is, it has not kept pace with the public spending. For decades we have piled deficit upon deficit, mortgaging our future and our children's future for the temporary convenience of the present. To continue this long trend is to guarantee tremendous social, cultural, political, and economic upheavals.

You and I, as individuals, can, by borrowing, live beyond our means, but for only a limited period of time. Why, then, should we think that collectively, as a nation, we're not bound by that same limitation? We must act today in order to preserve tomorrow. And let there be no misunderstanding: We are going to begin to act, beginning today.

The economic ills we suffer have come upon us over several decades. They will not go away in days, weeks, or months, but they will go away. They will go away because we as Americans have the capacity now, as we've had in the past, to do whatever needs to be done to preserve this last and greatest bastion of freedom.

In this present crisis, government is not the solution to our problem; government is the

---

SOURCE: *Vital Speeches,* years indicated.

problem. From time to time we've been tempted to believe that society has become too complex to be managed by self-rule, that government by an elite group is superior to government for, by, and of the people. Well, if no one among us is capable of governing himself, then who among us has the capacity to govern someone else? All of us together, in and out of government, must bear the burden. The solutions we seek must be equitable, with no one group singled out to pay a higher price.

We hear much of special interest groups. Well, our concern must be for a special interest group that has been too long neglected. It knows no sectional boundaries or ethnic and racial divisions, and it crosses political party lines. It is made up of men and women who raise our food, patrol our streets, man our mines and factories, teach our children, keep our homes, and heal us when we're sick—professionals, industrialists, shopkeepers, clerks, cabbies, and truck-drivers. They are, in short, "We the people," this breed called Americans.

Well, this administration's objective will be a healthy, vigorous, growing economy that provides equal opportunities for all Americans, with no barriers born of bigotry or discrimination. Putting America back to work means putting all Americans back to work. Ending inflation means freeing all Americans from the terror of runaway living costs. All must share in the productive work of this "new beginning," and all must share in the bounty of a revived economy. With the idealism and fair play which are the core of our system and our strength, we can have a strong and prosperous America, at peace with itself and the world.

* * *

So, as we begin, let us take inventory. We are a nation that has a government—not the other way around. And this makes us special among the nations of the Earth. Our government has no power except that granted it by the people. It is time to check and reverse the growth of government, which shows signs of having grown beyond the consent of the governed....

Now, so there will be no misunderstanding, it's not my intention to do away with government. It is rather to make it work—work with us, not over us; to stand by our side, not ride our back. Government can and must provide opportunity, not smother it; foster productivity, not stifle it.

If we look to the answer as to why for so many years we achieved so much, prospered as no other people on Earth, it was because here in this land we unleashed the energy and individual genius of man to a greater extent than has ever been done before. Freedom and the dignity of the individual have been more available and assured here than in any other place on Earth. The price for this freedom at times has been high, but we have never been unwilling to pay that price....

We have every right to dream heroic dreams. Those who say that we're in a time when there are no heroes, they just don't know where to look. You can see heroes every day going in and out of factory gates. Others, a handful in number, produce enough food to feed all of us and then the world beyond. You meet heroes across a counter, and they're on both sides of that counter. There are entrepreneurs with faith in themselves and faith in an idea who create new jobs, new wealth, and opportunity. They're individuals and families whose taxes support the government and whose voluntary gifts support church, charity, culture, art, and education. Their patriotism is quiet, but deep. Their values sustain our national life.

Now, I have used the words "they" and "their" in speaking of these heroes. I could say "you" and "your," because I'm addressing the heroes of whom I speak—you, the citizens of this blessed land. Your dreams, your hopes, your goals are going to be the dreams, the hopes, and the goals of this administration, so help me God. . . .

Can we solve the problems confronting us? Well, the answer is an unequivocal and emphatic "yes." To paraphrase Winston Churchill, I did not take the oath I've just taken with the intention of presiding over the dissolution of the world's strongest economy.

In the days ahead I will propose removing the roadblocks that have slowed our economy and reduced productivity. Steps will be taken aimed at restoring the balance between the various levels of government. Progress may be slow, measured in inches and feet, not miles, but we will progress. It is time to reawaken this industrial giant, to get government back within its means, and to lighten our punitive tax burden. And these will be our first priorities, and on these principles there will be no compromise.

On the eve of our struggle for independence a man who might have been one of the greatest among the Founding Fathers, Dr. Joseph Warren, president of the Massachusetts Congress, said to his fellow Americans, "Our country is in danger, but not to be despaired of. . . . On you depend the fortunes of America. You are to decide the important questions upon which rests the happiness and the liberty of millions yet unborn. Act worthy of yourselves."

Well, I believe we, the Americans of today, are ready to act worthy of ourselves, ready to do what must be done to ensure happiness and liberty for ourselves, our children, and our children's children. And as we renew ourselves here in our own land, we will be seen as having greater strength throughout the world. We will again be the exemplar of freedom and a beacon of hope.

To those neighbors and allies who share our freedom, we will strengthen our historic ties and assure them of our support and firm commitment. We will strive for mutually beneficial relations. We will not use our friendship to impose on their sovereignty, for our own sovereignty is not for sale.

As for the enemies of freedom, those who are potential adversaries, they will be reminded that peace is the highest aspiration of the American people. We will negotiate for it, sacrifice for it; we will not surrender for it, now or ever. . . .

Above all, we must realize that no arsenal or no weapon in the arsenals of the world is so formidable as the will and moral courage of free men and women. It is a weapon our adversaries in today's world do not have. It is a weapon that we as Americans do have. Let that be understood by those who practice terrorism and prey upon their neighbors. . . .

This is the first time in our history that this ceremony has been held, as you've been told, on this West Front of the Capitol. Standing here, one faces a magnificent vista, opening up on this city's special beauty and history. At the end of this open mall are those shrines to the giants on whose shoulders we stand.

Directly in front of me, the monument to a monumental man, George Washington, father of our country. A man of humility who came to greatness reluctantly. He led America out of revolutionary victory into infant nationhood. Off to one side, the stately memorial to Thomas Jefferson. The Declaration of Independence flames with his eloquence. And then, beyond the Reflecting Pool, the dignified columns of the Lincoln Memorial. Whoever would understand in his heart the meaning of America will find it in the life of Abraham Lincoln.

Beyond those monuments to heroism is the Potomac River, and on the far shore the sloping hills of Arlington National Cemetery, with its row upon row of simple white markers bearing crosses or Stars of David. They add up to only a tiny fraction of the price that has been paid for our freedom.

Each one of those markers is a monument to the kind of hero I spoke of earlier. Their lives ended in places called Belleau Wood, The Argonne, Omaha Beach, Salerno, and halfway around the world on Guadalcanal, Tarawa, Pork Chop Hill, and Chosin Reservoir, and in the hundred rice paddies and jungles of a place called Vietnam.

Under one such marker lies a young man, Martin Treptow, who left his job in a small town barbershop in 1917 to go to France with the famed Rainbow Division. There, on the eastern front, he was killed trying to carry a message between battalions under heavy artillery fire.

We're told that on his body was found a diary. On the flyleaf under the heading, "My Pledge," he had written these words: "America must win this war. Therefore, I will work, I will save, I will sacrifice, I will endure, I will fight cheerfully and do my utmost, as if the issue of the whole struggle depended on me alone."

The crisis we are facing today does not require of us the kind of sacrifice that others were called upon to make. It does require, however, our best effort and our willingness to believe that together with God's help we can and will resolve the problems which now confront us.

And after all, why shouldn't we believe that? We are Americans. God bless you, and thank you. ∼

State of the Union Address (1984)

Mr. Speaker, Mr. President, distinguished Members of Congress, honored guests, and fellow citizens:

Once again in keeping with time-honored tradition, I have come to report to you on the state of the Union, and I'm pleased to report that America is much improved, and there's good reason to believe that improvement will continue through the days to come.

You and I have had some honest and open differences in the year past. But they didn't keep us from joining hands in bipartisan cooperation to stop a long decline that had drained this nation's spirit and eroded its health. There is renewed energy and optimism throughout the land. America is back, standing tall, looking to the eighties with courage, confidence, and hope....

As we came to the decade of the eighties, we faced the worst crisis in our postwar history. In the seventies were years of rising problems and falling confidence. There was a feeling government had grown beyond the consent of the governed. Families felt helpless in the face of mounting inflation and the indignity of taxes that reduced reward for hard work, thrift, and risk-taking. All this was overlaid by an ever-growing web of rules and regulations.

On the international scene, we had an uncomfortable feeling that we'd lost the respect of friend and foe. Some questioned whether we had the will to defend peace and freedom. But America is too great for small dreams. There was a hunger in the land for a spiritual revival; if you will, a crusade for renewal. The American people said: Let us look to the future with confidence, both at home and abroad. Let us give freedom a chance.

Americans were ready to make a new beginning, and together we have done it. We're confronting our problems one by one. Hope is alive tonight for millions of young families and senior citizens set free from unfair tax increases and crushing inflation. Inflation has been beaten down from 12.4 to 3.2 percent, and that's a great victory for all the people. The prime rate has been cut almost in half, and we must work together to bring it down even more.

Together, we passed the first across-the-board tax reduction for everyone since the Kennedy tax cuts. Next year, tax rates will be indexed so inflation can't push people into higher brackets when they get cost-of-living pay raises. Government must never again use inflation to profit at the people's expense.

Today a working family earning $25,000 has $1,100 more in purchasing power than if tax and inflation rates were still at the 1980 levels. Real after-tax income increased 5 percent last year. And economic deregulation of key industries like transportation has offered more chances—or choices, I should say, to consumers and new changes—or chances for entrepreneurs and protecting safety. Tonight, we can report and be proud of one of the best recoveries in decades. Send away the handwringers and the doubting Thomases. Hope is reborn for couples dreaming of owning homes and for risk takers with vision to create tomorrow's opportunities.

The spirit of enterprise is sparked by the sunrise industries of high-tech and by small business people with big ideas—people like Barbara Proctor, who rose from a ghetto to build a multimillion-dollar advertising agency in Chicago; Carlos Perez, a Cuban refugee, who turned $27 and a dream into a successful importing business in Coral Gables, Florida.

People like these are heroes for the eighties. They helped 4 million Americans find jobs in 1983. More people are drawing paychecks tonight than ever before. And Congress helps —or progress helps everyone—well, Congress does too. In 1983 women filled 73 percent of all the new jobs in managerial, professional, and technical fields. . . .

The Congress deserves America's thanks for helping us restore pride and credibility to our military. And I hope that you're as proud as I am of the young men and women in uniform who have volunteered to man the ramparts in defense of freedom and whose dedication, valor, and skill increases so much our chance of living in a world at peace.

People everywhere hunger for peace and a better life. The tide of the future is a freedom tide, and our struggle for democracy cannot and will not be denied. This nation champions peace that enshrines liberty, democratic rights, and dignity for every individual. America's new strength, confidence, and purpose are carrying hope and opportunity far from our shores. A world economic recovery is under way. It began here. . . .

We can ensure steady economic growth. We can develop America's next frontier. We can strengthen our traditional values. And we can build a meaningful peace to protect our loved ones and this shining star of faith that has guided millions from tyranny to the safe harbor of freedom, progress, and hope.

Doing these things will open wider the gates of opportunity, provide greater security for all, with no barriers of bigotry or discrimination.

The key to a dynamic decade is vigorous economic growth, our first great goal. We might well begin with common sense in Federal budgeting: government spending no more than government takes in.

We must bring federal deficits down. But how we do that makes all the difference.

We can begin by limiting the size and the scope of government. Under the leadership of Vice President Bush, we have reduced the growth of Federal regulations by more than 25 percent and cut well over 300 million hours of government-required paperwork each year. This will save the public more than $150 billion over the next 10 years.

The Grace commission has given us some 2,500 recommendations for reducing wasteful spending, growth has been cut from 17.4 percent in 1980 to less than half of that today, and we already achieved over $300 billion in budget savings for the period of 1982 to '86. But that's only a little more than half of what we sought. Government is still spending too large a percentage of the total economy.

Now, some insist that any further budget savings must be obtained by reducing the portion spent on defense. This ignores the fact that national defense is solely the responsibility of the Federal Government; indeed, it is its prime responsibility. And yet defense spending is less than a third of the total budget. During the years of President Kennedy and of the years before that, defense was almost half of the total budget. And then came several years in which our military capability was allowed to deteriorate to a very dangerous degree. We are just now restoring, through the essential modernization of our conventional and strategic forces, our capability to meet our present and future security needs. We dare not shirk our responsibility to keep America free, secure, and at peace.

The last decade saw domestic spending surge literally out of control. But the basis for such spending had been laid in previous years. A pattern of overspending has been in place for half a century. As the national debt grew, we were told not to worry, that we owed it to ourselves.

Now we know that deficits are a cause for worry. But there's a difference of opinion as to whether taxes should be increased, spending cut, or some of both. Fear is expressed that government borrowing to fund the deficit could inhibit the economic recovery by taking capital needed for business and industrial ex-

pansion. Well, I think that debate is missing an important point. Whether government borrows or increases taxes, it will be taking the same amount of money from the private sector, and, either way, that's too much. Simple fairness dictates that government must not raise taxes on families struggling to pay their bills. The root of the problem is that government's share is more than we can afford if we're to have sound economy.

We must bring down the deficits to ensure continued economic growth. In the budget that I will submit on February 1, I will recommend measures that will reduce the deficit over the next five years. Many of these will be unfinished business from last year's budget.

Some could be enacted quickly if we could join in a serious effort to address this problem. I spoke with Speaker of the House O'Neill, Senate Majority Leader Baker, Senate Minority Leader Byrd, and House Minority Leader Michel. I asked them if they would designate congressional representatives to meet with representatives of the administration to try to reach prompt agreement on a bipartisan deficit reduction plan. I know it would take a long hard struggle to agree on a full-scale plan. So, what I have proposed is that we first see if we can agree on a downpayment.

Now, I believe there is basis for such an agreement, one that could reduce the deficits by about a hundred billion dollars over the next three years. We could focus on some of the less contentious spending cuts that are still pending before the Congress. These could be combined with measures to close certain tax loopholes, measures that the Treasury Department has previously said to be worthy of support. In addition, we could examine the possibility of achieving further outlay savings based on the work of the Grace commission.

If the congressional leadership is willing, my representatives will be prepared to meet with theirs at the earliest possible time. I would hope the leadership might agree on an expedited timetable in which to develop and enact that downpayment.

But a downpayment alone is not enough to break us out of the deficit problem. It could help us start on the right path. Yet, we must do more. So, I propose that we begin exploring how together we can make structural reforms to curb the built-in growth of spending.

I also propose improvements in the budgeting process. Some 43 of our 50 States grant their Governors the right to veto individual items in appropriation bills without having to veto the entire bill. California is one of those 43 States. As Governor, I found this line-item veto was a powerful tool against wasteful or extravagant spending. It works in 43 States. Let's put it to work in Washington for all the people.

It would be most effective if done by constitutional amendment. The majority of Americans approve of such an amendment, just as they and I approve of an amendment mandating a balanced Federal budget. Many States also have this protection in their constitutions.

To talk of meeting the present situation by increasing taxes is a Band-Aid solution which does nothing to cure an illness that's been coming on for half a century—to say nothing of the fact that it poses a real threat to economic recovery. Let's remember that a substantial amount of income tax is presently owed and not paid by people in the underground economy. It would be immoral to make those who are paying taxes pay more to compensate for those who aren't paying their share.

There's a better way. Let us go forward with a historic reform for fairness, simplicity, and incentives for growth. I am asking Secretary Don Regan for a plan for action to simplify the entire tax code, so all taxpayers, big and small, are treated more fairly. And I believe such a plan could result in that underground economy being brought into the sunlight of honest tax compliance. And it could make the tax base broader, so personal tax rates could come down, not go up. I've asked that specific recommendations, consistent with those objectives, be presented to me by December 1984.

Our second great goal is to build on America's pioneer spirit—I said something funny? I said America's next frontier—and that's to develop that frontier. A sparkling economy spurs initiatives, sunrise industries, and makes older ones more competitive.

Nowhere is this more important than our next frontier: space. Nowhere do we so effectively demonstrate our technological leadership and ability to make life better on Earth. The Space Age is barely a quarter of a century old. But already we've pushed civilization forward with our advances in science and technology. Opportunities and jobs will multiply as we cross new thresholds of knowledge and reach deeper into the unknown. . . .

America has always been greatest when we dared to be great. We can reach for greatness again. We can follow our dreams to distant stars, living and working in space for peaceful, economic, and scientific gain. Tonight, I am directing NASA to develop a permanently manned space station and to do it within a decade.

A space station will permit quantum leaps in our research in science, communications in metals, and in life-saving medicines which could be manufactured only in space. We want our friends to help us meet these challenges and share in their benefits. NASA will invite other countries to participate so we can strengthen peace, build prosperity, and expand freedom for all who share our goals.

Just as the oceans opened up a new world for clipper ships and Yankee traders, space holds enormous potential for commerce today. The market for space transportation could surpass our capacity to develop it. Companies interested in putting payloads into space must have ready access to private sector launch services. The Department of Transportation will help an expendable launch services industry to get off the ground. We'll soon implement a number of executive initiatives, develop proposals to ease regulatory constraints, and, with NASA's help, promote private sector investment in space.

And as we develop the frontier of space let us remember our responsibility to preserve our older resources here on Earth. Preservation of our environment is not a liberal or conservative challenge, it's common sense.

Though this is a time of budget constraints, I have requested for EPA one of the largest percentage budget increases of any agency. We will gain the long, necessary effort to clean up a productive recreational area and a special national resource—the Chesapeake Bay.

To reduce the threat posed by abandoned hazardous waste dumps, EPA will spend $410 million. And I will request a supplemental increase of $50 million. And because the Superfund law expires in 1985, I've asked Bill Ruckelshaus to develop a proposal for its extension so there'll be additional time to complete this important task.

On the question of acid rain, which concerns people in many areas of the United States and Canada, I'm proposing a research program that doubles our current funding. And we'll take additional action to restore our lakes and develop new technology to reduce pollution that causes acid rain.

We have greatly improved the conditions of our natural resources. We'll ask the Congress for $157 million beginning in 1985 to acquire new park and conservation lands. The Department of the Interior will encourage careful, selective exploration and production on our vital resources in an Exclusive Economic Zone within the 200-mile limit off our coasts—but with strict adherence to environmental laws and with fuller State and public participation.

But our most precious resources, our greatest hope for the future, are the minds and hearts of our people, especially our children. We can help them build tomorrow by strengthening our community of shared values. This must be our third great goal. For us, faith, work, family, neighborhood, freedom, and peace are not just words, they're expressions of what America means, definitions of what makes us a good and loving people.

Families stand at the center of our society. And every family has a personal stake in promoting excellence in education. Excellence does not begin in Washington. A 600-percent increase in Federal spending on education between 1960 and 1980 was accompanied by a steady decline in Scholastic Aptitude Test scores. Excellence must begin in our homes and neighborhood schools, where it's the responsibility of every parent and teacher and the right of every child.

Our children come first, and that's why I established a bipartisan National Commission on Excellence in Education, to help us chart a commonsense course for better education. And already, communities are implementing the Commission's recommendations. Schools are reporting progress in math and reading skills. But we must do more to restore discipline to schools; and we must encourage the teaching of new basics, reward teachers of merit, enforce tougher standards, and put our parents back in charge.

I will continue to press for tuition tax credits to expand opportunities for families and to soften the double payment for those paying public school taxes and private school tuition. Our proposal would target assistance to low- and middle-income families. Just as more incentives are needed within our schools, greater competition is needed among our schools.

Without standards and competition, there can be no champions, no records broken, no excellence in education or any other walk of life.

And while I'm on this subject, each day your Members observe a 200-year-old tradition meant to signify America is one nation under God. I must ask: if you can begin your day with a member of the clergy standing right here leading you in prayer, then why can't freedom to acknowledge God be enjoyed again by children in every schoolroom across this land?

. . .

During our first three years, we have joined bipartisan efforts to restore protection of the law to unborn children. Now, I know this issue is very controversial. But unless and until it can be proven that an unborn child is not a living human being, can we justify assuming without proof it isn't? No one has yet offered such proof; indeed, all the evidence is to the contrary. We should rise above bitterness and reproach, and if Americans could come together in a spirit of understanding and helping, then we could find positive solutions to the tragedy of abortion.

Economic recovery, better education, rededication to values, all show the spirit of renewal gaining the upper hand. And all will improve family life in the eighties. But families need more. They need assurance that they and their loved ones can walk the streets of America without being afraid. Parents need to know their children will not be victims of child pornography and abduction. This year we will intensify our drive against these and other horrible crimes like sexual abuse and family violence.

Already our efforts to crack down on career criminals, organized crime, drug-pushers, and to enforce tougher sentences and paroles are having effect. In 1982 the crime rate dropped by 4.3 percent, the biggest decline since 1972. Protecting victims is just as important as safeguarding the rights of defendants.

Opportunities for all Americans will increase if we move forward in fair housing and work to ensure women's rights, provide for equitable treatment in pension benefits and Individual Retirement Accounts, facilitate child care, and enforce delinquent parent support payments.

It's not just the home but the work place and community that sustain our values and shape our future. So, I ask your help in assisting more communities to break the bondage of dependency. Help us to free enterprise by permitting debate and voting "yes" on our proposal for enterprise zones in America. This has been before you for two years. Its passage can help high-employment areas by creating jobs and restoring neighborhoods. . . .

A lasting and meaningful peace is our fourth great goal. It is our highest aspiration. And our record is clear: Americans resort to force only when we must. We have never been aggressors. We have always struggled to defend freedom and democracy.

We have no territorial ambitions. We occupy no countries. We build no walls to lock people in. Americans build the future. And our visions of a better life for farmers, merchants, and working people, from the Americas to Asia, begins with a simple premise: The future is best decided by ballots, not bullets.

Governments which rest upon the consent of the governed do not wage war on their neighbors. Only when people are given a personal stake in deciding their own destiny, benefiting from their own risks, do they create societies that are prosperous, and free. Tonight, it is democracies that offer hope by feeding the hungry, prolonging life, and eliminating drudgery.

When it comes to keeping America strong, free, and at peace, there should be no Republicans or Democrats, just patriotic Americans. We can decide the tough issues not by who is right, but by what is right.

Together, we can continue to advance our agenda for peace. We can establish a more stable basis for peaceful relations with the Soviet Union; strengthen allied relations across the board; achieve real and equitable reductions in the levels of nuclear arms; reinforce our peacemaking efforts in the Middle East, Central America, and southern Africa; or assist developing countries, particularly our neighbors in the Western Hemisphere; and assist in the development of democratic institutions throughout the world.

Tonight, I want to speak to the people of the Soviet Union, to tell them it's true that our governments have had serious differences, but our sons and daughters have never fought each other in war. And if we Americans have our way, they never will.

People of the Soviet Union, there is only one sane policy, for your country and mine, to preserve our civilization in this modern age: A nuclear war cannot be won and must never be fought. The only value in our two nations possessing nuclear weapons is to make sure they will never be used. But then would it not be better to do away with them entirely?

People of the Soviet Union, President Dwight Eisenhower, who fought by your side in World War II, said the essential struggle "is not merely man against man or nation against nation. It is man against war." Americans are people of peace. If your government wants peace, there will be peace. We can come together in faith and friendship to build a safer and far better world for our children and our children's children. And the whole world will rejoice. That is my message to you.

How can we not believe in the greatness of America? How can we not do what is right and needed to preserve this last best hope of man on Earth? After all our struggles to restore America, to revive confidence in our country, hope for our future, after all our hard-won victories earned through the patience and courage of every citizen, we cannot, must not, and will not turn back. We will finish our job. How could we do less? We are Americans.

Carl Sandburg said, "I see America not in the setting sun of a black night of despair ... I see America in the crimson light of a rising sun fresh from the burning, creative hand of God ... I see great days ahead for men and women of will and vision." ...

Let us be sure that those who come after will say of us that in our time we did everything that could be done. We finished the race; we kept them free; we kept the faith.

Thank you very much. God bless you, and God bless America. ∼

41. National Conference of Catholic Bishops

THE NATIONAL CONFERENCE of Catholic Bishops is the principal vehicle for the American Catholic hierarchy to express itself, usually with respect to religious issues and church practices, but also with respect to policy questions involving moral dimensions. Such policy statements often take the form of a pastoral letter, made available publicly and through the Catholic churches of the country. Following the November 1980 general meeting of the Conference, a committee was appointed to draft a pastoral letter on the U.S. economy. The first draft was presented to the bishops in 1984 and discussed at length, after which subsequent drafts were presented and discussed in 1985 and 1986. Approval of the text was given and publication authorized by the plenary assembly in November 1986.

As might be anticipated, the pastoral letter proved highly controversial because it put the moral weight of the Catholic church behind redistributive economic principles. The letter explained itself as "a personal invitation to Catholics to use the resources of our faith, the strength of our economy, and the opportunities of our democracy to shape a society that better protects the dignity and basic rights of our sisters and brothers, both in this land and around the world." The bishops' central point was that it was appropriate, even necessary, to look at the workings of the economy in terms of the moral teachings of Christian faith. But many Catholic laypersons, and conservatives generally, clearly did not accept the bishops' principles nor their assumption of such a role in the public policy debates of the nation. ∾

Economic Justice for All: Pastoral Letter on Catholic Social Teaching and the U.S. Economy (1986)

PRINCIPAL THEMES
OF THE PASTORAL LETTER

12. The pastoral letter is not a blueprint for the American economy. It does not embrace any particular theory of how the economy works, nor does it attempt to resolve the disputes between different schools of economic thought. Instead, our letter turns to Scripture and to the social teachings of the Church. There, we discover what our economic life must serve, what standards it must meet. Let us examine some of these basic moral principles.

13. *Every economic decision and institution must be judged in light of whether it protects or undermines the dignity of the human person.* The pastoral letter begins with the human person. We believe the person is sacred—the clearest reflection of God among us. Human dignity comes from God, not from nationality, race, sex, economic status, or any

SOURCE: National Conference of Catholic Bishops, *Economic Justice for All: Pastoral Letter on Catholic Social Teaching and the U.S. Economy* (1986).

human accomplishment. We judge any economic system by what it does *for* and *to* people and by how it permits all to *participate* in it. The economy should serve people, not the other way around.

14. *Human dignity can be realized and protected only in community.* In our teaching, the human person is not only sacred but also social. How we organize our society—in economics and politics, in law and policy—directly affects human dignity and the capacity of individuals to grow in community. The obligation to "love our neighbor" has an individual dimension, but it also requires a broader social commitment to the common good. We have many partial ways to measure and debate the health of our economy: Gross National Product, per capita income, stock market prices, and so forth. The Christian vision of economic life looks beyond them all and asks, Does economic life enhance or threaten our life together as a community?

15. *All people have a right to participate in the economic life of society.* Basic justice demands that people be assured a minimum level of participation in the economy. It is wrong for a person or group to be excluded unfairly or to be unable to participate or contribute to the economy. For example, people who are both able and willing, but cannot get a job are deprived of the participation that is so vital to human development. For, it is through employment that most individuals and families meet their material needs, exercise their talents, and have an opportunity to contribute to the larger community. Such participation has a special significance in our tradition because we believe that it is a means by which we join in carrying forward God's creative activity.

16. *All members of society have a special obligation to the poor and vulnerable.* From the Scriptures and church teaching, we learn that the justice of a society is tested by the treatment of the poor. The justice that was the

sign of God's covenant with Israel was measured by how the poor and unprotected—the widow, the orphan, and the stranger—were treated. The kingdom that Jesus proclaimed in his word and ministry excludes no one. Throughout Israel's history and in early Christianity, the poor are agents of God's transforming power. "The Spirit of the Lord is upon me, therefore he has anointed me. He has sent me to bring glad tidings to the poor" (Lk 4:18). This was Jesus' first public utterance. Jesus takes the side of those most in need. In the Last Judgment, so dramatically described in St. Matthew's Gospel, we are told that we will be judged according to how we respond to the hungry, the thirsty, the naked, the stranger. As followers of Christ, we are challenged to make a fundamental "option for the poor"—to speak for the voiceless, to defend the defenseless, to assess life styles, policies, and social institutions in terms of their impact on the poor. This "option for the poor" does not mean pitting one group against another, but rather, strengthening the whole community by assisting those who are most vulnerable. As Christians, we are called to respond to the needs of *all* our brothers and sisters, but those with the greatest needs require the greatest response.

17. *Human rights are the minimum conditions for life in the community.* In Catholic teaching, human rights include not only civil and political rights but also economic rights. As Pope John XXIII declared, "all people have a right to life, food, clothing, shelter, rest, medical care, education, and employment." This means that when people are without a chance to earn a living, and must go hungry and homeless, they are being denied basic rights. Society must ensure that these rights are protected. In this way, we will ensure that the minimum conditions of economic justice are met for all our sisters and brothers.

18. *Society as a whole, acting through pub-*

lic and private institutions, has the moral responsibility to enhance human dignity and protect human rights. In addition to the clear responsibility of private institutions, government has an essential responsibility in this area. This does not mean that government has the primary or exclusive role, but it does have a positive moral responsibility in safeguarding human rights and ensuring that the minimum conditions of human dignity are met for all. In a democracy, government is a means by which we can act together to protect what is important to us and to promote our common values.

19. These six moral principles are not the only ones presented in the pastoral letter, but they give an overall view of the moral vision that we are trying to share. This vision of economic life cannot exist in a vacuum; it must be translated into concrete measures. Our pastoral letter spells out some specific applications of Catholic moral principles. We call for a new national commitment to full employment. We say it is a social and moral scandal that one of every seven Americans is poor, and we call for concerted efforts to eradicate poverty. The fulfillment of the basic needs of the poor is of the highest priority. We urge that all economic policies be evaluated in light of their impact on the life and stability of the family. We support measures to halt the loss of family farms and to resist the growing concentration in the ownership of agricultural resources. We specify ways in which the United States can do far more to relieve the plight of poor nations and assist in their development. We also reaffirm church teaching on the rights of workers, collective bargaining, private property, subsidiarity, and equal opportunity.

20. We believe that the recommendations in our letter are reasonable and balanced. In analyzing the economy, we reject ideological extremes and start from the fact that ours is a "mixed" economy, the product of a long history of reform and adjustment. We know that some of our specific recommendations are controversial. As bishops, we do not claim to make these prudential judgments with the same kind of authority that marks our declarations of principle. But, we feel obliged to teach by example how Christians can undertake concrete analysis and make specific judgments on economic issues. The Church's teachings cannot be left at the level of appealing generalities.

21. In the pastoral letter, we suggest that the time has come for a "New American Experiment"—to implement economic rights, to broaden the sharing of economic power, and to make economic decisions more accountable to the common good. This experiment can create new structures of economic partnership and participation within firms at the regional level, for the whole nation, and across borders.

22. Of course, there are many aspects of the economy the letter does not touch, and there are basic questions it leaves to further exploration. There are also many specific points on which men and women of good will may disagree. We look for a fruitful exchange among differing viewpoints. We pray only that all will take to heart the urgency of our concerns; that together we will test our views by the Gospel and the Church's teaching; and that we will listen to other voices in a spirit of mutual respect and open dialogue.

THE CHURCH AND THE FUTURE OF THE U.S. ECONOMY

1. Every perspective on economic life that is human, moral, and Christian must be shaped by three questions: What does the economy do *for* people? What does it do *to* people? And how do people *participate* in it? The economy is a human reality: men and women working together to develop and care for the whole of God's creation. All this work must serve the material and spiritual well-being of people. It influences what people hope for themselves

and their loved ones. It affects the way they act together in society. It influences their very faith in God.

2. The Second Vatican Council declared that "the joys and hopes, the griefs and anxieties of the people of this age, especially those who are poor or in any way afflicted, these too are the joys and hopes, the griefs and anxieties of the followers of Christ." There are many signs of hope in U.S. economic life today:

- Many fathers and mothers skillfully balance the arduous responsibilities of work and family life. There are parents who pursue a purposeful and modest way of life and by their example encourage their children to follow a similar path. A large number of women and men, drawing on their religious tradition, recognize the challenging vocation of family life and child rearing in a culture that emphasizes material display and self-gratification.
- Conscientious business people seek new and more equitable ways to organize resources and the workplace. They face hard choices over expanding or retrenching, shifting investments, hiring or firing.
- Young people choosing their life's work ask whether success and security are compatible with service to others.
- Workers whose labor may be toilsome or repetitive try daily to ennoble their work with a spirit of solidarity and friendship.
- New immigrants brave dislocations while hoping for the opportunities realized by the millions who came before them.

3. These signs of hope are not the whole story. There have been failures—some of them massive and ugly:

- Poor and homeless people sleep in community shelters and in our church basements; the hungry line up in soup lines.

- Unemployment gnaws at the self-respect of both middle-aged persons who have lost jobs and the young who cannot find them.
- Hardworking men and women wonder if the system of enterprise that helped them yesterday might destroy their jobs and their communities tomorrow.
- Families confront major new challenges: dwindling social supports for family stability; economic pressures that force both partners of young children to work outside the home; a driven pace of life among the successful that can sap love and commitment; lack of hope among those who have less or nothing at all. Very different kinds of families bear different burdens of our economic system.
- Farmers face the loss of their land and way of life; young people find it difficult to choose farming as a vocation; farming communities are threatened; migrant farmworkers break their backs in serf-like conditions for disgracefully low wages.

4. *And beyond our own shores, the reality of 800 million people living in absolute poverty and 450 million malnourished or facing starvation casts an ominous shadow over all these hopes and problems at home.*

5. Anyone who sees all this will understand our concern as pastors and bishops. People shape the economy and in turn are shaped by it. Economic arrangements can be sources of fulfillment, of hope, of community—or of frustration, isolation, and even despair. They teach virtues—or vices—and day by day help mold our characters. They affect the quality of people's lives; at the extreme even determining whether people live or die. Serious economic choices go beyond purely technical issues to fundamental questions of value and human purpose. We believe that in facing these questions the Christian religious and moral tradition can make an important contribution.

A. The U.S. Economy Today: Memory and Hope

6. The United States is among the most economically powerful nations on earth. In its short history the U.S. economy has grown to provide an unprecedented standard of living for most of its people. The nation has created productive work for millions of immigrants and enabled them to broaden their freedoms, improve their families' quality of life, and contribute to the building of a great nation. Those who came to this country from other lands often understood their new lives in the light of biblical faith. They thought of themselves as entering a promised land of political freedom and economic opportunity. The United States is a land of vast natural resources and fertile soil. It *has* encouraged citizens to undertake bold ventures. Through hard work, self-sacrifice, and cooperation, families have flourished; towns, cities, and a powerful nation have been created.

7. But we should recall this history with sober humility. The American experiment in social, political, and economic life has involved serious conflict and suffering. Our nation was born in the face of injustice to Native Americans, and its independence was paid for with the blood of revolution. Slavery stained the commercial life of the land through its first two hundred and fifty years and was ended only by a violent civil war. The establishment of women's suffrage, the protection of industrial workers, the elimination of child labor, the response to the Great Depression of the 1930s, and the civil rights movement of the 1960s all involved a sustained struggle to transform the political and economic institutions of the nation.

8. The U.S. value system emphasizes economic freedom. It also recognizes that the market is limited by fundamental human rights. Some things are never to be bought or sold. This conviction has prompted positive steps to modify the operation of the market when it harms vulnerable members of society. Labor unions help workers resist exploitation. Through their government, the people of the United States have provided support for education, access to food, unemployment compensation, security in old age, and protection of the environment. The market system contributes to the success of the U.S. economy, but so do many efforts to forge economic institutions and public policies that enable *all* to share in the riches of the nation. The country's economy has been built through a creative struggle; entrepreneurs, business people, workers, unions, consumers, and government have all played essential roles.

9. The task of the United States today is as demanding as that faced by our forebears. Abraham Lincoln's words at Gettysburg are a reminder that complacency today would be a betrayal of our nation's history: "It is for us, the living, rather to be dedicated here to the unfinished work ... they have thus far nobly advanced." There is unfinished business in the American experiment in freedom and justice for all.

B. Urgent Problems of Today

10. The preeminent role of the United States in an increasingly interdependent global economy is a central sign of our times. The United States is still the world's economic giant. Decisions made here have immediate effects in other countries; decisions made abroad have immediate consequences for steelworkers in Pittsburgh, oil company employees in Houston, and farmers in Iowa. U.S. economic growth is vitally dependent on resources from other countries and on their purchases of our goods and services. Many jobs in U.S. industry and agriculture depend on our ability to export manufactured goods and food.

11. In some industries the mobility of capital and technology makes wages the main variable in the cost of production. Overseas competitors with the same technology but with wage rates as low as one-tenth of ours put enormous pressure on U.S. firms to cut wages, relocate abroad, or close. U.S. workers and their communities should not be expected to bear these burdens alone.

12. All people on this globe share a common ecological environment that is under increasing pressure. Depletion of soil, water, and other natural resources endangers the future. Pollution of air and water threatens the delicate balance of the biosphere on which future generations will depend. The resources of the earth have been created by God for the benefit of all, and we who are alive today hold them in trust. This is a challenge to develop a new ecological ethic that will help shape a future that is both just and sustainable.

13. In short, nations separated by geography, culture, and ideology are linked in a complex commercial, financial, technological, and environmental network. These links have two direct consequences. First, they create hope for a new form of community among all peoples, one built on dignity, solidarity, and justice. Second, this rising global awareness calls for greater attention to the stark inequities across countries in the standards of living and control of resources. We must not look at the welfare of U.S. citizens as the only good to be sought. Nor may we overlook the disparities of power in the relationships between this nation and the developing countries. The United States is the major supplier of food to other countries, a major source of arms sales to developing nations, and a powerful influence in multilateral institutions such as the International Monetary Fund, the World Bank, and the United Nations. What Americans see as a growing interdependence is regarded by many in the less developed countries as a pattern of domination and dependence.

14. Within this larger international setting, there are also a number of challenges to the domestic economy that call for creativity and courage. The promise of the "American dream"—freedom for all persons to develop their God-given talents to the full—remains unfulfilled for millions in the United States today.

15. Several areas of U.S. economic life demand special attention. Unemployment is the most basic. Despite the large number of new jobs the U.S. economy has generated in the past decade, approximately 8 million people seeking work in this country are unable to find it, and many more are so discouraged they have stopped looking. Over the past two decades the nation has come to tolerate an increasing level of unemployment. The 6 to 7 percent rate deemed acceptable today would have been intolerable twenty years ago. Among the unemployed are a disproportionate number of blacks, Hispanics, young people, or women who are the sole support of their families. Some cities and states have many more unemployed persons than others as a result of economic forces that have little to do with people's desire to work. Unemployment is a tragedy no matter whom it strikes, but the tragedy is compounded by the unequal and unfair way it is distributed in our society.

16. Harsh poverty plagues our country despite its great wealth. More than 33 million Americans are poor; by any reasonable standard another 20 to 30 million are needy. Poverty is increasing in the United States, not decreasing. For a people who believe in "progress," this should be cause for alarm. These burdens fall most heavily on blacks, Hispanics, and Native Americans. Even more disturbing is the large increase in the number of women and children living in poverty. Today children are the largest single group among the poor. This tragic fact seriously threatens the nation's

future. That so many people are poor in a nation as rich as ours is a social and moral scandal that we cannot ignore.

17. Many working people and middle-class Americans live dangerously close to poverty. A rising number of families must rely on the wages of two or even three members just to get by. From 1968 to 1978 nearly a quarter of the U.S. population was in poverty part of the time and received welfare benefits in at least one year. The loss of a job, illness, or the breakup of a marriage may be all it takes to push people into poverty.

18. The lack of a mutually supportive relation between family life and economic life is one of the most serious problems facing the United States today. The economic and cultural strength of the nation is directly linked to the stability and health of its families. When families thrive, spouses contribute to the common good through their work at home, in the community, and in their jobs; and children develop a sense of their own worth and of their responsibility to serve others. When families are weak or break down entirely, the dignity of parents and children is threatened. High cultural and economic costs are inflicted on society at large.

19. The precarious economic situation of so many people and so many families calls for examination of U.S. economic arrangements. Christian conviction and the American promise of liberty and justice for all give the poor and the vulnerable a special claim on the nation's concern. They also challenge all members of the Church to help build a more just society.

20. The investment of human creativity and material resources in the production of the weapons of war makes these economic problems even more difficult to solve. Defense Department expenditures in the United States are almost $300 billion per year. The rivalry and mutual fear between superpowers divert into projects that threaten death, minds, and money that could better human life. Developing countries engage in arms races they can ill afford, often with the encouragement of the superpowers. Some of the poorest countries of the world use scarce resources to buy planes, guns, and other weapons when they lack the food, education, and health care their people need. Defense policies must be evaluated and assessed in light of their real contribution to freedom, justice, and peace for the citizens of our own and other nations. We have developed a perspective on these multiple moral concerns in our 1983 pastoral letter, *The Challenge of Peace: God's Promise and Our Response.* When weapons or strategies make questionable contributions to security, peace, and justice and will also be very expensive, spending priorities should be redirected to more pressing social needs.

21. Many other social and economic challenges require careful analysis: the movement of many industries from the Snowbelt to the Sunbelt, the federal deficit and interest rates, corporate mergers and takeovers, the effects of new technologies such as robotics and information systems in U.S. industry, immigration policy, growing international traffic in drugs, and the trade imbalance. All of these issues do not provide a complete portrait of the economy. Rather they are symptoms of more fundamental currents shaping U.S. economic life today: the struggle to find meaning and value in human work, efforts to support individual freedom in the context of renewed social cooperation, the urgent need to create equitable forms of global interdependence in a world now marked by extreme inequality. These deeper currents are cultural and moral in content. They show that the long-range challenges facing the nation call for sustained reflection on the values that guide economic choices and are embodied in economic institutions. Such explicit reflection on the ethical content of eco-

nomic choices and policies must become an integral part of the way Christians relate religious belief to the realities of everyday life. In this way, the "split between the faith which many profess and their daily lives," which Vatican II counted among the more serious errors of the modern age, will begin to be bridged.

C. *The Need for Moral Vision*

22. Sustaining a common culture and a common commitment to moral values is not easy in our world. Modern economic life is based on a division of labor into specialized jobs and professions. Since the industrial revolution, people have had to define themselves and their work ever more narrowly to find a niche in the economy. The benefits of this are evident in the satisfaction many people derive from contributing their specialized skills to society. But the costs are social fragmentation, a decline in seeing how one's work serves the whole community, and an increased emphasis on personal goals and private interests. This is vividly clear in discussions of economic justice. Here it is often difficult to find a common ground among people with different backgrounds and concerns. One of our chief hopes in writing this letter is to encourage and contribute to the development of this common ground.

23. Strengthening common moral vision is essential if the economy is to serve all people more fairly. Many middle-class Americans feel themselves in the grip of economic demands and cultural pressures that go far beyond the individual family's capacity to cope. Without constructive guidance in making decisions with serious moral implications, men and women who hold positions of responsibility in corporations or government find their duties exacting a heavy price. We want these reflections to help them contribute to a more just economy.

24. The quality of the national discussion about our economic future will affect the poor most of all, in this country and throughout the world. The life and dignity of millions of men, women, and children hang in the balance. Decisions must be judged in light of what they do *for* the poor, what they do to the poor, and what they enable the poor to do *for themselves*. The fundamental moral criterion for all economic decisions, policies, and institutions is this: They must be at the service of *all people, especially the poor*.

25. This letter is based on a long tradition of Catholic social thought, rooted in the Bible and developed over the past century by the popes and the Second Vatican Council in response to modern economic conditions. This tradition insists that human dignity, realized in community with others and with the whole of God's creation, is the norm against which every social institution must be measured.

26. This teaching has a rich history. It is also dynamic and growing. Pope Paul VI insisted that all Christian communities have the responsibility "to analyze with objectivity the situation which is proper to their own country, to shed on it the light of the Gospel's unalterable words and to draw principles of reflection, norms of judgment, and directives for action from the social teaching of the Church." Therefore, we build on the past work of our own bishops' conference, including the 1919 Program of Social Reconstruction and other pastoral letters. In addition many people from the Catholic, Protestant, and Jewish communities, in academic, business, or political life, and from many different economic backgrounds have also provided guidance. We want to make the legacy of Christian social thought a living, growing resource that can inspire hope and help shape the future.

27. We write, then, first of all to provide guidance for members of our own Church as they seek to form their consciences about economic matters. No one may claim the name

Christian and be comfortable in the face of the hunger, homelessness, insecurity, and injustice found in this country and the world. At the same time, we want to add our voice to the public debate about the directions in which the U.S. economy should be moving. We seek the cooperation and support of those who do not share our faith or tradition. ⌒

42. Carolyn Merchant

CAROLYN MERCHANT (b. 1936) is a leading scholar and ecofeminist whose current appointment is as professor of environmental history, philosophy, and ethics at the University of California, Berkeley. She earned her Ph.D. at the University of Wisconsin in 1967. Her scholarly work has brought together the fields of the history of science, gender studies, and ecology, in particular showing how the epistemological basis of "science" and the social ideology of male dominance are mutually supporting. In *The Death of Nature: Women, Ecology, and the Scientific Revolution* (1980) she shows that concepts of nature have always been female and that the task of (male) science is to find ways to dominate and exploit nature-as-female. In many ways, she is rewriting the environmental understanding of the early (Progressive era) conservation movement.

The excerpt here is from two chapters of Merchant's *Ecological Revolutions: Nature, Gender, and Science in New England* (1989), in which she develops a provocative theory of the succession of ecological revolutions that change human relationships to nature and the social relations that people have with one another. She sees economics, power structures, dominant worldviews, and gender relations as an integrated whole —changing together in linkage with ecological changes. She argues that an ecological revolution is under way in the 1990s, such that the nature of the American economy and social relations in the United States—and between the United States and the world—are entering a period of fundamental change. ᕼ

Ecological Revolutions (1989)

1. ECOLOGY AND HISTORY

Wherever [man] plants his foot, the harmonies of nature are turned to discords.... Indigenous vegetable and animal species are extirpated and supplanted by others of foreign origin ... with new and reluctant growth of vegetable forms, and with alien tribes of animals. These intentional changes and substitutions constitute indeed great revolutions.—George Perkins Marsh, *Man and Nature,* 1864

When Vermont statesman and author George Perkins Marsh took up his pen to write to botanist Asa Gray in 1849, he revealed the concerns that would spark his quest to understand the destruction of New England in a historical context. "I spent my early life almost literally in the woods. A large portion of the territory of Vermont was, within my recollection, covered with the natural forest.... Having been personally engaged to a considerable extent," he confessed, "in clearing lands, and manufacturing, and dealing in lumber, I have had occasion both to observe and to feel the effects resulting from an injudicious system of managing woodlands and the products of the forest." The changes that Marsh observed and docu-

SOURCE: Reprinted from Carolyn Merchant, *Ecological Revolutions: Nature, Gender, and Science in New England.* Copyright © 1989 by the University of North Carolina Press. Reprinted by permission of the author and publisher.

mented in *Man and Nature* were the culmination of a history of European interactions with the land. They were reflected only belatedly in the New World.

New England is a mirror on the world. Changes in its ecology and society over its first 250 years were rapid and revolutionary. Only through a historical approach can the magnitude and implications of such changes for the human future be fully appreciated. What took place in 2,500 years of European development through social evolution came to New England in a tenth of that time through revolution. This book delineates the characteristics of ecological revolution—colonial and capitalist—through the study of the New England exemplar. Yet the implications extend far beyond the confines of New England. As the American frontier moved west, similar ecological revolutions followed each other in increasingly telescoped periods of time. Moreover, as Europeans settled other temperate countries throughout the world, colonial ecological revolutions took place.

Today, capitalist ecological revolutions are occurring in many developing countries in a tenth of New England's transformation time. In the epilogue, it is suggested that human beings are now entering a third type of revolution—a global ecological revolution—that encompasses the entire earth.

Between 1600 and 1860 two major transformations in New England land and life took place. The first, a colonial ecological revolution, occurred during the seventeenth century and was externally generated. It resulted in the collapse of indigenous Indian ecologies and the incorporation of a European ecological complex of animals, plants, pathogens, and people. The colonial revolution extracted native species from their ecological contexts and shipped them overseas as commodities. It was legitimated by a set of symbols that placed cultured European humans above wild nature, other animals, and "beastlike savages." It substituted a visual for an oral consciousness and an image of nature as female and subservient to a transcendent male God for the Indians' animistic fabric of symbolic exchanges between people and nature.

The second transformation, a capitalist ecological revolution, took place roughly between the American Revolution and about 1860. It was initiated by internal tensions within New England and by a dynamic market economy. Local factories imported natural resources and exported finished products. Air pollution, water pollution, and resource depletions were created as externalities outside the calculation of profits. The capitalist revolution demanded an economy of increased human labor, land management, and a legitimating mechanistic science. It split human consciousness into a disembodied analytic mind and a romantic emotional sensibility.

Each of these "ecological revolutions" altered the local ecology, human society, and human consciousness. New material structures and technologies—maps, plows, fences, clocks, and chemicals—were imposed on nature. The relations between men and women through which daily life was maintained and reproduced were radically changed. And in turn the forms of consciousness—perceiving, symbolizing, and analyzing—through which humans socially constructed and interpreted the natural environment were reorganized.

My thesis is that ecological revolutions are major transformations in human relations with nonhuman nature. They arise from changes, tensions, and contradictions that develop between a society's mode of production and its ecology, and between its modes of production and reproduction. These dynamics in turn support the acceptance of new forms of consciousness, ideas, images, and worldviews. The course of the colonial and capitalist ecological revolutions in New England may be understood through a description of each society's ecology, production, reproduction, and forms of consciousness; the processes by which they broke down; and an analysis of the new relations between the emergent colonial or capitalist society and nonhuman nature.

Two frameworks of analysis offer springboards for discussing the structure of such ecological revolutions. In *The Structure of Scientific Revolutions* (1962), Thomas Kuhn approached major transformations in scientific consciousness from a perspective internal to the workings of science and the community of scientists. Scientific paradigms are structures of thought shared by groups of scientists within which problems are solved. When a sufficient number of anomalies challenges a scientific theory, scientists construct new paradigms, initiating scientific revolutions. The Copernican revolution in the sixteenth century, the Newtonian revolution in the seventeenth, Lavoisier's chemical revolution in the eighteenth, Darwin's evolutionary theory in the nineteenth, and Einstein's relativity theory in the twentieth are examples of major transformations within various branches of science.

One of the strengths of Kuhn's provocative account is its recognition of stable worldviews in science that exist over relatively long periods of time, but that are rapidly transformed during periods of crisis and stress. One of its limitations is its failure to incorporate an interpretation of social forces external to the daily activities of scientific practitioners in their laboratories and field stations. Internal developments in scientific theories are affected, at least indirectly, by social and economic circumstances. A viewpoint that incorporates social, economic, and ecological changes is required for a more complete understanding of scientific change.

A second approach to revolutionary transformations is that of Karl Marx and Friedrich Engels. Their base/superstructure theory of history viewed social revolutions as beginning in the economic base of a particular social formation and resulting in a fairly rapid transformation to the legal, political, and ideological superstructure. In the most succinct statement of his theory of history, in 1859, Marx wrote: "At a certain stage of their development, the material productive forces of society come in conflict with the existing relations of production. . . . Then begins an epoch of social revolution. With the change of the economic foundation the entire immense superstructure is more or less rapidly transformed."

For Marx, society is an integrated whole. A fabric of economic, political, and intellectual forces exists and evolves as a stable system for periods of time. But at particular times in history, changes are initiated in economic production that bring about rapid transformations in politics and consciousness. One weakness of this approach is in the determinism assigned to the economic base and the sharp demarcation between base and superstructure. But its strength lies in its view of society and change. If a society at a given time can be understood as a mutually supportive structure of dynamically interacting parts, then the process of its breakdown and transformation to a new whole can be described. Both Kuhn's theory of scientific revolution and Marx's theory of social revolution are starting points for a theory of ecological revolutions.

Science and history are both social constructions. Science is an ongoing negotiation with nonhuman nature for what counts as reality. Scientists socially construct nature, representing it differently in different historical epochs. These social constructions change during scientific revolutions. Similarly, historians socially construct the past in accordance with concepts relevant to the historian's present. History is thus an ongoing negotiation between the historian and the sources for what counts as history. Ecology is a particular twentieth-century construction of nature relevant to the concerns of environmental historians.

A scientific worldview answers three key questions:

1. What is the world made of? (the ontological question)
2. How does change occur? (the historical question)
3. How do we know? (the epistemological question)

Worldviews such as animism, Aristotelianism, mechanism, and quantum field theory construct answers to these fundamental questions differently.

Environmental history poses similar questions:

1. What concepts describe the world?
2. What is the process by which change occurs?
3. How does a society know the natural world?

The concepts most useful for this approach to environmental history are ecology, production, reproduction, and consciousness. The relations among animals (including humans), plants, minerals, and climatic forces constitute the ecological core of a particular habitat at a particular historical time. Through production (or the extraction, processing, and exchange of resources for subsistence or profit), human actions have their most direct and immediate impact on nonhuman nature. Human reproduction, both biological and social, is one step removed from immediate impact on nature: the effects of the biological reproduction of human beings are mediated through a particular form of production (hunting-gathering, subsistence agriculture, industrial capitalism, and so on). Population does not press on the land and its resources directly, but on the mode of production. Two steps removed from immediate impact on the habitat are the modes through which a society knows and explains the natural world—science, religion, and myths. Ideas must be translated into social and economic actions in order to affect the nonhuman world. . . .

How do reproduction and production interact? According to Engels in his *Origin of the Family, Private Property, and the State* (1884), "the determining factor in history is, in the last resort, the production and reproduction of immediate life . . . this itself is of a twofold character. On the one hand, the production of the means of subsistence . . . on the other, the production of human beings themselves." The reproduction of human beings is thus distinct from, but structurally related to, the production of the means of subsistence. A change in the mode of production from gathering-hunting to subsistence-oriented agriculture, or from subsistence agriculture to capitalist agriculture, will increase the capacity of the land to feed people. Intensification in agricultural production is made possible through advances in science and technology.

Production and reproduction interact dialectically. When reproductive patterns are altered, as in population growth or changes in property inheritance, production is affected. Conversely, when production changes, as in the addition or depletion of resources or in tech-

nological innovation, social reproduction and biological reproduction are altered. A dramatic change at the level of either reproduction or production can alter the dynamic between them, resulting in a major transformation of the social whole. Whereas the colonial ecological revolution in New England resulted from external impacts wrought by Europeans on Indian production and reproduction, the capitalist ecological revolution was initiated by internal tensions between production and reproduction. Because of the colonists' low person-land ratio, each family had to reproduce its own labor force in order to produce subsistence for the family. On the other hand, a partible system of patriarchal inheritance meant that farm sizes decreased over three or four generations to the point that not all sons could inherit enough land to reproduce the subsistence system. The tensions between the requirements of subsistence-oriented production (a large family labor force) and social reproduction through partible inheritance (all sons must inherit farms) helped to create a wage labor supply of landless sons needed for the transition to capitalist agriculture.

Socialist-feminists have further elaborated the interaction between production and reproduction. In her 1976 article, "The Dialectics of Production and Reproduction in History," Renaté Bridenthal argues that changes in production give rise to changes in reproduction, creating tensions between them. For example, the change from a preindustrial agrarian to an industrial capitalist economy that characterized the capitalist ecological revolution can be described with respect to tensions, contradictions, and synthesis within the gender roles associated with production and reproduction. In the agrarian economy of colonial America, production and reproduction were symbiotic; women participated in both spheres, since the production and reproduction of daily life were centered in the household and domestic communities. Likewise, children were socialized into production by men working in barns and fields and by women working in farm yards and farmhouses. But with industrialization, production of items such as textiles and shoes moved out of the home into the factory; while farms themselves became specialized and mechanized. Unmarried women were employed outside the home in textile production, or later in clerical work, while married women focused more of their efforts on the reproduction of daily life through housework. Production became more public, reproduction more private, leading to their social and structural separation. For working-class women, the split between production and reproduction imposed a double burden of wage labor and housework, while for middle-class women it led to an increase in domesticity and indoor housework.

Ecological revolutions are generated through tensions and interactions between production and ecology and between production and reproduction. Changes may be externally stimulated as in the colonial ecological revolution or internally stimulated (and aided by external market incentives) as in the capitalist ecological revolution. As society responds to change, inherent tensions in its legitimating worldview and forms of consciousness begin to widen. Some assumptions about nature are elaborated and developed to support and lead the new directions; others are rejected as irrelevant and become the ideas of subordinate groups.

Consciousness

Consciousness is the totality of one's thoughts, feelings, and impressions, the awareness of one's acts and volitions. Group consciousness is a collective awareness by an aggregate of individuals. Individual consciousness and group consciousness are shaped by both environment and culture. In different historical epochs, a society's consciousness is dominated by particular characteristics. These forms of consciousness, through which the world is perceived, understood, and interpreted, are socially constructed and subject to change.

A society's symbols and images of nature express its collective consciousness. They appear in mythology, cosmology, science, religion, philosophy, language, and art. Scientific, philosophical, and literary texts are sources of the ideas and images used by controlling elites, while rituals, festivals, songs, and myths provide clues to the consciousness of ordinary people. How are the ideas, images, and metaphors that legitimate human behaviors toward nature translated into ethics, morals, and taboos? Anthropologist Clifford Geertz holds that religious beliefs establish powerful moods and motivations that translate into social behaviors. Also, ideological frameworks or worldviews "secrete" behavioral norms. According to Charles Taylor, particular frameworks give rise to a certain range of normative variations and not others because their related values are not accidental. When sufficiently powerful, worldviews and their associated values can override social changes, but if weak or weakened they can be undermined. A tribe of New England Indians or a community of colonial Americans may have a religious worldview that holds it together for many decades while its economy is gradually changing. Eventually, however, with the acceleration of commercial change, ideas that had formerly existed on the periphery or among selected elites may become dominant if they support and legitimate the new economic directions.

For Native American cultures, consciousness was an integration of all the senses with the body in sustaining life. In this mimetic consciousness, culture was transmitted intergenerationally through imitation in song, myth, dance, sport, gathering, hunting, and planting. Oral-aural transmission of tribal knowledge through myth and transactions between animals, Indians, and neighboring tribes produced sustainable relations between the human and the nonhuman worlds. The primal gaze of locking eyes between hunter and hunted initiated the moment of ordained killing when the animal gave itself up so that the Indian could survive. The very meaning of the gaze stems from the intent look of expectancy when a deer first sees a fire, smells a scent, or looks into the eyes of a pursuing hunter. For Indians engaged in an intimate survival relationship with nature, sight, smell, sound, taste, and touch were all of equal importance, integrated together in a total participatory consciousness.

When Europeans took over Native American habitats during the colonial ecological revolution, vision became dominant within the mimetic fabric. Although daily life for most colonial settlers, as for Indians, was still guided by imitative, oral, face-to-face transactions, Puritan eyes turned upward toward a transcendent God who sent down his Word in written form in the Bible. Individual Protestants learned to read so that they could interpret God's word for themselves. In turn, the biblical word legitimated the imposition of agriculture and artifact in the new land. The primal gaze of the Indian was submerged by the objectifying scrutiny of fur trader, lumber merchant, and banker who viewed nature as resource and commodity. Treaties and property relations that extracted land from Indians were codified in writing. Alphanumeric literacy became central to religious expression, social survival, and upward mobility.

The imposition of a visually oriented consciousness by Puritans was shattering to the continuance of Indian animism and ways of life. The implications were similar to the loss of mimetic consciousness in Plato's Greece. According to philosopher Eric Havelock, Plato's critique of the oral mimetic heritage of Homer was devastating. The orator to Plato (as the shaman to the Puritan) was an imitator who

indulged in extremes extending even to the howls and cries of animals. The oral tradition was not the creative, individualistic medium appropriate to the virtuous, but the distortive chicanery of the trickster who presented appearance as reality. Myth and poetry stood for the illusions of appearance, not the truths discernible to reason. The oral tradition was merely a catalog of repeated, remembered examples that predetermined human responses. The person who repeated by rote memory through song, poem, or myth was not an individual with a unique psyche, but a victim of hypnosis. No "I" stood apart from the collective consciousness to examine or criticize its spell. No "self" asserted its own independence and authority. For Plato, the emergence of the autonomous psyche signified the separation of the knower from the known, the subject from the object, and the analytical from the oral.

Against poetry, Plato set his theory of pure forms, with mathematics as the exemplar par excellence of knowledge. The ideal forms of the triangle, the bed, and the good were exact, unchanging, and universal. The applied mathematician, the carpenter, and the philosopher attempted to copy these forms in matter, while the orator and the poet were content with word pictures. Mathematics, logic, and science, or *episteme*, were the true modes of knowing, and the self was the knowing subject. With the commercialization of the fur trade and the missionary efforts of Jesuits and Puritans, a society in which animals, plants, and rocks were equal subjects changed to one dominated by transcendent vision in which individual human subjects were separate from resource objects. This change in consciousness imposed by dominant elites characterized the colonial ecological revolution.

The rise of an analytic, quantitative consciousness was a feature of the capitalist ecological revolution. Capitalist ecological relations emphasized efficient management and control of nature. With the development of mechanistic science and its use of perspective diagrams, visualization was integrated with numbering. The printing press and perspective art linked the mental to the material through what sociologist of science Bruno Latour called "immutable mobiles." By reducing three-dimensional natural objects—oceans, rivers, beavers, birds, rocks, and ores—to two-dimensional inscriptions—maps, charts, drawings, diagrams, lists, graphs, curves, equations, papers, texts, files, and archives—quantitative features could be circulated unchanged. In a laboratory, observatory, or field station, they could be accumulated, arrayed, superimposed, compared, and reconstructed as a "natural" order. "The result," observed Latour, "is that we can work on paper with rulers and numbers, but still manipulate three-dimensional objects 'out there'.... Distant or foreign places and times [can] be gathered in one place in a form that allows all the places and times to be presented at once." The visual and material thus combined to produce power over nature through science. The capitalist ecological revolution was characterized by the superposition of scientific, quantitative approaches to nature and its resources. Through education analytic consciousness expanded beyond that of dominant elites to include most ordinary New Englanders.

Forms of consciousness are power structures. When one worldview is challenged and replaced by another during a scientific or ecological revolution, power over society, nature, and space is at stake. Symbol systems, metaphors, and images express the implicit ethics of elites in positions of social power. Debates over scientific theories, argues historian of science Donna Haraway, are contests for power over the terms of discourse. According to French philosopher Michel Foucault, the history of power over nature is a history of spaces, spatial metaphors (habitat, soil, land-scape, topography, terrain, region, and so on), strategies of control, and modes of mapping, tabulation, recordation, classification, demarcation, and ordering. Whereas space "used to belong to nature," when mapped by explorers and geographers, cataloged and inventoried by traders and naturalists, and coded by militarists and computer scientists, it can be controlled by an "eye of power" and subjected to unlimited surveillance. For Foucault, the vision obtained metaphorically through Jeremy Bentham's Panopticon, in which the radiating wings of an entire prison can be surveyed from a single central tower, is paradigmatic of the controlling scrutiny of the overseer. All things are made visible through the dominating, examining look of a cultural overseer located in a management center that controls not only social institutions, but also by extension nature, resources, national parks, wild rivers, endangered whales, herds of wild antelope, migrating warblers, and indeed the whole earth itself through satellite surveillance.

Human consciousness socially constructs nature in different ways in different historical epochs and cultures. Humans negotiate "reality" with nonhuman nature. Indians constructed nature as a society of equal face-to-face subjects. Animals, plants, and rocks were alive and could be communicated with directly. For eighteenth-century New England farmers, nature was an animate mother carrying out God's dictates in the mundane world. Plants and even rocks grew on the earth's surface, but were created for human use and could be harvested as commodities. Nineteenth-century scientists, industrialists, and market farmers reconstructed them as scientific objects to be analyzed in the laboratory and as natural resources to be extracted for profit.

Ecological thinking constructs nature as an active partner. The "nature" that science claims to represent is active, unstable, and constantly changing. As parts of the whole, humans have the power to alter the networks in which they are embedded. Nature as active partner acquiesces to human interventions through resilience and adaptation or "resists" human actions through mutation and evolution. Nonhuman nature is an actor; human and nonhuman interactions constitute the drama. Viewed as a social construction, nature as it was conceptualized in each social epoch (Indian, colonial, and capitalist) is not some ultimate truth that was gradually discovered through the scientific processes of observation, experiment, and mathematics. Rather, it was a relative changing structure of human representations of "reality."

Ecological revolutions, I argue, are processes through which different societies change their relationship to nature. They arise from tensions between production and ecology and between production and reproduction. The results are new constructions of nature, both materially and in human consciousness....

10. Epilogue: The Global Ecological Revolution

Twentieth-century New England is a product of the colonial and capitalist ecological revolutions. Its Native Americans have been reduced to small but resilient communities that have adapted to mainstream culture while retaining many tribal traditions. The region is deeply embedded in an interconnected modern world structured by capitalist forms of production, reproduction, and consciousness. As a member of a global ecological network, it is affected by the availability and scarcity of natural resources. It is an integral part of the Western capitalist core economies that depend on peripheral Third World economies for resources and cheap labor.

Most of the energy, food, and clothing needed to sustain the lives of New Englanders come from external markets. Roughly 80 per-

cent of its meat, vegetables, and fruit are imported from outside the region. The availability and the cost of food are affected by transportation strikes and midwestern droughts. Energy comes from imported oil and gas, augmented by wood-burning stoves and some locally generated nuclear energy. Energy availability is subject to global shortages and price variations. Clothing is largely imported from southern and foreign textile mills, where wage labor is cheaper and supplemented by local and cottage clothing industries. As in the country as a whole, fast food is often prepared from imported beef raised in Central and South America at the expense of tropical rain forests and served in styrofoam containers at the expense of the global ozone layer.

This dependence on outside markets has moved some types of environmental degradation beyond New England's boundaries, allowing portions of its own environment to recover. The twentieth-century decline in farming and the changeover to oil have resulted in the regrowth of the New England forest. Eighty percent of the land is once again forested, close enough to the 95 percent on the eve of colonization to provide a sense of how the original forest (minus its largest giants) might have looked. Maine, New Hampshire, and Vermont are among the four most heavily forested states in the nation. Sixty-two percent of New England's forested acreage, however, is held in small parcels by individuals, most of whom own less than fifty acres, and many of whom are urbanites with country retreats who are conscious of environmental preservation. The lumber industry owns only 32 percent of this acreage; the remaining 6 percent is public land. Major public policy issues are involved in deciding how the forests should best be used.

Yet this regenerated forest is itself the victim of industrial capitalism. Acid precipitation from the smokestacks of the East and Midwest has attacked New England's crops, trees, and shrubs. Acid rain leaches nutrients from leaves, makes plants more vulnerable to fungal and bacterial infections, and reduces tree seedlings and plant productivity. Between 700 and 1,400 wild species are thought to suffer from sulfur dioxide and ozone emissions. The effects are most visible in higher-elevation coniferous forests, but the damage is universal. Acid rain has raised the acidity of thousands of lakes all over New England and introduced mercury, cadmium, and lead into their ecosystems. With the reduction of zooplankton, phytoplankton, and mollusks, fish populations have declined, along with waterfowl such as herons, ducks, loons, and ospreys.

The growth of high technology and computer-based industries further connects New England to the rest of the planet, altering human perceptions of the earth. The Computer Age has mapped the earth's surface as a grid of Cartesian coordinates bounded by and enclosed within a communications network. Today, the "whole earth" image from a satellite's eye view is no longer an earth apple, but a two-dimensional photograph. Viewed from afar by the spectator, it has become a NATO object detached from human participation. Computer advertisements and popular media depict the earth variously as electronically wired; encircled by floating cars, calculators, and computers; enclosed within laboratory flasks; squeezed by human hands and lemon juicers; and dominated by oversized white males standing on its surface. The symbols of nature that permeate and structure modern consciousness present a mechanized, artificial, instrumental nature. It has become completely mechanical, having lost any semblance of organic life.

The adoption of the mechanistic paradigm throughout the Western world has implications that extend far beyond New England's borders. Based on the mechanistic model, capitalist agriculture over the whole globe has moved increasingly in the direction of artificial ecosystems, built on simplified monocultures that are vulnerable to pest outbreaks and catastrophic collapse. Identical rectangular and circular fields precisely laid out for efficient cultivation, irrigation, and harvesting replicate atomic and latticelike patterns, replacing the diversity of small, haphazard patchworks of fields within forests. Stimulated by urbanization and industrialization, agriculture has developed more efficient machines, genetically "improved" strains of crops and animals, artificial fertilizers, and chemical pesticides. The external energy needed to produce the chemicals, operate the farm machinery, and process, store, and transport the products often surpasses the calories the foods themselves supply. Most of this external energy comes from fossil fuels by way of industrial systems rather than from the sun by way of photosynthesis.

Ecological thinking, however, offers the possibility of a new relationship between humans and nonhuman nature that could lead to the sustainability of the biosphere in the future. The assumptions of the ecological paradigm contrast with those of the mechanistic, resting on a different set of assumptions about nature: (1) everything is connected to everything else in an integrated web; (2) the whole is greater than the sum of the parts; (3) nonhuman nature is active, dynamic, and responsive to human actions; (4) process, not parts, is primary; and (5) people and nature are a unified whole.

Ecology also offers a new ethic for grounding human relations with nature. Mechanism is consistent with a homocentric ethic of "natural rights" in which each individual uses nonhuman nature to maximize his or her self-interest. An egocentric ethic, however, is based on a network of mutual obligations rather than natural rights, and on values that are based on the ecosystem rather than on human interests. The land ethic of ecologist Aldo Leopold (1949) enlarges the boundaries of the community to include "soils, waters, plants, and animals, or collectively, the land." "A thing is right," according to Leopold, "when it tends to preserve the integrity, beauty, and stability of the biotic community. It is wrong when it tends otherwise."

Although much of scientific ecology has appropriated the reductionist approach of the mechanistic model, human ecology includes human beings as part of the natural world and recognizes their ability both to destroy as well as to live within the limits of local ecosystems. But for an ecological model to replace mechanism as the dominant paradigm for decision making would require not merely an intellectual, but a global, social, and economic revolution. The capitalist relations of production and the patriarchal relations of reproduction that support mechanistic consciousness would have to give way to new socioeconomic forms, new gender relationships, and an ecological ethic.

Nevertheless, the possibility exists that such a global ecological revolution may be occurring. A global ecological crisis that transcends national boundaries could trigger a transition to a sustainable earth. Global resource depletion and pollution have appeared at the intersection of capitalist (as well as Soviet) economic production and ecology. Nuclear war and nuclear power plant accidents threaten the earth with radioactive, cancer-causing emissions. The burning of fossil fuels for industrial production increases carbon dioxide in the atmosphere, while the cutting of tropical rain forests for grazing and crops reduces its conversion to oxygen, resulting in global warming and melting ice caps. This "greenhouse effect" alters weather patterns that affect agriculture, fishing, and the ecology of local habitats. Nondegradable industrial plastics pollute soils and oceans. As chlorofluorocarbons are produced for refrigerants

and styrofoam packaging, the earth's protective ozone layer is threatened. Toxic wastes from chemical industries enter ground water supplies, threatening human health. Acid rain from coal-burning "smokestack" industries crosses national boundaries, increasing the acidity of lakes and damaging forests. Habitat destruction from industrial expansion endangers hundreds of indigenous species around the whole globe.

Other disjunctions are occurring at the intersection of production and reproduction. Global population continues to grow exponentially despite declining reproductive rates in developed nations. Increased populations in developing countries put pressure on local economies and consequently on the land. Such pressures challenge traditional sex-gender roles and create new patterns in both production and biological reproduction. The emergence of worldwide "green" political parties is in part a response to the failure of the legal-political frameworks that reproduce capitalist society to regulate pollution and depletion. These tensions within production and reproduction are experienced as threats to the health and survival of both human and nonhuman nature.

The outcome of this global ecological crisis in production and reproduction could be negative or positive. A pessimistic scenario would be the crisis and collapse predicted by the "limits to growth" models of the 1970s and the Malthusian dilemma of exponential population growth outrunning the food supply. A positive outcome, however, could be the crisis and reorganization implied by the "order out of chaos" approaches of Ilya Prigogine and Erich Jantsch, moving the entire globe toward ecological and economic sustainability in the twenty-first-century. New forms of production, reproduction, and consciousness could structure the world differently for twenty-first century citizens.

The transition to a sustainable world

would entail changes in production and reproduction that emphasize ecodevelopment in both developed and developing countries. Colonial and capitalist forms of exploitation of nature and Third World peoples would give way to priorities that fulfill subsistence and quality-of-life needs. These would be enhanced by global efforts to conserve energy and renewable natural resources, recycle nonrenewable resources, and adopt appropriate technologies. Ecological and economic development, if sensitively structured by the developing countries themselves, could pave the way to the demographic transition that has lowered reproductive rates in developed countries. Changes in production would thus support changes in reproduction and both together would alleviate human pressures on the global ecosystem. This transition would be legitimated by changes in values and in ways that people perceive, know, and structure reality.

Supporting the emergence of a transformation of consciousness are calls by physicists, ecologists, feminists, poets, and philosophers for philosophical changes that would reintegrate culture with nature, mind with body, and male with female modes of experiencing and representing "reality." They suggest that nature as actor may now be breaking out of the mechanistic straightjacket in which human representations have confined it for the past three hundred years. Through the social construction of a new reality, future generations may learn a worldview that is nonmechanistic. When philosopher Max Horkheimer, writing in 1947, called for the revolt of nature, he invited it to speak in a language other than instrumentalist. "Once it was the endeavor of art, literature, and philosophy to express the meaning of things and of life, to be the voice of all that is dumb, to endow nature with an organ for making known her sufferings, or we might say, to call reality by its rightful name. Today nature's tongue is taken away. Once it

was thought that each utterance, word, cry, or gesture had an intrinsic meaning; today it is merely an occurrence." The voice with which nature speaks and is heard by humans is tactile, sensual, auditory, odoriferous, and visual—not disembodied reason, but visceral understanding.

"In the present crisis," Horkheimer continued, "the problem of mimesis is particularly urgent. Civilization starts with, but must eventually transcend and transvaluate, man's native mimetic impulses.... Conscious adaptation and eventually domination replace the various forms of mimesis ... the formula supplants the image, the calculating machine the ritual dances." To survive we must once again recover the meaning of mimesis, actively making ourselves "like" the environment, not as object, but in the deepest sense of visceral remerging with the earth.

Emerging from concerns over the earth's future is a spectrum of new sciences infused with an ecological perspective. At their root is mimesis in a new form—integrative thinking. Imitation, synthesis, and creative reciprocity between humans and nonhuman nature constitute a form of consciousness in which tacit knowing through the body and information networks ("mind") in nature links humans to the nonhuman world. The new theoretical frameworks challenge positivist epistemology through participatory forms of consciousness. Gregory Bateson's "ecology of mind" sees nature as a network of information moving from brain to hand to stick to rock to earth to eye to brain. "Mind" in nature integrates human subject and active object into a larger network of energy and information exchange. Nature is a changing whole consisting of interactions and processes interpreted by humans. The body's tacit knowledge is one with the mind.

Philosophers have proposed alternatives to the mechanistic framework based on nature's inherent activity, self-organization, permeable boundaries, and resilience. Deep ecologists argue that reform environmentalism is insufficient to deal with the magnitude of global environmental problems. They call for a fundamental transformation in Western epistemology, ontology, and ethics. Deep ecology represents a change from a mechanistic to an ecological consciousness rooted in biospecies equality, appropriate technologies, recycling, and bioregions as ecological homes. The new philosophy is infused with an environmental ethic oriented toward establishing sustainable relations with nature.

Structural changes within science itself may also be indicative of the emergence of a new paradigm. The new physics of David Bohm contrasts the older world picture of atomic fragmentation with a new philosophy of wholeness expressed in the unfolding and enfolding of moments within a "holomovement." His cosmology is one of the primacy of process rather than the domination of parts. The Gaia hypothesis of British chemist James Lovelock proposes that the earth's biota as a whole maintain an optimal chemical composition within the atmosphere and oceans that support its life. Gaia, the name of the Greek earth goddess, is a metaphor for a self-regulating (cybernetic) system that controls the functioning of the earth's chemical cycles. Chaos theory in mathematics offers tools for describing complexity and turbulence consistent with the idea that nature as actor offers surprises and catastrophes that cannot be predicted by linear equations and mechanistic descriptions.

Coupled with these changes in science, epistemology, and ethics are new applied sciences oriented toward effecting a transition to ecological sustainability. Restoration is the active reconstruction of pristine ecosystems (such as prairies, grasslands, rivers, and lakes). By studying and mimicking natural patterns, the wisdom inherent in evolution can be recreated. Rather than taking nature apart and simplifying ecosystems, as the past three centuries of mechanistic science have taught us to do supremely well, restorationists are actively putting it back together. Rather than analyzing nature for the sake of dominating and controlling it, restorationists are synthesizing it for the sake of living symbiotically within the whole.

Agroecology looks back to traditional agriculture and mimics its polycultural patterns. Traditional farming—developed over generations of trial and error through deep local knowledge and the transmission of successful adaptations from fathers and mothers to sons and daughters—is joined with an understanding of local ecology. The polycultures of traditional farmers often are more productive, are more resistant to pests, and use better-adapted varieties of crops than are monocultures of imported seed supported with herbicides and artificial fertilizers. In designing agroecosystems, the spatial arrangements and seasonal development of wild plant species are used as models. Arrangements of local species of grasses, vines, shrubs, and trees are simulated in designing integrated cereal, vegetable, fruit, and tree crop systems. Similarly, agroforestry restores the complementary arrangements of trees, crops, and animals in combination with ecological principles in order to maintain productivity without environmental degradation. Orchards planted with ground covers of legumes or berries and foraged by poultry, pigs, and bees keep down pests and produce well-mulched and manured soil.

The biological control of insects also uses natural ecosystems as models. Uncultivated land surrounding fields harbors birds and insect enemies as well as pests. Flowers along roadsides and fences are especially attractive to beneficial insects. Diversity in crops and surroundings and arrangements of beneficial plants mimic natural conditions, making crops less visible to insect enemies and acting as barriers to pest dispersal. By imitating nature, agricultural systems can be designed that both suppress pests and maximize total yield.

A global ecological revolution would also reconstruct gender relations between women and men and between humans and nature. The domination of women and nature inherent in the market economy's use of both as resources would be restructured. Both radical and socialist feminist theories present alternatives to patriarchal and capitalist ecological relations. But while radical feminism has delved more deeply into the woman-nature connection, socialist feminism is more consistent with the concept of the social construction of ecological revolutions.

For radical feminists and ecofeminists, human nature is grounded in human biology. Humans are biologically sexed and socially gendered. Sex-gender relations give men and women different power bases; hence the personal is political. The ontology and epistemology of the mechanistic worldview are deeply masculinist and exploitative of nature, which has historically been characterized in the female gender. Male-designed and produced technologies neglect the effects of nuclear radiation, pesticides, hazardous wastes, and household chemicals on women's reproductive organs and on the ecosystem. Often stemming from an antiscience, antitechnology standpoint, radical feminism celebrates the relationship between women and nature through the revival of ancient rituals centered on goddess worship, the moon, animals, and the female reproductive system. Its philosophy embraces intuition, an ethic of caring, and weblike human-nature relationships. Yet in emphasizing the female, body, and nature components of the dualities male/female, mind/body, and culture/nature, radical feminism runs the risk of perpetuating the very value hierarchies it seeks to overthrow.

Socialist feminism and socialist ecofeminism incorporate many of the insights of radical feminism, but view both knowledge and reality as historically and socially constructed. What counts as human nature is the product of historically changing interactions between humans and nature, men and women, social classes, races, ages, and national origins. Like Marxist feminists, socialist feminists see nonhuman nature as the material basis of human life, supplying the necessities of food, clothing, shelter, and energy. Nature is transformed by human science and technology for use by all humans for survival. Any meaningful analysis must be grounded in an understanding of power in both the personal and political spheres. Like radical feminism, socialist feminism is critical of mechanistic science's treatment of nature as passive and its male-dominated power structures. It deplores the omission of women's reproductive roles and gender analysis in history and would give reproduction a central place in theory construction. Socialist feminism views change as dynamic, interactive, and dialectical, rather than linear or incremental. Although as yet socialist feminism has had little to say about ecology, it is compatible with a view of nonhuman nature as a historical actor, with the ecological goal of developing sustainable, nondominating relations with nature.

An ecological transformation in the deepest sense entails changes in ecology, production, reproduction, and forms of consciousness. Ecology as a new worldview could help resolve environmental problems rooted in the industrial-mechanistic mode of representing nature. In opposition to the subject/object, mind/body, and culture/nature dichotomies of mechanistic science, ecological consciousness sees complexity and process as including both culture and nature. In the ecological model, humans are neither helpless victims nor arrogant dominators of nature, but active participants in the destiny of the webs of which they are a part.

Although many changes leading to a healthier, sustainable biosphere seem to be occurring, the forces that encourage the current patterns of global resource depletion and pollution are very strong. Patriarchy, capitalism, and the domination of nature are deeply entrenched and function to maintain the present direction of development. Yet one may hope that a sustainable global environment, society, and ethic will emerge in the twenty-first century. ∾

43. Glenn C. Loury

GLENN C. LOURY (b. 1948) is a prominent African American conservative whose current appointment is as professor of public policy at Harvard's John F. Kennedy School of Government. He earned his Ph.D. in economics at Massachusetts Institute of Technology in 1976 and taught economics at Northwestern University and the University of Michigan before joining the Kennedy School in 1982. He has won several awards including a Guggenheim Fellowship (1985–86) and the Leavy Award for Excellence in Free Enterprise Education (1987). In addition to his scholarly work in the field of resource management, he regularly contributes a conservative perspective on issues involving African Americans in contemporary journals of opinion.

The excerpt here was given as a lecture under the auspices of the Heritage Foundation, a conservative Washington, D.C., "think tank," on 12 February 1990, as part of a series observing Black History Month. He challenges both liberals and conservatives to find ways to achieve the "dream" that Martin Luther King Jr. set forth as a goal in 1963. In the process, he takes issue with King's approach by emphasizing the importance of individual responsibility rather than group entitlement. To Loury, African Americans cannot progress by asserting their role as victims or making claims as a racial group. They need to address the very real dysfunctional problems of the big-city ghettos and engage in "self-help" programs. But Loury's is a middle ground between today's left and right, and not a complete rejection of the civil rights movement. ∽

Achieving the "Dream": A Challenge to Liberals and Conservatives in the Spirit of Martin Luther King Jr. (1990)

Therefore, since we are surrounded by such a great cloud of witnesses, let us throw off everything that hinders, and the sin that so easily entangles, and let us run with perseverance the race marked out for us.— Hebrews 12:1, NIV

The struggle for freedom and equality is the central theme in the black American historical

SOURCE: Lecture given at The Heritage Foundation on 12 February 1990, as part of a lecture series observing Black History Month. Reprinted by permission of The Heritage Foundation.

experience. This struggle, in turn, has played a profound role in shaping the contemporary American social and political conscience. The trauma of slavery, the fratricide of the Civil War, the profound legal ramifications of the Reconstruction amendments, the long dark night of post-Reconstruction retreat from the moral and practical implications of black citizenship, the collective redemption of the civil rights movements—these have worked to make us Americans the people we are. Only the massive westward migration and the still continuing flow of immigrants to our shores rival this history of race relations as factors defining the American character. Beginning in the mid-1950s and culminating a decade later, the civil rights movement wrought a profound change in American race relations. Its goal was to achieve equal citizenship for blacks; it was believed by many that social and economic equality would follow in the wake of this accomplishment. The civil rights revolution largely succeeded in its effort to eliminate legally enforced second-class citizenship for blacks. The legislation and court rulings to which it led effected sweeping changes in the American institutions of education, employment, and electoral politics. So broad was the wake of this social upheaval that the rights of women, homosexuals, the elderly, the handicapped were redefined, in large part as a consequence of it.

FORCING A REDEFINITION

This social transformation represents a remarkable, unparalleled experience, graphically illustrating the virtue and vitality of our free institutions. In barely the span of a generation, and with comparatively little violence, a despised and largely disenfranchised minority descendant from chattel slaves used the courts, the legislature, the press, and the rights of petition and assembly of our republic to force a redefinition of their citizenship. One can begin to grasp the magnitude of this accomplishment by comparison with the continuing turmoil which besets those many nations around the world suffering under longstanding conflicts among racial and religious groups.

UNFULFILLED HOPE

Yet, despite this success, hope that the movement would produce true social and economic equality between the races remains unfulfilled. No compendium of social statistics is needed to see the vast disparities in economic advantage which separate the inner-city black poor

from the rest of the nation. No profound talents of social observation are required to notice the continuing tension, anger, and fear that shrouds our public discourse on matters concerning race. When in 1963 Martin Luther King Jr. declared his "dream"—that we Americans should one day become a society where a citizen's race would be an irrelevancy, where black and white children would walk hand-in-hand, where persons would be judged not by the color of their skin but by the content of their character—this seemed to many Americans both a noble and attainable goal. Today, even after having made his birth an occasion for national celebration, his "dream" seems naïvely utopian—no closer to realization than on that hot August afternoon when those inspiring words were first spoken.

Today black Americans, and the nation, face a crisis different in character though no less severe in degree than that which occasioned the civil rights revolution. It is not a crisis, however, which admits of treatment by use of the strategies that proved so successful in that earlier era. The bottom stratum of the black community has compelling problems which can no longer be blamed solely on white racism, which will not yield to protest marches or court orders, and which force us to confront fundamental failures in lower-class black urban society. This crisis is particularly difficult for black leaders and the black middle class. For this profound alienation of the ghetto poor from mainstream American life has continued to grow worse in the years since the triumphs of the civil rights movement, even as the success of that movement has provided the basis for an impressive expansion of economic and political power for the black middle class.

SOCIAL PATHOLOGIES

There is no way to downplay the social pathologies that afflict the urban underclass, just as it cannot be denied that vast new opportunities have opened for blacks to enter into the mainstream of American life. In big city ghettos, the black youth unemployment rate often exceeds 40 percent. Over one-quarter of young black men in the critical ages 20 to 24 years old, according to one recent study, have dropped out of the economy, in the sense that they are not in school, not working and not actively seeking work. In the inner city, far more than half of all black babies are born out of wedlock. Black girls between the ages of 15 and 19 constitute the most fertile population of that age group in the industrialized world. The families which result are most often not self-supporting. The level of dependency on public assistance for basic economic survival has essentially doubled since 1964; almost one-half of all black children are supported in part by transfers to the state and federal governments. Over half of black children in public primary and secondary schools are concentrated in the nation's twelve largest central-city school districts, where the quality of education is poor, and where whites constitute only about a quarter of total enrollment. Only about one black student in seven scores above the fiftieth percentile on standardized college admissions tests. Blacks, though little more than a tenth of the population, constitute approximately half of the imprisoned felons in the nation. Roughly 40 percent of those murdered in the United States are black men killed by other black men. In some big cities black women face a risk of rape which is five times as great as that faced by whites.

These statistics depict an extent of deprivation, a degree of misery, a hopelessness and despair, an alienation which is difficult for most Americans, who do not have direct experience with this social stratum, to comprehend. They pose an enormous challenge to the leadership of our nation—and to the black leadership. Yet, we seem increasingly unable to conduct a

political dialogue out of which might develop a consensus about how to respond to this reality. There are two common, partisan themes which dominate the current debate. One is to blame it all on racism, to declare that this circumstance proves the continued existence of old-type American racial enmity, only in a more subtle, modernized and updated form. This is the view of many civil rights activists. From this perspective the tragedy of the urban underclass is a civil rights problem, curable by civil rights methods. Black youth unemployment represents the refusal of employers to hire competent and industrious young men because of their race. Black welfare dependency is the inescapable consequence of the absence of opportunity. Black academic underperformance reflects racial bias in the provision of public education. Black incarceration rates are the result of the bias of the police and judiciary.

The other theme, characterized by the posture of many on the right in our politics, is to blame it on the failures of "Great Society liberals," to chalk it up to the follies of big government and big spending, to see the problem as the legacy of a tragically misconceived welfare state. A key feature of this view is the apparent absence of any felt need to articulate a "policy" on this new race problem. It is as though those shaping the domestic agenda of this government do not see the explicitly racial character of this problem, as if they do not understand the historical experiences which link, symbolically and sociologically, the current urban underclass to our long, painful legacy of racial trauma. Their response, quite literally, has been to promulgate a de facto doctrine of "benign neglect" on the issue of continuing racial inequality.

Competing Visions

These responses feed on each other. The civil rights leaders, repelled by the Reagan and now

Bush administrations' public vision, see more social spending as the only solution to the problem. They characterize every question raised about the cost effectiveness or appropriateness of a welfare program as evidence of a lack of concern about the black poor; they identify every affirmative action effort, whether it is aimed at attaining skills training for the ghetto poor or securing a fat municipal procurement contract for a black millionaire, as necessary and just recompense in light of our history of racial oppression. Conservatives in and out of government, repelled by the public vision of civil rights advocates and convinced that the programs of the past have failed, when addressing racial issues at all talk in formalistic terms about the principle of "color blind state action." Its civil rights officials absurdly claim that they are the true heirs of Martin Luther King's moral legacy, for it is they who remain loyal to his "color blind" ideal—as if King's moral leadership consisted of this and nothing else. Its spokesmen point to the "trickling down" of the benefits of economic growth as the ultimate solution to these problems; it courts the support and responds to the influence of segregationist elements; it remains at this late date without a positive program of action aimed at narrowing the yawning chasm separating the black poor from the rest of the nation.

There is, many would now admit, merit in the conservative criticism of liberal social policy. It is clear that the Great Society approach to the problems of poor blacks has been inadequate. Intellectually honest persons must now concede that it is not nearly as easy to truly help people as the big spenders would suggest. The proper measure of "curing" ought not be the size of budget expenditures on poverty programs, if the result is that the recipients remain dependent on such programs. Moreover, many Americans have become concerned about the neutrality toward values and behav-

ior which was so characteristic of the Great Society thrust, the aversion to holding persons responsible for those actions which precipitated their own dependence, the feeling that "society" is to blame for all the misfortune in the world. Characterizing the problem of the ghetto poor as due to white racism is one variant of this argument that "society" has caused the problem. It overlooks the extent to which values and behaviors of inner-city black youth are implicated in the difficulty.

Many Americans, black and white, have also been disgusted with the way in which this dangerous circumstance is exploited for political gain by professional civil rights and poverty advocates. They have watched the minority youth unemployment rate be cited in defense of special admissions programs to elite law schools. They have seen public officials, caught in their illegal indiscretions, use the charge of racism as a cover for their personal failings of character. They have seen themselves pilloried as "racists" by civil rights lobbyists for taking the opposite side of legitimately arguable policy debates.

IDEOLOGICAL BARRIER

Yet, none of this excuses (though it may help to explain) the fact that our national government has failed to engage this problem with the seriousness and energy it requires. It has permitted ideology to stand in the way of the formulation of practical programs which might begin to chip away at this dangerous problem. It has permitted the worthy goals of reducing taxes and limiting growth in the size of government to crowd from the domestic policy agenda the creative reflection which will obviously be needed to formulate a new, non-welfare-oriented approach to this problem.

Ironically, each party to this debate has helped to make viable the otherwise problematic posture of the other. The lack of a positive, high-priority response from a series of

Republican administrations to what is now a long-standing, continuously worsening social problem has allowed politically marginal and intellectually moribund elements to retain a credibility and force in our political life far beyond that which their accomplishments would otherwise support. Many are reluctant to criticize them because they do not wish to be identified with a Republican administration's policy on racial matters. Moreover, the shrill, vitriolic, self-serving, and obviously unfair attacks on administration officials by the civil rights lobby has drained their criticism of much of its legitimacy. The "racist" epithet, like the little boy's cry of "wolf," is a charge so often invoked these days that it has lost its historic moral force.

POLITICAL QUAGMIRE

The result of this symbiosis has been to impede the establishment of a political consensus sufficient to support sustained action on the country's most pressing domestic problem. Many whites, chastened by the apparent failures of 1960s-style social engineering but genuinely concerned about the tragedy unfolding in our inner cities, are reluctant to engage this issue. It seems to them a political quagmire in which one is forced to ally oneself with a civil rights establishment no longer able to command broad respect. Many blacks who have begun to have doubts about the effectiveness of liberal social policy are hindered in their articulation of an alternative vision by fear of being too closely linked in the public mind with a policy of indifference to racial concerns.

I can personally attest to the difficulties which this environment has created. I am an acknowledged critic of the civil rights leadership. There are highly partisan policy debates in which I have gladly joined on the Republican side—on federal enterprise zones, on a youth opportunity wage, on educational vouchers for low-income students, on stimulating

ownership among responsible public housing tenants, on requiring work from able-bodied welfare recipients, on dealing sternly with those who violently brutalize their neighbors. I am no enemy of right-to-work laws; I do not despise the institution of private property; I do not trust the capacity of public bureaucracies to substitute for the fruit of private initiative. I am, to my own continuing surprise, philosophically more conservative than the vast majority of my academic peers. And I love, and believe in, this democratic republic.

NEEDED COMMITMENTS

But I am also a black man, a product of Chicago's South Side, a veteran in spirit of the civil rights revolution. I am a partisan on behalf of the inner-city poor. I agonize at the extraordinary waste of human potential which the despair of ghetto America represents. I cannot help but lament, deeply and personally, how little progress we have made in relieving the suffering that goes on there. It is not enough, far from being enough, for me to fault liberals for much that has gone wrong. This is not, for me, a mere contest of ideologies or a competition for electoral votes. And it is because I see this problem as so far from solution, yet so central to my own sense of satisfaction with our public life, that I despair of our governments' lack of commitment to its resolution. I believe that such a commitment, coming from the highest levels of our government, without prejudice with respect to the specific methods to be employed in addressing the issue, but involving a public acknowledgment of the unacceptability of the current state of affairs, is now required. This is not a call for big spending. Nor is it an appeal for a slick public relations campaign to show that George Bush "cares" as much as Jesse Jackson. Rather, it is a plaintive cry for the need to actively engage this problem, for the elevation of concern for racial inequality to a position of priority on our government's domestic affairs agenda.

In some of my speeches and writing on this subject in the past I have placed great weight on the crucial importance to blacks of "self-help." Some may see this current posture as at variance with those arguments. It is not. I have also written critically of blacks' continued reliance on civil rights era protest and legal strategies, and of the propagation of affirmative action throughout our employment and educational institutions. I have urged blacks to move "Beyond Civil Rights." I have spoken of the difference between the "enemy without"— "racism"—and the "enemy within" the black community—those dysfunctional behaviors of young blacks which perpetuate poverty and dependency. I have spoken of the need for blacks to face squarely the political reality that we now live in the "post–civil rights era"; that claims based on racial justice carry now much less force in American public life than they once did; that it is no longer acceptable to seek benefits for our people in the name of justice, while revealing indifference or hostility to the rights of others. Nothing I have said here should be construed as a retraction of these views. But selling these positions within the black community is made infinitely more difficult when my black critics are able to say: "But your argument plays into the hands of those who are looking for an excuse to abandon the black poor"; and when I am unable credibly to contradict them.

It is for this reason that the deteriorating quality of our public debate about civil rights matters has come to impede the internal realignment of black political strivings which is now so crucial to the interest of the inner-city poor, and the political health of the nation. There is a great, existential challenge facing black America today—the challenge of taking control of our own futures by exerting the requisite moral leadership, making the sacrifices of time and resources, and building the needed institutions so that black social and economic development may be advanced. No matter how windy the debate becomes among white liberals and conservatives as to what should be done in the public sphere, meeting this self-creating challenge ultimately depends upon black action. It is to make a mockery of the ideal of freedom to hold that, as free men and women, blacks ought nonetheless passively to wait for white Americans, of whatever political persuasion, to come to the rescue. A people who languish in dependency, while the means through which they might work toward their own advancement exist, have surrendered their claim to dignity, and to the respect of their fellow citizens. A truly free people must accept responsibility for their fate, even when it does not lie wholly in their hands.

ONE INGREDIENT FOR PROGRESS

But to say this, which is crucial for blacks to consider at this late date, is not to say that there is not public responsibility. It is obvious that in the areas of education, employment training, enforcement of anti-discrimination laws, and the provision of minimal subsistence to the impoverished, the government must be involved. There are programs—preschool education for one—which cost money, but which seem to pay even greater dividends. It is a tragic error that those of us who make the "self-help" argument in internal dialogue concerning alternative development strategies for black Americans are often construed by the political right as making a public argument for a policy of "benign neglect." Expanded self-reliance is but one ingredient in the recipe for black progress, distinguished by the fact that it is essential for black dignity, which in turn is a precondition for true equality of the races in this country.

It makes sense to call for greater self-reliance at this time because some of what needs to be done cannot in the nature of the case be undertaken by government. Dealing with behavioral problems, with community values, with the attitudes and beliefs of black youngsters about responsibility, work, family, and schooling is not something government is well suited to do. The teaching of "oughts" properly belongs in the hands of private, voluntary associations—churches, families, neighborhood groups. It is also reasonable to ask those blacks who have benefited from the special minority programs—such as the set-asides for black businesses—to contribute to the alleviation of the suffering of poor blacks, for without the visible ghetto poor, such programs would lack the political support needed for their continuation. Yet, and obviously, such internal efforts cannot be a panacea for the problems of the inner city. This is truly an American problem; we all have a stake in its alleviation; we all have a responsibility to address it forthrightly.

PERMANENT VICTIMS

Thus, to begin to make progress on this extremely difficult matter will require enhanced private and public commitment. Yet, to the extent that blacks place too much focus on the public responsibility, we place in danger the attainment of true equality for black Americans. By "true equality" I mean more than an approximately equal material provision to members of the groups. Also crucial, I maintain, is an equality of respect and standing in the eyes of one's fellow citizens. Yet much of the current advocacy of blacks' interests seems inconsistent with achieving equal respect for black Americans. Leaders, in the civil rights organizations as well as in the halls of Congress, remain wedded to a conception of the black condition, and a method of appealing to the rest of the polity which undermines the dignity of our people. Theirs is too much the story of discrimination, repression, hopelessness, and frustra-

tion; and too little the saga of uplift and the march forward to genuine empowerment whether others cooperate or not. They seek to make blacks into the conscience of America, even if the price is the loss of our souls. They require blacks to present ourselves to American society as permanent victims, incapable of advance without the state-enforced philanthropy of possibly resentful whites. By evolving past suffering and current deprivations experienced by the ghetto poor, some black leaders seek to feed the guilt, and worse, the pity of the white establishment. But I hold that we blacks ought not to allow ourselves to become ever-ready doomsayers, always alert to exploit black suffering by offering it up to more or less sympathetic whites as a justification for incremental monetary transfers. Such a posture seems to evidence a fundamental lack of confidence in the ability of blacks to make it American, as so many millions of immigrants have done and continue to do. Even if this method were to succeed in gaining the money, it is impossible that true equality of status in American society could lie at the end of such a road.

Much of the current, quite heated, debate over affirmative action reveals a similar lack of confidence in the capabilities of blacks to compete in American society. My concern is with the inconsistency between the broad reliance on quotas by blacks, and the attainment of "true equality." There is a sense in which the demand for quotas, which many see as the only path to equality for blacks, concedes at the outset the impossibility that blacks could ever be truly equal citizens. For, aside from those instances in which hiring goals are ordered by a court subsequent to a finding of illegal discrimination, and with the purpose of providing relief for those discriminated against, the use of differential standards for the hiring of blacks and whites acknowledges the inability of blacks to perform up to the white standard.

DOUBLE STANDARDS

So widespread has such practice become that, especially in the elite levels of employment, all blacks must now deal with the perception that without a quota, they would not have their jobs. All blacks, some of our "leaders" seem proud to say, owe their accomplishments to political pressures for diversity. And the effects of such thinking may be seen in our response to almost every instance of racially differential performance. When blacks cannot pass a high school proficiency test as a condition of obtaining a diploma—throw out the test. When black teachers cannot exhibit skills at the same level as whites, the very idea of testing teachers' skills is attacked. If black athletes less frequently achieve the minimal academic standard set for those participating in intercollegiate sports, then let us promulgate for them a separate, lower standard, even as we accuse of racism those suggesting the need for a standard in the first place. If young black men are arrested more frequently than whites for some criminal offense, then let us decry the probability that police are disproportionately concerned about the crimes which blacks commit. If black suspension rates are higher than whites in a given school district—well, let's investigate that district for racist administrative practice. When black students are unable to gain admission at the same rate as whites to the elite public exam school in Boston, let's ask a federal judge to mandate black excellence.

The inescapable truth of the matter is that no judge can mandate excellence. No selection committee can create distinction in black scholars. No amount of circuitous legal maneuvering can obviate the social reality of inner-city black crime, or of whites' and blacks' fear of that crime. No degree of double-standard setting can make black students competitive or comfortable in the academically exclusive colleges and universities.

No amount of political gerrymandering can create genuine sympathy among whites for the interests and strivings of black people. Yet it is to such double-standard setting, such gerrymandering, such maneuvering that many feel compelled to turn.

WRONGS OF THE PAST

Signs of the intellectual exhaustion, and of the increasing political ineffectiveness of this type of leadership are now evident. Yet we cling to this method because of the way in which the claims of blacks have been most successfully pressed during the civil rights era. These claims have been based, above all else, on the status of blacks as America's historical victims. Maintenance of this claiming status requires constant emphasis on the wrongs of the past and exaggeration of present tribulations. He who leads a group of historical victims, as victims, must never let "them" forget what "they" have done: he must renew the indictment and keep alive the moral asymmetry implicit in the respective positions of victim and victimizer. He is the preeminent architect of what philosopher G.K. Minogue has called "suffering situations." The circumstance of his group as "underdog" becomes his most valuable political asset. Such a posture, especially in the political realm, militates against an emphasis on personal responsibility within the group, and induces those who have been successful to attribute their accomplishments to fortuitous circumstance, and not to their own abilities and character.

It is difficult to overemphasize the self-defeating dynamic at work here. The dictates of political advocacy require that personal inadequacies among blacks be attributed to "the system," and that emphasis by black leaders on self-improvement be denounced as irrelevant, self-serving, dishonest. Individual black men and women simply cannot fail on their own, they must be seen as never having had a chance. But where failure at the personal level is impossible, there can also be no personal successes. For a black to embrace the Horatio Alger myth, to assert as a guide to *personal* action that "there is opportunity in America," becomes a *politically* repugnant act. For each would-be black Horatio Alger indicts as inadequate, or incomplete, the deeply entrenched (and quite useful) notion that individual effort can never overcome the "inheritance of race." Yet where there can be no black Horatio Algers to celebrate, sustaining an ethos of responsibility which might serve to extract minimal effort from the individual in the face of hardship becomes impossible as well.

James Baldwin spoke to this problem with great insight long ago. In his 1949 essay "Everybody's Protest Novel," Baldwin said of the protagonist of Richard Wright's celebrated novel *Native Son:*

> Bigger Thomas stands on a Chicago street corner watching air planes flown by white men racing against the sun and "Goddamn" he says, the bitterness bubbling up like blood, remembering a million indignities, the terrible, rat-infested house, the humiliation of home-relief, the intense, aimless, ugly bickering, hating it; hatred smolders through these pages like sulfur fire. All of Bigger's life is controlled, defined by his hatred and his fear. And later, his fear drives him to murder and his hatred to rape; he dies, having come, through this violence, and we are told, for the first time, to a kind of life, having for the first time redeemed his manhood.

But Baldwin rejected this "redemption through rebellion" thesis as untrue to life and unworthy of art. "Bigger's tragedy," he concluded,

> is not that he is cold or black or hungry, not even that he is American, black; but that *he has accepted a theology that denies him life, that he admits the possibility of his being sub-human and feels constrained, therefore, to battle for his humanity according to those brutal criteria bequeathed him at his birth.* But our humanity is our burden, our life; we need not battle for it; we need only to do what is infinitely more difficult—that is, accept it. The failure of the protest novel lies in its rejection of life, the human being, the denial of his beauty, dread, power, in its insistence that it is his categorization alone which is real and which cannot be transcended. (Emphasis added.)

SELF-FULFILLING PROPHECY

While Baldwin's interest was essentially literary, mine is political. In either case, however, our struggle is against the deadening effect which emanates from the belief that, for the black man, "it is his categorization alone which is real and cannot be transcended." The spheres of politics and of culture intersect in this understanding of what the existence of systemic constraint implies for the possibilities of individual personality. For too many blacks, dedication to the cause of reform has been allowed to supplant the demand for individual accountability; race, and the historic crimes associated with it, has become the single lens through which to view social experience; the infinite potential of real human beings has been surrendered on the altar of protest. In this way does the prophecy of failure, evoked by those who take the fact of racism as barring forever blacks' access to the rich possibilities of American life, fulfill itself: "Loyalty to the race" in the struggle to be free of oppression requires the sacrifice of a primary instrument through which genuine freedom might be attained.

Moreover, the fact that there has been in

the United States such a tenuous commitment to social provision to the indigent, independently of race, reinforces the ideological trap. Blacks think we must cling to victim status because it provides the only secure basis upon which to press for attention from the rest of the polity to the problems of our most disadvantaged fellows. It is important to distinguish here between the socioeconomic consequences of the claims which are advanced on the basis of the victim status of blacks (such as the pressure for racially preferential treatment) and their symbolic, ideological role. For even though the results of this claiming often accrue to the advantage of better-off blacks, and in no way constitute a solution to the problems of the poor, the desperate plight of the poorest makes it unthinkable that whites could ever be "let off the hook" by relinquishing the historically based claims—that is, by a broad acceptance within the black community of the notion that individual blacks bear personal responsibility for their fate.

SOCIETAL PARADOX

The dilemmas of the black underclass pose in stark terms the most pressing, unresolved problem of the social and moral sciences: how to reconcile individual and social responsibility. The problem goes back to Kant. The moral and social paradox of society is this: we are on the one hand determined and constrained by social, cultural, not to mention biological, forces. Yet, on the other hand, if society is to work we must believe and behave as if we do indeed determine our actions. Neither of the pat political formulas for dealing with this paradox is adequate by itself. The mother of a homeless family is not simply a victim of forces acting on her; she is, in part, responsible for her plight and that of her children. But she is also being acted on by forces—social, economic, cultural, political—larger than herself. She is impacted by an environment; she is not

an island; she does not have complete freedom to determine her future. It is callous nonsense to insist that she does, just as it is mindlessness to insist that she can do nothing for herself and her children until "society" reforms. In fact, she is responsible for her condition; but we also must help her—that is our responsibility.

RESPONSIBILITY COIN

Now blacks have, in fact, been constrained by a history of racism and limited opportunity. Some of these effects continue to manifest themselves into the current day. Yet, now that greater opportunity exists, taking advantage of it requires that we accept personal responsibility for our own fate, even though the effects of this past remain with us, in part. But emphasis on this personal responsibility of blacks takes the political pressure off those outside the black community, who also have a responsibility, as citizens of this republic, to be actively engaged in trying to change the structures that constrain all the poor, including the black poor, in such a way that they can more effectively assume responsibility for themselves and exercise their inherent and morally required capacity to choose. That is, there is an intrinsic link between these two sides of the "responsibility coin": between acceptance among blacks of personal responsibility for their actions, and acceptance among all Americans of their social responsibilities as citizens. My point to conservatives should be plain. Rather than simply incant the "personal responsibility" mantra, we must also be engaged in helping these people who so desperately need our help. We are not relieved of our responsibility to do so by the fact that Ted Kennedy and Jesse Jackson are promoting legislation aimed at helping this same population with which we disagree.

My point to blacks should also be plain. What may seem to be an unacceptable political risk is also an absolute moral necessity. This is a dilemma from which I believe blacks can only escape by an act of faith—faith in ourselves, faith in our nation, and ultimately, faith in the God of our forefathers. He has not brought us this far only to abandon us now. As suggested by the citation from the book of Hebrews with which I began, we are indeed "surrounded by a great cloud of witnesses"—the spirits of our forebears who, under much more difficult and hostile conditions, made it possible for us to enjoy the enormous opportunities which we have today. It would be a profound desecration of their memory were we to preach despair to our children when we are in fact so much closer than were our fathers to the cherished goal of full equality. We must believe that our fellow citizens are now truly ready to allow us an equal place in this society. We must believe that we have within ourselves the ability to succeed on a level playing field, if we give it our all. We must be prepared to put the past to rest; to forgive if not forget; to retire the outmoded and inhibiting role of "the victim."

PROFOUND TRAGEDY

Embrace of the role of "the victim" has unacceptable costs. It is undignified and demean-ing. It leads to a situation where the celebration among blacks of individual success and of the personal traits associated with it comes to be seen, quite literally, as a betrayal of the black poor, because such celebration undermines the legitimacy of their most valuable political asset—their supposed helplessness. There is, hidden in this desperate assertion of victim status by blacks to an increasingly skeptical white polity, an unfolding tragedy of profound proportion. Black leaders, confronting their people's need and their own impotency, believe they must continue to portray blacks, as "the conscience of the nation." Yet the price extracted for playing the role, in incompletely fulfilled lives and unrealized personal potential, amounts to a "loss of our own souls." As consummate victims we lay ourselves at the feet of our fellows, exhibiting *our* lack of achievement as evidence of *their* failure, hoping to wring from their sense of conscience what we must assume, by the very logic of our claiming, lies beyond our individual capacities to attain, all the while bemoaning how limited that sense of conscience seems to be. This way lies not the "freedom" so long sought by our ancestors, but, instead, a continuing serfdom. ∽

44. Albert Gore Jr.

ALBERT GORE JR. (b. 1949), vice president of the United States, was assigned by President Bill Clinton to undertake a comprehensive review of the federal bureaucracy in search of economies and improvements in service delivery. The purpose of this National Performance Review was to find ways to implement the currently popular principles of "reinventing government," which call for changes in the direction of emphasizing outcomes and customer satisfaction, downsizing, decentralization, and market orientation. The goals were to make government more "businesslike" and explicitly emphasize that the problem was not *what* government should do but *how* it should work.

The excerpt here is from the report that emerged from the National Performance Review group in 1993. It bears some interesting comparison with the "scientific management" advocated by Frederick W. Taylor at the turn of the century because it seeks to reduce government to a set of methods that are good for all times and places—and purposes. And it reminds us that there is a recurring aspiration in American political thought, to the effect that government should be nothing but a neutral, allocative machine that runs from Madison to the present. ⌒

Creating a Government That Works Better and Costs Less: The National Performance Review (1993)

The National Performance Review is about change—historic change—in the way the government works. The Clinton administration believes it is time for a new customer service contract with the American people, a new guarantee of effective, efficient, and responsive government. As our title makes clear, the National Performance Review is about moving from red tape to results to create a government that works better and costs less.

These are our twin missions: to make government *work better* and *cost less*. The President has already addressed the federal deficit with the largest deficit reduction package in history. The National Performance Review can reduce the deficit further, but it is not just about cutting spending. It is also about closing the *trust* deficit: proving to the American

people that their tax dollars will be treated with respect for the hard work that earned them. We are taking action to put America's house in order.

The National Performance Review began on 3 March 1993, when President Clinton announced a six-month review of the federal government and asked me to lead the effort. We organized a team of experienced federal employees from all corners of the government —a marked change from past efforts, which relied on outsiders.

We turned to the people who know government best—who know what works, what doesn't, and how things ought to be changed. We organized these people into a series of teams, to examine both agencies and cross-cutting systems, such as budgeting, procurement, and personnel. The President also asked all cabinet members to create Reinvention Teams to lead transformations at their departments, and Reinvention Laboratories, to begin experimenting with new ways of doing business. Thousands of federal employees joined these two efforts.

But the National Performance Review did not stop there. From the beginning, I wanted to hear from as many Americans as possible. I spoke with federal employees at every major agency and at federal centers across the country—seeking their ideas, their input, and their inspiration. I visited programs that work: a Miami school that also serves as a community center, a Minnesota pilot program that provides benefits more efficiently by using technology and debit cards, a Chicago neighborhood that has put community policing to work, a U.S. Air Force base that has made quality management a way of life.

We also heard from citizens all across America, in more than 30,000 letters and phone calls. We sought the views of hundreds of different organizations, large and small. We learned from the experience of state and local leaders who have restructured their organizations. And we listened to business leaders who have used innovative management practices to turn their companies around.

At a national conference in Tennessee, we brought together experts to explore how best to apply the principles of reinventing government to improving family services. In Philadelphia's Independence Square, where our government was born, we gathered for a day-long "Reinventing Government Summit" with the best minds from business, government, and the academic community.

This report is the first product of our efforts. It describes roughly 100 of our most important actions and recommendations, while hundreds more are listed in the appendices at the end of this report. In the coming months,

we will publish additional information providing more detail on those recommendations.

This report represents the beginning of what will be—what *must* be—an ongoing commitment to change. It includes actions that will be taken now, by directive of the President; action that will be taken by the cabinet secretaries and agency heads; and recommendations for congressional action.

The National Performance Review focused primarily on *how* government should work, not on *what* it should do. Our job was to improve performance in areas where policymakers had already decided government should play a role.

We examined every cabinet department and ten agencies. At two departments, Defense and Health and Human Services, our work paralleled other large-scale reviews already under way. Defense had launched a Bottom-Up Review to meet the President's 1994–1997 spending reduction target. In addition, comprehensive health and welfare reform task forces had been established to make large-scale changes in significant parts of Health and Human Services. Nevertheless, we made additional recommendations regarding both these departments and passed other findings on to the relevant task force for review.

We also expect that the reinventions we propose will allow us to reduce the size of the civilian, nonpostal workforce by 12 percent over the next five years. This will bring the federal workforce below 2 million employees for the first time since 1966. This reduction in the workforce will total 252,000 positions —152,000 over and above the 100,000 already promised by President Clinton.

Most of the personnel reductions will be concentrated in the structures of overcontrol and micromanagement that now bind the federal government: supervisors, headquarters staffs, personnel specialists, budget analysts, procurement specialists, accountants, and auditors. These central control structures not only stifle the creativity of line managers and workers; they consume billions per year in salary, benefits, and administrative costs. Additional personnel cuts will result as each agency reengineers its basic work processes to achieve higher productivity at lower costs—eliminating unnecessary layers of management and nonessential staff.

In addition to savings from the agencies and savings in personnel, we expect that systematic reform of the procurement process should reduce the cost of everything the government buys. Our antiquated procurement system costs the government in two ways: first, we pay for all the bureaucracy we have created to buy things, and second, manufacturers build the price of dealing with this bureaucracy into the prices they charge us. If we reform the procurement system, we should be able to save $22 billion over five years.

As everyone knows, the computer revolution allows us to do things faster and more cheaply than we ever have before. Savings due to consolidation and modernization of the information infrastructure amount to $5.4 billion over five years.

Many of the spending cuts we propose can be done by simplifying the internal organization of our departments and agencies. Others will require legislation. We recognize that there is broad support in Congress for both spending cuts and government reforms, and we look forward to working with Congress to pass this package of recommendations. As President Clinton said when he announced the National Performance Review:

> This performance review is not about politics. Programs passed by both Democratic presidents and Republican presidents, voted on by members of Congress of both parties, and supported by the American people at the time, are being undermined by an ineffi-

cient and outdated bureaucracy, and by our huge debt. For too long the basic functioning of the government has gone unexamined. We want to make improving the way government does business a permanent part of how government works, regardless of which party is in power.

We have not a moment to lose. President Kennedy once told a story about a French general who asked his gardener to plant a tree. "Oh, this tree grows slowly," the gardener said. "It won't mature for a hundred years."

"Then there's no time to lose," the general answered. "Plant it this afternoon."

INTRODUCTION

Public confidence in the federal government has never been lower. The average American believes we waste 48 cents of every tax dollar. Five of every six want "fundamental change" in Washington. Only 20 percent of Americans trust the federal government to do the right thing most of the time—down from 76 percent 30 years ago.

We all know why. Washington's failures are large and obvious. For a decade, the deficit has run out of control. The national debt now exceeds $4 trillion—$16,000 for every man, woman, and child in America.

But the deficit is only the tip of the iceberg. Below the surface, Americans believe, lies enormous unseen waste. The Defense Department owns more than $40 billion in unnecessary supplies. The Internal Revenue Service struggles to collect billions in unpaid bills. A century after industry replaced farming as America's principal business, the Agriculture Department still operates more than 12,000 field service offices, an average of nearly four for every county in the nation—rural, urban, or suburban. The federal government seems unable to abandon the obsolete. It knows how to add, but not to subtract.

And yet, waste is not the only problem. The federal government is not simply broke; it is broken. Ineffective regulation of the financial industry brought us the savings and loan debacle. Ineffective education and training programs jeopardize our competitive edge. Ineffective welfare and housing programs undermine our families and cities.

We spend $25 billion a year on welfare, $27 billion on food stamps, and $13 billion on public housing—yet more Americans fall into poverty every year. We spend $12 billion a year waging war on drugs—yet see few signs of victory. We fund 150 different employment and training programs—yet the average American has no idea where to get job training, and the skills of our workforce fall further behind those of our competitors.

It is almost as if federal programs were *designed* not to work. In truth, few are "designed" at all; the legislative process simply churns them out, one after another, year after year. It's little wonder that when asked if "government always manages to mess things up," two-thirds of Americans say "yes."

To borrow the words of a recent Brookings Institution book, we suffer not only a budget deficit but a performance deficit. Indeed, public opinion experts argue that we are suffering the deepest crisis of faith in government in our lifetimes. In past crises—Watergate or the Vietnam war, for example—Americans doubted their leaders on moral or ideological grounds. They felt their government was deceiving them or failing to represent their values. Today's crisis is different: people simply feel that government doesn't work.

In Washington, debate rarely focuses on the performance deficit. Our leaders spend most of their time debating policy issues. But if the vehicle designed to carry out a policy is broken, new policies won't take us anywhere. If the car won't run, it hardly matters where we point it; we won't get there. Today, the central issue we face is not *what* government does, but *how* it works.

We have spent too much money for programs that don't work. It's time to make our government work for the people, learn to do more with less, and treat taxpayers like customers.

President Clinton created the National Performance Review to do just that. In this report we make hundreds of recommendations for actions that, if implemented, will revolutionize the way the federal government does business. They will reduce waste, eliminate unneeded bureaucracy, improve service to taxpayers, and create a leaner but more productive government. As noted in the preface, they can save $108 billion over five years if those which will be enacted by the President and his cabinet are added to those we propose for enactment by Congress. Some of these proposals can be enacted by the President and his cabinet, others will require legislative action. We are going to fight for these changes. We are determined to create a government that works better and costs less.

A CURE WORSE THAN THE DISEASE

Government is not alone in its troubles. As the Industrial Era has given way to the Information Age, institutions—both public and private—have come face to face with obsolescence. The past decade has witnessed profound restructuring: In the 1980s, major American corporations reinvented themselves; in the 1990s, governments are struggling to do the same.

In recent years, our national leaders responded to the growing crisis with traditional medicine. They blamed the bureaucrats. They railed against "fraud, waste, and abuse." And they slapped ever more controls on the bureaucracy to prevent it.

But the cure has become indistinguishable from the disease. The problem is not lazy or incompetent people; it is red tape and regulation so suffocating that they stifle every ounce of creativity. No one would offer a drowning man a drink of water. And yet, for more than a decade, we have added red tape to a system already strangling in it.

The federal government is filled with good people trapped in bad systems: budget systems, personnel systems, procurement systems, financial management systems, information systems. When we blame the people and impose more controls, we make the systems worse. Over the past 15 years, for example, Congress has created within each agency an independent office of the inspector general. The idea was to root out fraud, waste, and abuse. The inspectors general have certainly uncovered important problems. But as we learned in conversation after conversation, they have so intimidated federal employees that many are now afraid to deviate even slightly from standard operating procedure.

Yet innovation, by its nature, requires deviation. Unfortunately, faced with so many controls, many employees have simply given up. They do everything by the book—whether it makes sense or not. They fill out forms that should never have been created, follow rules that should never have been imposed, and prepare reports that serve no purpose—and are often never even read. In the name of controlling waste, we have created paralyzing inefficiency. It's time we found a way to get rid of waste and encourage efficiency.

The Root Problem: Industrial-Era Bureaucracies in an Information Age

Is government inherently incompetent? Absolutely not. Are federal agencies filled with incompetent people? No. The problem is much deeper: Washington is filled with organizations designed for an environment that no longer exists—bureaucracies so big and wasteful they

can no longer serve the American people.

From the 1930s through the 1960s, we built large, top-down, centralized bureaucracies to do the public's business. They were patterned after the corporate structures of the age: hierarchical bureaucracies in which tasks were broken into simple parts, each the responsibility of a different layer of employees, each defined by specific rules and regulations. With their rigid preoccupation with standard operating procedure, their vertical chains of command, and their standardized services, these bureaucracies were steady—but slow and cumbersome. And in today's world of rapid change, lightning-quick information technologies, tough global competition, and demanding customers, large, top-down bureaucracies—public or private—don't work very well. Saturn isn't run the way General Motors was. Intel isn't run the way IBM was.

Many federal organizations are also monopolies, with few incentives to innovate or improve. Employees have virtual lifetime tenure, regardless of their performance. Success offers few rewards; failure, few penalties. And customers are captive, they can't walk away from the air traffic control system or the Internal Revenue Service and sign up with a competitor. Worse, most federal monopolies receive their money without any direct input from their customers. Consequently, they try a lot harder to please Congressional appropriations subcommittees than the people they are meant to serve. Tax payers pay more than they should and get poorer service.

Politics intensifies the problem. In Washington's highly politicized world, the greatest risk is not that a program will perform poorly, but that a scandal will erupt. Scandals are front-page news, while routine failure is ignored. Hence control system after control system is piled up to minimize the risk of scandal....

Before long, simple procedures are too complex for employees to navigate, so we hire more budget analysts, more personnel experts, and more procurement officers to make things work. By then, the process involves so much red tape that the smallest action takes far longer and costs far more than it should. Simple travel arrangements require endless forms and numerous signatures. Straightforward purchases take months; larger ones take years. Routine printing jobs take a dozen approvals.

This emphasis on process steals resources from the real job: serving the customer.... Not all this money is wasted, of course. But the real waste is no doubt larger, because the endless regulations and layers of control consume every employee's time. Who pays? The taxpayer.

Consider but one example, shared with Vice President Gore at a meeting of federal employees in Atlanta. After federal marshals seize drug dealers' homes, they are allowed to sell them and use the money to help finance the war on drugs. To sell the houses, they must keep them presentable, which includes keeping the lawns mowed.

In Atlanta, the employee explained, most organizations would hire neighborhood teenagers to mow a lawn for $10. But procurement regulations require the U.S. Marshals Service to bid out all work competitively, and neighborhood teenagers don't compete for contracts. So the federal government pays $40 a lawn to professional landscape firms. Regulations designed to save money waste it, because they take decisions out of the hands of those responsible for doing the work. And taxpayers lose $30 for every lawn mowed.

What would happen if the marshals used their common sense and hired neighborhood teenagers? Someone would notice—perhaps the Washington office, perhaps the inspector general's office, perhaps even the GAO. An investigation might well follow—hindering a career or damaging a reputation.

In this way, federal employees quickly learn that common sense is risky—and creativity is downright dangerous. They learn that the goal is not to produce results, please customers, or save tax payers' money, but to avoid mistakes. Those who dare to innovate do so quietly....

The result is a culture of fear and resignation. To survive, employees keep a low profile. They decide that the safest answer in any given situation is a firm "maybe." They follow the rules, pass the buck, and keep their heads down. They develop what one employee, speaking with Vice President Gore at a Department of Veterans Affairs meeting, called "a government attitude."

THE SOLUTION: CREATING ENTREPRENEURIAL ORGANIZATIONS

How do we solve these problems? It won't be easy. We know all about government's problems, but little about solutions. The National Performance Review began by compiling a comprehensive list of problems. We had the GAO's 28-volume report on federal management problems, published last fall. We had GAO's *High-Risk Series,* a 17-volume series of pamphlets on troubled programs and agencies. We had the House Government Operations Committee's report on federal mismanagement, called *Managing the Federal Government: A Decade of Decline.* And we had 83 notebooks summarizing just the tables of contents of reports published by the inspectors general, the Congressional Budget Office, the agencies, and think tanks.

Unfortunately, few of these studies helped us design solutions. Few of the investigating bodies had studied success stories—organizations that had solved their problems. And without studying success, it is hard to devise real solutions. For years, the federal government has studied failure, and for years, failure has endured. Six of every ten major agencies have programs on the Office of Management and Budget's "high-risk" list, meaning they carry a significant risk of runaway spending or fraud.

The National Performance Review approached its task differently. Not only did we look for potential savings and efficiencies, we searched for success. We looked for organizations that produced results, satisfied customers, and increased productivity. We looked for organizations that constantly learned, innovated, and improved. We looked for effective, entrepreneurial public organizations. And we found them: in local government, in state government, in other countries—and right here in our federal government.

At the Air Combat Command, for example, we found units that had doubled their productivity in five years. Why? Because the command measured performance everywhere; squadrons and bases competed proudly for the best maintenance, flight, and safety records; and top management had empowered employees to strip away red tape and redesign work processes. A supply system that had once required 243 entries by 22 people on 13 forms to get one spare part into an F-15 had been radically simplified and decentralized. Teams of employees were saving millions of dollars by moving supply operations to the front line, developing their own flight schedules, and repairing parts that were once discarded.

At the Internal Revenue Service, we found tax return centers competing for the best productivity records. Performance on key customer service criteria—such as the accuracy of answers provided to taxpayers—had improved dramatically. Utah's Ogden Service Center, to cite but one example, had more than 50 "productivity improvement teams" simplifying forms and reengineering work processes. Not only had employees saved more than $11 million, they had won the 1992 Presidential Award for Quality.

At the Forest Service, we found a pilot pro-

ject in the 22-state Eastern Region that had increased productivity by 15 percent in just two years. The region had simplified its budget systems, eliminated layers of middle management, pared central headquarters staff by a fifth, and empowered front-line employees to make their own decisions. At the Mark Twain National Forest, for instance, the time needed to grant a grazing permit had shrunk from 30 days to a few hours—because employees could grant permits themselves rather than process them through headquarters.

We discovered that several other governments were also reinventing themselves, from Australia to Great Britain, Singapore to Sweden, the Netherlands to New Zealand. Throughout the developed world, the needs of information-age societies were colliding with the limits of industrial-era government. Regardless of party, regardless of ideology, these governments were responding. . . .

In the United States, we found the same phenomenon at the state and local levels. The movement to reinvent government is as bipartisan as it is widespread. It is driven not by political ideology, but by absolute necessity. Governors, mayors, and legislators of both parties have reached the sane conclusion: Government is broken, and it is time to fix it.

Where we found success, we found many common characteristics. Early on, we articulated these in a one-page statement of our commitment. In organizing this report, we have boiled these characteristics down to four key principles.

1. Cutting Red Tape

Effective, entrepreneurial governments cast aside red tape, shifting from systems in which people are accountable for following rules to systems in which they are accountable for achieving results. They streamline their budget, personnel, and procurement systems —liberating organizations to pursue their missions. They reorient their control systems to prevent problems rather than simply punish those who make mistakes. They strip away unnecessary layers of regulation that stifle innovation. And they deregulate organizations that depend upon them for funding, such as lower levels of government.

2. *Putting Customers First*

Effective, entrepreneurial governments insist on customer satisfaction. They listen carefully to their customers—using surveys, focus groups, and the like. They restructure their basic operations to meet customers' needs. And they use market dynamics such as competition and customer choice to create incentives that drive their employees to put customers first.

By "customer," we do not mean "citizen." A citizen can participate in democratic decision making; a customer receives benefits from a specific service. All Americans are citizens. Most are also customers: of the U.S. Postal Service, the Social Security Administration, the Department of Veterans Affairs, the National Park Service, and scores of other federal organizations.

In a democracy, citizens and customers both matter. But when they vote, citizens seldom have much chance to influence the behavior of public institutions that directly affect their lives: schools, hospitals, farm service agencies, social security offices. It is a sad irony: citizens own their government, but private businesses they do not own work much harder to cater to their needs.

3. *Empowering Employees to Get Results*

Effective, entrepreneurial governments transform their cultures by decentralizing authority. They empower those who work on the front lines to make more of their own decisions and solve more of their own problems. They embrace labor-management cooperation, provide training and other tools employees need to be effective, and humanize the workplace. While stripping away layers and empowering frontline employees, they hold organizations accountable for producing results.

4. *Cutting Back to Basics: Producing Better Government for Less*

Effective, entrepreneurial governments constantly find ways to make government work better and cost less—reengineering how they do their work and reexamining programs and processes. They abandon the obsolete, eliminate duplication, and end special interest privileges. They invest in greater productivity, through loan funds and long-term capital investments. And they embrace advanced technologies to cut costs.

These are the bedrock principles on which the reinvention of the federal bureaucracy must build—and the principles around which we have organized our actions. They fit together much like the pieces of a puzzle: if one is missing, the others lose their power. To create organizations that deliver value to American taxpayers, we must embrace all four.

Our approach goes far beyond fixing specific problems in specific agencies. Piecemeal efforts have been under way for years, but they have not delivered what Americans demand.... In recent years, Congress has taken the lead in reinventing these systems. In 1990, it passed the Chief Financial Officers Act, designed to overhaul financial management systems; in July 1993, it passed the Government Performance and Results Act, which will introduce performance measurement throughout the federal government. With Congress's leadership, we hope to reinvent government's other basic systems, such as budget, personnel, information, and procurement.

Our approach has much in common with other management philosophies, such as quality management and business process reengineering. But these management disciplines were developed for the private sector, where conditions are quite different.... Consequently, our approach goes beyond private sector methods. It is aimed at the heart and soul of government.

The National Performance Review also shares certain goals with past efforts to cut costs in government. But our mission goes beyond cost-cutting. Our goal is not simply to weed the federal garden; it is to create a regimen that will *keep* the garden free of weeds. It is not simply to trim *pieces* of government, but to reinvent the way government does everything. It is not simply to produce a more efficient government, but to create a more *effective* one. After all, Americans don't want a government that fails more efficiently. They want a government that *works*. To deliver what the people want, we need not jettison the traditional values that underlie democratic governance—values such as equal opportunity, justice, diversity, and democracy. We hold these values dear. We seek to transform bureaucracies precisely *because* they have failed to nurture these values....

OUR COMMITMENT: A LONG-TERM INVESTMENT IN CHANGE

This is not the first time Americans have felt compelled to reinvent their government. In 1776, our founding fathers rejected the old model of a central power issuing edicts for all to obey. In its place, they created a government that broadly distributed power. Their vision of democracy, which gave citizens a voice in managing the United States, was untried and untested in 1776. It required a tremendous leap of faith. But it worked.

Later generations extended this experiment in democracy to those not yet enfranchised. As the twentieth century dawned, a generation of "Progressives" such as Teddy Roosevelt and Woodrow Wilson invented the modern bureaucratic state, designed to meet the needs of a new industrial society. Franklin Roosevelt brought it to full flower. Indeed, Roosevelt's 1937 announcement of his Committee on Administrative Management sounds as if it were written only yesterday:

> The time has come to set our house in order. The administrative management of the government needs overhauling. The executive structure of the government is sadly out of date.... If we have faith in our republican form of government ... we must devote ourselves energetically and courageously to the task of making that government efficient.

Through the ages, public management has tended to follow the prevailing paradigm of private management. The 1930s were no exception. Roosevelt's committee—and the two Hoover commissions that followed—recommended a structure patterned largely after those of corporate America in the 1930s. In a sense, they brought to government the GM model of organization.

By the 1980s, even GM recognized that this model no longer worked. When it created Saturn, its first new division in 67 years, GM embraced a very different model. It picked its best and brightest and asked them to create a more entrepreneurial organization, with fewer layers, fewer rules, and employees empowered to do whatever was necessary to satisfy the customer. Faced with the very real threat of bankruptcy, major American corporations have revolutionized the way they do business.

Confronted with our twin budget and performance deficits—which so undermine public trust in government—President Clinton intends to do the same thing. He did not staff the Performance Review primarily with outside consultants or corporate experts, as past presidents have. Instead, he chose federal employees to take the lead. They consulted with experts from state government, local government, and the private sector.…

Nor did the effort stop with the men and women who staffed the Performance Review. President Clinton asked every cabinet member to create a Reinvention Team to redesign his or her department, and Reinvention Laboratories to begin experimenting immediately.…

The process is not easy, nor will it be quick. There are changes we can make immediately, but even if all of our recommendations are enacted, we will have only begun to reinvent the federal government. Our efforts are but a down payment—the first installment of a long-term investment in change. Every expert with whom we talked reminded us that change takes time. In a large corporation, transformation takes six to eight years at best. In the federal government, which has more than seven times as many employees as America's largest corporation, it will undoubtedly take longer to bring about the historic changes we propose.

Along the way, we will make mistakes. Some reforms will succeed beyond our wildest dreams; others will not. As in any experimental process, we will need to monitor results and correct as we go. But we must not confuse mistakes with failure. As Tom Peters and Robert Waterman wrote in *In Search of Excellence,* any organization that is not making mistakes is not trying hard enough. Babe Ruth, the Sultan of Swat, struck out 1,330 times.…

In times such as these, the most dangerous course is to do nothing. We must have the courage to risk change.…

CONCLUSION

Unlike many past efforts to change the government, the National Performance Review will not end with the publication of a report. We have identified what we must do to make government work better and cost less: We must serve our customers, cut red tape, empower employees to get results, and cut back to basics. Now, we will take action.

The task is immense. The federal government has 2.1 million civilian employees, 800,000 postal workers, 1.8 million military personnel, and a $1.5 trillion budget—more than the entire gross domestic product of Germany, the world's third-largest economy.

The National Performance Review has identified the problems and defined solutions. The President will issue directives, cabinet secretaries will change administrative practices, and Office of Management and Budget will issue guidance. We will work with Congress for legislation where it's needed. Senseless regulations will be repealed; mechanisms to enhance customer service will be created; change will begin.…

How we proceed will be as important as what we have done to date. We must avoid the pull of implementation models that are familiar and comfortable but poorly suited to today's world. We must avoid creating new bureaucracies to reform the old. We must actively involve government leaders at all levels. We must seek the guidance of those who have successfully transformed large organizations in both the private and public sectors.

The nature of our strategies will no doubt cause discomfort. They will be unfamiliar. They will not look like business as usual. They will challenge the current federal culture. And they will demand risk-taking.…

To succeed where others have failed, the President and Vice President have committed to specific initiatives that will create a culture capable of sustaining fundamental change. This shift in culture will not occur overnight. To bring it about, we will continue:

- a cascading process of education, participation, and ownership at the highest levels of the executive branch;
- two-way communication with federal employees and their organizations;

- bipartisan partnership with Congress;
- processes to listen to and use feedback from customers and citizens; and
- government-wide mechanisms to monitor, coordinate, and facilitate plans for reinvention.

The administration has already taken a number of steps to bring about the changes we are recommending.

First, we have launched Reinvention Teams and Reinvention Labs in every department to continue seeking ways to improve the government and put these ideas in practice.

Second, we have begun to work—and will continue to expand relationships with leaders and representatives of federal employees from throughout the government. Indeed, the National Performance Review is the first government-wide change initiative to be run and staffed by federal employees. Our actions will make employees' jobs better, and their participation will make our actions better.

Third, the President and Vice President have begun to work with the cabinet to develop performance agreements that will institutionalize a commitment to and establish accountability for change.

Fourth, we have developed a mechanism to spread our basic principles through our the government. The President will meet with the cabinet to develop strategies reflecting these principles and ideas, committing all involved to take responsibility for changing the way we do business. Cabinet members will then go through the same process with their senior managers, who will go through it with their senior managers, and so on.

Fifth, the President is establishing a management council to monitor change and provide guidance and resources to those working to bring it about. The President's Management Council will be charged with responsibility for changing the culture and management of the

federal government.

Sixth, the Federal Quality Institute will help agencies with access to information, education, research, and consultation on quality management. Like our other initiatives, this models a basic tenet of the behavior we recommend—encouraging managers to define their own missions and tasks, but providing the support they need to do a good job.

Seventh, we will launch future reviews of the federal government, targeted at specific problems. The National Performance Review was a learning experience; we learned what we could do in six months, and what we still need to do. We focused heavily on the basic systems that drive federal agencies: the budget, personnel, procurement, financial management, accountability, and management systems. In subsequent reviews, we will narrow our focus. For example, we plan a review of the antiquated federal field office structure, which dates from the 1930s and contains some 30,000 field offices. Other targets might include the abandonment of obsolete programs; the domination of unproductive subsidies; the redesign of failed programs; the redefinition of relationships between the federal government and state and local government; and the reinvigoration of relationships between the executive and legislative branches.

Finally, the National Performance Review will continue to rely on its greatest asset: the federal employees who made it happen. They have all worked hard for change and many will continue to work on reinvention in their own agencies. They constitute a network that will reach out to other employees, sharing their enthusiasm, energy, and ideas....

Despite all the horror stories and years of scorn heaped on federal employees, our government is staffed by people committed to their jobs, qualified to do them better, and hungry for the opportunity to try. The environment and culture of government have discouraged many of these people; the system has undermined itself. But we can—and will—change that environment and culture.

Over time, it will become increasingly obvious that people are not the problem. As old ways of thinking and acting are replaced by a culture that promotes reinvention and quality, a new face of government will appear—the face of employees newly empowered and newly motivated, and of customers newly satisfied.

WHAT REINVENTING GOVERNMENT MEANS FOR YOU

We have talked enough of what we will do and how we will change. The more important question is how life will change for *you,* the American people.

If we succeed—if the administration can implement our recommended actions and Congress can pass our legislative package—you will begin to see a different government. Your mail will be delivered more rapidly. When you call a social security office, you'll get through. When you call the Internal Revenue Service, you'll get accurate answers—and if you don't, you will no longer be penalized.

If you lose your job, a local career center will help you find a new one. If you want retraining, or you want to go back to school, you'll find counselors who can help you sort out your options, pick the best program, and pay for it. If you run a small business, you will have fewer forms to fill out.

If you live in public housing, your apartment complex might get cleaner and safer. Perhaps you'll even be able to move your family to a safer, quieter, more stable neighborhood.

Our workplaces will get safer because they are inspected more often. Our water will get cleaner. Your local government will work better because it is no longer hamstrung by silly federal regulations.

And perhaps the federal debt—that $4 trillion albatross around the necks of our children and grandchildren—will slow its rampage. Our federal agencies will begin to figure out, bit by bit by bit, how to cut spending, eliminate the obsolete, and provide better service for less money.

You will begin to feel, when you walk into a post office or social security office or employment service or veterans' hospital, like a valued customer. We will begin to spend more money on things you want and need—health care, training, education, environmental protection—and less on bureaucracy. One day you will be able to conclude that you are getting a dollar of value for every dollar of taxes you pay.

This is our vision of a government that works better and costs less. We know it will not come to be overnight, but we believe it is a vision we *can* bring to life. We believe this because we have already seen this vision come to life—in local governments, in state agencies, even in a few federal agencies. We believe it is the *right* vision for government as we approach the twenty-first century.

It will take more than a dedicated President and Vice President to make this vision a reality, however. It will take more than dedicated employees. It will take dedicated citizens, willing to work long and hard to improve their government.

It will take citizens willing to push their social security offices and unemployment offices to treat them like customers—and to demand that their voices be heard when they don't get satisfaction. It will take citizens willing to demand information about the performance of their federal organizations. And it will take citizens willing to act on the basis of that information.

As our President has said so often, the future is ours—if we have the courage to create it. ∾

45. Summary of an Era: Articles of Amendment Ratified and Not Ratified, and California Proposition 209

ALTHOUGH SOME are merely procedural (and therefore omitted here), amendments to the Constitution are often the symbol by which change is accepted into the ongoing constitutional consensus and civic religion of the country. Proposal to the states by a two-thirds majority of both houses of Congress followed by ratification by three-quarters of the state legislatures amounts to a powerful statement of American beliefs and intended practice. In the postwar period, there are several illustrations of this principle—and some in which nonratification of a proposed amendment nevertheless demonstrates the symbolic importance of formal constitutional change.

Amendment XXII of 1951, for example, is a clear statement of reaction against the four terms of Franklin Roosevelt as president, and perhaps against the war that made them possible. Amendment XXIII of 1961 allowed the District of Columbia to be represented in the Electoral College, but subsequent efforts to give the District voting representation in Congress have been rejected. Amendment XXIV of 1964 was obviously a product of the civil rights movement of the 1960s, and Amendment XXVI—an effort to address the problem of the anti–Vietnam war movement—set new records by proceeding from proposal to ratification in only three months, 23 March–30 June 1971. (Amendment XXV regarding presidential disability and succession has been omitted as merely procedural.)

The "equal rights" amendment that would have been Amendment XXVII was proposed in 1972 and nearly ratified before a vigorous movement arose to defeat it. Despite extension of the time for ratification to a total of ten years, it fell short and was recognized as defeated in 1982. In 1978 Congress proposed an amendment to make the District of Columbia the voting equivalent of a state in the Congress, but the seven-year time limit elapsed without ratification by the requisite number of states. Similarly, amendments to require balancing the federal budget and to prevent flag desecration have not been ratified or formally proposed, despite much discussion. One of Madison's original amendments submitted to the states in 1789, however, was resurrected and ratified in 1992, and stands as Amendment XXVII essentially as part of the reaction against the federal government of that period. Finally, as an indication of the continuing reaction of the 1990s, California's initiative-enacted Proposition 209, eliminating the state's affirmative action programs, has been included. ∾

Articles of Amendment Ratified

AMENDMENT XXII
(26 FEBRUARY 1951)

Sec. 1. No person shall be elected to the office of President more than twice, and no person who has held the office of President, or acted as President for more than two years of a term to which some other person was elected President, shall be elected to the office of the President more than once. But this Article shall not apply to any person holding the office of President when this Article was proposed by the Congress, and shall not prevent any person who may be holding the office of President, or acting as President, during the term within which this Article becomes operative from holding the office of President or acting as President during the remainder of such term.

AMENDMENT XXIII
(29 MARCH 1961)

Sec. 1. The District constituting the seat of Government of the United States shall appoint in such manner as the Congress may direct:

A number of electors of President and Vice-President equal to the whole number of Senators and Representatives in Congress to which the District would be entitled if it were a State, but in no event more than the least populous state; they shall be in addition to those appointed by the states, but they shall be considered, for the purposes of the election of President and Vice-President, to be electors appointed by a state; and they shall meet in the District and perform such duties as provided by the twelfth article of amendment.

AMENDMENT XXIV
(24 JANUARY 1964)

Sec. 1. The right of citizens of the United States to vote in any primary or other election for President or Vice-President, for electors for President or Vice-President, or for Senator or Representative in Congress, shall not be denied or abridged by the United States or any state by reason of failure to pay any poll tax or other tax.

Sec. 2. The Congress shall have power to enforce this article by appropriate legislation.

AMENDMENT XXV
(23 FEBRUARY 1967)

[Procedures for presidential succession: omitted.]

AMENDMENT XXVI
(7 JULY 1971)

Sec. 1. The right of citizens of the United States, who are eighteen years of age or older, to vote shall not be denied or abridged by the United States or by any State on account of age.

Sec. 2. The Congress shall have power to enforce this article by appropriate legislation.

AMENDMENT XXVII
(7 MAY 1992)

No law, varying the compensation for the services of the Senators and Representatives shall take effect, until an election of Representatives shall have intervened. ∿

Articles of Amendment Not Ratified

EQUAL RIGHTS AMENDMENT (PASSED BY CONGRESS, 22 MARCH 1972: NOT RATIFIED)

Sec. 1. Equality of rights under the law shall not be denied or abridged by the United States or by any State on account of sex.

Sec. 2. The Congress shall have the power to enforce, by appropriate legislation, the provisions of this article.

Sec. 3. This amendment shall take effect two years after the date of ratification.

[This amendment was proposed by Congress on 22 March 1972. In 1978 Congress extended the seven-year deadline for ratification to 30 June 1982. The deadline elapsed before the amendment could be ratified by the needed three-fourths of the states.]

D.C. STATEHOOD AMENDMENT: (22 AUGUST 1978: NOT RATIFIED)

Sec. 1. For purposes of representation in the Congress, election of the President and Vice President, and article V of this Constitution, the District constituting the seat of government of the United States shall be treated as though it were a State.

Sec. 2. The exercise of the rights and powers conferred under this article shall be by the people of the District constituting the seat of government, and as shall be provided by the Congress.

Sec. 3. The twenty-third article of amendment to the Constitution of the United States is hereby repealed.

Sec. 4. This article shall be inoperative, unless it shall have been ratified as an amendment to the Constitution by the legislatures of three-fourths of the several States within seven years from the date of its submission.

[This amendment was proposed by Congress on 22 August 1978. On 22 August 1985, the seven-year time limit elapsed.] ∾

California Proposition 209 (1996)

Section 31 is added to Article I of the California Constitution as follows:

SEC. 31. (a) The state shall not discriminate against, or grant preferential treatment to, any individual or group on the basis of race, sex, color, ethnicity or national origin in the operation of public employment, public education or public contracting.

(b) This section shall apply only to action taken after the section's effective date.

(c) Nothing in this section shall be interpreted as prohibiting bona fide qualifications based on sex which are reasonably necessary to the normal operation of public employment, public education or public contracting.

(d) Nothing in this section shall be interpreted as invalidating any court order or consent decree which is in effect as of the effective date of this section.

(e) Nothing in this section shall be interpreted as prohibiting action which must be taken to establish or maintain eligibility for any federal program, where ineligibility would result in a loss of federal funds to the state.

(f) For the purposes of this section, "state" shall include, but not necessarily be limited to, the state itself, any city, county, city and county, public university system, including the University of California, community college district, special district or any other political subdivision or governmental instrumentality of or within the state.

(g) The remedies available for violation of this section shall be the same, regardless of the injured party's race, sex, color, ethnicity, or national origin, as are otherwise available for violations of then-existing California anti-discrimination law.

(h) This section shall be self-executing. If any part or parts of this section are found to be in conflict with federal law or the United States Constitution, the section shall be implemented to the maximum extent that federal law and the United States Constitution permit. Any provision held invalid shall be severable from the remaining provisions of this section. ∼